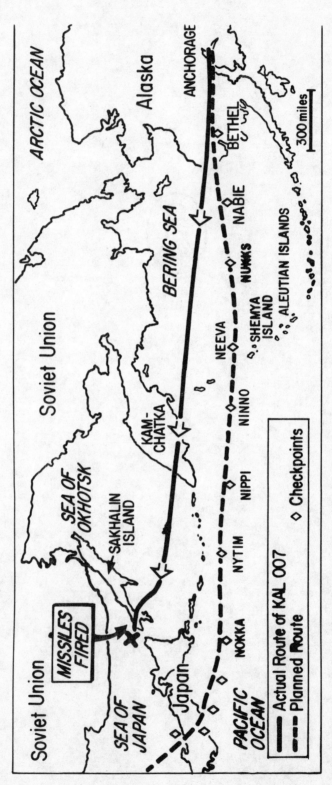

Actual course of KAL Flight 007, route Romeo-20, and checkpoints.

KAL 007
The Cover-Up

David E. Pearson

Summit Books
New York • London • Toronto • Sydney • Tokyo

Published by SUMMIT BOOKS
A Division of Simon & Schuster, Inc.
Simon & Schuster Building
Rockefeller Center
1230 Avenue of the Americas
New York, NY 10020
SUMMIT BOOKS and colophon are trademarks of Simon & Schuster, Inc.
Designed by Anne Scatto/Levavi & Levavi
Graphics by Virginia Simon
Manufactured in the United States of America

1 3 5 7 9 10 8 6 4 2

Library of Congress Cataloging in Publication Data
Pearson, David E. (David Eric).
KAL 007 : the cover-up.

Bibliography: p.
Includes index.
1. Korean Air Lines Incident, 1983.   I Title.
E183.8.S65P43   1987   909′.096454   87-10159
ISBN 0-671-55716-5

ACKNOWLEDGMENTS

A book such as this represents far more than individual effort. In a very real sense it is a group product, drawing upon thousands of hours of thought and research by an eclectic team whose common linkage has been a dedication to uncovering the truth about what actually happened on the night of August 31, 1983. The book has benefited immeasurably from their analyses, criticisms, and insights.

Victor Navasky and Hamilton Fish of *The Nation* had the courage to publish several articles on the incident in spite of occasionally sharp criticism. *Nation* editors Elsa Dixler and Zachary Sklar provided editorial skill and kind support throughout the writing of articles and book. Special thanks go to David Corn both for his many contributions throughout the investigation and especially for permission to use his material on the history of Korean Air Lines in the text.

Equally important has been the support of Anne B. Zill and the Fund for Constitutional Government, who made possible the acoustic analysis presented in these pages. The FCG has financed travel and numerous technical analyses, sponsored colloquia, arranged press contacts, and underwritten the publication of the *KAL 007 Information Bulletin & Newsletter*. FCG sponsor Stewart Mott was the moving force behind the memorial service and press conference by victims' families on the third anniversary of the tragedy. To those inquiring into the incident, the FCG has been a significant resource.

Information, criticism, translation, analysis, support—a full list of those who contributed in these and other ways would be long indeed. Larry Porter's analysis of Flight 007's transmissions has been especially valuable. Larry has given more hours of his highly professional attention to

6   ACKNOWLEDGMENTS

this material than could ever be recompensed. Thanks also go to Dr. Les Atlas and his colleagues at the University of Washington for their superb technical assistance in the acoustic analysis. Gwen Edelman, my agent, contributed to the project in numerous ways, resolving not a few crises in the process. The members of my family provided help and encouragement throughout what became a marathon. My sister Leslie helped with library research, and my father, to whom I extend the warmest gratitude and affection, helped in more ways than I can count. I gratefully acknowledge the support and many critical insights of my Yale advisers, Charles Perrow, Wendell Bell, and Garry Brewer. Translations were done by Ingrid Gray, Martha Humphreys, Kim Kap-heon, and Richard Torrence. Wolfgang Heim, the spokesman for the West German air traffic controllers' association Verband Deutscher Flugleiter, did an analysis of the flight paths of the Soviet interceptors, and Robert L. Williams of Yale did the cartographic work on the flight path of KAL Flight 007. Tom Gervasi, Director of the Brooklyn-based Center for Military Research and Analysis, provided a wealth of information and references about the military situation in Alaska and the Far East, as well as commenting on parts of the manuscript. Others who provided important technical assistance include Tom Bernard, Heino Caesar, Duncan Campbell, Harold Ewing, Jerry Fresia, Victor Jaffe, R. W. Johnson, Richard Kunkle, Yoshitaro Masuo, and Rupert Pengelley. Encouragement and critical comments were received from Jim Brazell, Oliver Clubb, Edward Herman, Sugwon Kang, and David Keppel. Those who aided the work by tracking down leads in the U.S., Europe, and the Far East include Mark Ackerman, Bob Bossin, Malcolm Brenner, Michael Chrisman, Anne Hurley, Andre Libik, Osamu Nakashima, and Shozo Takemoto. Beryl Normand of Yale's Sterling Library helped locate references ranging from the obvious to the unbelievably obscure, and Virginia Simon did the graphics for both the *Nation* articles and this book. Those whose names I have overlooked or who cannot be mentioned also have my special thanks.

The central figure in the case, and my understanding of it, has been retired U.S. Foreign Service officer John Keppel. John and I met just prior to the publication of the first *Nation* article, and we have worked closely ever since. His effort to bring out the truth in the case has been, in the very best sense of the term, an obsession. Working full-time and mostly at his own expense, John has been the FCG's Flight 007 project director as well as a source, author, lecturer, coordinator, tireless distributor of information, and gadfly. His contributions to this book have been numerous and essential. As counselor, critic, co-author, and friend, he has earned my deepest respect and gratitude.

Finally and most important, there is my beloved wife Paloma. Although I took too long and spent far too much on this inquiry, her encouragement and support were never lacking as the days drifted into years and the answers slowly came.

For Paloma

CONTENTS

INTRODUCTION   13

PROLOGUE   19

PART ONE THE FLIGHT
CHAPTER 1. TAKEOFF   27

CHAPTER 2. OFF COURSE   53

CHAPTER 3. SHOOTDOWN   65

CHAPTER 4. OVERFLIGHTS   81

CHAPTER 5. KOREAN AIR LINES   96

PART TWO AFTERMATH
CHAPTER 6. SAFE ON SAKHALIN   113

CHAPTER 7. MEETING THE PRESS   134

CHAPTER 8. SPEECHES AND THEORIES   146

CHAPTER 9. THE RUSSIANS RESPOND   160

CHAPTER 10. OUTRAGE   173

CHAPTER 11. MISSILES AND MEETINGS   182

CHAPTER 12. THE RUSSIAN CASE   197

CHAPTER 13. THE SECURITY COUNCIL   209

PART THREE COVER-UP
CHAPTER 14. DEBRIS   233

CHAPTER 15. THE BLACK BOX   240

CHAPTER 16. THE U.S. PRESS   258
CHAPTER 17. THE INTERNATIONAL CIVIL
AVIATION ORGANIZATION (ICAO)   266
CHAPTER 18. THE INVESTIGATION BEGINS   284
CHAPTER 19. IN COURT   302
CHAPTER 20. THE INVESTIGATION
CONTINUES   315
CHAPTER 21. THE THEORIES   328
CHAPTER 22. THE NEW EVIDENCE   345
NOTES AND REFERENCES   363
BIBLIOGRAPHY   442
INDEX   448

Who sees with eagle eye,
As God of all,
A hero perish
Or a sparrow fall.

—*Alexander Pope,* Essay on Man, *Epistle I*

INTRODUCTION

My interest in the downing of Korean Air Lines Flight 007 developed quite by accident. During my doctoral studies at Yale, I had become interested in how systems that are sufficiently complex and "tightly coupled" —interactive, that is, where things happen very quickly and can't be turned off, where redundancies are not available, and where failures in one part of the system have ramifications for the other parts—inevitably experience what sociologist Charles Perrow called "normal accidents."[1] The system I had in mind was the World Wide Military Command and Control System (WWMCCS, pronounced "Wimex"). WWMCCS is the central nervous system of the military, a series of computers, transmission lines and stations, electronic equipment, human beings, and their organizations. With tasks ranging from sending routine messages to providing early warning of nuclear attack, the system is critical to America's national security.

Over the course of its 25-year history, WWMCCS has experienced embarrassing and occasionally costly failures. These included a failure to convey timely information to the National Command Authorities (the President, Secretary of Defense, Joint Chiefs, and so on down through the military chain of command) during the 1967 Israeli attack on the intelligence ship U.S.S. *Liberty,* during the seizure of the electronic intelligence ship U.S.S. *Pueblo* by North Korea in 1968, and in 1969 when the North Koreans shot down an EC-121 reconnaissance plane. False indications of Soviet missile attacks and frequent breakdowns of WWMCCS's central computers have plagued our early-warning system. Communications breakdowns have hindered war-training exercises and created difficulties during crises such as when Congressman Leo Ryan and several others were killed by religious cult members in Jonestown, Guyana, in 1979, and during Operation Urgent Fury, the 1983 Grenada invasion.[2]

During the late fall of 1983, I was recounting to a friend the story of WWMCCS's failure at the time of the Jonestown incident, something he had not heard. (What happened was a thunderstorm in Florida caused a power outage that disrupted the computer linkage between the Joint Chiefs and relevant military personnel. They remained incommunicado for almost an hour.)[3] Chuckling, he replied, "You know what? At the time Flight 007 was shot down by the Russians, two of the WWMCCS's mainframes were down." "Really?" I responded. "What a system!" The conversation soon moved on, but I did not forget the remark.

Later, I decided to write up this most recent WWMCCS failure. Like most people, I had been surprised at the time by Secretary of State George Shultz's statement that the U.S. had no information about the downing for hours and that the President had not been fully informed until the next day. This seemed odd because I knew there were also independent intelligence communications channels available that were not a part of WWMCCS. But in any case, I thought I had been given a clue that would help me interpret information in the public record, so I began reading. And reading. But nowhere was there a reference to a computer failure on the night the Korean plane was shot down. There was a great deal of other information, of course, and my files soon began to swell with newspaper and magazine articles and reports of congressional hearings.

What started out as a small research paper soon ballooned to unforeseen proportions. As I continued to work, evidence began to accumulate that simply could not be explained by a couple of faulty computers. And the more the explanation of events advanced by U.S. officials was examined, the less satisfactory it appeared to explain many of the key aspects of the case. But having my own vested interest in documenting another "normal accident" in a complex system, these realizations were tardy in coming. It was only after many months of research that I sat myself down for a talk. Only then did I begin to entertain the possibility that more had taken place that night than the American public had been told. No, I never confirmed the fact of a computer outage or whether WWMCCS in any way played a significant role in the events of August 31, 1983, and by now I feel it does not matter. The case involves far more than just WWMCCS, the unlikely portal through which a scholar interested in complex organizations first entered the highly politicized world of Korean Air Lines Flight 007.

When my paper finally seemed publishable, one of my academic advisers sent a copy to Victor Navasky, the editor of *The Nation* magazine. On a

Saturday night in mid-June 1984, my wife and I were entertaining friends, lingering over glasses of Spanish brandy, when the phone rang. Navasky said he liked the piece and asked whether I was interested in publishing with *The Nation*. Perhaps it was the brandy. I said yes. Editing and fact-checking of the article, which became a special issue of *The Nation* for August 18/25, 1984, continued right up to press time. The piece described the substantial U.S. and allied intelligence presence in the area into which Flight 007 flew, some oddities about the flight itself, and discrepancies in the official version of events. It pointed out that Flight 007's persistence on its perilous course in an area watched by what is supposed to be an ever-vigilant U.S. and allied intelligence presence suggested one of two things—either an unprecedented, mind-boggling breakdown in the military early-warning and command and control systems or an intentional flight into Russia. The article concluded with a series of questions and called for a congressional investigation. Primarily because of its timing, the first anniversary of the downing, the *Nation* article became one of the principal points of reference in the case, both for those investigating the downing and their critics.

By now, the fourth anniversary of the tragedy, the world of KAL Flight 007 has become populated with a large number of experts, semi-experts, reporters, academics, government officials, bereaved family members, and a host of other highly interested parties. With few exceptions, these have divided themselves into two opposing camps: On the one side is the official position of the Reagan administration and its supporters who maintain that Flight 007's divergence from course was the result of an accidental error in navigation. They further claim that the U.S. did not know the plane was in danger until after it was shot down and that no blame of any sort adheres to the government in connection with the tragedy. On the other side are writers and independent investigators who hold that a substantial body of evidence suggests the flight over Soviet territory was intentional and that the United States bears some measure of responsibility for it.

Given such highly polarized perspectives, it is not unexpected that advocates, indeed crusaders, have arisen on both sides of the issue. Many of those supporting the official government position view themselves as defending the United States against dangerous or unwarranted criticism from Communists or conspiracy theorists. Investigative reporter Seymour Hersh, Thomas Maertens of the State Department, James Oberg, an employee of the major defense contractor McDonnell Douglas (which coproduces helicopters with Korean Air Lines), and Australian journalist Murray Sayle are perhaps preeminent on this side of the explanatory fence. All have published on the case, some of them providing elaborate theories for how Flight 007 could have accidentally come to be over the Soviet Union's Sakhalin Island to be shot down. To a man they say that the story of Flight 007 has already been told and that no further explanations from the Administration are due.

On the other side, those challenging the government's position have been equally kinetic. Viewing themselves as engaged in an endeavor of immense seriousness, trying to expose an egregious abuse of power by an increasingly unaccountable Executive that resulted in the deaths of hundreds of innocent people, they feel that a full, public exposition of the facts is essential so that further abuses can be avoided and our government brought back into accord with the precepts of the Constitution. Academic authors such as Oliver Clubb, Sugwon Kang, and R. W. Johnson, former State Department official John Keppel, a number of bereaved family members of those who died on board Flight 007, and others fall into this category. Many of these individuals have published analyses directly challenging the consistency and facticity of the official version of the downing. Some have gone a step further, providing detailed accounts of how an intentionally off-course commercial airliner could serve a purpose useful to U.S. intelligence. The persuasiveness and internal consistency of the arguments and the evidence presented by both sides are central concerns of this book.

Like other works that preceded it, *KAL 007: The Cover-Up* does not arrive at a definitive, fully elaborated picture of the downing of Flight 007 and its aftermath. Unlike many, it does not pretend to do so. Even after four years, some of the key evidence in the case remains contradictory, some no longer exists, and much continues to be shrouded in the "night and cloud" of official government secrecy, as Thorstein Veblen once engagingly put it.[4] Here, the impediments to understanding are a central concern of the analysis, whereas elsewhere they have been ignored or distorted as the facts were squeezed into preconceived versions of reality.

More of necessity than of choice, given the limitations imposed upon those investigating the case, mine has been an inquiry from the outside looking in. This book is not, then, so presumptuous as to suggest it tells the complete story of "what really happened" to Flight 007. Rather, what it does provide is the most comprehensive analysis of the evidence in the case to date, based on the most complete survey of the public record. It also introduces new and potentially important evidence, arrived at through both interviews and technical analyses. It examines the compatibility of the evidence with existing theories of the flight. It provides texture and nuances of understanding, stemming from the author's familiarity with many of the principal investigators in the case. It is skeptical and critical throughout.

This is not to say that I have avoided drawing conclusions from my review, nor would that be good practice. All too often in dealing with national security issues the notion of objectivity has been interpreted—misinterpreted, I feel—to mean that conclusions cannot follow from a presentation of the facts, even when the conclusions are obvious and implicit. All too often the idea of political neutrality has also come to mean that a study must not draw conclusions, since conclusions themselves can never be politically neutral.[5] What this has meant in the present case is that serious efforts to arrive at conclusions on the basis of the best available evidence have been dismissed, on both sides, as "polemics," "disinformation," "scrapbook scholarship," and "conspiracy theories." This is regrettable. It is the responsibility of an author, and certainly a scholar, to follow the facts where they lead, so where the facts appear to demand a particular conclusion, it has been presented for the reader's consideration. As the reader examines the evidence, he can decide for himself whether it has been fairly presented and whether the conclusions drawn from it are warranted.

It is appropriate, therefore, to acknowledge that I have arrived at two conclusions from my study of the KAL case. These reflect my own training, how I became involved in the case, and my evaluation and reevaluation of the evidence over the course of several years. The first of these is that what happened on the night of August 31, 1983, was not a random event—not just another "normal accident" in a highly complex system. Not only is the number of coincidences, errors, acts of incompetence, and so on that an accidental model of the flight has to incorporate unacceptably high, but it would also be necessary to accept that all of these problems occurred in redundant, independent components of that system. It is precisely this characteristic of redundancy—where buffers, slack, and alternative methods for detecting the plane off course existed—that leads the system analyst to question any accidental explanation. When we consider all the navigational equipment on board the airliner itself, the external air traffic control aids to navigation, and the fact of surveillance by a host of U.S., Japanese, and Soviet intelligence assets, the redundancies appear to have been more than sufficient for detecting the plane and guiding it safely back on course, even if one, two, or more of these failed simultaneously. That is, the system of which Flight 007 was a part was one where accidents are unlikely.[6] The second conclusion has to do with a clear pattern of obfuscation in how the case was, and continues to be, presented to the public, making it impossible for any investigator to get at the complete truth. A wealth of carefully documented examples supporting these conclusions is found throughout the book.

But if not an accident, why was Flight 007 off course? Was the airliner on an intelligence mission? If so, what was its purpose? Frankly, I have no definitive answer to these questions. No fully detailed, coherent theory has yet been advanced for what intelligence purpose the Korean airliner could have served, although many possibilities have been suggested, nor do I know precisely what the subsequent pattern of obfuscation was intended to obscure. But if the conclusions of intentional deviation followed by obfuscation can be supported, and I believe they can, this suggests that much remains to be explained before the tragedy of KAL Flight 007 is consigned to the history books. Thus, in the final analysis, *KAL 007: The Cover-Up* is a detective story in which the reader is invited to walk the labyrinthine trail of the evidence. If that evidence is sufficiently compelling, perhaps the Congress of the United States will decide to walk that trail as well.

New Haven, Connecticut

PROLOGUE

The area of the Far East overflown by Korean Air Lines Flight 007 on the night of August 31/September 1, 1983, is one of the most militarily sensitive in the world. In recent years, the Soviets have dramatically expanded their military forces in the Far East, causing both great interest and consternation in Western military circles. A 1983 Japan Defense Agency White Paper said that the Soviet Far Eastern Command had assigned to it a total of forty divisions—330,000 soldiers—plus 2,100 reconnaissance planes, fighters and bombers. At least seventy of the bombers were supersonic, long-range Tupolev "Backfires." Vital military facilities dot the region, including Soviet Pacific Fleet headquarters at Vladivostok and the major submarine base at Petropavlovsk on the Kamchatka Peninsula. The Soviets have constructed new military facilities on their islands and mainland, and many existing facilities have been expanded. There were at least 108 intermediate-range SS-20 nuclear missiles in the Soviet Far East in 1983, a number that Japan Defense Agency chief Kasuo Tanikawa, citing as evidence three launching bases under construction in Siberia, said he had reason to believe would soon be increased substantially. (In fact, by the summer of 1986 reports suggested that the Soviets had deployed as many as 165 SS-20s, each carrying up to three independently targetable nuclear warheads.)[1]

Soviet naval forces in the Far East have been expanded dramatically, indicating a shift from an essentially coastal defense force to a true "blue water navy" that now includes aircraft carriers, guided missile cruisers, and several new classes of attack and strategic missile submarines. According to Robert J. Hanks, a retired rear admiral and former director of strategic plans for the U.S. Navy, the Pacific Fleet, with its 830 vessels, is now the largest of the four Soviet fleets.[2] It operates 135 submarines, a number that includes a score of nuclear-powered ballistic missile submarines. Some of these are new Soviet Typhoons. With twin nuclear power plants driving their engines and life-support systems, the giant 25,000-ton Typhoons are 50 percent heavier than the largest U.S. submarine. Loaded on board in clips of two are twenty new-generation SS-N-20 submarine-launched ballistic missiles (SLBMs), their eighty nuclear warheads capable of striking targets in the United States.[3]

Geography does not work to Soviet advantage in the Far East. In order for the naval forces in the Sea of Okhotsk, those at Sovetskaya Gavan or Vladivostok on the Siberian mainland, or those at smaller facilities such as Korsakov on Sakhalin Island to carry out military operations, they have to pass through one of a series of so-called chokepoints, the most important of which is La Perouse Strait separating Sakhalin from the northern Japanese island of Hokkaido. In the event of war, the chokepoints would become the focus of American ships and planes attempting to block the deployment of the Soviet fleet into the northwestern Pacific. Consequently, the area is of great strategic importance to the Soviet Union.[4]

Like the Russians, the United States has placed increasing emphasis on the Far East in its strategic doctrine. Should the superpowers become embroiled in a conflict, even a non-nuclear one, the U.S. Navy has standing plans to attack Soviet ballistic missile submarines in the Sea of Okhotsk. The rationale behind this strategy is to use conventional weapons to quickly destroy a number of Soviet nuclear weapons, thus tipping the nuclear balance in favor of the United States without resorting to a nuclear strike. Just to make certain the Russians get the message, at the same time U.S. aircraft carriers and other surface vessels carrying nuclear weapons would be deployed around the periphery of the Soviet Union, off the coast from strategic places like Petropavlovsk on the Kamchatka Peninsula and Vladivostok on the Siberian mainland.[5] It is believed that such a show of force would compel the Soviets to end the conflict, without "going nuclear," on terms favorable to the United States.

Northeast Asia is also an especially attractive target in the Reagan administration's doctrine of "horizontal escalation." According to Defense Secretary Caspar W. Weinberger, should a Soviet attack take place in an area of Western vulnerability, such as the Middle East oilfields, the U.S. and its allies may "have to launch counteroffensives elsewhere to restore the peace." The most likely "elsewhere" is precisely the area overflown by Flight 007. As former Pentagon official and intelligence analyst William

Kennedy suggested, "That is the only place on earth where geography would permit the U.S. to marshal superior forces at points crucial to Soviet interests and objectives while making it difficult for the Soviets to respond in kind."[6]

The United States has been far from subtle in making its intentions in the area known. The year before the downing, Operation North Pacific Flexible Operations 1982 (NorPac Flexops '82, in military argot) brought two U.S. carrier battle groups to the waters off Kamchatka to practice an invasion. Moscow was obviously concerned; Backfire bombers were sent to shadow the fleet, and an intelligence satellite was deployed to keep an overhead watch on the maneuvers. In April 1983, another and even larger exercise by the name of Operation Fleetex '83 was held. As Michael Klare wrote, "No less than three U.S. carrier battle groups [were] deployed to the North Pacific, along with 300 combat aircraft and 23,000 sailors and soldiers." Commander-in-Chief of the U.S. forces in the Pacific Adm. Robert Long described it as "the largest fleet exercise conducted by the Pacific fleet since World War II. . . . It was a visible demonstration of the refocusing of the United States on the Pacific, particularly on the northern Pacific and Northeast Asia." It was also, as former CIA Director Adm. Stansfield Turner remarked, "part of an overall policy of showing the flag more, of being more visible, more willing to go into areas that are sometimes disputed." The exercises were intended to demonstrate to the Russians that the United States exercises control of the high seas.[7]

The geopolitical contest between the superpowers has produced a burgeoning American military and intelligence presence worldwide. Since the end of World War II, the United States has girdled the Soviet Union with literally thousands of its intelligence "assets" whose purpose is to eavesdrop on the Russians around-the-clock, 365 days a year. Located beneath the oceans, on the water's surface, on land, in the air, and in space, there are few areas on earth of greater interest to these assets, and few where they are more heavily concentrated, than the Soviet Far Eastern Command.

In the ocean depths, the hundreds of underwater microphones of the Navy's Sound Surveillance System (SOSUS) ceaselessly listen for the sounds of Soviet submarines and surface vessels. One array of these hydrophones, called Bronco, is strung from the southern tip of the Japanese island of Hokkaido northward along a line parallel to the Soviet Kuril Islands and Kamchatka Peninsula, and then along the Aleutian Islands to the northeast. A major purpose of this array is to detect Soviet submarines leaving or returning to their base at Petropavlovsk on Kamchatka. Other SOSUS arrays stretch from Japan southward toward the Philippines. Linked by fiber-optic cables buried beneath the ocean floor, the banks of hydrophones feed data to five computer centers operated by the Naval Security Group. The computer centers, including one on Adak Island in the Aleutians, are linked together by communications satellites to the master station on the island of Guam. With this setup, not only can the location of a ship or submarine thousands of miles away be determined to within a few miles but, as William Burrows noted, "the sounds that have been relayed by satellite are sorted out almost instantly by powerful computers such as the Illiac-4 and are then compared with other [prerecorded acoustic] 'symphonies' in the data bank." In this way the identity of every submarine and surface ship passing over the SOSUS line can be established, and in the process "its mission profile, capability, operational characteristics, and probable direction are determined."[8]

SOSUS is not the only underwater way the U.S. collects information about the Russians. American submarines with sensitive sensors lining their hulls listen in on communications and intercept other types of electronic signals as they play an unending game of hide-and-seek with Soviet vessels while patrolling the waters near the Soviet coast. Two nuclear submarines code-named Watchdog and Tomcat prowl the floor of the Sea of Okhotsk between Kamchatka and Sakhalin Island listening to Soviet military communications and monitoring the passage of submarines and surface vessels. On the water, specially equipped intelligence ships patrol off the Soviet coast collecting information.[9]

In Alaska, numerous listening posts and monitoring facilities dot the state's mainland and islands. Elmendorf Air Force Base in Anchorage is home to the 6981st Electronic Security Squadron, which operates huge installations with sophisticated electronic equipment for monitoring Soviet communications and other electronic transmissions. At Fairbanks is Eielson Air Force Base, home of the 6985th Electronic Security Squadron. Shemya Island in the Aleutians is home to several important radar facilities, their electronic eyes directed toward Kamchatka. At Clear, a pair of large radars make up part of America's Ballistic Missile Early Warning System (BMEWS).[10] Other intelligence facilities operated by the Army's Intelligence and Security Command (INSCOM), the Naval Security Group, Air Force Special Security (AFSS) squadrons, and the National Security Agency are at Adak, Amchitka, Annette Island, Attu Island, Fort Wainwright, Gambell, Kenai, King Salmon, Kodiak, North-East Cape, and at Point Barrow above the Arctic Circle. Dozens of smaller facilities and remote stations are located throughout the state.[11]

Farther to the south, many of America's most important intelligence assets are located in Japan, their white radomes sprouting on the landscape like giant surrealist mushrooms. There, a vast and complex system of sensitive electronic monitoring equipment, satellite relays, human operators, translators, and high-speed decoders monitor the Soviet Union "twenty-four hours a day, every day," as one Pentagon officer remarked. The most important of these are located at Wakkanai, on the tip of the northernmost island of Hokkaido, and at Misawa Air Base on the main island of Honshu, the largest listening post in the Far East. In addition, U.S. personnel operate radars, monitor communications, and perform cryptographic, cryptanalytic, and electronic warfare functions at Camp Fuchinobe, a heavily guarded 592-acre site about a dozen miles west of Tokyo, in Tokyo itself, and at Atsugi, Fuchu, Hakata, Johnson Air Base, Kamiseya, Kyoto, Kyushu, Moriyama, Sakata, Shiroi, Yokota Air Base, and elsewhere. Completing the electronic ring around the Russians, the United States operates intelligence facilities in Australia, the People's Republic of China, Okinawa, the Philippines, South Korea, and a host of other locations.[12]

Some of the most important monitoring takes place from the air. Reconnaissance flights near Soviet territory are conducted by planes called RC-135s, flying from their bases at Eielson AFB near Fairbanks, Alaska, Shemya Island in the Aleutians, Misawa Air Base in Japan, and Kadena Air Base on Okinawa. RC-135s are the workhorses of aerial reconnaissance, jammed with electrical equipment for intercepting radar and telemetry transmissions, and for eavesdropping on Soviet communications. Other reconnaissance planes known as P-3C Orions fly patrols out of Alaska, Japan, Okinawa, and other locations, their primary mission being surveillance of both Soviet surface and submersible vessels.[13] Finally, there are the thoroughbreds of aerial reconnaissance, the SR-71 "Blackbirds." Used primarily for photoreconnaissance, the SR-71 is the world's fastest aircraft, with a top speed of Mach 4—four times the speed of sound—and a maximum altitude in excess of 100,000 feet. Flying near the Soviet borders, the U.S. airborne reconnaissance fleet provides important coverage of target areas.[14]

Finally, there is another type of intelligence asset keeping watch on the Russians in the Far East, indeed the dominant type—the satellites. First, there are geosynchronous satellites such as Rhyolite, which has been described as a "multi-purpose covert electronic surveillance system." With orbital speeds that match the rotation of the earth so they remain stationary over its surface at an altitude of about 22,300 miles, each Rhyolite, as James Bamford wrote, carries

> a battery of antennas capable of sucking foreign microwave signals from out of space like a vacuum cleaner picking up specks of dust from a carpet: American intelligence agents could monitor Communist microwave radio and long-distance telephone traffic. . . . According to a former CIA official who was initially involved in the project, it is capable of "sucking up" a vast amount of both Soviet and Chinese military communications.

Geosynchronous satellites perform other tasks, such as relaying photos from lower-altitude satellites back to the continental U.S. and serving as a communications link between military forces and distant command centers. Data from the satellites are beamed down to top-secret ground stations, then electrically flashed to CIA headquarters at Langley, Virginia,

NSA headquarters at Fort Meade, Maryland, and elsewhere for processing.[15]

Flying in lower orbits are intelligence satellites called ferrets. Far smaller and lighter than the geosynchronous and photoreconnaissance varieties, these 125-pound octagonal satellites are normally launched "piggyback" on other, larger satellites. Ferrets are placed in circular orbits between 300 and 400 miles high. They circle the globe once every 90 to 100 minutes, collecting radar, radio, and other types of electronic transmissions. One of the major target areas for these satellites is the Soviet Far East. When the ferrets pass over ground facilities, such as the U.S. station at Pine Gap, Australia, the data they have collected are transmitted to earth in brief, highly compressed bursts.[16]

It was in the context of this multi-billion-dollar military buildup and aggressive thirty-year American effort to develop technical intelligence in the Far East that the Korean Airliner overflew the Kamchatka Peninsula and Sakhalin Island. The background of military tensions would prove fatal to the passengers and crew of Flight 007, for in this desolate corner of the world, the Cold War sometimes rages white hot.

PART ONE
The Flight

1

TAKEOFF

Korean Air Lines Flight 007 began routinely as one of more than 125 international flights that departed from John F. Kennedy International Airport in New York on a normal late-summer day.[1] KAL operates five passenger flights a week between New York and Seoul, South Korea, and by 10:00 P.M. on the evening of August 30, passengers had already begun crowding Gate 15 in the American Airlines terminal.[2] After a 19-minute delay, the Boeing 747 200-B jumbo airliner lifted off from Kennedy Airport's runway 31L and flew through the rain and clouds into the clear night sky above. The plane was en route to Seoul via Anchorage, Alaska, where it had a scheduled refueling stopover. The time was 12:24 A.M. It was a new day—August 31, 1983.

As on most flights, the passengers were a diverse bunch, traveling for diverse reasons. One passenger had won a vacation ticket in a golf tournament. Another, Columbia University researcher Dr. Jong Jin Lim, was flying to Korea with his brother to attend his mother's funeral. Yet another was on his way to lecture on advanced topics in research chemistry. A twenty-year-old Korean was returning home after a summer course at Yale University. On board was Dr. Michael Truppin, then-Congresswoman Geraldine A. Ferraro's physician of twenty-three years. The eighteen-year-old daughter of Kwon Jung-dal, a member of the South Korean parliament, was also a passenger. Another was listed simply as "King Kong." Still another passenger was U.S. Congressman Lawrence Patton Mc-Donald of Georgia, on his way to attend the anniversary celebration of the mutual defense treaty between the United States and the Republic of Korea.[3]

Captain Taek Yong-choi and his crew took the huge airliner and its 244 passengers over the northern United States, crossing the Great Lakes into central Canada. Before long, the ragged peaks of the Rockies and then the Coast Mountains passed invisibly below as Flight 007 flew to the north and west. For the passengers, it was seven hours and 3,400 miles of the usual airline routine of drinks, food, a movie, and boredom. After the movie, "Man, Woman, and Child," most passengers tried to sleep. It was late and there was little to see; the blinds were drawn and beyond was only darkness. The cockpit crew found the first leg of the trip equally uneventful; the weather was good and the ride was smooth, with all systems operating normally.[4] The plane's three inertial navigation systems (INS), those space-age devices designed to pilot a plane with extreme accuracy across great distances, worked without problem, as did the other navigational equipment.[5]

Flight 007 landed on runway 32 at Anchorage International Airport at 2:30 A.M., local time, and taxied to Gate 2N. Seven minutes later, the passengers were allowed to disembark, stretch their legs, and perhaps make a few purchases from the duty-free shops. Most did so, although some remained on board asleep, and four lucky passengers disembarked in Anchorage.[6] During the scheduled 50-minute layover, additional food, fuel, and drinks were brought on board by the contractor Servair Inc. The bottles, trays, and other refuse from the first portion of the flight were removed, and the plane was cleaned. Routine aircraft maintenance was performed by Servair under the supervision of a KAL maintenance engineer.[7]

Apparently none of this woke Congressman McDonald, who was asleep in his aisle seat in the first-class cabin. He was KAL Flight 007's most famous passenger—a forty-eight-year-old urologist, U.S. congressman, father of five, and chairman of the ultra-right John Birch Society.[8] One of the most reactionary members of the House of Representatives, McDonald was a Democrat in name only. He had voted against Justice Department enforcement of fair housing laws and for limiting food stamp funding. On Capitol Hill there was nobody more anti-Communist, anti-abortion, anti-homosexual, anti-gun control, or anti-big government (except where the military was concerned) than Larry McDonald. Yet, as the *Los Angeles Times* observed, McDonald was "long on rhetoric but short on effectiveness in his 8½ year congressional career."[9] His brand of reactionary conservatism assured ineffectual performance in the House.

Flight 007's most famous passenger wasn't supposed to be on the airliner at all. According to McDonald's press aide Tommy Toles, the congressman had been scheduled on an earlier flight to Seoul. McDonald's flight from Atlanta to New York had been rerouted to Baltimore because of bad weather over Kennedy Airport, causing him to miss his intended flight to Seoul by three or four minutes. McDonald then decided to stay in New York for two days and take Flight 007 early on August 31.[10]

Chance played a role in the presence or absence of other well-known travelers on Flight 007. ABC reporter Geraldo Rivera had been booked on the airliner, but a schedule change forced him to take a different flight. Representative Carroll Hubbard, Jr., of Kentucky had also been scheduled on Flight 007 but instead booked a flight through Nashville to Los Angeles. Republican Senator Steven Symms of Idaho, traveling with his wife Frances, had also considered taking Flight 007 to Seoul but had decided on the Los Angeles flight.[11] In Los Angeles, Hubbard and Symms rendezvoused with Republican Senator Jesse Helms of North Carolina. The three men boarded Korean Air Lines Flight 015 bound for Seoul via Anchorage. Like their friend Larry McDonald, the senators were flying to Seoul at the invitation of President Chun Do-hwan to attend a conference sponsored by the Asiatic Research Center, an organization affiliated with both the Korean government and Rev. Sun Myung Moon's Unification Church.[12] Although the formal reason for the trip was to celebrate the thirtieth anniversary of the U.S.–Korea mutual defense treaty, its real purpose was to strengthen military ties between South Korea and Japan, under the guidance of the United States. Former President Richard M. Nixon had also been invited to the conference but declined for reasons of health.

Twenty minutes after the arrival of Flight 007, KAL Flight 015 touched down at Anchorage International Airport. Its passengers, like those of Flight 007, were disgorged into the echoing, neon-lit hallways. Helms, Symms, and Hubbard looked for Larry McDonald but were told that he was asleep on board Flight 007. As Hubbard later observed, "If Larry had gotten off the plane, he would perhaps have suggested that we continue the journey in his plane because it was leaving sooner than ours, and we could have decided in favor of doing so."[13]

A new flight crew took over Flight 007 in Anchorage. The new pilot-in-command of Flight 007 was Chun Byung-in, a forty-five-year-old former colonel in the Korean Air Force. Chun had served for ten years in the military before joining Korean Air Lines in 1972. Part of his hitch was spent in Okinawa, and he reportedly had numerous American friends and colleagues. At KAL he moved rapidly through the ranks, receiving promotions to pilot-in-command of 707s in 1979 and to pilot-in-command of 747s in 1981. He had 10,627 hours of flying experience, 6,619 of those on 747 aircraft.[14] Chun was married, with a nine-year-old son and a daughter aged five.

Chun was a good pilot, one of the best. During his years with the Korean Air Force, he had served as a flight formation leader and had taken part in military air shows as a member of the aerobatics precision flying team.

Twice he had received Air Force citations for his aviation skills. Chun had on three occasions been selected as the backup pilot for ROK President Chun Do-hwan's state visits abroad and was scheduled to pilot President Chun on a six-nation tour in October 1983. KAL officials described him as a "model pilot," pointing out that in 1982 he had received a citation from the airline for his accident-free record. On instrument and proficiency checks in 1983, Chun received the overall rating "excellent." During an evaluation only a month and a half before he took command of Flight 007, it was noted that "he follows the regulations and specifications and has a good knowledge of INS operational procedures." [15]

His reputation among his colleagues was "strong-willed and bold." The holder of a black belt in the Korean national sport Tae Kwon Do, Chun demanded respect and obedience from subordinates in the cockpit. He was also described as zealous in his attention to detail. "He was the most careful man I've ever known," said Ahn Sang-jeon, who flew with Chun on the Korean Air Force precision flying team. According to his wife, Chun was so meticulous in his private life that if a picture on the wall was out of place by so much as the width of a nail, he would rehang it. [16]

Chun was no stranger to the route he was to fly, called Romeo-20. Romeo-20 is one of five parallel, 50-mile-wide commercial air routes running between Alaska and the Orient. Collectively, the routes make up what is known as the North Pacific composite route system (NOPAC) where, by international agreement, U.S. air traffic controllers exercise authority over flights on the half of the NOPAC routes closest to Alaska, and Japanese controllers on the portion nearest Japan. Between February 1973 and August 1983, Captain Chun had flown eighty-three times on the various NOPAC routes. Since February 1979, he had flown on route Romeo-20 twenty-seven times. His previous trip on the route had been on August 16, only two weeks earlier. [17]

According to a Chun family spokesman, the pilot said, "good-bye" and "see you soon" to his family when, on August 27, he left his home in an upper-middle-class suburb of Seoul, South Korea, on the trip that would end with Flight 007. Other accounts claim that Chun said a great deal more than that. In a discussion with the author, one of the attorneys representing Kim Ok-hee, Chun's wife, quoted her as saying that before Chun departed Seoul he confided that the "next flight will be particularly dangerous" and he "might not return." A similar claim has been made publicly by flamboyant San Francisco attorney Melvin Belli. And in what may have been a response to such a warning, it has been reported that a day before the tragedy Kim Ok-hee went to a Seoul insurance company and took out a supplementary insurance policy for 30 million won (about $38,000), paying the first premium of 106,740 won ($135). According to the report, Chun's son was named as the beneficiary of the policy. [18]

Flight 007's new first officer was forty-seven-year-old Sohn Dong-hwin. Sohn was a graduate of the Korean Air Force Academy and a Korean Air

Force veteran who served for nineteen years and attained the rank of lieutenant colonel. Only a week before Flight 007 he had passed KAL instrument, proficiency, and route checks. Sohn's total flight experience was 8,917 hours, of which 3,441 had been on board 747 aircraft.[19] He was married, with a son and twin daughters.

The third member of the cockpit crew was thirty-two-year-old flight engineer Kim Eui-dong, a graduate of the Korean Civil Aviation College. Kim had served in the Korean Marine Aviation Corps for four years before joining KAL in 1977. His total experience as a flight engineer was 4,013 hours, of which 2,614 had been on 747 aircraft. Kim had passed his annual flight engineer proficiency check about two months before the flight.[20]

In addition to the three members of the cockpit crew, an additional twenty-six Korean Air Lines employees were also on board Flight 007. Six of these were off-duty "deadheading" flight crew members returning to Seoul in the first-class compartment as passengers, including three captains and a first officer. That leaves a crew of twenty. For an airline like KAL with a reputation as a bargain-basement way to travel to the Far East, twenty cabin attendants seems excessive—more, in fact, than the normal complement of attendants on more expensive flights on Japan Air Lines. Press reports have identified thirteen of these as stewardesses, two as KAL sky marshals, and one as the plane's purser. The function of the remaining four crew members is not known.[21]

Chun, Sohn, and Kim had left Seoul on August 27, flying the NOPAC routes to Anchorage. After a rest stop of about 22 hours, they flew on to New York, where they rested another 31 hours. In New York, Chun took command of a nonscheduled Korean Air Lines cargo plane flying back to Anchorage via Toronto. The three crew members rested in Anchorage for 11 hours 43 minutes at the KAL hostel on the outskirts of town, slightly more than the minimum required by the KAL Operations Manual. One hour and twenty minutes before Flight 007's scheduled departure, they were taken by bus to Anchorage International Airport, where they proceeded directly to the KAL operation room for the mandatory preflight briefing.[22]

The crew had a lot of ground to cover. They received information from the KAL dispatcher about their departure time, route, assigned altitude, the weather they would encounter, alternate landing sites in case of emergency, and numerous other items. They also received a NOTAM (notice to airmen) that the Anchorage VOR beacon, a radio navigational aid normally used by pilots at the outset of their flight, had been withdrawn from service about eleven hours earlier.[23] Captain Chun reviewed and signed for the NOTAM. Each crew member received and reviewed the flight plan for the trip to Seoul. The flight plan is a computer printout containing useful information such as the geographic coordinates for the waypoints along their scheduled route. It had been prepared in Los Angeles earlier that evening and telexed to Anchorage by Continental Computer Services,

Inc., a subsidiary of Continental Airlines, to whom KAL had subcontracted the task. Making certain the coordinates on the flight plan are correct is a major responsibility for flight crews, since these numbers determine the course the aircraft will fly. Captain Chun approved the flight plan and the other documents.[24]

The preflight briefing was also the time when the maintenance status of the airplane was discussed. On the flight from New York to Anchorage, Captain Taek Yong-choi had noted several minor problems. First, one of the three very-high-frequency (VHF) radios was said to be noisy. Next, the warning flag on a cockpit instrument called the Horizontal Situation Indicator (HSI) was broken so that it was constantly in view, although the instrument itself was not affected. Finally, a spring on the cockpit map table was damaged. While the plane was on the ground in Anchorage, these problems were checked by a five-man KAL maintenance team. The broken map table spring was unimportant, and its repair was deferred until arrival in Seoul. The other problems were more important; in fact, were "no go" items unless corrected. "We checked the VHF communication," KAL Anchorage maintenance manager H. Park said. "We did a ground check and found all systems good, and the flight crew checked them and they were all normal." According to airport staff, Captain Chun himself checked the radio and found it to be operational. Park also checked the HSIs. "They were all normal as well," he said. "I checked them myself."[25]

KAL Flight 007 was originally scheduled to leave Anchorage at 3:20 A.M. local time, 50 minutes after it had arrived. From Anchorage, the trip to Seoul was scheduled to take another eight hours and twenty minutes. Yet the takeoff was delayed, reportedly because of favorable head winds on the route to Seoul that would speed up the flight. An official investigation of the tragedy later reported this was because "the routine practice of KAL was to reschedule the Anchorage departure time so that the flight would arrive in Seoul at [6:00 A.M. local time] since not only was that its scheduled arrival time but, in addition, passenger handling and customs services were not available prior to that time."[26] The waiting passengers were informed that Flight 007 was now scheduled to depart from gate 2N at 3:50 A.M. The plane took off 10 minutes later still.

Before takeoff, Captain Chun and his crew were required to go through a highly specific routine. Korean Air Lines procedures called for the first officer to turn on the Boeing 747's three inertial navigation systems. Using the computerized flight plan and a Jeppeson en-route chart for reference, he would then insert the aircraft's present (ramp) position in latitude and longitude into the INS, using a keyboard that looks something like a push-button telephone. As soon as the numbers went in, they appeared on the readout display of the INS. He would then go to the next INS and manually insert the ramp position coordinates, where they would be verified by the captain and the flight engineer. The other waypoints along the route—up to an additional eight sets of coordinates—would be inserted one by one.

Unlike the ramp position, these coordinates could then be "remoted" to the other two electrically linked inertial navigation systems, where they would be verified in the same way. If there was a discrepancy among the three systems, an alert light would come on and remain illuminated. When this task was completed, Korean Air Lines' procedures required the crew to do what is called a track and distance check, instructing the INS computers to run through the flight theoretically, using the figures just inserted. If some of the figures were wrong, the computers would show the plane ending up in the wrong place. These procedures, with their multiple checks, are explicitly designed to detect any errors in inserting the coordinates into the INS. With the information properly inserted, the system "knows" precisely where it is and can navigate the aircraft with a high degree of precision to the waypoints along its assigned route.[27]

The three systems on board a 747 are gyroscope-based and completely self-contained; two actively navigate the plane while the third functions as a "hot spare." Although electrically linked, the three inertial navigation systems on board Flight 007 operated completely independent of one another so that each system provided a backup and check on the other two. Each INS on board can be operated separately by the captain, first officer, or flight engineer to determine the plane's location, distance to the next waypoint, and a variety of other information. The guidance system for the INS is based on the same principle as that for ballistic missiles and in fact was a spinoff of that military research. The system's sensitive gyros can detect every movement of the aircraft in all three dimensions, even those caused by slight changes in wind direction and velocity. Seven times a second the INS computes direction, speed, and the effect of the wind on the plane. This information is then fed to the automatic pilot, which adjusts the throttles and directional controls. Properly programmed, the INS will keep a plane on course.[28] Thus, almost every theory that assumes Flight 007 to have accidentally gone off course begins with some type of "finger trouble" in the cockpit as the coordinates for waypoints on route Romeo-20 were being entered into the INS.

During the stopover in Anchorage, high-grade kerosene jet fuel for the remainder of the trip to Seoul was loaded on board Flight 007, and the total amount was listed on the aircraft's flight release sheet as its "ramp fuel." The ramp fuel is the sum of the fuel the plane needed to fly to its destination, plus enough extra fuel for 40 additional minutes of flying in the event of a landing at an airport other than Seoul, plus an additional 10 percent to cover contingencies such as greater-than-expected headwinds. The amount of fuel listed on the flight release sheet was 253,700 pounds, and Captain Chun signed the sheet.[29]

There was also a sheet called the weight and balance manifest, giving the plane's "total fuel." Here, the fuel total on board Flight 007 was listed as 263,700 pounds—10,000 pounds more than on the flight release sheet, although the figures should have been the same. As R.W. Johnson pointed out in his recent book, *Shootdown: Flight 007 and the American Connec-*

tion, "If Captain Chun had, for some reason, wanted extra fuel, he should have entered it under the 'extra' column on his papers—but this column was left deceptively blank." Discussing this point in an article on the downing, Sugwon Kang remarked, "What arouses suspicion about the reserve fuel on this flight is that there was no apparent justification for it." The weather was fine at Kimpo Airport in Seoul, and headwinds were so favorable that they had occasioned the 40-minute delay in departing Anchorage. As required, Captain Chun signed this sheet, thereby accepting the additional 10,000 pounds of jet fuel beyond that necessary for the scheduled trip to Seoul which had been loaded on Flight 007.[30]

Johnson and Kang view the fuel discrepancy with suspicion, and their reasons are worth noting. Some evidence suggests that the route actually taken by Flight 007 over Soviet territory involved turns and changes in speed and altitude. Such actions mean greater fuel consumption, of course, so if one entertains the idea that Captain Chun deliberately went off course, it is a logical step to conclude that the additional 10,000 pounds of fuel, a relatively minor amount, was loaded on board Flight 007 to compensate for these maneuvers.

Those advancing an accidental explanation of the flight have provided several rather different explanations for the fuel discrepancy. On the one hand, State Department officials have explained it as something quite normal: "Pilots frequently take on extra fuel for transoceanic flights," they said, "referred to as 'grandmother fuel.' " Others have claimed that the fuel discrepancy was just another in the long series of errors by Captain Chun and his crew, this time miscalculating the plane's weight and balance. If true, this represented a truly egregious error, since adding an extra five tons of weight to a fully loaded airliner could have resulted in an aborted takeoff or a disaster. These same writers say that an inquiry by Korean Air Lines concluded that no additional fuel was actually loaded on board, and it was all a mistake.[31]

Johnson also pointed out other anomalies in Chun's behavior. Although Flight 007 was only about two-thirds full, the crew scrubbed an 1,800-pound paying cargo item. In addition, Captain Chun made a number of longhand notations on his computerized flight plan, one of which was "ETP 1501 NM." As Johnson noted:

> ETP stands for Equal Time Point [a point demarking where, in the event of problems, the crew is either to return to the airport of origin or continue on to their destination] . . . an oddity, for there is no such point 1501 nautical miles along Romeo-20. What is striking is that 1501 nautical miles along the route that 007 actually took brings one exactly to the edge of Soviet airspace.

A number of other notations on the flight plan are also curious, such as the figure "250 NM." According to Johnson, "If one retraces the actual flight path of 007 across Kamchatka, one finds that the plane was inside Soviet airspace for approximately 250 nautical miles."[32] In preparing this book, a professional cartographer has confirmed Johnson's distance calculations, although his interpretation is not so easily evaluated and requires additional evidence.

Flight 007 received a "pushback" away from gate 2N at 3:51 A.M. by a small, squat tractor.[33] As the huge airliner rolled down runway 32, Captain Chun pointed its nose skyward and lifted off at 4:00 A.M.—1300 hours Greenwich Mean Time—August 31, 1983.[34] The passengers and crew of Flight 007 had almost exactly five and a half hours more to live.

Anchorage is home to a number of military installations, the most important of which is Elmendorf Air Force Base. In America's effort to keep an ever-vigilant eye on the Soviet Union, Elmendorf is one of our major intelligence centers. The Air Force base is headquarters for the Alaskan Air Command. A string of radars along the Alaskan coast feed information about everything airborne to the Regional Operations Control Center at Elmendorf. The base is home to a National Security Agency communications intelligence relay station and the 6981st Electronic Security Squadron (ESS). In the hills above Anchorage, the 6981st operates a huge antenna field used for eavesdropping on Soviet communications. Other remote antennas operated by the 6981st are located throughout the state, including one on Attu Island, the last island in the Aleutian chain, just a few hundred miles from the Soviet Kamchatka Peninsula. A variety of aircraft, including Airborne Warning and Control System (AWACS) planes, operate out of Elmendorf.

Rising over Knik Arm of the Cook Inlet, the plane gained altitude rapidly, the lights of Anchorage and the huge military installations at Fort Richardson and Elmendorf Air Force Base twinkling ever farther below. A minute after takeoff, air traffic controllers at Anchorage Tower radioed the airliner that it had been picked up on radar. Continuing the ascent, controllers then instructed the crew to turn left onto a heading of 220 degrees and to begin climbing to the assigned altitude of 31,000 feet. About two minutes later, Flight 007 was directed to head directly to Bethel, its first waypoint. "Roger, ah, proceed direct to Bethel, roger," came the reply from the cockpit. At that time, Flight 007 had circled over the blackness of Cook Inlet and was about seven miles west of the out-of-service Anchorage VOR beacon. The order to "proceed direct Bethel" meant that Flight 007's crew was to fly a straight line from their present location to Bethel, passing directly over the functioning VOR navigational beacon there.

In order to do this, Captain Chun engaged the inertial navigation system to guide the plane. There has been some speculation, notably by Australian journalist Murray Sayle, that perhaps he failed to do so, flying instead to Bethel using his magnetic compass. Yet, on closer examination, such speculations do not hold up. As a senior 747 captain pointed out, "The only means available to the crew to . . . proceed to Bethel was the INS. Also, it goes without saying that use of the INS in a case like this is such standard practice as to be virtually universal." [35]

Meanwhile, Korean Air Lines Flight 015, carrying senators Jesse Helms and Steven Symms as well as Representative Carroll Hubbard, was preparing for takeoff in Anchorage. The pilot-in-command of the airliner was veteran Captain Park Young-man. Captain Park, a senior pilot with KAL, had in the past been Chun Byung-in's superior officer in the Korean Air Force. He was also Chun's close personal friend. [36] Just after Flight 007 had taken off from Anchorage, communications between Flight 015 and air traffic controllers began. While Flight 015 was still on the ground, air traffic controllers confirmed information such as its assigned altitude, runway, transponder code, and other necessary items. When Flight 015's crew was informed that it had been assigned an altitude of 31,000 feet, the same as Flight 007, they immediately responded: "We're requesting flight level three three zero [33,000 feet]." This was an unusual request—most airlines accept the assigned level—and twice in the ensuing minutes the controllers noted the change.

Flight 015 took off from Anchorage 14 minutes later than Flight 007. Confirming Flight 015's departure, one controller told another, "Okay, he departed at one three one four, Bethel one four zero nine, three three zero." This meant that the airliner had taken off at 1314 Greenwich Mean Time, was expected to arrive at Bethel 55 minutes later (at 1409 GMT), and was assigned an altitude of 33,000 feet. "Three three zero?" the controller asked, surprised at the unexpected flight level. "Yes," was the reply. Flight 015 was off to an unusual start.

Douglas L. Porter was the controller working on the consolidated R-5/6 radar position at the Air Route Traffic Control Center (ARTCC) in Anchorage that night. He assumed responsibility for Flight 007 after the Tower at Anchorage International Airport cleared the airliner to "proceed direct Bethel." Porter's duties included monitoring all aircraft within the area of coverage of the civilian radar at Kenai, which extended 175 miles west of the city of Anchorage. It was his responsibility to issue a warning if a flight was on a course other than the one assigned. Porter sat in front of a radar screen displaying a video map of the various air routes in the area. During the time Flight 007 was under radar coverage, Porter's screen showed the airliner's location, flight number, altitude, and ground speed. Also displayed on the map were the locations of several navigational aids. [37]

Another of Porter's duties was to record on a flight data strip the "observed position" for all aircraft at a number of known locations, or "fixes." The only fix on Porter's radar that was applicable to Flights 007 and 015 was the nondirectional beacon at Cairn Mountain, and Porter was required to note the airliners' positions as they passed by. Against regulations, however, Porter did not do this for either Korean plane, although he did so for all other aircraft that night. By the time Flight 007 passed from Porter's area of radar coverage, about 28 minutes after takeoff, it was already more than 6 nautical miles (NM) north of its assigned direct course to Bethel.[38] This should have been obvious on his radar screen, but Porter did not issue a warning to Flight 007. "Korean Air zero zero seven, radar service is terminated. Contact Center one two five point two. Good morning," was all he said.[39]

By his own account, Porter did not issue a warning because the deviating track of Flight 007 was "perceived that night by me on the radarscope as being identical" to that of on-course airliners such as Flight 015.[40] Everything appeared "perfectly normal," he said, and there are a number of reasons why an aircraft deviating slightly from its course might not have been given much attention. First, the air lanes are fairly wide in that area and air traffic that night was negligible so that Flight 007's deviation posed no danger to other aircraft. Second, because the airliner had been cleared to fly directly to Bethel, it was not specifically required to be on an air route such as nearby J501. Finally, because the Anchorage VOR navigational beacon was out of service that night, a controller could have assumed that the Korean airliner would correct its course by using the VOR at Bethel when it came within its range.[41] But because Flight 007 did not come within range of the Bethel VOR beacon until it had just left the area of Porter's radar control, he could not tell if the airliner in fact used the Bethel signal to get back on course.

A major feature of aircraft navigation can be summed up by the term "redundancy." Using the language of systems analysis, the idea of redundancy can be addressed by looking at the "coupling" of elements within the system, whether they are loosely or tightly coupled. The processes occurring in loosely coupled systems are less invariant and time-dependent, meaning that delays are possible and there are a greater number of ways to produce the product (in the present case, navigational accuracy) than if the system were tightly coupled. Loosely coupled systems have more slack, meaning that if system components fail, substitutions—backups—can be used, and it is not necessary to shut down the entire system. For avoiding accidents as well as controlling their seriousness, then, whether the system is loosely or tightly coupled is of considerable importance.[42]

Fortunately, long-distance aircraft navigation is loosely coupled. In addition to the three independent inertial navigation systems, there are a variety of ways for a crew to determine the location of the airplane. Perhaps the most mundane of these is the plane's magnetic compass (two are carried on board). But there are far more sophisticated instruments as well. For instance, on board Flight 007 were two weather radars, located in the cockpit near the captain's and first officer's knees. These can be used in what is called "ground-mapping mode" to check the land and water masses below. Pilots flying from Alaska to the Far East routinely use their radars this way because practically all land masses are to be avoided: first the Kamchatka Peninsula, then the Kuril Islands, and then the northern Japanese island of Hokkaido.

The crew members of Flight 007 almost certainly used their weather radars in ground-mapping mode. A former Pan Am pilot with thirty-nine years' flying experience said of this route, "All you have to do is be awake and watch your radar. . . . Weather radar on a 747 like the South Korean plane is so good that the pilot looking at the radar screen can see the island chains just like he is reading a map. He can even make out details of the land masses." As the plane approached Soviet territory, the *New York Times* pointed out, the radar could have "clearly showed the tip of the Kamchatka Peninsula and the Kuril Islands to the right of the jet." Some pilots, think, however, that radar used for this purpose is erratic and far less useful as a navigational aid. But practically all pilots interviewed on this point agree it is inconceivable that Captain Chun and First Officer Sohn, flying a route that passed within 17 miles of Soviet airspace, with a peninsula and a string of islands to keep to their right, would not have used their radar in this fashion.[43]

In addition to the on-board radar, the Boeing 747 carried two horizontal situation indicators, one each for the captain and first officer. Located on the instrument panel directly in front of each crew member, the function of the HSI is to inform them if the plane is deviating to one side of its programmed course. There are still other aids to navigation outside the aircraft. Air traffic controllers have radars that they use to monitor aircraft for portions of their flight. There are old-style nondirectional beacons that serve as navigational checks for pilots, one of which was located at Cairn Mountain, at approximately the location where Flight 007 passed from the area of civil radar coverage. And then there are the modern VOR beacons.

VOR is the acronym for a Very-high-frequency Omnidirectional Range radio navigational beacon. The VOR is a ground-based transmitter which, as one writer described it, "broadcasts pencil-thin beams of radio waves that radiate like the spokes of a wheel and so are called radials." Flight 007 carried two receivers on board to capture the VOR's radio signals.[44] The VOR is an extremely accurate navigational aid. While in range of a VOR signal, pilots "ride a radial" by changing the automatic pilot switch in the cockpit from its normal INS setting to the VOR course setting they want to follow. The aircraft then follows the VOR navigational signal with a high degree of accuracy. This procedure not only allows for very precise navigation while in range of a VOR signal but also gives pilots a valuable cross-check on their inertial navigation system. In other words, the crew members of Flight 007 had a variety of means at their disposal with which to determine their location and course with great precision.

But the Anchorage VOR was not working, having been withdrawn from service for maintenance about twelve hours before Flight 007's departure.

So the first opportunity for the crew of Flight 007 to employ this accurate cross-check was at Bethel, a sleepy little fishing village about 400 miles west of Anchorage on Alaska's west coast, straddling the boundary between forested country and the treeless tundra. Bethel is the first required reporting waypoint on route Romeo-20, Flight 007's scheduled route to the Far East. The Bethel VOR beacon's area of coverage is considerable, extending 135 NM east and 160 NM west of the waypoint. At its assigned speed, Flight 007 had access to the navigational aid for well over half an hour. For Captain Chun and his crew to use the VOR was more than prudent, it was a Korean Air Lines required procedure. Employing it on August 31, 1983, was especially important because the Bethel VOR was the first opportunity for the crew to verify their course at the start of a long over-water flight. As one former 747 pilot remarked, "Bethel is a gateway station. Nobody goes past a gateway without checking the navigation."[45] Had the VOR been used, Flight 007 would have flown directly over Bethel.[46]

Instead, the airliner passed twelve nautical miles to the north.[47] This simply could not have occurred had the airliner been "riding a radial" from the VOR beacon; the deviation should have been in yards, not in miles. In order to have passed twelve miles to the north, Captain Chun and his crew could not have followed required company practice to use the VOR navigational aid. Instead, Flight 007 continued to be navigated by its inertial navigation system, into which the correct coordinates for Bethel had clearly not been inserted. Had they been, the airliner could not have been so far off course so early in its flight.

If some accident or series of errors put Flight 007 off course, practically every instrument in the cockpit would have warned the crew. Located on board the airliner were two DME (Distance Measuring Equipment) receivers.[48] These give the precise distance to a DME signal—at Bethel, part of an ultra-high-frequency system called TACAN, for Tactical Air Navigation. (At Bethel the TACAN is located with the VOR, producing the ponderous acronym VORTAC.) A glance at this instrument would have shown the crew that the airliner was twelve miles off course. It was required Korean Air Lines procedure to use the DME as well as the VOR at Bethel.

In addition, the horizontal situation indicators in the cockpit would be telling the crew that something was amiss. (It was the copilot's instrument with its broken warning flag that was checked at Anchorage and found to be fully operational.) An HSI display contains a needle above which is superimposed a little picture of an airplane. When the plane is on its proper course, the little airplane is centered directly over a vertical needle. If the plane flies to the left or right of the course, the needle swings to the left or right, and the little airplane is no longer lined up. The needles go off the scale when the plane is more than eight miles off course, so they would have been off the scale at Bethel when they should have been centered.[49]

Although the airliner was well off course even at this early stage of the

flight, that is not what its crew reported. Fifty minutes after takeoff, First
Officer Sohn radioed to Anchorage the required position report for Bethel:
"Zero zero seven, Bethel at four niner, Flight Level three one zero, estimate NABIE at one four three zero." Sohn was reporting that the airliner
had passed Bethel on course at 1349 GMT, 49 minutes after takeoff, although in fact it was already well off course. The plane's altitude, or flight
level, was given as 31,000 feet. The estimated time of arrival to the next
waypoint, called NABIE, was 1430 Greenwich Mean Time, 41 minutes
later. Not only was the plane off course, it had also picked up a little
speed. According to its computerized flight plan, Flight 007 should have
arrived at Bethel 53 minutes after leaving Anchorage, rather than 49 minutes.[50]

At the time it reported passing Bethel, Flight 007 had already exceeded
by more than six times the maximum permissible error for its inertial
navigation system, which is a drift of 2 nautical miles per hour. The Federal Aviation Administration reports that actual demonstrated performance of the INS on over 500,000 flights has shown that the average drift
using the INS is, in fact, about one nautical mile per hour.[51]

As Flight 007 headed out over the Bering Sea, the stewardesses in first
class, who had changed from their blue uniforms into a long multicolored
Korean skirt called a chima and a blouse called a chogori, served drinks
and passed out blankets and pillows. Passengers in first class were served
chicken florentine, zucchini au gratin, rice, and cheddar croquettes,
washed down with South Korean champagne with the unlikely name Pol
Pot. Sandwiches and juice were served in tourist class.[52] As the passengers
closed their eyes and tried to sleep, the only sounds were the hum of the
jet engines, the rush of air, and an occasional noise as people moved about
the cabin.

KAL Flight 007 had left the range of civilian radar coverage, but it did
not pass beyond military radar coverage for a much longer time. Back at
the Air Route Traffic Control Center in Anchorage, air traffic controller
Douglas Porter had transferred responsibility for Flight 007 to his colleague, Judy Nickell, immediately after informing the airliner that civilian
radar coverage had been terminated. Nickell was covering the consolidated D-2/3 sector, the next area into which Flight 007 passed, and immediately to her right was a fully operational radar screen. This was one of
fourteen radar scopes in the ARTCC that could receive data from seven
different radar antennas. These included not only the civilian radar at
Kenai but also military radars at King Salmon, Cape Romanzof, Tin City,
and Cape Newenham. The output from the military radars, naturally, was
also sent to military stations as well as to civilian controllers at the
ARTCC, which itself is located on the grounds of Elmendorf Air Force
Base in Anchorage.

What, if anything, Nickell saw is unknown. Although the radar screen
was on, she later said she had "no recollection" of which data from what

radar facility were displayed on it as Flight 007 flew its deviating course through her area of responsibility. Several years later in the lawsuit brought by the families of Flight 007's victims, their lawyers noted that while this mystery could readily be cleared up by information held by the U.S. Government, "it is unknown which radar was selected because the government has not produced that information which is solely within its control." [53]

The military radar at King Salmon covered an area including Flight 007's first required reporting waypoint at Bethel. It was the King Salmon radar that registered Flight 007 12 NM north of course about 50 minutes after takeoff. This deviation was unusual, and it seems unlikely that controllers such as Judy Nickell could have missed it. The explanation later offered by the Federal Aviation Administration was that . . . the radar was not certified for civilian air traffic control use, and the information from it was not presented to the controllers. But while it is true the King Salmon radar was not certified for civilian use, the controllers at the ARTCC frequently used it for controller functions, including "input of data information, handoff of data blocks, determining radar coverage at various altitudes, and as an aid in reducing communications for obtaining information to establish and maintain non-radar separation" of aircraft. [54]

Soon after Flight 007 reported itself at Bethel, Nickell received a position report from KAL Flight 015: "Passing Bethel at one four zero one. . . . " Using Greenwich Mean Time, Flight 015 was reporting passing Bethel 47 minutes after takeoff. Like Flight 007, KAL Flight 015 had flown the first leg of its journey at an accelerated speed. Normally this would have caused some worry among controllers since speeds are assigned so that adequate separation between aircraft can be maintained. (It is required that two planes on the same route at the same altitude be separated by a time gap of 20 minutes.) For both flights, 007 and 015, the assigned speed was the same: Mach .84, or 84 percent of the speed of sound. Yet less than an hour after takeoff, Flight 015 had, as far as the controllers knew, narrowed the gap between itself and Flight 007 by two minutes, or in distance terms about 16 to 18 miles. Had KAL Flight 015 not taken the unusual step of asking permission to ascend to 33,000 feet, this closing of the spacing between the two planes would probably have warranted comment from air traffic controllers. But because the two planes were at different altitudes, separation was less important.

Immediately after flights 007 and 015 reported passing Bethel, Judy Nickell transferred control of the planes to another controller, Kevin DeGarmo. DeGarmo was responsible that night for aircraft in the area of space adjoining that of Nickell's to the west, a sector known as D-10/11. Although he did not have a radar screen at his position, DeGarmo was sitting to the right of Nickell, with the radar screen between them. Occasionally, he covered for Nickell by working her D-2/3 sector. When he did, he would look at the radar screen to determine the position of the aircraft to which he was talking.[55] DeGarmo had received a flight progress strip for Flight 007 and knew that the airliner was supposed to arrive at its next waypoint on Romeo-20, NABIE, at 1430 Greenwich Mean Time.

Romeo-20, the route Flight 007 was supposed to follow, passes over the Bering Sea, crosses the Aleutian Islands, and enters the North Pacific. The route then parallels the Soviet-controlled Kuril Islands to Japan, where the NOPAC system ends. When the routes were set up, the sensitivity of the area was a major concern. An agreement with the Soviet Union guaranteed that no Soviet aircraft would enter the NOPAC system, and Federal Aviation Administration navigational charts covering the NOPAC routes plainly show the boundary of Soviet territory with the caution written in bold characters: "Warning: Aircraft Infringing Upon Non Free Flying Territory May Be Fired On Without Warning."[56]

While the warning is strong, it is by no means uncommon along commercial air routes. As one pilot noted, "The same wording can be found numerous times on maps of the Near and Far East or on maps of South America. Over India, for instance, there are prohibited areas right along the air route. Crossing that airspace and disobeying a command to land there would have the same consequences as doing it over the Soviet Union." One of the most heavily traveled air corridors in the world, between Bangkok and Hong Kong, comes closer to China than Romeo-20 does to the Soviet Union.[57]

There are a series of required reporting waypoints spaced along Romeo-20 with peculiar names like NABIE, NEEVA, NIPPI, and NOKKA. At these points the crew is required to inform air traffic controllers of their position, expected time of arrival at the next waypoint, remaining fuel, temperature, and the direction and velocity of the wind the airliner is encountering. In addition, there are a number of nonreporting waypoints along the route, so-called phantom stations that go by names such as NUKKS, NINNO, and NYTIM. At these places the crew is supposed to use the airliner's equipment to check their location, although no formal position report is required. After passing waypoint NOKKA, the last Romeo-20 reporting waypoint, Flight 007's route called for the plane to proceed on Oceanic Transit Route 1 to the east of the northernmost Japanese island of Hokkaido, turning to the west to cross over the main island of Honshu, passing over the Sea of Japan, and on to Seoul. Throughout this time the crew would continue to make position reports at other waypoints, some having strange names like Inkfish. The reason for all the waypoints and checking is to make certain the plane is on course.

But instead of following route Romeo-20, Flight 007 was deviating ever farther to the north, toward Soviet territory. About an hour and a half after takeoff, the crew of the airliner turned their aircraft to the right, directly toward the Kamchatka Peninsula, on a course that would pass over some of the Soviet Union's most sensitive military facilities. This turn was made in the area of coverage of several Air Control and Warning radars operated by the Air Force on the Alaskan coast, new FPS-117 radars installed in 1982, located at Cape Romanzof and Cape Newenham, and possibly another radar at Tin City. According to Air Force regulation 60-1, it is the duty of Air Force personnel to identify all aircraft, both military and civilian, if they are initially detected in or about to enter what is known as the "buffer zone" surrounding Soviet airspace. This area is analogous to the U.S.'s Aerospace Defense Identification Zone (ADIZ), which extends beyond actual U.S. airspace by as much as 200 miles. So this can be done, every military radar whose area of coverage includes the Soviet buffer zone is required to show it on its video map displays.[58] To identify Flight 007 was the Air Force's job on the night of August 31, 1983.

Flight plans for all commercial aircraft flying in the region are provided to the military as a matter of routine, and identification is done by checking the code number from the transponder carried by all commercial aircraft. To understand the transponder it is necessary to understand the difference between "primary" and "secondary" surveillance radar. Primary radar is the type seen in the movies. It sends out a powerful pulse of energy, receives an echo from the surface of remote objects, and displays them as blips on a radar screen. Secondary surveillance radar (SSR) uses a radio transmitter that sends out an "interrogator" signal which is received by a plane's transponder, a civilian adaptation of the military Identification Friend or Foe (IFF) system. When activated, the transponder responds by "squawking" a signal that is picked up and translated by a radar receiver. The transponder enhances a plane's image, provides a four-digit identification code, and gives information on altitude and course.[59] Since the Air Force received the transponder code for Flight 007 beforehand, its personnel had the capability to tell immediately not only that it was civilian but also which civilian plane it was.

For every plane flying in the buffer zone, the Air Force is also supposed to perform "normal surveillance and tracking procedures." This means they watch the plane and its course. If a nonmilitary plane is observed heading toward the buffer zone, Air Force regulations require personnel to contact it on emergency radio frequencies to warn it that it is near potentially hazardous airspace. Military personnel are also required to contact the Federal Aviation Administration, with whom they "work hand in hand," with a similar warning. As Flight 007 headed directly toward the buffer zone, military radar operators should have seen it, both at the individual radar stations and in the Regional Operations Control Center (ROCC) at Elmendorf Air Force Base. "It must have been noticed by the radar operators of the Air Force like a squadron of zeppelins," commented James Bamford, an expert on the super-secret U.S. National Security Agency. "Even with a skeleton staff, if they merely checked the screen every fifteen minutes or so, they should have noticed it."[60]

The Regional Operations Control Center is the nerve center of the Alaskan Air Command. The output from all thirteen Air Control and Warning radar stations strung along the Alaskan coast—collectively known as MARS, for Minimally Attended Radar System—is remoted to the Center. There, according to *National Defense,* the data are fed through state-of-the-art computers to consoles as well as being consolidated by computer and displayed on a large video map. Odis A. Carmon, the duty officer at the ROCC that night, stated, "We had several people that were performing surveillance and tracking duties." The Air Force personnel who watch the display perform a number of tasks, principal among which is to positively identify every aircraft within their area of responsibility. "It's correct to probably say," Carmon remarked, "that if individuals that were monitoring consoles at that time detected an aircraft in that vicinity, heading toward the buffer zone, [they] would advise me of such." "They were supposed to do that?" he was asked. "They should do that." "Whether it was military or civil?" "If it was an aircraft out there," Carmon replied. Carmon said he recalled receiving no such advisement that night. [61]

The time was now 1432 GMT, about an hour and a half after takeoff. Flight 007 had just entered the Soviet buffer zone, heading toward Kamchatka. The airliner's estimated time of arrival at waypoint NABIE had passed about two minutes earlier. During the next two minutes, air traffic controller Kevin DeGarmo tried five times to contact the airliner. Calling the airliner when it was only two minutes overdue at a waypoint was DeGarmo's technique, he said. Normally, a controller would wait until an aircraft was five or more minutes overdue before queries would be made. DeGarmo received no response from Flight 007.

KAL Flight 015 was talking to Flight 007 in Korean as Flight 007 deviated ever further from course:

> [Inaudible]
>
> [Inaudible]
>
> "Please switch it off as you proceed."
>
> "Please [try] it once again."
>
> "Three three zero won't do. Please wait."
>
> "Ours is three three zero." [62]

While it is difficult to determine the full meaning of a conversation by listening to only one side, Flight 015 seems to have been giving instructions to Flight 007: "Switch it off," "Try it again." A source knowledgeable about Air Force intelligence operations interpreted this conversation as suggesting that Captain Park Young-man of Flight 015, friend and colleague of Chun Byung-in, was establishing some sort of communications linkage between his airliner and Flight 007. If so, this would be quite unusual. Flight crews normally use specified "chatter frequencies" to speak with other planes.

Immediately after this exchange had taken place, KAL Flight 015 called the Air Route Traffic Control Center in Anchorage to relay a position report for Flight 007. The frequency assigned to Flight 015 was 127.8 MHz, and calls from airliners on that frequency were remoted to Anchorage from the radio transceiver located on St. Paul Island, one of the Pribilof Islands off Alaska's west coast. On its deviating course, Flight 007 had already passed out of radio range of St. Paul, but Flight 015 was within range and reported that Flight 007 had passed NABIE, the second waypoint, at 1432 GMT and would arrive at the next waypoint, NEEVA, at 1549. The plane's altitude was said to be 31,000 feet. "Korean Air zero one five, roger, ah, have Korean Air zero zero seven report NEEVA to Anchorage one two eight decimal two," Kevin DeGarmo radioed back. The final series of numbers referred to VHF channel 128.2, a frequency remotely controlled from Anchorage, whose transceiver is located on Shemya Island, near the end of the Aleutian chain.[63] The area of radio coverage for the Shemya transmitter was about 175 nautical miles for an aircraft at Flight 007's altitude. But by the time it made its next position report, Flight 007 was well over 200 miles off course.

Almost immediately, Kevin DeGarmo placed a call concerning Flight 007 to the International Flight Service Station, Anchorage Radio. The IFSS is a privately owned enterprise run by a company called Air Inc. "Four five nine," DeGarmo began, using the call numbers for the IFSS, "Center channel eleven reference, ah, Korean Air zero zero seven reports." The IFSS responded immediately, "Go ahead." But something or someone seems to have intervened at precisely this moment, and DeGarmo did not continue with his report about Flight 007. "Ah, you can cancel it," he said. Cancel what? What report was he about to make? Asked about this later, DeGarmo claimed he could not recall anything about the night in question.

The high-frequency (HF) radio channels covered by the IFSS offer one way for pilots to communicate with air traffic controllers. For aircraft on Romeo-20 and parallel routes, there is another, better way—very-high-frequency radio (VHF). A series of VHF transmitters and receivers (transceivers) are located on the Alaskan mainland and on the islands off the coast, allowing VHF radio communications at waypoints Bethel, NABIE, and NEEVA. Very high frequency is far and away the preferred means for pilots to communicate with air traffic controllers, and vice versa. Transmissions on VHF frequencies are much clearer than HF transmissions and have far less static and interference. More important, however, when using VHF, a pilot talks directly with the controllers.

HF transmissions, on the other hand, pass through a relay station—the IFSS—before they get to controllers, as do HF messages going from controllers to aircraft. Because many minutes can pass between a pilot's request and the delivery of a response, pilots don't use HF unless they have to. And an on-course airliner at this stage of its trip on Romeo-20 would have no need to use HF because it would have been within range of the VHF transceiver on St. Paul Island.

At 1443:08 GMT, Flight 015 gave its own position report for waypoint NABIE, which it said it had passed just moments earlier. Flight 015, unlike Flight 007, was communicating directly with controllers at the ARTCC (Anchorage Center) by VHF radio. The time that was reported as separating Flights 007 and 015 was continuing to shrink: from 14 minutes at take-off, to 12 minutes at Bethel, now down to 11 minutes.

At 1443:58 GMT, twelve minutes after Flight 007 reportedly had passed waypoint NABIE and nine minutes after Flight 015 had relayed Flight 007's position report to that effect, Flight 007 itself placed a call to the IFSS in Anchorage using its high-frequency radio. Although Flight 015 had just relayed a full position report for it, Flight 007 proceeded to give its own report, including a request for a higher altitude, 33,000 feet. The estimated time of arrival at the next waypoint, NEEVA, was also revised: "Estimating NEEVA one five five three." This new ETA was four minutes later than the estimate Flight 015 had forwarded for its companion. Flight 007 was now reporting going much more slowly than expected to its next waypoint.

Some commentators have suggested that Flight 007's deviation from course went undetected by its crew, meaning, among other things, that three experienced airmen failed to look at their instruments for hours on end. Most of these arguments fail precisely because of Flight 007's revised ETA. There is no way that a revised estimated time of arrival can be obtained except with the distance/time readouts that the INS can provide with the turn of a dial.[64] A revised ETA is proof that the crew members of Flight 007 were looking at the information displayed on their navigational instruments. How could they have missed that they were off course?

The revised ETA surprised the controller at the IFSS. "Korean Air zero zero seven, Anchorage, understand NABIE one four three two. . . . NEEVA one five five three, is that correct?" There were two reasons for the controller's surprise. The first was that Flight 007 was reporting needing an hour and 21 minutes to fly a leg of its route that normally should have taken an hour and 17 minutes. At the speed flown by a 747, this amounts to a distance of about 32 to 36 miles. "Affirmative," responded Flight 007, "Korean Air zero zero seven. That's affirmative."

The second reason for surprise was that Flight 007 was communicating by HF rather than VHF radio, and the controller at the IFSS was not going to authorize the airliner to ascend to the new altitude. "Uh, contact Anchorage Center now one two seven decimal eight, and make your request with them" was the IFSS's response. Like the earlier instruction given indirectly to Flight 007 by Kevin DeGarmo, this was a command to the jetliner to contact the Air Route Traffic Control "in person" via the VHF transceiver on Shemya Island. But Flight 007 was too far off course to "contact Anchorage Center now. . . ." Instead, Flight 007 would have to wait for Flight 015 to relay another position report for it.

Other anomalies mark this portion of the flight. Korean Air Lines crews are supposed to verify the position of the aircraft at NABIE by using what is called the NDB/DME (nondirectional beacon/distance measuring equipment) navigational aid located on nearby St. Paul.[65] But Flight 007 was so far north of its course that the navigational aid never came within range. Had Flight 007 been unwittingly straying, its crew should have been concerned about missing the beacon at St. Paul. But Flight 007 made no comment about this to air traffic controllers.

At about this time, says S. S. Yang, the pilot of another Korean Air Lines plane heading in the opposite direction on one of the North Pacific routes tried to establish radio contact with Flight 007 to share weather information. "His radio was very garbled," Yang said. "I tried to relay, but he couldn't hear me. I tried to call him several times."[66] Flight 007 was simply too far away.

As Flight 007 drew ever nearer to Soviet territory, it also approached the flight path of a U.S. Air Force RC-135 reconnaissance aircraft flying a series of long, lazy loops off the coast of the Kamchatka Peninsula, listening in on the activities of the Soviet air defenses. According to the Russians, their radar systems first detected the RC-135 at 1345 GMT, three quarters of an hour after Flight 007 departed Anchorage. It was south of Karaginskiy Island and north of the Commander Islands off the east coast of Kamchatka, they said, flying at an altitude of 8,000 meters (about 26,250 feet).[67]

The RC-135 is a modified Boeing 707, a version called a 717. An extremely sophisticated and capable aircraft, the RC-135 is powered by four turbofan engines and outfitted for aerial refueling, permitting it to remain aloft for missions of 18 to 20 hours, requiring only a single midair refueling. The planes normally carry a flight crew provided by the Air Force's Strategic Air Command (SAC) as well as a large staff of technicians and translators. RC-135s operate as "electronic security squadrons" under the direction of SAC and are based throughout the Pacific, including Alaska and Japan. While the aircraft is flown by the SAC crew, the intelligence equipment is manned by up to thirty Air Force Security Service personnel. All of those on board an RC-135 are under the operational authority of the National Security Agency.[68]

There are two general types of RC-135s, the first of which is called Rivet Joint. These planes are for normal surveillance missions and carry an impressive array of sophisticated sensors. On board are cameras and electronic equipment for surveillance and reconnaissance, including a high-resolution side-looking radar (SLAR) for all-weather reconnaissance and terrain-mapping. Among other things, the SLAR information is used to create maps that, stored in digital form in computer memory, could help bombers and cruise missiles navigate to their targets. Recent technical developments include real-time transmission of high-resolution television and SLAR imagery to ground stations, optical and infrared sensors for high-resolution images day or night, and automatic pattern recognition for detecting changes in the radar imagery between successive flyovers. These developments make it possible to monitor Soviet border areas from these airborne intelligence platforms under any environmental conditions.[69]

Rivet Joint planes fly what are called "peripheral missions," providing continuous coverage of target areas in a way that satellites cannot. The missions consist of collecting and analyzing the electronic signals, known as electronic intelligence (ELINT), within range of the aircraft. The United States wants to know where Soviet radar stations and antiaircraft missile bases are located and how the Soviets will react if their air defenses are penetrated. We want to know the power, pulse rates, and frequencies of the radars, the procedures used in operating them, and the ranges at which aircraft flying at different altitudes come under surveillance. When a plane is detected, we want to know who talks to whom. This information—what is known as the enemy's "electronic order of battle"—hopefully will also enable our bombers and missiles to evade Soviet air defenses on the way to their targets. "You don't want to shadowbox," said Gen. Russell E. Dougherty, a former Strategic Air Commander.[70]

While in the air, some of the gear on the RC-135s picks up radio signals from Soviet ground stations and aircraft, tipping the U.S. to any Soviet alert in the area. Other receivers and antennas are tuned to pick up radio transmissions between air defense installations and interceptor aircraft. The on-board technicians, called "ravens," watch the radar waves on their green oscilloscopes and monitor the radio transmissions as they take place. Some of the electronic information is recorded for later analysis on reels of 1-inch magnetic tape. But as the journal *IEEE Spectrum* pointed out, "In high-priority areas such as the Pacific Northwest, and particularly during intelligence-gathering missions, data can be acted upon almost immediately."[71]

The second type of RC-135, called Cobra Ball, is loaded with even more specialized electronic equipment, including electronic monitoring gear to intercept and record radio telemetry—data on the functioning of missiles and space vehicles relayed back to the test site.[72] For both superpowers, telemetry collection is critical in assessing military capabilities and verification of compliance with the provisions of arms control treaties.

Both to confound the Soviets and for self-protection, both classes of RC-135s carry electronic warfare equipment capable of "jamming" and "spoofing" enemy radars. Operated by SAC officers, the equipment can counter threats by surface-to-air missiles by jamming the signals of enemy air defense radars. It can pick up incoming radar signals and send them back amplified to make a small aircraft appear larger, create false radar images at incorrect distances and speeds, and multiply a signal into ghost images, the technique known as "spoofing." It has been reported that confusing radar signals can then be used to get the Soviets to scramble their fighters, permitting the crew of the reconnaissance plane to calculate how long it takes to respond to an attack. Once the interceptors were sent aloft, their air-to-air fire control radars would be in for the same treatment. As one observer put it, "No fighter can stand up to a good electronic-intelligence plane." [73]

Two former RC-135 crew members pointed out that the aircraft also has a super-advanced, ultra-secure communications system that ties into the most sophisticated communications network in the world. Operated by the National Security Agency, this system is called the Critical Intelligence Communications System (CRITICOM). Referred to as "backchannel," the system permits the instantaneous reporting of intelligence information to the highest levels of the U.S. Government from any location. Information from intelligence collectors around the globe is beamed on an "uplink" to a satellite in geosynchronous orbit 22,300 miles above the equator, then beamed back down to a set of giant dish antennas hidden in the woods behind NSA headquarters at Fort Meade, Maryland. From the Far East, information first makes its way to the NSA center at Pine Gap, in the desolate Australian outback. (And, by one account, that is just what happened: Australia's *Sydney Sun* reported that the Pine Gap station was able to make "detailed transcripts" of the conversations of the Soviet air defenses as they were alerted by the intrusion of Flight 007.) High-priority messages are given the designation "Critic," and NSA's goal is to have them on the President's desk within ten minutes. Testimony before the House Committee on Armed Services stated that messages designated for special Critic handling have been transmitted on the average within four to six minutes. [74] If there were some reason for him to do so, the President could speak directly with the crew of the RC-135.

RC-135s fly at altitudes from several thousand feet to over 35,000 feet. The higher the altitude, the greater the range of their electronic intelligence-gathering equipment. At an altitude of 35,000 feet the aircraft have excellent reception at a distance of 150 miles. As the *New York Times* noted, "That means, for example, that a plane flying at that altitude 150 miles over the Pacific off the coast of the Kamchatka Peninsula could monitor air-defense systems on the ground." Under some circumstances, RC-135s can monitor radio or microwave communications at distances ranging from 500 to 1,000 miles. [75]

But the Soviets won't always cooperate with the RC-135s by turning on all their equipment so that it can be monitored, so they have to be tricked into it. In his book about the National Security Agency, *The Puzzle Palace*, James Bamford notes that for many years the NSA has been "ferreting" the Soviet borders with aircraft jam-packed with the latest in electronic and communications eavesdropping gear. The aircraft fly close to the Russian border, picking up the electronic emissions of air defense radar, ground communications, and microwave signals. But Bamford noted that the Russians won't turn on many of their more important radars or use emergency communications nets except under emergency conditions. For this reason, he said, pilots occasionally engage in the dangerous game of "fox and hounds." They fly directly toward the border, setting off the radar, pulling away only at the very last second. Once in a while pilots would actually penetrate unauthorized airspace, both intentionally and unintentionally. This was confirmed by former NSA analyst Perry Fell-wock, who called overflights of Soviet territory "routine," and by former RC-135 crew members Tom Bernard and Ed Eskelson, who flew reconnaissance missions in the Far East out of Kadena Air Base on Okinawa. "It has been our experience," Bernard and Eskelson wrote, "that, on occasion, NSA adjusts the orbits of RC-135s so that they will intentionally penetrate the airspace of a target nation. This is ordered for the purpose of bringing a target country's air defense systems into alert. This allows NSA to analyze these fully activated systems for potential flaws and weaknesses." [76]

Such tactics might be especially important if the Soviets had recently altered their air defense procedures. A former Air Force intelligence officer who served in South Korea said that in such an instance "you would need some sort of aircraft to penetrate the air space significantly deeply" to fully activate the newly reorganized system so it could be examined. [77] And just a few months before the intrusion by the Korean airliner, the Soviets had reorganized their air defenses in the Far East.

Judging by both Soviet and U.S. claims, these manufactured "emergencies" occur with some frequency. The Soviet news agency Tass reported that "instances of deliberate violation of the state frontiers of the Soviet Union by American planes, including in the Far East, are far from rare" and that "protests were made to the U.S. Government over such border violations on more than one occasion." The United States makes similar charges against the Russians. According to military sources cited in the *Washington Post,* about 100 times each year Soviet aircraft, primarily the Tupolev TU-95 "Bears"—a bomber converted into a reconnaissance plane—intrude into U.S.-guarded territory, forcing U.S. fighters to scramble. In 1982 alone, Air Force planes were said to have scrambled 269 times. [78]

At times, this secret war of surveillance involves the use of civilian aircraft. Defense Department sources told the *Boston Globe* that RC-135s occasionally ride "piggyback" on the tail of commercial airliners passing near the Soviet Union to get an idea of what radar frequencies the Russians use to track civil aircraft. According to Lufthansa pilot Rudolf Braunberg, "Pilots who have flown international routes for more than two decades often notice U.S. military planes using civilian air routes and behaving like civilian planes. . . . On the North Pacific route one can detect the radio signals of similar planes." RC-135s also reportedly have the capability to mimic both civilian and military identification (transponder) codes. Spy planes "bristling with electronic apparatus . . . cling to passenger planes in flight, trying on the one hand to avoid discovery by ground radar and on the other to catch radio signals unhindered, to locate the position of radars, to establish the frequencies they work on, and to gather other data of an intelligence nature."[79] The Soviets say that RC-135s and other reconnaissance aircraft "constantly use civilian airliners of various companies of the world for 'covering up' reconnaissance flights near the territory of the USSR," and incidents involving the planes of the U.S. and its allies suggest there is some merit to the Soviet charge.[80]

There has been some controversy regarding whether the RC-135 operating off the Kamchatka Peninsula that night was of the Rivet Joint or the Cobra Ball type, but the question in fact is moot: Because of the equipment it carried, either type of RC-135 had the capability to determine the location, course, and identity of Flight 007, which had by now deviated from route Romeo-20 by about 200 miles. To keep out of danger as their aircraft is skirting Soviet airspace, the crew of an RC-135 closely monitors the Russians with an airborne electronic surveillance system that automatically acquires and identifies electromagnetic emissions over the known frequency band from surveillance and tracking radars, both ground-based and airborne. Warnings of possible danger are communicated both visually and aurally on a display unit. If the instruments detect the scrambling of interceptors or the firing of surface-to-air missiles, they transmit an alert code to the commander of the RC-135. As one knowledgeable source put it, "Not only do they know when a MiG has been scrambled, but they can also tell you exactly what the pilot's orders are and probably even what his name is." And military officers quoted in the *New York Times* said the Air Force plane would also have routinely "painted"—registered with radar—the Korean airliner as a matter of aerial safety, which would have divulged the civilian plane's location and course. James Bamford made a similar assessment: "On board the RC-135 . . . it would have been almost unthinkable for the intercept operators and radar specialists not to have tracked the bizarre flight path of the Korean airliner as it penetrated Soviet airspace or to have heard the Soviet air defenses go into various stages of alert or to have witnessed on radar the Soviet interceptors scramble skyward."[81]

Had the identity of the jetliner not been known, the crew of the RC-135 could have ascertained it simply by asking the ground stations with which, according to Air Force sources cited in the *Washington Post,* they maintain constant contact. Discovering that the plane was civilian, the crew of the RC-135 could have taken steps to notify civilian air traffic controllers in the United States or Japan, or they could have communicated directly with the Korean airliner itself since they had the capability of transmitting messages over an extremely broad range of radio frequencies, including those used by civilian and military aircraft, ships, ground stations, and air traffic controllers. Such warnings were frequently transmitted by crew members aboard RC-135s to U.S. pilots operating over North Vietnam. Irrespective of the plane's type and mission, then, it was standard procedure for the crew of the RC-135 to know precisely what other planes were near them off the northeast coast of the Kamchatka Peninsula. But the RC-135 transmitted no warning, and as Flight 007 flew directly toward the eastern coast of Kamchatka, the presence of the Air Force reconnaissance plane helped set off the sequence of events that led to the Korean airliner's destruction.[82]

2

OFF COURSE

According to a Soviet account in *Izvestia,* the watch officer on Kamchatka on the night of August 31 was Oleg Pakhomov. Pakhomov and his team had been watching the RC-135 on their radar screens for some time when, at 1551 GMT, radar operator Sergey Omipov sounded the alarm: "Target spotted!" The object of interest was a second plane "with a radar blip analogous to that of the RC-135 . . . in the same region and at the same height." By now, Flight 007 was about 500 miles northeast of the city of Petropavlovsk and on a heading north of Bering and Medny islands in the Bering Sea, together known as the Commander Islands. According to the Soviets, the altitude of both planes was 8,000 meters, or about 26,250 feet. At that time, Flight 007 was supposed to be operating at an altitude of 31,000 feet. As Pakhomov and his radar operators watched their radar screens, the blip that was the RC-135 turned in one of its lazy ovals and began converging with the second, unidentified blip. The blip that was Flight 007 was said to have twice altered heading during this period of time. At 1600 GMT, the two blips reportedly came so close that they merged together on Soviet radar screens, flying "on parallel headings maintaining communication."[1] The Soviets had some cause for concern: At that time the converging radar blips appeared to be heading directly toward the Petropavlovsk-Kamchatski Naval Base on Kamchatka.

Pakhomov and his comrades were members of the Soviet air defense command, called PVO, for the Russian *protivovozdushnaya oborona*, which translates to "anti-air defense." The nerve center of the system is PVO headquarters at Kalinin, about 100 miles northwest of Moscow, to which the PVO's various regional command centers report. As Andrew Cockburn noted in his book *The Threat: Inside the Soviet Military Machine*, "The whole air defense system comprises a network of 5,000 radar installations, 10,000 antiaircraft missile launchers, and 2,500 interceptor fighter planes." There are also some 12,000 antiaircraft guns to counter low-altitude threats. By some estimates, Flight 007 would have come within range of as many as fifty to sixty of these radar stations along the Pacific coast of the Soviet Union. Some of these are located on the mainland, while others are on islands including the Commander Islands in the Bering Sea.[2]

According to the position reports received by U.S. air traffic controllers, Flight 007 had really been losing time. Back when Flight 015 had relayed Flight 007's position report for waypoint NABIE, Flight 007's estimated time of arrival at the next waypoint, NEEVA, was said to be 1549 GMT. Twelve minutes after the relayed report, Flight 007 itself radioed in to revise that ETA to 1553, four minutes later. It was now seven minutes after that, and Flight 007 had still not reported its arrival at the waypoint. By all appearances something out of the ordinary was taking place on the NABIE-NEEVA leg of Flight 007's journey.

At 1600:39, precisely at the time the Soviets said they saw the blips of Flight 007 and the RC-135 coming together on their radar screens, KAL Flight 015 radioed Flight 007's waypoint NEEVA position report to Anchorage controllers:

> [Unintelligible]. Fortunately caught delayed report zero zero seven. Their position at NEEVA one five five eight, flight level three one zero, estimating NIPPI one seven zero eight . . . go ahead.

There are two oddities here; the first concerns the crew of Flight 015. It is unclear why they would have considered it "fortunate" to hear Flight 007's delayed position report since they later claimed to have been talking more or less continuously to their colleagues via the chatter frequency. In addition, Flight 007's position report contained weather information—temperature, wind direction, and velocity—that was substantially different from what Flight 015 was itself experiencing. This should have warranted comment from both crews and the air traffic controllers, but no mention of the discrepancy was made.

The second oddity concerns the air traffic controllers in Anchorage. As far as Kevin DeGarmo was concerned, Flight 007's tardiness in arriving at the waypoint should have been striking. The airliner was reported having arrived at NEEVA 5 minutes later than its revised ETA and 9 minutes beyond the time originally estimated. What could have caused such a dramatic slowdown of this leg of the flight to Seoul? If it were stronger than expected headwinds, wouldn't air traffic controllers have expected a similar slowdown for Flight 015, supposedly flying at the same speed on the same route? But when Flight 015 came in with its own position report for NEEVA, it beat its ETA by two minutes. Thus, the reported gap between the two airliners had now been narrowed to only four minutes, even though the planes should have maintained their original spacing of fourteen minutes.

DeGarmo did not remark on these oddities to either Korean airliner, but his remarks to controller Judy Nickell suggest that he found something unusual. At 1603:11 GMT, the following conversation took place in the Air Route Traffic Control Center:

DEGARMO: Look at this airplane. He goes from NABIE to NIPPI in ***.

NICKELL: That's pretty good.

DEGARMO: Yeah, I don't know who did that, but . . .

When an airliner passes waypoint NEEVA, it is required to report its position to air traffic controllers. Normally this is done "in person," via the VHF transceiver located on Shemya Island at the end of the Aleutian chain. But Flight 007 could not use the VHF transceiver because it was out of range. In addition, the crew of Flight 007 was required by Korean Air Lines procedures to use the VOR/DME navigational aid on Shemya to verify their position at NEEVA. It is exceedingly important to do so because immediately after passing the waypoint, Romeo-20 comes quite close to Soviet territory. As with the Bethel VOR and the St. Paul NDB/DME, the Shemya radio navigational beacon would immediately have told innocently errant crew members that they were off course. The Shemya VOR has an area of coverage extending about 175 nautical miles in all directions, and it was fully operative on the night in question.[3] But no reports from Flight 007 suggested that anything was wrong.

By the Soviets' account, the flight paths of Flight 007 and the RC-135 appeared "certainly coordinated" and "confused" their air defense forces. Since modern Soviet radar should be able to discern between two individual planes to within a quarter mile of each other, there are three possible explanations for this confusion. The first is simply that the Soviets were lying, but events would later demonstrate that their claim of confusion was genuine. The second explanation could be that, as the Soviets claimed, the two aircraft were physically very close to each other. The third explanation could be that the two planes, although farther apart, were lined up in such a way that their images merged. As the *Far Eastern Economic Review* pointed out, "Rough-and-ready maths show that the stated heights and range of probable cruising speeds make such transit of both aircraft with a ground-based radar possible."[4] Could this have been deliberate? Sometimes, according to former CIA agent Ralph McGehee, the Strategic Air Command sends multiple planes simultaneously into a target area, making it difficult for the Soviets to separate the blips—a tactic called "ghosting." Determining which plane is which after two targets have merged on a radar screen is, according to a naval radar expert, "a classic problem in radar tracking."[5]

According to one U.S. intelligence source, shortly after the blips merged on Soviet radar screens, the RC-135 went into a steep dive toward the sea, descending below the line of sight of Soviet radar coverage. It then popped up again some distance away. The sudden appearance of an aircraft apparently from nowhere was an additional factor in confusing the Soviet air defenses. The Soviet Defense Ministry newspaper, *Krasnaya Zvezda* (Red Star), made a similar claim. "The military call it a feint," *Krasnaya Zvezda* said.[6]

A source close to Air Force intelligence, whose experience led him to conclude that Flight 007's deviation was planned, suggested that "the dancers were to change leotards in mid-leap"—that is, the two planes deliberately confused their identities. "The RC-135 had to convince the Soviets it was not going home," the source said, "but was instead inbound in a common probe maneuver. When the RC-135 disappeared . . . it was solely out of sight long enough to emerge in a different area on a different heading." Flight 007, flying directly "down the throats" of the Soviet radar operators, was now considered to be the RC-135, and they expected that it would not actually enter their territory but would pull away at the last minute. "I can just see the [Soviet] duty officer looking over his operator's shoulder and agreeing that *must* be the RC-135," the source said.

The Soviets later described this "dance" with the RC-135 as one of many reconnaissance activities going on that night. The Soviets claimed that there were other RC-135s, P-3 Orion reconnaissance planes, and three naval vessels in the Sea of Okhotsk along Kamchatka's west coast and in the Karaginskiy Gulf off Kamchatka's northeast coast, a claim that has been partially verified. The U.S. later admitted that "there was a P-3 airborne from 31 August 1540 GMT to 2115 GMT operating over international waters north of 40 degrees north."[7] Western sources have also said that even as the RC-135 turned back toward Shemya Island, it was replaced by another RC-135 out of Misawa Air Base on the Japanese island of Honshu. This aircraft was said to have operated in the Pacific Ocean off the Kuril Islands.[8]

Flight 007 should have been identifiable to Soviet personnel by way of its transponder; when queried it provides the plane's four-digit identification number plus course and altitude information. Had Flight 007 been using its transponder at this stage of the flight, it would have been identified immediately as a commercial airliner. Not only that but the crew of Flight

007 woud have been aware somebody was using secondary surveillance radar to query their transponder. Whenever an interrogation signal is received, a blue radar sensing indicator light illuminates on the transponder panel, located behind the throttles in the cockpit. This light would have flashed repeatedly as the airliner approached Soviet territory and the Soviets sent out querying signals. The fact that the Soviets confused the RC-135 and Flight 007 suggests either that the Korean airliner had turned off its transponder or that the RC-135 had been intentionally using the same code as Flight 007.[9]

Imagine the scene at Soviet defense headquarters on Kamchatka. Two aircraft, one known to be a U.S. spy plane and the other of unknown identity, appear off the coast. Within minutes their radar blips appear to merge. One of the aircraft then drops below radar coverage, only to pop up a few minutes later in a different location. All the while the Soviets are hearing reports claiming that Flight 007 was out on Romeo-20. The result was that the Soviets had very little reason to believe the aircraft coming at them was a civilian airliner. They thought they were dealing with two reconnaissance aircraft, and they responded by moving their air defenses into a state of emergency.

The unfolding drama of Flight 007's "dance" with the RC-135 and the scrambling of the Soviet interceptors must have been noted with the greatest of interest by the U.S. intelligence facility on Shemya, a two-by-four-mile island near the end of the Aleutian chain. There is a variety of intelligence equipment located on the island, operated by approximately 570 military and 400 civilian personnel.[10]

Among the equipment on the barren, treeless island is the giant Cobra Dane phased-array radar. Sitting at an altitude of 270 feet, the radar is 95 feet in diameter and contains 15,360 active radiating elements. Cobra Dane has been described as so powerful that it can spot a baseball at a range of 2,300 miles. Its maximum range is on the order of 28,000 miles, giving it the capability to track satellites in their highest orbits in deep space. It can monitor simultaneously more than 100 objects. As Jeffrey Richelson observed, "The radar can search for unknown objects across 120 degrees of azimuth, from horizon to zenith, while simultaneously tracking several already acquired targets. In a typical twenty-four-hour period, it makes 10,000 observations." As with all radars, the function of Cobra Dane is to detect the position, motion, and nature of remote objects, the process known as tracking. Data on targets being tracked are transmitted back to the continental United States via satellite in real time, that is, as they are actually taking place. The data go to the Space Defense Center at the North American Aerospace Defense Command (NORAD), to the Air Force's Foreign Technology Division at Wright-Patterson Air Force Base in Ohio, and to the Defense Special Missile and Astronautics Center in National Security Agency headquarters at Fort Meade, Maryland.[11]

Cobra Dane operates in two modes: surveillance and tracking. In surveillance mode, the radar scans from the horizon to 80 degrees elevation over a horizontal area of 120 degrees of arc. In its tracking mode, Cobra Dane's area of coverage is less, only 44 degrees of arc, but highly detailed information about target objects can be assessed, such as the characteristics of Soviet reentry vehicles during a missile test. Cobra Dane's primary missions are to track Soviet reentry vehicles during missile testing, to track foreign satellites, and to serve as a component of the U.S.'s Ballistic Missile Early Warning System (BMEWS). Normally, the radar operates in its search mode to monitor the general radar environment. Tracking mode would be used during a missile test or other particularly interesting event.[12]

Could Cobra Dane have detected the deviating Flight 007 as it neared Soviet territory? Some have claimed that Cobra Dane's controlling computers are programmed to reject slow-moving objects such as aircraft, so as not to interfere with its primary function of watching fast-moving satellites and reentry vehicles. Such statements appear both true and false. Radar could in fact be programmed in such a manner, but that does not mean that slow-moving objects are not detected. As one expert put it, "The fact is, the 'raw return' from the radar sensor can be provided to several computer processors which work in parallel, some looking for missiles, some for aircraft; indeed, there could be a number of 'special interests' and processing technologies. One doesn't throw anything away!" A military expert out of government, when questioned directly about Cobra Dane's ability to detect aircraft, responded elliptically: "If you can see the fleas on the dog, one assumes you can see the dog as well." Did Cobra Dane detect Flight 007? According to Tom Gervasi, director of the Center for Military Research and Analysis in New York, the answer is yes. The radar's range, he said, "is limited only by the curvature of the earth. An aircraft at 30,000 feet would remain within line of sight of this radar for more than 400 miles. Cobra Dane saw [Flight 007] moving toward Soviet airspace."[13]

Even after the earth's curvature rendered a system like Cobra Dane ineffective, there were a number of other ways by which the Korean airliner could have been monitored by the United States. Gervasi writes that there is an over-the-horizon backscatter radar called Cobra Talon located on Shemya that can detect "anything airborne, at any altitude, between ranges of 575 and 2,070 miles away."[14] Military personnel in Alaska and elsewhere, working round-the-clock "trick shifts," continually monitor the radio, radar, and ground-based communications of Soviet air defenses on and near the Kamchatka Peninsula. The RC-135s provide further coverage.

Additional coverage comes from the sea. Stationed off the east coast of Kamchatka as Flight 007 approached was a sophisticated 563-foot U.S. Navy vessel, the U.S.S. *Observation Island*. On the ship's aft deck is a four-story-high, 250-ton, S-band phased-array radar whose octagonal face is seven meters in diameter and contains 12,288 antenna elements. Controlled by a large Control Data CYBER 175-112 computer, the radar, with the designation AN/SPQ-11, can rotate to keep its face toward an area of interest even as the ship moves beneath it. This ship-borne radar is called Cobra Judy. One of the U.S.'s "national technical means" of verifying Soviet compliance with arms control treaties, the *Observation Island* "prowls the neighborhood of the Soviets' Pacific test range," following warheads all the way to splashdown. In addition to the Cobra Judy radar, the *Observation Island* has on deck two 32-foot diameter radomes, containing microwave antennas capable of picking up missile telemetry and, almost certainly, ground communications.[15] (Given that both the RC-135 and the *Observation Island* were ideally suited as well as ideally located to intercept the numerous Soviet microwave transmissions as Flight 007 entered Soviet territory, some have suggested that the plane's deviation from course was intentional, to provide an opportunity both to record Soviet communications and to collect information on the microwave transmission network itself.[16])

So thorough is U.S. radar and electronic coverage of the Soviet Far East that sources resort to hyperbole in describing it. A former radar technician who had been stationed at the NSA listening post at Chitose on the island of Hokkaido commented, "U.S. radar coverage of the area from Kamchatka to Sakhalin is so complete that a plane's air wake can be detected." A former CIA officer disclosed that both the Soviet Union and the United States track every aircraft in this area. Another military officer remarked, "We know where every seagull is in the Far East." Tom Gervasi summed it all up: "There is no vertical or lateral portion of airspace in this entire area that American radar does not watch."[17]

The cold and humid Kamchatka Peninsula, a 750-mile-long land mass of 104,200 square miles, separates the Bering Sea and the Pacific Ocean to the east from the Sea of Okhotsk to the west. Kamchatka is a land of mountains—including twenty active volcanoes—forests, lakes, geysers, mineral springs, rivers, and valleys. The mountains create severe turbulence in the airspace above the peninsula that the crew of an innocently errant airliner would find both unusual and troubling.

Kamchatka is a sensitive military area for the Russians. There are nuclear weapons stockpiles, petroleum depots, underground ammunition storage facilities, and research, development, and test centers near the peninsula's principal city, Petropavlovsk. A relatively ice-free port with access to the open ocean, Petropavlovsk is a major naval base and is the headquarters of the Soviet Pacific submarine fleet. Ringed by a variety of sophisticated air defenses, the city is the home port for an estimated 130 ships, including more than thirty ballistic missile submarines and ninety attack submarines.[18] As the Soviets' land-based intercontinental ballistic missiles have become increasingly vulnerable to faster, more accurate U.S. missiles, the importance of the submarine fleet in Soviet strategic planning has increased. For this reason the Far Eastern Command has become increasingly important in recent years among the five Soviet theater commands.[19]

All of this hardware requires protection. Large phased-array radars have been constructed on Kamchatka.[20] Air defense forces have been expanded in recent years and include several airfields, radar tracking facilities, and surface-to-air missile batteries. Developmental work on the new SA-X-12 surface-to-air missile, suspected of having an antiballistic missile as well as an air defense capability, is underway on the peninsula. The Soviets have concealed the stage of development and capabilities of the new system by covering the antennas and service modules of the system with tarpaulins and sliding roofs.[21] Intermediate-range SS-20 nuclear missiles are deployed on Kamchatka.

This barren and frozen land is ideal for other military purposes as well.[22] Some missile tests begin on Kamchatka, the reentry vehicles splashing down in the waters of the Soviet Pacific range to the east. And reentry vehicles launched thousands of miles away in the western and cental Soviet Union, signaling their test information by radio telemetry to ground stations, smash into Kamchatka's bleak northern mountains.

The Kamchatka Peninsula is not the place a civilian airliner would wish to fly over without authorization. Soviet planes fly in the area, of course, relying on many of the same types of navigational aids that Western aircraft use. There are a number of navigational beacons on Kamchatka, at Kubaru, Kokutan, and Lopatka, among other locations, whose bearings can be taken by radio compass navigation if an interested pilot were flying nearby.[23] There are also beacons strung along the Kuril Islands. Although they are primarily for marine use, some Western pilots have used them for navigation and found them reliable. However, the price of error in this region can be high. According to Soviet émigré Dimitri K. Simes, the Soviet air defense forces in the Far East have standing orders to force down any unauthorized aircraft that penetrates their airspace.[24]

The Russians reacted slowly to the aircraft coming directly toward their territory. There are several possible explanations for this behavior. The first is that they thought the plane was playing the familiar game of "fox and hounds" and would promptly retreat according to script. A second possibility is simple incompetence or drunkenness. One Soviet official is said to have remarked, "It took us too long to sober up the pilots enough to get them to take off." A third possibility, perhaps in combination with other problems, is equipment failure. Official U.S. sources quoted in the *Los Angeles Times* reportedly said that two of the three long-range radar systems on the Kamchatka Peninsula were out of service that night, severely limiting coverage in precisely the area toward which Flight 007 was headed. Such breakdowns are apparently quite common. One source familiar with Soviet operations in the Kamchatka area during the 1970s said that "it was fairly common knowledge that what radar they had on the coast was often out of service." During the outages or when additional surveillance was considered necessary, he said, the Soviets rotated a pair of rehabilitated "Bear" class bombers in flight patterns designed to "augment their basic ground base [radar] net." Perhaps in confirmation of such a radar breakdown, it was later reported that several Soviet reconnaissance aircraft, "presumably on routine patrol missions, were flying in the area, the electronic eyes of their equipment stretching across the skies." A final possibility for the confusion could be electronic countermeasures —deliberate electronic interference by the RC-135, Flight 007, or someone else.[25]

Former Soviet radar specialist Yitzhak Tarasulo described how the air defense system on Kamchatka should have worked:

> Within the first five minutes, the command post of the Far Eastern Air Defense Army in Khabarovsk should have known about the airspace violation, and the state "Readiness No. 1" declared along the Soviet Pacific coast. . . . Within the next five minutes, the Central Command Post of the Soviet Air Defense Forces should have had the information necessary to bring the General Staff of the Soviet Army into action.[26]

Instead, air defense commanders reacted in confusion. Confusion rapidly turned into a frantic effort to get fighter aircraft off the ground. The first of four MiG-23 and Su-15 interceptors was scrambled at 1637 GMT, a full seven minutes after Flight 007 had physically entered Soviet airspace. Three other fighters were also sent aloft shortly thereafter in an attempt to find the intruder. According to the Soviets, at least one of these went off in the direction of the RC-135.[27]

At 1606, Flight 015 radioed to Anchorage that it had just reached a new altitude, 35,000 feet. Anchorage asked, "Would you ask Korean Air zero zero seven if he would like higher altitude prior to NIPPI?" NIPPI was the next waypoint on Romeo-20. "Ah yes," Flight 015 responded, "zero zero seven requested three three zero." The air traffic controller responded that Flight 007 was now cleared to climb and requested that Flight 015 relay this information to it. Without so much as a second's hesitation, and certainly without enough time to have contacted Flight 007 in the interim, Flight 015 radioed back, "Roger, they are now leaving three one zero for three three zero." The Soviets claim that Flight 007's altitude when it entered their airspace at 1630 GMT was 8,000 meters (about 26,250 feet), an unauthorized altitude for the airliner if the account is true.[28]

From the RC-135, the *Observation Island,* and from the ground-based electronic eavesdropping stations at Elmendorf, Shemya, and elsewhere, the United States was eavesdropping on the Russians as Flight 007 approached and entered their territory, intercepting their voice communications, Morse code, and radar transmissions as soon as they were broadcast. The result was a highly detailed and comprehensive picture of

Soviet inability to locate Flight 007. The sensitive U.S. monitoring equipment detected the sudden increase in air defense activity on Kamchatka, beginning with stepped-up radar surveillance as an unidentified aircraft approached the Soviet Air Defense Identification Zone. Air Force technicians listened as the Russians declared an alert and began charting the progress of the plane. They listened as one Soviet radar operator informed his superiors that he had sighted an "RC-135" and when another reported sighting an "unidentified plane." The eavesdroppers knew that later the Russians referred to the plane as an "intruder." The Americans listened as surface-to-air missile batteries on Kamchatka were put on alert to track the intruder. They knew that the missile batteries were unable to get a solid radar lock on the target. (This was because the path taken by Flight 007, either fortuitously or by design, managed to stay out of range of the SAM batteries.) And the Americans listened and watched as the four Soviet fighters that tried to intercept Flight 007 were plagued with difficulties. U.S. intelligence recorded conversations from the Soviet fighters that showed they never found the intruder over Kamchatka. So detailed was the information that U.S. intelligence knew none of the fighters came closer than 20 miles to the Korean airliner and that "as the airliner crossed the coast leaving Kamchatka . . . the closest fighter was still more than 25 nautical miles behind." [29] Is it possible that U.S. personnel did not understand the meaning of all these things so that a warning could be issued to Flight 007?

Some authors have argued that this was precisely the case. While acknowledging that U.S. intelligence was eavesdropping on the Russians in real time as Flight 007 intruded over Kamchatka, several accounts have suggested that all the activity was misinterpreted as the Russians simply "taking advantage of the quiet of the overnight shift to break in a new radar operator or to work on tracking technique by simulating an American intrusion into their airspace." [30] They claim that what really happened only became clear hours or days later, as the full play of events was slowly reconstructed by U.S. intelligence.

Such accounts are dubious because there was a wealth of information available to the Americans that the air defense flap over Kamchatka was quite real. Indeed, a familiarity with Soviet procedures suggests two reasons why it was virtually impossible for U.S. personnel to have believed that Flight 007's intrusion was simply a Soviet drill or exercise. First, we monitor a number of Soviet stations on Kamchatka, not just one. According to an intelligence source, when the Soviets are conducting an exercise —doing what is called "bogus tracking"—only one station does it, not all the stations. So the question is: What were the other stations doing? If they were all tracking the same thing, then U.S. personnel knew the activity was real, not an exercise. And of course all the Soviet stations were concerned with the same thing: the intruder that was Flight 007.

Second and even more compelling, the Soviets never mix real and bogus

radio traffic. Before the Soviets began tracking Flight 007, they were tracking the RC-135 up near Karaginskiy Island. Watching it go in and out of
the range of their radars, the Air Force plane was obviously very interesting to them. American intelligence personnel were eavesdropping as the
RC-135 was tracked, and they knew the RC-135 was quite real. Then Flight
007 entered the picture and started getting tracked as well. This should
have been conclusive proof that the new target was real since it is against
Soviet procedure to mix live and bogus traffic. So all the pieces are there
when the evidence is examined carefully: From the moment the Soviets
began tracking the Korean plane, U.S. intelligence operators knew they
had a live target and that it wasn't a drill. As an intelligence operator who
in the past had monitored the Soviet air defenses in the Kamchatka area
remarked, "That we thought they were doing an exercise is bullshit."

We also knew the target wasn't a Soviet plane because of how it was
first identified—as an RC-135. As the operator stated, "I remember listening to their bombers and cargo planes getting picked up by their radar
station at Ust'Bol'sherestsk on the west coast of Kamchatka as they came
across the Sea of Okhotsk. What the Soviets would always do is identify
the plane as one of their bombers, or whatever, or they would designate it
'unknown' until they figured out what it was. They didn't give a plane a
call sign until they were sure what they had." And here the Russians had
a plane that was originally designated as an RC-135, *then* unknown. That's
the reverse of what usually happens. Not to mention that the intruder
wasn't anywhere near the normal air routes for Soviet transports,
bombers, or anything else. For U.S. intelligence operators, these facts
should have been sufficient to eliminate the possibility that the target was
Soviet and make it mighty interesting to them. We knew it wasn't one of
theirs and we knew it wasn't an RC-135, so somebody would surely have
been interested in just what else it might be.

The Soviets claimed that during the Kamchatka overflight their radio
monitoring stations picked up periodically transmitted bursts of coded
signals of the type used in transmitting intelligence data originating from
Flight 007.[31] With this, they said, they had no remaining doubt that they
were dealing with an intelligence aircraft. The Soviets also claimed to have
repeatedly called to Flight 007 without success. Calls were almost certainly
attempted by air defense control units on Kamchatka which, like other
such units in the Far East, have equipment capable of transmitting on the
international hailing frequency 121.5 MHz. Col. Gen. Nikolay I. Moskvitelev, commander of aviation for the PVO, also claimed that calls to the
intruder were made by the interceptor pilots: "Our pilots continued to
close in on the intruder aircraft and attempted to communicate with the
crew on the international search and rescue frequency," he said.[32]

Flying in a southwesterly direction, the Korean airliner passed over
Soviet missile-testing areas, over the sites of several large phased-array
radars, and near the Soviet submarine pens at Petropavlovsk. Without

being intercepted, the airliner continued its flight in the direction of the Sea of Okhotsk. According to the Soviet account, Flight 007 exited Soviet territory at 1708 GMT. At that time it was said to be flying at an altitude of 9,000 meters—another unauthorized altitude, if true. Believing the intruder would exit from the Sea of Okhotsk by overflying the Kuril Islands, Russian air defenses prepared additional fighters for takeoff from Paramuschiv Island, one of the northernmost of the Kurils, to cover the exit route.[33]

Confusion in the Soviet air defense system continued as Flight 007 flew over international waters in the Sea of Okhotsk toward the area of Sakhalin Island. American intelligence sources citing top-secret reports on the flight noted afterwards that there was an abysmal lack of coordination between Soviet radar facilities on Kamchatka and those on Sakhalin. According to a high-ranking Japan Defense Agency source quoted in the *Japan Times,* after first confusing Flight 007 with the RC-135, the Kamchatka radar stations then lost track of the airliner and thus failed to "hand over" the intruder to their comrades on Sakhalin. Crucial time was lost before anyone realized it was the same plane. The possible outage of several of the long-range radars might have contributed to this confusion.[34]

At 1708 GMT, Flight 007's estimated time of arrival at waypoint NIPPI and precisely the time it left Soviet airspace, a call was received by both the IFSS, Anchorage Radio, and its equivalent in Japan, Tokyo Radio, from an aircraft identifying itself as Flight 007. Both were called because waypoint NIPPI is on the boundary between the U.S. and Japanese Flight Information Regions (FIR). Anchorage controllers transfer control to their counterparts in Tokyo as an airplane crosses the boundary. Flight 007 reported reaching NIPPI a minute earlier, at 1707, and estimated its time of arrival at the next waypoint, NOKKA, as 1826 GMT.

Flight 007 flew for about an hour and a half in international airspace over the waters of the Sea of Okhotsk. Now someone else was listening to the Russians. Some reports have suggested that the Japanese military had been aware of the heightened state of military alert on Kamchatka from the time Flight 007 was first detected by Soviet radar. Other accounts say that Japanese awareness began about an hour later, at approximately the time Flight 007 made its NIPPI position report.[35] In either case, when the airliner came within range of Japanese air defense radars, exquisite attention would be paid to the blip on the radar screens.

3

SHOOTDOWN

At the time that Flight 007 approached Sakhalin, the most important of the Japanese intelligence facilities were those at Wakkanai and Misawa. The 184-acre facility at Wakkanai, on the tip of the northernmost island of Hokkaido just 40 miles from Sakhalin, was built by the National Security Agency and run by the Army Security Agency under NSA auspices until 1971. It is now operated by the Japan Self Defense Force and the Nibu Besshitsu—the Annex Chamber of the Second Section, Investigative Division, of the Ground Self-Defense Forces—the Japanese equivalent of the NSA. Although officially a Japanese facility, the Air Force's 6920th Electronic Security Group, under NSA auspices, still works with the Japanese at Wakkanai. This facility collects radio signals from Soviet aircraft to ground stations. Other receivers are tuned in to the radio transmissions from the ground stations to the planes. These conversations and other data are flashed via secure communications links to the huge NSA listening post at Misawa Air Base. Satellite systems permit the instantaneous transmission of information to NSA headquarters at Fort Meade.[1]

Misawa is the largest American listening post in the Far East. Operating under NSA direction, Misawa employed about 1,600 Electronic Security Command and Naval Security Group personnel in 1980. Based at Misawa are E3A AWACS planes, F-16 fighters, and P-3C Orion reconnaissance planes. Among other intelligence-gathering hardware, Misawa is home to an AN/FLR-9 circularly disposed antenna array (CDAA)

> designed to locate and intercept signals from the low to high bands. Low-band traffic includes submarine traffic; radio-telephone traffic falls in the high band. . . . The outermost circle in an AN/FLR-9 is the size of about three football fields—875 feet[2]

The CDAA is a highly sensitive omnidirectional system, capable of picking up hundreds of signals simultaneously from all directions. Since a single station can provide only a rough idea of the exact source of the signal, a number of these facilities are electronically linked together, forming what is known as a high-frequency direction-finding net (HFDF, pronounced "huff-duff"). As James Bamford wrote, "The network of HFDF stations simultaneously plots the direction of the same signal. The point at which all lines intersect is the location of the target." A former NSA analyst who was stationed in Turkey and Vietnam explained that "we were able to locate [aircraft] exactly even though they weren't on our radar through RDF—radio direction finding. We did this by instantaneously triangulating reception coming through these gigantic antennas."[3] What these accounts suggest for the night of August 31, 1983, is that every time Flight 007, Flight 015, or any other aircraft used its radio, U.S. intelligence could plot its precise location, even if it was beyond radar range.

As Flight 007 proceeded toward and over Soviet territory, another type of intelligence asset, a ferret satellite, was on duty in the skies overhead. Circling the globe once every 98.6 minutes, its passages over the ground —its ground tracks—moved progressively to the west as the earth rotated beneath it. (Some have claimed that another intelligence satellite was also within range.) Shortly after Flight 007 reported passing waypoint NABIE, its first overwater reporting point, the ferret passed above. At almost precisely the moment the airliner first intruded into Soviet territory over Kamchatka, the ferret again appeared overhead, its area of coverage including the entire peninsula, the Kuril Islands, and the Sea of Okhotsk. And as Flight 007 approached Sakhalin Island, the ferret once again passed within range.[4] Ferret satellites collect radar and radio transmissions—precisely the type of information stimulated by the airliner's intrusion. Just minutes after each overhead pass, the ferret came within range of the satellite ground facility at Pine Gap, Australia, where the information presumably was transmitted to earth.

"I have seen Ceylon, which is paradise," wrote Anton Chekhov in 1890, "and Sakhalin, which is hell." Sakhalin is a narrow, mountainous island separated from the Siberian mainland on the west by the Tatar Strait and from Japan's Hokkaido island to the south by La Perouse Strait. To the north and east lies the Sea of Okhotsk. Covering a total area of about 30,000 square miles, about half the size of Florida, the island varies between 140 to only 16 miles wide at its thinnest. The northern half of the island is gently undulating taiga, or forest, while the southern part, also mostly forested, is cut by two rugged mountain chains. This former Czarist penal colony is cold, bitter, and inhospitable, and most of the island's approximately 600,000 inhabitants live on its southern tip. Until the night of August 31, 1983, its principal claim to American fame was as the birthplace of actor Yul Brynner.[5]

Pentagon officials say that the Soviets maintain a force of about 20,000 troops on Sakhalin, including two motorized rifle divisions (about 16,000 men) equipped with antiaircraft missiles and guns. In addition, there are 1,600 sailors stationed at seven naval bases and related facilities. The largest of these is the major naval base and shipyard at Korsakov, on the southern tip of the island. There are naval patrol craft and important radar and intelligence-gathering installations on the island. The air defense buildup has been particularly intensive on Sakhalin. The Soviets have also deployed more than 2,000 air force personnel and two squadrons (more than 100) jet fighters at Sakhalin's two principal air bases, Smirknykh and Dolinsk-Sokol. At Dolinsk-Sokol on southern Sakhalin are more than thirty Sukhoi-15 interceptors. Farther north, at Smirknykh, are numerous MiG fighters, including more than twenty of the new Mig-27s, all-weather fighters that can attack enemy airfields. In addition, there are maritime patrol planes, reconnaissance planes, and large numbers of attack helicopters. On Sakhalin is a squadron of supersonic Backfire bombers armed with nuclear weapons.[6]

The scene on Sakhalin as Flight 007 approached was probably similar to that described by Soviet defector Lt. Viktor Belenko. In the ready rooms at Dolinsk-Sokol, Smirknykh, and Kotikovo air bases, the duty pilots sat in their pressure suits throughout the night. They were not supposed to sleep or drink, although on occasion they probably did both. Outside in the darkness, 30 feet away, their supersonic MiG-23 and Su-15 fighters stood ready. When an unidentified aircraft was spotted by the air defense radar at Burevestnik on Etorofu Island in the Kurils, information was quickly sent to the headquarters of the Far East command in Khaborovsk, near the Soviet-Chinese border, and then to the National Command Center at Kalinin. As long as the aircraft was in the Soviet ADIZ, extending 100 kilometers beyond actual Soviet territory, its position, course, speed, and altitude were displayed at Kalinin on a huge screen, similar to the one at the Regional Operations Control Center at Elmendorf AFB in Anchorage.[7] If things went according to the book that night, the alarm sounded when Flight 007 entered the ADIZ. The duty pilots dashed out from the ready room and climbed into the tight cockpits of their interceptor fighters. Within minutes, six interceptors were airborne, climbing steeply to the intruding aircraft's altitude. From the moment of takeoff to the time of return to base, all the actions of the interceptors were strictly controlled by their ground stations.

According to the United Nations' guidelines for intercepting aircraft, ground controllers must first attempt to contact an intruding plane by radio. Controllers are supposed to be equipped with secondary surveillance radar that can trigger an airliner's transponder, ensuring immediate recognition. Should interceptor fighters be sent up, they are to approach the target from behind, taking up a position to the left side at the same altitude as the intruder but no closer than 1,000 feet. The pilots are to attempt to contact the intruder by radio on the international emergency frequency of 121.5 MHz. The intruder, in turn, is supposed to identify himself on 121.5 MHz and, if possible, communicate the nature of the flight. If the intercepting and intercepted pilots do not speak a common language, code words in English, the international language of the air, are available. Examples are "willco" for will comply and "am lost." All military and commercial pilots are trained in the use of these signals. If words do not work, however, there are nonverbal signals. At night the interceptor is supposed to rock his wings and flash his navigational lights at irregular intervals. This tells the crew of the intruding plane: "You have been intercepted. Follow me." The intruder is supposed to duplicate the procedure to signal; "Understand. Will comply." The fighter then breaks away in a slow, level turn onto the desired heading. The intruder is supposed to follow immediately. The pilot of the intruding aircraft is then supposed to turn his transponder to Mode A emergency code 7700.[8] But these are guidelines, not rules, and different countries adhere to them to different degrees.

The Soviets follow the guidelines, more or less. The Soviet Airman Information Publication (AIP) says that a number of the international signals are to be used by Soviet pilots. According to a Soviet military specialist familiar with their interception procedures, "Interceptors have instructions to identify themselves and make visual contact. If the intruder 'refuses to cooperate,' pilots fly in front of it to be absolutely certain the pilot is aware of what is going on." Specifically, the AIP states that at night the interceptors will signal to the intruding aircraft by rocking their wings, flashing navigational lights and, if available, landing lights at irregular intervals. Next come warning shots that, if unheeded, are followed by "wavering fire . . . to put the onus of decision on the [intruder's] crew. The assumption is that if the pilot has nothing to hide, he will land."[9]

As it passed over the Sea of Okhotsk, Flight 007 was flying on a course heading of 240 degrees, approximately parallel to route Romeo-20. This suggests that sometime earlier—the Soviets claim when Flight 007 was in proximity to the RC-135—it had altered its heading so as to fly a parallel rather than a diverging course. While the airliner was over the Sea of Okhotsk, the Soviets thought it would not overfly Sakhalin at all, passing instead south of the island, over La Perouse Strait, and on over the Sea of Japan. But as the intruder seemed about to pass to the south, it changed course sharply to the right, toward Sakhalin Island.

Problems attended the PVO forces on Sakhalin much as they had on Kamchatka. According to high-ranking Japan Defense Agency sources, the Soviet scramble was confused. Six interceptors were sent aloft, in pairs, and ground controllers initially gave one pair of fighters the wrong course, sending them to the east of Flight 007. They had to circle back, winding up behind the intruder. The other fighters moved in, and what ensued was a tail chase with very little time for identifying, signaling and, if necessary, taking action.[10] Sakhalin Island is not wide; the intruder would be over Soviet territory for only about 12 minutes.

Maj. Vasiliy Konstantinovich Kazmin was later identified by Soviet television as the Soviet pilot flying the close-pursuit role in a Sukhoi-15 fighter. The Sukhoi fighter is far faster than a 747 jumbo jet, having a top speed of over 1,500 miles per hour, but its combat radius—the distance it can cover before it must return if it is to land safely—is a relatively short 390 nautical miles.[11] As a consequence, fighter pilots are always concerned with how much fuel they have. Interceptions must take place quickly.[12]

In constant communication with his ground controller, called "Deputat," Kazmin made the following report

1805:53	On heading 240.
1805:56	Am observing.
1806:00	Roger. I'm flying behind.

Kazmin was flying behind the intruder, which he would refer to throughout the interception only as the "target." He reported the target to be on a heading of 240 degrees.

| 1807:50 | Roger. Say again heading. To the left, surely. Not to the right. |

Ground control had advised Kazmin that the target had suddenly changed course to the right. From his surprised reaction to the message, it is clear that the "am observing" comment two minutes earlier could not have been in reference to the target, since in that case he would have seen the turn with his own eyes. The turn was unexpected; the Soviet pilot assumed that any turn would be to the left, toward international airspace. Astonished to learn that the intruder had in fact turned to the right, toward Soviet territory, Kazmin suggested that the controller must be in error: "To the left, surely. Not to the right," he said, incredulous.

| 1808:06 | Am executing 260. On heading 260.... Roger. |

Deputat confirmed the right turn, and Kazmin changed his own course from 240 to 260 degrees, a right-hand turn, in order to follow the target.

But Flight 007 was not through maneuvering and shortly thereafter began another turn back toward the left.

1809:00	Affirmative, it has turned.... The target is 80 to my left.
1809:35	Executing 240.
1810:16	Executing 220.

Advised by Deputat that the target had begun turning back toward the left, Kazmin had no questions or hesitations this time. He promply executed a 40-degree turn to the left.

1810:44	I didn't understand.
1810:51	Roger. She is going with a blinking light.

Kazmin was closing in on the intruder. After bringing his Su-15 interceptor onto a course of 220 degrees, he received an instruction from Deputat. Misunderstanding the instruction, he asked the ground controller to repeat it. Deputat did so. Kazmin then reported, "She is coming with a blinking light." While it is not completely clear whether this referred to the Su-15's own lights on the intruder, given the context of the conversation, Kazmin's own lights appear to be the most likely answer.[13]

1812:10	Am observing it visually and see it on the screen.
1812:15	Roger.
1813:05	I see it. I'm locked onto the target.

Here, Kazmin reported that he had both visual and radar contact with the intruder. He then reported to Deputat that his air-to-air missiles had been locked on.

1813:16	Roger.
1813:26	The target does not answer my call.[14]

The precise nature of Kazmin's query is not clear from his transmission, and there is no record of any verbal call to Flight 007 in tapes and transcripts purporting to be complete records of what the Soviet pilots said on their ultra-high-frequency (UHF) military communications channels. This has given rise to speculation that the interceptor did not actually call the intruder by radio, instead using the military Identification Friend or Foe (IFF) procedure. However, it is almost certain that the call was on the international hailing frequency 121.5 MHz and not on IFF. This is because of the improbability that the Russians would use IFF at this stage of intrusion. As Yoshitaro Masuo pointed out, "The situation in which a Soviet fighter would employ the IFF procedure and judge that the unidentified object would return a prescribed signal is a case in which it was unclear whether the aircraft was a friend or foe, but that there was a strong possibility that it was a friend." It follows from this that the Russians may have used IFF at the time of Flight 007's first intrusion over Kamchatka, but almost two hours had passed since then, plenty of time for the Soviets to have determined that the intruder was not one of their own planes. As Masuo concluded, by the time Flight 007 again entered Soviet territory over Sakhalin, it was "unthinkable that one of the Soviet fighters might conclude that the plane 'was a friend' and employ the IFF procedure. . . . There is little doubt that the communication was probably carried out on the international emergency frequency." [15]

But focusing exclusively on the pilot's "call" begs the question of whether Flight 007 received warnings and orders to land from Soviet ground controllers. It is ground stations that normally issue orders to intruding aircraft, and almost always in English, a language all 747 pilots speak. (In the event that none of the Soviet ground personnel spoke English, they have available phonetic pronunciations of English words.) The Soviets claim their ground stations made repeated, unsuccessful efforts to communicate with the intruder. [16] This issue could easily be settled by examining the transmissions of the Soviet ground controllers, but both the United States and Japan deny they have this material. In any case, if the Soviet pilots and ground controllers called, Flight 007 did not respond.

> 1813:45   Affirmative. The target's heading is 240 degrees.
>
> 1814:10   Roger. It's on the previous course for now.

With this, Kazmin reported to Deputat that the target had resumed its original course of 240 degrees after having executed the second of its two turns.

From their stations on northern Hokkaido, the Japanese were listening as the events over Sakhalin unfolded. Conforming to what we know as their standard operating procedures, the Soviets were in all probability radioing information about the intruder from the local level up the chain of command as far as Moscow. This gave Japanese intelligence operators, as well as their American colleagues, several opportunities to record the various messages as they moved through the system. For instance, it was suggested that top military officials in Moscow had been consulted about the intruder but that the civilian leadership was only informed afterwards. [17]

The Japanese were also watching, although there is some dispute about when Japanese radar first detected Flight 007. The radar at Wakkanai has a certain range of 250 miles and a theoretical range of 300 miles for an aircraft at Flight 007's altitude, so Flight 007 was certainly picked up by 1800 GMT, and perhaps as much as 8 to 10 minutes earlier. But the Japan Defense Agency claims that the radar did not pick up the airliner until 1812 GMT, when it was only 190 miles away.[18] Thus the JDA has not released information regarding Flight 007's turn to the right on approach to Sakhalin, which it almost certainly has.

But even after 1812, the JDA learned a number of interesting things about Flight 007's passage over Sakhalin. At 1812, the airliner was on a course of 260 degrees. Over the next few minutes its course changed back to 240 degrees. This means that the airliner was being flown manually, since the INS cannot execute a slow turn of this kind. Second, according to early reports attributed to a Japanese radar operator and later confirmed by the Japan Defense Agency, at 1812 the airliner was flying at the unauthorized altitude of 32,000 feet. This would be difficult for a 747 crew to miss: If an airliner inadvertently strays from its assigned altitude, an alert light and buzzer go off in the cockpit, warnings that pilots say would be "impossible to miss." Next, information later released by the Japanese government suggested that just as Flight 007 was about to cross into Soviet territory, it began an unauthorized descent from 32,000 to 29,000 feet. Finally, as it was queried by Japanese military secondary surveillance radar, Flight 007's transponder squawked the code "1300," a number wholly inappropriate for a flight supposedly about to enter Japanese-controlled airspace. Unless explicitly instructed to do otherwise, proper procedures called for Flight 007 to be squawking the code number "2000." As an international investigative body later noted, "The reason for the use of SSR code 1300 is unknown."[19]

1814:16	Roger.
1814:34	Roger. I have speed. I don't need to turn on my afterburner.
1815:08	The target's heading is still the same ... 240.

Deputat ordered Major Kazmin to approach the target, and Kazmin responded by saying that he had sufficient speed to do so without turning on his fuel-guzzling afterburner. At 1815 GMT, Flight 007 entered Soviet territory for the second time over Sakhalin Island, with the Soviet pilot following behind. It was at this time, the Soviets say, that Deputat radioed Kazmin: "805, flash the lights on and off."[20] He responded as follows:

1818:12	Repeat.
1818:19	Executing.

| 1818:34 | She is turned on. The strobe is flashing. |

That is, misunderstanding the instruction from his ground controller, he asked Deputat to repeat the instruction. Deputat did so, and the pilot reported that he was executing. Fifteen seconds later he reported that the lights were on.

Some commentators have suggested that during this sequence Kazmin was remarking upon Flight 007's lights rather than his own. Although Kazmin does not specifically say to whose lights he is referring, the context of the passage suggests that either he had been instructed to turn on his own lights, as the Russians claim, and he promptly did so, or he executed some other interception procedure to which Flight 007 responded by flashing its lights. Some reports have explicitly claimed that it was only at this time Flight 007 first turned on its lights. One problem with this interpretation is that only the Soviet fighter had strobe lights. Flight 007 carried red revolving beacons.[21]

But the intruder kept flying across Sakhalin, and time was rapidly ticking down for the Russians. The interceptor pilots were working against time and the diminishing fuel supplies in their fuel-thirsty jet fighters, in a country where tight centralized command is coupled with local responsibility for failures—such as letting an intruder escape. Former MiG pilot Viktor Belenko said that these twin fears would have preoccupied the pilots as they chased the intruder in the darkness. "Will I execute properly? During all of his career, a Soviet pilot is taught: You may not think. You may not recommend. You may not judge. You may only execute. Your commander will think for you. The pilot, of course, does think to himself: I must do exactly as I am told. I must execute perfectly. If not, I and my family will be ruined." So limited is the discretion of Soviet interceptor pilots, in fact, that their American counterparts derisively refer to them as "guided missiles." The other fear for the pilots is equally salient: Will I have to ditch? Belenko says that Soviet pilots do not wear insulated, waterproof suits, so ditching the aircraft at sea means almost certain death.[22] Again and again the interceptor pilots reported their remaining fuel and asked the distance back to the airfield.

| 1819:02 | I am closing on the target. |
| 1819:08 | They do not see me. |

At this point, the Soviets say, Deputat issued a command to Kazmin: "805, a warning burst from guns." The instruction was repeated: "A warning burst from guns."[23] The pilot responded:

| 1820:30 | I'm turning lock-on off, and I'm approaching the target. |
| 1820:49 | I am firing a burst from the cannons. |

The Soviets later said that "four bursts of warning shots were fired from guns with tracer shells; a total of 120 shells were fired." [24] In the night sky, the brilliant tracer ammunition is visible for miles.

U.S. officials have suggested that the Soviets were lying when they said the cannon bursts contained tracers. Yet in this instance the Soviet claim can be reasonably accepted. The reason is simple: There could have been no other purpose to fire the bursts except as a warning, because the interceptor was out of cannon range. Had the Russians wanted to destroy the intruder at that point, why would the pilot have disengaged the lock-on for his air-to-air missiles just moments earlier? While out of cannon range, the Su-15 interceptor was well within missile range had the intention been to kill. The cannon bursts were clearly the next step in the interception procedure.

Time was ticking away, and Flight 007 was now only minutes away from international airspace, and safety, on a heading that would have taken it eventually over the Soviet military center at Vladivostok.

1821:24	Roger, I'm closing in on the target. I'm going in closer.
1821:35	The target is flashing the light. I have already approached the target to a distance of about two kilometers.

On orders from Deputat, Kazmin had closed the distance between himself and the intruder to just over a mile. It was only then, for the first time, he specifically reported to his ground controller that the target's lights were flashing.

1821:55	My instructions?
1822:02	The target is decreasing speed.
1822:17	Oh, God! I am going around. I have already moved in front of the target.
1822:23	Increased speed.
1822:29	No, wrong. It is decreasing speed.
1822:42	You should have [said it] earlier. I am already side by side with the target now.
1822:55	Not much now. I have to fall back a bit from the target now.

Flight 007 had abruptly reduced speed, causing Kazmin to go shooting by and leaving his rear vulnerably toward the enemy, a fighter pilot's nightmare.[25] For precisely this reason, cutting speed is a classic evasive action. Successfully executed, the maneuver buys time, since it takes a while for the fighter pilot to bring his plane around into firing position once more.

Now Major Kazmin was becoming desperate. His fuel was running dangerously low and he was far more preoccupied with getting back into position and executing his instructions than he was in moving close enough to positively identify the intruder. Identification, in any case, would not have been easy. As Gen. Goro Takeda, the former chairman of Japan's Joint Chiefs of Staff, remarked later, the Soviet pilot would have found it "extremely difficult—almost impossible—to have identified the type of aircraft or its emblem" given the conditions at the time of the interception. The sun did not rise over Sakhalin that day until 1950 GMT, an hour and a half later, and it was dark except for the light of the moon. But that would not have helped much, since the moon was waning, with only 23 percent of its surface illuminated. Under these conditions, the Soviet pilots would have had to be as close as one thousand feet to see the distinctive hump on the 747 fuselage. Kazmin, the pilot in close pursuit, never got nearer than about one and a quarter miles. At that range it might have been possible to identify the intruder as a "large aircraft," Takeda said, but with the shades drawn it would not have been easily recognizable as a passenger airliner. So Kazmin never brought his Su-15 fighter alongside the intruder as international guidelines recommend. For practically the entire time he was behind and below Flight 007, a position from which identification would have been difficult.[26] But in the final analysis it probably would not have mattered to the Soviet air defense forces if they had positively identified the intruder as a Boeing 747. From the time the intruder approached Soviet territory for the first time over Kamchatka through the final moments over Sakhalin, it changed course, speed, and altitude, appeared to take evasive action, and refused to identify itself or respond to signals, unlike an innocently off-course civilian airliner.

By this time, Flight 007 was rapidly approaching international airspace, the crew member at the controls pushing the airliner hard, increasing speed in what may have been an effort to make it over the boundary into international airspace. Little time remained for Soviet air defense commanders to make the decision whether to shoot it or let it escape, for Soviet fighters are not permitted to shoot outside their own territory. One U.S. official was quoted in the *Japan Times* as saying, "You can imagine those Soviet officers seeing their careers, maybe their lives, flash before their eyes if the airliner or whatever got away." The conclusion of the air defense commanders was foregone: The intruder must not be allowed to escape. Alexander Dallin, an expert on the Soviet Union, wrote that "shooting down the unknown intruder meant going by the book; it was a safe way for the Far East PVO commander to protect his *zadnitsa*." The Soviets say that their air defense commanders issued the final, fatal order because they had "proof" that the plane was transmitting information to U.S. intelligence installations. The proof was not specified.[27]

1823:37	I'm already dropping back. Now I will try a rocket.
1824:22	Roger. I am in lock-on.
1825:11	I am closing on the target, am in lock-on. Distance to target 8 [kilometers].
1825:16	I have already switched on.

Kazmin had dropped back into attack position, a minimum of 5 kilometers from the target in order to avoid fragments of metal from the missile impact. His Anab AA-3 air-to-air missiles already were armed, or locked-on. The Anab missile is one of the new generation of "smart" missiles, guided to their targets by either radar or infrared detection. The missiles travel at over two and a half times the speed of sound and have little fins that continually correct their course so evasive actions are less effective. Anabs have proximity fuses that cause their seventy pounds of high explosives to detonate when the missile comes within approximately 10 feet of its target.[28]

By now, time had run out for Pilot 805 and his ground controllers. The intruder was only about 90 seconds away from international airspace and escape. There was no time left to try any additional interception signals, to determine the identity of the intruder, or to place any more calls to Moscow. Over the small settlement of Pravda on the southwest coast of Sakhalin Island, Maj. Vasiliy Konstantinovich Kazmin received a "very definite order" from his ground control station. He was running low on fuel, and he did not hesitate:

1826:20	I have executed the launch.
1826:22	The target is destroyed.
1826:27	I am breaking off the attack.

But Flight 007 was still airborne. Some time after Major Kazmin reported to Deputat that "the target is destroyed," controllers at Tokyo Radio picked up a noisy, static-laden transmission, the only audible words being "zero zero seven." A controller in Tokyo tried to raise the airliner: "Korean Air zero zero seven, Tokyo." The words that followed were not understood and were later described as "noisy and weak."[29] Tokyo Radio then began a series of futile calls in an effort to raise Flight 007.

Major Kazmin had fired both of his Anab AA-3 missiles: "I launched both," he reported to Deputat. American intelligence analysts cited in London's *The Economist* later said that one of the Anab missiles launched was radar-guided while the other was a heat-seeking version. They said that the heat-seeking missile homed-in on the hot exhaust of one of the Boeing 747's four jet engines but the radar-guided missile missed. Three months later, Jack Anderson published an identical account based on information he said had been provided by intelligence sources, citing top-secret reports. In contrast, a confidential Soviet source claimed that the missile scored a near-miss. However, even a hit by a heat-seeking missile —especially if it hit one of the outer engines of the Boeing 747—would not necessarily destroy the plane.[30] The airliner could have survived the attack, said Robert Hutchinson, the defense correspondent of Britain's Domestic Press Association, "unless there was an explosion from vaporizing fuel."[31]

And Flight 007 was not destroyed. It survived for another twelve minutes, a time that must have seemed an eternity to the innocent passengers on board. Their horror and fear must have been unbearable. "What did the parents who were on board do with their children in the sudden chaos?" wondered pilot Bryce McCormick. "Did they simply clutch the children? Did they scream their love and fear to each other, inaudible in the noise, until they lost consciousness?"[32]

During those minutes, the crew of Flight 007 kept their airliner at substantial altitude. That they could do so meant the wings were essentially intact and no significant damage had occurred to any major control surface. Had Flight 007 plunged downward at its maximum level speed of about 600 miles per hour, it would have crashed into the sea in less than a minute. Maintaining altitude also meant that at least one of the 747's engines was functioning, and if an engine was working, there was electricity. An operating electrical system meant there was power for the three VHF and two HF radios carried on board the airliner. But no distress signals were sent. Air Force sources would later say they were "puzzled" by the lack of such signals.[33]

The strangeness of this behavior can be appreciated better by considering what would normally take place in the cockpit under the emergency conditions accompanying rapid decompression. Aviation expert Dr. Malcolm Brenner explained: "At an altitude of about 32,000 feet [Flight 007's altitude at the time of the attack], crew members and passengers would have about one minute of expected useful consciousness unless they successfully began receiving oxygen from an oxygen mask (in the event of a rapid decompression, this time gets cut to about thirty seconds since most of the air in the lungs gets sucked out during the decompression). The captain would then check with the flight engineer on the state of the pressurization system and, if the pressurization cannot be maintained, would declare an emergency descent." In addition, emergency messages should have been repeatedly radioed to air traffic controllers, and the plane's transponder should have been set to code 7700. As Brenner remarked, "There is a saying in aviation that 'one minute's flying is worth two days' rowing,' and for aircraft over water it would be critical to get the Mayday message started as soon as possible and lasting as long as possible. The ground station could then use the radio signal to take a fix on the aircraft's location and likely ditching site."[34] Emergency procedures call for saying "Mayday" three times, followed by other information about the nature of the emergency. The cockpit crew should have continued broadcasting until the last possible moment to help lead rescuers to the plane's location. But Flight 007's transponder was never set to the SSR emergency code 7700. There were no Mayday calls.

There are only two possibilities here: Either Flight 007's cabin decompressed as a result of the missile attack, or it did not. If it did, then it is difficult to explain the crew of Flight 007 staying at substantial altitude. At the height the plane was flying there is no air, and temperatures were on the order of minus 40 degrees Centigrade. If decompression occurred, staying up there meant freezing and suffocating the passengers. Yet even cabin decompression could not account for twelve minutes of silence. The pilots' oxygen masks have built-in microphones for use in precisely such emergencies. Thus, if the cabin decompressed, there seems to be no way to explain the behavior of Captain Chun and his crew.

But if the cabin did not suffer decompression, there are just as many questions. The members of the crew doubtless felt the impact of the missile or at least saw its explosion. Again, where were the emergency calls? And if the missile attack did not destroy the airliner, what did?

After Major Kazmin broke off the attack and headed back to Dolinsk-Sokol airfield, a MiG-23 fighter took up the close-pursuit role. In talking to his ground controller, Deputat, the MiG-23 pilot used the call sign "163." Pilot 163 was operating at an altitude of about 26,000 feet, receiving constant instructions from Deputat regarding the course he should take in order to intercept the intruder. For the next twelve minutes the Soviets tracked the intruder by radar, no doubt watching in fascination as it executed a series of turns, the final one of which brought it back toward Sakhalin Island (see map at end of chapter).[35] As each turn was made, pilot 163 was instructed to follow:

1827:29	I'm executing left heading 180 [degrees].
1827:53	But heading is 150. Roger.
1828:20	Roger, heading 150.
1828:29	Executing heading 210.
1829:21	Executing heading 360.
1832:12	Executing 210.
1835:15	Executing to the right heading 60.

At the same time another MiG-23 fighter was also closing in on Flight 007. The pilot of this fighter went by the call sign "731." Like his comrade

163, pilot 731 was operating at substantial altitude—about 23,000 feet—and was being directed toward the target by ground control. At 1837:45, pilot 731 abruptly rose in altitude by 6,500 feet. Immediately thereafter, the MiG-23 pilot 163 descended to an altitude of about 6,500 feet and began trying to locate openings in the clouds through which he could look earthward. Something had clearly happened to Flight 007 at about 1838 GMT.

The Japan Defense Agency high-altitude radar at Wakkanai was said to have followed the airliner until about 1829 GMT, when it went below its area of coverage. From that time on, Flight 007 was tracked by a separate, unpublicized low-level radar system at Wakkanai. At 1838 GMT, Flight 007 suddenly disappeared from the radar screens. As Japanese aviation expert Kunio Yanagida later commented, "The sudden disappearance from radar is very strange, as you would normally expect to track a plane even as it was falling to the earth. The only explanation would seem to be a very sudden explosion." A Japanese military spokesman in Tokyo cited by the *New York Times* said radar information in Japan's possession supported the idea that the plane exploded in midair. The spokesman said pulses received from Flight 007's transponder stopped at the same time that the plane disappeared from radar.[36] Soviet pilot 731 had apparently ascended to get out of the way of the exploding airliner's debris. Pilot 163 had descended shortly afterwards to see if there was anything left of the airliner. But they found nothing, and both fighters returned to base shortly thereafter. Twelve minutes after the missile attack, Flight 007 had, in fact, arrived at its destruction.

Thus, from beginning to end, numerous questions surround the tragic odyssey of Korean Air Lines Flight 007. Before the flight began, why did Captain Chun Byung-in allegedly tell his wife that he was embarking on a "particularly dangerous" flight? Is this the reason, according to some reports, she took out additional insurance on her husband? Is there any other evidence to suggest that KAL crews might engage in such dangerous flights? In Anchorage, why was additional fuel loaded on board the plane and paying cargo removed? Did Captain Chun's hand-scrawled notations on his computerized flight plan indicate innocent calculations to save fuel, as some have claimed, or did they have some other purpose? Could a 747 captain as meticulous as Captain Chun, not to mention his first officer and flight engineer, have violated all the regulations, failed to follow all the procedures, and made all the errors necessary to have gone off course accidentally? Is there a credible explanation for how the flight could have happened accidentally?

As the flight progressed, why did Flight 007 slow down while Flight 015 exceeded its authorized speed? Why do numerous U.S. air traffic controllers now say they recall nothing about the night in question? Is there any evidence that in fact they did know the plane to be off course yet failed to warn it? Why did the Air Force, which had the Korean airliner on radar for much longer than civilian controllers, fail to issue a warning as required by regulations? What happened to the radar data recorded by the Air Force? Over the Bering Sea, why did Flight 007 change course to the north, toward the Kamchatka Peninsula? Why did the airliner, as the evidence suggests, come sufficiently close to the RC-135 to confuse Soviet air defense forces? Did the RC-135, the U.S.S. *Observation Island,* and the intelligence facilities at Elmendorf Air Force Base, Shemya, Wakkanai, Misawa, and elsewhere have the capability to detect the off-course airliner? If so, did they understand events as they unfolded, or did the meaning of things only become clear hours or days later, as government officials and others have repeatedly claimed?

The questions multiply over Sakhalin Island. As the doomed airliner approached Sakhalin, why did it make a turn to the north? How could the crew of Flight 007 have failed to notice the signals of the Soviet interceptors? Did altitude and speed changes take place, as Japanese evidence suggests? If so, were these evasive actions? Is there any additional evidence that the crew members were aware of their situation or took other evasive actions? Why was Flight 007's transponder set to an incorrect code? What was actually said in the "noisy and weak" transmission by Flight 007 immediately after the missile attack? What is the meaning of the crew's silence during the twelve minutes of flight between the missile attack and the plane's destruction? Did the U.S. and Japan monitor the voices of Soviet ground controllers, which would provide important information about the airliner's final minutes, or should government officials be believed when they say that such monitoring was not possible?

These questions are intended to shed light on whether or not Flight 007 deliberately passed over Soviet territory and whether there is evidence of American complicity, the central issues in the KAL case.

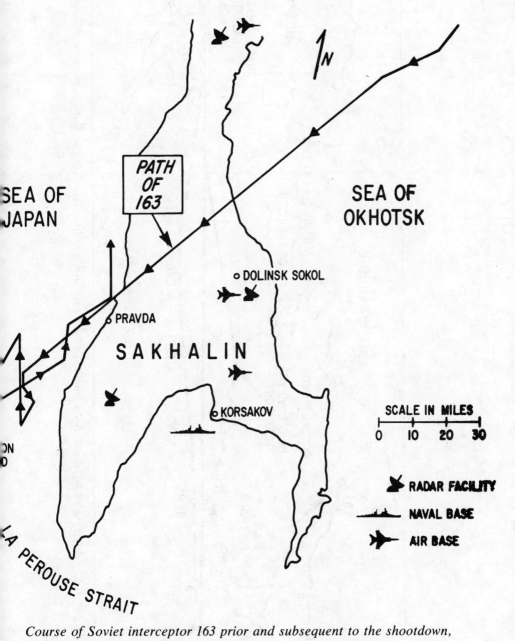

SEA OF
JAPAN

SEA OF
OKHOTSK

PATH
OF
163

N

DOLINSK SOKOL

PRAVDA

SAKHALIN

KORSAKOV

SCALE IN MILES

0   10   20   30

LA PEROUSE STRAIT

RADAR FACILITY

NAVAL BASE

AIR BASE

Course of Soviet interceptor 163 prior and subsequent to the shootdown, and Soviet military facilities.

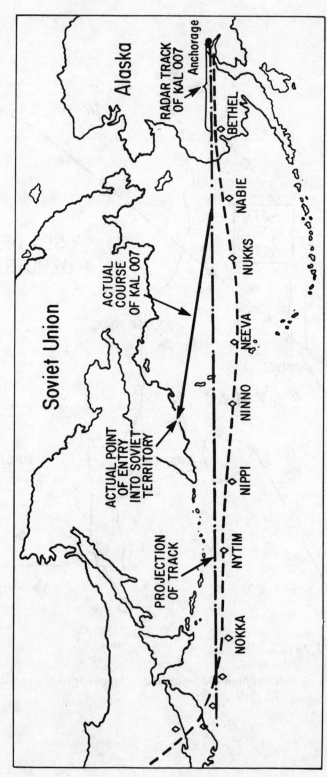

Projection of Flight 007's early course based on King Salmon and Kenai radar data, actual course flown, and route Romeo-20.

4

OVERFLIGHTS

Flight 007 was not the first airplane to fly without permission over Communist territory, and many of the intrusions in the past were quite deliberate. The 1950s were a decade of frequent intrusions by U.S. military aircraft, and since by no means do all intrusions into other countries' airspace result in shootdowns or diplomatic protests or otherwise come to public attention, only the most general idea of the full scope of such flights can be garnered. On April 8, 1950, a Navy B-29 patrol bomber with a ten-man crew was shot down by the Russians over the Baltic Sea. During 1951 an Air Force Superfortress was shot down over the Sea of Japan near Vladivostok after it failed to comply with the interception signals of Soviet fighters and then fired upon them. All ten crew members were lost. That same year a Navy reconnaissance plane was shot down off the coast of Siberia, and forced landings of U.S. military aircraft took place in Czechoslovakia and Hungary. In 1952, CIA agent John T. Downey was shot down on a spy mission over China. He was not released from prison until 1973.[1]

In 1953, there were at least two incidents involving U.S. aircraft. A four-engine Air Force RB-50 based at Elmendorf Air Force Base in Anchorage was attacked by two Soviet MiG fighters while it was collecting intelligence off the coast of the Kamchatka Peninsula near Petropavlovsk. Shots were fired, but the plane escaped unharmed.[2] An attack on another reconnaissance plane took place six months later in the Yellow Sea. In September 1954, a Navy Neptune P-2V reconnaissance plane was shot down over the Sea of Japan near Vladivostok, resulting in the death of one crew member. On November 7 of that year, an Air Force B-29 was shot down off the Kuril Islands near the Japanese island of Hokkaido. The crew managed to bail out safely, but one man died before rescuers arrived.

The remainder of the decade brought more of the same. In June 1955, two crew members of a Navy reconnaissance plane were forced to crash-land on St. Lawrence Island after being attacked by Soviet fighters over the Bering Strait. The next year brought intrusions into Chinese and Soviet airspace, the latter by three Air Force B-57 bombers in the area south of Vladivostok which resulted in a formal protest by the Soviet government. Numerous intrusions of East German and Soviet airspace were reported in 1958. An Air Force aircraft was forced to land in Soviet territory on June 27; the Soviets protested the violation of their airspace by an Air Force B-47 over the Caspian Sea on July 26; on October 16, the Soviets again lodged a protest of the violation of their territory in the area of the Bering Strait; and in November another Air Force plane entered Soviet airspace over the Baltic Sea.

However, the most costly violation that year took place on the afternoon of September 2, 1958, when an EC-130 electronic intelligence plane on assignment for the National Security Agency—part of what was euphemistically termed a "global Air Force project to study radio wave propagation"—was shot down near Leninakan in Soviet Armenia.[3] The EC-130's mission that day had taken it over areas of Turkey and Iran near the Soviet border. As it was returning to base, the plane entered Soviet airspace and was shot down by MiG fighters. The fate of the plane was immediately known to Air Force Security Service personnel at a listening post in Trabazon, Turkey, who had been continually monitoring Soviet radio communications as the reconnaissance plane entered their territory. The Soviets returned six bodies, but the fate of the other eleven was not known.

The downing of the U-2 spy plane in May 1960 was the first time many Americans discovered that their government would tell them a lie.

The first U-2 flight over the Soviet Union was on July 4, 1956, the 180th anniversary of the signing of the Declaration of Independence. Richard M. Bissell, CIA special assistant for planning and coordination, had hoped that the U-2, with its small radar "signature," would not be picked up on Soviet radar. The Soviet equipment proved to be more powerful than expected, however, and National Security Agency personnel in West Germany listened in as the Soviets tracked the U-2 along the entire course of its flight from West Germany to Moscow, to Leningrad, and then back to West Germany. They could track it but little else; at the U-2's operating altitude of about eighty thousand feet, neither Soviet fighters nor surface-to-air missiles could come anywhere close to the plane. Outraged at the intrusion, Soviet Ambassador Georgi Zaroubin delivered his government's formal protest to Secretary of State John Foster Dulles two days later. Dulles drafted a response to the Soviet note saying that no military aircraft had violated Soviet airspace (the CIA is not, of course, a military agency), and State Department spokesman Lincoln White assured reporters, "We know absolutely nothing about this."[4] The CIA overflights continued at irregular intervals throughout the following four years with the Soviets helpless to prevent them.

The most famous U-2 flight took place on May 1, 1960, the eve of a summit meeting between President Dwight D. Eisenhower and Soviet Premier Nikita S. Khrushchev. A U-2 plane piloted by Francis Gary Powers took off from Peshawar, Pakistan, on a flight that was supposed to carry it over the Soviet space center at Tyuratam, over the industrial complex at Sverdlovsk, on to the sensitive military areas of Plesetsk and Murmansk near the White Sea, finishing up at Bodø, Norway.[5] While there is still debate over precisely how it happened, Powers' plane went out of control over Sverdlovsk. Powers later testified to the Senate that he could not reach the destruct switches and was afraid to use the eject mechanism. Powers was promptly captured by the Russians but failed to use his poison suicide pin. Against CIA procedures, he carried an abundance of military identification, perhaps so that in the event of his capture he would be treated as a soldier rather than a spy. The Russians recovered the relatively intact wreckage of the U-2 plane and its camera.

Confident that neither the aircraft nor the pilot could have survived—U-2 pilots were under orders to destroy their planes and, if necessary, themselves—the CIA dusted off the prepared cover story. Acting on the instructions of CIA Director Allen Dulles, NASA chief T. Keith Glennan told the press on May 3 that a NASA high-altitude weather reconnaissance plane on a flight from Adana, Turkey, was "missing" and that "it might have accidentally violated Soviet airspace."[6]

With the U.S. confidently walking into his trap, Khrushchev pounced. On May 5, he announced to the Supreme Soviet that U.S. spy planes had been intruding into Soviet territory, that protests had been filed, but that the "United States offered formalistic excuses and tried in every possible way to deny the fact of aggression."[7] To thunderous applause, Khrushchev then announced that one of these spy planes had been shot down on May 1.

The Administration promptly waded deeper into the swamp of deception, announcing that NASA and the State Department were investigating the Soviet charges. On May 6, State Department spokesman Lincoln White emphatically told reporters, "There was absolutely no—N-O, no—deliberate attempt to violate Soviet airspace. There never has been."[8]

On May 7, Khrushchev announced to the Supreme Soviet and the world that the Soviet Union had the wreckage of the U-2 spy plane as well as a pilot "alive and kicking." Calling the American story about the U-2 a "complete lie," Khrushchev went on to describe Powers' equipment, mission, and confession in considerable detail. Khrushchev suggested that Powers might be put on trial in Moscow for spying. "The West is now accusing Khrushchev of wanting to sabotage the summit meeting," the Soviet Premier said. "No, we are not such a people. You have made a mess; smell it now yourselves."[9]

Even with the cover story collapsing on their heads, Administration officials continued the denials. Some State Department officials said they were, to say the least, "skeptical" of the story. Others called Khrushchev's claim "fantastic." Still other officials tried to shift the blame, suggesting that Khrushchev's announcement was motivated by a desire to place the failure of the upcoming summit on the United States and an almost pathological sensitivity over the integrity of Soviet borders.[10] Following the downing of KAL Flight 007 some twenty-three years later, these responses would be repeated almost verbatim.

On May 8, the State Department admitted that the flight had in fact been made but added that it had not been authorized in Washington—another lie. Since this approach had the unfortunate effect of making it appear as if the President was not in control of his government, Eisenhower finally announced on May 9 that the United States in fact conducted spy flights, took personal responsibility for them, and suggested that the flights were justified and would continue.[11] The prospects for peace offered by the summit meeting, now only a week away, were utterly destroyed. What Eisenhower had hoped would be a triumphant visit to the Soviet Union in June was cancelled.

A review of the historical record since the U-2 affair casts considerable doubt on the official Reagan administration contention at the time of the downing of Flight 007 that "since the 1960 U-2 incident the U.S. Government has never authorized or sent any aircraft to penetrate internationally recognized Soviet airspace."[12]

On the night of July 1, 1960, just two months after Powers' U-2 was shot down, an Air Force RB-47 reconnaissance plane left its base at Brize Norton, England, on what the State Department later alternately described as a "navigation research flight" and an "electromagnetic survey mission." The RB-47 is a six-man converted bomber, stripped of its armor and adapted for aerial reconnaissance. The plane was packed with long-range cameras, mapping cameras, and electronic equipment for checking sites and frequencies of Soviet air defense systems. Over the Barents Sea, the Air Force plane was attacked by two Soviet MiG-17 fighters. Two crew members were lost. The survivors were imprisoned by the Soviets for the remainder of President Eisenhower's term but released by Premier Khrushchev less than a year later as a gesture of goodwill toward the incoming Kennedy administration.[13]

During 1962, the U-2s were still very much in service. On August 30 of that year, the Soviets charged that a U-2 entered Soviet airspace near Sakhalin Island. And it was not only the Russians who were targeted. Less than two weeks later, another U-2 was shot down by China. Filing a formal protest with the United States, the Chinese claimed that various U.S. aircraft had violated China's airspace 213 times since 1958.[14]

On January 28, 1964, a U.S. Air Force T-39 jet trainer intruded into East German territory and penetrated at least 60 miles into East Germany before it was intercepted and shot down by Soviet MiG fighters. All of the crew members were killed. From the start the Soviets said that the T-39 had been on a reconnaissance mission. According to their account, the MiG interceptors gave the appropriate internationally accepted signals ordering the intruder to land. The U.S. plane was said to have ignored the signals, including warning shots fired along its path by the MiGs, and tried to escape. "We have all grounds to believe that this was not an error or mistake," the Soviets said.[15]

The U.S. account was predictably different. The Department of Defense said that Air Force operators had noted the aircraft heading into East Germany and had attempted to direct it westward, but the T-39 failed to respond to the warnings. This failure, Defense officials said, indicated that a malfunction must have occurred in the aircraft's radio or electronic navigational equipment. As with the U-2, the consequence of this incident was an increase in tensions between the United States and the Soviet Union. At the time, the two superpowers were actively involved in seventeen-nation disarmament talks in Geneva. The incident gave the proceedings a bitter flavor just as the session appeared to be off to a good start.[16]

Things soon would get worse. On March 10, 1964, just 42 days later, an Air Force twin-engine Douglas RB-66 reconnaissance aircraft attached to the 19th Tactical Reconnaissance Squadron at Toulrosires, France, also experienced "navigational trouble" and intruded into East Germany only 30 miles north of where the T-39 had entered. Allied air defense radars in West Germany reported an unidentified aircraft entering the ADIZ near the Berlin center air corridor and, according to the Air Force, instructions to reverse course were given. Allied regulations at the time specified that all aircraft within 50 miles of the East German frontier must identify themselves, but the RB-66 did not respond to the radio messages. The jet was intercepted and shot down by MiG fighters, but this time the crew parachuted to safety. There was no question in this instance that the downed aircraft was for aerial reconnaissance.[17]

On April 27, 1965, an Air Force RB-57 reconnaissance plane was attacked by two North Korean MiG-17s off the coast of North Korea. The RB-57, a modified version of the six-engine B-47 strategic bomber, was damaged but was able to return safely to its base in Japan.[18]

A final example involved an Air Force EC-121 reconnaissance plane that was shot down by two North Korean MiG fighters over the Sea of Japan on April 14, 1969. Prior to the flight, a top-secret message had been sent to all relevant facilities detailing the time and course the plane would follow. Throughout its flight the EC-121 was monitored by a number of facilities, including the Naval Security Group station at Kamiseya, Japan, and another in South Korea. When trouble occurred and two North Korean MiG fighters began stalking the reconnaissance plane, the U.S. station in South Korea dispatched four messages to the Joint Chiefs of Staff and other addressees describing the situation. A source familiar with Air Force reconnaissance operations noted, "We always had the Secretary of Defense and Joint Chiefs listed as 'parties on the line' to receive all data or advisories of events and emergencies." [19]

As the decade of the sixties drew to a close, the number of military intrusions began to drop off because spy satellites took over much reconnaissance work. While the need for reconnaissance flights by military aircraft was reduced, it was by no means eliminated. As *Air Force* magazine observed, reconnaissance flights induce the "other fellow" to react in a way that tells us things we want to know, something that can't be done with satellites.[20]

"I was stationed with the U.S. Air Force Security Service in Alaska," a source said. "I know firsthand our agencies *regularly* were told in advance, to maximize monitoring, of special air missions flown by scheduled foreign civil airliners and cargo aircraft, crewed by top-secret-cleared pilots, into foreign airspace and waters, mainly the USSR. I regularly saw communications that discussed preparations, plans, details, and approval for civilian aircraft penetration routes and plans for monitoring Russian communications nets prior to the 'accidental' flight into Russian airspace and radar fence.

"I learned it was a commonly held belief that 'so long as they cannot force the aircraft down, what can they do except bitch about it in the UN?' Everyone openly discussed the Department of Defense and Strategic Air Command awareness in advance and that the Secretary of Defense had the final approval or veto of an 'error in course,' which was jokingly changed to 'error, of course!' by staff." When a mission was approved, the source said, the next available crew and aircraft were given the mission directives. Air Force reconnaissance planes and ground monitoring stations were then notified that approval had been received and the mission was on. "We literally followed every relevant radio frequency until the mission was completed," the source said. "Rarely if ever did these missions *not* include some overflight of actual Russian soil. To my knowledge, no effort to determine who might be aboard the 'duck' aircraft was ever undertaken, even though the plans were instituted weeks in advance so that crews, aircraft, and routes could fit together into desired conditions for the mission. I once asked who gets rich from that, and the reply was that it was believed no money was involved, merely political cooperation between DoD, Secretary of Defense, and Japan, Korea, Thailand, and others.

"I am gravely and deeply concerned over our use of innocent civilians in what we very objectively believed to be a safe way to test and probe Russian radar and defense reaction capabilities," the source concluded. "We called those aircraft 'ducks.' " Ducks: Deep Undercover.

The use of commercial airliners for a variety of noncommercial purposes is well documented throughout the postwar era. In *The CIA and the Cult of Intelligence,* authors Victor Marchetti and John Marks noted that the CIA has owned, and most probably still owns, one of the largest fleets of "commercial" aircraft in the world. The airlines reportedly with past linkages to the agency include Air America, Air Asia, Air Ethiopia, Braniff Airways, Bird Air, China Air Lines (Taiwan), Civil Air Transport, Continental Airlines (a subsidiary of which was the company that prepared Flight 007's computerized flight plan), Evergreen Aviation, Fairways Corporation, Flying Tigers, Intermountain Aviation, the Korean Flying Tigers, Page Airways, Pan American World Airlines, Southern Air Transport, Transocean Air Lines, and others. "If I were sitting in a position where I was curious about what was going on in troubled areas, there are two things I would be damned well interested in," said Orvis Nelson, a businessman instrumental in setting up a number of the CIA airline connections. "The first is information. The second is transportation to get in and out, to get any information and, perhaps, to do some other air activities."[22]

While some have claimed that the CIA got out of the airline business in the 1970s following the Church Committee's investigation into the agency's illegal activities, a closer examination suggests that all that actually took place was a change in the form of its involvement—from direct to indirect. In its 1976 report, the Church Committee concluded that it was "nearly impossible" to determine whether the agency continued to maintain links to its former proprietaries. "In some cases," the report said, "even though formal and informal agency ties are discontinued, social and interpersonal relationships remain. The impact of such liaisons is difficult to assess." In several cases, however, the report noted that the agency's sale of the airline had as its condition that "the proprietary would continue to provide goods or services to the CIA."[23] Indeed, the same year that the committee's report appeared, a knowledgeable insider remarked that the agency's involvement in commercial airlines was as great as ever.[24]

The use of commercial airlines to perform "special missions" for governments is by no means limited to the United States. Other airlines said to do so include the Soviet national carrier Aeroflot; Czechoslovak Air Lines; Cubana, the airline of Cuba; the Israeli airline El Al; Finnair; Korean Air Lines; Libyan Arab Airlines; and the Polish airline Lot. Cubana is a frequent offender, with its planes veering from their authorized flight paths between Canada and Cuba in order to overfly U.S. military facilities. Finnair is said to "routinely" spy over Soviet territory. At the time of the launch of the first space shuttle, a Czechoslovak Air Lines (CSA) plane requested permission for a "special flight" over Cape Canaveral. Permission was denied. When the launch was postponed for unrelated reasons, CSA again applied for a "special flight" authorization. These plans too were denied. Reports say that Israel uses its national airline El Al to provide "deep cover" for agents of Mossad, the Israeli intelligence service, obtaining what has been described as "exquisite information" through use of the airline.[25]

Probably the worst individual offender in these regards, however, is the Soviet national carrier Aeroflot, and stories about Aeroflot's prodigious propensity to stray from course abound. The *Toronto Star* reported that Aeroflot flights to Montreal's Mirabel Airport often "take a wrong turn" and fly over the Air Force Base at Bagotville, Quebec. A West German television report showed films of Aeroflot planes with lens-shaped bulges on the fuselage parked at Frankfurt International Airport. Asked for comment, Bonn Defense Ministry spokesman Juergen Reichardt said, "Yes, that's well known. The entire transport capacity of Aeroflot and the East-bloc airlines also have military uses." Reichardt went on to say that Aeroflot planes often change course over West Germany to fly over NATO installations. The French newspaper *Le Monde* said that Aeroflot passenger planes taking off from Paris are frequently involved in aerial surveillance of France's strategic forces at Tavery. Aeroflot planes flying off the Atlantic coast of the United States often stray from their assigned air lanes into the ADIZ to trigger a U.S. response. In 1982, Aeroflot drew penalties from American aviation authorities for repeatedly flying over Air Force bases in New York State.[26]

The most famous incident involving an Aeroflot plane in the U.S. occurred on November 8, 1981, when an airliner bound for Washington's Dulles International Airport flew over the Strategic Air Command center at Pease Air Force Base in New Hampshire and the General Dynamics submarine construction facility at Groton, Connecticut. At first the overflight evoked no response by the Reagan administration because the Aeroflot plane had been given permission to fly the route. President Reagan had fired thousands of striking air traffic controllers, replacing them with relatively inexperienced personnel, and when the Aeroflot plane asked for permission to fly over the military bases, permission was granted. Departing Washington for its return flight to Moscow several days later, the same airplane flew the same route in reverse. As a result of the incident, a protest was lodged with the Soviet Union and Aeroflot service into Dulles Airport was suspended for two flights.[27]

On July 1, 1968, President Lyndon B. Johnson signed the treaty on the nonproliferation of nuclear weapons. He then made a surprise announcement that the governments of the United States and the Soviet Union had agreed to enter into discussions on the limitation and eventual reduction of both offensive strategic nuclear weapons delivery systems and ballistic missile defense systems.

That moment almost did not arrive. The previous day, June 30, a chartered DC-8 airliner filled with 214 GIs on their way to Vietnam had intruded into Soviet airspace over the Kuril Islands north of Japan. The aircraft was intercepted by Soviet MiG-17 fighters and took evasive action, risking being shot down. Only after the Soviet pilot had fired cannon bursts in front of the DC-8 did the airliner's pilot submit to the interception and make a forced landing on Soviet-controlled Etorofu Island.

Seaboard World Airlines Flight 253A, a DC-8 Super 63-F airliner chartered by the Military Airlift Command, originated at New York's John F. Kennedy International Airport. On board were American troops en route to Camranh Bay. The DC-8 then flew to McChord Air Force Base south of Seattle, where it took off on June 30 and flew to Seattle-Tacoma airport for refueling. Another refueling stop was scheduled at Tachikawa Air Base in Yokota, Japan. From there the plane would fly directly to Vietnam. The crew of Flight 253A filed a flight plan with air traffic control personnel at McChord Air Force Base; it called for the plane to follow a standard route to the Far East that took it off the southern coast of Alaska, then down alongside the Kamchatka Peninsula and Kuril Islands to Japan.[28]

A number of things about the flight seemed unusual. In addition to the one hundred seventy-four Army, thirty-one Navy, and nine Air Force personnel on board as passengers, Flight 253A carried seventeen crew members, a sizable crew for a chartered flight. In addition to the four regular cockpit crew members and six stewardesses, there were two additional Seaboard flight personnel on board, Captain Ralph Neary, Seaboard's director of flight, and Edward Acree, a flight engineer. A Seaboard spokesman later said that Neary was on board the flight as "check pilot" and Acree as "check engineer."[29] This still leaves five crew members who were described by the airline as "special checkers," although their function on board Flight 253A has never been disclosed.

Neary and Acree were reportedly on board because this was the maiden flight of this DC-8 for Seaboard. The aircraft had been acquired by the company on June 21, just a few days earlier, and new radar navigation equipment had just been installed.[30]

With new navigational equipment and a host of crew members, check pilots, navigators, and "special checkers" on board, it might seem remarkable, as the Department of Defense later reported, that during its flight the airliner "apparently strayed 80 to 100 miles off course," entering Soviet territory. This estimate of "80 to 100 miles" is rather inexact and unnecessarily so, for the Pentagon had in its possession intelligence data from both U.S. and Japanese sources that showed the precise deviation from course by Flight 253A. The estimate given by the Pentagon probably derived from the fact that Red One, the normal route the DC-8 was to have followed, skirted Kamchatka and the Kurils by about that distance.[31]

The DC-8 airliner may have been new, but many of its crew members were old hands. The captain of the flight was Joseph Tosolini, at the time of the incident a veteran with 17 years' flight experience. He had flown the North Pacific route a number of times, including seven times during the six months prior to the incident. Seaboard identified Earl Scott as the flight engineer and Henry Treger as the first officer. Lawrence Guernon, a veteran airman with 25 years' experience, was the navigator.

Guernon later recalled a number of oddities about the flight. Two days before the flight, Guernon said, he and Henry Treger had been deadheading from New York to McChord Air Force Base on a Seaboard cargo plane when Treger turned to him and said, "You know, Larry, I had the funniest dream last night. I dreamed that Russian airplanes were shooting at us." Guernon recalled the remark during the flight two days later when he observed Treger behaving exceedingly odd: "Hank was just sitting in his seat the whole time reading," Guernon said. "He didn't seem to care or want anything to do with the flight. I don't even remember him looking out the windows. He just sat there reading." As Guernon recalled, check pilot Ralph Neary was up front in the cockpit with pilot Joe Tosolini. "Neary was playing around with the instruments and giving instructions to Joe. I was taking fixes and knew we were going to the right of course. I kept saying, 'Joe, you're going to have to swing to the left, or we're going to go into Russian territory.' Joe and Neary would keep talking, and he would maybe turn to the left a few degrees, but never as much as I said." And the airliner continued to deviate toward Soviet territory.[32]

As the DC-8 flew along ever closer to the Kuril Islands, a number of electronic eyes and ears were watching and listening. On Shemya Island, personnel of the Air Force's 6981st Electronic Security Squadron and other military personnel watched events unfold in real time. Writing in the *Washington Post Magazine,* James Bamford described the recollections by Elwin Williamson, a military intelligence specialist who was stationed on Shemya during 1968–69, of the fascinated intercept operators who followed the entire incident involving the Seaboard DC-8.[33]

The Morse code intercept operators sat in front of radio receivers, headphones in place, and copied the intercepted Morse signals onto consoles resembling a typewriter. At the beginning of each shift, Shemya operators were provided with an up-to-date list of the frequencies on which the Soviets were transmitting and would "roll onto" their target, shifting to the frequency then being used.[34] In front of the operators was a large wall map of the Far East that included parts of Siberia, the Kamchatka Peninsula, and the Kuril Islands. A Morse intercept operator who was stationed on Shemya in the 1970s said at that time there were two principal radar transmitters on southern Kamchatka, his area of concern. He would flip a two-way switch on his equipment to change frequency to see what the stations were up to.

Each operator was responsible for covering one area of the map that corresponded to the "grid system" being used by the Soviets at that time. The Soviets divided up their airspace and surrounding waters into large areas, corresponding roughly to 5 degrees of longitude and latitude. This produced a number of essentially rectangular blocks, each of which was given a numerical designation. Each numbered block was divided into nine equal, numbered parts. Each of these was then further subdivided into nine even smaller parts, which were numbered in turn. The end result was a very fine-grained grid by which the locations of aircraft could be plotted.

For instance, if an aircraft's location was said to be "18536," it was located in large block 185, smaller block 3, and in smallest block number 6. Since the speed of an aircraft would rapidly carry it into new blocks, Soviet remote radar stations would transmit the locations of objects being monitored to their control center approximately every minute, prefixing the location numbers with several numbers describing the object being tracked as a fighter, a bomber, or "unknown." In this way the type and movement of aircraft could be very precisely described.

Every so often the Soviets changed the frequencies on which they transmitted so as to confuse the American listeners. Every month or so they also changed the numbers of the "grid blocks" for the same reason. Normally, it was easy for the Americans to adjust to these changes. On occasion, an RC-135 reconnaissance plane would be sent up so that its known position could be correlated with the grid positions reported by the Soviet radar stations. Sometimes these aircraft would actually enter Soviet airspace.

It should be emphasized that it was the Soviets who were actually tracking the aircraft. The operators on Shemya simply intercepted the Morse transmissions and plotted them out on the big wall map. This procedure is called "grid plotting" by operators, and it allows them to "see" precisely what the Soviets were in fact seeing on their radar screens. The consoles were connected to a tape machine so that, if desired, the information could immediately be printed out on magnetic tape. If the intercepted material was considered of importance, the contents of the tape could be instantly transmitted to National Security Agency headquarters at Fort Meade and to other locations.

Elwin Williamson recalled that through their earphones the operators on Shemya could hear as the Soviets began tracking the Seaboard DC-8 in international airspace midway between Shemya Island and the Kamchatka Peninsula. Excited operators began calling out the coordinates as Soviet fighters later took off to intercept Flight 253A as it intruded into their airspace. Other operators plotted the aircraft's dangerous course on the big wall map. "We had a line on our board which we left up for about two weeks where you could see the plane come and stop," Williamson said.[35] Etorofu Island, where the DC-8 eventually was forced down, lies over 1,000 miles from Shemya. This tracking seems quite a feat in an area described 15 years later by the Federal Aviation Administration as "beyond navigational coverage."

A former military watch officer who served in Korea said it is standard operating procedure to attempt to contact a civilian aircraft via air traffic controllers whenever it appears that it might precipitate a hostile reaction by going off course. Captain Tosolini of Flight 253A concurred: "When a plane flying this route strays off course toward Soviet territory, the U.S. Air Defense Command or the Japanese Self-Defense Forces normally signal it to turn away. *This happens all the time* [author's emphasis], but we were not warned by our Air Defense Command." [36]

The Seaboard World Airlines DC-8 was not alone as it drew close to Soviet territory. There were two other U.S. aircraft within Captain Tosolini's radio range as events unfolded. The first of these was a World Airways airliner that was flying some distance behind Flight 253A, also heading to Tachikawa Air Base at Yokota, Japan. The second plane was a Flying Tigers prop-jet heading toward an undisclosed location in Japan. Flying Tigers is a company reported to have long-standing connections to the U.S. intelligence community. [37] All of this took place near a sensitive Soviet military facility, the Vrevestinik Air Base on Etorofu Island.

The Soviets sent MiG-17 fighters aloft to intercept the intruder, and one of them appeared on the right side of the DC-8. "I was startled and took a second look and saw a red star on it," said Tosolini. As the captain looked, the Russian pilot motioned for him to turn his DC-8 toward Soviet territory. Tosolini twice asked his navigator to check the aircraft's position. As reported in the press at that time, Guernon replied both times that the DC-8 was not over Soviet territory. (In an interview in 1984, Guernon acknowledged to the author that the DC-8 probably had been in Soviet airspace.) [38]

In defiance of the instructions of the armed interceptor, Tosolini gently tried to steer his aircraft to the left, away from Soviet territory. Guernon later recounted that the MiG fighter then swooped beneath the DC-8, came up close on the port side to block the maneuver, and wiggled his wings in the international signal to "follow me." Tosolini then steered the DC-8 sharply to the left, "hoping," as he said, "to get out of [the MiG's] way." [39] This abrupt move was interpreted by the Soviet pilot as evasive action.

What happened next was described by Army Sp/5 (Specialist Fifth Class) Franklin Campbell, Jr., one of the military personnel on board the airliner. "We were sitting on the left-hand side of the plane looking out the window when a MiG appeared near the wing tip and fired a couple of cannon bursts in front of the plane. The pilot of the MiG began making hand motions with his thumb pointing downwards, apparently ordering our pilot to land." Two cannon bursts in all were fired parallel to the path of the airliner, according to several other of the military personnel on board the DC-8. [40]

Larry Guernon credits Captain Tosolini for dismissing check pilot Ralph Neary's suggestion at this point in the interception that he continue evasive actions. This seems an extraordinary suggestion since the MiG-17 had already given a number of interception signals, had fired cannon bursts when these went unheeded, was armed with air-to-air missiles, and was so close that, as Guernon remarked, "you could see the creases in the fighter pilot's face." Tosolini rocked his wings as a sign to the Soviet pilot that he acknowledged the interception and would comply with instructions. Had he not obeyed the instructions of the MiG to land, Tosolini commented afterwards, his airliner probably would have been shot down.[41]

Radar at the Japanese Air Force Station at Nemuro picked up Flight 253A at 8:12 A.M., Tokyo time, flying at an altitude of 21,000 feet at a distance of 250 miles. Although the plane was "immediately recognized," it was not promptly warned that it was 100 miles off course. At 8:17, the DC-8 radioed to civilian air traffic controllers at Narita International Airport in Tokyo, saying, "Soviet aircraft are interfering with our flight at 150 degrees east longitude." When controllers at Narita asked what was going on, Tosolini replied, "We are on course and don't know why they are interfering." At 8:20, 8 minutes after picking the plane up on radar and three minutes after the interception had begun, Nemuro radioed on the international emergency frequency: "If you continue as you are going, you'll enter Soviet territory, so take a southern course." Tosolini radioed back that the course could not be changed. Five minutes later he radioed, "It looks like we're over Soviet territory."[42]

Both before and during the interception, Captain Tosolini was in communication with the other two U.S. aircraft nearby. A number of communications between the DC-8 and the World Airways crew took place. Tosolini was also in continuous radio contact with Richard Rossi, the pilot of the Flying Tigers plane. Rossi's plane was behind the DC-8 by several miles but well within visual range. As the MiG-17s closed in, Rossi laughingly radioed to Tosolini, "What're those little mosquitoes next to you fellows?"[43] The Tigers plane was also in Soviet territory.

Prior to landing, Tosolini circled the airfield on Etorofu. According to his account, he wanted to make certain that the runway would accommodate an aircraft as large as a DC-8. As he circled, two other MiGs flew directly across his path to indicate he should touch down immediately. One report said that Tosolini communicated detailed information to Flying Tigers pilot Rossi, such as a description of the runway and facilities at Vrevestinik Air Base. According to the Pentagon, at 8:39 A.M., Japan time, Tosolini reported that he had landed his aircraft without injury or damage.[44]

The Soviets believed that the DC-8 was on an intelligence mission. The general who interrogated Tosolini on Etorofu said that Soviet air defense radar had been tracking two aircraft for some time prior to the interception. One was surely his DC-8, but Tosolini denied knowledge of any other plane.

The Pentagon quickly announced that its chartered troop transport was "apparently off course." William Evans, a spokesman for the FAA, said, "We have reliable information, including radar data, that there was a violation of Soviet airspace." He added, "This is something that's almost impossible to guard against because the route is almost out of range of ground-based navigational aids."[45] This is an interesting construction. While the radar data cited by Evans were military, the navigational aids to which he referred were civilian. Although reference to extensive radar tracking suggested extensive monitoring of the flight, the public face put on the incident was quite different.

The United States Government seemed eager to dispose of the incident. Shortly after Flight 253A was forced to land on Etorofu, Secretary of State Dean Rusk telephoned Soviet Ambassador Anatoly Dobrynin to explain the incident and ask for the immediate return of the aircraft, its passengers, and crew. The following day, U.S. Ambassador to the Soviet Union Llewellyn E. Thompson pleaded for the release of the downed airliner at the Moscow ceremony for the signing of the nuclear nonproliferation treaty. The Soviets demanded an apology for the intrusion, and the United States quickly complied, expressing regret and attributing the violation of Soviet airspace to "navigational error." On July 3, State Department press officer Robert J. McCloskey announced that the Johnson administration regarded the case as closed.[46]

Captain Tosolini and Seaboard World Airlines accepted no responsibility. In an interview three weeks after the State Department said it considered the incident closed, the DC-8 captain was emphatic: "I did not stray over Russian territory." However, the FAA conducted an investigation into the incident, and Seaboard World Airlines was fined $5,000 for violating six FAA regulations. The FAA report said that the aircraft "was operated carelessly so as to endanger lives and property of others by causing the flight to be performed with inadequate navigation equipment, permitting the aircraft to deviate from its course."[47] A remarkable finding considering the newness of the aircraft, the new navigational equipment installed, the experience of the crew, the presence of a senior check pilot and flight engineer, plus the presence of five additional "special checkers."

Joseph Tosolini is still flying as a captain for Flying Tigers. Other members of Flight 253A's crew, including head stewardess Patricia Parlette, are also with Flying Tigers. Several years after the 1968 incident, all of Seaboard World Airlines' operations were fully subsumed beneath the management of Flying Tigers, a company reportedly with connections to the Central Intelligence Agency.

The history of unauthorized flights over the Soviet Union and other Communist nations shares three similarities: Direct or indirect connections between the airline involved and U.S. intelligence services, a consistent pattern of obfuscation and denial on the part of the U.S. Government, and the troubling occurrence of these incidents at key moments in arms control negotiations.

5

KOREAN
AIR LINES

It was, by several accounts, a genuine Horatio Alger story, South Korean style.[1] After the liberation of Korea in 1945, Cho Choong-hoon—known as "Harry" to westerners—was driving along in his truck when he passed a jeep on the side of the road. Cho stopped his truck, offered a hand, and got the jeep started. One of the jeep's occupants, a U.S. military officer, was grateful and told Cho to come by and see him sometime. When Cho did, the result was a contract to haul goods for the U.S. military. The military was "the only game in town," according to a Korean lawyer familiar with Cho, "and Harry Cho had a truck." On November 1, 1945, Cho founded Hanjin Transportation, a truck company in Inchon. According to *Business Week,* Hanjin made tens of millions of dollars during these early years.[2]

During the Korean War, Hanjin hauled drinking water to U.S. troops, realizing substantial profits.[3] After the armistice, Hanjin thrived on business sparked by the U.S. shipments of military supplies and aid to South Korea. "Everyone was involved in getting his hands on as much of the U.S. aid as possible," said Merrill Hulse, who was the Seoul station manager of Civil Air Transport at that time.

The Vietnam war presented Harry Cho and his brother Cho Choon-kun (nicknamed "Charley") with their next business opportunity. South Korea sent its first combat troops to Vietnam in 1965, and the Cho brothers earned their share of the largesse, once again winning major contracts with the U.S. military. Hanjin earned the reputation, according to the *New York Times,* of delivering "ammunition to areas where other haulers were reluctant to go."[4] By several accounts, Hanjin's Vietnam ventures firmly established it as a corporate power. With the money they made in Vietnam, the Cho brothers were able to buy Korean Air Lines.

On January 9, 1962, the Supreme Council for National Reconstruction, the governing body of the junta led by Park Chung-hee, announced that a state-run airline would be established within a year. The privately owned Korean National Airline (KNA), started in 1951 with the help of Civil Air Transport, a wholly owned proprietary of the U.S. Central Intelligence Agency, was over $800,000 in debt and in financial ruin. On November 27, the Park government shut down the airline. At the same time, the junta cleared the way for the initial flights of Korean Air Lines, which had leased its first two airplanes from Japan Air Lines and All Nippon Airlines.[5]

KAL got off to a slow start. The airline had one DC-9 jet, which was rendered useless for several months after a flight attendant left the faucet running in a lavatory and the overflowing water ruined the electrical wiring of the plane. In 1966, the *New York Times* referred to the five-plane operation as "one of the world's smallest state-run airlines."[6]

KAL served as an asset to the Korean Central Intelligence Agency (KCIA), which was established, designed, provisioned, and trained by the U.S. CIA in the early 1960s to coordinate both international and domestic intelligence activities for the Park regime. Ever since, the American and Korean agencies have been described as "deep in one another's pockets." In June 1967, when the KCIA kidnapped over twenty anti-Park Korean intellectuals from West Germany and other European countries, the agency used KAL planes to bring them back to South Korea. An associate of Kim Hyung-wook, who was director of the KCIA from 1963 to 1969, maintained he learned from Kim that KAL planes overflew North Korea and, on occasion, the Soviet Union for intelligence purposes.[7] *Boston Globe* reporter Fred Kaplan noted that "a former U.S. Army intelligence officer remembers 'very clearly' being told in 1967 by an Air Force intelligence instructor that 'side-view cameras'—which take big, very clear pictures from long distances—were occasionally attached to commercial airliners flying along sensitive borders, and that Korean Air Lines was among those companies."[8]

In 1969, in a deal facilitated by Lee Hu-rak, the head of the Secretariat of the presidential mansion Chongwadae (called the Blue House) from 1963–69 and director of the KCIA from 1970–73, the interests of the government and the Cho brothers came together when Hanjin took over the airline. "It was a very, very special sweetheart deal," said a former Korean official close to the negotiations. "The fact that they were the ones to get the airline is one indication of how close they were to the Park regime," noted James Klemstine who was an economic officer in the U.S. Embassy in Seoul at the time. "It was a nice gift." Harry Cho was named president of KAL, Charley Cho vice-president, and the airline moved into a new twenty-three-story building, the largest in South Korea at the time, erected in downtown Seoul by Hanjin.[9]

Following the Cho brothers' takeover of KAL, they became an integral part of a power structure where the lines between corporate, political, intelligence, and military sectors were never clearly defined. According to a former U.S. intelligence official, the Chos "cooperated fully in anything the government wanted. KAL functioned as an arm of the KCIA. If the KCIA wanted to plant agents in the United States, they would be given phony documentation and brought over as KAL staffers. The KCIA used KAL pilots to smuggle money, operational supplies, and other things." According to the Korean attorney, "KAL is a means of transportation that is reliable for [the KCIA]. If it is asked to cooperate in matters of security, it can't say no." This relationship was, of course, highly advantageous: "No one at the Korean civil aeronautics board could supervise them," a former Korean government official said. "They would ignore the board and deal with higher political officials."

The airline developed a number of other operational links with Korean intelligence and the South Korean government. According to a company employee, when Korean intelligence agents fly to the United States on KAL, the airline's office at the airport receives a telex notifying it that a "Mr. So-and-So from, say, Room 201 of the Blue House is arriving on such a date. Please see to him." In these instances, a company employee would escort the agent through customs and immigration, avoiding searches and delays. The airline employee also said that on international flights there are two government security officers, usually in company uniform, and each plane carries a weapons box containing two or three guns, hand grenades, mace, and chloroform. While most airlines offer discounted travel to government officials, KAL provides free transportation to Korean government employees.

Korean intelligence has also used KAL as a front in its efforts to influence leaders in other countries. According to the associate of KCIA Director Kim Hyung-wook, Korean intelligence has, on occasion, requested that the airline invite a foreign journalist, businessman, or official to South Korea, luring him with free transportation and hotel accommodations and then acting as host during the trip. A Korean journalist in the United States said that KAL places advertisements in newspapers in the U.S. at inflated prices, with the implicit threat that it will pull the advertisements if the newspaper is critical of the South Korean government.

A former Korean government official familiar with KAL operations told *The Nation*, "If the airline was losing money overseas, the government subsidized some portion of the losses. That's why KAL grew up so fast— government subsidies. KAL was a special favor to Hanjin," he added.

"Many corporations started the same way. That means you have got to say yes to the president." And President Park Chung-hee did not hesitate to call on his friends when the need arose.

That need seemed to arise in 1973. On August 8, opposition leader Kim Dae-jung was kidnapped from his hotel room in Tokyo by KCIA agents. Five days later he was released near his home in Seoul. According to several sources, at the request of the Park regime Harry Cho dispensed payoffs to Japanese politicians after the kidnapping, presumably to smooth ruffled feathers. A former Korean government official confirmed that Harry Cho "was used undercover by Park" for political payoffs in Japan. The *Boston Globe* and other newspapers reported that in the early to mid-1970s, Charley Cho "passed money back and forth between the KCIA and Japanese businessmen, legislators, and opinion leaders" and that the money flowed most heavily after the kidnapping.[10]

Although the Lockheed scandal in Japan never drew in KAL or the Cho brothers, they came close to a similar scandal. According to an April 27, 1979, report in the *Wall Street Journal,* the U.S. Federal Trade Commission prepared draft complaints asserting that between 1971 and 1975 the Boeing Corporation paid $3.5 million to officers of KAL to sell two 747 and one 707 aircraft. "The payments were made by Boeing Corp. through a Japanese consulting firm," the draft complaints said. KAL denied the charge, and the FTC never filed the complaint in court because Boeing agreed to a consent order prohibiting future payoffs.

A number of mini-scandals involving KAL did come to light. On September 21, 1974, South Korean police arrested Charley Cho on charges of diverting $330,000 in funds earned by KAL in Japan and the United States to buy real estate abroad. In its rush to become one of the key players in Asian aviation, KAL has been extremely aggressive. In 1975 it was investigated, along with two other airlines, as to offering kickbacks to U.S. travel agents. Under a U.S.–Korean agreement, KAL can charge any fare it pleases. Since other airlines, notably Northwest and Pan American, match the low prices, KAL gave rebates to travel agents to undercut the published fares. One New York travel agent quoted in the *Wall Street Journal* said that KAL paid him a commission of 25 percent for "being a nice guy," while Pan Am paid him the usual 8 percent. The effect of this was that travel agents worked harder for KAL than for U.S. carriers. KAL denied such a policy: "Our commissions are pretty much in line with [those of] other carriers," a KAL spokesman in Los Angeles said. In 1976, it was one of thirteen airlines found guilty in the United States of providing illegal rebates to passengers and freight customers. That same year, the Japanese Transport Agency warned KAL and five other airlines against continued heavy discounting of trans-Pacific routes.[11]

As KAL expanded its routes in the 1970s, it also moved into a new line of work—contracting for both the South Korean and U.S. militaries. In 1976, the airline opened its Special Projects Division in a plant in Pusan to assemble Hughes helicopters for the Korean military. Over the next five years, KAL assembled 150 military helicopters in a series of contracts designed to take the airline from merely assembling helicopter kits provided by Hughes to completely manufacturing the helicopters in South Korea. "This was the seed activity to establish the Korean aerospace industry," said Rob Mack, a public affairs officer for McDonnell Douglas Helicopter, the company that acquired Hughes Helicopter in 1984. In 1980, KAL signed a joint-manufacturing agreement with Northrop to assemble F-5 jet fighters for the Korean Air Force.[12]

In 1979, KAL began repairing and servicing U.S. Air Force F-4 jet fighters at one of its maintenance facilities, the result of an initial Air Force contract of over $8 million. At the present time, KAL services Air Force planes throughout the entire Pacific theater. Included are F-4s, F-15s, F-16s, A-10 attack planes, and Navy C-130 cargo planes at the Kimhae Air Base.[13] The value of KAL's contract work for fiscal year 1985 was $27 million, according to Air Force figures. Peter Spriggs, a public affairs officer at the Air Force Logistics Command, states that of all the companies listed on the Contract Maintenance Center's roster of major Air Force contractors throughout the world (about forty-eight in total), only two civilian airline companies are noted: Philippines Air, whose contract is limited to C-130 corrosion control, and Korean Air Lines.

There are also suggestions that KAL is involved in the international arms trade. In 1983, *Time* magazine reported that U.S. Customs officials said KAL was registered with the U.S. State Department as "an exporter of arms, ammunition, and implements of war." KAL and several other South Korean countries made sixty separate purchases of Hawk missiles and parts, and diverted the weapons to Iran, despite a State Department ban on all weapons sales to that country. *Defense Week* reported, "The U.S. Customs Service is considering launching an investigation to find out how substantial amounts of military equipment, particularly spare parts for F-4s and F-5s, are winding up in Iran. The suspicion is that the supplies are coming in from South Korea and that Korea has replaced Israel as Iran's alleged major supplier of U.S.-origin equipment." KAL coproduces the F-5 and services both fighters.

KAL appears to have made another suspicious weapons purchase in 1982. According to Hughes Aircraft invoices, the airline bought twenty-five M65 tube-launched, optically tracked, wire-guided (TOW) missile systems. This is an antitank weapon designed for attachment to certain military helicopters, including the helicopters KAL coproduces with McDonnell Douglas Helicopter Company. The airline paid $3.9 million for the M65 TOWs, which are listed on an Air Force document as part of a Hughes deal that also involved sales to Israel. On the Hughes invoice, the destination to which the TOW systems were to be shipped was "OUR RECORDS ONLY." Since the invoice calls for information regarding a shipping address only if the goods are to be delivered to a location other than the purchaser's address, the suggestion is that the missile systems were destined for somewhere other than "Korean Airlines, Seoul, South Korea."

Several individuals familiar with the U.S.–South Korean weapons trade could not explain the purchase. "To my knowledge, no TOWs have been sold to KAL, which would have no use for an antitank weapon," remarked a Hughes official involved in the TOW program. "They have to be sold through governments and can't be sold to individual companies. . . . This doesn't make any sense to me." Clyde Bryant of the State Department's Office of Munition Control echoed the Hughes official: "No sales of TOW missiles can be made to a private corporation. It does not make sense. I cannot conceive of such a sale taking place if not directly to the South Korean government." When asked if KAL might have acquired the M65 TOW systems for the South Korean government, which is a large purchaser of TOWs, Col. Yoong Sam, Logistics Service attaché of the South Korean embassy, said, "If the Republic of Korea government purchases complete equipment, it doesn't use private companies. It makes direct contact with the U.S. supplier." But the invoices are real. All of these findings suggest that the White House's recent Iranian arms deals may have had a considerably earlier South Korean connection.

Given these activities as an intelligence asset, military contractor, arms broker, and conduit for political payoffs, the image of KAL as a civilian air carrier is difficult to sustain. While airlines in developing nations often have multiple government ties, KAL has many more than usual, and its symbiotic relationship with the South Korean government leads some observers to wonder if KAL is, *de facto,* an arm of that government.

The growth of KAL has been dramatic, with some of the most important financing coming from the U.S. Export-Import Bank in the 1970s, when William J. Casey was its president and chairman. By its own account it is now one of the top ten carriers in the world.[14] By any account it is the second largest carrier based in the Far East, after Japan Air Lines. In 1983, the carrier had a fleet of thirteen Boeing 747s, which included two 747SP (special performance) long-range versions, seven 747 200Bs, and four 747 200F freighters. The company had three other 747s on order. In addition, KAL owned five DC-10s, eight European Airbus A300s, seven vintage Boeing 707s, and five 727s. In the summer of 1985, Harry Cho announced that the airline's goal is to expand its business by 10 percent.[15] "Especially remarkable," Cho wrote, "is the fact that Korean Air has been designated as the official carrier for the 1986 Asian Games and the 1988 Olympic Games" to be held in Seoul.

A hint of SALT was in the air in the spring of 1978 as the United States and the Soviet Union renewed efforts to conclude the Strategic Arms Limitation (SALT 2) agreement. SALT 1 had expired on October 3 the previous fall, and Secretary of State Cyrus Vance was scheduled to travel to Moscow on April 19 for three days of meetings with Soviet leaders to try to iron out some of the remaining problems regarding the provisions of the new agreement. There was reason for some optimism. It was hoped that these initiatives would pave the way for a later summit conference between President Jimmy Carter and Soviet leader Leonid Brezhnev. That was before Korean Air Lines Flight 902.

At the beginning of the flight everything seemed normal to the passengers who boarded the KAL Boeing 707 321-B jet transport at Orly Airport in Paris. Nobody was especially upset when the airliner took off at 1:39 P.M., Paris time, either 9 or 39 minutes behind schedule, depending on the source. Some later claimed that Flight 902's delay was intentional. An article published by the Soviet-front U.S. Peace Council suggested that the delayed departure was necessary to coordinate the airliner's intrusion into Soviet airspace with one or more U.S. ferret electronic intelligence satellites.[16] Whether or not the delay was designed for purposes of "coordination" remains unsubstantiated, but the fact is that at least two satellites—one a newly launched ferret and the other a KH-11 "Keyhole" photoreconnaissance satellite—were in position several hours later to monitor Flight 902 when it intruded into Soviet territory.[17] It is also true that a delay of 40 minutes produced an overlap between the paths of a ferret satellite and KAL Flight 007 five years later.

Flight 902 was assigned a route that would take it to Anchorage, Alaska, where it was scheduled to arrive at 11:00 A.M., local time, 9 hours 20 minutes after takeoff. After a refueling stop, it was then to proceed to Seoul, South Korea, a total distance of 8,455 miles.[18] The flight plan called for a northwest course over the North Sea, making routine checkpoint reports along the way. At the plane's cruising altitude the weather was clear, with a cloud layer below. Flight 902 passed over the Faeroe Islands and later to the northeast of Iceland, swinging to the west to cross the coast of Greenland at Scoresbysund.

Both the aircraft and the crew were well equipped for polar flights. According to *Aviation Week & Space Technology,* the 707's navigational equipment included a dual Doppler radar and LORAN system in addition to its magnetic compass and sextant.[19] Although not as accurate as the more advanced inertial navigation system on board some planes, this equipment provided a reliable and redundant means of navigation. Neither the Doppler radar nor the LORAN (an acronym for Long-Range Navigation) is affected by the oddities that beset magnetic compasses in the polar regions.

The crew of Flight 902 was experienced. According to Korean Air Lines, forty-six-year-old Captain Kim Chang-kyu was a veteran who had logged more than 11,500 flight hours and had previously flown the polar route seventy times without incident. First Officer Cha Soon-do, also a veteran pilot, had been flying the polar route for more than five years.[20] Also in the cockpit was Lee Kun-shik, an experienced navigator whose job was to continually check on the plane's position.

As the flight progressed, Captain Kim radioed a position report to an air traffic control station at Spitzbergen in Svalbard, 400 miles off Norway's North Cape. He said that his airliner was over Greenland and requested that the Norwegian controllers relay his position report to a ground station at Keflavik, Iceland. Kim said he could not get through because of "atmospheric conditions." It was unusual for a plane in Flight 902's position to communicate with the ostensibly more distant Spitzbergen station rather than Keflavik, suggesting either that the airliner was out of range of very-high-frequency transmitters and thus off course or was experiencing radio problems, yet the relay was not questioned. According to the Federal Aviation Administration, the last report from Flight 902 was picked up by amateur radio operators in Canada when the plane radioed that it was near the Alert station of Canadian Defense Forces on Ellesmere Island, off the northwest coast of Greenland. This final message came 5 hours and 21 minutes after takeoff. (Other sources say the message was received at the intelligence facility at Bodø, Norway.) At about this point in the flight, approximately 3½ hours away from Anchorage, Captain Kim turned his aircraft around in what *Time* magazine described as a "180-degree turn back toward Europe."[21]

Canadian air traffic controllers reported Flight 902 overdue at 7:00 P.M., Paris time, 5½ hours after takeoff, when it failed to make a scheduled position report. The controllers repeatedly tried to contact the Korean plane, and a search was initiated shortly thereafter. Trying to understand what had happened to a civil airliner in an area under its control, the Canadian government then requested the North American Air Defense Command to play back its radar tapes to determine when the airliner actually disappeared from radar coverage. NORAD responded that it "had no information on the plane." It was only many hours later that the U.S. informed Canada the plane was down in Soviet territory.[22]

It was a remarkable navigational deviation, and the stories about its cause differ. Afterwards, Captain Kim would say that although his navigational equipment was giving him accurate readings for his course to Anchorage, his "sixth sense" told him that something was amiss. Kim also said that Lee, the navigator, repeatedly told him that the airliner was on course. First Officer Cha was quoted by the *Washington Post* as saying that "the crew somehow became disoriented. . . . Their instruments seemed to be indicating that they were in a safe flight path." Yet accounts from those on board Flight 902 have Kim telling terrified passengers after the crash landing that his compass had gone awry. In a different account, KAL President Cho later told reporters that the crew told him the deviation from course happened because "an electrical shock paralyzed the navigation system." Navigator Lee similarly claimed that the gyrocompass had failed as well as the LORAN—completely independent systems having nothing to do with the magnetic compass or on-board radios.[23]

Most news accounts of the incident obscured a key point. They noted that the plane took off from Paris in the early afternoon, made reports later in the afternoon, and entered Soviet territory as dusk was falling. Things seem chronologically in order until Flight 902's estimated time of arrival in Anchorage is known—11:00 A.M. As Oliver Clubb noted, Captain Kim turned away from the growing light and "flew for three hours toward the darkness encroaching from the east before entering Soviet airspace." This oddity was not lost on the passengers. Kishio Ohtani, a Tokyo camera shop owner, said he realized that something was wrong when he looked out the window. The Arctic sun, which had been on the right side of the plane, was suddenly on the left. According to the *Washington Post,* several of the other passengers said "they had become concerned when they noticed that the plane, which had been flying away from the setting sun, was suddenly flying toward it."[24] Captain Kim's "sixth sense" may have told him something was wrong, but what about his eyes?

According to the Russians, an unidentified aircraft was first spotted by their radar stations on Franz Josef Land, a group of islands in the Arctic Ocean about 700 miles north of the Soviet mainland. As the plane continued toward their territory, they said, numerous unsuccessful attempts were made by ground stations to contact the plane to ascertain its identity. Captain Kim later claimed his crew heard nothing and, as the *Washington Post* pointed out years later, "Western intelligence reports never cleared up this contradiction." The Russians had some reason to worry about the unidentified aircraft coming at them at 35,000 feet. The course flown by the plane was one frequently used by Rivet Joint RC-135s, monitoring electronic transmissions from the Kola Peninsula, a highly sensitive military region. The Soviets promptly concluded it was an American reconnaissance plane.[25]

Murmansk on the Kola Peninsula is the headquarters of the Soviet Northern Fleet, its port kept open by the combination of a warm current and icebreakers. Just a few miles to the north is the naval complex at Severomorsk and an important nuclear submarine base at Polyarnyy. Two mobile army divisions and a brigade of amphibious troops are said to be stationed along the border between the Soviet Union, Finland, and Norway. There are an estimated 900,000 soldiers and airmen based on the nearby Kola Peninsula alone. In the area are located medium-range missiles aimed at Western Europe, as well as the early-warning radar network that activates the antiballistic missile system surrounding Moscow. There are eight air bases in the area, reported to house between sixty and eighty long- and medium-range bombers. The air defense presence in the area is substantial and was undergoing a major buildup at the time. So sensitive is and was the area that maps, including those on board Flight 902, carried the notice, "Aircraft Infringing Upon Non Free Flying Territory May Be Fired On Without Warning."[26]

The Soviets were not the only ones watching as Flight 902 continued toward their airspace. Just as in the Far East, the Kola Peninsula area is ringed with U.S. and allied listening stations, some of the most important located in Norway. Antennas monitoring communications from Soviet submarines, surface ships, and aircraft are located at Vadsø, Jessheim, Randaberg, and Skage. William Burrows noted that there are UHF and VHF intercept facilities at Vadsø, Viksjøfjell, Vardø, Randaberg, and Fauske, most pointed toward the Murmansk area. There is a Satellite Data System (SDS) ground station at Vetan, and the stations at Vadsø and Viksjøfjell have sixty-foot-high concrete towers to intercept microwave telemetry from Soviet missile tests.[27]

The NATO tracking and listening station at Bodø, Norway, eavesdropped on the Russians as the southbound plane entered the Soviet air defense identification zone 200 miles to the north of the mainland. U.S. personnel at the station were attentive as it entered Soviet airspace over the Barents Sea and as Soviet interceptor fighters were scrambled in response. Stations at Vadsø and Barhauge monitored both Soviet ground- and air-based communications as the Russians reacted to the intruder. (That the Russians scrambled their fighters casts doubt on later suggestions that the NATO operators "thought [Flight 902] was a Soviet plane.") NATO sources later acknowledged that electronic surveillance units continued to track the airliner as it flew over the submarine base at Severomorsk, naval headquarters at Murmansk, and then continued south for another 200 miles over the radar facility at Olenegorsk and the bomber base at Malyavr. In addition to the personnel in Norway, American personnel at the intelligence facilities at Chicksands near London; Edzell, Scotland; Elmendorf Air Force Base, Alaska; Augsburg and Boerfink, West Germany; and at Marienfelde and Teufelsberg, West Berlin, monitored Soviet communications throughout the entire period. Information was relayed instantly via satellite to National Security Agency headquarters outside of Washington.[28]

According to Captain Kim's story, when he saw the lights of a city below he asked Lee, the navigator, to check the plane's location. Lee "checked and checked," according to Kim, "but finally he gave up. He didn't know." The Soviets say they sent up two fighters to intercept the intruder as it approached the air frontier. They also claim that the lights were turned on at the Murmansk airport to provide the intruder with an appropriate landing site.[29] As with the interception of Flight 007 five years later, the Soviet claim exaggerates the competence with which Flight 902 was eventually located and brought down.

In fact, Soviet incompetence appears to have been extreme. Although the high-flying airliner should have been visible to radar for hundreds of miles before actually entering Soviet airspace, it flew unchallenged through the 200-mile-wide air defense zone off the coast. It was over Soviet territory for almost 20 minutes before being successfully intercepted, another suggestion of problems with Soviet air defenses. The *San Francisco Examiner & Chronicle* reported that "according to U.S. sources who listened to the electronic intelligence tapes of Soviet responses, the first interceptor ordered in pursuit could not take off because of mechanical problems. Most of the pilots of the second unit ordered into action were drunk." Another report said that the recordings made by Western intelligence "reportedly reveal an atmosphere of chaos augmented by mounting panic as the 707 flew steadily deeper into Russia." It was only pilots from the third unit ordered in pursuit who finally made it into the air.[30]

According to the Soviet account, word of Flight 902's intrusion reached Moscow in 18 minutes. As Flight 902 continued south, unresponsive to radio queries from ground stations and to the signals from the interceptors, they became convinced that at any moment the intruder would turn to the west and try to escape over the Finnish border. (Several years later, the Soviets claimed that the Korean airliner had in fact turned toward the border in an effort to escape.) So a decision was made to fire on the airliner, not to destroy it, the Soviets said, but to bring it down in a condition that would permit a thorough examination.[31] The U-2 incident had demonstrated that catching spy planes can be an enormous propaganda coup.

At the time, many accounts in the American press claimed that the Soviets fired on the airliner without warning. An account in *Time* magazine is representative: "Radio contact was never established. None of the standard international signals to land, such as lowering wheels and turning on landing lights, were given. Instead, U.S. officials say, one of the Sukhoi-15s fired two missiles at the plane." After the downing of Flight 007 in 1983, South Korean Foreign Minister Lee Bum-suk harkened back to the incident involving Flight 902, telling newsmen that the airliner "was given no warning by his Soviet attackers."[32]

The Soviet account was dramatically different. The Soviet news agency Tass said that two Sukhoi-15 fighters circled the 707 and signaled it with landing lights. One of the fighters "fired a rocket trailing green smoke as a warning signal after no radio response to orders to follow the fighters to an airport." When that produced no response, the first fighter pulled away and another approached from behind, firing three bursts of cannon shells. The fighters were finally ordered to force down the intruder with a missile after it engaged in what were described as "evasive actions." As Soviet Premier Aleksei Kosygin remarked to Japanese Agriculture and Forestry Minister Ichiro Nakagawa shortly after the incident, Flight 902 was told to land at an airport on Soviet territory. "The crew did not follow the instruction," Kosygin said, and "took evasive action . . . in a vain attempt to get away."[33]

Additonal confusion would be created by Captain Kim himself five years later at the time of the downing of KAL Flight 007. Reflecting on his own experience, Kim said he saw the Soviet interceptor only once, off to the right and behind his aircraft, whereas international guidelines call for the interceptor to be on the left side. He said he slowed his speed and turned his landing lights on and off repeatedly. Kim also said he was unable to communicate with the interceptor because Soviet fighters are not equipped with radios capable of transmitting on the international hailing frequency, in order "to prevent Russian defections." Press reports at the time also made this suggestion, but they ignored the fact that Soviet ground stations can communicate on the international frequency.[34] And no response was received from Flight 902.

In trying to make sense out of the conflicting accounts, Flight 902 offered one source of information that Flight 007 did not: surviving passengers. According to their accounts, an interceptor followed the 707 on the right side in close formation for about 15 minutes. At one point the Soviet pilot pulled very close to the 707 and signaled it to land. First Officer Cha obliquely confirmed this later when he told reporters that the interceptor pilot pulled alongside and made "a threatening sign" which he said he "did not understand." The Sukhoi-15 was so close that passengers and crew alike recalled seeing the red star on the Soviet aircraft. Some passengers even took pictures. The interceptor then fell back. What happened next was described by Japanese passenger Seiko Shiozaki, who noted that she saw "many lights" suddenly flashing close to the left side of the airliner —tracer bullets. As Zbigniew Brzezinski, President Carter's national security adviser, noted, the fighter had opened fire in order to force the Korean airliner to land only when other means had failed. Former CIA Director Stansfield Turner remarked that "when the Soviets gave the signals, the pilot didn't obey." In spite of the crew members' subsequent protests that they saw nothing, the interception procedure appears to have been proceeding step by step, with signals and cannon bursts. But the plane did not respond and continued flying south.[35]

Then came an explosion. Two missiles had been fired. According to U.S. officials, the first missed and the other exploded on the left side of the airliner, shearing off about 15 feet of the left wing and damaging the fin, rudder, and brake system. The attentive intelligence personnel at Bodø, Norway, later said the missile that hit was a radar-guided Anab, a type designed to explode with a proximity fuse when it gets sufficiently close to its target. The force of the explosion tore a hole in the fuselage and sent pieces of shrapnel into the cabin. Two passengers were critically injured. One was killed instantly; the other bled to death a few minutes later. Thirteen others were wounded. One man had twenty small pieces of shrapnel in his left foot. "There was smoke everywhere," Captain Kim recalled afterwards. "The emergency bells were ringing, and the plane was bucking and rocking all over." The wind was rushing in the passenger cabin. The oxygen masks had dropped down with the loss of pressure, and Captain Kim put his aircraft into a steep dive. "It was sudden, like a lift," recalled Karlheinz Schwaken, a passenger from Düsseldorf, West Germany.[36] Over a period of about five minutes the 707 descended to 3,000 feet.

But as far as is known, Captain Kim never did the obvious. He never issued a "Mayday" call to signal his serious condition. This was certainly not for lack of time, since the 707 continued to fly for nearly an hour at 3,000 feet. According to U.S. intelligence experts who monitored the Soviet radio traffic, at this point the Soviets lost track of Flight 902 completely. It was said the Soviet pilots even radioed to their base that the plane had been shot down.[37] NATO personnel monitored the confusion and heightened level of military activity occasioned by the continued flight of KAL 902, a flight said to have produced great intelligence gains for the attentive Western services. At no time did they attempt to contact the plane, presumably to avoid letting the Soviets know the extent of Western intelligence monitoring in the region.

The attack had taken place at 8:43 P.M., Paris time, and for the next hour and 42 minutes Captain Kim flew a meandering course over this militarily sensitive region. (It has been suggested that this may have been to continue exciting Soviet air defenses.) Finally, with fuel running low, Captain Kim made the decision to land his plane on a frozen lake.[38] The landing was gear-up, tearing off part of a wing, and shattering the ice. The time was 10:25 P.M., Paris time, almost ten and a half hours after takeoff. Over the microphone Kim shouted, "We have survived!" and the passengers burst into applause.[39]

Captain Kim emerged from the cockpit to speak with the passengers, explaining how his "sixth sense" told him the course was in error, although his navigational equipment was supposedly giving on-course readings. The passengers and crew did what they could for those who were wounded. About an hour later, Soviet troops arrived and surrounded the Boeing 707 airliner. After building a bonfire as a signal for the helicopters that were on their way, they boarded the plane and took passports from the passengers and crew. As the hours passed, helicopters arrived to take the passengers to Kem, the nearest town of any size. The seriously wounded were put on a plane for transport to a hospital in Leningrad.[40]

Senior U.S. officials were called to the White House within half an hour of the plane's landing to discuss and consider the situation. It was reported that President Carter did not participate in the meeting, although he did receive a 20-minute briefing on the latest developments later in the evening. Overall, the atmosphere was cautious, and the White House seemed to be trying to head off an atmosphere of crisis. Secretary of State Cyrus Vance had just that day concluded a meeting on the SALT 2 treaty with Soviet Chief of Staff Nikolai V. Ogarkov, although they reportedly did not discuss Flight 902.[41] Calming messages were sent to Congress and members of the press.

Negotiations for the release of the passengers and crew were organized by the United States. While the Soviets agreed to the prompt release of the passengers and most of the crew, they detained both Captain Kim and navigator Lee for an additional eight days of questioning. "They kept on insisting to me that I intentionally flew over the Soviet Union," Kim recounted later. "No, no, no, I kept saying." The Soviets announced later in Tass that both Kim and his navigator eventually pleaded guilty to "violating the USSR's airspace." They had "confirmed" to Soviet authorities that they had "understood the orders of the Soviet interceptors but did not obey these orders." (The Soviets released the statement by Captain Kim, dated April 22, 1978, after the downing of KAL Flight 007 five years later.) After Kim and Lee made these admissions, Tass said, they were pardoned and released.[42]

Arriving in Copenhagen, Kim and Lee were immediately surrounded by KAL officials and agents from Korean Central Intelligence. In a formal talk with reporters, Kim made his comments through an official of the Korean embassy, although he both speaks and understands English. Kim refused to say if he had seen or heard any of the signals of the interceptors or if he ever saw the Soviet planes. He acknowledged awareness of an explosion but refused to confirm that he was fired upon. He refused to comment on the Tass report.[43]

The odyssey of KAL Flight 902 may have resulted in the loss of the aircraft and the deaths of two passengers, but it was a major intelligence boon for the U.S. and allied intelligence services that followed it every step of the way. Every detail was known: when and where the airliner entered the Soviet territory, when the interceptors were scrambled and from which bases, what orders were given, by whom and using what channels, and when the orders were executed. They knew that the Soviet pilot in close pursuit identified the plane as civilian and was ordered to force it down. They even knew how many missiles had been fired, that one had missed, and that the order to fire was intended to cripple, not kill, the intruder. Recalling the incident afterwards, former U.S. Ambassador to the Soviet Union Malcolm Toon commented, "The thing that really surprised us about that incident was the fact that the Soviet defense forces reacted so sluggishly to the penetration of their airspace by the Korean airliner."[44] In closed-door briefings, the CIA bragged to the Senate Intelligence Committee about how much intelligence had been collected, while failing to mention that Flight 902 had been on a course flown by RC-135s and had, in fact, been identified as an American reconnaissance plane. According to Adm. Bobby Inman, then deputy director of the CIA and later director of the National Security Agency, the details of this humiliating episode were leaked "by some U.S. officials who wanted to goad the Soviets." There was, he said, "a deliberate attempt in Washington to embarrass the Soviets."[45]

For the Russians, the result of all this was first embarrassment and later changes in air defense procedures. "It was very clear in the aftermath that the Soviets were very unhappy with the performance of their defense system," Inman said. In the wake of the incident, resolve stiffened in the Soviet air defense command to the point that "the Soviets will absolutely not tolerate any intrusion into their airspace."[46]

Subsequent reports suggested this in fact was the case. Writing in the *Washington Post* in 1983 after the downing of Flight 007, former Defense Secretary James R. Schlesinger said that following the 1978 incident reprimands were issued by the Soviets, court-martial proceedings were instituted, new rules of engagement were established, and warnings unquestionably issued that such an incident "must not be allowed to occur again." Other accounts attributed to Western intelligence sources reported that a number of senior Soviet air defense officers were sacked for permitting the Korean airliner to penetrate so far before it was downed. There were even rumors that six air defense colonels were shot as a result of the incident, although these have been dismissed by some Soviet experts in the West.[47]

And what of the pilot whose extraordinary deviation from course resulted in the death of two passengers, the injury of a number of others, and the loss of his aircraft? Kim is now a 747 captain, the most prestigious assignment for a Korean Air Lines pilot. During a trip to the West Coast early in 1985, I interviewed a person personally acquainted with Kim and other crew members of Flight 902. Not long after the 1978 incident, Kim was in command of a cargo flight with a scheduled stopover near this person's home town. During dinner the conversation came around to the Murmansk overflight. Kim was asked how it could happen that he, an experienced pilot, could turn his aircraft around in broad daylight, fail to make required reports, and fail to notice that he was flying toward the setting sun rather than away from it. Glancing at his copilot, Kim is said to have responded, "I just do what the government tells me."[48]

The history of Flight 902 is, to say the least, ambiguous, but for Reagan administration officials it became an object lesson in Soviet callousness and brutality. In a televised address to the nation after the downing of Flight 007, Ronald Reagan told the public, "In 1978, the Soviets also shot down an unarmed civilian airliner after having positively identified it as such. In that instance the Soviet interceptor pilot clearly identified the civilian markings on the side of the aircraft, repeatedly questioned the order to fire on the civilian airliner, and was ordered to shoot it down anyway. The aircraft was hit with a missile and made a crash landing. Several innocent people lost their lives in this attack—killed by shrapnel from the blast of a Soviet missile."[50] The Soviets did shoot it down but only after Flight 902 failed to respond to the attempts at interception. Until the full story is known, however, it might be wise to keep the jury out on KAL Flight 902. It seems there may be more to the story than just another example of Soviet callousness.

PART TWO
Aftermath

6

SAFE ON
SAKHALIN

The confused pattern of events during the first twenty or so hours following the downing of Flight 007 is not easy to unravel. Administration officials and their supporters say that information about the shootdown took hours for intelligence personnel to sort out and was thus quite tardy in arriving in Washington. Other evidence contradicts this, suggesting that things were understood far more quickly, that information about the shootdown arrived in Washington far sooner than has been acknowledged, and that a pattern of obfuscation began almost immediately concerning what the Administration knew and when it knew it.

In the early morning hours of September 1, the *Chidori Maru,* No. 58, a 99-ton cuttlefish boat was in the Sea of Japan about 36 kilometers west of Moneron Island off the coast of Sakhalin Island, heading in an east-northeasterly direction. The fishermen said that at approximately 3:30 A.M., Tokyo time (1830 GMT), they heard a noise like that of a jetliner followed by a great explosion. Then they saw a brilliant flash of light over the east-southeast horizon: a "glowing orange-colored, expanding fireball." The flash lasted for about five seconds, the fishermen said, then faded. A second explosive sound was heard, not as loud as the first explosion, followed by a series of successive flashes of orange light of less intensity than the original fireball. Some accounts reported a third explosion. The captain of the vessel said he noticed a strong smell of oil or gasoline about five minutes later.[1] Thinking the smell might come from their own boat, the crew looked for an oil slick but found none.

The *Chidori Maru* reported the flashes and explosions to another boat operating nearby, which relayed the message to the Japan Maritime Safety Agency (JMSA) office at Wakkanai. One of the patrol boats dispatched to the area found an oil slick off Cape Menushin on the southern tip of Sakhalin Island.[2]

Other indications of trouble would appear shortly. There is a Japanese air traffic control radar unit at Jyobonzam, on the eastern end of Hokkaido. The radar has a range of approximately 200 nautical miles, extending to waypoint NOHO on Romeo-20, and marks the beginning of civilian radar coverage from the Japanese islands. Based on its estimated time of arrival at waypoint NOKKA, its earlier obligatory reporting waypoint, Flight 007 should have arrived at NOHO at 1847 GMT. When Flight 015 showed up on the radar screens a few minutes later without Flight 007 in front of it, the Japanese air traffic controllers—reputedly some of the best in the world—knew they had a major problem on their hands. Within half an hour of the shootdown, Tokyo controllers notified both civilian and military agencies that Flight 007 had not appeared as scheduled and requested that the Japan Defense Agency, the Sapporo Air Control Center, and other agencies try to contact the missing airliner. Notification that Flight 007 was missing was also communicated shortly thereafter to the Air Route Traffic Control Centers in Tokyo and Anchorage.[3]

While there is disagreement over precisely when the Japan Defense Agency understood the meaning of the events over Sakhalin, all accounts agree that the JDA monitored those events as they took place. At the time of the shootdown, the intelligence stations at Wakkanai and Misawa had been monitoring the Soviet air defense flap for at least 1½ hours, and by some accounts for an hour beyond that—since the time of Flight 007's initial intrusion into Soviet territory.[4] Later on, the Japanese had the means to determine that the intruder causing all the commotion over Kamchatka, the Sea of Okhotsk, and Sakhalin was Flight 007. This is because the Japan Defense Agency operates what is called the BADGE system, an acronym for Base Air Defense Ground Environment. The BADGE system receives computer flight plans for all commercial planes and "can supervise simultaneously from several centers" all aircraft flying in Japan's air defense identification zone.[5]

That should have included KAL Flights 007 and 015. Flight 007's flight plan had been sent to the Japan Defense Agency at 1614 GMT and was put into the BADGE system shortly thereafter, more than two hours before the attack.[6] The military radar at Nemuro would have picked up Flight 007 at approximately 1800 GMT, had the Korean airliner been on Romeo-20. The JDA also received Flight 015's flight plan, and military personnel knew that it was supposed to be flying on Romeo-20 a few minutes behind Flight 007. The appearance of Flight 015 at 1805 GMT without Flight 007 in front of it should have alerted them that something was seriously wrong. Since the JDA was also monitoring the Soviet air defense commotion over Sakhalin at just that time, caused by an intruder flying a course parallel to Romeo-20, it should have been possible for the JDA to have added two and two together at least twenty minutes before the missile attack.

At 1915 GMT, about forty-five minutes after the downing, Tokyo controllers informed the Rescue Coordination Center (RCC) at Haneda Airport in Tokyo that Flight 007 was missing. The RCC is responsible for search and rescue operations within an area covering all of Japan and a large body of water east and south of the islands. At 1922, Tokyo controllers declared an "alerting phase." This step, one step below the more serious "distress phase," meant that messages regarding the airliner's disappearance were transmitted to "relevant units" in Japan and the United States, including Anchorage and Honolulu Air Route Traffic Control Centers, as well as the headquarters of the military air defense watch at Yokota Air Base near Tokyo. Aircraft flying on the NOPAC routes were requested to try to establish radio communications with Flight 007, and two Japan Air Lines flights en route from Anchorage to Tokyo on Romeo-20 repeatedly attempted to do so on the emergency hailing frequency of 121.5 MHz.[7]

At 2000 GMT, officers from the Defense Agency's Northern Warning Intelligence Corps at the Wakkanai monitoring station contacted on-call personnel at the Defense Agency in Tokyo about the events that had taken place over Sakhalin an hour and a half earlier. By 2020, Japanese officers at the Misawa intelligence station informed their American colleagues about Japanese knowledge of the incident. According to Kim Yong-kuk, a KAL spokesman, at 2019 GMT, Tokyo air traffic controllers informed the KAL traffic department at Seoul's Kimpo Airport that "something is very wrong." Five minutes later, Korean Air Lines was said to have issued an alert to the South Korean Transportation Ministry and its staff.[8]

Two conflicting accounts later emerged concerning when the Rescue Coordination Center in Tokyo first learned of events over Sakhalin. According to one informed source, two hours after the attack, at 2030 GMT, the Japan Defense Agency released to the RCC part of the Wakkanai radar information covering an unidentified aircraft's passage over southern Sakhalin. To the contrary, official accounts say that the radar information was given to the RCC at 2330 GMT, five hours after the shootdown. Some support for the first account comes from the fact that shortly after 2030 GMT, the RCC contacted the Soviet air control center in Khabarovsk, Siberia, to inquire if they had any information on Flight 007. For an hour and 20 minutes the Soviets made no response to the inquiry. By 2050 GMT, Tokyo controllers declared a "distress phase" regarding the missing flight and alerted civilian and military stations in the United States, Japan, the Soviet Union, and the Republic of Korea. With this step, the Tokyo Rescue Coordination Center became the principal focus of the search effort.[9]

By now, September 1 had fully dawned over the Far East. At about 6:00

A.M., Tokyo time (2100 GMT), the RCC requested that the Japan Maritime Safety Agency, the Japan Defense Agency, and the United States military forces in Japan help in a search for the missing airliner around reporting point NOKKA on route Romeo-20, where civilian controllers believed Flight 007 to have radioed its last transmissions. In response, the JMSA, the Japanese coast guard, sent a total of twelve ships and five aircraft, including helicopters, to the area.[10] But neither the American nor Japanese militaries dispatched any aircraft to the area of Romeo-20. One interpretation of this could be that they already understood the meaning of the scrambling of Soviet fighters, their attempts to intercept an intruder plane over Sakhalin, and the plane's disappearance over the Sea of Japan near Sakhalin's west coast. That is, perhaps they understood there was nothing to be found in the waters beneath Romeo-20.

The first report that comes in of an accident almost always is wrong, and Flight 007's downing was no exception. Some of the inaccurate stories probably resulted from the inevitable confusion that accompanies a major disaster; others may have been of quite a different order. Virtually all early press reports of Flight 007's disappearance contained the assertion that the airliner had made its last position report at waypoint NOKKA, the set of overwater geographic coordinates about 115 miles southeast of the Japanese island of Hokkaido. Flight 007 was due at NOKKA at 1826 GMT, ironically almost precisely the time at which it was struck by one or more Soviet missiles over Sakhalin, more than 300 miles to the north and west. Both the Japanese government and other official sources now say that no position report was made by Flight 007 for NOKKA, yet the story found its way into the news stream and persisted for some time. About six hours after the shootdown, Frederic N. Smith, an administrative assistant to Congressman Larry McDonald, was told by the State Department that the U.S. Embassy in Seoul was reporting that the airliner was in the water 120 miles southeast of Hokkaido. Numerous press accounts about the NOKKA position report appeared, some highly specific. The story even made its way into President Reagan's September 5 television address to the nation. "At one point," Reagan said, "the Korean pilot gave Japanese air control his position as east of Hokkaido, Japan, showing that he was unaware they were off course by as much or more than 100 miles."[11] But all of these accounts would be subsequently denied.

The early belief in a NOKKA position report had its effects. The Tokyo Rescue Coordination Center established a search area around checkpoint NOKKA. The JMSA ships contacted fishermen operating in that region of the North Pacific to determine whether they had any information on the airliner. Thus, one effect of the NOKKA position report was that civilian ships and aircraft were sent off in the wrong direction, leaving the actual search area to the military. According to one source, following the shootdown the United States promptly dispatched several military ships and aircraft to the actual crash area west of Sakhalin. A U.S. submarine was said to have been on the scene within an hour of the downing.[12]

SAFE ON SAKHALIN   117

Another story which gained wide circulation in the press and persisted for a number of days was that Flight 007 made a radio report after crossing over the Kamchatka Peninsula. Early accounts to this effect originated from Tokyo air traffic control sources. The message—"We passed safely south of Kamchatka"—was said to have been received by Tokyo controllers about an hour and a half before Flight 007 was shot down. This was just the time when Flight 007 in fact made its position report for waypoint NIPPI.[13] There apparently was no such report, but the error corresponded to the reality: at 1708 GMT, Flight 007 had in fact just reentered international airspace after passing safely over the Kamchatka Peninsula.

The most interesting story, however, came out hours after the downing. This was a report, attributed to the U.S. Central Intelligence Agency and subsequently denied, that the Korean airliner had landed on Sakhalin Island and the passengers were safe.

Just as contradictory accounts appeared about when the American and Japanese militaries learned of the shootdown, two radically different accounts emerged regarding when officials of the Reagan administration learned of it. The first of these was in the West German magazine *Der Spiegel*, where authors Wilhelm Bittorf and Anthony Sampson described a series of events completely at odds with the story told by Administration officials. According to their sources, within moments of the attack on Flight 007, the National Security Agency at Fort Meade learned of it through its dedicated intelligence communications network. NSA promptly passed on to the U.S. leadership the information that the airliner had either crashed or landed on Sakhalin; according to this account, NSA did not know which at that time. The downing of the plane was said to have been fully confirmed within two hours.[14]

President Reagan was at his ranch outside Santa Barbara. With him on the West Coast were William P. Clark, the national security adviser, and Edwin Meese III, Reagan's friend and White House counselor. Clark and Meese were staying at the Pacific Biltmore Hotel, on the ocean about 30 miles from the President's ranch. According to the account in *Der Spiegel*, as soon as NSA confirmed its intelligence that Flight 007 had been shot down, Clark was notified through a special secure communications channel. Within minutes, Clark and Meese began a coast-to-coast telephone conversation with several top officials in Washington: Assistant Secretary of State for European Affairs Richard Burt, Undersecretary of State for Political Affairs Lawrence S. Eagleburger, Secretary of State George Shultz, and CIA Director William Casey. The President was not awakened from his nap. *Der Spiegel*'s source, who was with the presidential party at the Biltmore, maintains that the participants made some important decisions.[15]

According to Bittorf and Sampson, intelligence reports coming in by the minute were making it increasingly clear that the Soviets had been grossly inept in their interception and that they had not, in fact, positively identified the airliner before they shot it down. But a story of bungling and ineptitude did not serve the purposes of the Administration. "We had a good issue, and we were going to use it as a club," one source remarked. And the most effective club was maintaining that the Soviets had knowingly downed a commercial airliner.[16]

Der Spiegel reported that Casey, Shultz, Burt, Eagleburger, Clark, and Meese decided to slow the flow of news until a proper strategy could be worked out. "Time had to pass to make the public believe that the warning and listening stations of the United States were aware only hours after the catastrophe. Time had to pass to correlate the stories with the Japanese and the Koreans, to check the Japanese material, and to feel out the reactions by the Soviets," *Der Spiegel* speculated. Time to decide how to use the incident to its fullest propaganda effect. As a result, the false report that Flight 007 had landed safely on Sakhalin Island began to circulate. This story, which would soon appear worldwide, was said to have been distributed through CIA liaison officers in Seoul, Tokyo, and Washington.

Not surprisingly, the official version of events was substantially different. It also went through two distinct versions. The first, provided by Richard Burt at the time of the downing, was that the State Department was alerted on Wednesday night between 10:00 and 10:30 that Flight 007 was off course. This was between 7½ and 8 hours after the shootdown. Burt said that "within the hour" after receiving the first notification, the State Department had received "other indications that much more tragic circumstances had taken place." During the next several hours, Burt said, reports were coming in that made it "increasingly apparent the plane had been forced down."[17]

Perhaps because evidence eventually surfaced that showed the State Department had actually learned of the incident sooner, a revised version of the story later appeared. In this account Washington did not receive its first indication that the plane was missing until almost five hours after the shootdown. Another three hours passed before the first tentative assessment that Flight 007 might have been shot down was forwarded to the Administration, and an additional 3½ hours before "a more certain assessment" about the downing was made. Only then, this version goes, did Burt telephone Eagleburger, although Shultz was not informed until later still. The idea that a teleconference took place soon after the shootdown "appears to be fiction," U.S. officials say.[18]

As to the report that Flight 007 had landed safely on Sakhalin, U.S. officials at first suggested that perhaps the story had originated with the Soviets or had referred to Korean rather than American CIA. Later on, some writers portrayed the story as the result of a gigantic misunderstanding. By this account, Dennis H. Wilham, the FAA's Asian representative stationed at the U.S. Embassy in Tokyo, had received calls from the press about the missing airliner. Wilham reportedly suggested that it could have landed in the Kuril Islands, where there are a number of airports, and newsmen supposedly misquoted him as saying Sakhalin Island. When the first stories to this effect hit the Japanese press, the information was relayed to Washington, where the CIA in turn relayed it to Jangnai Sohn, the Washington station chief for the Korean Central Intelligence Agency. Sohn supposedly had been receiving periodic updates on the missing flight from the CIA because his sister-in-law was a passenger on the plane. Sohn quickly telephoned this information to the KCIA in Seoul, this account goes, mistakenly attributing it to American Central Intelligence. KCIA passed the story to the Foreign Ministry, who in turn passed it on to Korean Air Lines, who made it public.[19]

In deciding the credibility of each account, it is first necessary to consider how likely it is that top U.S. officials initially heard about the missing plane five hours after the shootdown. This seems improbable for two reasons. First, the American intelligence presence in the area made it possible to convey relevant information to Washington in minutes, not hours, and a number of press reports suggested this in fact was precisely what occurred. Thus, the *Der Spiegel* account far more accurately reflects U.S. intelligence capabilities than the official version of events. The second reason to question the official story is that members of the media already had the same information hours before. Cable News Network ran an item that the airliner was missing at 6:00 P.M. EDT, only 3½ hours after the downing, and CBS and NBC ran reports on their evening news broadcasts shortly thereafter. The official account argued unconvincingly that these news stories beat the first intelligence reports by several hours. And not everyone was convinced. When asked about the official chronology, Adm. Eugene Carroll of Washington's Center for Defense Information replied, "Certainly the basic information on the entire incident was available to everybody in the power structure within two hours. There is no doubt about that."[20]

In addition, an account lending support to *Der Spiegel*'s allegations appeared shortly thereafter in *New York* magazine. Based on the report of an intelligence source in Washington—not the source for the *Der Spiegel* article—it was reported that "just hours after the downing" Shultz, Eagleburger, Burt, Casey, Clark, and Meese "decided in a video conference that the incident could be used to quell European opposition to Pershing missiles."[21]

The other point to consider has to do with the origin of the story that Flight 007 landed safely on Sakhalin. Was it a deliberate ploy to buy time, or was it all simply a big mistake? To get a clearer idea, the trail of the story has to be traced from the beginning.

The crowd began gathering at 5:00 A.M. at Seoul's Kimpo Airport to await the arrival of Korean Air Lines Flight 007 from New York and Flight 015 from Los Angeles, even though many of the facilities at Kimpo did not open for another hour. Flight 007 was scheduled to arrive at 6:05 A.M. As arrival time drew near, the crowd of approximately 400 people began to move toward the customs area. Among the crowd in the terminal were officials from the United States Embassy in Seoul, including political counselor Harry Dunlop. Dunlop and others were there to greet the four members of the United States Congress: Larry McDonald on Flight 007 and Jesse Helms, Steven Symms, and Carrol Hubbard on Flight 015.[22]

KAL Flight 015 arrived at Kimpo on schedule at approximately 6:20 A.M. Flight 007 had not appeared, and its arrival was listed on the screens as "delayed." Anxiety began to build as the passengers from Flight 015 passed through customs and left the airport. At the end of an hour, Korean Air Lines officials announced that something was wrong with Flight 007, but those waiting in the terminal were told not to worry. When it left Anchorage, they were told, Flight 007 had enough fuel to fly for twelve hours. The inevitable rumors began to circulate—that the plane had been hijacked or had exploded in midair. The 1978 odyssey of KAL Flight 902 was recalled and discussed. To calm the crowd, KAL invited the friends and relatives into a separate room where tea and snacks were served. KAL Vice-President Charley Cho came in to reassure them, saying that Korean Air Lines was doing everything in its power to find out what had happened.

At 7:20 A.M., Seoul time, on September 1, less than four hours after the downing, the Korean Broadcasting System broke into its regular morning programming with a news bulletin that Flight 007 had disappeared. In the United States, where it was still the evening of August 31, 1983, Cable News Network ran its item that the airliner was missing some 3½ hours after the downing, and CBS and NBC ran similar reports shortly thereafter. Although these are the reports that supposedly prompted the FAA's Dennis Wilham to speculate that Flight 007 might have landed in the Kurils, a speculation that allegedly was distorted as it passed from Japan to CIA to KCIA to Seoul and back to Washington, this does not jibe with the facts. By this time, less than four hours after the downing, the South Korean government had already asked the Japanese to find out through their embassy in Moscow if Flight 007 had been forced down over Sakhalin.[23]

Three hours later, at 10:45 A.M., James Kim, the Seoul bureau chief for United Press International, was watching a televised press conference with Charley Cho. Newsmen were asking Cho about a story, said to originate with the ROK Ministry of Foreign Affairs, that at 10:00 A.M. South Korea had received information from a "friendly government"—meaning the United States—that Flight 007 had landed safely on Sakhalin. Cho told the newsmen he had heard the account and went on to say, "I cannot tell how the plane came to land on Sakhalin. It does not matter as long as the passengers are all right." He continued, "The aircraft had all modern navigation equipment and was in perfect shape. Thus, I am inclined to think that it was forced out of normal flight against its intention. I cannot tell exactly what actually happened to it." As Cho was speaking, an aide ran in with a message. Cho then jubilantly announced, "Ah, well, now it's confirmed. The Republic of Korea Ministry of Foreign Affairs has been told by the United States Central Intelligence Agency that the plane is down on Sakhalin and the passengers are safe."[24] Kim said that an identical scene took place at the Seoul conference attended by the American congressmen. Senator Jesse Helms was discussing the rumor that the passengers of the missing plane were safe when an aide handed him a note. Helms read it quickly and announced that it was now confirmed.[25]

James Kim immediately called the Foreign Ministry in Seoul. To Kim and others, officials at the Foreign Ministry cited the U.S. CIA as their source for the report. Kim filed this story, which became the basis for many of the reports in the United States that said the airliner had landed safely on Sakhalin, and attributed the story to the United States Central Intelligence Agency.[26]

Shungi Taoka is a senior military correspondent for the Tokyo newspaper *Asahi Shimbun*. By 9:30 A.M., six hours after the downing, he had learned through his military sources that Flight 007 had been pursued over Sakhalin Island by Soviet interceptors and shot down. Taoka wrote a report and was ready to break the story half an hour later, but at approximately 10:45 A.M., he heard a television report that the Republic of Korea Ministry of Foreign Affairs had been told by the United States Central Intelligence Agency that Flight 007 had landed safely on Sakhalin. With that report, the flow of news came to a standstill. Although their sources disputed it, no newspaper, radio, or television reporter could present the story he or she had heard. The journalists suspected the "safe on Sakhalin" story from the first, Taoka said, but "we had to wait for official clarification."[27]

Journalists were not the only ones perplexed by the story about the CIA. A Japan Defense Agency source told the Reuters news service that top Japanese officials knew of the attack on Flight 007 soon after it occurred and instantly supplied information about the downing to U.S. forces in Japan and to the National Security Agency via satellite. Officials were thus described as "bewildered" when a Foreign Ministry official in Seoul said that the CIA had reported the airliner to have landed safely on Sakhalin. According to journalist Kunio Yanagida, Japan's Chief Cabinet Secretary Masaharu Gotoda heard the story on television, laughed, and said, "Somebody is trying to control the news." Gotoda reportedly instructed the Foreign Ministry to check with the United States, the Republic of Korea, and the Soviet Union on the matter.[28]

The public attribution of such a story to the CIA was highly unusual, so much so that some journalists suggested the attribution represented a major breach of security. Others have argued that there was no way for the Koreans to make a mistake about the origin of the message because diplomatic messages contain a code number on the message form. For the Koreans to have said "U.S. CIA" meant, this reasoning goes, that a message was received with the CIA identification number on it. But whether the CIA label was intentional or the result of a gigantic string of misunderstandings, its effect was precisely as described by *Der Spiegel:* Had the safe-on-Sakhalin story come from a less authoritative source, or had it merely been unattributed, reporters such as Taoka would have broken the news of the downing. Instead, with American officials in Seoul, Tokyo, and Washington unwilling to confirm or deny the report, the flow of news came to an abrupt halt.[29]

At Kimpo Airport an announcement was made over the public address system at 11:00 A.M. that, according to reliable sources in the United States, Flight 007 had landed safely on Sakhalin Island and that additional information would be available soon. In trying to explain to the families assembled in the terminal how this could have occurred, KAL Vice-President Cho emphasized the proximity of Romeo-20 to Soviet territory: "The usual flight course is only 80 miles off Soviet territory," he said, "so it is where the crewmen get tense." Anxious family members were told they could go home on KAL-provided buses to await further information.[30]

No reason was given why the plane had landed on Sakhalin. Y. S. Lee, a KAL spokesman, said that pilots had been given standing instructions to obey interceptors' orders to land. "If you are flying a jumbo airliner when you are ordered to land or fly somewhere, the pilot would obey rather than jeopardize passengers," he said. KAL New York spokeswoman Bonnie Villarico told reporters that it had been a forced landing and said that arrangements were being made to send another airplane to Sakhalin to bring the passengers to South Korea. KAL Vice-President Cho flew to Tokyo to commence negotiations for the release of the passengers, crew, and aircraft, he said.[31]

By now it was about 10:00 P.M. on August 31 on the East Coast of the United States. Larry McDonald's press officer Tommy Toles, who had called the State Department after hearing the initial television reports of Flight 007's disappearance, picked up the phone at his home in Georgia:

> This is Duty Officer Orville Brockman at FAA headquarters in Washington, D.C. We have just received information from our FAA representative, Mr. Dennis Wilham in Tokyo as follows: He has been advised by the Japanese Civil Aviation Bureau headquarters, Air Traffic Division, Mr. Takano—T-a-k-a-n-o—who is his counterpart in Japanese aviation, as follows: Japanese self-defense radar force confirms that the Hokkaido radar followed Air Korea to a landing in Soviet territory on the island of Sakhalinska—S-a-k-h-a-l-i-n-s-k-a—and it is confirmed by the manifest that Congressman McDonald is on board.[32]

This casts further doubt on the contention that Wilham was the original source for the safe-on-Sakhalin story. At 10:50, Reed Clark of the State Department called Toles to confirm that the plane had landed safely on Sakhalin. According to Toles, Clark made reference to news reports and said, "We have confirmed the plane is safe." Toles later remarked, "I was delirious with joy and relayed that to everyone."[33]

So did the Department of State. Dr. Harold P. McDonald, Jr., the congressman's brother, received a call telling him that the flight had landed safely on Sakhalin. "We've just heard from the State Department that the plane is down and apparently the passengers are safe," McDonald told the Associated Press's Atlanta bureau. "We're just going to wait and pray." AP immediately contacted the Department of State and confirmed that the phone call had in fact taken place. According to a report in the *Washington Post*, it was also almost precisely at this time that an unidentified official from State called Kathryn McDonald, telling her that Flight 007 had landed on Sakhalin and the passengers were safe. (This account would later be disputed by State Department officials, who insisted that it was KAL, not State, that had contacted Kathryn McDonald.)[34]

Tommy Toles then called the National Military Command Center at the Pentagon to ask about the FAA report; he said he "was told they couldn't tell me anything unless the phone was secure." The duty officer at the Pentagon, Col. Thomas Roundtree, suggested that Toles send over someone with a top-secret clearance for a briefing. Toles dispatched Frederic N. Smith, an administrative assistant to Larry McDonald. After Smith had left for the Pentagon, however, Roundtree called Toles back. About the FAA report that Flight 007 had landed on Sakhalin, Roundtree said that Japanese news broadcasts were saying the same thing. "That's as good information as we've got," Roundtree said, "and we believe that to be true." Roundtree told Toles not to bother sending anyone over for a briefing. Tommy Toles was angry. "You mean that's what you wanted a secure phone for?" he snapped, saying that Smith was already en route. "Well, we'll give him a tour of the place," the Pentagon officer said.[35]

When doubt later began to be cast upon the safe-on-Sakhalin story, Toles called the State Department to speak with Reed Clark, the person who had first told it to him. Clark was not available, and instead Toles's call was put through to Richard Burt. Toles demanded to know why Clark had said the airliner was safe when it apparently was not. "That's not what I told him to say," Burt replied. Toles responded, "Your man said it was." According to Toles, Burt became agitated and repeated that he had instructed people not to give out the safe-on-Sakhalin story. "I later got that individual [Reed Clark] and asked him why he did that," Toles said. "I had notified friends and families."[36] The State Department official offered Toles no explanation, however, and provided no additional information.[37]

The story that the airliner had landed safely on Sakhalin quickly spread across the globe. Late-night viewers of ABC's "Nightline" were told: "The state-run Korean Broadcasting System reports that the U.S. Central Intelligence Agency informed South Korea's foreign minister of the landing of [*sic*] Soviet-occupied territory, of the landing of the plane on that territory." ABC's Barry Dunsmore came on to say, "We do understand from Korean sources that there were no injuries and that they are in fact about to send a plane to that island to pick up passengers.''[38]

The morning newspapers on September 1 carried the safe-on-Sakhalin account but noted that military officials in Honolulu, where U.S. Pacific operations are based, had declined comment. The CIA was equally unhelpful. Agency spokesman Dale Peterson told reporters in Washington: ''I can neither confirm nor deny that story at this time. I just don't have any information.'' With nobody willing to confirm the story, qualifications soon began to appear. *New York Times* Tokyo correspondent Clyde Haberman had been roused out of bed by his editors in New York. He had repeatedly called the U.S. Embassy in Tokyo to confirm the story that Flight 007 had landed safely, but without success. Unable to get a straight answer, Haberman came to distrust the story and switched his line to say that the fate of the airliner was uncertain.[39] Newspapers with later filing deadlines, such as the *Los Angeles Times,* reflected even greater levels of uncertainty in their stories.

When Larry McDonald's assistant, Frederic N. Smith, arrived at the Pentagon shortly before midnight, he was read intelligence intercepts from the Soviet fighters that had been sent by telecopier from Japan. Smith was told that the plane was in the water and that this was secret information. He was instructed, however, to tell the news media that ''no U.S. source is able to confirm that the passengers are alive.'' After the briefing, Smith would do his best to help the Pentagon keep its story secret for another few hours, telling reporters ''indications are'' that Soviet authorities had forced the jetliner to land. Asked if he knew why the plane had landed on Sakhalin, Smith responded, ''We can't confirm that, but indications are that it got too close to Soviet airspace.''[40]

At 1:48 A.M., Washington time, Robert Rappleye of Mutual Radio called Tommy Toles with the report that Mutual's Frank Rogers in Tokyo was reporting Japanese military radars on Hokkaido had watched three Soviet fighter squadrons converge on Flight 007 before it dropped from radar screens. Listening stations had picked up radio transmissions from the Soviets saying they had scored a hit on their target.[41] Rogers said his information came from the Japanese broadcasting giant NHK, which apparently had gotten it in a leak from the Japan Defense Agency. Toles immediately called the State and Defense departments. Both said they had no information at that time regarding the NHK story.

As news of the downing of Flight 007 exploded during the following hours, the early reports of the airliner landing safely on Sakhalin Island disappeared. Also lost were critical questions about the attribution of the false story to the Central Intelligence Agency, the effect of that attribution, and the fact that at least some people in the United States appeared to know the story was false at the time it was introduced. ABC's Ted Koppel had told his audience the story on the night of August 31. The following evening Koppel apologized, saying, ''Senior U.S. officials led us to believe, and we led you to believe, that the plane had landed safely on Soviet territory. Sadly, that was not true.''[42] Yet his lack of curiosity about the reasons behind the story was the norm. The result was that the false safe-on-Sakhalin story quietly faded away, never to return.

By all indications the Japanese were efficient in sorting out the information about Flight 007 but rather reluctant to disclose what they knew. Sources in the Japan Defense Agency told writer Kunio Yanagida that the Japanese radar operators at Wakkanai understood almost immediately the significance of the events they had witnessed. By 1900 GMT—within half an hour of the downing—the communications specialists had, at least on a preliminary basis, sorted out the intercepted voice transmissions among the Soviet planes and their ground stations on Sakhalin. The highest levels of the Defense Agency were then promptly informed. As the information came in, Kazuo Tanikawa, head of the JDA, was roused from bed, and he quickly assembled a working group.[43]

For many months after the downing, the Japanese government claimed in public statements that it received no information whatsoever until 1956 GMT, a full 90 minutes after the downing, when the Japan Transport Ministry informed the military that Flight 007 was missing. When the December 1983 International Civil Aviation Organization report said that the Transport Ministry had in fact called the military an hour earlier, the Japanese government maintained silence. It was not until February 15, 1985, that officials of the Defense Agency acknowledged under questioning by a member of the Diet that the conversation with the Transport Ministry had indeed taken place at the earlier time. The government of Japan seemed to want to distance itself from suggestions Japan had monitored the flight and to have the public believe that no Japanese was aware of Flight 007 until long after the downing had taken place.

The Japanese official story is further eroded by reports that by the time the Transport Ministry called the JDA about the missing airliner, Japan's air defense forces had already declared an elevated state of military alert. In addition, by this time Japanese officers at Misawa Air Base were reportedly already discussing the situation with their American counterparts.[44]

Other elements of the Japanese official chronology are equally suspect. It was said that only after receiving the report from Transport Ministry at 1956 GMT did the JDA retrieve the radar and communications tapes at Wakkanai and begin to analyze them. The analysis was said to have been completed at 2330 GMT, five hours after the downing, when the results were forwarded by JDA Chief Tanikawa to Chief Cabinet Secretary Masaharu Gotoda. This was the same time, according to later official reports, that the information was released to the Japan Maritime Safety Agency.[45] The Japanese official line continues by saying that Tanikawa reported to Prime Minister Yasuhiro Nakasone even later still, after which Nakasone called a 9:30 A.M. (2430 GMT) Cabinet meeting. So much in the same way as with the American leadership, the public is asked to believe that the highest levels of the Japanese government remained in the dark about the incident for a considerable length of time.

But although the JDA analysis was said not to have been completed until 8:30, half an hour earlier two P2J submarine surveillance aircraft from Aomori Prefecture's Naval Defense Corp at Hachinoe Base and five warships from Ominato Base had already gathered off the coast of Hokkaido, having been alerted hours earlier. If the JDA had no knowledge of the shootdown, how can this be explained? *Der Spiegel* reported that by this time officials in Washington had already spoken with Prime Minister Nakasone and Foreign Minister Shintaro Abe via secure "back channel" communications, urging the Japanese leaders to make statements and take actions only in consultation with the United States.[46]

Between 10:00 and 10:30 P.M., Washington time, about 8 hours after the downing of Flight 007, a State Department special operations group was formed to deal with the incident and determine the U.S. official line on all points of relevance. Working out of the State Department's seventh-floor operations center, the group worked nearly around the clock. Headed by Assistant Secretary of State Richard Burt, the group contained representatives from a variety of branches of government including the Defense and State departments, the CIA, and the White House. Burt had emerged as the key figure in the group for several reasons. One of these was Burt's hard-line approach to the Russians. Another reason was that the propaganda value of the shootdown would be realized most strongly in Europe. Specifically, one of Burt's principal concerns at the time was ensuring the successful deployment of Pershing II and Cruise missiles with NATO forces later in the year. The deployment was facing considerable resistance among the Western European peace movement and public, and Burt recognized the propaganda value of the downing of Flight 007 at once.[47]

The working group's primary task was to collect all information relating to the downing and to coordinate and disseminate the official U.S. response. The group soon learned, through its access to recordings of the conversations between the Soviet fighters and their ground control stations on Kamchatka, that Soviet fighters never found the Korean jetliner during its first intrusion into Soviet territory. The group also concluded early on that the Soviet fighters had not been able to locate Flight 007 until shortly before they attacked it. But in spite of this information, the theme of Soviet culpability was repeatedly stressed in official statements. At Burt's direction, the Department of State sent requests to all U.S. posts abroad asking for information about Aeroflot's landing rights in each country, and U.S. posts were instructed to forward reports on local press coverage. Burt wanted to know what kind of beating the Soviets were taking in world opinion. "We've got 'em! We've got the bastards!" Burt reportedly exclaimed.[48]

To use the incident to its fullest propaganda effect, Burt's group began a campaign of major proportions to centralize all information about the downing in the Department of State. (In a secret Department memorandum a week later, it was stated, "The effort to coordinate action within the U.S. Government is proceeding quite smoothly"), and it was not long before that effort focused on Alaska. At 1:45 P.M., local time, on August 31 in Anchorage, a little over three hours after the downing, the duty officer of the National Transportation Safety Board (NTSB) was notified by the Federal Aviation Administration that the airliner was missing. Within three minutes, James Michelangelo, the chief of NTSB's Anchorage field office, had assembled his staff in his office in the Federal building on C Street in downtown Anchorage. An NTSB staff member was sent immediately to the airport to retrieve the airline's passenger list, manifest, and other relevant information.[49]

The passenger list had revealed that Larry McDonald was on board Flight 007. By 3:30 P.M., Michelangelo had placed two calls with all this information to NTSB headquarters in Washington. According to Michelangelo, his calls were the first time that anyone had alerted the government that McDonald was on board the airliner, although it was already known that Flight 007 was missing. The information about McDonald was promptly relayed to the White House. Michelangelo said he received congratulations and a "feather in his cap" for being the first to inform Washington about McDonald's presence on the flight.

Michelangelo's records indicate that precisely nine hours after Flight 007 disappeared from radar, word was received by the NTSB in Anchorage that the airliner had been either "forced down or shot down." With this information, Michelangelo and his staff swung into gear. Investigators were booked on flights to Tokyo and Seoul, where they planned to collect crew training records, maintenance records, and all other information relevant to the case. In Tokyo, the NTSB planned to interview Japanese air traffic controllers about procedures for directing aircraft within the Japanese Flight Information Region. Other staff members began gathering information about Flight 007 from Anchorage International Airport and the Air Route Traffic Control Center at Elmendorf Air Force Base. In short, the NTSB was planning to investigate fully the downing of Flight 007. They had the authority to do so because the flight had U.S. passengers on board and had originated in a United States Flight Information Region.

By 6:30 in Anchorage the following morning, September 1—almost precisely the time that Secretary of State Shultz broke the official silence on the incident by denouncing the Soviets—NTSB headquarters in Washington called Anchorage at the behest of the Department of State. Michelangelo was instructed to forward to Washington all the information he had collected. He sent everything: the passenger list, the manifest, the fuel report, the load list, the crew list, the flight release sheet. Raising his arms in a sweeping gesture toward his files, Michelangelo later said, "There are absolutely no documents in this room."

A few hours after the relay of documents began, Michelangelo received another call telling him that his office was off the case. NTSB headquarters in Washington had received instructions that the Department of State "would handle matters" from that time forward. State said the shootdown was not "technically an accident" and thus not the responsibility of the NTSB.[50] It was the first time that a case had ever been taken away from the Anchorage field office by the NTSB chief. The next day, State Department officials told the NTSB that they might require "technical assistance" in conducting their own investigation. Yet when asked if to his knowledge State had ever sent any investigators to Anchorage or had taken any other actions to investigate the case, James Michelangelo responded with an emphatic "No!"

NTSB investigators tend to be aggressive, thorough, and independent. Their reports and files are quickly released to the public. All told, the NTSB is a poor organization to deal with if one's purpose is to limit and control an investigation. Far better a relatively timid bureaucracy like the FAA. Or, better still, an organization like the United Nations' International Civil Aviation Organization, which has no independent investigative powers at all. Whether limiting the investigation was State's intention, it was certainly the result of pulling the National Transportation Safety Board off the case. No investigation by either the NTSB or the Department of State has been conducted. As *The Nation* later observed, "Eighteen months after the airliner was shot down, when asked if the State Department ever conducted such an inquiry, a high-level State Department official [Lynn Pascoe] replied, 'How is the State Department going to investigate?'"[51]

The search for the wreckage from Flight 007 off Sakhalin Island, one of the most extensive in history in terms of number of vessels and time expended, began almost immediately. One source said that within an hour of the downing a U.S. submarine had arrived in the general crash area. Later, when Japanese vessels showed up, they were said to have found the skies full of U.S. aircraft. When asked about that report, State Department spokesman John Hughes had no comment. The Japan Defense Agency reported that on the afternoon of September 1 a large number of Soviet military aircraft had also been detected in the area off Sakhalin, flying in what appeared to be search patterns. Soviet ships were also seen zigzagging as they searched the waters. Japanese fishing ships operating in the area had quickly been warned away by the Soviets, as had the newly arrived Japanese search ships. By the afternoon of September 1, the Soviets had assigned at least eleven ships to the search effort, and their aircraft were continually overflying the area. Administration officials in Washington received what they considered to be "reliable reports" from the commander-in-chief of U.S. Pacific Forces "of the strong possibility the Soviets had located the crash site."[52]

Even as the hours passed and hope of finding survivors in the 50-degree water faded, the efforts to recover the wreckage intensified. The objective of the rapidly intensifying effort, according to official explanations reported in the media, was the recovery of the flight recorders, the "black boxes," that could, it was believed, provide information about the cause of Flight 007's deviation from course and the actions of its crew.

In Moscow, both the Japanese and American embassies had been trying to find out additional information about the report that Flight 007 had landed safely on Sakhalin Island. At 7:00 A.M., Moscow time, some eight and a half hours after the downing, Hasashi Owada of the Japanese embassy was told by a Soviet Foreign Minister duty officer that Flight 007 had not landed on Sakhalin Island but that no further information was available. A report of the Soviet denial was relayed to Washington. An hour later, Richard Burt, already well aware of what had happened to Flight 007, woke the Soviet chargé d'affaires, Oleg M. Sokolov, and asked for information and an explanation of the plane's fate. The Soviets later said that during the conversation Burt told Sokolov he knew the plane was located somewhere in the area of Sakhalin. At almost precisely the same time, Warren Zimmerman, U.S. chargé d'affaires in Moscow, made a formal inquiry to the Soviet Foreign Ministry's Aleksandr Bessmertnykh. Bessmertnykh was no more forthcoming with Zimmerman than Sokolov had been with Burt. Later, Sokolov met at the State Department with Lawrence Eagleburger, who demanded that the Soviets provide a full explanation of the incident. Sokolov offered few facts.[53]

The first information from the Soviets came at 11:00 A.M., Moscow time, when Hasashi Owada was told by a senior official of the Soviet Foreign Ministry that the Korean plane had not "landed" in the Soviet Union. Owada asked if this meant that the plane was not in Soviet territory at all, and the Soviet official was said to have replied, "Yes." Shortly thereafter, Kazuhiko Togo, a counselor at the Japanese embassy, met with an unnamed official at the Soviet Foreign Ministry, who bluntly denied that the plane had landed on Sakhalin. When Togo asked for clarification, the official said it was not in Soviet territory "because it had not landed there." By midday in Moscow, the Soviet Foreign Ministry had expanded on its statement to say that the missing plane was not "on or over" Soviet territory, interpreted in some reports to mean that the airliner had been downed over the sea.[54]

The first account of the incident in the Soviet media came ten and a half hours after the downing in a Tass report over Moscow Radio. In a brief dispatch, Tass said, "A South Korean Boeing 747 passenger plane on a regular flight from New York to Seoul has disappeared without a trace. On board were 269 passengers and crew. The last time the plane was in contact was eighty kilometers east of Hokkaido. Searches mounted by Japanese produced no result." [55]

Reporters were now trying their best to confirm or deny that the airliner had landed on Sakhalin. In a telephone interview with the Kyodo news service, airport officials at Yuzhno Sakhalinsk Airport on southern Sakhalin Island said that no such aircraft had landed there. The Kyodo dispatch appeared 12 hours 42 minutes after Flight 007 had been shot down.[56] But this was well beyond the deadline for the morning newspapers in Europe and the United States. The news, when it was broken, would come from other, official sources.

Television crews and newspaper reporters had gathered at Kimpo Airport in Seoul. Several hours after the announcement that Flight 007 had landed safely on Sakhalin, KAL told the news media there was a possibility that the airliner had exploded in midair. Similar reports had already come from the Japan Broadcasting Corporation via the Japan Defense Agency. JDA sources had told the press they had tracked a plane flying near Sakhalin that suddenly disappeared from their radar screens after several other aircraft were observed flying nearby. According to the JDA, the airliner had been flying at an altitude of approximately 33,000 feet when it vanished from radar, suggesting an explosion.[57] Upon hearing such reports, many of the family members who had returned to their homes after Charley Cho announced that the airliner had landed safely on Sakhalin hurried back to the airport.

After the Soviets denied the airliner was on Sakhalin, the government of South Korea said that a formal announcement regarding the plane's fate would be made in Seoul at 3:30 P.M., local time, 12 hours after the missile attack. The time came and passed. Finally, a little before 7:30 P.M., Seoul time, Korean Minister of Culture and Information Lee Jin-hee appeared on national television. Lee told his countrymen a slightly confused tale of radar and radio monitoring, in which Flight 007 was last observed at an altitude of 30,000 feet at 3:23 A.M., local time. As South Korean government officials would later say, Lee's information "flowed out of either U.S. intelligence sources or results of the Japanese Defense Agency's analysis of its tracking of the plane." Lee explained that "judging from information on the situation gathered so far from various sources with regard to the missing passenger plane, we are almost certain that the civilian passenger plane in question has crashed after having been attacked by a third country," an apparent reference to the Soviet Union. Lee said that South Korean Prime Minister Kim Sang-hyup would shortly call an urgent meeting of Cabinet members to discuss the incident.[58]

During the afternoon of September 1, top Japanese officials met at Prime Minister Nakasone's residence in Tokyo. They decided to see what the United States and the Soviet Union did before Japan acted, which meant maintaining official silence. Although the Nakasone government was not talking, there was a great deal of rumor and speculation, some of it quite accurate, about Flight 007's fate in the Japanese press. But details remained sketchy since it proved impossible to have reports officially confirmed.[59]

At 8:15 P.M. in Tokyo, some 17 hours after the downing, the official silence was finally broken. Foreign Minister Shintaro Abe announced that "the possibility is very high" Flight 007 had been shot down by the Soviets. "We are concerned about the fate of twenty-seven Japanese aboard the plane," he said. "Therefore, we would like to request information as soon as possible. . . . If this [attack] is true, it should be regarded as very regrettable indeed." Abe's concern was reiterated shortly thereafter by Chief Cabinet Secretary Masaharu Gotoda, who told reporters that the government of Japan "judges" the airliner to have been shot down. An emergency meeting of the Nakasone Cabinet was planned for the following morning.[60]

Fifteen minutes after Abe had spoken, Soviet Ambassador to Japan Vladimir Y. Pavlov was called to the Foreign Ministry to meet with Yoshiya Kato, the director general of the Ministry's European and Pacific Affairs Bureau. Pavlov was asked to provide the government of Japan with the Soviet Union's information on Flight 007. Kato also requested that Soviet ships not disturb the Japanese vessels already searching for the airliner in the waters off Sakhalin. Pavlov promised to convey the requests to Moscow but said he was surprised by the "anti-Soviet campaign" being conducted by the Japanese media before all the facts were in, including Foreign Minister Abe's "unfriendly comment" that Flight 007 had been shot down by Soviet aircraft.

In the early morning hours of September 1 in Washington, D.C., Tommy Toles was still trying to find out what had happened to his boss, Larry McDonald. At 3:30 A.M. Toles spoke to some of the staff of McDonald's organization, Western Goals, who were in Seoul. They told Toles they had just been informed by Korean intelligence officials that Flight 007 had been shot down by either Soviet or North Korean fighters. Fifteen minutes later, a Defense Department official advised Toles that all information pointed to a "catastrophic failure." However, CIA spokesman Dale Peterson told him that the agency had "absolutely no information" about the incident at that time. At 6:23 A.M., Toles received a call from an official at the Department of Defense telling him that the Pentagon now believed the plane was in the water, but the official refused to elaborate on how it got there.[61] This was a full 6½ hours after Pentagon officials had told Frederic N. Smith the "secret" information that the airliner had been shot down.

The continuing obfuscation and confusion were by no means limited to Tommy Toles and the members of Larry McDonald's family. Hans Ephraimson is a New York City businessman whose daughter, Alice, was booked on Flight 007 to Seoul, where she was scheduled to catch a connecting flight to Hong Kong. While waiting for an early train from the New Jersey suburbs, he picked up a copy of the New York Times for September 1. On the cover he saw the story that Flight 007 was down on Sakhalin and the passengers were safe.

Ephraimson is a methodical man who keeps a telephone log. At 7:04

A.M. he called the Hong Kong hotel where his daughter had reservations. Ephraimson said that his daughter's plane was down on Sakhalin and it was not clear when she would arrive in Hong Kong, but he asked the manager to hold her room. The manager replied that of course he would do so, but he was afraid that Ephraimson had the story all wrong. The airliner had been shot down, he said, and everyone on board was dead. Ephraimson took a few minutes to recover his composure. At 7:20 he called the Department of State for information, and his call was put through to a member of Richard Burt's task force. Ephraimson asked whether Flight 007 was safe but was told that State had no information at that time. This was a full seventeen hours after Flight 007 had been shot down and was, by any account, well after Administration officials had assembled all significant details about the incident.[62]

According to White House spokesman Larry Speakes, Ronald Reagan did not fare much better. Speakes said the President received his first notice that the plane was missing from National Security Adviser Clark at 10:30 P.M., EDT, a full eight hours after the downing. "It was regarded as a missing aircraft for a long period of time," he explained, "and we were monitoring, trying to make assessments." By the "wee hours" U.S. intelligence was said to have agreed that the plane had been shot down. Reagan was said to have received additional details from William Clark at 1:30 A.M., EDT, including that some officials had "reason to believe" Flight 007 was "in the water." But according to Speakes, it was still not completely clear at this time what had happened. "It seemed so incredible to us through the night," Speakes said, that there was a need for checking and rechecking of all available data on the incident.[63] Although U.S. and Japanese military forces were on alert and the fate of the plane had been known for hours, the President supposedly went to bed without knowing the whole story.

At 2:15 A.M., Secretary of State Shultz reportedly spoke with Clark to clear the statement that Shultz planned to make on national television later that morning. According to Larry Speakes, by 3:00 A.M., EDT, White House officials received confirmation that the airliner had been downed, "but . . . we did not know whether it had been forced down or whether it had actually been fired upon." Speakes said he could not cite a precise moment when the U.S. Government finally reached the conclusion that Flight 007 had been shot down.[64] President Reagan was not awakened.

Larry Speakes later told reporters that Secretary of State Shultz gave National Security Adviser Clark the latest details the following morning at 8:00 A.M., EDT. When President Reagan woke up at 10:10 A.M. (7:10, Pacific time), so the story goes, he was thoroughly briefed about the crisis —19 hours 46 minutes after Flight 007 was shot down. The briefing was said to include a written transcript of radio conversations between the Soviet pilots and their ground controllers during the interception over Sakhalin, prepared by U.S., not Japanese, intelligence sources that had monitored the radio transmissions. "That's incredible," Reagan was said to have responded.[65]

Administration officials insisted that Reagan was not out of touch. Larry Speakes went on to say, "As soon as we had the facts, the President was given an update. When the facts became certain, we apprised the President of it." However, at 10:45 A.M., EDT, Secretary of State Shultz went before the world to denounce the Soviets in the harshest terms without even having spoken to the President of the United States.[66]

7

MEETING THE
PRESS

It was 10:45 A.M., Washington time, on September 1, the forty-fourth anniversary of the beginning of World War II, when Secretary of State George P. Shultz went before the press to present the official American version of the downing of Korean Air Lines Flight 007. Shultz was grim-faced, his voice occasionally breaking as he reconstructed the drama in the skies over the Soviet Far East. "The Soviets tracked the commercial airliner for some two and a half hours," Shultz explained. "A Soviet pilot reported visual contact with the aircraft at 1812 hours. The Soviet plane was, we know, in constant contact with its ground control. . . ." Shultz was angry, and it showed. He went on to emphasize what would become the central assertion in the official U.S. response to the incident—the Soviets' culpability for the deaths of the passengers on board an innocent, unarmed, civilian airliner. "The United States reacts with revulsion to this attack." Shultz concluded: "We can see no excuse whatever for this appalling act." [1]

The statement by Shultz contained some revelations. While focusing on the Soviet action, it also showed that both the United States and Japan had been monitoring the progress of the airliner.

At the Pacific Biltmore, the President's men were busy. Larry Speakes and Edwin Meese drafted the first White House statement on the incident, calling Reagan for his approval. It was at 1:05 P.M., EDT (10:05 A.M. on the West Coast) when Speakes took the podium in front of reporters at the Santa Barbara Sheraton. "I have two statements," Speakes began, "the first on the Korean Air Lines incident." The press was told that Reagan was "very concerned and deeply disturbed about the loss of life" on Flight 007 and that he saw "no circumstances that can justify the unprecedented attack on an unarmed civilian aircraft." When Speakes finished reading the first part of the statement, he was asked if Reagan was going back to Washington. Speakes ignored the question and proceeded to read the second portion of the statement, which dealt with the situation in the Middle East. When he finished, the question was repeated. "There are no plans for the President to return to Washington earlier than anticipated," Speakes shot back. Reagan was planning to "horseback ride this morning and will generally work around the ranch in the afternoon." But the questions of when, how, if, and by whom the President had been informed about the downing of Flight 007 persisted. Exasperated by the reporters' doggedness, Speakes lost his cool. "As soon as they [White House officials] were certain of it, they informed the President of it," he said. "Now, that was 7:10 A.M. for you tick-tock fanatics."[2]

As Speakes faced reporters in Santa Barbara, it was evening in Moscow. About halfway through the Soviet evening news program *Vremya* (Times), after several routine reports, a Tass news item was read without commentary.[3]

> An unidentified plane entered the airspace of the Soviet Union over the Kamchatka Peninsula from the direction of the Pacific Ocean and then for the second time violated the airspace of the USSR over Sakhalin Island. The plane did not have navigation lights, did not respond to questions, and did not enter into contact with the [Soviet] dispatcher services. Fighters of the antiaircraft defense, which were sent aloft toward the intruder plane, tried to give it assistance in directing it to the nearest airfield. But the intruder plane did not react to the signals and warnings from the Soviet fighters and continued its flight in the direction of the Sea of Japan.[4]

As admissions go, it wasn't much. The Soviets said they had intercepted the airliner but not that they had shot it down; however, they did not explicitly deny they had shot it down either. The report was incomplete, leaving viewers with the impression that the Soviet interceptors took no action aside from a few warnings and that the unidentified plane continued on its course unmolested. One possible explanation for the slow and guarded statement was the absence from Moscow of Soviet leader Yuri V. Andropov, who was in ill health and said to be vacationing in the northern Caucasus at the time of the downing. An additional reason could be that the Politburo needed more time to assess what information the U.S. had and what its likely reaction would be. Support for this latter interpretation came from the Soviet State Committee for Television and Radio Broadcasting, which quickly refused to permit foreign television correspondents access to satellite transmission facilities in Moscow. This has happened in the past when the Kremlin has wanted to block Western television reports on especially sensitive topics, and the television studios, usually available, were mysteriously either "fully booked" or else "equipment was being repaired." While this strategy of playing for time might have worked at home, it would prove to be nothing short of a disaster for Soviet public relations beyond its borders. From the very first, the Soviets would be decidedly on the defensive.[5]

The *Vremya* news item was repeated the next day in *Pravda* under the title "Tass Report." Diplomats in Moscow were quoted in the Western press as saying that the Tass statement "seemed to suggest that an attack on the airliner . . . was a justifiable act of self-defense."[6] By this time the essential difference between the U.S. and Soviet approaches to the incident was already apparent: The Soviets would focus solely on what the plane was doing, while the Americans would focus solely on what was done to it.

In Washington, the incident was being treated as a full-scale international crisis. The State Department ordered American embassies around the world to report the reactions of foreign governments and press to the incident. Richard Burt's original working group had grown and was using both American and Japanese intelligence information in its analysis of the downing. Conferences between top Administration officials, from the President on down, continued throughout the day.

Throughout the day on September 1, Larry Speakes suffered a continuous headache in responding to headlines such as that in the *Baltimore Sun*: "Reagan Was Out of Touch with Situation All Night." Speakes kept pushing the story that Reagan had been informed as soon as "U.S. officials were certain" about the fate of the airliner and continued to defend and justify the decision that the President would not return to Washington. Speakes told the press, "At the ranch the President has every facility, every capacity, every capability to perform any function that he could perform in Washington. He has at his disposal the same information he would sitting in the Oval Office of the White House, and he is fully capable of having detailed discussion with his advisers." Indeed, it was reported that Reagan's foreign policy advisers met during the day on Thursday and sent the President a "number of options and recommendations." Speakes further noted that Reagan "may talk on the telephone from wherever he is on the ranch." However, newsmen at the ranch spotted Ronald and Nancy Reagan on horseback, riding, as the *New York Times* poetically put it, "in brilliant afternoon sunshine."[7]

By midafternoon in Santa Barbara (5:33, EDT) on September 1, Larry Speakes appeared before reporters in what *Newsweek* described as "dress quite unusual for the western White House, a coat and tie."[8] Speakes read the President's statement, which said that Reagan was speaking "for all Americans and for the people everywhere who cherish civilized values in protesting the Soviet attack on an unarmed civilian passenger plane. Words can scarcely express our revulsion at this horrifying act of violence." Demanding an explanation for what was termed an "appalling and wanton misdeed," Reagan concluded: "Mrs. Reagan and I want to express our deepest sympathy to the families of the victims. . . . They have my personal assurance that I will make every effort to get to the bottom of this tragedy."

The President's message defined a stark and highly artificial choice: Either join the United States in condemning the Soviet Union or side with uncivilized barbarians who wantonly shoot down unarmed civilian passenger planes. From the very first, there was no room for skeptical reporters, politicians, or citizens to say, "Wait a minute. Let's take a look at the facts."

When Speakes had finished reading the President's statement, a reporter asked whether the President would cut short his vacation. Speakes said yes, Reagan had decided to return to Washington on Saturday, September 3, for meetings with the National Security Council and congressional leaders. At 6:15 that evening, Speakes called reporters back to the briefing room at the Sheraton. The President, he announced, would return to Washington earlier still, on Friday morning. The official reason for the early return was the "general urgency of the situation" regarding Flight 007 and Lebanon. "All of these matters, the President believes, must be addressed now," Speakes concluded. A reporter asked if this was a public relations effort. "No," Larry Speakes replied.[9]

Reagan's return to the capital was unusual. The President had never been one to cancel his vacations or even cut them short.[10] But as international outrage against the Soviet action mounted, Reagan's aides saw in his low-key response the makings of a public relations disaster. There was a precedent for their concern. As the *Washington Post* recalled, in 1981 Reagan had suffered bad press when his aides did not bother to awaken him after U.S. fighter planes shot down two Libyan jets. Ever since that time, the *Post* continued, Reagan's aides had been sensitive to any suggestion that the President is not "in touch" with late-breaking world events. Explaining that "the President's continuing his vacation at his ranch might be misunderstood" by both the Soviets and the American people, Reagan's staff rushed him back to Washington.[11]

The official U.S. response to the Tass statement came a day later in the form of a written statement by Secretary of State Shultz. Read to the press by State Department spokesman John Hughes, the statement, not unexpectedly, focused on the Soviet reluctance to admit shooting down Flight 007 rather than asking how the plane might have come to Sakhalin in the first place. "The Soviet Union," Shultz insisted, "will not admit the truth

—that they shot down an unarmed civilian airliner." By this time, however, questions concerning what the U.S. knew about the airliner and when it knew it were beginning to appear in the media, including discussions of the sophisticated array of U.S. military and intelligence hardware in the neighborhood of the Soviet Far East. So, a new argument appeared in Shultz's statement, one that would become central to the official line: The United States was not aware that the Korean airliner was in jeopardy until after it was shot down. "Our first knowledge of the incident," Shultz said, "was based on subsequent analysis of Soviet defense activity." [12]

There are two key terms in Shultz's statement: "United States" and "jeopardy." Who exactly is the "United States"? The Secretary of State? The President? The military and intelligence personnel who were manning the intelligence platforms in the area? All of these? Not only does Shultz's statement not tell who was informed and on how timely a basis but it also defines "the incident" as the downing of the airliner, not as all the things that led up to its getting shot in the first place. Next, just what is meant by "in jeopardy"? All the secretary's statement says is that some unspecified people did not know the airliner was likely to get shot down until after it happened, not that they had no idea it was over Soviet territory. This is not surprising unless one is to argue that the downing was somehow foreseen. A year later a U.S. official, speaking with the Associated Press on condition he not be identified, said that Flight 007 probably was not warned because none of the individuals who observed its deviation thought that the Russians would react by shooting it down. The general belief was that they would simply direct the plane out of their territory or, at worst, force it down, he said. Just as they did with intruding planes in the past. [13]

On the afternoon of September 1, Federal Aviation Administrator J. Lynn Helms and Transportation Department General Counsel James H. Burnley were called to the State Department for a meeting with high-ranking Administration officials. Principal among these was Undersecretary of State for Political Affairs Lawrence S. Eagleburger. Following the meeting, Helms ordered the closing of Romeo-20 and had the FAA telephone its centers around the country to inform them that planes would not be able to use that route. Westbound traffic was transferred to route A-90, a parallel route that had previously been used for both east and westbound flights at different times of the day. The closing was strictly a "precautionary measure" rather than for reasons of safety, according to FAA spokesman Edmund Pinto. "We don't think there's any real safety problem because thousands of planes have flown along that route without any problem," said another FAA spokesman, Fred Farrar, "but we thought this was a good idea to do this until we clarify some of the issues surrounding this tragedy." Korean Air Lines apparently did not feel there was any safety problem with Romeo-20 either. Until Helms closed the route, KAL had scheduled one of its planes to fly Romeo-20 that night. [14]

Before September 1 had passed into history, President Reagan also took his first action in response to the downing, ordering "the flags of the United States flown at half staff at all Federal installations and U.S. military bases around the world." The governments of Canada and the Republic of Korea lowered their flags from September 2 to 4.[15]

On the first leg of his trip back to Washington, Ronald Reagan flew by helicopter from Rancho del Cielo to Point Mugu Naval Air Station, northwest of Los Angeles, receiving an en-route briefing on the international reaction to the downing of Flight 007 by National Security Adviser William Clark, presidential counselor Edwin Meese, and White House Chief of Staff Michael K. Deaver. Ronald and Nancy Reagan disembarked from the helicopter at 9:35 A.M. and, holding hands, walked grim-faced to a makeshift podium. Standing there on the tarmac, Reagan spoke for two and a half minutes on national television in what was perhaps the harshest public denunciation of the Soviet Union of his Administration to date. "What can we think of a regime," the President asked, "that so broadly trumpets its visions of peace and global disarmament and yet so callously and quickly commits a terrorist act to sacrifice the lives of innocent human beings? . . . What can be said about Soviet credibility when they so flagrantly lie about such a heinous act? . . . What can be the scope of legitimate mutual discourse with a state whose values permit such atrocities?" [16]

Arriving in Washington, Reagan, Clark, and Meese flew by helicopter from Andrews Air Force Base to the White House and proceeded directly to the Situation Room, where members of the National Security Council had already assembled. An extraordinary session of the council was convened at 6:30 P.M., Washington time. In attendance were the President, Vice-President George Bush and his Chief of Staff Adm. Dan Murphy, Secretary of State Shultz, Defense Secretary Caspar Weinberger, CIA Director William Casey, Attorney General William French Smith, Treasury Secretary Donald T. Regan, Office of Management and Budget Director David A. Stockman, Chairman of the Joint Chiefs of Staff Gen. John W. Vessey, Jr., U.S. Information Service Director Charles Z. Wick, Federal Aviation Administrator J. Lynn Helms, and Transportation Department General Counsel James H. Burnley. In addition, there was an assortment of White House officials, including Clark, Meese, Deaver, and White House Chief of Staff James A. Baker. One of the main items on the agenda was reviewing a list of possible options for dealing with the Soviets, with Defense Secretary Weinberger advancing the hardest-line approaches. The expanded NSC session ended two hours after it began. Larry Speakes told reporters later that the response strategy was intended to "focus international outrage on the Soviet Union." It was, Speakes said, a "positive approach" to the downing, a "measured response." [17]

The Administration had settled on a boycott of Aeroflot, the Soviet national carrier. In practice, however, suspending Aeroflot flights to the United States amounted to very little because they had been suspended

since December 1981, almost two years earlier, in response to the imposi-
tion of martial law in Poland. An effective boycott, therefore, required
action by the U.S.'s allies and by international organizations such as the
U.N.'s International Civil Aviation Organization and the International
Federation of Air Line Pilots Associations (IFALPA).

Late on Friday, September 2, in Moscow, the official Soviet news
agency Tass issued the second of what would be a continuing series of
statements on the incident. The statement was released simultaneously in
Russian and English at 8:53 P.M. (12:53 P.M., EDT) and read on Soviet
television shortly thereafter. Accompanying the television report was a
map reportedly showing the course of Flight 007 during the entire period
of Soviet radar tracking. The map showed the airliner making a course
adjustment as it approached Kamchatka and a sharp turn to the north-
northwest as it neared Sakhalin. The statement of September 2 went much
further than earlier reports in describing the actions of the airliner and
laying responsibility for the incident at the door of the United States: "In
violation of international regulations the plane flew without navigation
lights, did not react to radio signals of the Soviet dispatcher services, and
made no attempts to establish such communications contact. Anti air-
defense aircraft were ordered aloft; they repeatedly tried to establish contacts with the plane using generally accepted signals and to take it to the
nearest airfield in the territory of the Soviet Union. The intruder plane,
however, ignored all this." [18]

Then came a new allegation, one that would be vigorously denied by the
United States at the time but later shown to be true: "Over Sakhalin
Island, a Soviet aircraft fired warning shots and tracer shells along the
flying route of the plane. Soon after this the intruder plane left the limits of
Soviet airspace and continued its flight toward the Sea of Japan." Calling
the U.S. response to the downing a "hullabaloo," Tass said, "The relevant
U.S. services followed the flight throughout its duration in the most attentive manner. . . . The intrusion . . . cannot be regarded in any other way
than a preplanned act. It was obviously thought possible to attain special
intelligence aims without hindrance using civilian planes as a cover."

The battle had been joined. The Soviets posed their own rhetorical questions, in reverse, to the Americans: Why were no steps taken to warn the
plane of its danger and get it back on course? Why didn't the U.S. contact
the Soviet side to try to explain things? Although Tass made no direct
mention of the destruction of the Korean airliner, this was implicit in the
statement: "In leading circles of the Soviet Union regret is expressed over
the loss of human life and at the same time a resolute condemnation of
those who consciously or as a result of criminal disregard have allowed
the death of people and are now trying to use this occurrence for unseemly
political aims." [19]

The second Tass statement was issued as a direct result of a meeting of
the Politburo on Friday, September 2. Soviet leader Yuri Andropov was

in attendance, having returned to Moscow the day before.[20] There was speculation from Western sources in Moscow that Andropov initially intended to acknowledge the downing but backed down under pressure from the military, which viewed any such admission as tantamount to "submitting to international pressure."

Secretary of State Shultz blasted the Tass report: "They still do not want to admit the truth—that they shot down an unarmed civilian airliner." Shultz said the Soviet pilots "came close enough to see" that Flight 007 was a civilian airliner, and emphasized that the passengers "included a number of women and children." As to the Soviet claim, accurate as it would turn out, that warning shots were fired, Shultz said, "There is no indication the Soviets tried to warn the plane by firing tracers." The assertion that the airliner was on an espionage mission was said to be a "false claim." Shultz then repeated his earlier line that the United States was not aware the Korean airliner was in jeopardy until after it was shot down. "No cover-up, however brazen and elaborate, can change this reality—or absolve the Soviet Union of its responsibility to explain its behavior," Shultz said. "The world is waiting for the Soviet Union to tell the truth."[21]

On September 1, Charles M. Lichenstein, the acting permanent U.S. representative to the United Nations, forwarded a letter to Ambassador Noel G. Sinclair of Guyana, the president of the Security Council, requesting that an "urgent meeting" of the Security Council be convened to discuss the downing of Flight 007. The request for an extraordinary session of the Security Council was made in association with the Republic of Korea, a nation that has "permanent observer" status in the United Nations. The letter to Sinclair was almost a verbatim transcript of Shultz's comments about the Soviet tracking and destruction of Flight 007. "This unprovoked resort to the use of force by the Soviet military authorities in contravention of International Civil Aviation Organization standards and the basic norms of international law," Lichenstein said, "must be deplored and condemned by the international community and by world public opinion."[22] That is, Lichenstein hoped the session would serve as a forum for condemning the Soviets, for coordinating a Western response, and as an impetus to have the U.N.'s International Civil Aviation Organization (ICAO) conduct an inquiry into the matter.

At 4:15 P.M. on the afternoon of September 2, the fifteen-member Security Council convened before a capacity crowd in the hall normally used by the Economic and Social Council. The opening address of the session was by South Korean Ambassador Kim Kyung-won, who demanded from the Soviet Union, a "full and detailed" account of the circumstances surrounding the downing of the airliner plus an apology and compensation for the loss of the aircraft and also to the families of those killed. He further demanded that search and recovery crews be permitted to enter Soviet territorial waters in their search for wreckage. During the session Kim was joined by the representatives of thirteen other countries who rose to demand apologies, compensation, explanation.[23] With the exception of the Soviet representative himself, no speaker rose in defense of the Soviet Union.[24]

It was the American delegate, however, who stole the show. Charles Lichenstein, a political appointee, was brought to the U.N. by Ambassador Jeane J. Kirkpatrick. A longtime friend of Kirkpatrick and her husband, Lichenstein had distinguished himself in the past as a senior vice-president of the Public Broadcasting Service and as a ghostwriter for former President Nixon's book *Six Crises*. In a speech described by the *New York Times* as "ranging from biting contempt to harsh anger," Lichenstein said, "The crime committed was, indeed, calculated; and indeed, it was deliberate; and it was wantonly irresponsible. Let us call the crime for what clearly it is: wanton, calculated, deliberate murder." He called the Soviet Union "a ruthless totalitarian state [that has been] responsible . . . for killing more people and enslaving more nations than any state, any regime, in the history of mankind."[25]

Soviet envoy Richard Ovinnikov sat impassively through Lichenstein's address and the opening statement by South Korean envoy Kim Kyung-won, puffing on his pipe. Then in a monotone, Ovinnikov read a prepared text extremely similar to the September 2 Tass statement. Like that account, Ovinnikov's statement included the regret of Soviet leading circles over the loss of life. But it also accepted no Soviet responsibility for the downing and called the Administration's reaction "a propaganda display" designed to fuel the "militarist policy in the U.S."[26]

Toward the end of the session, Lichenstein read into the record a statement by Secretary of State Shultz denouncing the Soviets and describing "the facts" of the case as portrayed by Washington. Lichenstein then paused "to comment on the suspicion which the Soviet representative expressed at the fact that United States services followed the flight throughout its duration in the most attentive manner. No, I would remind the representative of the Soviet Union: We followed you following the flight."[27]

This aside was an explicit admission that U.S. military and intelligence services were actively intercepting radar and communications throughout the 2½ hours of Soviet tracking of the airliner. In fact, it was far too much of an admission. The Security Council session's verbatim transcript contains Lichenstein's remark, but the offending passage has been expunged from many accounts of Lichenstein's statement made public by the Administration. (When asked to comment on Lichenstein's remark later, a U.S. official told the *Washington Post,* "We have never explained that because it gets into intelligence information. The obvious implication is that we have information indicating what the Soviets saw.")[28]

The meeting adjourned at 6:40 P.M., almost 2½ hours after it began. The language employed on all sides was extreme and uncompromising, reducing the middle ground for dispassionate discussion of the incident.[29] No resolutions were offered, and debate was scheduled to resume on September 6.[30]

By September 2, reactions to the downing were being heard throughout the West. British Foreign Secretary Sir Geoffrey Howe, meeting with Soviet Ambassador to Britain Victor Popov, demanded a "full explanation" for the downing and expressed his government's "strong condemnation." In Bonn, West German government spokesman Juergen Sudhoff told a news conference that the downing of Flight 007 was "an inconceivable act of unsurpassed brutality." The French Foreign Ministry said the incident "puts into question the principles that govern international relations and respect for human life." Swedish Foreign Minister Lennart Bodstrom said that his nation was "deeply shocked" by the tragedy. Italian Defense Minister Giovanni Spadolini remarked how the incident horrified "every civilized conscience and brings disgrace to its perpetrators."[31]

Members of Congress quickly joined the worldwide condemnation of the Russians. "We cannot have détente with a dictatorship which willingly kills innocent people," said Representative Newt Gingrich of Georgia. "Attacking an unarmed civilian plane is like attacking a school bus," said Representative Thomas Hartnett of South Carolina. "They just tracked them down and shot them out of the sky like you would track a mad dog and shoot it," Representative William Dickinson of Alaska remarked. Senator Patrick Leahy of Vermont agreed, saying, "If that's not cold-blooded, outrageous murder, I don't know what is." Speaking on ABC's "Nightline" from Seoul, South Korea, Senator Jesse Helms commented, "I think we ought to review all of our relationships, including the negotiations with respect to arms control and so forth, because obviously this was a premeditated, deliberate murder of 265 [sic] people. I think it's incumbent upon all of us to have the civilized world wake up and smell the coffee."[32]

The Administration's response to the downing combined passionate rhetoric with an unwillingness to let the crisis get in the way of business. On September 1, the very day Shultz and Reagan were condemning the Soviets, the Agriculture Department announced that the Soviets would buy 900,000 tons of grain from the United States, the first purchase under a new long-term agreement signed in Moscow the week before. Reagan had always opposed grain embargoes and had campaigned in 1980 on a promise to lift the embargo put into effect by the Carter administration. "A contract is a contract," Secretary of Agriculture John R. Block explained.[33]

However, the U.S. was trying to sell its allies on a boycott of Aeroflot for not more than 90 days. As the *New York Times* put it, Reagan had "seemingly chosen the path of strong rhetoric without irrevocable and harsh retaliation. The strategy seems to be to seek a propaganda victory in the United Nations and, with world opinion, to embarrass and isolate the Soviet Union, but not to rupture the dialogue nurtured in recent months."[34]

None of this sat well with the Right. Unhappy with Reagan's "measured response,'' the extreme Right had from the first perceived the downing of Flight 007 as a golden opportunity to advance its political agenda. As ABC's "Nightline" commentator Ted Koppel noted, the National Conservative Political Action Committee (NCPAC) "whipped out a television commercial that was nothing if not direct": "On August 31, the Soviet Union shot down an unarmed civilian jetliner, murdering 269 innocent people, including Congressman Lawrence P. McDonald," began the NCPAC commercial message. "Yet some congressmen still want to appease the Soviet Union by supporting a nuclear freeze that would make the Soviets more powerful and allow them to kill more innocent people. To find out if your congressman is willing to appease the Soviet Union with a nuclear freeze, call 1-800-331-1000." [35]

Invoking Neville Chamberlain became a favorite device for those demanding stronger action against the Russians. NCPAC's executive director Terry Dolan said those who contend both superpowers share responsibility for their high level of tensions "are very reminiscent of Neville Chamberlain telling us that we could negotiate with monsters." Howard Phillips, chairman of the Conservative Caucus, noted, "This crisis is the moment of truth for Reagan. . . . He has been using the rhetoric of Superman and the policies of Neville Chamberlain. Unless he takes stronger action than it now appears, he will make Jimmy Carter look like Charles Atlas." Richard A. Viguerie, publisher of *Conservative Digest* and an active fund raiser for right-wing causes, described Reagan's proposed sanctions against the Soviets as "namby-pamby" and asserted that Reagan had "just walked away from the town bully without drawing his gun." "I don't think this is going to wash with the American people," Viguerie said. So outraged was the Right that the National Conservative Political Action Committee, having already spent $1.5 million on rallies, fund-raising events, direct-mail efforts, and a 30-minute television film for the President's reelection bid, threatened to drop the rest of its $5 million campaign. [36]

The Administration's harsh and uncompromising words began to be reflected in actions across the country. At about 7:30 A.M. on September 4, a crowd organized by the Korean Association of New York gathered at the high school in Glen Cove, a town about 20 miles east of New York City on the northern shore of Long Island. In Glen Cove is the home of the Soviet Permanent Mission in New York, a 36-acre compound known as Killenworth. Senator Alfonse D'Amato was reported to have addressed the crowd before it marched from the high school to Killenworth. The Soviet news agency Tass noted that "a team of American TV reporters arrived in advance at the gate." [37]

Once there, new arrivals continued to swell the crowd until it numbered about one thousand. Angry protesters shouted denunciations of the Soviet Union and shook their fists in the air. A number carried baseball bats and signs reading "Kill the Russians." At about 10:00 A.M., the Korean Association led sixty people in a successful charge over the compound's 8-foot-high wrought-iron gates. Once inside, the demonstrators attempted to force entry into the main building and held a brief rally in a sunken garden in front of the mansion. South Korean flags were unfurled, and yells of "Kick them out" were heard. Eventually, four plainclothes detectives and two uniformed officers escorted the group back through the gates. A secret State Department memorandum noted that "Soviet embassy duty officers were in touch with the [State Department KAL] working group throughout the incident."[38]

As was becoming Soviet practice, a Tass statement was released just prior to the evening television news bulletin at 9 P.M., Moscow time, the third such statement in as many days. Like official U.S. statements that stayed close to the central theme of who shot down the airliner, the Tass statement stuck to the Soviet point of emphasis, asking how the plane could have veered so far off course and why the U.S. military and intelligence services that monitored the flight did not warn it. It was a strong counterattack, composed, as the *New York Times* observed, "in a belligerent and hostile tone." Ridiculing assertions that the airliner might have had a communications or navigation problem, Tass called the intrusion a "provocation staged against the Soviet Union," an act in which the United States was said to have had a "direct relation." "The purpose of this provocation is more than obvious," Tass said. The Reagan administration was "feverishly covering up traces of the provocation . . . going out of its way to disrupt the process of the normalization of the situation in the world," and "shedding hypocritic tears over what happened." The White House and State Department were said to be "mounting a worldwide rabid anti-Soviet campaign," the tone of which was "set by the U.S. President."[39]

Employing a variety of rhetorical devices, the Tass statement played on the nationalism, patriotism, and fears of the Soviet public. As with the earlier statements, the *Washington Post* concluded, the most recent missive appeared "aimed at convincing an intensely patriotic Soviet public that what happened" was justified.[40] Since the Soviets use precisely the same approach when they are telling the truth as when they are lying, it is difficult at times to figure out which is which.

8

SPEECHES AND
THEORIES

Col. Gen. Seymon F. Romanov was chief of the main headquarters
staff of the Soviet air defense forces. Romanov joined the military in 1940
and rose through the ranks. He won the Hero of the Soviet Union medal,
the country's highest military award, and became the sixth-ranked general
in the Soviet air defense forces, the PVO.[1] On Sunday, September 4,
Romanov spoke to Soviet journalists about the downing of Flight 007, the
first specific individual in the Soviet Union to comment on the incident.

Romanov spoke on the main Soviet television news program on Sunday
night, following a special news commentary that accused the CIA of sac-
rificing the KAL airliner and its passengers for an espionage mission over
sensitive Soviet military installations. Soviet political commentator Vitaly
I. Kobysh told viewers for the first time that "peaceable people" have
been lost on board the airliner. "That is the awful thing," Kobysh said.
"That knowing this, the responsible services used it for their dirty aims."[2]

Romanov told viewers that the Soviet pilot "failed, despite all his attempts, to establish radio contact with the intruder." At one point, he said,
the Korean plane rocked its wings in apparent recognition of the Soviet
signals but continued its flight. "At that, our interceptor flew with its lights
on, flashing them in order to attract the attention of the intruder's crew.
Neither waggling nor flashing, however, brought the necessary result."

The airliner did not respond to these "repeated attempts" to get it to land or to radio signals, and it exhibited other "strange behavior." Romanov then gave a brief history of U.S. intrusions into Soviet airspace. He concluded his remarks by explaining that the airliner "flew with extinguished lights, and its outlines resemble much those of the American reconnaissance plane RC-135." [3]

Compared to earlier Tass statements, Romanov's speech was relatively moderate in tone. It appeared the following day in *Pravda* in a half page. [4] In response, Pentagon officials cited by the Associated Press said the chance "is almost nil" that the Soviets thought they were shooting at an RC-135 rather than the Korean jetliner. [5]

President Reagan and his top advisers met with members of Congress to discuss the downing of Flight 007 in an unusual Sunday meeting on September 4. As the congressmen gathered together around an oval table in the White House Cabinet Room, Reagan opened the meeting with a moment of silent prayer for Flight 007's 269 victims. Other Administration officials present included Vice-President George Bush, Secretary of State George P. Shultz, Defense Secretary Caspar W. Weinberger, Director of Central Intelligence William J. Casey, Attorney General William French Smith, Chairman of the Joint Chiefs of Staff Gen. John W. Vessey, Jr., Office of Management and Budget Director David A. Stockman, and special Middle East envoy Robert C. McFarlane. From the Congress came Senate Majority Leader Howard H. Baker, Jr., Senate President Pro Tempore Strom Thurmond, Senate Minority Leader Robert C. Byrd, House Majority Leader James Wright, House Minority Leader Robert H. Michel, and Speaker of the House Thomas P. O'Neill, Jr. [6]

In order to convince the legislators of the Administration version of the tragedy and secure their approval for retaliatory steps against the Soviet Union, Reagan played a highly edited portion of the intercepted transmissions from the Soviet fighter pilots over Sakhalin Island. As the congressmen listened, the pilots' words were played on a tape recorder in Russian and then translated into English. UPI commented, "The playing of the tape heightened the drama during Reagan's discussions." [7]

The most interesting disclosure made at the meeting was that the RC-135 had passed in close proximity to Flight 007. House Majority Leader Wright later said he had "asked if it were possible that the pilot who shot down the Korean airliner had confused it with an RC-135. The answer from General Vessey and from Secretary Weinberger was no, because on the tape that was played, that particular pilot referred to having been within two kilometers at one point of the plane." Vessey added that in the time available to them, the Soviet pilots should have been able to identify Flight 007 as a passenger airliner. [8]

The President was unequivocal in his presentation, describing the downing as "a barbaric, uncivilized, cold-blooded act committed by the Soviet regime." He told the congressmen, "We have definite proof that they intentionally shot down that unarmed, civilian airplane. The evidence is irrefutable.'' Beyond the playing of the tape, however, no ''irrefutable evidence'' was adduced to prove that the Soviets knew the identity of the intruder at the time they shot it down. Indeed, it would later be acknowledged by the Administration that the Soviets did not, in fact, identify the airliner before the attack. The unusual Sunday meeting, which included a briefing on the situation in Lebanon by Middle East envoy Robert Mc-Farlane, lasted 2 hours and 40 minutes rather than the 90 minutes originally scheduled. Larry Speakes later remarked that the meeting produced a ''genuine consensus on the President's approach'' toward dealing with the Soviet Union.[9]

The way in which the news leaked out about the RC-135's proximity to Flight 007 prior to its downing is an interesting story. As the *New York Times* put it, ''The disclosure of the presence of the American reconnaissance plane in the general area appeared to come almost by accident.'' Almost by accident, but not quite. Speaking with reporters after the White House briefing, House Majority Leader Wright was describing the communications of the Soviet interceptor pilots over Sakhalin Island. One of the reporters asked Wright if the Soviet pilots had ever referred to the Korean airliner as an RC-135. ''Yes, that's true,'' Wright replied. ''At at least one point they referred to it by that designation.'' Wright apparently had confused the intercepted communications from the time of the Kamchatka overflight, where Flight 007 had in fact been referred to as an ''RC-135,'' and the intercepts over Sakhalin, where it was simply called the ''target.'' But Wright's leak had two consequences. First, it prompted a mildly rebuking call from White House Chief of Staff James A. Baker III.[10] Second, Wright's mention of the presence of the RC-135 touched off a flurry of activity by Administration officials.[11]

Both the Soviets and the Americans were fully aware that an RC-135 had been operating off the east coast of Kamchatka Peninsula as Flight 007 approached. The statement just issued in Moscow by General Romanov had moved the Soviet official line a significant step toward disclosing its presence. For all the Administration knew, the Russians might be preparing to disclose the paths of the RC-135 and Flight 007, as they later did. Such a release could cast doubt on the U.S. official version of events, not only for having an intelligence plane in the area but for having concealed its presence. After distancing themselves from the leak by rebuking Wright, Administration officials practically threw themselves in front of the press to get out their account of the role of the Air Force plane. Consequently, the Wright leak was almost certainly intentional, on the Administration's part if not on Wright's. It assured that the press would hear about the RC-135 from U.S. officials before they heard about it from the Russians. Facts could then be presented to suggest that there was no connection between the two aircraft.

It was not long before Larry Speakes, in the company of National Security spokesman Robert B. Sims, told reporters that Representative Wright had been mistaken. The segment of tape played by the White House contained no reference to an RC-135. Another Administration official later assured reporters that there was no such reference during the entire 55 minutes of tape, which was true since the tape played was from the Sakhalin period. Speakes told reporters that the U.S. does operate reconnaissance flights "in international waters off the Soviet coast to monitor missile tests and other actions." But "if there was any reference" to an RC-135, he said, "it took place well in advance" of the downing of Flight 007. Speakes refused to answer reporters' questions about when President Reagan learned of the presence of the RC-135 for the first time.[12]

Speakes then presented the U.S. interpretation of the presence of the RC-135. Knowing that Soviet radar had tracked both the RC-135 and Flight 007 prior to the latter's entry into Soviet airspace, Speakes asserted that "it was not long" before they should have discovered they were dealing with "two separate aircraft." "With the visual and radar information available to them," he continued, "when they shot it down, they should have known irrefutably that it was a civilian airliner."[13] Thus, the deputy press secretary opened the possibility of misidentification of the airliner by the Soviets.

After Speakes's briefing, Administration officials began talking about the RC-135 on condition that they not be identified. The officials said the mission of the RC-135 was "routine" and that the RC-135 picked up no information suggesting that the airliner was in trouble. They said that the RC-135 was "based in Alaska," although they declined to provide more specific details about the intelligence plane's flight path or the duration of its mission.[14] These statements are not as straightforward as they sound. A Korean airliner intruding into Soviet territory that is successfully avoiding interception is not "in trouble," per se. The "based in Alaska" formulation, which would appear in more developed form in a televised speech by the President the following evening, also obfuscated the situation. While Shemya Island, near the tip of the Aleutian chain, is technically Alaska, it is only about 400 miles from the Kamchatka Peninsula, closer than it is to the Alaskan mainland.

Then more complex geography crept in. The press was told that the RC-135 flew no closer than 50 miles to the Soviet coastline, although this tells nothing about its proximity to Flight 007. Another of the unnamed high-ranking Administration officials added that at one stage the RC-135 came within 75 miles of the Korean jumbo jetliner. Others corrected this to 75 nautical miles (about 86 statute miles). Others said it was not the planes themselves but their tracks that came within 75 nautical miles. Still other accounts noted that the two aircraft had crossed paths but were "never closer than 300 miles to each other." It was then said that the RC-135 was 1,000 miles away from the area where the Korean airliner was shot down.

The geographic *coup de grace* was administrated by Lawrence Eagleburger, who said, "The U.S. aircraft never came any closer to the shootdown site than 1,200 NM, a distance equal to that from New York to Florida or to the width of Europe from the English Channel to the Russian border." [15] It was not surprising that the press was confused.

Next, the White House released a statement describing the activities of the RC-135, and it merits some attention because of the large number of deceptive phrases it contains. When Flight 007 was first detected by radar, the statement began, "a U.S. RC-135 aircraft was in the vicinity. Both aircraft were then in international airspace, and the U.S. aircraft never entered Soviet airspace." [16] The statement explained that both the U.S. and Soviets routinely operate reconnaissance aircraft near each other's borders. These claims are true but irrelevant to what happened on the night of August 31.

The White House statement went on to say that the Soviets "know that our aircraft do not enter their airspace," a statement that a large body of evidence suggests is untrue. Further, "The closest point of approach [for Flight 007 and the RC-135] was 75 nautical miles, while the U.S. aircraft was in its mission orbit." That clears up the mystery of miles and nautical miles, but the sentence refers only to the RC-135's mission orbit. The mission orbit of a reconnaissance aircraft is a very specific portion of its flight path. What the statement fails to address is how close the two planes might have come while the RC-135 was outside of its mission orbit. The Soviets did in fact confuse the two planes, and it is hard to see how that could have occurred if they had been separated by 75 nautical miles. Not even the worst of the worst of the Soviet radars are that bad. The only other possibility is that the planes had been lined up with a high degree of precision, making their radar blips appear to merge. The chances of this happening by chance are exceedingly remote. One of these explanations must be true, however, for as Larry Speakes suggested, the Soviets had reason for believing that there were not "two separate aircraft" at one point.

"Later," the statement continued, "the U.S. aircraft crossed the path taken by the Korean airliner, but by then the airliner was almost 300 miles away." This implied an even further separation between the two planes, but the 300-mile figure refers to the second time the path was crossed, which is a completely irrelevant statement. "Approximately 2½ hours after the U.S. and Korean aircraft were near each other in international space, the Soviets shot down the Korean airliner." This took place "some 1,000 miles and 2½ hours flight time from the scene of the shoot-down."

We have now arrived at a stunning irrelevancy. Where the RC-135 was when Flight 007 was shot down has nothing to do with where it was when the Korean jet was about to enter Soviet airspace for the first time. By suggesting this temporal and spatial dissociation, the White House directed attention away from where the two aircraft were and what they were doing when Flight 007 first approached Soviet territory. And the press did not call the Administration on this point.

On the contrary, the media focused not on what the two planes were doing but on how they looked. Administration officials emphasized that the "RC-135 reconnaissance plane is a converted 707 that has a completely different configuration from the Korean jet," and virtually all major newspapers carried silhouettes of the two airliners stacked on top of each other. When the planes are compared that way, the differences between them are clear. A converted Boeing 707, the RC-135 has an overall length of 152 feet 11 inches, compared to 231 feet 4 inches for a 747. They have heights of 42 feet 6 inches versus 63 feet 5 inches. Their wingspans are 145 feet 9 inches and 195 feet 8 inches, respectively.[17] The comparisons reinforced the belief that the Soviets could not have mistaken a 747 for an RC-135. Anyone could tell the difference.

The problem for the Soviet fighter pilots was that they had no RC-135 alongside for comparison. It was dark, the airliner was no closer than a mile and a half away, and its lights were only occasionally visible. The spy plane and the jumbo jet are both four-engined, swept-wing aircraft of generally similar form, and the interceptor aircraft was flying below so that the distinctive hump on the front of the 747's fuselage could not be seen. But newspaper accounts did not consider the circumstances of the interception, and the silhouettes appeared everywhere.

In spite of all this, Administration officials were beginning to suggest that maybe the Soviets did not properly identify the airliner after all, although they should have. The New York Times cited anonymous Administration officials as saying it was "conceivable" that the Soviets had initially confused the two planes. "If indeed it was a mistake," said Larry Speakes, "they should tell the world it was a mistake. If they wanted off the hook on this, they could at least admit they made a mistake."[18]

The reason for the change in the official line was simple. President Reagan was planning to play portions of the intercepted transmissions from the Soviet fighter pilots to their ground controllers in his address to the nation the following day. United Nations Ambassador Jeane Kirkpatrick would play even more extensive portions at the United Nations the day after that. And at no time did the Soviet pilots ever refer to Flight 007 as anything other than the "target."

On the morning of September 4, Assistant Secretary of State for European Affairs Richard Burt appeared on CBS television's "Face the Nation."[19] Burt's agenda that day was to push the three elements of the Administration's approach to the incident: First, any actions contemplated by the United States were to be "international," which would implicate the allies in supporting the official U.S. explanation of events. Second was to promote an inquiry into the downing by the International Civil Aviation Organization. Third, Burt would use the incident to push for increased support for the Administration's entire wish list of military hardware and spending.[20]

At first, the White House had not planned to have the President make a national speech dealing with the downing. The original plan was for Reagan to inform congressional leaders of the actions he planned to take. But as the *Washington Post* noted, "Reagan has always had extraordinary faith in his own ability to shape U.S. public opinion with a speech," and a televised speech it would be. The speech had been prepared by White House speech writer Benjamin Elliott on the basis of suggestions made by Reagan's national security staff, the State and Defense departments, and the CIA.[21] During the day of September 5, Reagan worked for several hours on his speech, now in its third draft, making notations and changes in his own handwriting.

The speech was broadcast from the Oval Office at 8:00 that evening. "My fellow Americans," the President began, "I am coming before you tonight about the Korean airline massacre—the attack by the Soviet Union against 269 innocent men, women, and children aboard an unarmed Korean passenger plane." Reagan's speech writers had decided to use the word "massacre" instead of "murder" because it conjured up the slaughter of innocents more effectively, and the *Los Angeles Times* pointed out that Reagan referred to the downing as a "massacre" six times.[22]

Ronald Reagan turned to history, noting that in 1978 "the Soviets also shot down an unarmed civilian airliner after having positively identified it as such. . . . Several innocent people lost their lives in this attack." Reagan did not mention that this plane had also been a Korean airliner—the coincidence might be hard for some to swallow—nor did he mention that the unarmed civilian airliner took evasive action, endangering the innocent people on board and provoking the shootdown.

Reagan's speech was also important in the development of the official U.S. line. New arguments appeared in the speech, and some older ones were discarded. One new element that would become a durable part of the official line was the eternal mystery of the case. "No one will ever know," said the President, "whether a mistake was made in giving the computer the course or whether there was a malfunction."[23] This was an unusual comment, coming only five days after the downing, when American, Japanese, Korean, and Soviet vessels were still busily searching the Sea of Japan for the airliner's "black box" flight recorders, which could have solved many of the mysteries of the case. In addition, this formulation limited the possible causes of Flight 007's deviation to an error in programming the INS or some unspecified technical malfunction. In fact, the number of logical possibilities is much larger.

Reagan was by no means through. "Despite the savagery of their crime," he continued, "and the universal reaction against the evidence of their complicity, the Soviets still refuse to tell the truth. They have persistently refused to admit that their pilot fired on the Korean aircraft." This was contrasted with the actions of the Administration where, "as you know, we immediately made known to the world the shocking facts as honestly and completely as they came to us." Recent additions to the official line were incorporated into Reagan's speech[24] Reagan mentioned the presence of the RC-135 but carefully avoided explaining its relation to Flight 007 except to reiterate misleadingly that it "had been back at its base in Alaska, on the ground, for an hour when the murderous attack took place."[25]

To dramatize his points, the President played a tape of the voices of two of the Soviet interceptor pilots, designated 805 and 163, as they pursued Flight 007. Lasting for only a few seconds, the audio material was a condensation of six different radio exchanges that took place over an 8-minute period and was not translated for the television audience. Even so, some found the performance convincing. A U.S. official quoted in the *Wall Street Journal* said, "The absolute lack of emotion is chilling. The pilot has just blown up 269 people and he's not excited or depressed, just flat, a professional doing his job. It's a good illustration of the kind of people we're dealing with in the Soviet Union."[26]

Although Administration officials were now admitting there was no absolute proof that the Russians knew they were firing at a commercial jetliner, Reagan asserted that the Soviets knew Flight 007 was a civilian airliner when they shot it down.[27] "The 747 has a unique and distinctive silhouette unlike any other plane in the world," he said. "There is no way a pilot could mistake this for anything other than a civilian airliner." Reagan even gave a weather report from the area. The tragedy took place, he said, "on what we know was a clear night with a half moon." This was not true. There was extensive cloud coverage over Kamchatka, scattered low clouds over the Sea of Okhotsk, and overcast with low clouds and some scattered medium and high clouds over Sakhalin.[28]

The President's speech reached its crescendo on the theme of the nature of the Soviet Union. "They deny the deed," the President said, "but in their conflicting and misleading protestations, the Soviets reveal that, yes, shooting down a plane—even one with hundreds of innocent men, women, children, and babies—is a part of their normal procedure if that plane is in what they claim is their airspace.[29] He added, "We shouldn't be surprised by such inhuman brutality."[30]

It might seem that severe sanctions against the Soviets would surely be forthcoming, but Reagan was asking for very little. First, the President said he would ask Congress to pass a joint resolution condemning the Soviet Union. This was followed by three unilateral actions to be taken by the United States, described by one official as a "symbolic flyspeck": the suspension of negotiations on a cultural agreement with the Soviets, on new U.S.–Soviet consulates in New York and Kiev, and on a transportation agreement that the *Washington Post* described as "of so little consequence it could not be described by a senior Administration official who briefed reporters before the President's speech." Reagan also "reaffirmed" the suspension of Aeroflot's landing rights in Washington which had been in effect since 1981 and said that the United States would institute claims through diplomatic channels on behalf of the families of the sixty-one Americans who died on board Flight 007.[31]

As the finale, Reagan turned to the defense budget, the largest in the nation's history, that was being considered in Congress. "The Congress will be facing key defense issues when it returns from recess," he said. "There has been legitimate difference of opinion on this subject, I know, but I urge the members of that distinguished body to ponder long and hard the Soviets' aggression as they consider the security and safety of our people, indeed all people who believe in freedom."[32]

The press had accolades for the September 5 speech. "President Reagan tried on the mantle of statesmanship," a *Los Angeles Times* editorial gushed. "It is a surprisingly good fit." Admitting that the language used was perhaps a bit strong, the *Times* observed that "the words were not the message, which was restrained." In a similar laudatory vein, a *Christian Science Monitor* editorial praised Reagan's "balanced response," noting that the Administration wanted to "avoid any comparisons with the previous administration's futile efforts at modifying Soviet behavior."[33]

After Reagan's television speech, the inevitable Tass response was broadcast on Radio Moscow. Calling it "an aggressive, hateful speech . . . to arouse an outburst of anti-Soviet sentiment in the American nation," Tass said that Reagan "attempted, clumsily, to make it appear as if the violation of the Soviet Union's sovereignty had been merely the result of a mistake with which the CIA and other U.S. espionage agencies allegedly had nothing to do." Questioning the origin and authenticity of the tapes of the Soviet interceptor pilots, the report concluded by noting that Reagan "urged Congress to approve his giant military program, using the [Flight 007] incident . . . as a pretext."[34]

The press devoted considerable space to analyzing the Soviet mindset that led to the attack. Articles, editorials, and television commentaries in the United States frequently noted the xenophobia of the Soviet system, its unthinking bureaucratic rigidity, its aggressive and secretive tendencies, and its profound insecurity. Columnist James Reston was representative: "The Soviet response has been so bizarre," he said, "so indifferent to the human tragedy, and so vicious in its charges against the U.S. and the South Koreans that it can be explained only by the Russians' pathological fear of freedom."[35] History was invoked: the precedents of intrusion and invasion that produced an extreme defensiveness, a militaristic, trigger-happy defense of the Motherland. These were said to be the cause of the downing of Korean Air Lines Flight 007.

It was an image of unmitigated darkness. By September 5, Flight 007 had already become a symbol. "In the symbol," Walter Lippmann once wrote, "emotion is discharged at a common target, and the idiosyncrasy of real ideas blotted out." The target, of course, was the Soviet Union as the ideological differences between the two superpowers were trumpeted in newspaper headlines and the leads of the nightly news programs. Fears were deliberately evoked: fear of the Soviets; fear of the unseen enemy; fear of technologies only imperfectly understood; the vivid image of decompression and cold, and then the spiraling down into the abyss; the utter lack of control as events unfold, unable to do anything more than clutch at the imagined oxygen mask in the freezing silence of altitude. All of the fears of the modern world, from which we are normally so carefully shielded, focused to the flashpoint by the downing. A White House spokesman said that as of noon on September 7, the White House had received 734 telephone calls favoring Reagan's "measured response" toward the Soviet Union; however, 1,526 callers wanted even tougher action.[36]

Shortly after President Reagan's disclosure that an intelligence aircraft had been in close proximity to Flight 007 as it approached Soviet territory, military officials began talking about the super-secret spy plane's mission. Two completely different stories about the RC-135 came out at approximately the same time.

The first was that the RC-135 in question was an air defense monitor, code-named Rivet Joint, equipped with a classified scientific and technical intelligence system for intercepting a broad range of electronic signals. In an article entitled "U.S. RC-135 Was Assessing Soviet Air Defenses," sources cited by the *Washington Post* said that the plane "flew out of Eielson Air Force Base, 26 miles southeast of Fairbanks, Alaska, where it is part of the 6th Wing of the Strategic Air Command." This account was seconded by *The Guardian,* which attributed the story to "a senior Administration official who briefed reporters on condition that he would not be identified." Equipped with the "most elaborate electronic devices to ensure that they do not cross into Soviet airspace," the RC-135 was said to be on a "routine" mission, operating off the Kamchatka coast either to find out more about the Soviets' "electronic order of battle" or "to calibrate its radar on a milk run." The sources said that the Air Force technicians in the rear of the RC-135 "were listening to and recording Soviet voice and electronic communications" throughout the duration of its mission. This almost certainly included the communications between the Soviet fighters scrambled over Kamchatka and their ground controllers.[37]

The second story was also quite specific. According to anonymous U.S. officials cited in the *New York Times,* the RC-135 in question was part of a fleet operated by the Strategic Air Command "to seek information on Soviet missile deployments, communications, and test shots," the type known as Cobra Ball. This plane has a crew of about seventeen and is equipped with electronic devices to monitor missile telemetry, although it is also capable of monitoring radio, radar, and other types of electronic emissions. The RC-135 was said to have been flying "in a monitoring orbit that our planes normally occupy," off the Kamchatka coast, "to listen and tape Soviet communications about missiles."[38] Cobra Ball telemetry planes are based on Shemya Island, and unnamed Administration officials said that the RC-135 in question was based on Shemya.[39]

Military officers said that "so far as had been determined, the reconnaissance crew heard neither radio transmissions from Soviet ground stations to the fighter pilot who reportedly shot down the Korean plane nor conversations between the Korean pilot and a Japanese ground station." Of course they didn't—the RC-135 was back at its base when Flight 007 was shot down. The officers' statement, however, avoids mentioning what the intelligence personnel on board the RC-135 heard from the Soviet fighters and ground controllers over Kamchatka. It does not disclose whether Flight 007's communications with American air traffic controllers were monitored, saying only that "Air Force planes on such missions rarely listen in on commercial airline radio frequencies."[40]

According to James Bamford, however, "The RC-135 is designed for one purpose—it's designed for eavesdropping." That involves the monitoring of "Soviet voice communications, such as MiG pilot communications, ground station communications . . . [and] naval communications; virtually anything that goes through the air the NSA tries to collect." He said that "there's almost no way that that aircraft could not have picked up the indications of Soviet activity: Soviet fighters taking off, Soviet air defense stations going to higher states of readiness, higher states of alert."[41] Although some accounts have erroneously suggested otherwise, both Rivet Joint and Cobra Ball planes can, and do, monitor Soviet communications.[42]

Was the RC-135 a Rivet Joint or a Cobra Ball plane? On September 8, William Safire's column in the *New York Times* told readers: "Here is what happened near the Soviet-Japanese border. Our electronic ears told us that a major Soviet missile test was in its beginning stages; as usual, one of our RC-135 spy planes was sent up to observe the test from a position well outside the Soviet Union. At the same time, the Korean civilian jumbo jet wandered off course into the area. Preparations for the missile test were promptly shut down; as that mission was scrubbed, our reconnaissance plane returned to its base."[43] Safire, a former aide in the Nixon administration, maintains good contacts within the intelligence community. Asked to comment on his missile test story, Safire said, "I had that report from an intelligence source that has been accurate in the past."[44] (In fact, in all the time since the downing it has never been established if in fact there was a test scheduled for that night, although apparently a series of missile tests was taking place during that general period of time.)

The way the story about the missile test was subsequently used by the Administration evokes even greater skepticism. After the appearance of Safire's column, reporters asked Larry Speakes about the reported missile test. Speakes hemmed and hawed and said he would not discuss the matter because it involved intelligence-gathering capabilities. But then he quickly added, "I don't doubt the reports."[45] The story about the missile test was quickly picked up worldwide. Now there was an excuse for the presence of the RC-135 and an explanation for how its crew could have missed the air activity accompanying the intrusion of the 747 into Russian airspace.

The missile test soon began to assume a life of its own. The missile acquired a name: PL-5. The "PL" designation denotes an experimental type of Soviet missile undergoing testing at the facility at Plesetsk. Since February 1983, American intelligence had detected tests of a new three-stage, single-warhead missile at that facility, located about 150 miles south of the White Sea port of Arkhangel'sk.[46] As testing and development progressed, the designation of the missile was changed to "SS-X-25."[47]

During the spring of 1983, intelligence reports were accurately predicting that the SS-X-25, a fifth-generation, solid-propellent ICBM, would be mobile-based, the first such ICBM on either side. A senior Administration official noted that the Soviets had on three previous occasions tried to hide the missile's tests by camouflaging the launchers, launching the missiles at night, and encrypting missile test telemetry data. The United States believed that this secrecy was intended to conceal at least two violations, or "breakouts," of arms control treaties. First, the U.S. thought that the throw-weight of the SS-X-25 had increased by more than the 5 percent permitted under the unratified provisions of SALT II. In addition, the warhead was believed to weigh less than 50 percent as much as the warhead dispenser, or "bus." This is not permitted under SALT II because a big bus could make possible a treaty breakout if warheads were added later.[48] If such a test was being conducted that night, it would explain the presence of the RC-135 in a way unconnected to the intrusion of Flight 007.

Despite the convenience of the missile test story, it may have some basis in fact. In the original stories, the missile carried no designation. The inference drawn by the media after Safire's column was that the test had to do with a long-range missile that would fly from west to east across the Asian continent to smash into the hills of Kamchatka. But what if the test was of some other type of missile? What if the missile wasn't an ICBM but one intended for air defense? What if the Russians had figured out ways to hide the missile from U.S. reconnaissance satellites so that the United States would have to resort to other ways to get information on it? What if the guidance for such a missile consisted of radars that the Soviets were reluctant to turn on because they did not want to disclose their capabilities to the ever-vigilant U.S. watchers and listeners? What if they might do so only under conditions of actual emergency? In such an instance, the presence of the RC-135 and the intrusion of Flight 007 might be interpreted in a dramatically different way.

Reports suggesting this alternative to the PL-5 soon began to appear. On September 11, a story in the *San Francisco Examiner & Chronicle* observed that the area into which Flight 007 intruded contained "targeting sites for a secret new missile system capable of destroying U.S. nuclear missiles in midair." The newspaper continued, "Work on the weapons system at sites *on the Kamchatka Peninsula and Sakhalin Island* [author's emphasis] has been shrouded—sometimes with sliding roofs and tarpaulins —to conceal it from U.S. spy satellites." The report also mentioned the U.S.'s consuming interest in the new missile: "One government official with close ties to the intelligence community described as 'extravagant' recent American attempts to learn more about the missile and its targeting radar." This new missile was called the SA-12, and some officials in the Reagan administration felt it was a violation of the 1972 antiballistic missile treaty.[49]

From the beginning, the Reagan administration has had an active interest in trying to pin arms control violations on the Russians. The U.S. interest was further piqued by a new Soviet phased-array radar located near Abalakova, in Siberia, with suspected antiballistic missile capabilities. Discovery of the radar in the spring of 1983 had prompted the U.S. to launch a number of photoreconnaissance satellites to get more information on the new system. It had also prompted the formation of a top-level arms control verification panel, headed by staunchly anti-Communist National Security Adviser William P. Clark, a former Army counterintelligence officer. Clark's group included a number of officials who would assume central roles in managing the Flight 007 crisis, such as Richard Burt and Lawrence Eagleburger. At their first meeting on July 19, 1983, Reagan instructed the group to "explore every possible angle" in its efforts to expose Soviet cheating on arms control agreements.[50]

A number of possibilities are worth examining. First, either there was a missile test scheduled for the night of August 31/September 1 or there wasn't. On this, the evidence is contradictory. If there was a test, either it was the SS-X-25 (a.k.a. PL-5) or it was not, and there is no evidence that the SS-X-25 was being tested at that time. Administration officials said that three days after the downing of Flight 007 the Soviets tested an SS-X-24 ICBM.[51] The test of the SS-X-24 was a failure and the missile exploded, the seventh such failure in ten test flights. The officials said they did not know for certain if this was the missile supposedly planned for testing on the night Flight 007 was shot down. To add to the confusion, other reports noted that a modified version of the huge SS-18, the Russians' so-called monster missile with the capability of carrying up to thirty nuclear warheads, was also scheduled to be tested two days after the downing of Flight 007.[52]

Sorting through the contradictory evidence, the most plausible conclusion is that a series of Soviet tests was taking place at the general time of Flight 007's intrusion. On the night in question, however, there is no firm indication that there was a scheduled test of the SS-X-25 or any other missile. This in turn suggests that the presence of the RC-135 cannot be explained by an impending test, nor would its attention have been wholly consumed by monitoring missile telemetry that was never transmitted.

Successful propaganda is not "based on lies but rather on truth interpreted in a particular way," wrote William Dorman. While the Reagan administration's presentation of the Flight 007 case did contain outright falsehood, limited truth and irrelevancy were much more common. As Anthony Marro put it, half-truths are "a specialty at the State Department" and for a reason Tennyson described a century ago:

> That a lie which is half a truth is ever the blackest of lies,
> That a lie which is all a lie may be met and fought with
>   outright,
> But a lie which is part a truth is a harder matter to fight.

The Reagan administration's statements about the RC-135 did not deceive the Soviets, but that was not their purpose. The intention was to rally domestic and world support behind the Administration's agenda. And support was gained, but at the cost of deceiving the American and world publics.[53]

9

THE RUSSIANS
RESPOND

The *Pravda* story of September 6 was the fullest discussion of the downing of Flight 007 yet to appear in the Soviet Union. *Pravda* said that KAL Flight 007 radioed to air traffic controllers in Tokyo that it had successfully overflown Soviet territory, telling Tokyo controllers, "We successfully crossed over southern Kamchatka. Maintaining course normally."[1] The statement added that the Soviet fighter who fired tracer shells did so only after the intruder had altered course in order to pass over a Soviet air base on southern Sakhalin Island. Another new twist in the Soviet account was that their air defense forces had been tracking seven RC-135 reconnaissance aircraft on missions off the coast of the Soviet Far East between 1145 and 1649 hours GMT, that is, during the five hours prior to Flight 007's first intrusion into Soviet territory (Flight 007 came into close proximity to the RC-135 at 1600 GMT). *Pravda* also claimed that during this period of time three U.S. naval vessels were just outside Soviet territorial waters.[2]

By Soviet standards, the *Pravda* item contained a remarkable amount of specific information about their air defense capabilities. It explicitly mentioned that the RC-135 was observed from 1345 to 1649 GMT flying at an altitude of 8,000 meters. Then a second aircraft (Flight 007) was picked up at 1600 hours flying in the direction of the Kamchatka Peninsula, producing a radar blip "analogous" to that of an RC-135. The second plane was said to be flying at an altitude of 8,000 to 9,000 meters, not Flight 007's assigned altitude.[3] Specific information like this gives one's adversaries an idea of radar range and tracking capabilities, which the Soviets are normally very reluctant to make public. Clearly, the Soviets felt there were overriding concerns in presenting their case about the relationship of the RC-135 and KAL Flight 007.

Although moving decidedly in the direction of stating that the Soviets had in fact downed Flight 007, the *Pravda* statement did not go that far. Rather, it mentioned that the Soviet air forces used the "utmost restraint" in dealing with the intruder. "If they had the goal of destroying the plane, as claimed by President Reagan, they could have done so many times over. . . . They could have done so over Kamchatka, using heat-seeking missiles fired from the ground."[4] The *Pravda* statement was also the first acknowledgment in the Soviet press of Western charges that the Soviets downed Flight 007.

The United States was quick to respond. Pentagon spokesman Lt. Col. Peter Friend emphatically denied to reporters the Soviet charge that there were seven RC-135s flying off the coast of the Soviet Far East during the time in question. He failed to mention, however, how many there actually were.[5] Friend also appeared to deny the Soviet claim that there were three Navy warships off the coast of the Soviet Far East as Flight 007 intruded: "Not to my knowledge," he said. This could mean that there weren't that number of vessels there and they did not do what the Soviets claimed, or simply that Friend did not have personal, firsthand knowledge of them. Such apparent attempts to disclose only the barest essentials without blatantly lying were once called a "policy of minimum candor" by a spokesman for President Lyndon Johnson.[6] A final statement by Friend concerned the Korean airliner's alleged radio message that it had successfully overflown the Kamchatka Peninsula. Friend responded, "I have nothing on that."[7]

President Reagan had used a brief excerpt from the tapes of the transmissions of the Soviet pilots in his speech on September 5, but far bigger plans were afoot. Working all through the weekend of September 3–4 at the headquarters of the U.S. Information Agency in Washington, officials from the USIA, the State Department, and the White House were preparing the big show: Ambassador Jeane J. Kirkpatrick's September 6 presentation at the U.N. Security Council. A team of six State Department translators went over every word on the tapes. Did the Soviet pilot really say "fiddlesticks," or was it something stronger like "holy shit"? Did a pilot say "roger," or was "yes, sir" closer to the meaning? How should ambiguous passages be treated? As USIA counselor John L. Hedges put it, the group was instructed to come up with a presentation "that would make it clear, very clear, what exactly the transcript of the Soviet pilots represented."[8]

As the planning proceeded, there was a fear that the Soviets would try to block the playing of the tapes in the Security Council. This would be the first time such material would be used to support a case being argued in the council. There was a precedent, of sorts: More than two decades earlier, then U.S. Ambassador Henry Cabot Lodge brought into the council the Great Seal of the United States from the American embassy in Moscow to show members how it had been bugged by the Russians. But in the event the Soviets were able to block the playing of the tapes, other plans were also carefully worked out. The tapes would be played on TV monitors set up in the U.N. hallways, in the U.N. garden, and in the U.S. Mission across the street.[9]

On Monday morning, September 5, the finished tape was played at a State Department planning session. The officials present included Ambassador Kirkpatrick, Undersecretary of State Lawrence Eagleburger, and U.S. Information Agency Director Charles Z. Wick, a close personal friend of Ronald Reagan. Wick wanted the translations of the tapes to appear on television screens, and the task force came up with a Cyrillic typewriter for the Russian subtitles. Wick's plan was to provide a riveting visual image for the press. A television monitor was deliberately placed behind Soviet chief delegate Oleg A. Troyanovsky in order, as the State Department put it, to "drive home the point of Soviet responsibility." Eagleburger would later describe Wick's efforts as "superb."[10]

The tape played by President Reagan on September 5, which would be more fully presented in the Security Council by Ambassador Kirkpatrick the following day, relied exclusively upon information collected by Japanese, rather than U.S., intelligence. The information had been collected by the Nibu Beeshitsu, Japan's NSA, at their intelligence stations at Wakkanai and Abashiri.[11] This material was of considerable sensitivity because it revealed the intercept capabilities of the Japanese. In the world of intelligence, the ability to collect information is often much more secret than the actual material collected. While the Soviets knew perfectly well what they said on the night Flight 007 was downed, they did not know how much their adversaries could monitor.

The CIA had asked the Japanese for copies of the Soviet transmissions they had intercepted. According to British journalist Anthony Sampson, the request for the tapes led to heated arguments along military-civilian lines at the highest levels of the Nakasone government. Ultimately the military was overruled, and the "family jewels," as the tapes were called by the Americans, were handed over to the CIA and flown by a special military flight to NSA headquarters. However, the material came with several strings attached: The tapes could be made public only with the approval of the Japanese government, and American tapes (which the Japanese knew to be extensive) had to be made public at the same time.[12]

But contrary to its promise, the Administration released the tapes without Japanese approval, compromising Japan's intelligence-monitoring capabilities in the process. Further, the much more extensive U.S. tapes were kept secret.[13] As might be expected, the Japanese were embarrassed and angered by the unauthorized release of their intelligence material. "We should have known from the name of the White House spokesman," one Japanese official complained bitterly. "The trouble with Larry Speakes is . . . he speaks." Within days, a Foreign Ministry source said that Japan's intelligence collection abilities had been adversely affected. After the tapes were made public, the Soviets promptly changed the codes and radio frequencies used by their aircraft. According to a source cited in the *Los Angeles Times,* the Japanese monitoring capability was reduced to only 60 percent of what it had been before the downing. "Our peepholes have been closed in the last several days," he said.[14]

The Security Council chamber was jammed on the morning of Tuesday, September 6, as the debate on the Korean airliner that had left off on September 2 was resumed. In addition to representatives of the fifteen Security Council member nations, dozens of other diplomats, aides, and members of the press were present.[15] The chamber was hushed as the first speaker, U.S. Ambassador to the United Nations Jeane J. Kirkpatrick, rose to denounce the Soviet action.

The U.S. permanent representative reiterated all the harsh language and vitriolic invective that had been expressed by Administration officials from the President on down. Then came the punch line: "The U.S. Government, in cooperation with the government of Japan, has decided to spread the evidence before this council and the world. It is available on the video tape I am about to play. On this tape you will hear the voices of the pilots of Soviet interceptors—which included three Su-15 Flagons and one MiG-23 Flogger, including the Su-15 pilot who pulled the trigger which released the missiles that destroyed Korean Air Lines number 007. . . . Nothing has been cut from this tape."[16]

Five large video screens with loudspeakers were set up in the Security Council chamber, and the words spoken by the four Soviet fighter pilots were transcribed both in English and in Russian and shown on the screens. Interpreters read the transcript, covering slightly over 10 minutes of time, into the audio system in all six of the official languages of the United Nations.[17]

Soviet Permanent Representative to the United Nations Oleg Troyanovsky sat glumly through Kirkpatrick's speech and the videotape, reading a transcript provided by the U.S. delegation. His country's chief delegate since 1977, Troyanovsky had studied at Swarthmore College in the late 1930s, and his father, Aleksandr A. Troyanovsky, had once served as the Soviet ambassador to the United States.[18] At first Troyanovsky paid close attention to the spectacle but later appeared to lose interest, passing papers to his deputy, Richard Ovinnikov, seated behind him. From time to time both men would look up at the television monitor behind them.

Although Russian-speaking Westerners present at the session complained that they could not understand the voices of the Soviet pilots (aviation tapes are often noisy and unintelligible on first listening), the Soviet diplomats did not challenge their authenticity. The United States claimed the tape showed, in Kirkpatrick's words, "that the Soviets decided to shoot down this civilian airliner, shot it down, murdering the 269 persons aboard, and lied about it." [19] The key elements of Kirkpatrick's denunciation rested on several points: First, that "contrary to what the Soviets have repeatedly stated, the interceptor pilot saw the airliner's navigation lights and reported that fact to the ground on three occasions." An examination of the tapes would later show that there was only a single unequivocal reference to the lights of the "target"; the other two references may be to the lights on the Soviet interceptors. For these two ambiguous transmissions, however, the U.S. transcript gratuitously included bracketed references indicating that the lights belonged to the "target."

The next assertion was that "contrary to Soviet statements, the pilot makes no mention of firing warning shots." Less than a week later, however, it would be admitted that the U.S. translation had been in error and the Soviets had, in fact, fired warning shots as they claimed from the outset. Kirkpatrick then noted that "contrary to Soviet statements there is no indication whatsoever that the interceptor pilot made any attempt either to communicate with the airliner or to signal it to land." The U.S. delegate made much of the Soviet interceptor pilot's supposed reliance on Identification Friend or Foe, the military technique for identifying aircraft. "Of course, the Korean airliner could not have responded to IFF because commercial aircraft are not equipped to do so," she informed the Security Council. As to why the Soviets did not use some other form of communication such as calls on the international emergency frequency: "Perhaps," Kirkpatrick said, "the Russians feared giving their pilots a system to communicate with civilians because they fear defections." Yet as with the cannon bursts, it would later be "discovered" that the U.S. version of what was on the tape was again in error. It is not without interest that U.S. translators had the greatest apparent difficulty with precisely those transmissions that showed the Soviet pilots following some of the internationally accepted interception procedures.

Kirkpatrick admitted the Soviets may not have known the identity of the aircraft they were pursuing, but she denounced their policy of "fire now, identify later." As to the Soviet statements on the incident: "None of these lies, half lies, and excuses can withstand examination," she said. "The fact is that violence and lies are regular instruments of Soviet policy."

After Kirkpatrick concluded what London's *Daily Telegraph* described as her "moving and convincing diplomatic tour de force," Soviet Ambassador Troyanovsky took the floor to denounce the U.S. "propaganda campaign" as a deliberate effort to advance the Reagan administration's agenda for increased defense spending. The flight path of the airliner was deliberate, he said, so that Soviet air defense reactions could be monitored. "These people lost their lives not because of the Soviet Union but because of the Cold War." Troyanovsky observed that the council had just been subjected to "a provocative anti-Soviet spectacle . . . an instrument of psychological warfare mounted by the U.S. against the U.S.S.R. It is well known," Troyanovsky concluded, "that in the job of disinformation, American propaganda has no equal." [20]

After the Troyanovsky/Kirkpatrick exchange, the permanent representatives from Japan, the Philippines, Liberia, and Sweden availed themselves of the opportunity to condemn the Soviets. Then the American delegation made available audio cassettes and transcripts of the air-to-ground transmissions of the Soviet pilots to all interested delegations. Although the White House had issued a statement earlier saying that a 55-minute tape would be released, Kirkpatrick's tape covered only 49 minutes and 11 seconds of time, and the tape was only slightly more than 10 minutes in length because the time between the pilots' transmissions was omitted. Of this, Kirkpatrick had played only the first 6 minutes during the Security Council session, to the point where the pilot of the Su-15 that fired the missiles reported to his ground controller that the "target is destroyed." The meeting was adjourned until 4:15 that afternoon. [21]

In a coordinated move in Tokyo, Defense Vice-Minister Haruo Natsume released the transcripts and tapes of the Soviet pilots simultaneously with Kirkpatrick's release of the material at the United Nations. The Japanese transcript was virtually identical to that released by Kirkpatrick, but there were two minor differences. One was that the U.S. transcripts referred to the Soviet ground stations to whom the Soviet pilots were speaking by name (Karnaval, Deputat, Trikotazh), while the Japanese version did not. The second was that the U.S. transcript contained a reference saying "the strobe light is flashing," while the Japanese version again did not. Natsume stressed, however, that both versions were authentic. [22]

None of this pleased the Russians. The Soviet Union filed a protest with the government of Japan for what it called a "totally forged" document, a "fabrication." The Soviets also said that the transcript released by the U.S. was forged and the material presented by Ambassador Kirkpatrick "only an extract, a gist" that does not cover what was transmitted to the plane "and what instructions it received." [23]

It was "six days to the hour," *The Times* of London said, that the Soviets finally admitted what the world had known with certainty for days: A Soviet fighter was ordered to "stop the flight" of the intruding Korean airliner. The admission came in the form of a Soviet government statement issued by the official news agency Tass and read as the lead item on the television evening news in Moscow. This was, in fact, the first time that the Soviet government had directly commented on the incident. It was a strong statement, approved at the highest levels of the Politburo. [24]

In part, the Tass report was a response to the events of the day. It was probably also intended to facilitate Andrei Gromyko's appearance at the Conference on Security and Cooperation in Europe to be held in Madrid. Yet the Soviet statement indicated an official line that was becoming increasingly harsh and a leadership that had no intention of apologizing for the incident. The report stated that the Soviet interceptor that fired the missiles at Flight 007 was equipped with a radio capable of broadcasting on the emergency frequency of 121.5 megacycles, "contrary to the false contentions of the United States President." The interceptor was said to have radioed to Flight 007 on that frequency. "These signals had to be received by the intruder plane," Tass said, "but it did not respond to them." Tass also maintained that the RC-135 was "in the same area near the Soviet border at the same altitude" as Flight 007 and that it had been the focus of attention of Soviet fighters; it repeated the charges that the intruder's lights had been extinguished and that the Soviets did not know the intruder was a civilian aircraft. The statement also contained the first suggestion that the decision to stop the flight of the intruder had been made locally rather than in Moscow. "The antiaircraft forces command of the area, having analyzed thoroughly the actions of the intruder plane, . . . concluded that a reconnaissance aircraft performing special tasks was in the airspace of the USSR," Tass said. This information was submerged beneath a flood of invective reminiscent of that of the Reagan administration. The U.S. Embassy in Moscow said that the Soviet statement was "much too little and much too late," and the Japanese called it "deceptive and unsatisfactory." Larry Speakes commented afterwards, "It's about time they owned up to what they have done."[25]

When the debate in the United Nations Security Council resumed at 4:45 P.M., Soviet Ambassador Troyanovsky was the first speaker. Having been briefed during the recess on the most recent Tass statement, Troyanovsky repeated many of its formulations word for word. Troyanovsky was followed by a parade of speakers from Bangladesh, Italy, Libya, Malaysia, Nigeria, the Republic of Korea, Sierra Leone, and Togo. With the exception of Libya, all were more or less vehement in their condemnation of the Soviet action.[26]

Japan's permanent representative Mizuo Kuroda responded to the Soviet charge that Flight 007 had been involved in espionage, telling the Security Council that the Japanese radar station at Wakkanai had followed the passage of the airliner over Sakhalin for 17 minutes, but he contended that the personnel had no way of knowing the blip on their radar scopes was Flight 007. This was, he said, because the plane was not using its transponder in a way that would have allowed it to be identified. Civilian radars, Kuroda continued, were too far away to pick up the deviating airliner.[27] Kuroda did not mention that the Japanese had monitored the Soviets' communications for a substantial length of time before the downing or that Flight 007's flight plan had been put into the BADGE system, allowing the Defense Agency to know it was not on Romeo-20. Thus,

Kuroda downplayed Japan's capabilities while not mentioning that Japan had substantially more information than simply an unidentified blip suddenly appearing on their radar screens.

When the Security Council session finally broke up about an hour later, Ambassador Kirkpatrick held a conference with members of the press in which, according to the *Washington Post,* she "denied charges that American reconnaissance planes had 'systematically' violated Soviet airspace, maintaining that U.S. policy opposes such intrusions." (Of course, "policy" can be radically different from practice. For example, take the Reagan administration's oft-expressed commitment to reduce the deficit.) When asked about tapes of the ground-to-air transmissions from Soviet ground controllers to their fighters, Kirkpatrick said she had "received no explanation for the absence" of the recordings. Asked why no attempts had been made to correct the course of the airliner, Kirkpatrick said that Japanese air traffic controllers were not aware the plane had strayed "because the only radar covering the area was Soviet radar." This, of course, was completely untrue since the military radars at Wakkanai and elsewhere had tracked the airliner for at least half an hour. Afterwards, the U.S. Mission informed the State Department that "the press conference . . . following Jeane's remarks went well. There were no hard questions. . . . The RC-135 story has not weakened our message." [28]

Both the United States and Japan went to considerable length to deny their capabilities with respect to radar, communications, and other forms of intelligence. The point of the denials was to make it appear as if neither nation had knowledge of Flight 007's deviation from course prior to the downing. Yet these denials do not appear credible. It is worth considering one element of this denial—the claim that neither the Japanese nor the Americans have the ground-to-air transmissions from Soviet controllers to the fighter planes which were dispatched to intercept the intruding airliner over Sakhalin Island.

Although the Japanese now claim not to have the ground-to-air transmissions, the Kyodo News Service, quoting Japan Defense Agency sources, reported a day after the downing that Japanese military intelligence had recorded the following conversation:

"Take aim at the target."

"Aim taken."

"Fire."

"Fired."

Similar accounts, also based on the JDA, appeared in a number of media around the globe. [29] Could all these accounts have been in error? [30]

On September 6, the Kyodo News Service quoted a statement by Masaharu Gotoda, chief secretary of the Japanese Cabinet, head of the Cabinet Information Agency, and principal spokesman for Prime Minister Nakasone, that Japan had "monitored communication from the ground to the fighter but will not release it." Asked why the Japanese government chose only to release the air-to-ground communications, Gotoda replied, "This will be enough evidence to prove the Soviet shooting down of the South Korean jet." Two hours later, Japan Defense Vice-Minister Haruo Natsume told reporters that Japan had no such recordings.[31] Masaharu Gotoda, however, never publicly retracted his comments.

Natsume notwithstanding, accounts of the Japanese possession of this material continued to appear. On September 7, in the process of denying that the United States had the ground-to-air tapes, White House deputy press secretary Larry Speakes said the Japanese had them, but it was up to them to make them public. *The Sunday Times* of London announced on September 11 it had confirmed that "Japan's Air Self-Defense Force *did* intercept ground control transmissions." The following day the *New York Times* wrote, "Publicly, [Japanese] government officials say no such ground-to-air recordings exist. However, some have suggested privately that there are tapes but that Japan does not wish to aggravate what it believes has been a compromising of its intelligence-gathering abilities."[32] Despite all this, the government of Japan now firmly denies it has the recordings.

What about the United States? The President himself told the American people and the world on September 5 that "we only have the voices from the pilots; the Soviet ground-to-air transmissions were not recorded." But all the evidence suggests otherwise. It seems that much of the talk about the separation of U.S. and Japanese intelligence assets—"U.S. information" versus "Japanese information"—was merely a pretext for not having to make information available to the public. The United States not only collects its own information in this region of the world but has access to a great deal of the Japanese intelligence "take" because of the three-way working arrangements among the United States, Japan, and South Korea, called "triangular security cooperation," of which the U.S. is the senior partner.[33]

And many press accounts argue that the U.S. not only received Japanese information but had its own. As *The Sunday Times* observed, the Japanese "supplied tape recordings [of ground-to-air transmissions from Soviet ground facilities] to the Americans. The Americans maintain, however, that they have only the pilot's transmissions." As early as a day after the downing, reports from Japan said that the Japan Defense Agency was monitoring the action over Sakhalin "at the same time that U.S. monitors heard the radio transmission." Japan's *Asahi Evening News* noted that the Japanese had monitored the communications between Soviet fighters and ground controllers, and that "such information was checked against information obtained by the U.S. from satellites and American facilities within Japan and confirmed as accurate." Jack Anderson reported that the Air

Force's 6920th Electronic Security Group at Wakkanai monitored the entire course of events, including ground-based transmissions, and that Russian-speaking personnel were on hand.[34]

Accounts of the Kamchatka portion of the Korean airliner's overflight give further evidence of U.S. monitoring of Soviet ground-based transmissions. After the downing, U.S. Government officials presented a chronology of events including a statement that the Soviets picked up Flight 007 on radar at 1600 hours GMT and that the Russians continued to track the airliner for the ensuing 2½ hours, until the time it was shot down. Many of the accounts were highly specific about the nature of U.S. monitoring. The *New York Times* reported intelligence officials as saying that highly sensitive U.S. monitoring equipment detected a sudden increase in Soviet air defense activity over Kamchatka, including stepped-up radar surveillance and the scrambling of interceptor aircraft. It was reported that "a radar operator at an early point in the incident informed the air defense command in Kamchatka that he had sighted an RC-135. Another radar operator later said he had sighted an 'unidentified' plane." *Newsweek* told its readers it had learned that U.S. evidence included messages intercepted from air defense commanders at Soviet ground stations, notifying a surface-to-air missile battery that an RC-135 had penetrated Soviet airspace. According to *Aviation Week & Space Technology,* however, the missile batteries were never able to get a solid radar lock on the target.[35] That's fairly extensive coverage, a lot of which came from leaks from the intelligence community based on ground-originated communications.

The public record also provides a number of additional statements that suggest the United States intercepted ground-based communications subsequent to the downing of Flight 007 in the Sakhalin area. NBC's "Nightly News" reported on September 7 that less than an hour after the airliner was shot down, "highly sensitive U.S. intelligence equipment" picked up communications between Soviet ground crews on Sakhalin in which the downing of the airliner was discussed. This report jibed with an earlier report in the *New York Times* that quoted an Administration official as saying the U.S. had intercepted some "chatter" by Soviet ground crews referring to the downing. A similar report about U.S. monitoring of conversations between Soviet ground stations appeared in the *Washington Post.* Secretary of State Shultz told the world, "About an hour [after the downing], Soviet controllers ordered a number of their search aircraft to conduct search and rescue activity in the vicinity of the last position of the Korean airliner reflected by Soviet tracking."[36]

Military personnel confirm that such coverage exists. A Pentagon officer quoted by the *Omaha World-Herald* stated, "Surveillance work [in the area of Sakhalin Island] routinely includes the eavesdropping by U.S. and Japanese intelligence personnel on Soviet military radio transmissions, both *ground-to-air* [author's emphasis] and air-to-air." He said "it's a sure bet" that U.S. intelligence officers were listening. "They listen to everything. They listen twenty-four hours a day, every day." A former radar technician who was stationed at the National Security Agency listening base at Chitose on Hokkaido asserted that "Soviet ground-to-air transmissions are routinely monitored" in the Kamchatka-Sakhalin area. Even Larry Speakes told reporters that the United States had the ground-to-air tapes but some of the transmissions were "unintelligible."[37] Speakes later denied making this statement.

The denials notwithstanding, the ability of American and Japanese intelligence to intercept ground-based transmissions is demonstrated, and it is equally clear that both the U.S. and Japan used that ability on the night of the shootdown. As proof, it is sufficient to note that some of the information made public by both governments originated from Soviet ground stations. But for some reason, both governments denied intercepting a key series of transmissions—from Soviet ground stations to their interceptor pilots over Sakhalin. Were these available, it is likely they would shed additional light on the actions of Flight 007's crew over Sakhalin, including evasive actions or other signs of awareness of their peril, as well as on the thoroughness of Soviet interception procedures. Some have argued that the tapes have been withheld precisely because they do not support the official version of events in these respects. But the denials by both governments stand, logic and previous statements by officials notwithstanding. Is there any additional evidence that what the public is being told is false?

In fact, there is proof that the ground-to-air transmissions were recorded because a few can still be found on the tape of communications from the Soviet pilots to their ground controllers made available by Ambassador Kirkpatrick at the United Nations on September 6. The Soviet pilot known as 121 was searching for Flight 007 while talking to Deputat, his ground control station, about 9½ minutes after the firing of the missiles. In the course of the search, pilot 121 put out a call to another ground station called Trikotazh. The following exchange then ensued:

FROM	TO	MESSAGE
121	TRI	(Call)
TRI	121	(Answering)
121	DEP	Trikotazh answered me.
121	TRI	Do you see the target?
TRI	121	No, I don't see it.
121	TRI	But I see it [for myself].

Since it was obviously possible to record the ground-based transmissions from Trikotazh, it is prudent to ask just where all of the other ground-based transmissions went.

According to the statements of U.S. officials, carried in the *New York Times,* "The United States did not receive the recordings [of the conversations of the Soviet interceptors], which were made by the Japanese, until almost twelve hours after the incident." The U.S. supposedly did not have the ability to monitor ground-based transmissions, "to monitor the conversations as they were taking place, or to warn the plane that it was in jeopardy." The American and world publics were told that the delay in making information available about the downing was because "it takes an extensive search of recordings made by surveillance radars to first find the data, then it took more time to translate it [*sic*] from Russian into Japanese and then English." [38] This portrayal of an intelligence-poor Uncle Sam, hat extended, begging for whatever few scraps of intelligence the Japanese might choose to provide, is dramatically at odds with actual U.S. capabilities.

September 6 was drawing to a close when, at 6:00 P.M., Undersecretary of State Lawrence S. Eagleburger read an official Administration statement to the press in reply to that day's Tass announcement. "Today the Soviet government at last admitted that its forces shot down KAL 007," he said. "Their confession comes only after the truth was known everywhere that the U.S.S.R., without any justification, shot down an unarmed civilian airliner with 269 people aboard." [39] Eagleburger called upon the Russians to make an "unequivocal apology" and pay reparations to the families of the victims.

As had become the norm in official U.S. statements, Eagleburger did not assert that the Soviets consciously ordered the downing of a commercial airliner, although "it strains credulity," he said, "to accept the argument that the Soviets, after more than two and a half hours of tracking and after the Su-15 that later shot down KAL 007 had moved to approximately one mile from the Korean aircraft, failed to identify the KAL airliner." Eagleburger's statement also addressed many of the issues raised in the Tass statement on a point-by-point basis. It said that Soviet statements about trying to contact Flight 007 on the emergency frequency of 121.5 megacycles were not borne out by the material released by the United States and Japan. "Even if the Soviet aircraft had that capability, which we do not believe," Eagleburger said, "there is no evidence on the tapes of the Soviet pilots' making any such transmission." Yet within days it would be learned that the U.S.'s translation of a critical passage of the Soviet pilots' transmissions was erroneous and that Major Kazmin in fact had reported to his ground controllers that the target "is not responding to the call." Eagleburger said it was "clear" that Flight 007 had its navigation lights illuminated. While that certainly seems true toward the end of the interception over Sakhalin, there is no evidence this was the case throughout the flight.

After the U.N. Security Council session concluded, the United States and its allies set to work trying to put together a resolution condemning the downing of Flight 007. The major points being considered were a call for compensation, the proposal that an inquiry into the downing be conducted by the U.N.'s International Civil Aviation Organization, and the establishment of guarantees against recurrence of such an incident. In drafting the resolution, the U.S. wanted to denounce the Soviet Union by name but was warned by its allies that this might cost supporting votes. Several of the Third World members of the Security Council were prepared to condemn the act but not the actor, and might abstain if the Soviet Union was named in the resolution.[40]

On Wednesday, September 7, the Security Council resumed the debate on Flight 007 it had left off the previous day. The agenda was essentially to permit a parade of speakers from non-Security Council U.N. member nations to express their feelings about the downing of Flight 007. When the session resumed, the Soviet Union came under severe critical attack by Colombia, Fiji, Guatemala, Ireland, Kenya, and Singapore. As might be expected, Bulgaria, East Germany, and Poland placed responsibility for the downing on the United States. Tass later reported that the Soviet Union's allies "proved convincingly during the Security Council meeting that this abortive CIA-planned espionage action is being used by Washington for increasing international tension, stepping up the nuclear arms race, and thwarting measures to achieve real disarmament. A vote was expected the following week.[41]

10

OUTRAGE

Korean Air Lines Vice-President Charley Cho arrived at Chitose Airport in Sapporo, Japan, on the afternoon of Sunday, September 4, on board a chartered KAL airliner. Cho was leading a group of more than forty South Koreans, including five KAL executives, several officials from the Korean embassy, thirty journalists, and members of three bereaved families. The group was scheduled to travel to Wakkanai, where the officials and reporters would collect information about the recovery effort. While still at the airport, Cho announced that Korean Air Lines would pay $75,000 to each bereaved family. Earlier, it had been reported that KAL officials said they would "probably include other compensation that could bring the average total to about $100,000." [1]

At Wakkanai, the group was met by municipal government officials who briefed them on what little progress had been made in the search for wreckage from the airliner. That afternoon, forty-eight bereaved relatives from fourteen families boarded the chartered 790-ton ferry *Soya Maru No. 5* for a 7-hour round trip journey to a point about 23 kilometers south of Moneron Island. Oriental custom dictates that relatives try to get as close to the scene of death as possible. Tears welled and chrysanthemums, the mourning flower, were thrown into the Sea of Japan. Some of the bereaved relatives threw clothing into the sea to help keep the dead warm beneath the cold waters. "Father, father!" cried Mai and Mei Osaka, sisters eleven and eight years old. A man called out to his son, "Answer me!"[2]

Not all aboard were bereaved relatives, however. Television crews and reporters were on board to bring the tragic scene to millions around the globe. Also present were lawyers who hoped to capitalize on the sorrow. As one bereaved relative recalled, "They talked to all these people trying to get their case. . . . They try to attract business. And they were there, handing their business cards out."[3] The *Soya Maru* lingered near Moneron Island for about an hour before beginning the 3-hour journey back to the port at Wakkanai.

On the morning of September 5, another thirty-six people sailed to the waters off Moneron Island. Among those on board were eight KAL officials and South Korean journalists, as well as three relatives each of American and Japanese victims of Flight 007. That evening, about thirty family members of Japanese victims who had been staying in Wakkanai returned to Tokyo to join another group of bereaved relatives at the Imperial Hotel. There, Charley Cho told them he was very sorry for the incident. According to the *Japan Times,* "The families were apparently not content with Cho's statement, saying [instead] that the prime responsibility rests with KAL, whose plane veered off course and intruded Soviet airspace."[4]

Day after day the families continued their pilgrimages onto the Sea of Japan. On September 6, sixty more relatives went out on the ferry to a point off Sakhalin about five miles outside Soviet territorial waters. As the relatives cried, a Soviet reconnaissance plane repeatedly flew overhead. "You murderers, get lost!" one relative shouted. "You damned Russians," another cried, "why did you shoot down the passenger plane?"[5] Then the roar of the engines faded, and the only sounds were those of the wind, the sea, and crying.

The first day of the search and rescue effort had passed, and it was now the early morning of Friday, September 2, Tokyo time. The seas were relatively calm, and a fog had lifted, although the skies were still overcast. The winds were blowing at 15 miles per hour, and visibility was limited to about 6 miles as the First Regional Maritime Safety Headquarters in Otaru sent six patrol boats to the waters west of Sakhalin Island. Six vessels had gone out the previous day, and four additional patrol boats would join in the search by early evening. Isamu Imura, the head of the Maritime Safety Agency office in Wakkanai, said that the Japanese search effort was focused on an area extending 150 kilometers north to south and 110 kilometers east to west around Moneron Island. The suspected crash site lay about 36 kilometers to the northeast of Moneron Island, in or near Soviet territorial waters. A number of Soviet ships were patrolling the area. At about 6:30 A.M., the commanding patrol ship *Rebun* approached to within 30 yards of a Soviet coast guard ship. Using a loudspeaker and speaking in Russian, the *Rebun* asked the Soviet vessel whether anything had been found. "Nothing, so far," the Russians responded. The Japanese then requested that the Soviets cooperate in the search effort. "Understand" was the reply.[6]

Throughout the day, the Japanese had repeatedly contacted the Soviets trying to get news of their progress in recovering the wreckage from Flight 007. Their vessels radioed the Soviet coastal station at Holmusk, but no reply was received.[7] Hours after the shootdown, the Japan Maritime Safety Agency began asking permission for Japanese vessels to enter Soviet territorial waters to search for the wreckage from the airliner. These requests also went unanswered.

At approximately 3:40 A.M. on September 2, Soviet Ambassador to Japan Vladimir Y. Pavlov visited the Foreign Ministry in Tokyo. Pavlov told Minoro Tanba, director of the Foreign Ministry's Soviet Division, that the Soviets were searching for the "unidentified aircraft and later found signs of an aircraft crash west of Moneron." Pavlov was unable to say whether the debris was from Flight 007. Tanba asked Pavlov about an Associated Press report that Administration officials in Washington had learned the Soviets had recovered some bodies. Pavlov replied that he knew nothing about the recovery of any bodies.[8]

According to confidential sources, the Soviets recovered much more than they publicly admitted. A Soviet fisherman of Japanese origin, a resident of one of the islands near Sakhalin, claimed he had watched some of the Soviet recovery efforts. By his account, many bodies were brought ashore on southern Sakhalin, where their shoes were removed and their clothes were changed. The purpose of removing the clothing, apparently, was for cleaning and analysis. The Soviets eventually did return a number of pairs of shoes, all of which had been dry-cleaned and some of which were later identified as having been worn by Flight 007's victims.[9] The story appeared confirmed in a State Department internal memorandum that noted the commander-in-chief of the U.S. Pacific Forces had "transmitted a brief report indicating that Soviet units are recovering bodies and wreckage from the crash."[10]

While the Japanese continued to request permission to enter Soviet territorial waters, the United States was rapidly building up its search and rescue presence in the Sea of Japan. Shortly after the downing, U.S. submarines and aircraft arrived at the crash site. Within 24 hours of the downing, an E3A Airborne Warning and Control System (AWACS) surveillance plane, one of three stationed at Kadena Air Base in Okinawa, was sent to Misawa Air Base on the island of Honshu accompanied by an escort of six F-15 fighters. The AWACS plane and its escort were immediately sent to the Sakhalin area. Although according to the Navy the AWACS plane was sent to "provide additional communications support and any other support as necessary" for the U.S. search and recovery effort, it was believed that one of its unstated missions was to keep watch on Soviet warships and other military activities with its 400-kilometer surveillance radius. There were reports that another unstated mission was to try to provoke an incident with the Russians.[11]

With every passing day, the U.S. presence off Sakhalin grew. In addition to the AWACS plane and its fighter escort, the United States, officially at the request of the government of Japan, sent a Lockheed P-3 Orion reconnaissance aircraft and a Lockheed C-130H aerial recovery plane to assist in the operation. The Navy dispatched the 3,800-ton frigate U.S.S. *Badger* and the 7,800-ton helicopter destroyer U.S.S. *Elliott* to the search area. By September 3, the U.S. force in the area was so large that the U.S. Embassy in Moscow passed to the duty officer at the Soviet Ministry of Foreign Affairs formal notification of the U.S. search and recovery operation.[12]

The Japanese were also active, their search and recovery efforts continuing in spite of rain, poor visibility, and their inability to enter Soviet territorial waters. By September 3, fourteen Japan Maritime Safety Agency patrol boats had been brought to the waters west of Sakhalin. The vessels were not permitted by the Russians to come anywhere near Sakhalin, and Soviet aircraft continually overflew the area, buzzing Japanese vessels on several occasions.[13]

The early results of the Japanese effort were disappointing. A 330-foot-long oil slick was discovered by the patrol boat *Sarobetsu* about 18½ miles off the southwest coast of Sakhalin, about 14 miles from where the plane was believed to have gone down. Some 27 ounces of the oil were collected by crew members of the ship *Chitose* for later analysis at Wakkanai. Bits of fiberglass insulation were found by the ship *Sorachi*. Along with the insulation, some plastic bags containing bread and other materials with Korean writing on them were found in an area about 18 miles north of Moneron Island. These were also taken to Wakkanai for analysis. (It later turned out that the oil was ship's oil and the insulation material was too thick to have come from Flight 007.) No wreckage from the airliner was recovered, although the sea in the search area was only 200 meters deep on the average. Had the airliner crashed in that area, its wreckage would have been located easily. Isamu Imura of the Maritime Safety Agency clearly was frustrated with the agency's lack of success: "Unless any trace of the airliner is found in the area soon," he said, "it should be assumed that the aircraft did not crash in the area."[14]

The next several days brought more frustration for the fourteen Japanese vessels involved in the recovery effort in spite of improved weather and visibility. Patrol boats found chunks of insulation with an L-shaped piece of metal attached floating on the sea about 95 kilometers north of Moneron Island. Japanese officials said that the insulation could be significant—a "key clue" to the fate of Flight 007. In addition, they pulled from the sea some charred styrofoam, bags of ramyon (Korean instant noodles) and pieces of white polyurethane covered with shreds of woolen yarn and human hair. Officials in Tokyo said the polyurethane might have been part of a seat cushion. The objects were flown to Chitose for analysis but, as before, the findings were negative. The polyurethane object entangled with human hair and the singed styrofoam board turned out to have nothing to do with Flight 007. KAL's Charley Cho announced that the noodles were not from the airliner. The piece of insulation with the piece of metal attached also turned out not to be from the downed plane. Sources at the Japan Maritime Safety Agency reiterated their feeling that they were conducting search operations in the wrong area.[15]

But the number of vessels involved in the search continued to rise. By September 5, the Soviets had increased the number of vessels in their search fleet to four patrol boats, four trawlers, and an ocean survey ship. A day or two later, the number had increased to thirteen.[16] The increase in Soviet activity fueled speculation in Japan that they were making progress.

This enormous military presence increased the chances of a confrontation. On September 6, the U.S. destroyer *Elliott* cruised very close to Soviet territorial waters, shadowed by a Soviet destroyer and patrol boat. Additional P-3 Orions and C-130s based at Yokota and Misawa air bases flew continuous missions in the area, often flying right to the boundary of Soviet airspace. As they did, they were shadowed by Soviet Ilyushin reconnaissance aircraft and fighters. Soviet air defense units and surface-to-air missile batteries were at what a U.S. official described as a "very aggressive" level of readiness and activity. Tensions were so high that, by one account, the Soviets almost shot down one of their own planes, stopping only when visual identification was made. A car ferry carrying thirty-six members of families of those who died on board Flight 007 was buzzed by a Soviet patrol plane, which flew as close as 30 meters overhead.[17]

Still the number of ships in the Sea of Japan continued to grow. Stepping up its efforts, the Japan Maritime Safety Agency replaced two of its patrol boats with two larger vessels: the 3,800-ton patrol boat *Tsugaru,* equipped with helicopters, and the 495-ton ship *Bihoro.* Another ship, the *Yamagiri,* was dispatched to the area to work as a messenger, bringing the Japanese total to fifteen. South Korea had by this time committed four naval vessels and several fishing boats to the search and recovery effort. To augment the American effort, the Coast Guard cutter *Munroe,* in Japan on a good-will mission to encourage cooperation between the U.S. and Japanese coast guards, left Tokyo for the waters off Sakhalin Island with several Japanese officers on board in addition to its normal crew.[18]

By all appearances, all those ships were doing more than looking for the wreckage of KAL Flight 007. Military sources in Tokyo cited by the *Japan Times* noted that Japan "monitored communications conducted between Russian surface ships and military bases and headquarters." This was in addition to monitoring the Soviet reports on their search activities.[19]

Back in the United States, many people wanted to take action against the Russians. In a unanimous 3–0 vote on September 6, the State of New

Hampshire Liquor Commission ordered the cessation of sales of Stoli-chnaya vodka—an action having no real impact since Stolichnaya only ranked ninth in total vodka sales at the state-run liquor outlets.[20] Commis-sioner Lyle Hersom explained, "I feel it's the least I could do." The New Hampshire ban followed an earlier action by Ohio Governor Richard Ce-leste, who ordered his Liquor Control Agency to stop selling the two brands of Russian vodka and one of brandy normally carried by the state's 427 liquor stores.[21]

As the days rolled by, boycotting Russian vodka became the symbol of what the little guy could do to protest the downing of Flight 007. When there was a chance for media attention, all the stops—or more accurately, all the corks—were pulled out. With the press watching, a pub owner in Bar Harbor, Maine, poured out twenty-seven bottles of Russian vodka. "I plan to talk to every tavern owner from here to Bangor," he said, "and see how much product I can take off the shelves." Likewise, James Le-hane, the manager of Rip's Restaurant outside Detroit, poured out a case of Stolichnaya. "This is just a statement from a small person to a large nation that we don't like their actions," Lehane told reporters. More rhe-torically, Los Angeles Assemblyman Michael Roos called upon the entire world to impose an international boycott of Russian vodka. Both houses of the California legislature unanimously endorsed an anti-Soviet resolu-tion that called the downing "an unprovoked and cowardly attack."[22]

Across the continent, other symbolic actions took place. Donald Kerr, director of the Los Alamos National Laboratory in New Mexico, banned visits by laboratory scientists to the Soviet Union and forbade Soviet scientists from visiting Los Alamos. Richard Rosenfeld, head of Interna-tional Weekends Charter Vacations, Inc., a company that had reserved thirteen of the seats on board Flight 007, said it would not provide travel to the Soviet Union the following summer. Los Angeles auto parts shop owner Rafael Suarez bought a Soviet flag to use as a doormat in his store. The Atlanta Ballet cancelled an October tour of Moscow and Leningrad. The seven-game basketball series between the Soviet national team and the universities of Maryland, Kentucky, Houston, Alabama, Oklahoma, Vanderbilt, and Kansas was cancelled. California journalists planning a conference with their Soviet counterparts put off the meeting. The Rever-end Jesse Jackson announced that he had postponed his trip to the Soviet Union indefinitely because of the downing. In Austin, Texas, a video ar-cade owner reprogrammed his games so that patrons could shoot down Soviet missiles, battle against ostrich-mounted Russians, and destroy So-viet leader Yuri Andropov. The reason for the reprogramming, he said, was to give the games "a little social relevance."[23]

From the East to West coasts, anti-Soviet demonstrations took place. In New York, Mayor Ed Koch told a crowd that the Soviets "should get down on their knees and apologize for what they have done." Excited by the mayor's words, the crowd broke through a police line and began to head toward the Soviet Mission on East 67th Street, between Lexington and Third avenues, but police reinforcements stopped the surging demonstrators. In San Francisco, a crowd composed mainly of Koreans and refugees from Iron Curtain countries fought briefly with police and moved toward the Soviet consulate in San Francisco. They were stopped only when police reinforcements arrived.[24]

In the midst of the passion there were moments of gallows humor. According to *Adweek* magazine, within hours of the downing Korean Air Lines contacted its advertising agency, the Los Angeles-based firm of Ogilvy & Mather, to request that all its advertising be suspended temporarily. But it was too late to stop an ad from appearing in the September 5 issue of *Travel Weekly,* a trade journal for travel agents. "It was the standard ad the airline had been running for some time," recalled Paul Crehan, the advertising director for *Travel Weekly*. The headline for the KAL advertisement read: "Our flights not only seem shorter, they are shorter."[25]

The response in the Republic of Korea to the downing of Flight 007 was both emotional and well orchestrated. In the days following the downing, tens of thousands of students, workers, and government employees turned out to condemn the Soviet action. On September 2, some 40,000 middle, high school, and university students gathered on their school grounds and campuses for protest rallies. The students carried signs and shouted anti-Soviet slogans in a steady rain. The following day, thirty social organizations and universities held rallies throughout the country. In Seoul, workers burned the Soviet flag in front of the city hall, and a similar flag-burning demonstration took place at the Korean Air Force academy. On September 4, a Sunday—the only day off for Korean workers—all of South Korea's major business associations and combines staged rallies. The *Los Angeles Times* described the scene: "Flags of the Soviet Union . . . were burned in heavily photographed and televised demonstrations, their participants arrayed in military-like formations."[26]

Calls for action against the Russians were particularly fierce in the Korean National Assembly, where, on September 3, members of the Korean Democratic party said: "We should counter the deliberate Soviet action with deliberate actions." Said Representative Lee Han-ki, "We should strike Soviet ships that pass through the Korea Strait camouflaged as fishing boats." If possible, some assembly members were even blunter: "I even feel like declaring war," said Representative Yu Chi-song. "It is . . . a time to forge the people's will." Members of the National Assembly's Foreign Affairs Committee called upon their government to "urge the United States not to make its retaliatory measures against the USSR a flash in the pan."[27]

Criticism of the supposedly mild U.S. response to the Russians was particularly sharp in the government-controlled Korean press. The *Korea*

Herald moaned that Reagan's response was "by all standards milder than what the previous administration did against Moscow by interrupting grain exports." The newspaper *Kyonghyang Sinmun,* circulation 773,000, called the U.S. response "soft" and "lukewarm," and concluded, "We cannot repress the feeling that the retaliatory measures announced by President Reagan do not meet the expectations of American citizens." The Seoul newspaper *Choson Ilbo* agreed: "It is very clear that such measures are not sufficient."[28]

In the aftermath of the downing, ROK President Chun Do-hwan followed a script remarkably similar to that of Ronald Reagan: a fierce rhetorical attack on the Soviets coupled with an apparent moderation of actions.[29] Chun called the downing a "savage, inhumane, barbaric act," but beyond the rhetoric the Korean position was to "keep the door open for more Soviet contacts." Before a week had passed, officials were telling reporters, "Our open-door policy has a long history, and there is good reason to continue that policy."[30]

From the first, Chun had explicitly ruled out provocative actions such as closing the Korea Strait between South Korea and Japan. He ruled out sanctions and proceeded with efforts to normalize relations with the Soviet Union. Thus, the South Korean response fell into precisely the same three categories as the U.S. response: caustic rhetoric, maintenance of economic and business links with the Soviets and, most important, increasing the nation's military buildup.

The government-sponsored memorial ceremony and demonstration took place on September 7 in the Seoul soccer stadium. Ostensibly organized by fifty-four private organizations, primarily civic groups and corporations, the mass rally was in fact ordered by the government of President Chun Do-hwan, who had personally ordered that the service be "well prepared." Schools and companies were told to turn out specific numbers of people, and by 10:00 A.M. more than 100,000 people, most from the business and school delegations, had packed into the stands and onto the playing field. The ceremony began with a moment of silent prayer as a siren blared throughout the country for one minute. The members of Chun's Cabinet were present at the stadium in places of honor. Standing before the assembled masses, Roman Catholic Cardinal Kim Su-hwan offered up a prayer for the dead. President Chun did not attend the mass ceremony but issued a statement that was read over the loudspeakers. He called the downing of Flight 007 a "barbarous, criminal act" and informed his people that defense spending would have to rise so that the Republic of Korea could ensure its "national self-esteem."[31]

Chun elaborated on the need for more weapons in a television speech live from the Blue House that was broadcast simultaneously with the ceremony. "The strength to punish and chastise injustice does not come from grieving to oneself or from a sense of defeat but is developed by the resolute will and practice to directly counter injustice and to smash it in the end,'' Chun said. "We must cultivate our own strength so that we can defend our airspace and guarantee the safety of our aircraft. We should build without fail a firm and powerful country. . . .''

Koreans are sometimes called the "Irish of Asia," and for the bereaved family members present the rally was an emotional event.[32] Korean women dressed in traditional garb collapsed in the huge crowd. A mourner savagely bit his own finger, writing in blood, "Soviets, apologize, repent, and compensate." The thirteen-year-old daughter of Flight 007's First Officer Sohn Dong-hwin gave a farewell address: "To my dear father and his friends who are now with him under the chilly waters." Some of the sorrow was intensified by the Buddhist tradition that unless the departed's remains are recovered and placed in a shrine, the ghost is never at peace. And the television cameras rolled throughout the emotional outpourings. As the *Los Angeles Times* noted, "Although the South Korean government controls the mass media here and usually restricts movements of photographers, cameramen were permitted to climb onto the altar as mourning relatives placed wreaths and burned incense at the end of the ceremony."[33] The Seoul government would use this genuine suffering as a vehicle for its political message.

The ceremony lasted 70 minutes, and then grief gave way to other emotions. The participants began a massive anti-Soviet outpouring, not even paying lip service to peace. On cue from the loudspeakers, fists were raised, shouts of denunciation rang out, and signs were displayed reading "Down with Russian Murderers," "Soviet Is a Mad Butcher," and "Red Bear Back to the Zoo." All the shouts and chants were coordinated; indeed, as the *New York Times* observed, they were "executed with military precision."[34] As hatred and patriotism fused, it was all too easy to forget that hundreds of ordinary, innocent people had died.

11

MISSILES
AND MEETINGS

Secretary of State George Shultz was scheduled to meet with Soviet
Foreign Minister Andrei Gromyko at the final session of the Conference
on Security and Cooperation in Europe (CSCE) held in Madrid, Spain.
The session, lasting from September 6 to 9, was the culmination of three
years of discussions between thirty-three European nations plus the
United States and Canada. The conference was intended to serve as a
follow-up to the 1975 session that produced the Helsinki accords on human
rights, security, and cooperation in Europe. Many hoped that the talks
would serve as a catalyst for improvements in East-West relations, con-
tribute to progress in arms control negotiations, and pave the way for a
superpower summit meeting in early 1984.

The three years of discussions and hard bargaining had produced the
Madrid agreement, a lengthy document "designed to foster détente mainly
through future accords on human rights and disarmament." The comple-
tion of the agreement had been announced on July 15, 1983, and the three-
day September session was to be the formal signing and conclusion.[1]

After the National Security Council meeting on September 2, it had been
decided that Shultz would not, as Defense Secretary Caspar Weinberger
had urged, abandon his plans for a meeting with Soviet Foreign Minister
Gromyko in Madrid. As originally envisioned, the purpose of the meeting

182

was a comprehensive review of many aspects of Soviet–U.S. relations. During a 20-minute meeting with Reagan before his departure on September 6, it was determined that Shultz would "raise only subjects related to the [KAL] incident or other matters of concern dealing with Soviet behavior." The President quipped to his advisers, "In the eyes of the other nations there, won't Gromyko be the proverbial skunk at a Sunday picnic?!"[2] Madrid was now viewed as little more than a major propaganda opportunity for the United States.

Flying from Washington to Madrid, George Shultz held an in-flight press conference. Asked why it was necessary for him to go to Madrid simply to chastise the Russians, Shultz responded, "I consider it an opportunity to confront directly a member of the Politburo—the person who must have been involved heavily in the decision about all of this. I think it's important to put it to their high authorities directly. What is their explanation? Why don't they tell the truth?"[3]

"We are now immersed in a sad crisis that casts a dark shadow over our meeting," Spanish Foreign Minister Fernando Moran ruefully remarked as the concluding session of the CSCE began on Tuesday night, September 6. That night, all thirty-five participants of the conference formally adopted the Madrid document, but what was supposed to be the culmination to years of hard work to improve security and cooperation had become, *The Guardian* observed, a "tense, morose affair [with] little attempt during private meetings between the foreign ministers from East and West to resolve some of their long-standing differences."[4]

On the morning of September 7, the foreign ministers of the NATO countries began the day with a working breakfast to coordinate a joint response to the downing of Flight 007, but the meeting was inconclusive about what sanctions might actually be taken. There was a strong desire to avoid fiascoes such as the U.S. boycott of the 1980 Olympic Games in Moscow. "Western spokesmen," the *Los Angeles Times* commented, "seemed more interested in the principle of action than in actually planning for it."[5]

Andrei Gromyko took the podium in Madrid that afternoon following speeches by the foreign ministers from fifteen other countries. Beginning with Foreign Minister Pierre Aubert of Switzerland, all the speakers raised the issue of the downing of Flight 007. Then it was Gromyko's turn, the first time a member of the Politburo had publicly discussed the incident. He gave a rambling talk restating the Soviet Union's standard peace rhetoric and calling for a renewal of both the spirit and the letter of détente. The Madrid conference was a "noticeable success," Gromyko said, demonstrating that the prospects for détente were not exhausted.[6] Yet Gromyko's mind seemed to be elsewhere.

Near the end of his 25-minute speech, Gromyko seized the offensive. Continuing what a member of the U.S. delegation described as "the outrageous Soviet line on KAL," the Soviet Foreign Minister accused the

United States of using the KAL jetliner to spy on the Soviet Union, violating its "sacred" borders in the process. "As has become perfectly clear," Gromyko said, "the South Korean aircraft was on special duty for American authorities and their relevant services," flying for hours over some of the Soviets' most important strategic facilities. "Why was it there and what was it doing?" he asked the assembled dignitaries. "Anyone who had recourse to this sort of provocation must know he will bear full responsibility for it."[7]

At first, George Shultz sat impassively in the front row of the cavernous hall, listening to the Soviet Foreign Minister. Toward the end, however, the secretary appeared increasingly angry as Gromyko condemned the behavior of the United States. Once Gromyko had finished speaking, Shultz went into the corridors of the Palace of Congresses looking for reporters, something he seldom does. He told the press that "the implication of [Gromyko's] remark was that if anyone strays over the border, they are ready to shoot it down again."[8]

Both Gromyko's speech and Shultz's comments to reporters afterwards indicated that the meeting between the two foreign ministers the following day would be, as the *Washington Post* commented, "one of the toughest top-level Soviet-American encounters in years." The two sides' positions appeared irreconcilable. Originally, the two foreign ministers planned to have a luncheon before their meeting, but the United States had cancelled it because it "seemed inappropriate." When Gromyko arrived at the site of the meeting, the residence of U.S. Ambassador to Spain Thomas O. Enders, Shultz did not turn out to greet him. The *Wall Street Journal* observed, "The Americans did everything possible to create a climate of incordiality" for the meeting between Shultz and Gromyko.[9]

It was, ABC's Bob Schieffer remarked, "a stage being set with icicles." Shultz and Gromyko sat without smiling on opposite sides of a large oval table in the ambassador's dining room while photographers took the customary pictures. There were no glasses of water on the table and no pads or pencils. The two foreign ministers did not speak until the photographers had left. Shultz and Gromyko then went off to speak in private, accompanied only by their interpreters.[10]

They returned to their delegations in half an hour and the meeting began. Initially, Gromyko tried to keep to the initial agenda, opening with a statement on the Soviet position on arms control, the militarization of space, and human rights. Shultz defended the U.S. positions, arguing it was the United States that had taken all of the serious initiatives toward progress and peace. Returning Shultz's diplomatic snubs, Gromyko chose to answer Shultz's points in Russian, although he speaks perfectly good English. Finally, the focus of discussion moved to the airliner incident. Gromyko tried to avoid the subject, but Shultz reportedly "made him" discuss it. While some in the State Department may have hoped Gromyko would be less strident in private than he had been in his public speech the day before, he was even more aggressive in his denunciation of the United States than he had been in public.[11]

Shultz decided to end the meeting after 2 hours and 6 minutes because "further discussion wouldn't be productive" if the Soviet minister would not change his position about the downing of the Korean airliner. As he left the U.S. ambassador's residence, Gromyko, the foreign minister of the Soviet Union for 26 years, waved to reporters and said, "I have nothing to say at this moment." Shultz did not accompany Gromyko to his car. Instead, Gromyko walked with U.S. Ambassador to Moscow Arthur Hartman. The two men did not shake hands.[12]

Gromyko did not have much to say to the press, but George Shultz did not at all display the same reticence. A grim-faced Shultz called reporters to read a statement condemning the Soviets that had been prepared largely before the meeting. His voice was described by reporters at the scene as "tight with fury" as he outlined the session with Gromyko, whose private positions had been "even worse" than his public positions the day before. "This is not the end of the matter," Shultz threatened.[13]

Secretary of State Shultz gave one of the closing speeches at the CSCE in Madrid. "The fate of Korean Air Lines Flight 007 once again reminds us," he said, "that the Soviet Union defines its security in a way so absolute, so self-centered and cynical that it poses a danger to all other countries." The assembled delegates listened in silence. "And from this rostrum," Shultz said, "its foreign minister shamelessly insisted that the Soviet Union would do so again." Gromyko was not there to hear his words, having already departed for Paris for meetings with Foreign Minister Claude Cheysson and President François Mitterrand. After presenting a litany of grievances against the Russians, Shultz concluded: "We must be disappointed but we cannot be surprised" by the "blatant acts of defiance against the spirit and the letter of the Helsinki accords." "For our part," he said, "we will continue to negotiate patiently in good faith and will consider any proposals that meet our basic objective of enhancing true security and cooperation."[14] Shultz's speech drew practically no applause from the audience.

Thus ended the Conference on Security and Cooperation in Europe. President Gerald Ford and Soviet leader Leonid Brezhnev had signed the 1975 Helsinki accords as the capstone to the era of détente. Now, in 1983, quite a different legacy was being created to take its place.

Aeroflot is the world's largest airline. Formed in 1923 as a company called Dobrolet, in 1983 the airline was headed by Boris Bugayev, an under-minister of Civil Aviation and a retired general. Aside from commercial air service and an occasional espionage flight, Aeroflot performs a variety of other tasks, ranging from running airfields, training centers, an airport-design institute, and a hospital, to crop dusting an estimated 7 million hectares a year and volcano-watching over the Kamchatka Peninsula. It employs approximately half a million people. Each year it carries an estimated 108 million passengers to more than 3,000 foreign and domestic destinations. Aeroflot travels to more than ninety-three countries, and about a third of its 600,000 daily flight miles are logged abroad. Within the Soviet Union it serves about 3,600 cities, towns, and outposts. All U.S. airlines combined fly about twice as many daily miles as the Soviet monopoly carrier.[15]

Aeroflot, a symbol of the Soviet Union's power and influence, became a lightning rod for anti-Soviet gestures. On September 5, the government of Canada suspended Aeroflot's landing privileges for a period of 60 days, affecting the twice-weekly flights by Aeroflot Ilyushin-62s between Moscow and Montreal's Mirabel Airport, as well as Aeroflot's refueling rights in Gander, Newfoundland.[16] The Canadian foreign minister said he hoped the suspension "will prompt a review by the Soviet authorities of the merits of continuing to evade their responsibility for the death of Canadians and of so many other innocent passengers."[17] Ten Canadian citizens had died on Flight 007.

Boycott fever was promoted by pilots, who felt particularly threatened by the shooting down of a commercial airliner. Almost immediately after the downing, pilots' groups and other aviation professionals began expressing their disgust at the Soviet action. On September 2, ground crews at London's Gatwick Airport refused on their own initiative to work on two Aeroflot Tupelev 154 jets, delaying one plane's departure for an hour as supervisory personnel were forced to do the work. In the United States, Henry Duffy, the president of the Air Line Pilots Association, a group representing 34,000 U.S. pilots, said that the group planned to provide support for the Reagan administration in its response to the Soviets."[18]

On September 6, the six-member governing board of the International Federation of Air Line Pilots Associations (IFALPA) met in a six-hour emergency session in London. Otto Lagerhus, IFALPA's deputy president, said that the meeting had been called by the organization's American members. The result of the session was a call for a 60-day ban on flights to Moscow by the 57,000 pilots from IFALPA's sixty-seven member countries. After 30 days, the ban was to be reviewed to see whether it should be extended in duration or scope.[19]

Australia followed with its own 60-day ban. New Zealand's Minister of Civil Aviation, George Gair, also called for sanctions and expulsion of the Soviet Union from the International Civil Aviation Organization. Captain Robert Tweedy, the Irish president of IFALPA, said that pilots from Great Britain, France, Sweden, Denmark, and Norway were in favor of boycotting flights to Moscow. West German pilots negotiated with the government in Bonn for a similar 60-day ban. "We are getting more support by the minute," said Tweedy. The effect of a comprehensive boycott on Aeroflot flights would be severe, forcing the airline to take costly, circuitous routes to places such as South America.[20]

But pilots are not governments. While the IFALPA ban in theory applied to all sixty-seven member countries, in fact it affected only pilots of the seventeen non-Communist airlines that provide commercial service to Moscow. Twelve of these, Japan included, are in the so-called Western bloc of nations. One of these, Finnair, seemed certain from the outset not to join a boycott because of its treaty obligations with the Soviet Union. Further, some pilots would not be able to participate because, as an IFALPA spokesman pointed out, "some countries do not permit industrial action." Finally, the federation had no power of enforcement. "We're not pretending this is going to be easy," Captain Tweedy said. "There are a lot of legal and political problems for some of our associations." [21]

In spite of their outrage over the downing of Flight 007, most Western European nations valued their trade with the Soviet bloc, saw little practical value in sanctions, and feared reprisals for any sanctions they might impose. Of the Western nations, the three with the greatest number of flights to the Soviet Union were Britain, France, and Germany. Both British Airways and Air France had five scheduled weekly flights to Moscow, and five Aeroflot flights per week arrived in Great Britain and France. West Germany received eleven Aeroflot flights, and Lufthansa planes flew to Moscow ten times each week. West German officials and business leaders were concerned about banning Aeroflot flights because of almost certain Soviet retaliation against Lufthansa, which could disrupt traffic to West Berlin, located 110 miles inside East Germany. The editor of the West German newspaper *Die Zeit* commented, "There's a natural reluctance of our business people to lose business." An Air France spokesman in Paris said that sanctions such as a boycott "won't work," and an informed source in London observed, "If we close Heathrow Airport to Aeroflot, the Soviets will retaliate against British Airways flights to Moscow and possibly against its flights to Warsaw and Bucharest. That means jobs and money lost. . . ." The Italian government made known its "unwillingness to do anything that might cost Alitalia routes or money at a time of recession and industrial strikes." [22]

The problems in trying to achieve coordinated action among the Western nations were amply demonstrated in meetings of NATO foreign ministers in Madrid on September 8. The United States had been actively pushing for sanctions, but many of the Western Europeans wanted nothing to do with them. In a breakfast with Secretary of State Shultz, West German Foreign Minister Hans-Dietric Genscher argued that boycotts and sanctions were not a realistic response to the Flight 007 incident. Shultz countered with a five-point plan for joint action, designed, its supporters said, to prevent recurrence of such incidents in the future. The first element of the plan was to "ban attacks on civil airliners in time of peace" in all international civil aviation agreements. Second, there was a call for greater cooperation between civil and military air traffic controllers. The third point was a demand for compensation for Korean Air Lines and the families of the passengers who had been on Flight 007. Fourth, there was a call for an inquiry into the downing to be conducted by the ICAO. The final point was a call for some "demonstrative political signal," such as a ban for 10 to 14 days on flights to the Soviet Union.[23]

While most of the members of NATO tentatively agreed to a relatively brief moratorium on flights between their countries and the Soviet Union, the five-point plan was insufficient for some and too drastic for others. All NATO members agreed to press the ICAO for new rules to outlaw the shooting down of civilian airliners. But the NATO members and other Western nations (including Australia, Japan, New Zealand, and South Korea) agreed to postpone a final decision until the following evening in Brussels, at a meeting of NATO delegates. There, it became clear that unanimous action by all NATO countries was not possible. The representative from Turkey said his country could not endorse the NATO sanctions because of bilateral agreements between Turkey and the Soviet Union. France said it was bound by the terms of a civil aviation agreement with the Russians that prohibited unilateral cessation of flights. Greece opposed the ban outright, and Spain was still undecided. Most individual members of the organization agreed on a two-week ban on civil flights to and from the Soviet Union to begin on September 15. With NATO unable to reach agreement, Secretary General Joseph Luns declared that it simply wasn't a NATO problem. "All members agreed this is not an East-West problem —it covers the whole community of nations," he said. "NATO does not take these decisions. It's for governments to announce them."[24]

NATO may have been unable to coordinate a response, but there were a number of independent actions. Although no Australian airlines flew to Moscow, Australian pilots announced they would not permit Soviet diplomats or government officials to travel on domestic flights for a period of 60 days. Four Australian citizens had been on board Flight 007. The Association of British Pilots announced on September 7 that its 4,500 members would boycott flights to Moscow for a 60-day period beginning Friday, September 9. However, the stoppage did not affect Aeroflot flights between Britain and Moscow, only British Airways flights, leading to increased bookings for the Soviet carrier. Further, while British Airways had cancelled its own flights to Moscow, it was busily helping its passengers make connections through other airlines in Prague and Budapest.[25]

The Japanese were exceedingly cautious in balancing their national interest with any actions they might take against Moscow. On September 8, U.S. Ambassador to Japan Mike Mansfield called on Foreign Minister Shintaro Abe to renew the U.S. call for punitive sanctions against Moscow. This was followed up by a call to Abe from Secretary of State George Shultz, urging Japan to take joint measures with the Western European nations.[26]

The following day, Nakasone chaired a 30-minute Cabinet meeting called to make a final decision on the Japanese response to the Soviet downing of Flight 007. After the session, Chief Cabinet Secretary Gotoda announced a three-point plan "in line with actions taken by other nations in the West" but not in a way that Japan would "stand out as particularly severe against the Soviets." First, all Aeroflot charter flights to Japan would be suspended, although regularly scheduled flights would not be affected.[27] Second, Japanese officials would be instructed not to use Soviet flights. Third, the number of Soviet flights to Japan would not be increased beyond the present level. In addition, there was an informal fourth point: "As an expression of national protest," Gotoda said, "I appeal to the nation to refrain from using the Soviet airline."[28]

Dissatisfied with the inaction of governments, pilots' groups around the globe began to take actions ranging from stating support for IFALPA's goals to actually boycotting Soviet planes. Against the expressed position of their government, the Finnish pilots' association began a two-month boycott of Finnair flights to Moscow. As a result, Finnair was forced to cancel its flights to Moscow but continued its daily service from Helsinki to Leningrad. Italian pilots announced a two-week boycott of Alitalia flights to Moscow. Commercial pilots in the Netherlands, Norway, Denmark, and Sweden voted to join IFALPA's ban. So did Spain, although Iberia was planning to phase out its Madrid-Moscow flights before the end of 1983. French pilots belonging to the pilots' group SNPL said they would boycott Air France flights to Moscow. This did not affect the airline, however, for 20 percent of France's pilots are not members of the pilots' federation, and they flew the Moscow-Paris runs. Swedish air traffic controllers announced a boycott of all flights between Sweden and the Soviet Union for one week, to begin on September 19. Norwegian controllers had already taken a similar action, and Danish controllers were meeting with officials from their Transport Ministry to discuss one.[29] But already it seemed clear that a number of countries would not support IFALPA's call for a boycott.

The Reagan administration decided as a symbolic gesture that all U.S. airlines would sever commercial links with Aeroflot. In a letter to Daniel McKinnon, the chairman of the Civil Aeronautics Board (CAB), the President requested that five measures be implemented against the Soviet carrier: Aeroflot's right to sell tickets in the U.S. be suspended; U.S. airlines be forbidden to sell tickets in the United States for transportation on Aeroflot; U.S. airlines be prohibited from carrying passengers to, from, or within the United States when an Aeroflot flight is listed on the ticket; U.S. airlines be directed to suspend any interline service arrangements with Aeroflot; and, finally U.S. airlines be forbidden to accept any tickets issued by Aeroflot for travel to, from, or within the United States. Reagan gave McKinnon instructions to "take appropriate immediate action" to implement the sanctions, which would begin on September 12 and "remain in effect until further notification." The CAB voted 4 to 0 to approve Reagan's recommendation for sanctions against Aeroflot and claimed that its actions would cost the Soviets about $1.5 to $2 million annually. The board was realistic, however, noting that the actions would probably have a greater negative effect on the United States than on the Soviet Union. According to one CAB official, "There is a symbolism involved, and the sanctions will underline that the Soviets do not belong in the world of civil aviation."[30]

President Reagan deepened the symbolism in a number of ways. Larry Speakes announced that the President had "reaffirmed" the suspension of Aeroflot flights to and from the United States which had been in effect since 1982, when martial law was imposed in Poland. Reagan also ordered that Aeroflot's two U.S. offices, in New York and Washington, be closed by September 15, and he ordered three Aeroflot officials to leave the country by that date. As one Administration official, who refused to be identified, put it, "It is hard to imagine a more minimal operation" than Aeroflot's in the United States.[31]

One of the few things on which the Western nations could agree was the need to bring the matter of the downing before the U.N.'s International Civil Aviation Organization. The United States had been mentioning the ICAO practically from the start. In his September 5 television address, President Reagan told the nation, "We have joined with other countries to press the International Civil Aviation Organization to investigate this crime at an urgent special session of the council." An investigation by the ICAO was called for in the NATO foreign ministers' five-point plan. Organizations as diverse as the International Confederation of Free Trade Unions and the International Transport Workers Federation urged that "urgent and appropriate steps" be taken against the Soviet Union, and pilots' groups called on the ICAO to do something. In response, the ICAO governing council announced on September 6 that it would hold an emergency meeting on September 15 at its headquarters in Montreal.[32] The timing was propitious: The next triennial session of the ICAO was scheduled for September 20.[33]

There were two considerations for the United States in putting the matter before the ICAO: its usefulness as a forum for condemning the Soviets and its utility as the locus for an inquiry into the downing. As a stage for condemning the Soviet Union and distracting attention from the details of the flight itself, the ICAO surely had its advantages. Unlike the Security Council where the ever-present Soviet veto could block any unfavorable resolution, the Soviets had no such power in the ICAO. The ICAO charter rejects the use of weapons in the event of the interception of an off-course civil airliner that has violated a nation's territorial airspace. Therefore, although there would be no binding power in the call, some form of condemnation of the Soviets seemed assured.[34]

As the locus for an inquiry into the downing, the ICAO, from the perspective of the U.S. Government, seemed equally ideal. The ICAO has no independent investigative powers and must rely solely on the information presented to it by member governments. It has no power of subpoena and, by charter, cannot extrapolate beyond the limits of the information in its possession. Because of its dominance in air transport, the United States has considerable influence in the ICAO. All these factors make it an eminently controllable organization. But even a limited inquiry is still an inquiry, of course, and an inquiry conducted by an international aviation body at that. This suggests still another reason for involving the ICAO. If the limited inquiry concluded, strictly on the basis of information provided it by member governments, that a navigational error of some kind was the most likely explanation for Flight 007's deviation from course, who could argue?

The Republic of Korea made a formal motion for an emergency session of the ICAO council, and things were quickly arranged. When the meeting took place, the Koreans planned to introduce a resolution forcefully condemning the Russians, and by September 9, U.S. Secretary of Transportation Elizabeth H. Dole had cabled seventeen countries seeking support for such a resolution. On the opposite side of the Iron Curtain, the Soviet news agency Tass castigated the call for an ICAO investigation as "unlawful."[35]

The rhetoric that has surrounded arms control negotiations over the past several decades follows an odd logic—that there is no way to reduce nuclear arms until their numbers are increased. In the fall of 1983, NATO was preparing to deploy 572 U.S. Pershing II and Cruise missiles at bases in West Germany, Great Britain, Belgium, Italy, and the Netherlands, and a series of demonstrations between September 1 and October 22 was planned throughout Europe. Stressing the need for the new missiles at the Intermediate-range Nuclear Forces (INF) talks in Geneva, Reagan administration officials publicly expressed the belief that Moscow would not be prepared "to bargain substantively until the United States and its allies show that they can begin deploying the Pershing and Cruise missiles in December despite militant antinuclear demonstrations."[36] In support of this effort, the downing of Flight 007 would prove a powerful argument.

It was, however, only the most recent argument in a major U.S. influence campaign designed to justify the deployment of the 572 new missiles. Tom Gervasi wrote that well before the downing "the Reagan administration created a special cabinet-level interagency group, chaired by the National Security Adviser [William Clark] . . . to develop a public relations strategy to sell the deployment." The group's objectives were obtaining "more favorable media coverage and influencing younger Europeans to adopt sympathetic attitudes toward the presence of nuclear weapons and U.S. nuclear policy in Europe."[37] Strobe Talbott quoted Defense Secretary Caspar Weinberger as saying, "We've got to make them think that what we're doing is good for them. Not just that, but we've go to make them think that they're going to *like* it and that it's what they've been asking us to do." Weinberger denied making the comment.[38]

Manipulation was only one element of the "strategy to sell" the new missiles; distortion and deception also played a role. This was done by obscuring the missiles' actual capabilities, insisting upon the dubious distinction between "strategic" and "theater" weapons, and consistently inflating Soviet force levels while minimizing those of NATO. Other elements came into play as well, including threats and intimidation. After repeatedly warning that opposition to the missile deployments would end in violence, the conservative government in Bonn introduced legislation to try to stop the protests by "holding that a person's mere presence at a demonstration where there is violence as participation in that violence unless the person can prove he tried to stop the violence." As Gervasi remarked, "It was clear whose interests would be best served if violence did occur and equally clear who was therefore most likely to employ it." [39]

Still another tactic was deligitimation. Numerous official statements suggested that those opposed to the deployment of the new missiles were either prone to emotionalism, ill-intentioned, ill-informed, or had their ideological or actual roots in the Soviet Union, and these suggestions were widely disseminated by the media. Speaking at the U.S. air base at Ramstein in 1983 in a ceremony marking the opening of the annual NATO exercises, NATO Secretary General Joseph Luns said, "We cannot condemn strongly enough what the peace movements are trying to do. They are trying to achieve an imbalance and weakening of the credibility of deterrence." NATO's decision to deploy the new missiles was "peace-promoting," he said, "and those opposing it are war-promoting." In an effort to link the upcoming demonstrations to the Soviet Union, Gen. Bernard Rogers, Supreme Allied Commander in Europe, told the Ramstein audience he believed that right up to the moment of missile deployment, "the Soviet Union will believe its campaign of disinformation will keep us from putting those missiles on our soil." [40]

A final tactic was to underline the supposed futility of mass protests while simultaneously shifting the blame for failure in the arms control talks to the Soviet Union. Official statements were issued which declared the only thing that could prevent the deployment, from the NATO perspective, would be an unexpected, last-minute breakthrough in the upcoming talks in Geneva. On the one hand, this implied that the demonstrations would have no impact upon NATO's decision in any case. On the other hand, it implied that any lack of progress in Geneva was the Russians' fault.

Some informed observers disagree with this portrayal, however, saying it was NATO that was putting forth what former Secretary of State Alexander M. Haig, Jr., once called "absurd and non-negotiable proposals," virtually guaranteeing that the Soviets would have to turn them down. Adm. Eugene Carroll of the Center for Defense Information pointed out that "the whole goal of this Administration has not been arms control. It has been modernization of the nuclear forces and the creation of a nuclear warfighting capability. And arms control gets in the way of that." But this is not what the public is told. "This is a public relations program of major proportions that's going on now," Carroll concluded. "The public is being misled by a deliberate and knowing misrepresentation of the facts about arms control." It appears that official statements stressing the West's commitment to arms control were merely declaratory policy, what U.S. INF negotiator Paul H. Nitze once called "policy statements," made for their "political and psychological effects." [41] When it comes to arms control, it seems that the linkage between rhetoric and reality has come completely unglued.

The peace movement understood much of this, and in Europe the Hot Autumn had arrived: The season of the missiles. The Hot Autumn's opening-day salvo was dubbed "Anti-War Day," recalling Hitler's commencement of World War II on September 1, 1939.

The peace movement in Western Europe was a very broadly based coalition of groups and political positions, its opposition to nuclear weapons extending without hesitation to such Soviet systems as the SS-20. The movement developed in response to several important international events: the interest by both superpowers in "winnable" nuclear wars that would presumably be limited to Europe, the general deterioration in their relations, the erosion of détente, and a profound and increasingly widespread awareness that more than two decades of arms control talks had achieved no arms reduction at all. [42] Since their governments apparently had no intention of seriously pressing for arms control and, indeed, routinely disregarded public opinion when it came to matters of the NATO alliance, those in the peace movement decided to carry their grievances to the streets.

In West Germany, the polls showed fully 70 percent of the population opposed deployment of the new NATO missiles, yet this overwhelming expression of concern was dismissed by government spokesmen who dryly observed that "democracy functions by elections, not by opinion polls." [43] However, in an effort to influence precisely the public opinion it derided, the Bonn government conducted a $3 million public relations campaign to try to sell its people on the merits of deploying the new missiles on West German soil. [44]

The first wave of demonstrations came at the American base at Bitburg —the town about 50 miles southwest of Bonn made famous in 1985 by Ronald Reagan's controversial visit to a Nazi cemetery—and at the Mutlangen Army base in Bavaria. About 2,000 people from a number of European countries, as well as a number of Americans including anti-Vietnam war activist Daniel Ellsberg, gathered in Bitburg near the gate of the U.S. Air Force base. At Mutlangen, a crowd of 1,500 led by Gerd Bastian, a former general in West Germany's army, and Nobel laureate Heinrich Boll blocked traffic at the U.S. Army base. There was no violence or arrests, yet the prospect of continued Europe-wide protests weighed heavily on the United States and its NATO allies. [45]

And then the news broke that a Soviet Sukhoi-15 interceptor had shot down a South Korean commercial airliner. The United States, previously on the defensive about the missile deployments, facing massive demonstrations and under pressure from its allies to show greater flexibility in the upcoming INF talks in Geneva, took the offensive. As an adviser to President Reagan told the *New York Times,* "It's going to make things easier for us." Among members of the peace movement, the almost universal first reaction to the downing was shock and horror. A spokesman for the West German Green Party described the downing as "a cold-blooded mass murder carried out with military precision." The antinuclear demonstrators disrupting traffic at the U.S. Army base in Mutlangen issued a similar statement. "Against which missiles must we protest now?" asked Montreal's major French language daily *La Presse:* "Those that NATO plans to install at the end of 1983 in Germany and Britain, or those that the Soviets are firing against a commercial carrier off Sakhalin Island?" *The Times* of London informed its readers, "A continuing arms race with all its dangers is better than accepting an imbalance which would leave us at the mercy of the cold-blooded murderers of Sakhalin." [46]

As world outrage mounted, the peace movement found itself increasingly isolated. The *Wall Street Journal* commented, "The President is benefiting politically from Moscow's action. . . . Those who oppose his deployment of new U.S. nuclear missiles in Europe this fall . . . have been undercut." [47]

Preliminary talks on intermediate-range nuclear forces began in Geneva in October 1980 in the waning days of the Carter administration but were discontinued upon the inauguration of Ronald Reagan. The stalled talks were finally resumed on the last day of November 1981, but things went slowly. By the time the talks recessed on July 14, 1983, the two sides were still very far apart, each loudly blaming the other for blocking progress. Until the downing of KAL Flight 007, there had been considerable pressure on the United States from its allies to show some signs of flexibility and good faith in Geneva. Afterwards, negotiator Paul H. Nitze was ordered to toughen up the U.S. stance, and the onus for flexibility was shifted to Moscow. [48] As Nitze noted, "It will take greater cooperation on [the Soviet] side to get a deal." Yes, he would mention the KAL incident to the Soviet negotiating team, for there was an "unavoidable linkage" between the jetliner's downing and the new round of talks. Soviet negotiator Yuli A. Kvitsinsky had already said that as far as the Soviets were concerned, the downing had no bearing on the discussions. [49] Nitze traveled to Geneva by way of West Germany, where Chancellor Helmut Kohl told him that the United States had West Germany's "strong support" for the U.S. negotiating position. In a statement issued after the meeting, Kohl said that Washington and Bonn "will not be discouraged in their patient efforts for armament reduction." [50] The statement appeared designed to assure the nervous West German public that in spite of the crisis over the downing of Flight 007 the Geneva talks would go forward.

Soviet negotiator Yuli A. Kvitsinsky arrived in Geneva for the eighty-seventh plenary session of the INF talks with a new arms proposal from Yuri Andropov, announced by Moscow on August 26. It offered to "destroy part of the Soviet intermediate-range missile force in return for U.S. renunciation of the planned deployment of 572 Cruise and Pershing II missiles." Although this represented a major concession on the Soviets' part, Nitze had already described it as "only a limited step forward."[51]

At 11 A.M. on Tuesday, September 6, the American delegation arrived at the Soviet compound in Geneva, Villa Rosa. It was the Soviets' turn to host the session, and Nitze was welcomed with a handshake by Kvitsinsky. Although on the surface it was all smiles and pleasantries, it appeared to be forced bonhomie. The downing of Flight 007 hung heavily over the proceedings. The first session of the new round of talks lasted for an hour and 50 minutes, about usual for an opening session. Two days later another meeting was held in the U.S. Mission in Geneva. Even as the two negotiators were talking, the penultimate test of the Pershing II was being conducted at Cape Canaveral, Florida. The 34-foot 6-inch missile arced 200 miles skyward in its ballistic trajectory, covering a distance of over 1,000 miles in less than 12 minutes before its reentry vehicle splashed into the Atlantic Ocean south of Bermuda. Still other talks were held over the ensuing days, but none produced an agreement, and the NATO deployment of the Euromissiles began on schedule in December. When that happened, Kvitsinsky walked out of the talks in protest.[52]

Both the Soviets and some Americans have charged that the entry of the airliner into Soviet territory, or its downing, was a "provocation" by the other side to scuttle the Geneva talks. Both arguments assume that the adversary did not really want to stop the arms race and would sacrifice lives to maintain its military buildup.

The provocation theme was a central element of the official Soviet line virtually from the outset. The Tass statement of September 2 suggested that part of Flight 007's purpose in overflying Soviet territory was to aggravate tensions between the superpowers. A day later, Tass said the "purpose of this provocation is more than obvious . . . to disrupt the process of normalization of the situation in the world." The Soviets reiterated this theme at the United Nations and after President Reagan's television speech on September 5. Moscow's *Literaturnaya Gazeta* concluded in a September 7 article that "the aim of this whole act of provocation was not only once more to discredit the Soviet Union and socialism but also to poison (to a far greater extent!) the international atmosphere."[53]

Accusations of a Soviet provocation, to the contrary, were almost entirely unofficial. One example came in *The Times* of London on September 3: "Senior members of the Soviet military command, who are opposed to any deal with the U.S. which could result in a reduction of Soviet intercontinental ballistic missiles, may have seen this as an opportunity to torpedo the Geneva arms talks." This theme was reiterated several days later: "Some sources assert that senior armed forces commanders, suspicious of Mr. Andropov's attempts to mend fences with the West, may have used the incident to impede the revival of détente." Richard Pipes, writing in the *Los Angeles Times,* implied that the downing was attributable to a Soviet desire to undercut the normalization of relations between the super-powers.[54]

Could the downing have been a Soviet provocation? This claim says nothing about how Flight 007 got to Sakhalin in the first place. In fact, such a claim, like the official U.S. line, carries the implicit assumption that the flight was innocently off course. This argument, not surprisingly, comes almost exclusively from those on the political Right. However, the Soviets' principal concern at the time—both for military and political reasons—was to prevent deployment of NATO's new intermediate-range missiles in Europe. Its principal vehicles in this effort were the peace movement in the West, which opposed the missiles for its own good reasons, and the Geneva talks. As a result of the downing, the United States became appreciably more intransigent at Geneva, and the Western European peace movement was dealt a crushing blow. While the Soviets are fully capable of engineering a provocation to advance what they consider their state interests, they were clearly not served by the downing of Flight 007.

For the United States, however, the outcome was considerably different. By a number of accounts, the U.S. reaped significant intelligence benefits from the intrusion.[55] There were also substantial gains realized from the downing itself. Opposition to deployment of American missiles was swept away, and relations between the United states and its allies were improved by the reaffirmation of the "Evil Empire" image of their common adversary. The downing proved to be the final, visible sign that Yuri Andropov's battle for Western European public opinion was lost.[56] In short, the Soviets took a serious beating as a consequence of the incident, and the U.S. and its allies benefited considerably (at least from a tactical, short-run perspective). Thus, if one is to entertain the fanciful possibility that the downing of Flight 007 was a calculated "provocation" designed to provide advantage to one side or the other, then one must also concede it was not the Soviet Union that was doing the calculating.

12

THE RUSSIAN
CASE

American observers initially speculated that the downing of Flight 007 had been ordered at the very highest levels of the Soviet hierarchy, with good reason. In the rigid, centralized Soviet system, an action as serious as an attack on an intruding aircraft would be carried out only with the approval of headquarters. Standard procedures called for local air defense commanders to try to contact the Soviet Far Eastern regional command center at Chita. Authorization at Chita would have come from fifty-eight-year-old Army Gen. Vladimir I. Govorov, the son of a Soviet World War II hero and since 1980 the commander of the Far Eastern Theater.[1] Moving up the chain of command, Govorov would have reported the intrusion to Commander of Air Defense Forces Marshal Aleksandr Koldunov at air defense headquarters at Kalinin. Koldunov, in turn, would have notified Deputy Minister of Defense Marshal Pavel Kutakhov, the commander-in-chief of Soviet air defenses. From there, word would have gone to Defense Minister Dimitri Ustinov and other top officials, up to and including Yuri Andropov himself. The time from the initial detection of Flight 007 to the attack over Sakhalin Island was some 2½ hours, more than sufficient for a relay of messages all the way up the chain of command —to Chita, Kalinin, and Moscow.

By September 3, however, reports began to appear that the decision to

197

down the intruder was made at a fairly low level. According to sources cited in the *Washington Post*, "Intelligence information suggested that the authorization [to down the intruder] could be traced at least to fairly high military officers, probably a senior colonel or one-star general." This appeared confirmed several days after the downing when several sources in Moscow said the order to fire had been given by General Govorov at the Far Eastern regional command center at Chita. The sources denied that higher-ups, such as marshals Koldunov or Kutakhov, or Defense Minister Ustinov, had prior knowledge of the attack. Numerous subsequent reports noted that the decision to shoot down the intruder was made entirely within the military chain of command, without consulting the civilian leadership. Some accounts explicitly reported Andropov, said to be vacationing at the Caucasian spa of Kislovodsk but in fact seriously ill, was not consulted.[2]

This account contains a measure of logic. It seems unlikely that political leaders would have approved action that would risk an angry world reaction and upset their remaining hopes for preventing deployment of NATO weapons in Western Europe. An experienced diplomat quoted by the *Japan Times* noted that if the shootdown had been a deliberate act planned in advance, the Soviet civilian leaders "would have had their story ready. Instead, they look like they've been stumbling around trying to collect information from their military on what happened."[3]

That a regional commander made the decision to fire suggests a serious problem in the management of the Soviet military system occurred that night. After the downing, the *Washington Post* cited an Administration official as saying there had been a mistake in the Soviet command structure, and a number of sources remarked that the command and control of Soviet forces was a "key question to be reviewed by everyone in the period ahead." One possibility suggested by a high-ranking source in the Pentagon was that several of the Soviet military's command and control system computers were down at time of the intrusion. Unable to get through, General Govorov would have followed standard orders to repel intruding aircraft. When the surprised civilian leaders finally found out what was happening some 6,200 miles and nine time zones away from Moscow, the deed was done.[4]

Another possible explanation, suggested by several informed observers of the Soviet Union, is that information about the intruder did reach the civilian leadership before the shootdown, but afterwards they found it politically expedient to deny any prior knowledge. This logic argues that when word arrived in Moscow there was a U.S. reconnaissance plane overflying Soviet territory, the military was ordered to go by the book. This meant trying to force the intruder to land, or if that was unsuccessful, to shoot it down. When the identity of the intruder became clear hours later, the civilian leaders, shocked at the political implications of the incident, tried to distance themselves from it by portraying the shootdown as a strictly military decision and action.

Whatever the cause of the Russians' difficulties, Govorov apparently made the decision to fire on the intruder and subsequently took responsibility for it. Under Soviet rules of engagement local commanders are empowered to use military force if national security is endangered. Semiofficial Soviet sources said Govorov's decision was based on his firm belief that the intruder was on an espionage mission, and he had ample reason to think so.[5] The intruding airliner had arrived from well outside the commercial air lanes. It had passed in close proximity to a U.S. Air Force reconnaissance plane. The Soviets claimed it had emitted "short, coded bursts" of intelligence information. It had passed near sensitive military facilities on the Kamchatka Peninsula. It had altered course as it approached Sakhalin Island. It did not respond to the ground-based queries that almost certainly were transmitted. It ignored interception signals by the Soviet fighters trying to force it to land. Based on the actions of the intruder, Govorov had no reason to believe he was dealing with an innocent commercial airliner.

The shootdown has far-reaching implications. We make plans for war and peace on the assumption that Soviet political leaders would be in control of their military machine and informed of events as they occurred. Yet it apparently took only routine failures in this exceedingly complex human and technical system to shatter this assumption. Errors were compounded and unexpected interactions came into play as the Russians tried to understand what was taking place in the skies over the Far East. Believing he was dealing with a reconnaissance plane and lacking instruction from above, Govorov acted by the book: He shot down the intruder.[6]

In Moscow's *Literaturnaya Gazeta* on September 7 appeared the name of a pilot who supposedly was involved in the attempts to intercept Flight 007—Maj. Vasiliy Konstantinovich Kazmin. According to the journal, Kazmin was the pilot on duty at an air defense station on Sakhalin when the action began. "The alarm sounded in one of the control points in our Far Eastern air defense system, which has been for a long time the target of attention by uninvited U.S. visitors. Maj. Vasiliy Konstantinovich Kazmin, duty air defense pilot, immediately took off in the air above his zone to intercept the violator aircraft." *Literaturnaya Gazeta* claimed that "Major Kazmin did everything possible and necessary so that the crew of the violator aircraft could land at one of our airports. This failed to produce any results, however. With its lights switched off, the violator maintained its illegal course over Soviet territory."[7]

It was not clear from the story if Kazmin was the pilot who eventually fired the missiles at Flight 007, although that was certainly the suggestion. However, for whatever reason, the Russians had selected Kazmin as the face of the Soviet air defense forces. In an accompanying article, *Literaturnaya Gazeta* extolled and glorified the role of pilots like Kazmin. "In an hour of possible tragedy, this shining bowl of skies will be pierced by armadas of alien bombers, the cruel weapons of total war. . . . The winged pack, released from the pods, will scream toward our rivers and valleys. . . . To prevent this, long before the missiles are launched . . . the bombers must be annihilated." That's where heroes like Kazmin come in. "In front of you is the hulking, smoking mass of the enemy, shooting back in flashing bursts, raising dense screens of interference. And behind you is the Motherland and its cities. And you alone have the power to protect and to save them."[8]

On September 10, Moscow Domestic Service correspondent Aleksandr Tikhomirov interviewed an unnamed man who claimed to be the Su-15 pilot who fired the missiles at the Korean airliner. He wore no uniform or rank, and was dressed in a brown leather jacket, blue cotton pants, and a blue shirt. He was in his early forties, stocky and swarthy, his tousled hair streaked with gray. Slouched in a chair, he described to Tikhomirov in a raspy voice the events that took place in the skies over Sakhalin. "Pilot X," *The Sunday Times* of London dubbed him.[9] It was probably Major Kazmin.

"It is difficult to explain what my emotions were at that moment," the pilot said, recalling the interception. "I had a certain task assigned to me, and I was trying to fulfill it as well as I could—a combat task, which is what gives meaning to my whole life." "And your actions?" Tikhomirov asked. "The first thing I did, I went forward, up to this aircraft, and winked my onboard lights. The second thing is that I fired four bursts of tracer shells right across his nose. I dipped my wings . . . but he continued to fly on the same course. I was also sure that this was clearly an intruding aircraft flying on some specific espionage mission or perhaps with a bomb on board that might be dropped on my house." Finally: "I received an order," he said, "a precise and definite order to destroy the plane." The pilot then told how he had fired his two air-to-air missiles at the intruder.[10]

Aleksandr Tikhomirov concluded the six-minute interview by telling the audience that he and his television crew had traveled to both Kamchatka and Sakhalin in preparing the broadcast. The inside of what was said to be an air defense forces radar tracking station on Kamchatka was shown. While the television crew was on Sakhalin, Tikhomirov said, an American reconnaissance plane flew "a direct course toward our territory, appeared briefly close to it, and rapidly moved away." The Soviet television correspondent remarked that this happens as often as ten times a day in this bleak and militarily important area of the world.[11] For a Soviet public that seldom heard such discussions, this was heady stuff.[12]

Kazmin and his colleagues would again be called into service a day or so later in the Soviet Defense Ministry newspaper *Krasnaya Zvedzda*. Kazmin was quoted as saying here: "Seeking to get away from the aircraft in pursuit, the South Korean pilot had recourse to a trick that is often used by American pilots manning RC-135 reconnaissance planes. He lowered all his flaps, and the intruder plane began to lose speed. This was done in the hope that the Soviet aircraft would dash past and, while it was turning to make another approach, the intruder would be able to slip away."

Kazmin boasted, "I did not fall for that trick, and the pilot of the intruding plane recognized this immediately." Another pilot who was said to have been involved in the interception attempt over Kamchatka said, "That South Korean colonel who was at the controls knew his onions very well. You know how he maneuvered after spotting me? He began wildly changing course, altitude, and speed. He saw me perfectly well, and he knew what he was doing." [13]

On September 9, representatives of the world press were invited to a high-level press conference in Moscow, conducted by sixty-five-year-old Marshal Nikolai V. Ogarkov, the chief of the general staff of the Soviet armed forces. Ogarkov also held the rank of first deputy minister of defense under Defense Minister Marshal Dimitri Ustinov. A bright, aggressive soldier who had been called the "father of the modern Soviet army," Ogarkov was one of the new generation of technically skilled officers who advanced rapidly during the regime of Nikita S. Khrushchev. He was considered by Western observers as an adept politician in the labyrinthine Soviet bureaucracy and a hard yet flexible negotiator in arms control talks. Like his American adversaries, Ogarkov publicly subscribed to the idea that his side could win a protracted nuclear war. [14]

The announcement that a soldier of Ogarkov's stature would appear before the world's journalists was unexpected. The *Washington Post* observed: "The decision to allow Ogarkov to be questioned by Western journalists was seen as a measure of the Kremlin's concern over the airliner disaster's effect on the Soviet Union's international image at a time when it is trying to win support for its policies on arms control." The *New York Times* noted that Ogarkov was a man "normally so remote that most Westerners had only glimpsed him in the twice-yearly appearances of the Soviet hierarchy atop the Lenin mausoleum in Red Square." Western diplomats said they had no recollection of any previous news conferences attended by the chief of the Soviet general staff. [15]

The press conference was held in the Foreign Ministry Press Center, built for the 1980 Olympic Summer Games, and it was open to all accredited journalists and diplomats in Moscow. As the time for the conference drew near, the seats filled to capacity and beyond with hundreds of reporters and diplomats from around the world. The top journalists from the Soviet press, senior reporters from *Pravda* and *Izvestia,* had reserved seats in the front row. [16]

The conference began at 2:00 P.M. after a short delay, due to what Cable News Network's Daniel Schorr described as "haggling" with the Soviet television authorities over who would do the English translations heard in the press center. Moscow wanted the translation done by a Russian from the Foreign Ministry. The United States wanted U.S. Embassy personnel to translate. To strengthen their hand, U.S. officials began talking ominously about whether or not the conference would be carried live in the

United States, something the Soviets very much wanted. The solution was that U.S. Embassy personnel would translate and CNN would broadcast the press conference live, as planned. None of the major American networks carried the conference.[17]

Accompanying Marshal Ogarkov was Georgy M. Kornienko, a first deputy minister of foreign affairs, who was responsible for the Kremlin's handling of Soviet-American relations. Also present was Leonid M. Zamyatin, the head of the International Information Department of the Communist party's Central Committee, one of the principal architects of the Soviet propaganda response to the downing of Flight 007.[18] The three officials thus represented military, government, and the Communist party, respectively. Ogarkov was the principal speaker, which made sense because the military had the most information about the downing. For a time, however, this fueled speculation in the West that the downing of Flight 007 and subsequent response represented a new ascendancy by the military in Soviet affairs.

The three officials sat behind a long table on the raised front stage of the center. Behind them was a huge map of the Soviet Far East, 6 by 3 meters, on which the flight paths of Flight 007, two RC-135s, and a U.S. Navy P-3 Orion reconnaissance aircraft were drawn. A red cross on the map indicated the spot where the intruding aircraft's flight had been "terminated." A dotted line showed the intruder's flight path as the Soviets believed it would have continued had they not shot it down—heading straight for Vladivostok, a sensitive naval base closed to all foreigners and most Soviet citizens.[19]

Nikolai Ogarkov was an impressive figure: rugged and self-assured, in his olive drab military uniform, with the large gold stars of a marshal on the shoulder boards and double red piping on the pants. Above nine rows of campaign ribbons was the medal of a Hero of the Soviet Union. The information about to be presented, Ogarkov began, resulted from an investigation into the incident by a Soviet expert investigative commission, including experts from the State Aviation Agency that "had access to all materials relevant to the incident." The commission had, he said, conducted interviews with the pilots, ground controllers, and other personnel involved, and had access to tapes of all conversations that had taken place during the time in question. Commission members had traveled to Kamchatka, Sakhalin, and the Kuril Islands in the course of the inquiry.[20]

The first issue was motive. "It has been proved irrefutably," Ogarkov said, "that the intrusion of the plane . . . was a deliberate, thoroughly planned intelligence operation. It was directed from certain centers in the territory of the United States and Japan. A civilian plane was chosen for it deliberately, disregarding or, possibly, counting on the loss of human life."[21]

Although Ogarkov had prepared notes, he hardly used them. Using a steel pointer, he indicated on the map where the events he was describing had taken place. He pointed to the locations of various American and Japanese beacons and air control stations.[22] The Soviet marshal divided the intrusion into three stages:

The first stage was the beginning of the flight. Flight 007 had gone off course almost immediately after departing Anchorage, Ogarkov said. How was it, he asked, that air traffic controllers did not correct the airliner's flight when it failed to pass over its numerous required waypoints? Rather, it was heading straight for Kamchatka. "I want to draw your attention to the fact that the South Korean plane entered the zone covered by Soviet radar systems precisely in the area that is constantly patrolled by American reconnaissance aircraft, specifically RC-135 planes. We detected an intelligence plane, RC-135, in the area [at 1345 GMT]. It was on a somewhat strange patrol. At [1551 GMT], another plane with a radar blip analogous to that of the RC-135 was detected in the same region and at the same height—8,000 meters [about 26,250 feet]." At that time, Flight 007 was assigned an altitude of 31,000 feet and reported that to be its altitude. "The planes approached each other and flew together for some time, about 10 minutes. Then one of them . . . headed for Alaska while the second one headed for Petropavlovsk-Kamchatski." "Naturally," Ogarkov said, "the conclusion was made at Soviet antiaircraft defense command posts: An intelligence plane is approaching the USSR's airspace."[23]

Ogarkov continued, "The second stage is actions above Kamchatka." At 1630 GMT, "the intruder plane approached Kamchatka. He was heading straight toward a major base of the USSR's strategic nuclear forces." This was the naval base at Petropavlovsk. "It did not respond to any inquiries by Soviet ground control and air defense planes. At the same time, radio monitoring stations detected periodically transmitted brief coded signals, which are usually used for transmitting intelligence data." (Although Ogarkov did not specifically state that the signals originated from Flight 007, the official Soviet news and feature service Novosti announced on the same day that the signals originated with the Korean airliner.) "During the period," Ogarkov continued, "actions of the Anti-Aircraft Defense Forces were directed exclusively at establishing contact with the plane, including with the help of general call signal at the fixed international distress frequency of 121.5 megahertz, and compelling it to land at the nearest Soviet airfield." The radio queries on 121.5 MHz were said to have been undertaken both by Soviet aircraft and ground stations. "But these attempts failed," Ogarkov said, and "the intruder flew toward the Sea of Okhotsk."[24] Earlier Soviet accounts had claimed that wing waggling and other interception procedures had taken place over Kamchatka. These claims were untrue, for the interceptors had never found Flight 007. Ogarkov was dropping an earlier false part of the Soviet official line.

The third and final stage was played out in the skies over Sakhalin Island. There, Ogarkov said, "the actions of the intruder plane became outrageous. . . . It had not responded to the warning shots of Soviet interceptor planes. Moreover, it began to change simultaneously the direction, altitude, and speed of flight, obviously trying to evade the air defense planes." These were damning charges, all of which would eventually be borne out. "It was rather characteristic," Ogarkov said, "that at [1802 GMT] the intruder plane, sharply changing its course, circumvented the positions of our air defense missile units and passed over important military facilities in the southern part of Sakhalin Island. There remained no doubt that a reconnaissance plane was in the air. When the intruder plane reached the southwestern part of Sakhalin Island, the last attempt was made to force it to land on an airfield, for which purpose four bursts of warning shots were fired with a total of 120 tracer shells at 6:20, local (Sakhalin) time [1820 GMT]." This charge, vehemently denied by U.N. Ambassador Jeane Kirkpatrick and other U.S. officials, would also later be shown to be true. "Since even after that the intruder plane did not obey the demands but tried to escape," Ogarkov continued, "an interceptor plane was given the order to stop the flight of the intruder with missiles, the order which was fulfilled." [25]

As to the U.S. charge that the Soviets wanted to destroy the airliner from the outset, Ogarkov called this a "bizarre accusation" and claimed that "if this aim indeed had been set, we could have destroyed the intruder many times over and with certainty when it was over Kamchatka, even without scrambling fighter planes but with air defense missiles known in the United States as SAM-5," a 30-foot surface-to-air missile designed for use against targets at medium to high altitudes. Ogarkov finished on a legal note, claiming that the actions of the Soviet air defense forces had been consistent with the Law of the Soviet Border. "That's all I wanted to say," the marshal concluded. "Thank you very much." [26]

Then followed a period of questions and answers during which Kornienko and Zamyatin joined in. The three officials responded to written questions, but a number of spontaneous questions from the floor were also entertained. "Who gave the order to cut the flight short?" read the first question. Ogarkov fielded this one: "The order to the pilots was given by the commander of the Biya region." [27] In Soviet terms, this makes sense: This is how the system is supposed to work. By answering in this fashion, Ogarkov protected Moscow, suggested that Soviet commanders have the right to make decisions, and dodged the question of how much discussion between Moscow and the regional command center had actually taken place before the decision to down the intruder was made.

This was news in the West, and baseless fears of a local commander initiating nuclear war were fueled by headlines quoting this statement. A follow-up question to Ogarkov asked, "Does that mean the Soviet Union is willing to risk war with the United States on the decision of a district commander?" Unruffled, the marshal replied, "To derive an analogy based on this leading to a war between the United States and the Soviet Union is simply unacceptable, in my opinion." [28]

Then questioning turned to the RC-135. Asked by *Izvestia* about the role of the U.S. aircraft, Ogarkov referred to the huge map behind him. The Air Force plane was near Soviet airspace "with the aim to test the capabilities of the Soviet air defense system," he said. "But we believe that was not the only aim. Both planes acted concertedly. Their flights were performed so as to complicate the air situation and confuse our air defense systems." To make his point, Ogarkov indicated the broad loops representing the RC-135's course and the area of proximity between the two aircraft. And confusion, the Soviets had now admitted, was the result. According to Ogarkov, the two planes "confused our Air Defense Forces." The RC-135 "obviously played the control" in the initial phase of Flight 007's intrusion into Soviet territory.[29]

As the journalists listened, the questions were translated for Ogarkov, Zamyatin, and Kornienko. They responded in Russian, with their answers translated for the journalists through the headphones. As agreed, the English translations heard in the Foreign Ministry Press Center were done by U.S. Embassy personnel. The CNN audience in the U.S. heard a different translation, done in Washington by free-lance translator Victor Litvinski. The CNN format had Litvinski speaking as a voice-over as the Russian officials spoke. At almost all times during the conference it was possible to hear the Russian speaker behind Litvinski—with one peculiar exception.

Ned Temko of the *Christian Science Monitor* stood to ask two questions of Marshal Ogarkov. The first followed up the earlier questions regarding how the decision to terminate the flight was made. As always, it was possible to hear Ogarkov speaking in the background while Litvinski translated. Temko's second question was more interesting: "Both the Japanese and Americans have released transcripts of conversations between Soviet pilots, and at one point these transcripts refer to the Soviet pilots having noted the flashing of lights on what is called the 'target plane' several minutes before its flight was terminated. Could you comment on this, please?" The question was then translated for Ogarkov. When the translator had finished, Ogarkov raised his head and, looking straight toward the packed hall, said, "Yes, I can comment on that." Those watching the show in the United States did not hear him finish. No sooner did he begin speaking than his voice was entirely drowned out by static. Litvinski's voice with its distinctive Slavic accent disappeared, to be replaced by a male voice speaking in a midwestern English. The new voice was also familiar with U.S. military jargon. For instance, at one point there was a reference to the Intermediate-range Nuclear Forces (INF) talks in Geneva. The voice pronounced INF as "Eye-naff," this being the military's pronounceable form of the acronym. The interference went on for several minutes.

At one point, CNN technicians in Atlanta could be heard asking, "Are we doing that here, or is that Moscow?" But the source of the interference was not in the press center in Moscow. CNN technicians said the problem was not in Atlanta, either. Suddenly, 2 minutes 25 seconds after it had begun, the interference abruptly ceased. The audio portion of the conference from the press center in Moscow could again be heard, but not Litvinski's translation. After another 1 minute and 20 seconds, the earlier pattern of translation resumed. Questioned later, Litvinski said that "the interference clearly must have been caused in Washington. The technicians gave me no sign throughout the conference that anything out of the ordinary was happening. . . . I remember translating this part with no interruptions, with the voices of the participants coming loud and clear." [30]

In fact, Ogarkov's response to Temko's question caused a stir. "The second fighter that followed the first fighter," he said, "saw these lights on the first Soviet plane and reported so to the Soviet command post." After Ogarkov said this, murmurs of disbelief swept through the press center. The U.S. Government transcript had the pilot saying, "Roger. [The target's] strobe light is blinking." [31]

Ogarkov remained cool throughout, but Kornienko and Zamyatin displayed more emotion. When asked why it took the Soviets six days to officially acknowledge the downing, Zamyatin said that the information had been made available from the outset. "We understand our own language better than you, particularly the political overtones," he said. "You should read the Soviet press and Tass statements better." When he said this, another audible murmur went up among the journalists. Then a reporter from The Times of London asked whether it would have made any difference to the Soviets if the airliner had carried 2,000 people instead of 269. With this, Zamyatin became red-faced and agitated. "If the Soviet Union had any antihumanistic feelings," he replied, "the airliner could have been destroyed earlier." [32]

Kornienko said bluntly and unequivocally that the Soviet Union would pay no compensation. "The financial responsibility must be borne by those who sent the passengers to their deaths," he said. "How would you react?" asked Zamyatin. "What if a Soviet plane appeared over Los Alamos—would you greet it with flowers?" As to the reaction in the West, "It is a fairly old and primitive method that is being applied: the outcry that the guilty person raises in order to divert suspicions from his own person." To find the person responsible for the downing, Kornienko suggested that Ronald Reagan "look in the mirror." [33] He was still raging at the United States when the conference ended two hours after it had begun.

There was some accurate information in the Soviet account, but there was also a number of distortions. The "humanistic" character and competence of the interception over Kamchatka were exaggerated; in fact, the Soviets never found the airliner. "We don't exactly know the area in which the plane came down," Ogarkov had told the audience, and this was also probably false. Ogarkov said that "no bodies have been found and no survivors," which is half true. No survivors were found, but the Soviets very likely recovered a number of bodies. Finally, there was the statement that the local commander had made the decision to down the airliner and informed the higher-ups in Moscow "at an appropriate time."[34] That may or may not have been true. Given the political embarrassment the downing was now causing, the Soviet leadership would almost certainly have denied knowing about the plane before the shootdown, whether that was true or not.

The Ogarkov press conference fixed the basic outline of the Soviet official version of the downing of Flight 007. While this would be elaborated and slightly modified in the coming days and weeks, the essential framework had been established. Further, Ogarkov had presented the Soviet case with consummate skill and poise. At the end of the conference, as security officers pushed back reporters who wanted to ask additional questions, Ogarkov smiled and shouted answers to those he heard. "As the crowd slowly dissolved at the end of the news conference," the *New York Times* reported, "Foreign Ministry press officials milled about anxiously asking foreign correspondents, 'Well, what do you think?' " The Soviet Foreign Ministry wanted to know if the extraordinary press conference had worked.[35]

There were several important discrepancies between the U.S. and Soviet accounts. First was the Soviet claim that warning shots had been fired across the path of Flight 007. Another was that they had tried to contact it. A final bone of contention was whether or not Flight 007 was flying with its navigational lights illuminated. While the final question would never be satisfactorily answered, the other two soon would be.

Later that day, State Department spokesman Alan Romberg specifically addressed the Soviet charges. Romberg repeated earlier Administration claims that when Flight 007 passed beyond radar coverage about 200 miles after takeoff, there was "no indication that it was off course or that anything was seriously wrong." This was one of those plausible denials possible only until it became known that the U.S. military had tracked the airliner for a far longer time. Also according to Romberg, the transcript of the Soviet pilots' conversations contained "no indication" that 120 cannon rounds, including tracer shells, were fired as a warning to the airliner, and the Soviets were denounced for this supposed falsehood. Romberg was right: The transcript contained no such reference. The tape from which the transcript was made most certainly did, but few people knew this at the time. Ogarkov's contention that the RC-135 and Flight 007 had "rendezvoused" was said not to be supported by intercepted Soviet radar data, but these data were not made public. Romberg concluded, "The Soviets offered no evidence that they attempted to identify or force down the KAL plane" or that the Korean airliner was on a spy mission.[36]

At the White House, Deputy Press Secretary Larry Speakes said he was not impressed by the performance of the three Soviet officials. Without mentioning specifics, Speakes said that numerous elements of the Soviet charges were "inaccurate" and "wrong." Speakes noted that the Soviets still owed the world an apology, an explanation. When asked what he thought of the Ogarkov press conference, President Reagan responded, "I haven't had an opportunity to look into it or hear it." [37]

13

THE SECURITY COUNCIL

On Friday, September 9, President Ronald Reagan and his wife Nancy joined other dignitaries in Washington's National Cathedral for a memorial service for the victims of Flight 007. As with much else, the idea for the service had originated in the Department of State. Ambassadors of countries with citizens among the victims and the entire diplomatic corps were invited. To ensure a packed house, the department gave all its employees wishing to attend the ceremony two hours off from work.[1] The ceremony was scheduled to begin at noon.

The President entered with his wife and took a seat in the front pew in the cathedral's main nave. Across the aisle were about sixty family members of those who died on Flight 007, including Larry McDonald's son Tryggvi. The congressman's widow did not attend the service, and there were suggestions in the press that Kathryn McDonald intended this as a snub to the President for what she considered his inadequate response to the Soviets. Accompanying Reagan were a number of members of his Administration: presidential counselor Edwin Meese, Undersecretary of State Lawrence Eagleburger and his wife Marlene, White House Chief of Staff James A. Baker III, and National Security Adviser William P. Clark. Immediately behind them were about 150 members of Congress and dark-suited members of the diplomatic corps, including the ambassadors of

209

South Korea, Canada, Japan, Sweden, and Thailand, plus a number of lower ranking diplomats from Australia, Malaysia, India, the Philippines, and other countries.[2] Behind the dignitaries sat the tourists and the curious, about 750 people in all.

Together they sang "A Mighty Fortress Is Our God." Then Bishop John T. Walker of Washington rose to address the congregation. The bishop's words were both stern and conciliatory. "We cannot accept that the people of the Soviet Union are inherently immoral," Walker told the President and other top Administration officials. "Rather," he said, "we must believe that the context for this action is suspicion, distrust, and fear."[3] The ceremony lasted 26 minutes, and the President did not speak.

Following the service, Reagan met privately with the sixty relatives of Flight 007's victims downstairs in the cathedral's Bethlehem Chapel. According to Larry Speakes, before he departed Reagan told the families, "No words can compensate for the burden of sorrow you carry. At times like this we can only trust in God for his mercy and wisdom. We are determined to do everything we can to see if things can't be done so that events like this never happen again. I promise we'll do everything we can."[4]

Back at the White House, the President signed a proclamation designating Sunday, September 11, as a national day of mourning for the victims of the "Korean Air Lines Massacre." The signing took place in a one-minute ceremony for photographers in the Oval Office. "September 1, 1983," the proclamation began, "will be seared in the minds of civilized people everywhere as the night of the Korean Air Lines Massacre. Two hundred sixty-nine innocent men, women, and children, from thirteen different countries, who were flying aboard KAL Flight 007, were stalked, then shot out of the air and sent crashing to their deaths by a missile aimed and fired by the Soviet Union." The proclamation concluded, "This was a crime against humanity that must never be forgotten, here or throughout the world." Afterwards, Reagan told reporters that his proclamation was only the sixth day of mourning in U.S. history, but "I don't know of anything that would be more fitting." In fact, as the *Washington Post* pointed out later, it was the seventh day of mourning in the United States during the past twenty years.[5]

During the morning of Saturday, September 10, the President met with members of the National Security Council at the White House. Secretary of State George Shultz, recently returned from the CSCE meeting in Madrid, briefed the council on his meeting with Soviet Foreign Minister Gromyko. The council then discussed what the United States would propose at the meeting of the International Civil Aviation Organization's governing council. The question of whether Shultz should cancel an upcoming meeting with Gromyko at the United Nations, tentatively scheduled for September 27, was examined. Finally, there was consideration of the President's scheduled speech to the U.N. General Assembly on September 26.[6] In all of these discussions, Flight 007 figured prominently.

Flight 007 also predominated when Ronald Reagan gave his weekly Saturday radio address to the nation. "I hope the Soviets' recent behavior will dispel any lingering doubt about what kind of regime we are dealing with," he said, "and what our responsibilities are as trustees of freedom and peace." While not specifically mentioning the Ogarkov press conference, Reagan accused the Russians of "mobilizing their entire government behind a massive cover-up, then brazenly threatening to kill more men, women, and children should another civilian airliner make the same mistake as Flight 007."[7]

By this time, practically everyone in the Administration except the President himself had stopped using the words "crime" and "massacre." Listening to the President ten days after the downing, it was as if time had stood still, as if the revelations of the past week had not occurred and things were still as simple as the President suggested. The difference between what the President said and the revelations at lower levels of the Administration that qualified his remarks suggested two distinct levels of public information. Reagan was putting forth an emotional and simplistic "profane truth" for what must have been considered the masses of relatively uninformed, TV-fixated Americans. The qualifications and elaborations, to the contrary, were for a quite different audience: the relatively informed business, professional, and intellectual elites. This "esoteric truth" was far more complex, yet it still embraced the twin tenets of the innocence of the flight and the lack of involvement of the U.S. Government.

Reagan devoted more than half of his speech to a plug for more money for the worldwide string of government-supported radio stations that were in the midst of a vigorous campaign broadcasting the official U.S. version of the Flight 007 incident behind the Iron Curtain. The principal vehicle for this was the radio—the Voice of America (VOA), Radio Free Europe, and Radio Liberty. "The KAL story became the 'Must Lead' item on each newscast in all forty-two languages broadcast during every on-air hour." The Voice of America doubled the number of transmitters beamed at the Soviet Union, and by September 4, the weekly number of hours of broadcast time had increased by fifty-six. Each day for two weeks after the tragedy, according to Laurien Alexandre, an expert on VOA, the Voice of America met with representatives from the departments of State and Defense, the National Security Council, the United States Information Agency, and the Agency for International Development. "A liaison from the State Department's Korean Working Group consulted daily with VOA personnel. Policy directives for coverage of events drew from both White House and State Department sources. And the State Department had heavy input into the station's frequently aired editorials."[8]

Things were similar at Radio Liberty. Morning after morning it gave the story heavy play. To do this, it was necessary to reduce the commentary section of the program, but, as a Radio Liberty official put it, "there is little need for commentary. The facts speak for themselves." As Alexandre noted of the programming, "Excerpts from an interview with U.S. Ambassador to the Soviet Union Arthur Hartman were broadcast frequently. Secretary of State George Shultz's day-after speech was translated into Russian and Ukrainian and repeatedly aired. So were President Reagan's speeches of September 5 and 10 (the full text of the latter was translated into forty-one languages)." Statements by Shultz and Reagan were sent to fifty-one posts worldwide. To play on the emotions aroused by the downing, VOA carried "heart-wrenching stories about the victims' families." The reason, according to United States Information Agency director and longtime Reagan Hollywood crony Charles Z. Wick, was that the Russians were "giving their own people even less than they are giving us."[9]

The Russians jammed the broadcasts, but despite approximately 2,500 jamming transmitters installed throughout the Soviet Union, their efforts met with the usual limited success. James Buckley, then president of Radio Free Europe and Radio Liberty, said that the broadcasts reached about 50 percent of the adult population in East European countries—an impressive 38 million people. The broadcasts were considerably less effective, however, in reaching audiences in the Soviet Union. According to Buckley, there only about 8 or 9 percent of the adult population, about 18 million listeners, heard the broadcasts.[10]

The massive efforts of the Voice of America, Radio Free Europe, and Radio Liberty did not go unnoticed. In an appeal to Congress to support the Administration's efforts to modernize and expand the U.S. global radio network, Ronald Reagan said, "Truth is mankind's best hope for a better world. That's why, in times like this, few assets are more important than the Voice of America and Radio Liberty, our primary means of getting the truth to the Russian people." The President's efforts paid off handsomely. Following the downing of Flight 007, appropriations for 1985 were approximately $160 million, and Congress allotted $1.3 billion for expansion and modernization.[11]

During the meeting of the U.N. Security Council on the evening of September 8, a resolution was introduced by the Netherlands that "deeply deplores the destruction" of Flight 007 by "Soviet military aircraft."[12] It was, everything considered, a mild statement. There was no direct condemnation of the Russians and no direct demand that compensation be paid to the families of Flight 007's victims. The strongest paragraph in the resolution read: "Use of armed force against international civil aviation is incompatible with the norms governing international behavior and elementary considerations of humanity." The resolution concluded by asking U.N. Secretary General Javier Perez de Cuellar to conduct a full investigation into the incident and to report back to the Security Council in two weeks.[13]

Support from nine of the fifteen Security Council members was required, so the resolution was worded to attract the maximum number of votes. Even so, with vote time on Friday, September 9, approaching, the U.S. could count on only its own vote, plus those of the Netherlands, Britain, France, Togo, Zaire, and Pakistan—seven in all. In that instance, a negative Soviet vote would not have counted as a veto, and the U.S. and its allies would have suffered a "crushing, humiliating defeat" in their attempt to demonstrate Moscow's isolation on the airliner incident.[14]

Just 45 minutes before the session was to begin, Sir John Thompson, the British envoy, asked Security Council President Noel G. Sinclair of Guyana to put off the vote on the resolution until Monday, September 11. According to U.S. Ambassador Jeane J. Kirkpatrick, the delay was requested as "a result of the failure of some council members to receive instructions from their capitals on how to vote."[15] In fact, this was face-saving and buying time by the U.S. and its allies. Sinclair postponed the session. Both the U.S. and the Soviet Union would be lobbying the undecided nations very hard over the weekend.

Howard Phillips was the driving figure behind the ceremony memorializing Larry McDonald that took place at 2 P.M. on Sunday, September 11. He headed the sponsoring organization, the Conservative Caucus, which claimed a membership of some 400,000. When the ceremony was first announced, a group spokesman said that Soviet journalists would not be permitted to attend. Tass Washington bureau chief Evgeny Egorov quickly responded that the Conservative Caucus "need not bother, because we were not going to cover it anyway." Although Kathryn McDonald personally invited him, President Ronald Reagan also did not attend. The ceremony would be a bombastic, extremist affair, and the President's aides thought it wise for him to stay away.[16]

The memorial was held in Constitution Hall, the property of the Daughters of the American Revolution, just a few blocks away from the White House. Reporters watched as those arriving for the ceremony were handed bumper stickers that read "Remember Flight 7" and "Honk If You Hate Massacres." More than 3,700 people packed into the hall, among them Kathryn McDonald, her children, and Larry McDonald's mother.[17] Beneath the arching ceiling of Constitution Hall were hung banners reading "Victory Over Communism" and "This Time We Will Not Forget." The United States Navy Band opened the ceremony with what the *New York Times* described as a "rousing medley of martial airs," and Tryggvi McDonald led the crowd in the pledge of allegiance.[18]

More than a dozen speakers walked up to the flower-festooned platform —one of the floral arrangements had been sent by South Korean President Chun Do-hwan—to extol McDonald and his conservative vision. The first applause of the day came when Howard Phillips strongly criticized the Reagan administration for what he called its limited response to the Soviets and demanded "simple justice and godly retribution."[19]

The mention of godly retribution set the stage for the Reverend Jerry Falwell, the head of the Moral Majority. To Falwell, the downing of Flight 007 was a watershed, a moment of truth when the blinders about the Soviet Union fell away and when holy war against the infidel began. Falwell likened Larry McDonald to the biblical Samson who brought the walls down upon the Philistines and himself. "Amen!" shouted a man in the audience. The applause was thunderous.[20]

Then came the generals. First was retired Army Gen. John K. Singlaub, head of the World Anti-Communist League and the United States Council for World Freedom, who, in the fall of 1986, would come to public attention for his role in funneling money and weapons to the Nicaraguan *contras*. He was followed by Adm. Thomas H. Moorer, former chairman of the Joint Chiefs of Staff. Both Singlaub and Moorer are members of the advisory board of Western Goals, Larry McDonald's organization dedicated to spying on the political left.[21] "Let the peaceniks and the freezeniks and the unilateral disarmers and the better-red-than-dead crowd get the word," Moorer said. The word, of course, was money for the military to combat the Russians. Two and a half hours later, with the Navy band playing, the crowd filed out of Constitution Hall. On the way, many picked up placards that read "We wouldn't trade with Hitler. Why trade with Communists?"[22]

On Sunday, September 11, the State Department made an unexpected disclosure about the tapes of the Soviet pilots, and another announcement was simultaneously made in Tokyo at the Japan Defense Agency. "As part of the policy of the U.S. Government to develop full information on the tragic shootdown," the statement began, "U.S. Government experts have continued to review the tape which was played at the U.N. Security Council September 6." This was the famous tape played by Jeane Kirkpatrick which was said to have demonstrated unequivocally that the Soviets failed to use any accepted interception procedures before firing missiles at Flight 007. "Contrary to Soviet statements," Kirkpatrick had told the council, "the pilot makes no mention of firing any warning shots." The Soviets had disputed this.[23] Now the U.S. Government admitted that the Russians had been right all along. The revisions of the transcript of the Soviet pilots' communications showed that cannon bursts had in fact been fired.

The reason for the admission was the Russians, who had been dropping hints for some days. During his press conference on September 9, Marshal Ogarkov had not only mentioned that "four bursts of warning shots were fired," he also mentioned when they had been fired: "At 6:20, local time [1820 GMT]." Soviet U.N. envoy Oleg Troyanovsky had been mentioning the discrepancies between the U.S.'s transcript and the actual tape to undecided council members over the weekend of September 10–11 in his effort to block the resolution condemning the Soviet Union. It appeared likely that Troyanovsky would publicly drop this bombshell before the

Security Council vote on the resolution on Monday, badly embarrassing and damaging the U.S. position.[24] As with the disclosure of the RC-135, the Soviet release of embarrassing information had to be preempted.

The State Department explained that the transmissions from which the transcripts were made were of "poor quality," and it was only "after efforts at electronic enhancement and hundreds of replays of the tape" that "U.S. Government linguists were able to interpret three passages more clearly." The impression that the passages were inaudible was incorrect.

One series of transmissions by the Soviet pilot was originally rendered as:

> 1818:34   The ANO [air navigation lights] are
>   burning. The [strobe] light is flashing.
>
> 1819:08   I have enough time.

This seemed to suggest that Flight 007's lights were on and that the Soviet pilot reported he had "enough time" to sneak up on the helpless airliner to make the kill. With the revision, however, things appeared quite different:

> 1818:34   The ANO are burning. The light is
>   flashing.
>
> 1819:08   They do not see me.[25]

Now, the transmissions can be interpreted as meaning that the Soviet pilot turned on his lights—part of the interception procedure—reporting half a minute later that the intruders "do not see me," meaning they are not responding to the signal. This is the interpretation presented at Marshal Ogarkov's press conference.

Also of interest is the bracketed reference to a strobe light in the original manuscript. The word "strobe" was not actually spoken, but it established a connection to an earlier series of remarks in the U.S. transcript:

> 1810:44   I didn't understand.
>
> 1810:51   Roger, [the target's strobe] light is
>   blinking.

The bracketed comment again suggests that the Soviet pilot reported Flight 007's strobe light blinking. However, Flight 007 was not equipped with white strobe anticollision lights, but with red anticollison beacons.[26] And without the helpful insertion of the words "the target's strobe," it is problematic as to just whose lights the interceptor was referring. What was actually said was:

1810:44	I didn't understand.
1810:51	Roger. She is going with a blinking light.[27]

This could as easily refer to the Soviet pilot himself—an instruction to turn on his lights followed by his report that they were on. Thus, the blinking strobe and its presence on Flight 007 are interpolations with no definitive basis in the actual transcript.

The final change in the transcript was the most sensational. With this change, a passage at 1820:49 GMT—said to be "previously unintelligible" —was now rendered "I am firing cannon bursts," as the Soviets had said all along (see Chapter 3). This transmission was equally or more intelligible than those that preceded and followed it. How could all the expert linguists miss this?[28] The revised transcript read:

1820:30	I'm turning lock-on off and I'm approaching the target. [*The Soviet pilot turned off his missile guidance system and moved in closer.*]
1820:49	I am firing cannon bursts. [*The next step in the interception procedure.*]

The cannon bursts no doubt came as a shock to many. The *Washington Post* had informed its readers that the Sukhoi Su-15 "does not carry guns," and London's *Daily Telegraph* made an identical claim under the byline of its veteran aviation reporter Air Commander G. S. Cooper.[29] Anticipating that the disclosure would be big news, the Department of State informed U.S. diplomatic posts abroad that "the transcript does not indicate whether the cannon shots were aimed at the KAL plane or were tracer rounds" and to "avoid speculation or interpretation" of the revised materials. In an interview with the BBC, Richard Burt went on the offensive with this peculiar line of reasoning, saying, "All we know was that the pilot did fire his cannon and, for all we know, he fired his cannon to shoot down the aircraft, not to give it a warning shot." (As if to add currency to this new interpretation, just hours before the revised transcripts were released, media reports from Japan noted that pieces of metal from Flight 007 had been discovered with "bullet holes" in them. However, police officials in charge of the recovery operation on Hokkaido could not verify the report.)[30]

Burt's comments appear completely disingenuous when the Soviet fighter pilot's transmissions are carefully read. Since the pilot was well out of effective cannon range when the bursts were fired, the only possible purpose would have been to fire tracer ammunition—visible as a bar of light in the sky for many miles.[31] More to the point, if he had wanted to destroy the aircraft, why would the pilot have turned off his missile lock-on? When the order to destroy the airliner was finally received, it was the Su-15's Anab air-to-air missiles, not cannons, that were fired.

Keeping up the offensive, the State Department then claimed that Captain Chun's apparent lack of response to the cannon bursts indicated that he must have been unaware of the interception in progress. "The evidence indicates that the pilot was totally unaware of the fact that he was off course, that he was intercepted by Soviet fighters, nor was he aware that any warning was given."

Flight 007's response to the interception had been disputed for some time. On September 3, the *New York Times* quoted senior intelligence officials who said that Flight 007 had "tried to signal it would comply with established interception procedures" before it was shot down. "Soviet communications," the officials went on to say, "include conversations that indicate the Korean plane either rocked its wings, flashed its navigational lights, or took some other form of action to show that it knew it was in trouble." Identical reports appeared in other media worldwide. Similarly, the French newspaper *Le Monde* reported that Flight 007 had been flying with its lights extinguished until about 1818 GMT, about 8½ minutes before the missile attack, at which time it flashed its lights as a signal to the Soviet fighter. Afterwards, *Le Monde* said, Flight 007 began zigzagging to avoid being intercepted.[32]

While Deputy Press Secretary Larry Speakes could not be reached for comment on the revisions, and Kim Hoggard, the press duty officer, simply said, "The White House doesn't have anything to add to it or clarify it with," the Soviets had a field day with the story of how the transcripts had been revised. "The State Department was forced officially to admit that the Soviet pilot had really fired, as it had been pointed out at the press conference in Moscow, warning shots," said Tass political analyst Yuri Kornilov. "All this hullabaloo, from beginning to end, is built on lies, on a crude, brazen distortion of facts. . . . We shall see what happens next."[33]

It was going to be close at the U.N. Security Council session that Monday afternoon, September 12. Right up until the last minute there were only eight certain votes for the resolution condemning the downing of Flight 007 out of the minimum nine required to force the Soviet Union to use its veto. Over the weekend, the resolution's sponsors had been working feverishly, first to revise the resolution to make it more palatable to some of the undecided nations and then to twist whatever arms could be twisted to get the needed votes.[34]

The session was convened at 4:48 P.M. by Council President Noel G. Sinclair. Johan H. Meesman of the Netherlands submitted the revised resolution and spoke first. He was followed by speakers from a number of countries that were not Security Council members.[35] Then it was the Soviet Union's turn. Permanent representative Oleg Troyanovsky recited the points outlined by Marshal Ogarkov in his Moscow news conference the previous week. Then Troyanovsky turned to the tapes. Until the previous day, he said, U.S. officials had denied the existence of the cannon bursts "with foaming mouths." Now, transcripts of the tapes played on September 6 in the Security Council were in need of revision. Could one expect other such revisions in the future? he asked. Troyanovsky went on to say that there were still other discrepancies between the U.S. transcripts and what the Soviet pilots actually said. For example, Major Kazmin told his ground controller that the plane he was pursuing did not respond to his "call." In the transcript provided by the U.S., there was no such transmission. Reiterating that Flight 007 had been an espionage flight and a provocation, the Soviet envoy said his delegation would vote against the resolution.[36]

When the vote was taken, the final count was nine in favor (France, Jordan, Malta, the Netherlands, Pakistan, Togo, the United Kingdom, the United States, and Zaire), two votes against (Poland and the Soviet Union), and four abstentions (China, Guyana, Nicaragua, and Zimbabwe). U.S. officials quoted in the *Washington Post* expressed their dismay that in spite of all the lobbying over the weekend, Guyana, China and Zimbabwe had refused to join the majority. It was only at the last minute and under intense U.S. pressure that Malta decided to vote for the resolution, sparing the U.S. a political humiliation. "They got nine votes by the skin of their teeth," Soviet Ambassador Troyanovsky said: "It was a Pyrrhic victory." The Soviets vetoed the resolution.[37]

The results were far from the complete isolation of the Soviet Union that the United States had hoped. Particularly annoying was Zimbabwe, whose president, Robert Mugabe, was at that moment in Washington discussing increased U.S. aid to his country. While Zimbabwe's reasoning for abstaining appeared sound—"We are not satisfied that all the facts and circumstances about the matter have been made known and fully explained to the international community"—this did not sit well with members of the Reagan administration, especially Ambassador Kirkpatrick. Under Kirkpatrick, as one diplomat noted, "for the first time, it became U.S. policy that if you want to be a friend of America outside the U.N., you have to be a friend inside the U.N." Following Mugabe's visit, the U.S. aid program to Zimbabwe was cut from $75 million to $40 million.[38]

Amid the furor over the Security Council vote, Oleg Troyanovsky's reference to another error in the transcript of transmissions from the Soviet pilots to their ground controllers was all but overlooked, although it was perhaps equally important. In the original transcript presented by the Administration, it was reported that the Soviet fighter pilot in close pursuit made the following transmissions to Deputat, his ground control station:

1813:16	Roger.
1813:26	The target isn't responding to IFF [Identification/Friend or Foe].[39]

IFF involves sending out an electronic signal to activate a transponderlike piece of equipment on other aircraft. Some aircraft can return the signal, identifying them as friendly, while hostile aircraft cannot. Administration officials made much of the IFF business, with Ambassador Kirkpatrick and others claiming that Soviet interceptor aircraft "may be technically incapable of communicating by radio with civilian aircraft, presumably out of fear of Soviet pilot defections." [40] It was a grim picture—Soviet pilots could not communicate with civilian airliners because Moscow feared they would defect if given the chance.

If one accepts the Administration's claims, Major Kazmin must have queried the intruder with IFF, but the Soviet pilot never said anything of the sort. As Dimitri Simes, a Soviet émigré and senior fellow at the Carnegie Endowment for International Peace, pointed out, "There is nothing about IFF, repeat, absolutely nothing about IFF in the Soviet text. In the English translation, it is somehow found there." Instead, what was actually said was:

> 1813:16   Roger.
>
> 1813:26   The target does not answer my call.[41]

From the very first, the Soviets had claimed that both their aircraft and ground stations had tried to communicate with the intruder on 121.5 MHz. (For example, the official Soviet information agency Novosti claimed that during the interception over Sakhalin the fighter pilot had activated equipment on board his fighter that "automatically emits internationally recognized signals" on 121.5 MHz.) A number of Western experts went on record to state definitively that Soviet pilots could, in fact, communicate with civil aircraft on the international hailing frequency. When asked by the British Broadcasting Corporation about the fighters' ability to do so, former head of Air Force intelligence Gen. George Keegan replied, "I have seen the radio equipment installed in the [Sukhoi] 15 and MiG-23 and the answer to your question is yes, the Soviet fighters of those two classes are equipped to so communicate." And had the Russians attempted such radio calls, they should have been immediately apparent to the crew of Flight 007 since they were required by Korean Air Lines procedures to continually monitor the international channel on one of their three VHF radios.[42]

However, the most compelling reason to believe that the call was on the international hailing frequency 121.5 MHz is the improbability that IFF would be used at this stage of the intrusion. By the time Flight 007 entered Soviet territory over Sakhalin, the Russians had been tracking and trying to contact it for over two hours. They had had plenty of time to determine that the intruder was not one of their own aircraft. As Yoshitaro Masuo remarked, it was thus "unthinkable that one of the Soviet fighters might conclude that the plane 'was a friend' and employ the IFF procedure. . . . There is little doubt that the communication was probably carried out on the international emergency frequency.''[43]

So the transcripts were again revised. The Administration now acknowledged that the Soviet pilot reported making a ''call'' to the intruder, rather than saying he was using IFF, but the Administration quickly moved to question what kind of call it was. Perhaps the call referred to IFF anyway, some officials argued. Undersecretary of State Lawrence Eagleburger told the press that ''even if the Soviet aircraft had that capability [to communicate on 121.5 MHz], which we do not believe, there is no evidence on the tapes of the Soviet pilots' making any such transmission.'' Perhaps this was because the tapes to which Eagleburger referred included only UHF transmissions; 121.5 MHz is a very-high-frequency channel and may have been excluded.

But the confusion about what type of call was made and questions as to whether or not Soviet pilots could make calls to civilian planes obscured a central issue: The Reagan administration had presented an incorrect and misleading interpretation of what the Soviet pilots had said in the first place. The tapes and transcripts purporting to be complete and accurate records of what the Soviet pilots said on their ultra-high-frequency military communications channels were neither accurate nor, as would become clear later, complete.

On September 12, Oleg Sokolov, the chargé d'affaires at the Soviet embassy in Washington, was summoned to the State Department. When he arrived, he was met by acting Assistant Secretary of State John H. Kelley, who read to him in full the contents of a diplomatic note demanding that the Soviet Union pay compensation for the downing of Flight 007. Sokolov refused to accept a copy of the note and Kelley, in return, refused to accept Sokolov's rejection of the U.S. note. Kelley then tried to present a similar diplomatic note on behalf of the government of the Republic of Korea. Sokolov refused to accept the Korean note, and Kelley again refused to accept the refusal. Sokolov left the State Department without any of the notes.[44]

The second act of this bitter comedy came several days later when Assistant Secretary of State Richard Burt called in Sokolov and presented him with a second set of diplomatic notes from the United States and South Korea. The notes pointed out that a Soviet refusal to accept them would be regarded as an additional delict giving rise to a ''right to additional redress under international law.'' Sokolov refused to accept the notes. Burt said that because of this the two notes would be delivered to the Soviet embassy.[45]

Similar actions were taking place around the globe. In Melbourne, Australia, a diplomatic note demanding compensation for the lives of the four Australians on board Flight 007 was rejected by Soviet Ambassador Yevgeniy Samoteykin. In Canada, a diplomatic note demanding compensation for the ten Canadian citizens who died on board the airliner was refused. On September 15, Canada's External Affairs Department again summoned an official from the Soviet embassy to present the note a second time, and it was refused again. When the note was hand-delivered to the Soviet embassy, the embassy returned it to the External Affairs Department. Things were no better in Japan. Yoshiya Kato, the director general of the Foreign Ministry's European and Oceanic Affairs Bureau, summoned Soviet Ambassador Vladimir Pavlov to the Foreign Ministry to present him with a diplomatic note demanding compensation for the twenty-eight Japanese passengers on board Flight 007. Pavlov rejected the note outright and left the Foreign Ministry. The Kyodo news service reported that the Japanese embassy presented a similar note to the Soviet Foreign Ministry in Moscow, which was refused as well. After Pavlov refused to accept the diplomatic note, the Japanese Foreign Ministry sent it to the Soviet embassy in Tokyo via "verification of contents" mail, similar to registered mail in the United States. Japanese courts regard a signature as proof of receipt. But on September 17, the Soviet embassy returned the note to the Japanese Foreign Ministry, also by verification of contents mail.[46]

Returning from the summer, Congress faced a $187.5 billion defense authorization compromise that represented a 10 percent real increase in defense expenditures for the new fiscal year. Congress was also scheduled to act on a conference report put together by a joint House-Senate team authorizing a number of controversial weapons, including the B-1 bomber, new nerve gas weapons, and the new MX missile with its ten extremely accurate Multiple Independently-targeted Reentry Vehicles (MIRVs). A nuclear freeze resolution had already passed the House and was scheduled to go before the Senate Foreign Relations Committee later in September. Several other bills before Congress had to do with the U.S. financing of covert operations in Central America.[47] The Department of Defense had wanted to proceed with all of the programs, with the obvious exception of the freeze, but for the most part met stiff resistance in the Senate and action stalled in the House.

The MX was the most visible of the programs, and the Administration wanted $4.6 billion for twenty-seven of the new missiles. Before leaving town, House and Senate budget conferees had approved production only of the first twenty-one missiles—six fewer than the Administration believed necessary to assure the national defense during fiscal year 1984. Not only that but Congress had linked production of the MIRVed MX to the design, development, and testing of the small, single-warhead ICBM known as "Midgetman." (The MX had never gained the constituency in Congress that the Administration thought it deserved, largely because it was too expensive to be useful as a bargaining chip in arms control talks and too provocative to be useful as a deterrent. Midgetman, to the con-

trary, was a far less expensive, ostensibly less provocative weapon. Midgetman had few friends in the Department of Defense.) [48]

During August 1983, the chairman of the Presidential Commission on
Strategic Forces, retired Air Force Lt. Gen. Brent Scowcroft, had pri-
vately warned the White House that the MX would not survive its next
vote in the House unless the Administration began to be more flexible with
the Soviets on arms control at the upcoming talks in Geneva. And then
Flight 007 was shot down by the Russians. Whereas just a month earlier
House Speaker Tip O'Neill had said the MX was "in deep, deep trouble,"
feelings in the House abruptly changed. "Now we'll get more votes for the
MX," said Representative Les Aspin of Wisconsin, a member of the
House Armed Services Committee and a supporter of the MX. Representative Norman Dicks of Washington felt the downing meant that "a lot of
people who were shaky [on MX] are going to firm up." Representative
Joseph P. Addabbo of New York, chairman of the House Appropriations
Subcommittee on Defense and an opponent of the MX, said the missile "is
a big visible vote and you can say, 'Well, I got back at the Russians, I
voted for this MX.' " [49]

What before had been questionable was transformed overnight into essential national security. In June 1983, the House had rejected resuming
production of binary nerve gas, nicknamed "Bigeye," by the narrow vote
of 216 to 202.[50] The Senate favored the program but not by much. The vote
there had been 50 to 49, with Vice-President Bush casting the tie-breaking
vote. And then came the airliner, and resistance crumbled. Commencing
production of Bigeye weapons "will send a clear message to the Kremlin
that we have the will and we have the resolve to be strong," said Representative John R. Kaisch, Republican of Ohio.[51]

Flight 007 also cast its long shadow over Central America. On October
1, two legal restraints on the Administration's actions were set to expire:
the Boland Amendment, which outlawed U.S. aid for overthrowing the
government of Nicaragua, and the congressional requirement that the Administration certify every six months that human rights progress was being
made in El Salvador as a condition for continued U.S. aid.[52] The Administration loathed the restrictions and saw the downing of Flight 007 as an
opportunity to deal them a fatal blow.

The Administration immediately went to work on a Congress now more
receptive to its arguments. Representative Michael D. Barnes of Maryland, chairman of the House subcommittee on Latin America, observed,
"I think there will be some spillover effect from the Korean airliner downing. The intensity of feeling is so strong that it's bound to affect other
issues." A House aide quoted in Newsweek said, "Those who have been
beating up on Reagan's 'freedom fighters' in Nicaragua will be quieter for
a while now." And resistance to the Administration's covert war in Nicaragua was at least temporarily silenced. Secretary of State George Shultz
and CIA Director William Casey lobbied the Senate Intelligence Commit-

tee for support, securing what the *New York Times* called a "down payment" on the Administration's request for continued funding of the *contras,* and U.S. covert activities and bombings of civilian targets by the *contras* were stepped up.[53]

As with the MX, so with the freeze. In the Senate, a number of Democrats, including Senator Edward Kennedy of Massachusetts, plus several Republicans, supported a nuclear arms freeze. A key vote on a resolution to support the measure was coming up. The resolution had only a prayer of passing before September 1, but whatever support there was waned rapidly in the wake of the downing. As one conservative Capitol Hill staff member told the *Christian Science Monitor,* "The Soviets melted the nuclear freeze movement in about 30 milliseconds."[54]

The Administration also won a victory over the deployment of 1,600 U.S. Marines in war-torn Lebanon. The Marines had already been in Beirut longer than the 90 days specified under the War Powers Resolution—a legacy of what President Reagan derisively called the "Vietnam Syndrome"—and some thought a constitutional crisis was brewing. But after Flight 007 was shot down, a compromise with Congress authorized the President to deploy the Marines for a full 18 months.[55]

The attack on Flight 007 advanced the Administration's agenda along a broad front. The attack removed much of the pressure to make concessions in the Geneva talks on intermediate-range missiles, aided the Administration's fiscal year 1984 request for $463 million for Pershing II missiles, and ensured that the missile deployment in Western Europe would take place as scheduled. The downing meant that the controversial military and naval exercises to take place that month in Central America and the Caribbean—the largest in history in that area of the world—could all but escape congressional and public attention. It meant it was no longer even necessary to maintain pretenses about the desire for a military buildup. In one instance, Administration officials flatly told Congress that they were not interested in a comprehensive test ban (CTB) treaty. Up to the time of the downing there had been the usual talk about lack of "verifiability," but now the masks came off. It meant, as conservative writers Rowland Evans and Robert Novak happily pointed out, that some "detour from détente" was possible.[56] The extensive public outpouring of anti-Communist, anti-Soviet sentiment emboldened the Administration, setting the stage for increasing involvement in Central America and the invasion of Grenada less than two months later. A more active interventionist policy, increased defense expenditures, less arms control—these were the legacy of Flight 007.

The U.S. Congress convened on Monday, September 12. In the Senate, Majority Leader Howard H. Baker, Jr., and Minority Leader Robert C. Byrd introduced a resolution denouncing "one of the most infamous and reprehensible acts of aviation history." Senator Henry "Scoop" Jackson, an inveterate anti-Communist who died just a few hours after denouncing the downing of Flight 007, was eulogized. In the front row of the chamber of the House, twenty-two members lined up to make one-minute speeches denouncing the Russians.[57]

Members of the House and Senate had already worked out a joint resolution condemning the Soviets' "murderous conduct" and "wanton act" in shooting down "the unarmed, clearly marked civilian airliner with 269 innocent men, women, and children from fourteen nations aboard." It called for a "full and frank explanation from the Soviet Union for this brutal massacre," demanded that compensation be paid to the victims' families, and called for an international investigation into this "heinous incident" (although it had already been concluded that the airliner had wandered "inadvertently into Soviet airspace").

It was in this atmosphere that the Senate voted emphatic final approval to the $187.5 billion defense authorization bill the following day, in spite of a projected $189 billion budget deficit. Following numerous references to the downing of Flight 007, the vote was a lopsided 83 to 8. The bill, a 5 percent increase in real terms over the previous record-breaking year, gave the Administration practically everything it wanted.[58] It was sent to the House, where it would be taken up right after the voting on the resolution to condemn the Soviet Union.[59]

On Wednesday, September 14, the House voted on the joint resolution following two hours of debate in which everyone tried to outdo everyone else in denouncing the Russians. "You can dress them up and put them on television, but the fact is we are dealing with murderers, thugs, and outlaws," said Representative Sam B. Hall, Jr., of Texas. In what the *New York Times* described as "a rare display of bipartisan unity," the House of Representatives voted 416 to 0 to pass the resolution. (Two members, both from the Detroit area, voted "present.") Some conservatives were miffed that there was no call for sanctions. However, the main disagreement was that most conservatives felt the downing of Flight 007 provided justification for a U.S. arms buildup, while many liberals said that it should give added impetus to bring the arms race under control.[60]

The Senate was scheduled to vote on the resolution the following day, but the prospects for its swift passage came under attack from the Right. "The President will be missing a golden opportunity if he doesn't nail the Soviets' hide to the wall," Jesse Helms said. He wanted the resolution coming out of Congress to have "some teeth." In the days before the Senate vote, Helms and some half-dozen other senators began introducing amendments. Helms wanted the President to recall the U.S. ambassador to Moscow for consultations. He wanted to reduce the number of U.S. diplomats in the Soviet Union and reduce the number of Soviet diplomats in the United States to a deputy chief of mission and a skeleton staff. Poland would be declared in default in repaying its farm loans from the Commodity Credit Corporation. A ban would be placed on loan guarantees and credit to the Soviet Union. Controls would be tightened over the export of U.S. high technology to the Eastern bloc, and a ban would be placed on importation of goods produced by "forced labor." Helms wanted to call on the President to conduct a "comprehensive reappraisal" of all U.S.–Soviet relations, including a temporary suspension of arms control negotiations with the Soviets "until they withdraw their claimed right to shoot down *U.S. military reconnaissance aircraft*" [author's emphasis].[61]

The Administration viewed Helms's activity as a threat. Controversial amendments would prevent the resolution from passing in the Senate unanimously, whereas unanimous support in both houses of Congress would provide powerful public relations support for the Administration's handling of the incident. In addition, there was the embarrassment of Congress being tougher on the Russians than the White House. Most important, the Administration opposed Helms's sanctions as counterproductive to its main response to the Soviets, which was its military buildup.[62]

To try to get the Senate in line, Secretary of State Shultz invited all members to a closed two-hour meeting on Tuesday, September 13. Shultz explained that it was not up to the United States to unilaterally impose sanctions against the Soviets. Without the support of the rest of the world, Shultz said, such sanctions would be an exercise in futility. Talk was heated at a closed-door Senate Republican lunch that afternoon, as Senator Baker and other members of the Republican leadership tried to persuade their colleagues not to support Helms's amendments. "It is more important to speak with one voice than to argue among ourselves about shades of opinion," said Charles H. Percy of Illinois, the Foreign Relations Committee chairman.[63]

The Senate vote on the joint resolution was scheduled on September 15, a day after it had passed unanimously in the House. During the hours of often heated debate, all of Helms's amendments were rejected. The White House had lobbied against the sanctions up until the time of the vote, including a last-minute memo to the Senate leadership outlining its opposition. After eight hours of debate, the Senate passed the resolution, shorn of amendments, by a vote of 95 to 0.[64]

Even before the final vote had taken place, President Reagan had praised Congress for its action. "The Kremlin is on notice," he said. "When it comes to responding to its aggression, there are no Republicans or Democrats, only Americans—united and determined to protect our freedom and secure the peace." After its unanimous approval, the joint congressional resolution went to the President for signature, but Reagan did not get around to signing it until the last week in September, and when he did, it was with no public ceremony. A written statement, released by the White House afterwards, repeated that "the American people are united in their condemnation of this dreadful act."[65]

With the vote taken and the Congress showing unprecedented support for the Administration's policies, it was time for the House vote on the defense authorization bill. Backers of the bill argued that the 416–0 House and 95–0 Senate votes would ring hollow unless followed up by concrete actions. "The referendum today is whether we really meant what we said yesterday," said Representative Ike Skelton of Missouri. "We sent them a message 416 to 0 yesterday," said Representative Marvin Leath of Texas. "but that doesn't mean a cotton-pickin' thing unless we pass this." The defense authorization bill—nerve gas, MX, and all—was approved by a vote of 266 to 152.[66]

The actions of the U.S. Congress paralleled those that had already taken place in Japan and other countries. On September 11, a plenary session of the Upper House of the Japanese Diet unanimously adopted a resolution deploring the Soviet downing of Flight 007. The following day, the Lower House of the Diet, also in a rare show of unanimity, passed a similar resolution.[67] In Canada, the House of Commons unanimously approved a motion condemning the "unwarranted attack," demanding a "full and truthful" explanation and demanding "full and generous compensation" for the victims' families.[68]

The Reagan administration had successfully linked its defense buildup and the downing of the Korean airliner, but as columnist William Raspberry pointed out, the reasoning employed by the Administration was a logical absurdity. The Administration said that the "massacre" exposed the Soviets as murderers and barbarians, and argued that only a sufficiently strong America could keep them in check—thus the need for the MX, Bigeye nerve gas, the B-1 bomber, and all the rest. But on the night in question, the Soviets were not deterred by the Minuteman III, the Trident submarine, the M1 tank, or any of the other hardware possessed by the world's greatest military power. "The more you think about it," Raspberry wrote, "the less reasonable it is to suppose that U.S. military preparedness was any factor at all in what the Soviets did to KAL 007."[69]

On the international front, the United States had been pushing hard for an international response to the Soviet Union, urging the governments of its allies to take action against Aeroflot. Bans of various types were enforced by thirteen NATO countries including the United States, by the U.S.'s ANZUS treaty allies Australia and New Zealand, and by Switzerland and Japan, which decided under pressure from the United States to invoke additional sanctions against the Soviet Union along the lines being considered by the NATO countries. Various bans by pilots in several other countries were also in effect. During the two-week ban, 80 out of a scheduled 156 flights in and out of the Soviet Union were cancelled. "We are very gratified," a senior State Department official said. "This won't destroy Aeroflot, but that was never the purpose. We wanted to provide a strong political signal."[70]

The Soviets responded to the signal in the predictable way. Individual governments were warned that their actions might be illegal and that the

Soviet Union "reserved the right to take measures in response." The Soviets also began pulling out of a variety of conferences, performances, and competitions in the United States.[71] On September 14, an Aeroflot spokeswoman in Moscow announced that "Aeroflot is accepting all tickets from capitalist countries except the United States." The refusal to accept U.S.-issued airline tickets had the effect of temporarily stranding hundreds of Westerners in the Soviet Union.[72]

Promises that more evidence relevant to the downing would be adduced came and went. In the U.N. Security Council on September 6, Ambassador Jeane Kirkpatrick said that the tapes of communications between Flight 007 and Tokyo air traffic controllers would be released shortly. A day later, the State Department backed away from this, saying that the tapes were "under the control of Japan's Ministry of Transportation, and any decisions on release of tapes or transcripts were for the Japanese to make." On September 12, the government of Japan released to the press written transcripts of these communications.[73] The actual tapes themselves were not released for another two years.

There were several points of interest in the transcripts. First, almost all of the communications seemed routine—asking permission to climb, receiving permission, acknowledging that a new altitude had been reached, and so on. More interesting, however, was a gap of over half a minute between the time the Japanese military said Soviet missiles were launched and the time that the final radio communication from Flight 007 was received by Tokyo air traffic controllers. As the *Daily Yomiuri* remarked, "There should be no time difference between the Transport Ministry and the Defense Agency since both communication lines are connected to the time signal cable of Nippon Telegraph and Telephone." The gap seemed especially odd since officials of the Transport Ministry's Civil Aviation Bureau, who had heard the actual tape, said that the final message had been made in a calm voice. A calm message half a minute after the missile attack?[74]

At the same time the Japanese released their transcript from Narita Airport, the U.S. was also releasing transcripts and tapes from Anchorage, continuing the close coordination the two countries had established for dealing with all aspects of the case. "These tapes and transcripts indicate that no one was aware the KAL Flight 007 was off course," announced State Department spokesman Alan Romberg. However, "since the communication covers a period of several hours," he continued, "both the transcripts and the tapes have been compressed by eliminating all material that doesn't relate in any way to the flight of KAL 007."[75] It would later be argued that information on the tape showing that U.S. air traffic controllers had been aware of Flight 007's deviating course was information eliminated in the State Department's abridged version.

"One thing I should note," Romberg said. "The tapes show that KAL 007 was relaying its position reports, after it left the mainland, through another Korean airliner in the general vicinity. The chief of FAA control center in Anchorage says, 'It is not unusual for an aircraft to relay information through another aircraft. In itself, this relay would not alert a controller that an abnormal situation exists.' "[76] But while one such relay might not be unusual, Flight 007 relayed its reports through Flight 015 for a protracted period of time, even at places where air traffic controllers should have expected it to be able to forward its own position reports without difficulty. Thus, another of the many oddities of the flight was quickly dismissed as "routine" by the Administration. And as before, the press did not have the time or inclination to fully evaluate the Administration's claims.

The two key points around which the Reagan administration built its case against the Soviet Union—that the Soviets had identified Flight 007 as a civilian airliner and that they did not bother with interception procedures before shooting it down—continued to unravel in the second week after the downing. On September 13, "senior intelligence officials" (as they were described by the *New York Times*), speaking on condition that they not be identified, disclosed that highly sensitive U.S. intelligence equipment had monitored the heightened level of activity by Soviet air defense forces in the Far East for some time prior to the downing of Flight 007. By intercepting Soviet communications, U.S. personnel knew that the Soviets had misidentified Flight 007 as an RC-135. The existence of the information had been shielded, it was said, in order to protect U.S. intelligence sources and methods. This seemed confirmed in a *Times* interview the following day with Air Force Chief of Staff Charles A. Gabriel, who said information available to him suggested it was "quite possible" that the Soviets did not know they were shooting at a civilian airliner. The poor Soviet performance, Gabriel added, "gives us a little more confidence" in the ability of the U.S. Air Force to successfully penetrate Soviet air defenses in the event of war.[77]

After making these disclosures about the extent of U.S. monitoring, however, the officials then went to considerable lengths to deny that U.S. personnel understood the meaning of the events while they were monitoring them. But even if the activity had been understood, the officials said, "there's no system of merging the day-to-day work of the intelligence community with the day-to-day work of the airline control people."[78]

As with most limited truths, the language was revealing. Nobody had ever suggested "merging" the intelligence community with the day-to-day civil air traffic control system. What was at issue was the ability of military and intelligence personnel to correctly understand events as they took place and to communicate, either directly or indirectly, with the Korean airliner or air traffic controllers. The intelligence officials cultivated the impression that it was impossible to do either, although such contacts in fact take place regularly. Since there were numerous reasons why U.S. personnel would not have believed the Soviet air defense activity to be a drill exercise, all that was required to communicate with the airliner was the flip of a switch on a radio or a telephone call to civilian air traffic controllers.

But in spite of these obfuscations, the new story served several purposes: First, it prevented the military and intelligence services from appearing totally incompetent. Second, it was an attempt, albeit a modest one, to put the brakes on the deteriorating relations with the Soviet Union. Finally, the changes in the official line in response to the new information posed no threat to the main line of argument—an innocently off-course airliner without U.S. involvement. Intelligence officials concluded that the new revelations "completely supported the version of events presented by President Reagan and other senior officials."[79]

During the first two weeks following the downing, the official rhetoric had a strong effect on public opinion. In an early poll conducted by *Newsweek*, 86 percent of the respondents said they were convinced that the Soviets knew they were shooting down a civilian plane. But by the end of the second week, the polls also showed that 61 percent of Americans now believed that the Administration was holding back information the public ought to know.[80]

Not for two weeks did another story command the headlines of the nation's major newspapers. The Conference on Issues and Media said that the downing of Flight 007 had occupied an overwhelming portion of national media coverage. CBS led the networks with 120 minutes of coverage during the two weeks, while ABC and NBC trailed far behind with 64 and 60 minutes, respectively.[81] Dozens of pages were devoted to the incident in the major news magazines, as were hundreds of column inches in the nation's newspapers. While the quantity of coverage was staggering, questions remained as to its critical quality. The incident was reported and reported, yet the focus was almost exclusively the version of events presented by the Reagan administration.

PART THREE
Cover-Up

14

DEBRIS

On Thursday, September 8, Soviet Ambassador to Japan Vladimir Pavlov told the Foreign Ministry that debris believed to be from Flight 007 had been found at four locations and documents had been recovered "in the northeastern part" of the Sea of Japan.[1] Although he said he was unable to give details, Pavlov promised that the items would be turned over to Japan and that the Soviets would report on their progress in the search in accordance with "international practices."[2] This seemed to be good news for the Japanese, for as the Foreign Ministry's Yoshiya Kato remarked the following day, "not a single piece of debris has been found in nine days of intensive search."[3]

Rumors that objects from the airliner had been found continued to circulate. Late on the evening of September 8, a report by the Paris Domestic News Service said that both human remains and the front of the fuselage from Flight 007 had been recovered by an East German ship, apparently one of the vessels utilized by the Soviets in their search operation. The coordinates for the recovery were said to be near Rebun Island, off the west coast of Hokkaido.[4] Paris Domestic News Service got the story from an employee of Onda Pesquera (Fisherman's Wavelength), a Spanish maritime radio channel, who claimed to have monitored a conversation between a British ship and a Liberian tanker in which the two ships discussed

233

overhearing an East German freighter radioing a report to the Russians that it had found human remains in the Sea of Japan. The Russians, it was said, immediately ordered the freighter to sail to Vladivostok. This report, also carried by CBS News on September 8, has never been confirmed.[5]

On September 8, a Japanese fisherman found a gruesome object floating in the Sea of Okhotsk about 125 yards offshore, near the town of Abashiri at the base of Hokkaido's Shiretoko Peninsula.[6] It was the body of a child between six and eleven years of age, so badly decomposed that neither race nor sex could be determined at first. The legs and the top half of its head were missing. It was not immediately apparent whether the child had been a passenger on Flight 007, but autopsy results confirmed that the child had been dead between one and two weeks and that there were metal fragments embedded in the head and glass fragments in the chest. As the *New York Times* remarked, this was "the first tangible evidence that an explosion had occurred in the air."[7]

Other objects were discovered as well. A piece of the tail section of an aircraft was found on a Hokkaido beach near the town of Hamatombetsu on the Sea of Okhotsk. The piece of metal measured about 32 by 28 inches, with a white letter "L" on a red background and what appeared to be parts of the letter "H" and the number "7." Flight 007's serial number, painted on the tail of the aircraft, was HL7442. Korean Air Lines representative Park Chung-hong confirmed that the piece of metal was from the airliner. In addition, a sponge seat cushion, a plastic "please fasten safety belts" sign written in both Korean and English, and an oxygen mask were found on the beaches near Hamatombetsu. The tail section appeared to be the one truly identifiable part from Flight 007. With these discoveries, the Japan Maritime Safety Agency sent six aircraft and seven ships to search the area east of La Perouse Strait.[8]

That flotsam was being found on the northern Hokkaido beaches adds weight to other testimony that the airliner crashed in Soviet waters. The ocean currents in the Tatar Strait off Sakhalin's west coast are such that only if the airliner had crashed close to shore would the debris be carried south, through La Perouse Strait into the Sea of Okhotsk and on to Hokkaido. Alternatively, had the plane gone down just a few miles further offshore, where the U.S. and Japan were concentrating their search efforts, the debris would have been carried north, not south.

On and near the Hokkaido beaches, things continued to turn up. The Japanese search effort was intensive over the weekend of September 10–11, involving more than four hundred policemen from twenty-two stations in the thinly populated area of northern Hokkaido, seventeen patrol boats, and seven aircraft. Despite heavy winds and rain, more human remains were discovered. Near the town of Abashiri, a factory worker who was angling found the torso of a female, missing the upper left arm and the face. The torso was believed to be Caucasian because of the long auburn hair attached to what remained of the head. Police said the body appeared to have been torn apart by a blast. Later, pieces of what were believed to be parts from a human thigh and back were found in the Sea of Okhotsk. Body parts washing ashore were temporarily laid to rest in the Ryotokuji Temple in Wakkanai.[9]

Over the weekend, Japanese searchers found about 220 pieces of flotsam, bringing the total number to about 420. These included pieces of metal, shoes, camera cases, and blouses. Other debris included a scorched, twisted plastic water bottle of the type used by young children and a bottle of dish-washing liquid with the label in Hangul, the Korean alphabet. Searchers also found eight paper cups with the inscription "KAL." [10]

The identification card of twenty-five-year-old Mary Jane Hendrie of Sault Ste. Marie, Canada, was among the first objects definitely believed to be from Flight 007. Yet Hendrie's parents wondered how her identification card, which should have been tucked away tightly inside her wallet, came to be floating on the waters of the Sea of Okhotsk. Could it be that during the long minutes between the missile attack and the eventual destruction of the airliner this bright young woman had the presence of mind to take out her card, casting onto the winds this small memento of her life? "I'm convinced she took it out at the last minute," said Margaret Hendrie, her mother. "She knew she wasn't going to get out." [11]

The beginning of the third week of searching brought the recovery of large quantities of additional debris from Flight 007. On Tuesday, September 13, searchers found another eighty-five items from the plane, including shoes, sandals, boots, a vest, and other personal belongings. A human ear was found by a policeman walking in a downpour on a Hokkaido beach. On Wednesday, a skull fragment attached to a piece of flesh and a piece of flesh from a human back were recovered. Thursday's principal find was the business card of Kathy Brown-Spier of New York, the first piece of identification belonging to a U.S. citizen on Flight 007. But as the third week drew to a close, the earlier torrent of debris had turned into a trickle.[12]

With debris from the airliner beginning to turn up, U.S. officials began making statements in apparent preparation for the eventuality that the Soviet Union might produce the airliner's flight recorders. On September 9, Defense Secretary Caspar W. Weinberger accused the Soviets of keeping Western search vessels out of their waters. "I think the reason they're doing that," Weinberger warned, "is because they are going to try to manufacture some sort of evidence and come up with some black box dripping with seaweed and claim that the Korean pilot was a spy or some nonsense like that." [13]

This claim was repeated at the highest levels of the Administration. In a rare public appearance at the Air Force Association convention in Washington on September 14, National Security Adviser William Clark predicted that the Soviets would try to fabricate some evidence to prove the "big lie" that Flight 007, "an innocent, stray plane, was on a spy mission in the dark of night over [the] Soviet Union." Copies of Clark's speech were distributed by the White House press office, indicating that his remarks reflected official Administration policy. Briefing reporters on the condition that he not be identified, a State Department official said on September 16 that "it wouldn't be surprising" for the Soviets to release some disinformation in connection with the wreckage from Flight 007. Specifically, the official suggested that Moscow might try to fabricate documents, a flight plan, or even a black box so it could claim the airliner had been on a spy mission.[14]

The black box was actually not black at all but high-visibility yellow. And it was really two boxes—the digital flight data recorder (DFDR) and the cockpit voice recorder.[15] The DFDR is a rectangular box measuring approximately 20 by 5 by 8 inches. On its metallic tape are recorded a variety of data for the previous 25 hours of flight—heading, airspeed, altitude, pressure, acceleration, engine power, VHF and HF radio selection, navigation mode switch, autopilot alignment, and about thirty other variables. As Boeing spokesman Jack Gamble pointed out, the DFDR "could provide information about where the Korean airliner was hit, and its altitude and heading." The voice recorder, measuring about 12 by 5 by 8 inches, contains a magnetic tape on which the previous 30 minutes of cockpit conversation, air-to-ground radio exchanges, and sounds such as engines and the moving of switches are recorded. The tape is a closed loop, meaning that previous recordings are automatically erased as new recordings are made. The voice recorder might contain conversations revealing whether or not Captain Chun and his crew knew they were off course and were aware of the Soviet interception procedures. Built like safes and fireproof, the recorders were located in the aircraft at fuselage station 2300, above the coat rack in front of the rear left lavatories. This is where the tail section of the aircraft rounds into the fuselage, an area that usually survives a crash relatively intact. The recorders were equipped with water-activated acoustic locator beacons, effective to depths of 20,000 feet, to aid in their recovery in the event of a crash at sea. The signals emitted by the boxes have a range of about 5 miles and can be detected by submarines, surface vessels, and even helicopters trailing a sonar buoy. The batteries powering the locator beacons are guaranteed for a minimum of 30 days and usually last considerably longer.[16]

The official expressions of fear that the Soviets could successfully fake the flight recorders were disingenuous. U.S. officials and representatives of Sunstrand Data Control, Inc., and Collins, Inc., the makers of the digital flight data recorder and the cockpit voice recorder, discussed this point at length. It would be easy for the Soviets to open the flight recorders undetected—they were held together by only two screws—but it would be virtually impossible to fake their contents successfully. Forging the 30-minute voice tape would be extremely difficult, for there were recordings of Chun's and Sohn's voices made in both Tokyo and Alaska for comparison. Replacing and faking the entire 25-hour flight data tape would be an even more monumental task.[17] But while the official fear of forgery was unfounded, it suggested something else—the belief that the Soviets had recovered significant debris from Flight 007.

A report radioed from the Japanese patrol ship *Rishiri* on September 8 said that there were eleven Soviet patrol ships and fishing boats operating in an area about thirty kilometers to the northwest of Moneron Island. The vessels were accompanied by a Soviet intelligence ship that was observed lowering two cables into the sea. According to Japan's Maritime Safety Agency, the twelve Soviet ships were moving in a double line, combing the area for debris. Other patrol boats and minesweepers were seen dropping buoys with red flags into the water, and sonar was being used. Five Soviet aircraft were participating in the operation, and an additional forty-three Soviet fishing boats and trawlers were also sighted in the general area.[18] It seemed as if the Russians were up to something.

On September 13, the 226-foot Navy tug U.S.N.S. *Narragansett* arrived in the search area and began looking for the flight recorders in depths of 600 to 900 feet.[19] The ship carried an electronic locator system, a kind of underwater microphone, to detect the faint pinging of the flight recorders. In addition, it carried a side-looking sonar system, designed to be pulled along underwater behind the surface ship, using reflected sound waves to map the sea floor and locate objects. The pinger locator and side-looking sonar system were provided by Ocean Search, the company hired by the Navy to oversee the search and recovery operation.[20]

Even as the *Narragansett* neared the search area, Navy spokesmen announced that the U.S. salvage ship *Conserver* and the Japanese oiler *Hassayampa* were also on their way. The *Conserver* was bringing with it a remote-controlled deep-diving drone built by Eastport International. When a target object was detected beneath the surface, the drone would be sent down. Equipped with lights, acoustic sensors, and three television cameras, the drone was designed to retrieve objects up to 350 pounds from depths in excess of 6,000 feet. For larger objects, the support crew of three could attach cables so that they could be raised by surface vessels. It was one of only two such submersibles in the world. According to a Navy spokesman, Soviet warships and aircraft were "watching very closely" as the new vessels arrived and began their activities.[21]

As the second week drew to a close, the Soviets began stepping up their search operations. Japanese officials reported that the *Georgi Kozumin,* a 12,000-ton Soviet rescue vessel carrying two onboard cranes capable of lifting the wreckage of Flight 007 from the sea floor, was anchored about 25 miles north of Moneron Island. This was the first large rescue ship to be mobilized by the Soviets. Japan Maritime Safety Association officials said that by this time at least fifty-five Soviet ships had gathered off the coast of Sakhalin Island in several areas.[22] And as the number of vessels and their level of activity increased, so did the tensions between the searchers.

The Soviets continued to harass the foreign searchers who were near, and on occasion in, their territorial waters. Soviet MiG-21s and Su-15s from the same units that had scrambled to intercept Flight 007 made a number of low passes over the growing flotilla of U.S., Japanese, and South Korean ships. (By the end of the second week, the Koreans had five vessels searching the waters off Sakhalin, as well as naval officers and frogmen on board several U.S. vessels.) In one case, a Soviet fighter was said to have come within 150 feet of a U.S. reconnaissance helicopter from the frigate U.S.S. *Badger*. In what *Aviation Week & Space Technology* described as a "deterrent to the harassing actions of the Soviets," U.S. Air Force McDonnell Douglas F-15 Eagle jet fighters were scrambled on several occasions from their base at Misawa. On September 14, reports out of Tokyo said that the Japanese patrol boat *Etomo* had spotted a Soviet ship raising a deep-sea exploration submersible craft from a spot in international waters about 20 miles north of Moneron Island. A red and orange buoy was seen in the area, leading to increasing speculation that the Soviets had found parts of the wreckage from Flight 007. But it was hard to tell precisely what the Soviets were up to because they conducted most if not all of their search operations at night, allowing their ships to drift during the day.[23]

Although U.S. ships had been in the area for two weeks, the United States did not formally announce its participation in the race to recover the black boxes until September 15. Asked about the delay, Rear Adm. William A. Cockell, commander of the U.S.S. *Sterret,* replied, "I am not going to comment other than to note that preparation time was needed."[24]

The Soviet vessels were busy. At 11:10 P.M. on Friday, September 16, the JMSA patrol ship *Daisetus* reported that the Soviet oil-drilling ship *Mikhail Mirchinsk* had winched up a 30-foot-long object. At the time, the Soviet ship was in international waters off Moneron Island, where the ocean depth was about 500 feet. The Japanese were not able to confirm if the object was picked up from the sea floor or was something belonging to one of the twenty-four other Soviet vessels that had gathered within a circle with a radius of about 5 miles. The Japanese watched as the *Georgi Kozumin* hauled up one of the small undersea submersibles into the ship's hold, a process that took about 20 minutes. The Soviets knew they were being watched but wanted the watchers to steer clear. When the *Daisetus* approached to a distance of 500 yards to get a better look, a Soviet coast guard ship quickly intervened, flashing an optical signal warning the Japanese ship against approaching any closer.[25]

The search procedures of the Soviets and the Americans were, at this stage, very different. The Soviets employed a large number of vessels and an organized formation over a large expanse of ocean. The Americans were using a far smaller number of vessels in what was described as a "pinpoint approach," targeting smaller areas considered most likely to contain the wreckage from Flight 007.[26]

Over the weekend of September 17–18, tensions continued to mount as ships of the four nations converged in a 12-mile-wide area in international waters north of Moneron Island. A JMSA official reported that the Soviet flotilla included the guided missile cruiser *Petropavlovsk,* the *Georgi Kozumin,* a rescue ship, one "intelligence-gathering ship," two ocean-going research vessels, a small coastal patrol boat, and a "special mission" vessel used for communications. The Soviets also were operating their mini-sub for the second straight day. The Japanese had as many as twenty vessels and ten aircraft involved in the effort. Additional U.S. vessels such as the destroyer *Stark* arrived to join in the search. When several reporters based in Japan tried to get a look at the operations for themselves by hiring a plane to take them to the search area, they were turned back by Soviet aircraft.[27]

On Monday, September 19, sixteen Soviet and four U.S. ships were clustered in an 8-mile-wide area about 25 miles north of Moneron Island. The Soviets were using at least two undersea submersibles and setting up 6-foot-high red buoys. The buoys, indicating that salvage operations were underway, marked sonar equipment that had been placed on the ocean floor. A South Korean fishery research ship left Wakkanai for the search area, carrying a team of six divers. Three U.S. ships, including the Coast Guard cutter *Munroe,* were spotted dropping wire into the sea.[28] The activity seemed to be moving toward some sort of climax.

Quoting U.S. officials, the *Washington Post* reported that equipment on board the *Narragansett* had picked up the pinging from the flight recorders —what was described as a "strong fix" on the signal—for about an hour. The signal was said to be lost but recovered later by the *Conserver* for about 30 minutes. Pentagon press spokesman Benjamin Welles said that there was little doubt the sounds were from Flight 007's black box. "We're quite certain that what we've got is what we're looking for," Welles said. The Soviets were presumed to have heard the sounds as well. Pentagon sources told the *Post* that it was "almost certain" the wreckage from Flight 007 was located in international waters rather than within the 12-mile limit around Soviet territory. The sources further disclosed that there appeared to be several large pieces of wreckage strewn over a wide area with a depth between 600 and 1,200 feet—easy pickings for the sophisticated equipment on board the search ships. "There is one helluva race going on out there," the official said.[29]

15

THE BLACK BOX

After all the pressuring and pleading with its allies to impose a two-week ban on Aeroflot flights to their countries, it looked as if the United States might have to permit just such a flight to land. Foreign Minister Andrei Gromyko and a delegation from the Soviet Union were scheduled to arrive in New York for the convening of the United Nations' thirty-eighth General Assembly while the two-week ban on Aeroflot flights would still be in effect. The Administration was determined that the Aeroflot boycott would not be bent for Gromyko even though his was not a regular commercial flight.[1]

The official story went like this: On Wednesday morning, September 14, a State Department protocol official called the Port Authority of New York and New Jersey requesting the customary approval for the landing of the Soviet delegation at John F. Kennedy International Airport. The airport, like numerous other facilities in the greater New York area, is operated by the Port Authority of New York and New Jersey. The following morning, Peter C. Goldmark, Jr., the executive director of the Port Authority, said that Gromyko's landing presented a "virtually impossible situation." At 5:30 P.M., the Port Authority issued a two-sentence statement saying it had determined that the arrival of the Soviet delegation would pose "major security and safety problems" as well as create the possibility of "massive anti-Soviet demonstrations." At 7:00 P.M., governors Mario M. Cuomo of New York and Thomas H. Kean of New Jersey issued a joint statement that they had "instructed" the Port Authority to deny the State Department request to let the Soviet diplomats land at either Kennedy or Newark International airports.[2] As an alternative, it was suggested that Gromyko's plane land at a military base that would be "better equipped to handle the security and safety requirements" of the flight.[3]

The suggestion came as no surprise to the Reagan administration, since the State Department had already decided that Gromyko could not come to the United Nations session on Aeroflot. That meant that he either could fly to New York on a non-Soviet airliner or he could come on a Soviet military plane and land at a U.S. military air base. Suspecting that Gromyko would reject the former option, the State Department, according to spokesman John Hughes, decided that Gromyko would have to land at a military field in the New York area. It thus seemed more than a little convenient that governors Cuomo and Kean would ban Gromyko's flight, as the State Department wanted, as well as suggest precisely the alternative already conceived by State. This was denied, of course. The *New York Times* noted that "Federal officials said they had not connived with the local authorities in blocking the landing," and the *Christian Science Monitor* quoted a senior State Department official as saying, "The landing affair was not a subtle, clever, manufactured thing involving the Administration."[4] But the Administration voiced no objections whatever to the governors' action.

At the State Department on September 16, Richard Burt informed Soviet chargé d'affaires Oleg Sokolov of the flight ban. Sokolov reported this to Moscow, and the Soviet response appeared in Tass the following day: Gromyko's trip to New York had become "impossible" because U.S. authorities failed to give adequate guarantees for his safety. Viewing the failure by the Administration to overturn the governors' ruling as a major diplomatic affront, the Soviets decided that Gromyko would not attend the opening session of the United Nations' thirty-eighth General Assembly.[5]

Administration officials immediately suggested that Gromyko was using the flight ban as an excuse to avoid running a diplomatic gauntlet of criticism. It wasn't the U.S.'s restrictions that had led to the cancellation, the State Department said, but rather the "beating up" Gromyko had taken a week earlier in Madrid. Jeane Kirkpatrick told reporters that Gromyko's cancellation was "a decision to keep a low profile in the wake of three resounding defeats in United Nations arenas," referring to the U.N. Security Council, the CSCE in Madrid, and the recent resolution by the ICAO. Shifting the blame to the Russians, she said, "For the Soviet Union to provide lower than usual representation was probably an attempt to cast a pall over the proceedings."[6]

On the afternoon of Saturday, September 17, U.N. Secretary General Javier Perez de Cuellar sent a representative to the U.S. Permanent Mission to the U.N. to advise the United States that under the 1947 United Nations Headquarters Agreement the U.S. had no right to prevent the landing of Gromyko's plane. This was well known to officials at the State Department, who wrote that the agreement "prohibits Federal, state, and other authorities from impeding the transit of representatives of other states to and from the U.N. headquarters on U.N. business." As one unnamed State Department official told the *New York Times,* "you could make a good argument" that the state authorities were in violation of the law.[7]

But this was not the public position. "We absolutely disagree with the officer who said they were in violation," Larry Speakes roared to reporters the next day. "We'll find out who he is and see how long he lasts." The State Department told the press that charges of a U.S. violation of the headquarters agreement were "baseless." "We believe our actions have been fully consistent with our obligations under international law," a spokesman said.[8]

Tass raised the question of whether the United States, which refused to permit foreign representatives to travel unhindered to the United Nations, "should be the site of the U.N. headquarters." U.S. deputy representative Charles Lichenstein replied, "The United States strongly encourages member states to seriously consider removing themselves and this organization from the soil of the United States [if] they feel they were not welcome and treated with the hostly consideration that is their due. We will put no impediment in your way," he concluded, "and we will be at the dockside bidding you a farewell as you set off into the sunset." In response to heavy criticism of Lichenstein's remarks, Administration officials quickly said that Lichenstein was speaking only for himself: "It was not a White House approved statement," a White House official said. But two days later, Ronald Reagan seconded Lichenstein's remarks, saying he had spoken with "the hearty approval of most people in America." It was against this background that the United Nation's General Assembly began its 3-month-long session on Tuesday, September 20.[9]

Meanwhile, and practically unnoticed, information about the incident continued to trickle out. On September 16, the semi-governmental Japanese radio and television giant NHK presented the first attempt to decipher the final radio transmission from Flight 007. NHK had managed to get the section of tape containing the final transmission through its contacts in the Nakasone government and conducted an acoustic analysis at its Technical Research Center. The central figure in the analysis was consultant Matsumi Suzuki, director of the Japan Acoustics Research Center.

Acting quickly to accommodate the TV station's desire to get out a story, Suzuki rendered the transmission as follows:

Radia ... Korea Air 007 ... repeater ... all engine ... [repeat or rapid] decompression ... 101 ... 00 ... Delta.[10]

In spite of the analysts' uncertainties, this rendering made it sound like Flight 007 was in trouble. "Judging from the basic voice pattern," Suzuki said, "there is almost no change in pitch between when the plane left Anchorage and when it communicated with Narita [Airport in Tokyo] on the way to inform the Narita center of its position—rather—of the change in its altitude. But the final communication shows an extremely high pitch. This means that tension was high and the pilot was in a state of agitation." [11]

Another, far more fragmentary rendering of the final transmission was released almost simultaneously by the Japan Ministry of Transport's Aviation Bureau. In this version, the message was somewhat different:

> ... puter ... all engine ... rapid decompression ... one-zero-one
> ... delta.

A ministry spokesman helpfully suggested that the syllable "puter" might mean computer, which in turn might mean that there was something wrong with the inertial navigation systems on board Flight 007. [12]

Nobody seemed to agree on what was said or even on what Suzuki had said. An Associated Press report appearing in the *New York Times* on September 17 said that the final transmission contained the words " 'one-zero-one,' apparently a reference to loss of pressure, and 'two delta.' " "Delta," AP incorrectly informed its readers, "is a word used by pilots to describe change in speed or altitude." That same day, *Los Angeles Times* Tokyo correspondent Sam Jameson reported how Suzuki's analysis had rendered Flight 007's final radio transmission as follows:

> Korean Air zero zero seven ... Rapid ... [unintelligible] ... all
> engine ... a rapid decompression ... one zero one zero delta.

Jameson reported how neither Suzuki nor he had any explanation or interpretation for the final "one zero one zero delta." [13]

On September 19, the official Soviet news agency Tass presented its most extensive report to date about the intelligence nature of Flight 007's passage over Soviet territory. Tass said that the intrusion of the Korean airliner was part of a "large-scale intelligence operation" involving several military aircraft and vessels. Then a new element was added: Flight 007's passages over Soviet territory had been coordinated with a U.S. spy satellite. [14]

Stories about U.S. eavesdropping by satellite as Flight 007 intruded into Soviet territory were not new. On "Nightline" on September 1, ABC Washington correspondent Jack Smith told viewers, "One source today claimed the National Security Agency was even listening in from its headquarters outside Washington, D.C., via satellite as the tragedy occurred." Japan's *Asahi Evening News* reported on September 3 that communications between the Soviet fighter jets and their ground controllers had been intercepted and "checked against information obtained by the U.S. from satellites and American facilities within Japan and confirmed as accurate." [15]

Charges that the United States had used satellites to monitor Soviet forces in the Far East during the Korean airliner's intrusion appeared in the Soviet media soon after the downing. During the September 4 evening news on Moscow Domestic Television, a commentator said that both the U.S. and Japan had monitored Flight 007's progress, and "observations of the flight were also conducted by space satellite." Tass reported on September 6 that the U.S. "closely followed the actions of the intruding plane with the help of a satellite." In *Literaturnaya Gazeta* the same day it was said that observation of sensitive military installations "was conducted, inter alia, by satellite from space." [16]

On September 20, an article by Marshal of Aviation Piotr Kirsanov appeared in *Pravda* under the title, "The Facts Expose Washington." The appearance of the Kirsanov article in *Pravda* indicated that it was an authoritative official statement approved at the highest levels of the Kremlin. According to Kirsanov, Flight 007's 40-minute delay in departure from Anchorage was deliberate, "in order to strictly synchronize the time of the plane's approach to the shores of Kamchatka and Sakhalin with the flight of the American intelligence satellite 'Ferret-D.' This satellite is intended for carrying out radiotechnical reconnaissance in a broad range of frequencies used by the radiotechnical means of the Soviet Union." The satellite was said to be capable of collecting the Russians' electronic signals and pulses within a swath of land some 3,000 kilometers wide. [17] Kirsanov said the time required by the satellite to make a revolution of the earth was 96 minutes. The article in *Pravda* was accompanied by a map showing the passes of the satellite in relation to the Korean airliner's flight path. [18]

Kirsanov then described three orbits of the satellite which, he said, paralleled three stages of the Korean airliner's flight. The first revolution was said to give the satellite the "opportunity immediately before the intrusion of Soviet airspace by the South Korean plane, to monitor the Soviet radio-electronic means on Chukota and Kamchatka, working in the normal regime of combat duty." The second revolution was "precisely at the moment of the intrusion of the trespasser plane into Soviet airspace. The violation," Kirsanov continued, "had forced about a doubling of the intensiveness of the work of our radiotechnical means. . . . All of this was being recorded by the 'Ferret' spy satellite." The third revolution of the satellite was said to coincide "with absolute accuracy with the last, third stage of the Boeing 747 flight over Sakhalin. . . . As was to be expected, [the ferret] monitored the work of our additionally switched-on air defense radiotechnical means on Sakhalin Island, the Kuril Islands, and the Primorskiy territory." Kirsanov concluded, "It is doubtless that the moment of the penetration by the intruder plane of the airspace of the USSR in the area of Kamchatka and its appearance over Sakhalin had been carefully planned in advance so as to assure the maximum information by the U.S. 'Ferret' intelligence satellite.''

Kirsanov also implicated a whole array of other U.S. assets which he claimed were in the area at the time of Flight 007's intrusion. In addition to the now-famous RC-135 that had been operating off the northeast coast of the Kamchatka Peninsula, Kirsanov said that there had been another RC-135 flying near the Kuril Islands. There was also a Navy P-3 Orion reconnaissance plane over the Sea of Okhotsk north of Sakhalin and another Orion over the Sea of Japan. The frigate *Badger* was said to be off the Soviet coast in the area of Vladivostok. "There are also other convincing data," Kirsanov said, "giving grounds to assert that an E-3A AWACS plane monitoring the flights of both the intruder plane and our fighters operated in the area where the violation of the Soviet airspace had occurred." It was "a whole intelligence complex," which included Flight 007, "several specialized intelligence planes, a number of U.S. Navy vessels, the ground tracking stations in the Aleutian Islands, Hawaii, Japan, South Korea and, finally, the radiotechnical intelligence satellite 'Ferret.' ''

Kirsanov also examined the behavior of Flight 007 itself. He said that the Korean airliner was "maneuvering along the route, in speed and in altitude. The crew saw the warning measures of Soviet air defense planes and tried to evade them." He pointed out that "ordinarily the normal complement of a Boeing 747, including the crew and ancillary personnel, is up to eighteen people. In this particular case there were twenty-nine crew members." The lengthy *Pravda* article concluded by noting that both Captain Chun and First Officer Sohn had "links to" and engaged in "collaboration with the U.S. special services."

In Washington, State Department spokesman John Hughes said the Kirsanov charges were "the kind of nonsense and lying that has characterized Soviet statements from the beginning." White House spokesman Les Janka said that the Soviet charges were "nonsense," Anson Franklin called them "without foundation," and Larry Speakes reiterated that the plane "was not on a spy mission." National Security Adviser William P. Clark cautioned that the U.S. must be braced for a Soviet "disinformation" campaign designed to place the blame for the incident on the United States.[19]

But while the truth or falsehood of several of Kirsanov's statements has not been determined, his central point—the passage of the ferret electronic intelligence satellite at the times Flight 007 was violating Soviet airspace —was quite correct, although this was not known at the time. Yet another charge that was dismissed by U.S. officials as Soviet "disinformation" would later turn out to be true.

NBC Nightly News on September 21 reported that Flight 007 was already some 15 to 17 miles off course about an hour after it left Anchorage, as observed by a U.S. Air Force radar in Alaska. Prior to this time, most accounts had speculated that Flight 007's deviation from course began at approximately waypoint NEEVA, near Shemya Island. Sgt. William Bruu, the information officer for the Alaskan Air Command at Elmendorf Air Force Base in Anchorage, declined comment on the report and referred all inquiries to Washington. At the Pentagon, Air Force spokesman Capt. Daniel Wooley remarked, "To our knowledge, we do not track outgoing aircraft. Therefore, we wouldn't have any comment on the report." [20] The argument that "we do not track outgoing aircraft"—as if radars could selectively filter out objects traveling in one direction—seems strange, but the press never pursued the point. The Reagan administration had defined the central questions as whether or not the Russians shot down the plane and, later, whether or not they knew it was a civilian airliner when they did so. Details such as the point of initial deviation or how radars work did not seem relevant to a press that accepted the Administration's framework.

It was a tactic the Soviet leadership had used in the past—to authorize Soviet academics attending an international conference to say something the Kremlin wanted said but didn't want to say itself, what the journal *Aviation Week & Space Technology* referred to as "reinformation." But this time things did not go quite as planned. Viktor A. Linnyk, a staff member of the Soviet Institute of the United States and Canada (an advisory group to the Soviet leadership on international issues) and a consultant to the Communist Party Central Committee's department of internal information, was attending a conference on East-West relations at Edinburgh University in Scotland. During an interview with reporter Tim Sebastian of BBC-TV, Linnyk claimed that the Soviets "never thought it was a civilian plane. If they did, the decision would have been totally different, I am absolutely certain of that." Linnyk emphasized that Flight 007 was spying but added, "Had we known [it was civilian] we wouldn't [have shot it], never, no—even though it was spying." Linnyk concluded, "The tension that the pilots in that area are telling about is so intense, is so high, that I was not surprised they reacted in this trigger-happy manner." If the expression "trigger-happy" seems a bit colloquial for a Russian, it was because it was helpfully supplied by the BBC's Tim Sebastian. Sebastian then posed the question as to whether the airliner "had not been spying," to which Linnyk replied, "Yes, there is very strong evidence supporting that." [21]

After the BBC broadcast the statement the damage was apparent, and Linnyk immediately retracted his statement. In an interview with Independent Television News, Linnyk complained, "My bad knowledge of your language, and the awkward way the questions were phrased, made it sound as if I was saying the converse of what I intended." Linnyk also objected to the word "trigger-happy." "The wrong word was used—he gave me the word," Linnyk complained. "I am very angry at the way the BBC treated it."[22] In spite of the obvious mistake and subsequent retraction, the erroneous statements attributed to Linnyk gained wide coverage in the Western press.[23]

Swirling around the tidal wave of facts, partial truths, and disinformation were a number of rumors. Some of them have never been successfully confirmed or discredited, assuming their place in the shadowy lore of the case. One such story was that a Korean airliner—some say Flight 007— had been outfitted with electronic equipment at Andrews Air Force Base near Washington several weeks before the downing.

The story was unusually specific. The Korean Air Lines plane was said to have arrived at Andrews at 10:30 A.M. on August 11, followed by an RC-135 reconnaissance aircraft. Upon arrival it was taken to the far end of the field to building 1752, operated by E-Systems. E-Systems is a Dallas-based defense and CIA contractor specializing in electronic warfare equipment. There, the Korean airliner was said to have been outfitted with unspecified electronic gear. At 6:40 P.M. on August 14, the Korean plane was said to have departed Andrews, again in the company of an RC-135. According to initial accounts, the identification number on the tail of the aircraft was HL7442—that of Flight 007—although subsequent versions say this was not the case.

A reporter for a major U.S. newspaper was in Washington when his office called to inform him of the Andrews story. Later that day, in a restaurant with a member of National Security Adviser William P. Clark's staff, he mentioned the story. The staff member immediately left the table and called Clark. Almost before the story was out of his mouth, however, Clark blew his head off for spreading "Soviet disinformation."

Later that day, National Security Agency Director Lt. Gen. Lincoln Faurer called a number of editors and publishers to his office to tell them the Andrews story had been fabricated by the Russians. The State Department took the similarly unusual step of advising Washington-based editors that stories of Flight 007's alleged connection to U.S. intelligence were Soviet "disinformation." Some members of Congress received a classified State Department briefing, from which most congressional staff members were excluded because they did not have the right security clearance. Congress was told that intercepted East-bloc embassy messages proved the Andrews story was Soviet disinformation.[24] The briefings at State and NSA imbue the whole affair with a level of seriousness that seems inconsistent with the later claim that one inexperienced reporter had invented the entire story.[25]

While the origin and truth of the Andrews story are still unknown, its effect is more readily assessed. When the story began making the rounds of the news services, excitement was predictably high. But after investing considerable resources in investigating the story, editors were told that it was Soviet disinformation. This was "proof" that the entire "spy plane" line of speculation was an expensive dead end. The result was that whatever interest there had been in investigating the possibility of espionage dropped perceptibly. The press had been burned and in the future would be reluctant to investigate similar claims.

President Reagan delivered his customary Saturday radio address on September 24 in a novel way. Normally, the Saturday chat originates from the Oval Office in the White House. This Saturday, however, the White House had provided the Voice of America with a text of Reagan's speech, and translations had already been prepared when the President arrived unannounced at the VOA's studios. Broadcast live and simultaneously translated into seven languages—Russian, Ukrainian, Rumanian, Bengali, Hausa (an African dialect), Lithuanian, and Urdu—the President's address was aimed in particular at the Soviet people. Kenneth Y. Tomlinson, VOA's director, said that the secrecy of the broadcast was an attempt to minimize Soviet jamming.[26]

"I'm attempting to speak directly to the people of the Soviet Union," Reagan began. "I will speak to the U.N. General Assembly in two days for a cause that people everywhere carry close to their hearts—the cause of peace." This referred to a "package of steps" recently put forward in Geneva by U.S. arms control negotiator Paul Nitze, the specifics of which Reagan would publicly announce at the United Nations. Ineluctably, the President's speech drifted toward Flight 007. "If you're hearing the truth," he asked the Soviet people, "why has the outcry been so intense from members of the United Nations, the International Civil Aviation Organization, and why are pilots all over the world boycotting flights to Moscow?" Aeroflot had violated U.S. airspace "scores of times," he said, "but we would never fire on one of your planes . . . and risk killing your loved ones." United Press International described the broadcast afterwards as a "long-planned and highly secret bit of diplomatic one-upmanship," while Tass called it "a propaganda performance on an international scale."[27]

On Wednesday, September 21, another pathetic procession of bereaved family members departed from the port city of Wakkanai by ferry to travel to the crash site in the Sea of Japan. The group consisted of sixty-two family members from the Republic of Korea, Taiwan, the Philippines, and the United States. In the Buddhist tradition, many of the bereaved relatives threw clothing, favored books, and other personal articles—and of course the chrysanthemums—into the cold waters. This was the eighth, and final, party to venture out onto the Sea of Japan.[28]

In the afternoon on Sunday, September 25, seven Japanese and American officials set out from Otaru, Hokkaido, aboard the 3,218-ton JMSA patrol boat Tsugaru on a 15-hour trip to Sakhalin. Their mission was to retrieve from the Russians what the State Department described as "items and documents" from Flight 007. Heading the American contingent was Lynn Pascoe, deputy director of the Office of Soviet Affairs at the Department of State. Accompanying Pascoe were Dennis Wilham, the FAA representative at the U.S. Embassy in Tokyo, and Capt. Burt Terry of the U.S. Navy's Pacific forces. Four Japanese officials also attended the transfer, headed by Minoru Tanba, the director of the Soviet Union division of the Foreign Ministry's European and Oceanic Affairs bureau.[29]

At 8 the following morning, the team arrived at the Sakhalin port town of Nevelsk, described by one of the Americans as a quiet, "somewhat dilapidated" fishing community set against a backdrop of mountains. They were met at the docks by a six-man Soviet delegation headed by Maj. Gen. A. I. Romanenko, the commander of the Sakhalin and Kuril Islands frontier guard.[30]

The Soviets wanted to get the business over as quickly as possible, but the Japanese and Americans persisted in questioning the Russians to learn more about their salvage operations. "I used as many angles as I could," Minoru Tanba recalled. "We asked Romanenko persistently, and I looked him straight in the face and asked if they really hadn't found any [bodies]. . . . His response was, 'My mission is limited to delivery of these goods.' "[31]

The goods were seventy-six objects stowed in five wooden boxes. They consisted primarily of aircraft wreckage and personal belongings, and no human remains were included among them. There were women's slacks, a windbreaker, newspapers, oxygen bottles, seat cushions, a life raft, a Boeing 747 technical manual, an application for a course at Tsukuba University in Japan, and twisted pieces of metal. All of the clothing had been dry-cleaned and, contrary to expectations, there were no suitcases. None of the objects showed any evidence of fire. Some of the structural pieces of the aircraft were severely twisted. In a later comment, a spokesman from the Boeing Company said the forces that produced such damage must have been considerable. The Soviets offered no explanation, saying only that all of the items had been found floating in the water or had washed up onto the shores of Sakhalin and Moneron islands.[32] After verifying the items and issuing a disclaimer that accepting them did not attest to their completeness or authenticity, the Western delegation took possession. Five hours after it had arrived, the *Tsugaru* departed Sakhalin on its return trip to Japan.[33]

The vessel anchored in Wakkanai that evening to show the items to members of the press as well as officials from the Republic of Korea and Korean Air Lines. "They said it was everything, but do you believe in Santa Claus?" asked a member of the U.S. delegation. The items "are only a small part of what was on the plane," Minoru Tanba said. "The general feeling among those involved in the search operation is that the Soviets have apparently recovered human remains and disposed of them secretly because the bodies look too ghastly." Shortly after Tanba made this statement, deputy chief Cabinet Secretary Takao Fujinami went before reporters to say that it did not represent the official Japanese government position on the Soviet recovery effort.[34]

After the stopover in Wakkanai, the *Tsugaru* returned to its home port at Otaru, where bereaved family members of Flight 007's victims had assembled. "This is their coming home," one family member said. "Somebody should be here to receive them." When the relatives saw the items, however, their disappointment was evident. "I was hoping to see more," said Kensuke Nakazawa, who lost his twenty-five-year-old son on Flight 007. "I can't believe this is all. I wish we had something worn by the victims, or passports or bodies." But aside from a very few articles that the Soviets would recover in the coming months, that was all there was.[35] From Otaru, the items were taken to the local JMSA headquarters at Chitose Air Base near the city of Sapporo, where they were displayed and made available to bereaved family members for six months, beginning on October 1.[36]

In all, 373 personal effects believed to be from Flight 007 were recovered by Japan and the Soviet Union. These included 6 identification cards, 42 pieces of clothing, 207 shoes, 16 bags, 6 sports shoes, a hat, and 3 leather items. Eighteen of the objects were recovered by the Soviet Union.[37] The Japanese policy was to turn over the items to family members who could positively identify them.

On Thursday, October 7, forty-eight boxes containing the remainder of the objects from the airliner were turned over to a Korean delegation headed by Cho Chin-u, the head of the Seoul International Airport customs office. After a brief ceremony at Chitose Airport near Sapporo, Cho and his team took possession of 334 items collected by Japanese police, plus an additional 409 that had been recovered by the JMSA and the Soviet Union. The boxes were put on board a Korean Air Lines plane bound for Seoul. Cho said that the objects would be used by the Korean government and the International Civil Aviation Organization to probe into the incident.[38]

Defense Secretary Caspar W. Weinberger was in Japan to promote defense cooperation between the U.S. and Japan, and to encourage Japanese officials to undertake a military buildup. In a September 21 interview with the Tokyo newspaper *Yomiuri Shimbun,* Weinberger intoned ominously, "Confrontation in the Far East and northern Pacific is likely only if the Soviets feel they can effectively apply pressure against a weak, innocent, or disinterested party. I don't know how much time we have in the Far East."[39]

The government of Prime Minister Yasuhiro Nakasone agreed. For quite some time Nakasone and other officials had been pushing for increased expenditures for defense. But according to Secretary Weinberger, the proposed 6.88 percent rise in the defense budget "would not enable Japan to achieve its self-defense goals as early as may be necessary." Weinberger invoked Flight 007, which, he said, underscored the nature of the Soviet threat confronting Japan.[40]

The downing of Flight 007 significantly strengthened the defense lobby in Japan's Diet as it had in the U.S. Congress. A number of groups had strongly resisted Nakasone's drive to increase the level of defense spending, but as one pro-defense Diet member said, it was now "unthinkable to roll back the targeted figure. It would mean we didn't learn anything from the KAL incident." Shintaro Ishihara, a Liberal Democratic party member of the Diet's lower house, summed up the effect of the downing: "This incident made Japanese more aware of the danger surrounding them much faster than anyone could have expected."[41]

On September 25, the United States and Japan commenced a large-scale joint military exercise close to sensitive Soviet areas in and near the Sea of Japan. The Japan Defense Agency called it the largest-scale exercise in the past five years. The purposes of the exercise were to practice transferring Japanese forces from the southern islands to Hokkaido, the likely point of invasion in the event of war with the Soviet Union because of its proximity to Sakhalin Island and La Perouse Strait, and to practice defending the sea lanes near Japan, thus bottling up the Soviet fleet.[42] As the *Christian Science Monitor* commented, "The timing of the exercise could not have been better chosen to aggravate Soviet anxieties and suspicions, even though it was planned long before the airline tragedy."[43]

In this effort, Japan contributed 117 aircraft, 150 ships, and some 30,000 men from all branches of their armed forces—almost one-eighth of their total military force. The U.S. Seventh Fleet sent 10 warships (including the 7,800-ton destroyer U.S.S. *Elliott*), 2 nuclear-powered submarines, and an undisclosed number of aircraft. The 81,600-ton nuclear-powered aircraft carrier U.S.S. *Carl Vinson*, docked at Sasebo in southern Japan, provided communications and air control. "Never has Japan thrown itself so wholeheartedly into military exercises with the U.S. so close to Soviet territory," the *Christian Science Monitor* remarked. The Soviets sent at least five warships and two intelligence ships to keep an eye on the exercise.[44]

The Sea of Japan was rough and stormy as the search for the black box entered its fourth week, and tempers were short. "We believe every effort is being made to hamper our search in international waters," said Pentagon spokesman Benjamin Welles. The Soviets charged in return that the U.S. was obstructing the Soviet search effort. The Defense Ministry newspaper *Krasnaya Zvezda* reported that "on 16, 17, 18 and 19 September the U.S. ships *Badger, Narragansett, Sterrett, Conserver,* and others repeatedly created serious obstacles to Soviet ships and vessels. . . . " Each superpower charged the other with violating the 1972 Incidents at Sea Agreement, which established norms to prevent incidents on the high seas and the airspace above them.[45] Protests were lodged by both sides.[46]

But it was not easy to get straight answers about what was actually taking place. As the *New York Times* reported, naval authorities had not answered any questions about their progress since the time of the downing, being fully as close-mouthed as the Russians. Throughout the search effort, the Navy consistently refused to discuss the movements of its ships.[47]

The question was whether the pinging sounds of the black box had been picked up. After initial denials, the Navy admitted that the vessels *Narragansett* and *Conserver* had heard the signal. According to Navy spokesman Lt. Cmdr. Mark Neuhart, it was between 30 and 40 kilohertz, apparently a positive sign, for the flight recorders' frequency was 37.5 kilohertz. Yet Navy sources soon began telling the press that the Soviets were deliberately transmitting on the pinger frequency in order to confuse the U.S. searchers. Patrick Rock, the third mate of the *Narragansett,* told the Oakland *Tribune* that the Soviets had dropped pingers as decoys. And U.S. searchers may also have been dropping pingers to confuse the Soviets. Dan St. Martine, the *Narragansett*'s second mate, said, "We heard a ping, sure, but the Russians could have dropped it. *We could have dropped it*" [author's emphasis].[48]

Contradictory and suggestive reports fueled speculation as the search entered its fourth week. In Wakkanai, Rear Adm. Masayoshi Kato of the Japan Maritime Safety Agency said, "There is a possibility that the United States has located crucial portions of the aircraft far away from where the Soviet fleet is operating," but Pentagon duty officers said they had received no such information. Rear Adm. William A. Cockell, commander of the U.S.S. *Sterrett,* said that he "would not preclude the possibility" of recovering the flight recorders. Asked whether the pinging sound from the flight recorders was still being picked up, a Navy source responded, "It could be." But other U.S. officials cited by the Associated Press said that no wreckage had been found on the sea floor and that no further sounds were being heard from the pingers.[49]

Rumors began running wild. A report in Seoul's *Hanguk Ilbo* said that the U.S. was making significant progress in the search effort and "will soon recover the black box of the downed KAL airliner." According to *The Times* of London, "Reliable sources said Washington has told Seoul that the black box would be recovered soon." Adding fuel to the speculation, the commander-in-chief of U.S. Pacific Forces (CINCPAC) announced that two observers from the International Civil Aviation Organization would be allowed to accompany the U.S. searchers on board the supply ship U.S.S. *Wichita.* CINCPAC also invited two official observers from each of the countries that had citizens on board Flight 007. To satisfy the press, a dozen Japanese and foreign reporters were allowed onto the guided missile cruiser U.S.S. *Sterrett* on September 22. But the hours and days passed and nothing happened. Stormy weather set in on the weekend of September 24–25, slowing down but not halting search operations by both Soviet and U.S. vessels.[50]

On September 27, six officials from Japan, Canada, Britain, Thailand, and the Philippines plus two officials from ICAO left Wakkanai by Navy helicopter for the *Wichita*. The two Japanese officials, both communications experts, said that their mission was to cooperate with the ICAO in the recovery of the flight recorders, although they pointed out they had been given no detailed information about the recovery effort. Japanese Chief Cabinet Secretary Masaharu Gotoda told members of the press that the U.S. had requested the officials be present so that there could be international witnesses when the black boxes were recovered. "We've narrowed the area of search," announced White House spokesman Larry Speakes, saying that the Navy was again receiving the signals from the flight recorders in international waters.[51] The sea floor in the area was said to be mountainous, with depths ranging from 300 to 2,500 feet. Sound-emitting buoys anchored to the sea floor marked off the area.[52]

Reports from Japan attributed to Foreign Ministry sources said that the United States had pinpointed the location of the flight recorders in international waters west of Moneron Island at a depth of 700 to 800 meters (about 2,300 to 2,600 feet), well within the limits of recovery operations. At precisely this time, a State Department official in Washington heard that the flight recorders had been recovered by the U.S. Navy. Figuring that the story would soon be all over the front pages of the world's newspapers, he called a friend, the publisher of a Silicon Valley defense industry magazine called *Microwave Systems News*, to give him a scoop. The result was an extraordinary dispatch in the magazine's "Intelligencer" column:

> Reports from usually reliable sources indicate that the flight recorders belonging to Korean Air Lines' ill-fated Flight 007 . . . have been found by the U.S. Navy. According to these sources, a Navy submersible located and recovered the so-called "black box" from the bottom of the Sea of Japan, and the South Korean government was immediately informed about it. The find was about to be publicly announced in front of official Japanese witnesses, when Washington was privately approached by Seoul with the request that the discovery be kept secret. . . . As far as the United States is concerned, KAL Flight 007's flight recorders continue to be officially listed as lost.

Similar rumors continued to spread. A sailor who had been assigned to the *Wichita* claimed that the portion of wreckage containing the flight recorders had been found by the U.S. Navy and brought to within a few feet of the surface by a submersible craft. Navy frogmen were said to have constructed a crate around the wreckage, which was airlifted by helicopter to an aircraft carrier. Helicopters were regularly coming and going, so this attracted no attention, he said. Sailors, who were told that the airliner had intentionally entered Soviet territory because the Koreans were trying to save fuel on their way to Seoul, were instructed not to mention to reporters what happened, the sailor concluded. In a similar account, a source close to CIA said, "You know, we recovered the black box." [53]

Such accounts are difficult to square with the evidence. The Administration's concern that the Soviets would produce a "fake" black box, the early reports that the Soviets found bodies, and the distribution of floating debris all suggest that the plane went down in Soviet rather than international waters. In addition, it is important to remember that the black box would not have been found all by itself in some isolated location but instead among a great quantity of other debris from the airliner. While it is surely possible to imagine U.S. officials not owning up to finding the black box if it contained damaging information, it is far less credible to imagine that the recovery of the accompanying wreckage, luggage, and bodies could have successfully been denied. [54]

Denials of the recovery of the black box began immediately. Japanese Chief Cabinet Minister Masaharu Gotoda said that Tokyo had received no word about the U.S. recovery of the flight recorders. U.S. Embassy spokesmen denied that the invitation to the observers was linked to the imminent recovery of the flight recorders, and Navy spokesmen denied that the flight recorders had been located. As September ended, weather conditions took a turn for the worse and the wind picked up on the Sea of Japan. [55]

"Once again I come before this body preoccupied with peace," said Ronald Reagan as he began his address to the thirty-eighth session of the U.N. General Assembly. It was Monday morning, September 26, and Reagan's speech opened the working portion of the General Assembly. The decision to have Reagan address the General Assembly had been made on September 9, in the heated aftermath of the downing of Flight 007, because, as deputy press secretary Larry Speakes told the press, "the President believes that the overall world situation requires a statement at the highest level." [56]

Reagan began by discussing the arms control talks that had recently reconvened in Geneva. Recounting the history of the arms control talks, the President said the Russians were utterly recalcitrant in the face of honest, well-meaning U.S. proposals: "The door to an agreement is open," Reagan said. "It is time for the Soviet Union to walk through it." It was the type of speech he gives best—general statements delivered in personal and moralistic tones—and inevitably it moved on to Flight 007. "Reactions to the Korean airliner tragedy are a timely reminder of just how different the Soviets' concept of truth and international cooperation is from that of the rest of the world," he said. [57]

In contrast to his earlier positions, Reagan declared that "a nuclear war cannot be won and must never be fought" and that "we support a policy to disengage the major powers from Third World conflict." He praised the

United Nations, telling his audience that all nations must "commit ourselves to a new beginning, a beginning fresh with the ideals of the U.N.
Charter." The speech appeared to be a propaganda offensive aimed at
convincing the world, and the American voter, that the President, despite
his bellicose image, really wanted peace. When the speech concluded 23
minutes later, the applause was heavy, although not from the Soviet delegation. U.N. deputy envoy Richard Ovinnikov bitterly complained that
Reagan's speech seemed little more than "a sugar-coated [missile] deployment."[58]

Almost everyone was relieved that the ban on Aeroflot was drawing to
a close. On Tuesday, September 20, both Japan Air Lines and Aeroflot
had begun accepting advance reservations on flights between Tokyo and
Moscow, to commence as soon as the two-week flight ban ended. On
September 25, the Japan Foreign Ministry announced that it would not
extend the ban beyond the two weeks already scheduled. On Thursday,
September 29, the two-week ban expired and most major carriers resumed
their flights to Moscow. The exceptions were Alitalia, British Airways,
and Finnair, companies still held up by their pilots' boycotts. No European
government had volunteered to extend the two-week ban, although Canada
tenaciously held to the full 60 days of its suspension of Aeroflot flights to
Montreal.[59]

On September 30, the International Federation of Air Lines Pilots
quietly called for an early suspension of its 30-to-60-day boycott of flights
to Moscow. That action removed virtually all of the remaining obstacles
to a return to normal. "There have been indications from technical aviation sources that the Soviet Union is willing to cooperate in methods to
prevent a recurrence of such an event," said Captain Thomas Ashwood,
the first vice-president of ALPA, the American subsidiary of IFALPA.[60]
Flights would resume on Monday, October 3.

The U.S. Government said very little about the lifting of the ban and the
end of the pilots' boycott. In a response to an inquiry by the Los Angeles
Times, the State Department described the pilots' boycott as "an impressive demonstration of international outrage." Asked for comment about
the refusal of everyone but Canada to extend the two-week ban, the department responded, "Obviously, the duration and extent of this boycott
is up to those private-sector organizations." In a four-page memo to the
President, Secretary of State Shultz summed up the ban's effect, saying
that "governments and private groups imposed an unprecedented series of
concrete measures against the U.S.S.R."[61]

Tass celebrated the end of the boycott by reporting how "Ronald Reagan's latest 'sanctions' against the U.S.S.R. have exploded like the rain
bubbles that are bursting these fall days on the tarmac of the Moscow
airport. . . . Japan Air Lines, Air France, Swissair, and Lufthansa airliners are landing one after another at Sheremetyevo [International Air-
port], and the Soviet airline, Aeroflot, has resumed flights to West

Germany, Sweden, Italy, Spain, France, Belgium, and other Western countries." Any calls by Reagan for continuing the boycott, Tass poetically said, "are lost in the roar of airliners landing at Sheremetyevo."[62]

More than 100,000 commercial flights had safely traveled from Alaska to the Far East along the edge of Soviet territory without incident for over a decade until Flight 007. As the weeks wore on and Romeo-20 remained closed, however, commercial airline companies began to complain. Pan American and Northwest Airlines requested to the FAA that the route be reopened because limiting flights to the remaining four NOPAC routes was causing delays, and an official of ALPA, the Air Line Pilots Association, pointed out that many U.S. carriers flying the NOPAC routes were having scheduling problems. "We would encourage the FAA to open the route, since safety is not a major factor," the official said. Everyone wanted the route opened before winter, when unfavorable changes in the prevailing winds made flying the more southerly routes more difficult and expensive.[63]

The FAA, to the contrary, said that the closing of Romeo-20 was "not causing any real hardship" and the route would not be reopened until preliminary investigations into the downing of Flight 007 were completed. Since that time, FAA personnel had flown the airway to check the signals from the various navigational aids along the way. They considered increasing the number of times a pilot must report an airliner's position. They had asked Air Force personnel on Shemya Island in the Aleutians, near waypoint NEEVA, to monitor the flights of commercial aircraft as they passed nearby. The FAA announced that it planned to put a new radar facility on St. Paul Island, one of the Pribilof Islands off the Alaskan coast that was currently the site for the nondirectional beacon/distance measuring equipment navigation aid that Flight 007 should have used to verify its position at waypoint NABIE. The proposed station was intended to provide an additional area of civil radar coverage for the NOPAC routes.[64] What the FAA found as a result of all its discussions, checks, and deliberations was that the safety of the route was just fine.

On September 27, FAA spokesman Dennis Feldman announced that route Romeo-20 would be reopened as of 3:00 P.M. on Sunday, October 2, a month after it had been closed. Since the closing, Feldman said, "the FAA verified the accuracy of the route." The FAA spokesman also announced that the Japanese would reopen their end of Romeo-20 at the same time. According to Feldman, no problems had been found with the route and no problems with its reopening were foreseen.[65] "We already know those routes are safe," said Raymond J. Van Buren, director of FAA's air traffic services.[66]

Sixty-nine-year-old Yuri Andropov, secretary general of the Communist Party of the Soviet Union and chairman of the Presidium of the U.S.S.R.

Supreme Soviet, had been seriously ill at the time of the downing of Flight 007. Throughout the month of September, the Western media remarked repeatedly that Andropov's name had been assiduously kept out of the press, permitting the military to assume the burden of explanation for what was portrayed as a strictly military action. But on September 27, Andropov's silence on the incident was finally broken. Speaking for the Soviet leadership, Andropov issued a statement, the first by an indentifiable political leader, that was read twice in full on television and printed in the main newspapers the following day. "The importance attached to the statement by the Kremlin," the *New York Times* observed, "was indicated by the fact that it was made by itself, without the context of a dinner speech for a visiting dignitary or an interview with *Pravda*." [67]

In a statement apparently intended for both foreign and domestic audiences, Andropov dismissed U.S. professions of flexibility in Geneva as "prattle" and criticized the Reagan administration for its arms buildup and the growing U.S. military presence worldwide. And then, of course, there was the airliner. According to Andropov, "The sophisticated provocation organized by the U.S. special services using a South Korean plane is also an example of extreme adventurism in policy. . . . The loss of life is on the conscience of those who . . . conceived and implemented this provocation and who literally the next day hastened to force colossal military appropriations through Congress and are now rubbing their hands with satisfaction." Andropov's statement was followed on October 1 by a government-sponsored rally in which tens of thousands of Muscovites marched against the impending deployment of Pershing II and Cruise missiles in Western Europe. On Soviet television, a rock 'n' roll group sang "Stop Mr. Reagan, Stop, Stop, Stop," and folk groups sang "We Shall Overcome" against a backdrop of U.S. fighter planes taking off from aircraft carriers and nuclear explosions bursting. [68]

16

THE U.S. PRESS

The American media did a grossly inadequate job of covering the downing of Flight 007. Instead of addressing the inconsistencies and questioning dubious assertions in the official version of events, instead of actively investigating the downing, journalists in the fall of 1983 simply reported what officials said.

Where were the veteran reporters who most certainly knew that the official explanation of when the U.S. Government knew about the incident was false? Where were the critical analyses of the belated acknowledgments about the RC-135, the cannon bursts, and the call by the Soviet pilots? As far as I am aware, not a single news organization actually bothered to check the official rendering of the Soviet statements by having a Russian speaker translate them. Finally, where were the hard questions about why the Administration told us that the Soviets had knowingly shot down a civilian airliner when they had not? What we got instead, as one journalist remarked, "was the Richard Burt/Lawrence Eagleburger/Jeane Kirkpatrick show, complete with compliant newspeople who regularly served up simplistic queries and declined to follow up on hazy answers." [1]

In the aftermath of the downing of Flight 007, members of the press occasionally contributed to the confusion and misinformation. One example: Veteran *New York Times* reporter Leslie Gelb, dismissing the allegation that Flight 007 was a spy plane, told his readers that the United States doesn't need to take photographs from airplanes and, anyway, it was night and infrared cameras "are ineffective above a few thousand feet." Gelb wrote that the "only imaging system that works at higher altitudes at night is something called synthetic aperture radar," something that is "fairly large and is said to take up a lot of space." (But if infrared cameras are so ineffective, Andrew Cockburn wondered in the *Village Voice,* why do spy satellites carry them? And if synthetic aperture radar is so large, why is it carried inside the nose of F-15 fighters?) But Gelb, other newsmen, and a host of Administration officials were dismissing charges about spy equipment that had never been made. As Sugwon Kang pointed out, "The truth is, no one was making such an allegation with any seriousness, yet government officials seemed to derive much satisfaction from denying it."[2] Dismissing claims of cameras on board Flight 007 obscured questions of what else the plane might have been up to.

Part of the compliance of the press can probably be attributed to a lack of knowledge, in turn attributable to the Reagan administration's vigorous efforts to restrict information. To an unprecedented degree, the "night and cloud" of government secrecy has been extended to new areas of American life. The Administration has moved the system of classification toward greater restrictions on information. Efforts to reclassify information already in the public domain have been undertaken. It has sought to impose lie detector tests on all federal employees, and to make government officials sign nondisclosure agreements and agree to submit speeches and manuscripts for prepublication review as a condition of employment. It has monitored media coverage of government actions and castigated those journalists who were critical. It has imposed restrictions on publications and films coming into the United States, limited travel abroad, and restricted travel to the U.S. of persons the Administration considers undesirable. The Administration has expanded the range of covert operations, including the financing of an illegal war. Finally, it has refused to share information with Congress by asserting executive privilege, stonewalling requests, forcing Congress to threaten subpoenas and court action to get basic information about the actions of the Executive branch. As Floyd Abrams noted, the Administration has acted as if "information were in the nature of a potentially disabling disease which must be feared, controlled, and ultimately quarantined."[3]

Another reason for press compliance probably lay in its experience of pervasive official dishonesty. As Anthony Marro wrote, "Washington reporters over the years have had to deal with a steady barrage of deceptions, half-truths, and outright lies."[4] Under the present Administration, repeated, egregious "misstatements" by officials from the President himself on down have become the norm. Selective truths are offered up, apparently to help explain reality but in fact with the opposite intention, and the public is left to draw obvious, and incorrect, conclusions from them. Other information is omitted entirely, perverting the information that is provided by modifying its context and weakening the reporters' ability to reason effectively. Lying has become institutionalized through a deliberate policy of disinformation—putting knowingly false information into the public domain—regarding CIA programs such as support of the Nicaraguan *contras* and the Department of Defense's Strategic Defense Initiative. Perhaps the sensibilities of the press, and those of the public, have been so dulled or their minds so jaded that another lie just didn't seem important.

Other explanations have to do with the nature of journalism—reporters must rely on sources. This Administration is especially hostile to critics.[5] Raising questions about Flight 007 when the Administration had clearly declared the topic off-limits could end the career of a Washington-beat reporter. Sources would dry up, invitations would cease, and interviews would be denied. Not to mention that in a case such as this the sources with the highest rank and therefore the greatest apparent credibility were also the ones with potentially the most to conceal. Thus, reliance on official sources derailed investigation.

Finally, there are constraints on how deeply newspapers and television news departments can cover stories. When they are following major news stories, seldom is there time for journalists to review and analyze previously reported statements and information. New information is constantly breaking, previous accounts are rapidly relegated to the trash heap of "incomplete" understanding, and the news, like an irresistible force, moves on. News organizations also reach a point of diminishing returns with long-running stories, where new bits of information do not merit the repeated explanations, space, and expense their presentation would require. Thus, complex stories requiring a great deal of digging, synthesis, and expense are less likely to be fully investigated. "It is not impossible to reconstruct the whole," Jacques Ellul wrote in his classic study of propaganda. "With much patience, work, and research, one can bring order into such facts and relate them to each other. But the job is for a specialist, and the results would not appear until long after the propaganda action had obtained its effect. Besides, they would be published as a technical study and be seen by only a handful of readers." This is not in the nature of today's news business.

The result of these and other forces has produced in some members of the press a new brand of "political realism." Concerns such as responsible, accountable government and the public's right to know are believed by the new realists to be holdovers from an earlier naive era that has vanished forever. In their place has been constructed a new set of values more consonant with the demands of the power structure. The jaded members of the press who play this game deride as unsophisticated and sentimental those who do not accept the new realities. It is a game where, by some alchemy, political realism and their own career interests come out equal. So the press took the easy road and reported what the Administration said without a great deal of analysis or criticism. Serious efforts to evaluate the Administration's version of events were never attempted.

Instead, the press gave free rein to the Administration. The most obvious of the emotional buttons pressed by the Administration was hostility to the Russians, by now a deeply American cultural theme. Pictures appeared in the *New York Times* of U.N. ambassadors Kirkpatrick and Troyanovsky not looking at each other, of Shultz and Gromyko staring across a vast blank expanse of table, devoid of ornamentation and human comforts: the existential gulf between Us and Them. In reporting the downing and its aftermath, the press was swept up in the Administration's emotionalism, embroidering it with animal and hunt imagery, with sexual imagery, and with the themes of revenge and death. As one writer described this Freudian landscape, "This is a world inhabited by the primitive, a world of distortion and destruction, both inside and out."[6] By no means did all members of the press corps believe the Administration's caricatured view of the Soviet Union, and not all embellished that vision. But even those who did not generally reported official statements uncritically. Through repetiton, the caricature was gradually accorded the mantle of facticity.

"During those first days in September," Asa Baber wrote, "my own government was passing out contradictory and incorrect information, yes, but what was even more frightening was the way in which the media cooperated with that exercise in news management. . . . Don't tell me that we're living in a society that can be as controlled as Russia's during a crisis and that the control is voluntary, that the censorship is born inside the pack; don't tell me that the pack fears alienating its official sources more than it loves the truth, that it prefers to play the game sedately even when it knows it's being manipulated and lied to and that it sticks together in rough weather, never even asking the burning questions. No, don't tell me that. I mean, you don't have to. I've seen the evidence of it."[7]

Although a number of Administration officials had been saying privately, and not so privately, for more than a month that the Soviets did not know Flight 007 was a civilian airliner when they shot it down, a story to that effect in the *New York Times* on October 7 seemed to catch everyone by surprise. In a lengthy front-page article, the first front pager on the case for quite a while, *Times* correspondent David Shribman reported, "Five weeks after a Soviet fighter shot down a South Korean airliner, United States intelligence experts say they have reviewed all available evidence and found no indication that Soviet air defense personnel knew before the attack that the target was a commercial plane."[8]

According to Shribman's sources, the White House received these conclusions from the intelligence community about two weeks after the downing. They were "very careful to point out," the *Times* said, that the Administration did not know these things on the day of the incident. The two-week period of ignorance was convenient for the Administration because it means that all the inflammatory speeches by the President, Secretary of State, various assistant secretaries and U.N. ambassadors were made in good faith. The two-week framework allowed the Administration to deny deceiving Congress by using the shootdown as an argument for new weaponry.

The story that the Administration did not find out the facts of the incident for two weeks was not only convenient but also unbelievable. As early as September 3, Administration officials began qualifying their accusations, saying the Russians were guilty either of "enormous callousness" or "incredible incompetence." By September 4, Administration officials told the *Washington Post* that they could not "be certain that the Soviets did not make a mistake." But official statements and U.S. policy were slow in catching up with this perception.[9]

The Administration's presentation of the incident rested on three claims: that the Soviets had positively identified Flight 007 as an unarmed civilian airliner, that Soviet interceptors had not warned Flight 007 before shooting it, and that the Korean airliner had overflown Soviet territory because of some unspecified combination of human and/or mechanical errors.[10] With the appearance of the Shribman article in the *New York Times,* the first of these three claims was shown to be false: The Soviets had not identified Flight 007 as a civilian airliner. The second claim, that the Soviets failed to warn Flight 007, had already been called into question by the disclosure that cannon bursts had been fired and a call made to the intruder. The third claim, that the airliner was off course owing to human and/or mechanical error, continues to generate controversy.

"So the Soviet Union has been telling the truth," wrote William Pfaff in the *Los Angeles Times.* "There are probably people in Washington and the other Western capitals who will say, so what? It has all produced a glorious victory for the West in the propaganda war. So it has, so far. . . . None of this should necessarily surprise anyone who is a witness of contemporary history. But it still commands the power to make a citizen of that side which professes to represent justice as well as truth feel diminished." U.S. Information Agency counselor John L. Hedges quickly penned a letter to the *Times* saying that "Pfaff's column must delight Soviet propagandists who have been trying to obscure the issues raised by that tragic event." It was more than a response to Pfaff; it was a warning to anyone who might consider criticizing the Administration's version of events. Distressed by this heavy-handed approach, Stephen Rosenfeld asked in the *Washington Post,* "Is there not one person in the United States Government who can talk straight about this affair?"[11]

As if to add credibility to Shribman's description of their poor performance, the Soviets began a shake-up in their Far Eastern air defense command. Sources in Moscow said that the purge reflected unhappiness at the top levels of both the military and civilian leadership over the "massive failure" of the air defense forces to halt the flight of the Korean airliner. Sources in the Reagan administration confirmed the report, although they declined to discuss with the press how they knew about the shake-up.[12]

The names of the supposedly ousted officers were not given, and some speculated that the rumor of a shake-up was a plot to exonerate the civilian leadership in Moscow. The evidence cited in support of this theory was that military officials had carried the ball in explaining the incident from the very first. Those who believed the purge was genuine repeatedly raised the name of Marshal of Aviation Aleksandr I. Koldunov. Koldunov, a hard-baked professional soldier, had become PVO chief after Marshal Pavel Batitsky was ousted following the intrusion of KAL Flight 902 in 1978. Western intelligence sources had speculated that Koldunov's career had been under a cloud since the downing because he had not played a role in the almost exclusively military Soviet propaganda campaign and had not received routine state recognition on his sixtieth birthday on September 20. But speculation quieted when the marshal appeared at the annual parade in Red Square on November 7, 1983, his standing apparently undiminished, and was stilled forever a year later when an article in *Krasnaya Zvezda* announced his promotion to chief marshal of aviation. "If there was any doubt in anybody's mind about Koldunov being in the doghouse after KAL," a Japanese expert on the Soviet military observed, "he came out of that one all right." [13]

In fact, the scapegoat turned out to be Col. Gen. Seymon F. Romanov, the first identifiable Soviet official to make a statement on the downing. Eight months later, a report from East Germany said that Romanov had died "in the line of duty," a formulation, as the *New York Times* pointed out, that is normally used when an officer is killed in an accident. Officially, Romanov had been assigned to the Warsaw Pact forces as a representative of Marshal Viktor G. Kulikov, a move considered to be a demotion. However, reports from confidential military sources indicated that Romanov died in an East German hospital after being wounded in a rocket attack in Afghanistan, where he had been sent as punishment for the poor performance of the air defense forces on the night of September 1, 1983.[14]

Even Soviet chief of staff Nikolai Ogarkov may not have escaped from the incident untouched. A year after the downing, the Soviet press announced that Ogarkov had been made head of the Voroshilov Academy of the General Staff in Moscow. "It was a demotion," said William Jackson, a senior fellow of the Fulbright Institute of International Relations. "It is quite conceivable that the buck stopped with Ogarkov on the night of the shooting down." [15] Some Kremlinologists disagreed, however, suggesting that Ogarkov had gotten out of line by acting with excessive autonomy and making decisions without adequately consulting the civilian leadership.[16]

Events in the Soviet Union may have had their parallel in the United

States. At the time of the downing of Flight 007, few, if any, in the Administration could compare in power and influence to Assistant to the President for National Security Affairs William P. Clark. In an exceedingly brief time, this former California Supreme Court justice, rancher, and seventeen-year Reagan crony had risen from obscurity to a position of enormous influence. During the summer of 1983, there was talk that Reagan would almost certainly appoint Clark to the Supreme Court if an opening occurred. Clark enraged the State Department by authorizing military maneuvers in Central America without consultation and by otherwise subordinating many of State's traditional foreign policy prerogatives to the White House. In mid-July 1983, the implacably hard-line, anti-Communist Clark was appointed by the President as the leader of the Senior Arms Control Policy Group, which supplanted interagency groups headed by officials from the State and Defense departments. (Other members of this group were Richard Burt and Lawrence Eagleburger.) As Steven Weisman wrote in the *New York Times Magazine,* "Seldom has a man so inexperienced become so powerful in helping to shape United States foreign policy." [17]

On October 18, the Assistant to the President for National Security Affairs resigned, amid considerable secrecy, to be replaced by his assistant, Robert McFarlane. The official story was that Clark, a fourth-generation rancher, ached to take over the Department of the Interior after James Watt was forced to resign. Such accounts were certainly false: Clark, who had repeatedly said that he would stay on as National Security adviser as long as Reagan wanted him to, showed no enthusiasm for the Interior job and a year later drifted out of government altogether. Some writers have suggested that Clark may have lost a power struggle over Flight 007. [18]

In early October, just after the black boxes from Flight 007 were reported to have been recovered and the reports were denied, the U.S. vessels operating in the Sea of Japan were said to have entered a new phase of activity—scanning and mapping the sea floor. [19] Although the world's attention had turned from Flight 007, there was still a substantial flotilla in the Sea of Japan. The U.S. continued to operate seven of its own ships plus three leased Japanese vessels. There were about half a dozen Soviet ships operating in the area as well, and tensions in the area were still running high. [20]

As the second month after the downing drew to a close, there were increasingly high seas and winds, as well as rain, sleet, and snow. On November 5, the search for the wreckage from Flight 007 officially ended. The commander-in-chief of Pacific forces reported that "a painstaking search of all likely areas in international waters has been completed. Using every technical means at our disposal, we have exhausted any reasonable chance of finding the wreckage." A Pentagon spokesman reiterated,

"We've looked everywhere we think it might be, and we haven't found a thing. Maybe it's lying within Russian waters. But that's another thing. They won't let us in." On November 9, the Japanese followed the American lead and stopped all search efforts. The Soviets stopped theirs a day later.[21]

It had been a costly effort. By the end of the operation, more than 3,000 hours had been flown by U.S. aircraft and more than 320 ship-days steamed by Navy vessels. The cost of the operation to the American taxpayers was estimated to be $22.4 million. Yet, according to all public accounts, the location of the main wreckage was never determined. Not a single piece of flotsam was recovered by the U.S. No aircraft fragments or personal effects were said to have been recovered during those thousands of flight hours and hundreds of ship days.[22]

The implausibility of the official story was shown on June 23, 1985, when an Air India Boeing 747, Flight 182, exploded in midair as the result of a bomb. The airliner crashed about 90 miles off the coast of Ireland, killing all 329 people on board. The wreckage scattered over a 4-mile stretch of seafloor at a depth of 6,700 feet—well over twice the depth of the very deepest part of the search area in the Sea of Japan. With far fewer vessels participating in the search and with considerably less equipment, the airliner's black boxes were quickly located. Within two weeks of the tragedy they were raised from that great depth using a Submersible Craft for Assisting Repair and Burial (SCARAB—an unmanned sub normally used for laying and repairing undersea telephone cables). In addition, more than 100 bodies were recovered, along with a wide assortment of floating debris, much of it from the baggage hold of the aircraft. Most if not all of the flotsam from Flight 007, to the contrary, appeared to have come from the passenger compartment.[23] As the *New York Times* wondered at the time, "If the Air India flight recorders can be recovered from 6,700 feet, why not those from the Korean Air Lines 747?"[24]

17

THE INTERNATIONAL CIVIL AVIATION ORGANIZATION (ICAO)

The United Nations' International Civil Aviation Organization was organized in 1947 to encourage the orderly growth of international civil aviation. A specialized agency, the ICAO usually addresses issues such as aviation noise standards, uniform standards for aircraft markings, standards for airworthiness, international navigation rules, and the licensing of pilots. ICAO also renders technical assistance to member nations, especially in aviation training. The organization is governed by an assembly, composed of one representative from each of its 151 member nations, which meets every three years. A 33-member governing council oversees the affairs of the ICAO between meetings.[1]

Because of its technical orientation, the ICAO has not generally been used as a forum for international bombast and deception, as so many other U.N. agencies have. Only rarely has it found itself embroiled in issues transcending its technical focus. During the late 1960s and early 1970s, the ICAO spent a great deal of time considering effective international responses to the problem of airline hijackings. Prior to 1983, the only ICAO investigation involving the downing of an airliner was when Israeli fighters shot down a Libyan airliner over the Sinai in 1973. The Israeli action was condemned, although then, as now, ICAO had no power to impose sanctions.[2]

For the Reagan administration, there were several benefits to presenting the downing of Flight 007 before the ICAO. First, the U.N. agency was an international forum, serving the Administration's desire to portray the incident as "the Soviet Union versus the world." Because in the ICAO there is no veto power and a resolution can pass with a simple majority, the U.S. could reasonably expect to push through a resolution condemning the downing similar to the one vetoed by the Russians in the Security Council. In addition, the ICAO had very limited facilities to conduct an inquiry. Any "investigation" could in fact be no more than an analysis based on whatever information member nations chose to provide. The reason the ICAO served these purposes springs from the essential nature of the United Nations itself. As Conor Cruise O'Brien wrote in *The New Republic,* "The United Nations cannot do anything, and never could. It is a place, a stage, a forum, and a shrine. . . . If there is something you are expected to do, but don't want to do, or even have done for you, you can safely appeal to the U.N. in the comfortable certainty that it will let you down." The only way an inquiry by the ICAO could hope to get at the truth would be if member nations cooperated fully and had nothing to hide.[3]

The nations with relevant information about the downing of Flight 007 were the United States, Japan, the Republic of Korea, and the Soviet Union. Japan and the U.S. were members of ICAO, and along with South Korea had a strong vested interest in limiting the investigation to those facts injurious to the Soviet Union. While the Soviets, also members of ICAO, might have had abundant reason to produce evidence supporting their claims that Flight 007 was part of an intelligence operation, doing so would disclose details about the capabilities and limitations of their air defense systems. This they were extremely unlikely to do.

Almost immediately after the shootdown, calls for a meeting of ICAO's governing council were heard. Even before Secretary of State Shultz made his statement on the morning of September 1, South Korean consul general to the ICAO Kim Chang-hun met in Montreal with Assad Kotaite, the secretary general of the ICAO council. Kotaite said that the ICAO would give the South Korean government "full assistance" in ascertaining the fate of the missing airliner. After the fate of the airliner became known, Kotaite responded to a South Korean request to schedule an extraordinary session of the governing council for 10:00 A.M. on September 15. The Republic of Korea was invited to attend the meeting as an observer.[4]

On numerous occasions during the next two weeks, U.S. officials emphasized the importance of the upcoming meeting. On September 14, President Reagan met in the Oval Office with his key transportation aides to set the strategy for the upcoming session. FAA Administrator J. Lynn Helms was selected to head the U.S. delegation, temporarily replacing Edmund Stohr, a former executive of United Airlines, the U.S.'s permanent delegate to ICAO. Helms would be accompanied to Montreal by

Transportation Secretary Elizabeth H. Dole. Helms had attended the expanded National Security Council session on September 2, when much of the strategy for the U.S. response to the downing had been formulated. During the meeting, Reagan instructed Helms to "keep ICAO focused on Soviet responsibility and not get bogged down in details" and to "achieve passage of a solid resolution that condemns the act of violence," with an investigation to follow.[5] This continued the approach used by the Administration from the outset: limit discussion of the incident, pronounce the Russians guilty, and then investigate that guilt along lines established by the Administration.

As the meeting opened on the morning of September 15, the United States, Japan, Canada, France, West Germany, Brazil, and several other council members denounced the Soviet Union and called for an inquiry into the downing of Flight 007. Dr. Kun Park, head of the ROK Foreign Ministry's Foreign Affairs and National Security Institute, compared the downing of Flight 007 to "a little deer being stealthily trailed and hunted down by a savage animal." Not unexpectedly, the Soviet Union took a somewhat different approach, and there were few surprises during their turn to address the council. No new information was offered, with their arguments turning on the information already made public in official statements.[6]

Soviet permanent representative to the ICAO Ivan Orlovets restated the Soviet position that Flight 007 had been coordinated with an RC-135 reconnaissance aircraft and that both U.S. and Japanese military officials had known the airliner was off course but did nothing to direct it back. In making his points, Orlovets used an overhead projector to display a chart similar to the one used by Marshal Ogarkov at his September 9 press conference. As members of the council looked on, Orlovets traced the series of events off the Kamchatka coast with a pointer. J. Lynn Helms busily took notes, at one point jumping up to point out a technical error in one of the charts that suggested an impossible flight speed for the Korean airliner. The Soviet delegate concluded that the ICAO had no business conducting an inquiry into the downing since a Soviet special commission had already been formed. "We believe those guilty should be punished," chimed in V. I. Sazhin, the executive secretary of the Soviet Union's Commission on International Civil Aviation. Sazhin said that a list of U.S. and Korean air violations would also be made public when the Soviet special commission had finished its inquiry into the incident.[7]

Then it was the Americans' turn. J. Lynn Helms strongly condemned the downing of Flight 007, calling it "a grave threat to the safety of the international civil aviation system" and "terrorist action." In a dramatic gesture, Helms held up a piece of paper. "I have here in my hand a detailed list of over a page of Aeroflot violations of U.S. airspace, showing the date and the aircraft," he said. At a press conference afterwards—a press attaché had been assigned to the delegation to help coordinate the media interest in the ICAO council meeting—Helms told reporters that there were twelve or fourteen such violations. (However, members of Helms' staff would not release copies to the press.)[8]

The next morning, the ICAO council met to consider a resolution introduced by Canada and sponsored by ten other countries, including the United States. The resolution, referred to by J. Lynn Helms as "the strongest pre-investigation resolution in the history of ICAO," "deeply deplored" the Soviet action, which was "incompatible with the norms governing international behavior and elementary considerations of humanity." In addition, there were calls to permit the bereaved families access to the crash site and to study international navigational rules to prevent recurrence. Finally, the resolution directed ICAO's secretary general to investigate the incident, provide an interim report to the council at its meeting a month later, and prepare a final report by the middle of December.[9]

The Soviet delegation tried to delay indefinitely a vote on the resolution but lost by a vote of twenty-five to two, with five abstentions. When Secretary General Kotaite called for a vote, the resolution was overwhelmingly adopted. Of the thirty-three member nations of the ICAO governing council, twenty-six voted for the resolution.[10] Only Czechoslovakia and the Soviet Union opposed it. Algeria, China, and India abstained from voting because they felt the language of the resolution was too strongly political. Iraq and Lebanon were not present at the time of the vote. The vote effectively blocked a vote on the competing Soviet resolution condemning the crew of Flight 007 and ground personnel in Japan and the United States. Kotaite requested that "all information related to this incident . . . be handed over to the ICAO as soon as possible."[11]

Reactions to the voting were predictably mixed. "We are pleased," J. Lynn Helms told reporters afterwards, "at the very, very strong support that has been evidenced by the world civil aviation community as reflected by the strong positive vote." The Russians felt otherwise. Ivan Orlovets remarked that the Soviets had been beaten by a "voting machine," and *Pravda* commented afterwards that a "lopsided resolution was adopted under the pressure of the United States and some of its allies, which sidestepped the main issue." "No one has talked about anybody being responsible except the USSR," Orlovets complained.[12]

A central need in the propaganda battle between the superpowers over the downing of Flight 007, both inside and outside the United Nations, was to assert the legality or illegality of the Soviet action. From the outset, the downing was described by President Reagan as a "murder" and a "crime against humanity" without legal justification. Charles Lichenstein noted in a letter to the president of the U.N. Security Council on September 1 that it was "the considered position of the Government of the United States of America" that the downing represented a "contravention of International Civil Aviation Organization standards and the basic norms of international law."[13]

Similarly, the Soviets described the intrusion as a violation of the regulations in the 1947 Chicago Convention on International Civil Aviation and said the behavior of Flight 007 was "contrary to ICAO standards." They claimed that the United States and Japan had violated international treaties which require the proper control of aircraft in their area of flight responsibilities. While the intrusion was a "criminal action," the Soviet response was "fully in keeping with the Law of the State Border of the USSR." This law, enacted nine months before the downing, was described by the *New York Times* as "one of the harshest such laws anywhere." Article 38 "specifically provides for the air defense forces to use 'weapons and combat equipment' against aircraft that intrude into Soviet airspace that cannot be detained by any other means." No distinction between civilian and military aircraft was made. A parade of Soviet legal experts defended the downing as "in full accordance with the established international regulations of flight." [14]

Some experts in the West argued that downing the airliner was illegal even if it had intentionally entered Soviet airspace to gather intelligence because the reaction was too severe, violating the principle of "proportionality" in international law. Others disagreed. "You can never say that anyone is entitled to kill another 269 human beings," said a spokesman for the Geneva-based International Air Transport Association, "but the Soviet Union followed the standard recognized procedure and, leaving aside the humanitarian and moral case, they have a pretty sound case in law." [15]

The resolution passed by the governing council directed ICAO Secretary General Yves Lambert to determine the facts of the flight. Time was short: An interim report was due on October 16, and a completed report at the 110th session of the council, scheduled to conclude on December 16. Lambert immediately formed a probe team, composed of members from Lebanon, Finland, the Netherlands, Pakistan, Sweden, and Britain. The team provided its first progress report to the governing council on September 20. One of its first decisions was that the flight recorders, if they were recovered from the Sea of Japan, should be examined by an impartial nation. Lambert selected France and promptly made arrangements for the transport and extraction of data from the flight recorders in a French laboratory if they were recovered. Observers from the nations directly involved would be invited to be present during the entire operation. [16]

The United States and its allies attempted to embarrass the Soviets at the session of the ICAO general assembly beginning the first week in October. A few nations, led by New Zealand, suggested submitting a proposal that would bar the Soviet Union from membership on ICAO's thirty-three-member governing council. This approach was publicly endorsed by several U.S. congressmen, notably Senate Foreign Relations Committee Chairman Charles H. Percy and Senate Minority Leader Robert C. Byrd, and privately reaffirmed in letters to the President and Secretary of State. A strategy more likely to succeed, however, was advanced by the Republic of Korea. This was to try to influence the voting for the top eleven spots on the council, an implicit statement that the Soviet Union was not among the world's top aviation nations. The initiative failed.[17]

On Thursday, October 20, the ICAO inquiry team delivered its confidential interim report to a closed session of ICAO's thirty-three-member governing council. It was a six-page description of a fact-finding trip originating in New York, with stops in Anchorage, Seoul, and Tokyo, to interview air traffic controllers and other relevant personnel. The team members were received on U.S. and Japanese vessels operating on the Sea of Japan. Since October 10, the team had been assembling its material at the ICAO regional office in Bangkok, Thailand.[18]

ICAO Secretary General Yves Lambert had formally requested that the governments of Japan, South Korea, the Soviet Union, and the United States cooperate fully with the inquiry team. The interim report noted that the United States, Japan, and South Korea were cooperating but that "no answer has yet been received" regarding the team's request to visit the Soviet Union. In an effort to deflect criticism, Soviet delegate Ivan Orlovets extended an offer to the secretary general to visit the Soviet Union the following month. Lambert promptly accepted the offer and designated Mohammed Y. Wazirzoda of Pakistan, a member of ICAO's Bangkok regional office, to accompany him on the trip.[19]

Between November 11 and 17, Lambert traveled to the Soviet Union, where he received what he described as "specific information" about the destruction of Flight 007. Although Lambert refused to make the information public upon his return, Western diplomatic sources said that Lambert had received a copy of the report of the State Commission for Civil Aviation Flight Safety in the USSR (Gosavianadzor), which contained no new evidence and continued to blame the United States for using the Korean airliner for espionage. In their continuing bid to deflect some of the criticism they expected when the ICAO report was released, the leadership in Moscow announced on December 2 that a new unified air traffic control system for the Soviet Union was being created "in connection with the implementation of the provisions of the air code of the USSR."[20]

On December 5, advance copies of the ICAO inquiry team's report were distributed to the thirty-three members of the organization's governing council, and it was not long before the press had copies. Before the report's findings could be analyzed or verified, the media immediately jumped onto the ICAO bandwagon. *The Far Eastern Economic Review,* a journal that had been trying for months to figure out how the airliner could have arrived at Sakhalin accidentally, announced that "a lengthy technical report by a team of experts . . . is probably the last word on what led to the disaster. . . . It lays firmly to rest any possible suspicion that the airliner was on a spying mission for the United States or anyone else." The *Washington Post* concluded that the report "supports the theory that human error in operating navigation equipment led the airliner to stray off course."[21]

The report's biases and limitations went unreported. Take, for example, the assertion that the ICAO report, in the words of the *Washington Post,* "rejects the Kremlin's contention that the plane was on a spy mission." But the ICAO inquiry team did not conclude that. The report rejected the Soviet claim that Flight 007's "departure time from Anchorage was . . . delayed by forty minutes to coincide with certain satellite orbital positions or passages." For this reason alone, "the investigation did not consider further the hypothesis" of "a premeditated deviation from the flight plan route for intelligence gathering purposes." Alexander Dallin quite correctly pointed out that this "cannot be characterized as anything but a whitewash on this issue. The reasons for this," he says, "are a matter of speculation," although "the influence of the United States in the ICAO is not likely to be irrelevant." As Dallin wrote, "It is of course possible— indeed, even sensible—to dismiss the forty-minute-delay argument and still entertain the 'secret mission' alternative." [22] But that was not done by the ICAO team, which ruled intentionality out of court as one of the inquiry's ground rules. It is hardly surprising, therefore, that an intentional course deviation did not emerge as the report's conclusion.

Without compelling theoretical reasons, a refusal to consider alternative causes for an event is known, in scientific investigation, as bias. For example, the report states the following:

> Since the aircraft's flight progress was routinely reported by the flight crew as if it were proceeding along the assigned route and since no transmissions from the aircraft were received in Anchorage and Tokyo other than routine reports and requests for a change in cruising level, there was no indication that the pilot knew or suspected that the aircraft was off track. [23]

Assuming that the airliner's deviation was accidental, as the ICAO team did, then routine reports would obviously indicate a lack of knowledge by the pilot. However, a pilot flying a deliberately illegal course could offer routine reports to controllers in order to disguise his actions. Had the ICAO inquiry team considered this possibility, its conclusion might have read: "Since the aircraft's flight progress was routinely reported by the flight crew, they were either unaware they were off track or were intentionally falsifying their reports." Other evidence would then have to be examined to determine which explanation was more likely.

Presuming the innocence of the flight from the start rather than making that a subject of analysis produced some curious results. In discussing the interception of the airliner over Kamchatka and Sakhalin, for example, the ICAO report noted, "In the absence of any indication that the flight crew of KE007 was aware of the two interception attempts, it was concluded that they were not." [24] There are two problems with this: First, there is a problem of logic. The statement is logically indistinguishable from saying,

"In the absence of a confession from the accused, it was assumed he was innocent." Second, the statement that there was no indication that Flight 007's crew was aware of the interception is not true. The remarks of the Soviet fighter pilots provide precisely such indications.

Just how comprehensive was the ICAO team's inquiry? A Department of State white paper called it an "authoritative account" of the incident. Not even the U.S. delegates to the ICAO, however, made such a claim. As Duane Freer, the director of the Air Navigation Bureau, pointed out, the ICAO has investigated only two aviation disasters in its 41-year history. "We're not in the business of doing that," Freer said in an interview with *The Nation*. "We had a short time frame to determine the technical aspects of the accident. A full-fledged state investigation goes into greater detail." Freer compared the ICAO inquiry with the National Transportation Safety Board's investigation following the crash of a DC-10 airliner at Chicago's O'Hare Airport in 1979, on which a team of more than one hundred people worked for seven months. In contrast, the ICAO inquiry employed just five full-time and three part-time investigators, and completed the report in just 60 days.[25]

Did the team have access to all relevant information? The ICAO has no power to subpoena witnesses or documents, and had to rely wholly on the information presented to it by member governments, all highly interested parties. The ICAO report itself notes that the inquiry team "was not provided any radar recordings, recorded communications, or transcripts associated with the first intercept attempt [over Kamchatka] or for the ground-to-intercept portion of the second attempt [over Sakhalin]; therefore it was not possible to fully assess the comprehensiveness or otherwise of the application of intercept procedures, signaling and communications." The State Department would later claim that the information withheld from ICAO by Japan and the U.S. "did not pertain to the Flight of Korea 007." As would become clear later, the team was also not provided with Japanese radar data, publicly released by the Nakasone government more than a year later, which suggest that the airliner changed altitude and speed over Sakhalin. The team was not informed that military radar data from Alaska pertinent to the incident had been destroyed by the Air Force. In fact, so limited was the information provided to the inquiry team that frustration occasionally set in. At the ICAO's year-end session, one of the U.S. delegates was denouncing the Soviets for not having participated in the inquiry. "And what government is it," he asked, pointing a rhetorical finger at the Soviet Union, "that has withheld information from this inquiry?" The answer came from an unexpected quarter: Yves Lambert, the normally cautious ICAO secretary general. He responded, "The governments of the Soviet Union, the United States, Japan, and the Republic of Korea."[26]

Not only was material withheld from the ICAO, but there are also questions about the materials that were produced. Perhaps the most serious of these concerns the transcript of the transmissions by the Soviet fighter pilots over Sakhalin. Since a major concern of the ICAO team was to assess the interception procedures used by the Soviet air defense forces, it would seem important to consider whether warning shots were fired. But the transcript produced by the ICAO team did not include the revision announced by the State Department on September 11. The team's conclusion: " These monitored communications contained no reference to firing of warning bursts of tracer shells." [27]

The second misrepresentation is more serious. This has to do with the Sukhoi-15 pilot's remark at 1810:51 GMT. The original U.S. transcript released to the press rendered this passage as: "Roger, [the target's strobe] light is blinking," using brackets to create the impression that the Soviet pilot referred to Flight 007's lights rather than his own, although that is by no means certain. When properly translated, this remark reads, "Roger. She is going with a blinking light." But the passage in the ICAO report is rendered: "Roger. Target is flying with strobe light, with strobe light." [28] The bracketed remarks about strobe lights, which do not appear in the Soviet pilot's transmissions, were given new life by the ICAO report.

A final example of misrepresentation is the conversation, beginning at 1835:27, between the pilot of the Soviet MiG-23 interceptor known as 121 and the ground controller Trikotazh. In the transcript released at the United Nations by Ambassador Kirkpatrick, the following conversation appeared:

121—	(Call)
Trikotazh—	(Answering)
121—	Trikotazh answered me.
121—	Do you see the target?
Trikotazh—	No, I don't see it.
121—	He doesn't see the target.

In this passage, interceptor 121, hunting for the "target," called his ground controller Deputat (whose remarks are not included), but another ground station, Trikotazh, unexpectedly answered. Pilot 121 reported to Deputat that "Trikotazh answered me." The MiG-23 pilot then directly asked Trikotazh whether he could see the target. Trikotazh said no, and 121 so informed Deputat. [29] The conversation on the original Russian tape includes two distinctly different voices, one much deeper than the other, talking back and forth.

But the ICAO transcript attributed all of the remarks by Trikotazh to the MiG pilot 121:

121—	(Call)
121—	(Call)

121—	Trikotazh is answering.
121—	Do you see the target?
121—	No, I don't see it.
121—	He doesn't see the target.[30]

The conversation was rendered as a monologue. This suggests both that the ICAO did not listen to the original voice tapes and that it was attempting to avoid challenging the Reagan administration's contention that ground controllers' voices could not be recorded.

The closer one looks at the transcript, the worse things get. Take pilot 805. Concerned about how much fuel he had left, he reported the amount to his ground controllers on several occasions. At 1807:50, he had 3 metric tons of fuel. At 1814:41 he had 2.7 tons. By 1826:53, just after the missile attack, he was down to 1.6 metric tons. Airplanes burn fuel, of course, but how much? During the earlier parts of the interception, the aircraft was climbing and accelerating to catch up to the target, which increases fuel use. Later, the fighter was flying at a relatively constant altitude and speed and weighed less, since some fuel had been burned off. Thus, it should have been using less. But a little simple arithmetic shows that the fighter was burning 97 pounds of fuel per minute during the first period of time and 199 pounds per minute later on.[31] The only way this could happen was if the pilot was using his fuel-guzzling afterburner, but he explicitly reported to his ground control station that he was not. This seemingly impossible situation raises the possibility that there is something wrong with the sequence or timing of the transmissions found on the audio materials used by the ICAO.[32] Could the tapes themselves have been altered?

The ICAO report is full of sloppiness, carelessness and inconsistencies. For example, the body of the report says that the VOR/DME navigational aid in Anchorage was out of service from 2217 hours on August 23 until 0039 hours on September 2. This is an error. In one of the appendices, the outage was correctly dated from 0139 hours on August 31 until 0039 hours on September 2.[33] The effect of this error was to make it appear that the outage—which was never adequately explained—began days before Flight 007 arrived in Anchorage. In fact it went out of service just 11 hours earlier. Furthermore, the ICAO report contains a transcript of the communications between Flight 007 and air traffic controllers in Alaska and Japan that is absolutely plagued with inaccuracies.

The final radio transmission from Flight 007, a critical passage, was also handled badly. "After extensive analysis and filtering of noise," the report says, "the following words were discernible. 'Korean Air zero zero seven . . . (unintelligible) . . . rapid   compressions . . . (unintelligible) . . . descending to one zero thousand."[34] An appendix to the report states that this was only a "best interpretation" of the transmission, but in the body of the report there are no brackets around the words "rapid compressions" or "descending to one zero thousand." However, an independent analysis of this material concludes that they do not appear on the tape. Once again, the ICAO report presented as a certainty something that was in reality extremely problematic.

The ICAO investigation's attempts to explain how Flight 007 got to Kamchatka and Sakhalin are the basis of the Administration's claim that "human error in operating navigational equipment led the airliner to stray off course." The simulations were conducted by the Boeing Company of Seattle, Washington, working with consultants from Litton Industries, Korean Air Lines, and the Korean and U.S. governments. Although best known as the maker of commercial airplanes like the 747, Boeing is one of the nation's top defense contractors, realizing more than twice as much profit from military as from commercial sales. Litton, the maker of the INS, is also a major supplier of electronic warfare and other equipment, with annual sales to the Department of Defense of about $360 million.[35] Thus, a case could be made that the simulations were not objective, since the participating parties were all highly interested in the outcome.

Actually, the ICAO team presented six simulations, but four of them were either so implausible or led the aircraft to places so far from where it actually went that they were never seriously considered. This left only two others. The first "convincing scenario," as the *Far Eastern Economic Review* called it, did not even convince the ICAO team. This model of the flight posited that the INS automatic pilot selector switch in the cockpit was improperly set to "heading mode," an error that allowed the aircraft to be navigated by its magnetic compass instead of the INS. The major problems with this scenario noted in the ICAO report were that under these circumstances the airliner would have passed only 6.5 nautical miles north of Bethel, its first waypoint, rather than the 12 nautical miles actually observed, and that a 246-degree magnetic heading would not have taken the plane to Sakhalin Island but about 100 miles farther south.[36]

In addition, the 246-degree magnetic heading theory requires that we accept an unbelievable string of failures, errors, negligence, and gross incompetence.[37] Although the ICAO report does not discuss them, these include:

1. That the flight crew did not notice for five and a half hours that the automatic pilot mode selector switch, located at eye level on the airliner's instrument panel, was in fact improperly set to "heading mode";

2. That the crew forgot to use the VOR/DME (Very High Frequency Omni Range/Distance Measuring Equipment) beacon at Bethel, although it is required Korean Air Lines procedure to do so. Since the VOR in Anchorage was out of service, Bethel was an important opportunity for the crew to verify their position before a long overwater flight;

3. That the crew somehow failed to notice that none of the normal course adjustments made by the INS at waypoints occurred;

4. That for a full five and a half hours neither Captain Chun nor First Officer Sohn bothered to check the "cross track distance/ track angle error" readout on the INS, which would have shown them how far off course they were, although this is a customary and prudent practice;

5. That the pilots never bothered to use their on-board radar in ground-mapping mode, although to do so is customary practice and many pilots consider it a valuable cross-check on their navigation;

6. That the crew never thought it unusual that they could not receive the signal from the NDB/DME (Non-Directional Beacon/ Distance Measuring Equipment) navigational aid at waypoint NABIE, although KAL procedures required them to use the aid as a cross-check on the INS;

7. That the crew never bothered to compare the waypoint coordinates on their computerized flight plan to those displayed on the INS when they arrived at a waypoint, although this is required —indeed, that is what waypoints are for;

8. That the crew never thought it unusual that they could neither send nor receive messages from air traffic controllers over their VHF (Very High Frequency) radios for a protracted period;

9. That they somehow neglected to notice that they did not receive signals from the VOR/DME navigational aid located on Shemya Island. Verifying one's position by the Shemya beacon is especially important because it is immediately thereafter that route Romeo-20 passes close to Soviet territory, and, as with the other aids, the crew was also required by company procedures to use the beacon;

10. That the crew never bothered to look at their Horizontal Situation Indicators, another instrument in the cockpit that would have shown for the entire flight that the plane was off course. Both the captain's and first officer's HSIs are located in conspicuous positions;

11. That nobody ever bothered to look at the "distance/time" reading that is normally displayed continually on one of the INS systems. This information provides a "countdown" in time and distance to the next waypoint. Because Flight 007 never actually

arrived at its waypoints, the distance and time would never tick down to zero, as they should. For example, when Flight 007 reported its position at NEEVA, the INS would have indicated that there were still several hundred miles and about half an hour to go, instead of giving readings of zero;

12. That, finally, the scenario cannot account for any turns, changes in speed, and changes in altitude which were made by Flight 007.

The most convincing argument against the 246-degree magnetic heading scenario, however, comes from the fact that from the moment Flight 007 was cleared "direct Bethel" shortly after takeoff, it was the INS, not the magnetic compass, that navigated the airplane. As 747 pilot Harold Ewing explained:

> Use of the INS in a case like this is such standard practice as to be virtually universal . . . [and] any model involving the crew of KE007 attempting to fly to Bethel at this point using any navigational means other than the INS is not tenable. Such a model would: require the crew to ignore the simple and easy way of getting to Bethel, for no identifiable reason; posit them imposing upon themselves, again for no clear reason, additional workloads associated with a task which they had no physical means of accomplishing anyway, i.e., navigating to Bethel without the INS; involve a technical violation of their ATC [Air Traffic Control] clearance; presume that a crew of a carrier well known for its high degree of interest in fuel savings would deliberately choose a significantly less fuel efficient method of operation than another equally available to them, and so on.[38]

That the INS was indeed used is more than speculation about good airmanship; it can be demonstrated. This is because Flight 007 was tracked by two radars whose data were made public: the civil radar at Kenai and the military radar at King Salmon. Properly analyzed—something the ICAO team apparently did not do—the data show Flight 007 to be flying an absolutely perfect great circle course from the time it was cleared "direct Bethel" until the Alaskan coast, a distance of approximately 400 miles.[39] As Ewing observed:

> The probabilities of an aircraft flying a constant magnetic heading, while climbing through and laterally transiting a windfield which is thus changing both as a result of altitude and distance, achieving this level of congruity with a perfect great-circle course, are vanishingly small.[40]

Although some writers, notably Australian journalist Murray Sayle, have embraced and vociferously defended this explanation, on the basis of the evidence it can be safely rejected.

The second scenario advanced by ICAO was equally dubious. This involved inserting a single incorrect number into one of the three inertial navigation systems, with the result that Flight 007 began deviating from course upon takeoff. The suggestion was that the longitude for Anchorage, the point of origin, was entered into the INS as 139 degrees 58 minutes, instead of the correct 149 degrees 58 minutes. Such an error would have had the effect of displacing the entire course flown by the airliner, taking it more or less to where it actually flew. "It is a very real possibility," declared FAA Administrator J. Lynn Helms. "I have not seen any that are more likely."[41]

However, although this course would have gotten Flight 007 to Sakhalin, it wouldn't have gotten it to Bethel. Flight 007 would have passed not 12 nautical miles north of Bethel, as we know it did, but rather 38 nautical miles. While this point alone should have been enough to throw the scenario out, there are still other problems. With the triply-redundant INS, an error in one machine will be spotted by the others. As the ICAO report noted, "The INS comparator system would automatically detect the difference between the units." This would be apparent to the crew because "the data display of the affected unit would flash."[42] Since the erroneous number posited by this scenario would have been the first of a long series of numbers entered into the INS, the flashing data display would have been difficult to miss. It would not have stopped flashing until the error to which it referred was corrected.

The principal problem with this scenario, however, has to do with its effect on the position reports offered by Captain Chun and his crew. If the coordinate 139 degrees 58 minutes W longitude was inserted as the aircraft's point of origin, the INS would "think" it was beginning its flight at that point, located in the Gulf of Alaska off the Alaskan panhandle, about 300 miles from Anchorage. But the scenario also requires that all the other coordinates—including those for Bethel, the first waypoint—were entered correctly into the INS. The INS computer would thus believe that the first leg of the trip was from the Alaskan panhandle to Bethel, a distance of about 650 nautical miles, 300 nautical miles greater than the distance between Anchorage and Bethel.

The results of such an error would have been apparent to the crew as they approached Bethel. They had flown the route before and knew that flight time to the waypoint was about 50 minutes. In case they forgot, they also had their computerized flight plan in the cockpit with the estimated travel time to Bethel written on it. The crew should have been especially alert at this time since they were required to make their first position report at Bethel. Imagine the surprise of an innocent crew when the waypoint alert lights failed to illuminate (because the INS believed the waypoint to still lie some 300 miles away). Imagine their surprise when they looked at the "distance/time" reading on their INS, showing about 300 nautical miles and half an hour to the waypoint! If they were using their instruments, an innocent crew would have had no reason to make a position report at that time. But the crew of Flight 007 did, right on time.

To these considerations, it is also necessary to add virtually all of the errors, failures, and oversights listed for the 246-degree magnetic heading theory as well. Under this scenario the crew still is assumed to have forgotten to use the VOR/DME navigational aids at waypoints Bethel and NEEVA, and the NDB/DME aid at NABIE. The same lack of interest in why their radios did not work and the same failure to use their weather radar are required. Like the other scenario, this is, to say the least, extremely unconvincing.

The ICAO team did find it difficult to understand "the causes of and duration of the divergence," listing the failure to use the Bethel VOR, the failure to receive the navigational signals at waypoints NABIE and NEEVA, and the lack of use of the weather radar. In fact, their report explicitly stated that "in all of the scenarios it must be appreciated that . . . information would be readily available to alert the flight crew that their navigation was not in accordance with the flight plan." The investigators concluded that "in the absence of the flight data recorder and the cockpit voice recorder, there was insufficient information to draw firm conclusions." A stronger statement was later made in court testimony by a representative from Litton, producer of the INS and one of the participants in producing the scenarios: "Certain simulated flight paths were run on the Boeing simulator at the request and under the direction of ICAO," he said, "and at best, these are hypothetical flight paths. They are not by any stretch of the imagination a recreation of an actual flight path flown by this airplane." [43]

Then why were the scenarios even presented? And how could State Department officials claim that the ICAO report concluded there was "no evidence of any deliberateness in KAL 007's deviation"? Part of the answer may be that most members of the press and public never read the report, which was hard to obtain. Another reason is that a narrow, out-of-context reading of some of the report's passages seems to support the Administration's claim. For example, the report says that the scenarios it presented "assumed a considerable degree of lack of alertness and attentiveness on the part of the entire flight crew but not to a degree that was unknown in international civil aviation." [44] All official comments on the ICAO investigation refer to this passage. The report says that accidents *can* happen, so the Administration and its defenders say this therefore must have been an accident.

The ICAO report quickly became the Administration's "last word" on the downing and the centerpiece of its effort to silence those who continued to raise questions, a rubber stamp for its official line. A State Department official wrote to the congressman of one of Flight 007's victims:

> [The ICAO] final report, meticulously drawing on all available evidence, provides the clearest and fullest explanation to date of what

happened to the KAL civilian airliner . . . . The ICAO report clearly establishes that there was no indication that the pilot of KAL 007 ever knew he was off course or that he was aware of any Soviet efforts to warn his aircraft. . . . The report concludes that KAL 007 was not on an intelligence mission.[45]

As another State Department official put it, once those conclusions were accepted, it followed that "no useful purpose would be served by additional investigation."[46]

The thirty-three-member ICAO governing council began its two-week, closed-door consideration of what J. Lynn Helms called "a meticulously researched report" on Monday, December 12. Lobbying for the report's release at the start of the session, the U.S. delegation wrote to Washington that it had "scored a major victory" in the council's decision to declassify and release the entire report to the public. Included in the report, however, was a submission by the Soviet Union, and this came under sharp attack as soon as the session was underway. Helms said the Soviet report lacked the minimum standards of credibility because of its lack of supporting data, and suggested that it be viewed solely as a political tract. The Russians were lambasted for their "noncooperation" in the ICAO team's inquiry, and Secretary General Yves Lambert, who opened the session, was hotly criticized by the U.S. delegation because "at several points [he] appeared to give equal credence to the Soviet claims as to the conclusions drawn by the ICAO team."[47]

The fifteen-nation Air Navigation Commission (ANC), the ICAO's technical evaluation panel, was directed to provide a report "as early as possible" to the ICAO council. As with the ICAO inquiry itself, the U.S. wanted to circumscribe the ANC's evaluation, and before long the U.S. delegation reported to Washington that "the U.S. was instrumental in restricting the ANC's review to . . . the subject of identification and interception of civil aircraft. . . . As originally drafted, the ANC would have been able to 'second guess' all aspects of the ICAO report." The group completed its report on February 2, 1984.[48] Final delivery to the council of the fifteen-page document, translated into the U.N.'s four official languages, took place on February 27.[49]

The language of the ANC report was hotly debated. The Russians wanted the report to stress that Anchorage air traffic controllers should have known something was amiss with the flight, while the U.S. and its allies preferred emphasizing that the flight "was not intentional [and] the allegation that it was engaged in intelligence gathering has no ground whatever." Soviet representatives contested every sentence that implied criticism of the USSR. The U.S. recommended that the word "allegedly" precede all Soviet claims. In ambiguous cases, such as the rendering of Flight 007's final radio transmission, the U.S. delegation's recommended interpretation included words that supported the official U.S. version of events.[50]

The ANC final report confirmed that the information available to the ICAO inquiry team had been limited: "The commission recognized that the team of specialists, for reasons beyond its control, was unable to obtain all the information it needed," the report said.[51] And it noted that there was "insufficient information" to determine whether the Soviets had properly followed internationally accepted procedures in intercepting Flight 007. The conclusion of the ANC report, however, was damning:

> The Air Navigation Commission is unable to establish the exact cause for the significant deviation from track. The magnitude of the diversion cannot be explained, particularly as the aircraft was equipped with navigation equipment which should have enabled the crew to adhere to its track. . . . Furthermore, the commission found it difficult to validate and endorse the conclusions connected with the scenarios postulated in the Secretary General's report because any one of them contained some points which could not be explained satisfactorily.[52]

In other words, the ICAO's expert technical panel was dubious about the navigational scenarios offered in the ICAO report.

Unlike the ICAO report, which the U.S. delegation actively sought to make public, the ANC report was ignored for as long as possible. When word of the ANC's refusal to endorse the scenarios contained in the ICAO report finally began leaking out in print, Administration officials used selective and out-of-context quotations to claim that the Air Navigation Commission's findings supported their official version of events. It was noted, for example, that the ANC report said "the handling staff at New York and Anchorage had free access to all parts of the aircraft, and none of these personnel reported any unusual equipment or structural changes."[53] The implicit suggestion was that the ANC had investigated the possibility of espionage and found none, but this is false. And an aircraft used as a passive probe to test Soviet air defenses would not require "unusual equipment or structural changes."

The ICAO governing council met from February 29 to March 6 to consider the Air Navigation Commission's findings and a U.S. resolution, cosponsored by a number of Western nations including Japan and Canada, that "condemns the use of armed force which resulted in the destruction of the Korean airliner and the tragic loss of 269 lives." The resolution "deeply deplores the Soviet failure to cooperate in the search and rescue efforts of other involved states and the Soviet failure to cooperate with the ICAO investigation of the incident" and strongly endorsed the ICAO report.[54]

In an effort to defeat the resolution, Soviet delegate Boris Rygenkov repeated that the airliner was on a spy mission and that his country's "measures to protect its airspace were in accord with the rules and procedures of international law." The Russians distributed a brochure to buttress their case and showed pictures of an airborne radar display showing what the crew of Flight 007 would have seen on Romeo-20 versus what they would have seen during their actual flight over Soviet territory. They said the ICAO report was based on distorted data and at some points on openly counterfeited documents, such as the transcript of the Soviet pilots' transmissions, which "taken in isolation from the ground commands become meaningless and create a wrong impression of the interception process." The entire ICAO inquiry, the Soviet representative said, ignored the "true causes" of the tragedy and was simply a regurgitation of the U.S. official line.[55]

The U.S. resolution was passed, by secret ballot, by a vote of 20 to 2 with nine abstentions. As before, negative votes were cast by the Soviet Union and its ally Czechoslovakia. One council member, Iraq, was not present for the voting, and another vote was apparently not cast.[56] The effect of the resolution was purely political—the ICAO had no power to impose sanctions—but it was a victory of some importance for the United States. By "condemning" the downing, a formula stronger than earlier versions that had "deplored" it, the resolution focused on what the Soviets did to the airliner, not how it arrived at Sakhalin. And the resolution pointed to the ICAO report as "proof" that human error was the most likely cause for the Korean airliner's deviation from course.

Between April 24 and May 10, the ICAO Assembly held the fifth extraordinary session in its forty-year history. Representatives from 107 contracting states, one noncontracting state, and eleven international organizations attended the session, a total of about 400 delegates in all. At the opening of the session, speeches were made by thirty-four state delegates and five of the invited observers.[57] Given the reason for convening the extraordinary session, it was hardly surprising that almost all mentioned the downing of Flight 007.

The purpose of the session was to amend the Chicago Convention, the shorthand name for the Convention on International Civil Aviation, which came into force on April 4, 1947. This agreement (to whose provisions the Soviet Union adhered on October 15, 1970) says that every state has "complete and exclusive sovereignty over the airspace above its territory" and gives states the right to establish prohibited flying zones and deal with intrusions in the manner they choose. The amendment under consideration prohibited the use of weapons against civilian aircraft. As things stood, the Chicago Convention neither explicitly authorized nor explicitly prohibited the use of such force. On May 10, the ICAO Assembly unanimously approved the amendment.[58]

18

THE INVESTIGATION BEGINS

The first major assault on the Reagan administration's official line on the downing of Flight 007 came in June 1984, in the obscure British defense journal *Defence Attaché*. The cover of the magazine was sensational—solid black with only the name of the magazine and the words "Korean 'Spy' Plane: The New Evidence," in bold white lettering. In an editor's introduction, Rupert Pengelley wrote, "The aim of this appraisal is purely to try and understand what might have happened, and the method is to introduce some new and hitherto unpublished perspectives." Although the editor said he "does not necessarily agree with all the author's views," he called for further investigation and noted, "Scientific inquiry is needed, not name-calling and mud-slinging."[1]

The article, "Reassessing the Sakhalin Incident," was written under the pseudonym P. Q. Mann. Pengelley described the author as a person "who for professional reasons must remain anonymous." Mann was, however, well known to the editor. Misidentified in the *Daily Telegraph* as Tom Devereux, he is Anthony Devereux, an executive with an advertising firm whose clients included several of the largest defense contractors in Britain. At the time of the Grenada invasion in October 1983, Devereux came to public attention because one of his company's clients, Plessey Airports, headed the construction of Grenada's new airport at Point Salines, a facility the Reagan administration considered its strongest piece of evidence that the Communists were "bent on transforming the little island into a strategically placed anti-Western base."[2] Devereux is a fellow of the British Interplanetary Society and has written extensively about space flight. If not an "expert," Devereux is, by any acceptable criteria, an informed observer.[3]

Defence Attaché was an unlikely forum for a controversial article on a hot topic. As London's *Observer* noted, "The magazine is well regarded in the Ministry of Defense Sales Organization and the British defense industry." British officials told the *Washington Post* that the magazine was widely read within the Ministry of Defense (MOD) and was regarded as a "sober and responsible publication."[4]

Devereux asserted that two intrusions into East Germany by U.S. Air Force planes in 1964 had been attempts to "light up" air defenses. On January 28, 1964, a U.S. Air Force T-39 reconnaissance jet was shot down after penetrating about 100 kilometers into East Germany. Nine days earlier, the U.S. had launched a ferret satellite from Vandenberg Air Force Base in California. Had the aircraft's penetration lasted just another two or three minutes longer, he wrote, the satellite would have been in "optimum position" to record the air defense flap caused by the intrusion. However, the East German air defenses quickly shot down the T-39, killing the crew. The U.S. Government claimed that the aircraft experienced an unspecified malfunction in its radio or navigational equipment.[5] On March 10, 42 days later, the satellite had orbited to almost the same location. And on that day, remarkably, a U.S. Air Force RB-66 reconnaissance aircraft experienced similar "navigational trouble" and penetrated into East German airspace about 30 miles north of the earlier intrusion. It was also shot down, but this time the crew parachuted to safety.

The *Defence Attaché* article then argued that Flight 007 had also been coordinated with the orbit of a U.S. intelligence satellite. Using a version of the map presented by Marshal Pyotr Kirsanov in *Pravda* on September 20, 1983, Devereux suggested that Flight 007 was, in many respects, a rerun of the earlier intrusions in East Germany. There were, however, some new twists and turns. The presence of the RC-135 was designed to confuse Soviet air defense forces about the identity of the intruder, therefore forcing them to operate under conditions of actual emergency. Observing the Soviet air defense response from space along with the "Ferret-D" satellite, Devereux said, was the ill-starred Space Shuttle Challenger (Mission STS-8), which was orbiting the earth at the time of Flight 007's intrusion.

The Challenger had been launched at night from pad 39-A at the Kennedy Space Center, about 36 hours before the downing of Flight 007. (It landed at night at Edwards Air Force Base in California on September 5.) The night launch, the first for a space shuttle, took place after a 17-minute delay, putting the liftoff precisely in the center of a 34-minute launch "window."[6] Launch windows are established so the spacecraft will be at a certain place at a certain time, determined by the nature of the mission —photography, for example, or the deployment of satellites. In this case, the night launch was said to be necessary for the deployment of an Indian communications satellite, Insat-1B.[7]

Another task for Challenger on mission STS-8 was to communicate through the Tracking and Data Relay Satellite (TDRS), using an encryption technique that was being tried for the first time. The technique was designed to permit secret communications during military shuttle missions. (Although there were some problems with the satellite's ground station at White Sands, New Mexico, Challenger was able to send data through TDRS at a rate of 300 million bits per second, a rate the Los Angeles Times equated with roughly 100 volumes of an encyclopedia.)[8]

Other aspects of Mission STS-8 were unique. Put on board Challenger at the last minute was a 7,600-pound Payload Flight Test Article (PFTA), also called a "dummy payload." The official purpose of the PFTA was to test the mechanical muscles of a Canadian-built manipulator arm extending from the spacecraft's cargo bay. It was practice, NASA said, to prepare crews for retrieving satellites so they could be brought back to earth for repairs. Since carrying a huge dead weight into space seemed an expensive luxury the financially troubled shuttle program could ill afford, some have argued that the PFTA served other purposes. For instance, a former senior Lockheed engineer who worked on intelligence satellite programs noted that the PFTA had the same dimensions as some communications antennas.

That the shuttle is a military as well as civilian spacecraft is well established. The Air Force provided part of the funding for shuttle development and, as Donald C. Latham, the deputy undersecretary of defense for communications, command, control, and intelligence, pointed out, "The Department of Defense is [NASA's] biggest customer and always has been." The connections between NASA and the Department of Defense extend well beyond the space shuttle program. The Department of Defense and NASA provide technical assistance to each other, exchange technologies, and cooperate on special projects. For instance, the Defense Mapping Agency acquires pictures from NASA's earth resources satellites (Landsats) to help locate military targets. NASA's Geodetic satellite supplies gravity measurements that support actual and planned weapons projects. Experts have noted that civilian space programs cannot be ruled out as a source of data for arms control inspection. The space shuttle's military uses include satellite deployment and retrieval, and orbital refueling of maneuvering reconnaissance satellites such as the KH-12. Another example of the shuttle's military potential was apparent in a 1984 issue of Aviation Week & Space Technology. A photograph taken by Mission 9 three months after the downing of Flight 007 clearly showed the city of Petropavlovsk on Kamchatka, the ballistic missile submarine port, a fighter base, and a number of clearings used as staging areas for surface-to-air missiles. As William Burrows remarked, "There is not, and never has been, a clear line separating 'military' and 'civilian' space activities, as many in the nation's space program like to pretend."[9]

Anthony Devereux concluded his article by proposing a plausible explanation for why a civilian airliner would be useful in an intelligence operation:

> If U.S. intelligence services planned the Korean incident, they would have been in no doubt that they could not achieve their aims with a military aircraft. Equally, they would not achieve their aims with a manifestly civilian aircraft, because a manifestly civilian aircraft would not have the effect of turning on all manner of military radars and electronics. They would need to offer an aircraft of initially apparently military character, which would turn out later to be apparently civilian. This would be the explanation for the co-incident flight of KAL 007 with a U.S. military aircraft of similar profile, an RC-135, within range of Soviet radars, less than half an hour before the first Soviet landfall.

The article had its origins in an account of the U.S. military aircraft intrusions into East Germany that Devereux had written some years earlier. When the Korean airliner was shot down, he immediately saw the similarity. He composed what eventually became the *Defence Attaché* article with the intention of submitting it to the London *Sunday Times*. He distributed several copies of the manuscript for comment to high-level officials in British intelligence and the Ministry of Defense, and received written comments attesting to the essential accuracy of the article's main points. They recommended, given the potential embarrassment the article might cause for Britain's principal ally, the United States, that Devereux find a less-conspicuous outlet for the piece.

Thus, the selection of *Defence Attaché*. Editor Rupert Pengelley was well acquainted with Devereux and respected his reputation. As part of the magazine's fact checking process, copies of the manuscript were sent to friends and associates in the British defense and intelligence communities. No written comments were received this time, but Pengelley was told, "If you publish this, you won't be far wrong."

The piece caused an immediate stir in Washington. The State Department developed a set of technical questions and answers refuting the article and sent these to all diplomatic posts abroad. The United States Information Service sent guidance to overseas posts suggesting that the article must be Soviet inspired. Reagan administration officials issued denials to the press and hinted darkly that it was part of a "well-planned Soviet disinformation campaign." Defense Secretary Caspar W. Weinberger said that the magazine had "picked up lock, stock, and barrel the total set of lies that the Soviet Union published after the Korean jetliner was shot down." "Had we wanted to test Soviet radar," the defense secretary said, "there are a lot better ways to do it than with a 747 jumbo jet full of civilians." (This remark is interesting in light of other officials' remarks that "the Soviet electronic activity provoked by Flight 007's intrusion provided Western intelligence with its biggest coup for many years.") [10]

Almost immediately, the problems started for Rupert Pengelley and *Defence Attaché*. During the days following the publication of the article, Pengelley began receiving calls from defense contractors wondering whether they should continue to advertise in a magazine espousing "pro-Soviet" sentiments.[11] Devereux was told by his employer that his job would be in jeopardy if he continued to expound his thesis publicly.

According to Pengelley, a source in the Ministry of Defense informed him shortly after the article appeared that an angry call had been placed from the White House to the office of the prime minister asking why things were "getting out of hand." The prime minister's office then reportedly called the Ministry of Defense to see if there wasn't some way to discredit the article or *Defence Attaché*. According to Pengelley's account, MOD replied that the magazine was a reputable defense journal.

Attacks on the P. Q. Mann article soon appeared in the Western press, virtually all emanating from James E. Oberg. Oberg, a former mission controller for NASA, now works for the McDonnell Douglas Corporation —one of the nation's largest defense contractors and a company that co-produces helicopters with Korean Air Lines. The relationship between NASA and McDonnell Douglas is exceedingly cozy. McDonnell Douglas is intimately involved with many aspects of space shuttle launches, for example, and as one NASA official remarked, "we work so closely together that we jokingly call ourselves 'partners in crime.' " It became Oberg's personal crusade to debunk the charge that the Challenger had anything to do with the intrusion of Flight 007. Rushing to the attack, Oberg called the *Defence Attaché* article "yet another example of widespread passion to rush to publish the vilest slanders as long as they are anti-American."[12]

Oberg first attacked the claim that the 1964 intrusions were coordinated with a ferret satellite. He insisted that the satellite to which Devereux referred was a weather satellite, of no use for electronic intelligence-gathering, and its passes overhead were simply coincidence. Oberg then stated that the passes of the U.S. satellite over the Far East as Flight 007 was making its intrusions were also coincidental. It was a ferret, he acknowledged, but "the skies are full of ELINT satellites, of course, and the chance is excellent that every night they pass over airliners on the Anchorage-to-Far East air routes."[13] The logic here is elusive. It is like claiming that because a car was used as a getaway vehicle in a robbery and the roads are full of innocent cars, this particular car must have been innocent as well.

Then there was the Challenger. It was, Oberg admitted, about where

Devereux said it was, but the shuttle could not have played a role in the incident because it was not in line-of-sight range. *Time* seconded this, saying that NASA officials had told the magazine that the shuttle was never close enough to the Korean airliner to monitor radio or radar activity. This is true, but line-of-sight is only one way to communicate. Other satellites in the area can serve as intermediaries, and the military and intelligence services frequently use them in this way. "We are establishing a *tactical* satellite system," the former Lockheed engineer remarked, a tactical system by which ground- and space-based commanders can accept, evaluate, and act immediately upon orbital surveillance.[14]

None of this proves that the Challenger in fact played the active command and control role that Anthony Devereux claimed, but it suggests that such use would by no means be impossible.

Defence Attaché was to make headlines again. On August 28, 1984, just in time for the first anniversary of the tragedy, Korean Air Lines filed suit against the magazine in High Court in London. According to David Clark, one of the attorneys representing KAL, the company was "claiming damages for libel as a result of suggestions that Korean Air Lines might have committed Flight 007 on September 1, 1983, to be used for the purpose of espionage."[15]

Defence Attaché's decision to settle the libel suit out of court was announced on November 20. The *New York Times* reported that lawyers representing *Defence Attaché* confirmed that "there is no foundation for any suggestion that either Korean Air Lines or any of its staff on the aircraft concerned took part in a spy mission" and that KAL had accepted a public apology and a "substantial" amount of money in damages. Unable to hide his pleasure, a South Korean official said, "We hope the court settlement will put an end to the seemingly endless speculations about unauthorized missions of Flight 007." Department of Defense spokesman Michael I. Burch announced to the press, "I think that the magazine admitting that the story was a fabrication and that they're willing to set the record straight, plus pay a substantial amount for damage and legal claims, is noteworthy."[16]

The implication of these statements was that *Defence Attaché* had admitted error and wanted to set the record straight. U.S. officials have since cited the apology as proof of the innocence of the flight. But this, according to editor Rupert Pengelley, is not the case. *Defence Attaché* is a small publication with a circulation of about 3,500. Not in the business of publishing potentially libelous material, the magazine had no insurance. When Korean Air Lines filed suit for libel, Pengelley asked his anonymous author for assistance. But Anthony Devereux, who had been warned by his employer against public discussion of the article, refused to participate in the defense. (He was later fired nonetheless.)

British libel law is much harsher than its American counterpart, placing the burden of proof on the accused. It is not necessary to show malicious intent as well as false information, and a defendant who is found guilty can be charged with libel for statements made during the defense. In addition, the party who loses a libel case is responsible for the other party's legal costs. KAL made it clear that even if it lost the first round, it would appeal and appeal again. Even defending itself in the first round of legal actions would probably have bankrupted *Defence Attaché*. It is not surprising, therefore, that the magazine settled. The truth or falsity of the article, said Pengelley, had nothing to do with the decision.

As part of the out-of-court settlement, *Defence Attaché* agreed to publish an apology and a "rebuttal" by James Oberg.[17] The magazine also agreed to pay legal expenses for KAL through that time (about 1,000 pounds). But the "substantial amount for damage" mentioned by Pentagon spokesman Burch was zero. KAL seems to have been seeking a victory in the media.

Within two months of the downing, British space expert Anthony Kendon confirmed that a satellite was in approximately the location claimed by Marshal Kirsanov. This satellite had the international launch number 1982-41C.[18] Ironically, this confirmation of one of P. Q. Mann's central contentions first appeared in the *Defence Attaché* "apology issue." Kendon's conclusions were subsequently verified by Dr. Bhupendra Jasani and Geoffrey Perry in a report published in the Stockholm International Peace Research Institute's 1985 Yearbook.[19] Looking at the satellite's passes over the Far East, it is clear that satellite 1982-41C was the satellite to which Marshal Kirsanov referred, although the ground tracks do not match perfectly.[20]

With the "absurd" Soviet charge that a satellite had been passing overhead as Flight 007 intruded into Soviet territory now shown to be true, U.S. officials, echoing James Oberg, pronounced the presence of the satellite to be a coincidence. "It is possible to charge that practically any event was coordinated with a satellite," one State Department official explained. "NASA's most recent Satellite Situation Report shows that the United States has more than 2,700 military and civilian satellites in orbit, although not all are operational. . . . During any given time period, at least a few are likely to pass overhead."[21] Yes, but how many are operational? How many are ferrets? And how many had orbits that corresponded to Flight 007's route at precisely that time? The answer is not 2,700, but one.

After P. Q. Mann's, the next article on Flight 007 to cause a stir was my article in *The Nation,* appearing at the time of the first anniversary of the tragedy. It was a lengthy critical examination of the Reagan administration's official version of the downing of Flight 007. Its central thesis was that such an explanation, based on a remarkable set of coincidences, was extremely difficult to believe given the facts already in the public record. Among these were the anomalies of Flight 007's known flight path, the U.S.'s considerable military and intelligence capabilities in the region, and the technical systems which should have kept top Administration officials informed of the developing situation. The article concluded by asking a number of specific unresolved questions about the case, suggesting the U.S. Government release a wealth of data that could help answer those questions, and calling for a congressional inquiry into the tragedy.[22]

The response was not long in coming. Vermont Senator Patrick J. Leahy, a member of the Senate Select Committee on Intelligence, appeared on the "Today Show" to respond to the charges that had appeared in *The Nation*. Before he did so, he received what the *Washington Post* called an "extensive briefing by U.S. intelligence officers at CIA headquarters." Leahy told "Today Show" host Bryant Gumble that he had "reviewed still-classified information" on the airliner's shooting and "found nothing in it that would relieve the Soviet Union of its responsibility." "The article is a fascinating compendium of coincidences and hypothesis," Leahy said, "but it comes out false in the end, it really makes no sense at all."[23]

The *Nation* article was only one of several investigations to appear on the first anniversary. Although most television coverage was superficial, several companies devoted considerable resources to the case and presented their findings in lengthy programs. These were ABC Television in the United States, Thames Television in Britain, and the West German network ARD.

The West German program, "Missiles Launched—Target Destroyed: The Deathflight of Flight 007," was a wide-ranging summary of many of the lingering issues in the case.[24] It included interviews with a number of air traffic controllers, State Department officials, intelligence experts, airline pilots, and others, among them flamboyant San Francisco attorney Melvin Belli. "I flew to Seoul and talked with the flight captain's and the copilot's widows," Belli said. "They told me that the captain and the copilot were paid to intentionally take this shortcut over Russian territory. They made this statement voluntarily in the presence of three other American attorneys and thirty bereaved persons. The widows said that KAL paid its pilots special bonuses for flying over Russian territory. The widows, furthermore, stated that the pilots had become so afraid of these flights that they wanted to discontinue them."[25]

As early as December 1983, Belli told *People* magazine that Captain Chun "was so frightened of flying over Russia that he was going to quit." In an interview with the Canadian Broadcasting Corporation, he remarked, "The United States knew very well that this Korean plane was going to be flying over Russian territory at the time it did, so did the Japanese, and so did the Koreans. And this pilot was told to fly over that territory, and he said before he left, when he came back he was going to resign from the airline: He'd had it." When I asked Belli about this, he not only confirmed he had said these things but suggested that there was far more to the story than had yet been told. Belli referred me to three other attorneys, and I was able to speak with two of them. One of them confided to me that prior to his departure from Seoul, Captain Chun Byung-in had told his wife that he was departing on an "especially dangerous mission" and that he "might not return."[26]

Michael Chrisman and Mark Ackerman were the two principal researchers for a program on Flight 007 that appeared on the Thames Television investigative series "TV Eye" entitled "007—Licensed to Spy?" Getting wind of the program during its preparation, the U.S. Embassy in London forwarded word to Washington. The State Department wired back that it "appreciates early warning on scurrilous allegations" expected in the program and directed the embassy to "vigorously refute" the charges by "direct contacts" with leading journalists, interviews, and press conferences. The department had said earlier that there was going to be no "free ride for the other side." (After the program, State used heavy-handed tactics with members of the British media who reported the findings of "TV Eye." For example, *The Guardian* received a letter from the U.S. Embassy in London saying that its report "suggests something about the bias of your writer.")[27]

A number of U.S. officials and analysts appeared on the "TV Eye" program, as they had on the West German show, and several expressed their grave doubts about the official U.S. version of events. The Thames researchers were themselves skeptical. On a trip to Anchorage, Michael Chrisman had investigated the King Salmon radar, which had provided the data from which the ICAO had determined that Flight 007 was off course at Bethel. He asked FAA officials where the King Salmon data were displayed in the Air Route Traffic Control Center and was told that the radar signals go to a recorder in the basement and are not available to air traffic controllers. (The U.S. had wanted to include a statement to this effect in the ICAO report.) Then Chrisman learned that there was a screen "down the hall." Finally, FAA officials acknowledged that the radar information was displayed on a screen near where the air traffic controllers sat. FAA personnel hastened to add, however, that they were "not certain" whether or not it had been turned on the night of the incident.[28] Chrisman also learned in Anchorage that the Department of State had called off an investigation into the incident by the National Transportation Safety Board.

The last new allegation to be offered by the "TV Eye" team had to do with the black box. " 'TV Eye' has learned," program host Denis Tuohy reported, "of a leak from a U.S. State Department official claiming that the box was recovered by the U.S. Navy, that the South Koreans asked the Americans to hand it over, and that the U.S. Government refused." The official in question was said to be a "middle-ranking" official who found out about the discovery of the black box while in Washington and tipped off Alexander Braun, the editor of the Silicon Valley electronics journal *Microwave Systems News*. It was duly noted on the "TV Eye" program that the State Department had denied the story.[29]

Thames Television soon joined *Defence Attaché* in legal hot water. On August 28, 1984, a writ of summons arrived at Thames Television from the offices of Beaumont and Son, the legal firm representing Korean Air Lines in London, claiming the "TV Eye" program to be "malicious" and a "damaging libel." KAL asked for an injunction against Thames from re-broadcasting the show, plus damages and legal costs. But this time, how-ever, the airline had a more powerful opponent than *Defence Attaché*. Thames, the largest and richest of Britain's independent television com-panies, is contesting the suit, and legal machinations are still underway.[30]

The final program was produced by Don Thrasher on ABC Television's "20/20 Newsmagazine." It focused on the human element of the tragedy and included a number of statements by family members of those who died on the ill-fated airliner. Relatives, intelligence experts, and airline pilots all asked the same question: How could the plane stray so far off course with all the military and intelligence hardware the U.S. and Japan had in that area? As James Bamford remarked on the program, "The area in which that airliner was shot down is the most heavily listened to, most heavily watched area in the entire world." Such statements were balanced by the denials of U.S. officials.[31]

Although the program raised questions about the incident, host Geraldo Rivera downplayed anything that suggested intentionality on the U.S.'s part, although the program seemed intended to raise questions about the incident. He concluded: "Even though questions are now being asked about why the plane was flying over Soviet territory and whether the United States had the knowledge and ability to warn it away, we should never forget that central point: The Soviet Union had no right to kill 269 people."[32]

This was not how the program had been planned. Since U.S. officials had been asked for their reactions to allegations offered by other interview-ees, the Administration was well aware that ABC was preparing the pro-gram. According to both published reports and a high-level ABC source, Defense Secretary Caspar Weinberger telephoned ABC's top management to try to stop the airing of the program. "Cap phoned ABC and he tried to kill that story," the Dutch magazine *Panorama* quoted Administration officials as saying. ABC reportedly refused, and Weinberger expressed his hope that the program would contain the appropriate measure of "bal-ance." The statements by Rivera were said to be the result of this top-level Administration intervention.[33]

Nor was this the only example. A similar story was recounted by a high-ranking official of the Independent Society of Literary Representatives. The official had been told by a senior editor at a major U.S. publishing house that two writers had submitted a manuscript on the Flight 007 case, and it was being seriously considered for publication. This was at the time the libel trial was going on in New York between CBS and Gen. William Westmoreland. One of the witnesses in the trial was a former high-ranking military and intelligence official. While in New York, the official stopped off at the publishing house. At the conclusion of the meeting, the company was no longer interested in the manuscript.

Yet even in those instances where top-level intervention has failed to kill or add "balance" to a particular story or program before it appeared, another goal was achieved by complaining afterwards—putting the media organizations on notice that they had treaded on dangerous ground. NBC President Julian Goodman once remarked that an administration applies this kind of after-the-fact pressure for much the same reason that a baseball player argues with the umpire: "They don't expect to win the argument, but they hope to make us think twice the next time." [34]

The Republic of Korea observed the first anniversary of the downing of Flight 007 by dedicating a 26.9-meter-high granite monument to the memory of the 269 passengers and crew. Designed by a South Korean university professor, the monument is situated on a hill in Manghyang Gardens in Chonan, about 50 miles south of Seoul. Homeland Longing Hill, as its name translates, is a cemetery for Koreans who die overseas." [35]

The ceremony at Manghyang Gardens on Saturday, September 1, 1984, was sponsored by the Korean Anti-Communist League, a government-backed organization. Korean Air Lines officials estimated that 1,200 people attended, including several ROK Cabinet officials and 160 members of victims' families. KAL had offered to fly any foreign victims' family members to the ceremony and dedication of the monument without cost, and many accepted. As the families huddled under their umbrellas in a driving rain, a military band played funeral music and hymns, including "Nearer My God to Thee." Prayers were offered by a Buddhist monk, a Protestant pastor, and a Catholic priest. "All I can do now is pray that the soul of my husband may rest in peace," said Kim Ok-hee, Captain Chun's wife. "My heart aches every time I hear my son saying he would like to become a pilot." [36]

No mass demonstrations or services were planned for the anniversary in South Korea, and Foreign Minister Lee Won-kyung's statement on the anniversary was exceptional in its soft approach. These and other actions were viewed by many as a move by the ROK government to improve ties with Moscow in light of Seoul's position as host of the 1988 Olympic Summer Games. [37] So eager were the Koreans to avoid a boycott of the games that they backed out of a deal to help finance an American movie based on the Flight 007 incident—"The Aftermath"—because Korean sponsorship "might upset the Soviets." [38]

Korean Air Lines celebrated the anniversary of the downing by changing its name to Korean Air and replacing its bird logo with a new red, white, and blue yin-yang type symbol. Shortly after the downing, Flight 007 had been renamed Flight 017. A year after the tragedy there was no more Korean Air Lines, no more Flight 007.

The first anniversary brought a sad reenactment for many of the bereaved relatives of those who died on Flight 007. At 5:00 on the morning of September 2, seventy-nine bereaved relatives from twenty-one Japanese families and a diplomat from the Australian embassy boarded the ferry *Soya Maru No. 7* for the 5½-hour trip to the Sea of Japan between Moneron and Sakhalin islands. The ferry was accompanied by a patrol boat from the Japan Maritime Safety Agency. The weather was calm and gentle when the vessels departed the docks in Wakkanai, but a drizzle began on the open sea. By the time the vessels arrived in the vicinity of Sakhalin, fog had set in, muffling sounds and obscuring the five Soviet naval vessels that appeared to keep a watch on the activities. The memorial service, like a service the previous day on a hill overlooking the sea near Wakkanai, was sponsored by the KAL Incident Victims Association.[39]

There was anger as well as grief that day. A number of families issued a statement saying that Flight 007 might have been part of an "elaborately preschemed plot on the part of a certain country." The country was not named, according to spokesman Professor Shozo Takemoto, who had lost his wife and son on the plane, because the allegation could not as yet be proved. "When you think back on the last year," Takemoto observed, "nothing has been solved at all." In a ceremony that lasted only an hour, the bereaved relatives, as they had a year before, threw flowers and other personal items into the sea. "Daddy, how are you?" cried nine-year-old Mei Osaka, who had lost her father on the doomed airliner. "Sister and I are studying hard, and Mommy is working until late at night. Sometimes I massage her shoulders. Come back early, Daddy." Candy and fruit and chrysanthemums were thrown overboard. As the rain began falling, the *Soya Maru* began the journey back to Japan.[40]

Across Pennsylvania Avenue from the White House, the Ad-Hoc Coalition to Commemorate the Korean Airline Massacre gathered on August 31 to condemn the downing of Flight 007 in particular and world Communism generally. Approximately 100 demonstrators set up 269 paper and wire headstones bearing the names of all those who died on the airliner. "What we are protesting is not a single incident," one demonstrator told the *Washington Post*. "What we are protesting is the fact that it is a mere example of what [the Soviets] have been doing every day since 1917."[41]

Similar observances took place in other cities as well. In Canberra, Australia, a man placed 270 crosses in front of the Soviet embassy: 269 for those who died on Flight 007 and one for an additional casualty, the truth. In New York, Senator Alfonse D'Amato unveiled a plaque near the United Nations. This was an appropriate place for the plaque, D'Amato said, because the United Nations had left a "dark stain" on history by refusing to excoriate Moscow.[42]

In order to coordinate the Western response at the time of the anniversary, the State Department sent a long memorandum to U.S. embassies around the globe and non-American NATO officials advising them how to answer questions about the incident. Materials describing the official line were disseminated to editors and reporters, and the State Department arranged a series of briefings for reporters to deny the new charges that were cropping up throughout the world. Assistant Secretary of State and former *New York Times* reporter Richard Burt wrote an article for the *New York Times* on August 31, debunking, in exceedingly general terms, those reports that continued to question the veracity of the U.S. official line. Burt savagely derided "conspiracy buffs" and "spy plane theorists" who bought the "baloney" turned out by "the Russians' propaganda and disinformation machine." As *The Nation* commented, "So much for their evidence, acquired, Burt neglects to say, through painstaking independent research and analysis. So much for the questions they raise, which Burt dismisses peremptorily." [43] The skillfully constructed piece was a strained exercise in journalistic balance, where the Soviet charges and U.S. replies were presented with Richard Burt doing the summing up.

As Burt explained, two schools of criticism had emerged with regard to the incident, and the State Department had responses for each. The first was that Flight 007 was on an intelligence mission of some nature for the United States. The State Department dismissed this: "The United States does not use civilian airliners for intelligence purposes." The other school of thought posited that Flight 007 was a "target of opportunity"—an innocently errant airliner that U.S. personnel saw yet permitted to fly into Soviet airspace to see how their air defense systems would react. "No agency of the U.S. Government even knew the plane was off course and was in difficulty until after it was shot down" was the response to this. "Only the Soviets . . . knew where it was before it was shot down because they had tracked it for 2½ hours." [44]

The official line was echoed in the press. *Time* magazine noted that the "inevitable conspiracy theories," such as that found in "the leftist U.S. magazine *The Nation*," were part of a "massive overt disinformation campaign" orchestrated by the Soviet Union. *U.S. News & World Report* reported that "examination of the evidence . . . indicates that most of it was planted by the Soviets." The *Washington Times* complained that questions about the official account "are being repeated and embellished both by the Kremlin's covert agents-of-influence around the world and by independent writers who for their own reasons question the slightest semantic inconsistency in the U.S. exposition of fact, without applying similar rigorous standards toward the Soviet position." [45]

The complaint about dual standards was true, and for good reason. Democratic governments, unlike totalitarian ones, must hold themselves accountable for their actions. Yet with increasing frequency the argument is made that the Soviet threat justifies deception by our own government. The Reagan administration's lies about Iran, Nicaragua, Libya, and its policy decision to disseminate disinformation about some 15 to 20 CIA and Department of Defense programs, including the "Star Wars" Strategic

Defense Initiative, are only the most recent manifestations of this mindset. As one government official remarked, "It was not until recently that, after watching the Soviet Union practice this philosophy for years, the U.S. decided it would benefit by creating a similar program."[46] Those critics who believed the Administration knew a great deal more about the downing of Flight 007 than it had acknowledged were concerned about precisely to whom those "benefits" accrued.

Sugwon Kang summarized the Reagan administration's handling of criticism of the official U.S. line:

> What the press has characterized as government "denials" have rarely been anything other than one-liner dismissals. Instead of reasoned rebuttals to these charges, the public has gotten evasions, half-truths, irrelevant clarifications, calculated leaks, and selective release of data. When confronted with carefully defined factual questions that did not lend themselves to the usual disposition by obfuscation, the government seemed to retreat into silence as if it could make the problem go away by ignoring it. . . . As questions of judgment and loyalty were brought into the discussion, the press too retreated into silence, thus abdicating its investigative responsibility.[47]

The result was that most press coverage of the first anniversary of the downing of Flight 007 lacked critical analysis and understanding of the issues involved. Not only did the American press do very little investigative reporting, it also failed to discuss such reporting when it appeared in the foreign press. Perhaps the best example of this was the lack of U.S. press coverage of a four-part series in the West German magazine *Der Spiegel*. In the final installment of the series, dated October 15, authors Wilhelm Bittorf and Anthony Sampson accused the Reagan administration of a major deception of the American and world publics.[48]

The story had to do with when the Administration knew about the downing. Bittorf and Sampson alleged that National Security Agency facilities had been fully aware of the events transpiring over the Kamchatka Peninsula, the Sea of Okhotsk, and Sakhalin Island in real time, as they occurred. Within half an hour of the downing, they said, NSA headquarters in Fort Meade, Maryland, was informed by its Misawa station that Flight 007 had either crash-landed or crashed. NSA passed this information to the Administration, both in Washington and in Santa Barbara.

Within the next two hours, according to Bittorf and Sampson, an NSA analysis of its intelligence information confirmed that the airliner had been shot down. National Security Adviser William P. Clark, at the Pacific Biltmore Hotel near Santa Barbara, received this information through secure channels from Washington. Then, Bittorf and Sampson claimed, Richard Burt, Lawrence Eagleburger, Secretary of State George Shultz, CIA Director William Casey, Clark, and presidential counselor Edwin Meese conducted the conference call described in Chapter 6.

As NSA continued to provide updated information to the American leadership, Bittorf and Sampson went on, the picture of Soviet incompetence and overreaction became clearer. "In order not to turn the downing into a confirmation and justification for the peace movement," the authors wrote, "it was decided to use it as a weapon so that there would be no mistakes about the nature of the Soviets. . . . The Soviets had to be described as fully aware that they had shot down a commercial jetliner filled with women and children like sitting ducks and, while so doing, were filled with satisfaction about the act."

Wanting to avoid a situation such as the downing of the U-2 in 1960 where insufficient information produced disaster, Bittorf and Sampson said, the President's men decided to buy time. A press blackout was imposed in Washington. Hours before official accounts admit, officials in Washington had already contacted Japanese Prime Minister Nakasone and Foreign Minister Shintaro Abe via secure CIA "backchannel" circuits. The time was needed to coordinate cover stories—Japanese and Korean leaders were "urgently asked to speak and act in matters regarding the airliner only in strictest unity with the U.S. Government"—and to feel out the reactions by the Russians. The result, Bittorf and Sampson claim, was the false report that Flight 007 had landed safely on Sakhalin, passed out through CIA liaison officers in Seoul, Tokyo, and Washington.

The charges were sensational. Given what we knew of the time schedule of events in Japan and the United States, my colleagues and I were confident that something of the kind must have happened. We immediately had the article translated and began calling everyone in the media with whom we had contact, trying to get the story into the news stream. Within a few days we had mailed out dozens of copies of the translated article. The result was a deafening silence. The presidential election was only a few weeks away, and a Reagan victory appeared certain. With the Administration's demonstrated vindictiveness toward criticism, which it called "liberal bias," and its track record of ostracizing and denouncing journalists who "willingly, willfully, and knowingly" publish information "harmful and damaging to the country," the likely outcome of publishing even a word about the *Der Spiegel* story as the election drew near was clear.[49] As a senior producer at one of the major TV networks explained, "When you step on a rattlesnake, you'd better make certain you kill it."[50]

"The depressing complicity with government into which the free American press has sunk since Vietnam and Watergate has seldom been more visible than it was at the first anniversary of the Soviet destruction of Korean Air Lines Flight 007," wrote columnist Tom Wicker in the *New York Times* a week after the anniversary. Wicker had read the *Nation* article and had been impressed. "The press effectively ignored an authoritative article in *The Nation*," he continued, "establishing to a reasonable certainty that numerous agencies of the U.S. Government knew or should have known, almost from the moment Flight 007 left Anchorage, Alaska, that the plane was off course and headed for intrusion in Soviet airspace.''

With this, the campaign to discredit critics of the official line expanded to include Tom Wicker.[51] Former Assistant Secretary of Defense Henry E. Catto, Jr., asserted in a letter to the *New York Times* that "we don't monitor flight pattern accuracy for civilian planes."[52] He then put in the inevitable plug for the ICAO report: "The International Civil Aviation Organization carefully investigated the incident," he said, "and concluded that pilot error was the most likely cause of the plane going off course." Catto finished by noting, "We have here a classic example of two facets of the American psyche—love of the idea of conspiracy, no matter how flimsy the evidence, and the peculiar readiness of many to assume the worst of our people and our government." In just a few words, questioning the U.S. official line about Flight 007 had been transformed not only into "conspiracy theory" but into hatred of the American people. Wicker responded a few weeks later. To Catto's assertion that "we don't monitor flight pattern accuracy for civilian planes," Wicker correctly noted, "But nobody said they did." He detailed a number of the ICAO report's limitations and concluded by repeating his call for the U.S. Government to answer the questions raised in *The Nation*.[53]

The next act in this back-and-forth drama came from former Federal Aviation Administrator J. Lynn Helms, who, a year earlier, had joined the scores of Reagan administration appointees to leave office under a cloud of scandal when the Securities and Exchange Commission accused him of fraud in a multimillion-dollar industrial development bond issue. Helms sharply attacked Wicker in the *New York Times,* calling his article "the latest of a series, none with substance, written around innuendo, speculation, 'unanswered questions,' and allegations, but unfortunately falling directly in line with the extensive Soviet disinformation effort." Because Flight 007 was "more than 1,000 miles from any air traffic control radar," Helms said, it was "impossible to monitor the flight. The laws of physics, as we now know them, just won't allow it." Helms did not mention that nobody had ever claimed that civil air traffic control radar could monitor Flight 007 the whole way; the critical question was the area of coverage for military radars. Helms presumably knew this, but most readers of the *New York Times* probably did not. He then said that "only one [military] radar station showed the aircraft barely off course." (Only one radar whose data had been released, that is. It would soon emerge that the data from other Air Force radars, systems that followed the off-course airliner for a far longer time, had been destroyed.) The former FAA administrator concluded, "There is no more to the story, and no Administration denial is due."[54]

After publication of Helms's letter in the *Times,* the laws of physics began to be cited with astonishing frequency. Calling the *Nation* article a "plot," a writer in *Discover* magazine denied the existence of over-the-horizon (OTH) radar on Shemya Island in the Aleutians and said that Cobra Dane could not have tracked the Korean jetliner because "the airliner's 33,000-foot altitude was far below the radar's horizon." The article concluded, "If the conspiracy theorists want to be believed, they will have to do better than rely on flat-earth physics." Identical assertions appeared both in the writings of other supporters of the official line and in those of active State Department officials.[55]

No over-the-horizon radars? In the civil suit being brought by victims' families in Federal District Court in Washington, D.C., attorney Donald Madole remarked, "We do know that an Air Force general testified in the Senate this past year that there is over-the-shoulder, over-the-horizon radar at Shemya, Alaska, and that it goes out over the horizon throughout the area where this plane flew. We know that." In his book *America's War Machine,* defense analyst Tom Gervasi noted the existence of a radar system called Cobra Talon, "an over-the-horizon backscatter radar based on Shemya since 1972. Reflecting its beam off the earth's ionosphere, Cobra Talon detects anything airborne, at any altitude, between ranges of 575 and 2,070 miles away." A vice-president for flight training of a major U.S. commercial airline told me he had firsthand knowledge of OTH radar on Shemya. James Michelangelo, the chief of the National Transportation Safety Board's Anchorage office, told me in an interview that there is over-the-horizon radar at Elmendorf Air Force Base in Anchorage.[56]

Indeed, there is OTH radar around the world. *Jane's Weapons Systems* reported that other Cobra Talon radars were built at Dijar-Bakir in Turkey and Koka in Thailand. There was reportedly an OTH radar named Cobra Mist at Orford Ness in Suffolk, England, which was closed in June 1973 because "something better had become available." A new OTH system code-named Cold Witness is now being built in Orford Ness to complement an operational station in nearby Cricklade. Similar radars have been built in France, Cyprus, and at Chitose and Tokovozawa in Japan. The *New York Times* reported that U.S. facilities in Australia include "an over-the-horizon radar post." *Jane's* reported that the Navy has had working shipboard OTH radar since the mid-seventies. What this means is that the American military has "over-the-horizon radar and radio navigational ability that can track planes in their flights most places around the world."[57]

A final point to consider when Administration officials state that the United States has no OTH radars is that the Soviets have had such systems for some time. In the Pentagon's glossy publication on the Soviet threat, *Soviet Military Power,* several operational OTH systems are shown. In fact, both superpowers are experimenting with OTH radar in an effort to detect at considerable ranges "the minute variations in the wave pattern" caused by a submarine as it cruises beneath the sea, and much thought has been given to the problem of "ionospheric modification," a euphemism for OTH countermeasures.[58]

But like most top-secret programs, the existence of over-the-horizon radars can be plausibly denied. Published reports of congressional hearings delete key details about OTH systems. In congressional hearings after the downing of Flight 007, Captain Henry A. Duffy, president of the Air Line Pilots Association, mentioned that "defense radar has over-the-horizon capabilities." In response, Donald C. Latham, deputy undersecretary of defense for communications, command, control and intelligence, said, "I don't know what over-the-horizon radar they're talking about. No such radar exists in the Far East. As Jacques Ellul once noted, "well-known facts are simply made to disappear." [59]

"Letters to the editor and State Department spokesmen have since accused me of being 'far out' and of helping along Soviet 'disinformation,' " Tom Wicker wrote at the end of 1984, "but have not answered those questions to my satisfaction. So in due course and in the spirit of what I hope will be an invigorating 1985, I aim to ask them again, along with others perhaps as intriguing." [60]

19

IN COURT

Almost as soon as the Korean airliner went down, the lawyers began moving in. On September 2, Melvin Belli filed a $52 million suit charging "wanton negligence" against both Korean Air Lines and the Soviet Union on behalf of Michael Kole, a forty-year-old therapist from Albany, New York, who had lost his wife on the airliner. The following day, Belli and attorney David Sabih filed a class action lawsuit against KAL and the Soviet Union, calling for $99 billion in punitive and exemplary damages. In this second filing, the attorneys said that Korean Air Lines endangered its passengers and that the Soviets had launched a "barbaric, reprehensible, cowardly, deadly attack" on the plane.[1]

Other lawyers were also busy. On September 6, attorneys for Hans Ephraimson of Saddle River, New Jersey, who had lost his daughter on Flight 007, filed a $60 million suit against KAL, the Soviet Union, the Boeing Company, Litton Industries, and the estates of the three KAL cockpit crew members. Two weeks later, Betty Lim, the widow of Columbia University physicist Dr. Jong J. Lim, filed a $2 billion suit in New York against Korean Air Lines and Litton Industries. The suit also named the Soviet Union as a defendant.[2]

KAL Flight 007's airframe was insured for $35 million. The policy covered war risks, which meant that a claim would be paid even if the airliner was shot down. On September 13, Lloyd's of London and other insurance companies paid Korean Air Lines $26.8 million for the loss of the aircraft. Lloyd's was the underwriter for 76.64 percent of the plane's insured value, while the remainder was carried by Oriental Fire & Marine of Seoul. The South Korean company in turn was reinsured by several other companies, including the U.S. insurance firm Frank B. Hall & Co., which held 8 percent of the insured value, an amount that translated into $2.3 million. In addition to the coverage of the airframe, Korean Air Lines carried $365 million in insurance on the passengers and cargo. But determining the value of the people who were lost on the airliner was by no means as simple as calculating the value of a Boeing 747.[3]

In Japan, discussions with Korean Air Lines about compensation began almost immediately. The first meeting between Korean Air Lines and about eighty bereaved relatives of the Japanese who died on Flight 007 took place on September 11, 1983, at Tokyo's Imperial Hotel, as described in Chapter 10. A KAL official offered to pay $75,000 for each victim, as required under the terms of the Warsaw Convention. The families refused the money. As a result of the meeting, an association to press the families' claims against KAL was formed. Offices were opened in the hotel, and Yasukaza Kawana, whose twenty-year-old daughter had been on the flight, was elected the group's spokesman.[4]

On September 24, Korean Air Lines President Harry Cho met with Japanese Transport Vice-Minister Takaya Sugiura to discuss the issue of compensation. Sugiura thought the offer of $75,000 per victim was inadequate because the primary cause of the downing was the intrusion of Flight 007 into Soviet territory. Later that day, Cho told the families of the twenty-eight Japanese victims after a joint memorial service held at Aoyama Funeral Pavilion in Tokyo that KAL should probably not be held responsible for the violation of Soviet airspace. He suggested that the Soviets had electronically lured the airliner off course with false radio signals, a tactic known as "meaconing."[5] Asked why the Korean pilot would not have radioed that he was being lured off course, Cho offered the unconvincing explanation: "We were brought up on Confucian principles: When victims are suffering, we should not try to defend ourselves." Cho promised to present KAL's compensation plan to the Japanese families by December.[6]

The second meeting, on December 11, produced an additional offer of $25,000 for "special condolences." The Japanese families again demanded that KAL raise the amount of compensation.[7] The third round of talks with the Japanese families was in May 1984, but no new offer was made by KAL, which continued to insist that the airliner had been lured off course by "meaconing." Later, families of twenty-six Japanese victims filed a lawsuit in Tokyo court asking a total of $2.75 billion.[8]

In the United States, eighty-one claims resulting from the incident were consolidated, and pretrial proceedings began during the week of December 5, 1983, in U.S. District Court, Washington, D.C., with Chief Justice Aubrey E. Robinson, Jr., presiding. The plaintiffs were the families of those who died on board the airliner. The defendants were Korean Air Lines, Litton Industries, the Boeing Company, and the United States Government. Jeppesen Sanderson, Inc., the maker of the charts used on board Flight 007, had been named as a defendant, but Judge Robinson dismissed the company on the grounds that no causal link was established. The Soviet Union had also been named as a defendant in the case, but initial efforts to serve papers had met with failure, with the Russians refusing letters sent via certified mail. Later, the Soviets sent a diplomatic note saying that the court had no jurisdiction, and charges against the Soviets were formally dropped in August 1985. The steering committee for the plaintiffs' lawyers were Donald W. Madole of the Washington, D.C., firm of Speiser, Krause & Madole; Milton G. Sincoff of the New York firm of Kreindler & Kreindler; George E. Farrell of the Washington firm of Healey, Farrell & Lear; and F. Lee Bailey of the New York firm Bailey & Broder.[9]

From the outset, Justice Department attorneys argued that the United States should be dismissed as a defendant. Justice Department attorney Mark Dombroff told the court: "The United States has no role in this." In response to plaintiffs' charges that U.S. personnel had seen the deviating plane but had not notified it, Dombroff responded that even if they had seen the airliner going off course, they had no obligation to issue a warning. Dombroff also said that the court had no legal authority to act on "political questions" such as where military aircraft and intelligence assets were deployed.[10] Although it would take over two years, the request for dismissal would eventually be successful.

The U.S. also attempted to limit the scope of the case. At a pretrial hearing on December 9, 1983, George Tompkins, an attorney representing Korean Air Lines, requested a gag order that "prohibits the attorneys involved in this case and their clients from expressing views and opinions about this case in the press and in the news media." No compelling reasons or claims of "national security" were given for such an order. But on December 22, 1983, Judge Robinson prohibited divulging not only "information or documents" but also "any opinions with respect thereto." This order reduced media attention in the civil litigation, and hence to the case of Flight 007 more generally, blocked the flow of information developed in the civil case to outside investigators and kept other investigators from obtaining information from any party to the case, including Korean Air Lines, Litton Industries, the Boeing Company, and the United States Government.[11]

A month later, J. Lynn Helms's Federal Aviation Administration announced that the gag order "applies to all FAA employees" and insisted that "no person shall divulge any information or documents obtained in connection with the KAL 007 disaster to any person who is not a party to the lawsuit."[12]

In October 1984, attorneys for the *Washington Post* successfully challenged the scope of the gag order on constitutional grounds, as a violation of First Amendment rights of freedom of the press and the freedom of the public to information. Judge Robinson modified the order to cover only those documents (maps, charts, and so forth) and exact testimony of witnesses obtained during the pretrial "discovery process." But the blanket internal gag order on FAA employees still stands. "We have fifty thousand employees," said James Dillman, an assistant chief counsel for litigation at the FAA. "We can't allow each the latitude [Robinson's] order may contemplate." In fact, so little latitude was given to FAA personnel that they now even refuse to answer technical questions about the functioning of aircraft equipment in commercial use, such as the INS, even when the question has no direct connection to the KAL case.[13]

Justice Department attorney Mark Dombroff successfully argued that Judge Robinson should discourage parties in the suit from filing Freedom of Information Act (FOIA) requests. Robinson could not legally prohibit FOIA requests, but he said that attorneys who chose to do so could not participate in the consolidated suit and would have to "go their merry way" and initiate individual legal action. "I can ask for no more," said Mark Dombroff.[14]

The civil case was also limited by the invocation of national security. The State Department anticipated early on that "plaintiffs will demand all USG [U.S. Government] documents and may attempt to depose USG officials," and Justice Department attorneys argued successfully to limit the case in these respects. "We don't want to open up that can of worms as to whether this is a military intelligence, whether it is foreign surveillance, what are the capabilities of NASA [sic], what satellites you have got up there and what they are doing," Robinson said. As to whether the RC-135 or other planes in the vicinity could have contacted the Korean airliner, Robinson said, "That is out of the case once and for all." Thus Robinson effectively barred the attorneys representing the victims' families from exploring the possibility that Flight 007 had been on an intelligence mission. In response to protests, he decided on April 18, 1984, to allow questions to the military, "but only with respect to uncovering the existence of a legal duty [for the military] to warn or advise civilian aircraft."[15]

In the final analysis, however, the civil case was not intended to find the cause of Flight 007's deviation from course. A tort case, as any lawyer knows, is about money. If the lawyers could prove that the crew of the airliner was guilty of "willful misconduct" rather than an unintentional error in judgment, then the $75,000 limit set by the Warsaw Convention would not obtain, and there would be no limit to the damages that could be claimed. Working on a contingency basis, attorneys receive no payment unless they win; but if they do, they get one-third, and in some instances one-half, of the damages awarded. So success in such a case does not necessarily mean bringing out the whole truth; it means obtaining an acceptable settlement for one's clients.[16]

Unlike the lawyers, the families of Flight 007's Japanese victims wanted to find out why the airliner had gone off course. On March 20, 1984, the bereaved association issued a statement saying, ''We cannot but have a deep and grave suspicion that the aircraft, in close association with American intelligence agencies, deliberately intruded on important Soviet military installations on several occasions.'' By this time the association had joined with a group of technicians from Japan Air Lines and had published pamphlets entitled ''Pursuing the Truth in the KAL Affair'' and ''Deepening Doubts on the ICAO Report.'' [17] Beginning on May Day 1984, the association began sending monthly letters to President Reagan, demanding he tell ''the truth should you know it.'' Month by month, additional letters followed, each becoming angrier and more accusatory. By August 1984 the letters called Reagan an ''accessory to murder.'' [18]

On September 1, 1984, a new group including bereaved family members, members of the Japanese Diet, and Japan Air Lines personnel set up offices in Tokyo.[19] The Association for Inquiry into the Truth of the KAL Incident pointed out that the explanations for the tragedy offered by the United States, Japan, South Korea, and the Soviet Union were unconvincing and incomplete. ''We demand again that the governments of the four countries and officials of Korean Air Lines disclose to the public all information on the incident without manipulation of the facts,'' the founding announcement read. As Hideyuki Seya, a Socialist senator in the Diet and member of the association, added, ''The fact that the plane was shot down by the Soviets has been much played up. But the reason why the plane violated Soviet airspace has not been fully pursued.'' [20]

As 1984 drew to a close, the families of seven Japanese victims filed suit against Korean Air in Tokyo District Court, arguing that Korean Air was responsible for damages in excess of the Warsaw Convention limit of $75,000 because the crew of Flight 007 had either willingly trespassed into Soviet territory or had committed grave negligence in navigating their aircraft. Lawyers representing the airline continued to claim that their client bore no responsibility for the incident because the jetliner flew off course because of Soviet ''meaconing.'' They also argued that bereaved relatives of passengers who had purchased a round-trip ticket between New York and Seoul were not in a position to bring suit in a Japanese court because the destination on the tickets had not been Japan.[21]

Other Japanese families were taking a different approach. In mid-December, the families of nineteen Japanese victims filed suit in United States District Court in Los Angeles. After some preliminaries, the suit was transferred to U.S. District Court for the District of Columbia. In Washington, attorneys from the law firm of Speiser, Krause & Madole would represent the Japanese, and in January 1985, several attorneys flew to Japan to explain the progress of the court case to their new clients. The group had filed suit in the United States because its members wanted a forum where the U.S. Government would be one of the defendants.[22]

The plaintiffs' steering committee soon discovered that not only had the scope of the pretrial "discovery" process been severely limited, but there was no cooperation from the Administration even on those topics on which the investigation could legally proceed. Requests for information were delayed or refused, and it became increasingly clear that a number of agencies, the Department of State in particular, were not cooperating. As veteran aviation lawyer Donald Madole remarked in court, "This is the only accident investigation that I have ever been involved in in the thirty years that I have been involved in this business where the release of accident investigation information is from the Department of State. It does not come from the FAA. It's not with the National Transportation Board. . . . Therefore, we were not in a position at this time as we are normally in an aviation case to look at the facts involved. . . . [W]e have a motion to produce documents with the United States Government—and we have received no information except we have obtained a copy of the ICAO report." [23]

The discovery process in a trial involves gathering sworn testimony from individuals considered relevant to the case. One of those scheduled to appear was Captain Park Young-man, the pilot of KAL Flight 015. A former Korean Air Force pilot, Park had been Chun Byung-in's superior officer and close personal friend. He had been in communication with Flight 007 throughout the fateful flight and had relayed its position reports. Some of the lawyers representing the victims' families said that Park had been extremely upset by the death of his friend and had made some disparaging remarks about Korean Air Lines. Park was being kept away from the press, and there were suggestions that he was under an informal "house arrest" in the Republic of Korea.

On the day he was slated to testify, KAL lawyers announced that Park would not appear. Attorney George N. Tompkins blamed "personal reasons." "It's a family matter," he averred. Tompkins then explained that the reasons were also professional: In a recent reorganization of Korean Air Lines, Captain Park had been assigned to a desk job. In what Tompkins called a "power play," Park refused to testify unless he was put back on full flight status. KAL turned him down, Tompkins said, "and he resigned." The convenient result of all this was that KAL was no longer obliged to produce the allegedly disgruntled Park as a witness. In his place appeared Flight 015 First Officer Hwang Duk-sun. [24]

Following Park's failure to appear, Justice Department attorneys suggested to the plaintiff's lawyers that taking testimony was too cumbersome and time-consuming a procedure. Instead, they suggested that plantiffs' counsel submit a series of written questions, called interrogatories, to which the government would reply. Attorney Donald Madole responded on October 29 with a set of questions that asked, among other things, for data from two U.S. Air Force radars located on the coast of Alaska. The data were of interest because on its deviating course Flight 007 had passed through the area of coverage for each. But as Madole angrily remarked, the government promptly "lost the interrogatories for four months." By mid-February 1985, Madole had still not received the answers to his questions and had to insist that they be provided.[25] When the answers finally arrived, Madole and his colleagues were shocked.

The radar data had been destroyed. The Regional Operations Control Center at Elmendorf Air Force Base in Anchorage had in fact tracked the Korean airliner and recorded a far longer portion of its flight path than had previously been acknowledged. As the *Washington Post* pointed out, "The Air Force, which customarily impounds any information relating to an aviation disaster," destroyed the tapes. Justice Department attorney Jan Van Flatern explained that the radar data in question were "just Air Force data" that were recycled every 15 days. The data had not been preserved, it was said, "because within 15 days of this incident, the Air Force, the Regional Operations Control Center, had no idea that it was going to be involved or that that data would be useful in the litigation at any point."[26]

Van Flatern then went on to assure the court that Air Force personnel had not seen anything unusual on their radar scopes when Flight 007 was shot down. Of course they hadn't; nobody said that the Air Force radars in question could monitor Flight 007 when it was shot down. What was at issue was what the radars had monitored four hours before the shootdown, when Flight 007 was within their area of coverage. "Outbound aircraft such as 007 would have been are not monitored," Van Flatern continued, "or were not particularly at that time."[27]

The Justice Department attorney's remarks were characteristic of the way government officials had handled information about radar from the very beginning. At first, they claimed that only civil air traffic control radars could track Flight 007, and these only for the first half hour of its flight. Beyond that, "we would have no way of knowing if the aircraft was not where a pilot said he was." In addition, the State Department said that the military "did not detect the plane going off course." After the disclosure that the airliner was detected off course by the U.S. Air Force radar station at King Salmon, FAA personnel claimed that nobody would have known about it because the screen on which the data were displayed was "in the basement." When that could no longer be sustained, the display was said to be "down the hall." Finally, when it could no longer be denied, it was admitted that the data in fact were fed to a screen next to the controllers in charge of the airspace leading to Bethel.[28]

Radar coverage was now admitted through Bethel, but no farther, and government officials quickly moved to downplay its importance. Hank Elias, assistant manager of the Air Route Traffic Control Center in Anchorage, said that he did not know if the controllers had looked at the radar. The controllers themselves professed to recall nothing about the night in question. Other officials said the radar could not have been used anyway because it lacked certification from the FAA. The ICAO report repeated that the radar was not "certified for use in civil air traffic control,'' then went on to add "nor was information from it presented to the controller."[29] (When the ICAO team examined the radar, however, they found it sufficiently accurate to show a 12-nautical-mile divergence by Flight 007 at Bethel.)

What about coverage beyond Bethel? The ICAO report flatly said that once Flight 007 passed that waypoint, "there was no means by which the controllers could have independently determined its position. From Bethel to KE007's destruction near Sakhalin Island, controllers had to rely on pilot reporting, the only available information."[30] Now it had come to light that several additional military radars had the capability to track Flight 007 on its deviating course well beyond Bethel, but the data from those radars had been destroyed.

The admitted destruction of evidence did not seem to bother Judge Robinson. "Your Honor, excuse me," Van Flatern continued. "I have been advised that I misspoke myself, and I mixed up the air traffic service and the Air Force. Actually the radar tapes are kept for thirty hours and not for fifteen days." "In any event, we don't have them," Robinson replied. "We do not have them," Van Flatern affirmed. "And we have not had them since shortly after the accident," the judge continued. "That is correct," said Jan Van Flatern.[31] The fact that the fate of Flight 007 was known well prior to either 15 days or 30 hours apparently struck nobody as important.

The Air Force explained its actions by more or less repeating what Justice Department lawyers had said in court. Pentagon spokesman Michael Burch told reporters that the tapes had been "routinely erased" for reuse some 24 to 30 hours after they were recorded. "The tapes would have shown the Korean airliner only up to the limits of the radar," Burch noted, and the site where the plane was shot down was "beyond the Air Force's radar range."[32]

"Routine," "no idea" the data would prove useful—the language sounded uncomfortably familiar, indeed identical to that used by the Air Force in another incident several years earlier.[33] In an effort to humanize the U.S.'s withdrawal from Vietnam in the spring of 1975, President Gerald Ford ordered that a number of Vietnamese war orphans be brought to the United States in what was called Operation Babylift. At a press conference announcing the operation, Ford said that the plane to be used was the Lockheed C5A, a flying building of a plane—the world's largest—and an aircraft already legendary for its serious mechanical problems.

Even on the face of things the C5A seemed an unlikely choice. It was a cargo plane, not a passenger airliner. There were no on-board provisions for the orphans, especially the infants among them. The Air Force had medical planes on hand, and a charter passenger jet could easily have been hired, but Ford's choice was the giant C5A. The reason, as television producer Danny Schechter put it, was "to rehabilitate the aircraft's image at a time when Lockheed was on the ropes financially and politically, a time when Congress was being asked to spend millions more on repairing the plane.''

Repairs were not a bad idea because the plane's cargo doors kept falling off in flight. An Air Force study in 1971 had called the doors a "monster system" that could lead to a catastrophe, but nothing was done. Lockheed engineers had recommended improvements, but management vetoed the work until the Air Force agreed to pay the costs of the repairs. The doors of one C5A had fallen off just two months before Operation Babylift commenced in April 1975.

Captain Dennis Traynor lifted the giant plane into the air, climbing to an altitude of 23,752 feet twelve minutes later. That's when the doors fell off. In less than a second, all the air was sucked out in an explosive roar. Many of the children and crew members in the cargo hold were sucked out as well. For many of the children in the passenger compartment on the upper deck, the oxygen masks did not fit; they were for adults, not small children. Most of the children still in the plane lost consciousness.

When the doors fell off, they severed several of the plane's control cables. With only partial control, Captain Traynor turned his aircraft, as best he could, to make an emergency landing in Saigon. The C5A touched down in a rice paddy two miles short of the runway, bounced back into the air, crossed the Saigon River, and hit an irrigation dike. It came apart in four sections. Although the crew walked away from the wreckage, only six children and a few adults who had been in the cargo hold survived. One hundred and fifty-three people died.

The Air Force and Lockheed fought hard to limit their liability, spending an estimated $10 million on their legal defense. The multiple neurological problems subsequently experienced by some of the survivors were dismissed by Lockheed's doctors as unrelated to the accident. But things were not going well for the defendants and, as Schechter wrote, "it emerged later that the Air Force had destroyed 'hundred, perhaps thousands of photographs, negatives, and slides of the crash scene and wreckage.' One Air Force official who admitted burning the documents said he didn't know why they should have been saved as evidence. He said the destruction was 'routine.' The trial judge would later call this destruction 'intentional' and 'questionable.' ''

Things were equally questionable in the destruction of the tapes covering the flight of the Korean airliner. Although the destruction of the tapes was publicly portrayed as a routine action, Air Force sources report that standard operating procedures were not followed and the destruction was anything but routine. According to the sources, radar tapes at Elmendorf Air Force Base are always given to the radar watch officer, who puts them in a vault for safekeeping. But on the night Flight 007 was shot down, the tapes were not put in the vault. They were erased "by mistake."

Although the destruction of the Flight 007 radar tapes was reported in the media, the U.S. press did not ask questions. But Tass picked up the story, arguing that "the tapes would have supplied further proof that the deviation of the plane from its course had been preplanned" and that the tapes were not erased "by chance." [34]

What might have been on the tapes that the Air Force found necessary to destroy? On March 1, 1984, the Russians told the ICAO Council that "Soviet experts processed the data contained in the [ICAO] report and came to a conclusion that prior to reaching [waypoint] NABIE the airplane made an approximately 20-degree turn to the right of the route and headed for Kamchatka." The Russians offered no evidence to back up their claim, and it went unmentioned in the press and is reported here for the first time.[35] I and other investigators had been pondering this issue for some time and had reached the tentative conclusion that the Soviets were right: Flight 007 probably made some sort of course change during the time it was in the radars' area of coverage. The problem was to prove it without the radar data the Air Force had destroyed.

In fact, such a turn can be logically demonstrated. In the course of the investigation, I had met a pilot who flew 747s for a major U.S. cargo carrier. He was interested in the case and was very excited to learn that I had the data from the civil radar station at Kenai, west of Anchorage, and from the Air Force station at King Salmon (the data the ICAO inquiry team used in determining that Flight 007 had been 12 nautical miles north of course when it reached Bethel). I sent the pilot copies of the data, and he called back several weeks later with an important finding: The course flown by the Korean airliner during the time of radar coverage had been perfectly straight—a "Great Circle" course. As the pilot explained, the probability was infinitesimal that an aircraft could fly such a perfectly straight course in any other way than by its inertial navigation system. "I therefore take this as very strong evidence," he said, that Flight 007 "was being navigated by reference to INS virtually from the moment that it was cleared direct to Bethel." [36]

Based on the pilot's finding that Flight 007 had followed a great circle course—a straight line—between Anchorage and Bethel, the next step was to project that course to see where it went. But to plot a straight line on the surface of a globe requires more than an atlas and a straightedge. I contacted Dr. Robert L. Williams, the retired director of the Yale University Map Studies Laboratory, and asked him two questions: Was Flight 007 in fact flying a perfectly straight course? If so, where would that course have taken the airliner? The issue was whether or not the airliner had made a turn in order to enter Soviet territory where it did.

Williams' answers were unequivocal: The course flown by Flight 007 was, he said, a near-perfect Great Circle.[37] This meant the airliner was being directed by its INS because given the airliner's changes in altitude and the variable windfield it encountered, no other mode of navigation could have produced such a course. It was an INS-directed course, but the question was to where? Projecting the early track flown by the airliner led to a course that entered Soviet territory for the first time over the Commander Islands off the coast of Kamchatka, missing the peninsula entirely. Projecting the course even further showed a route that crossed the Kuril Islands and eventually wound up near Tokyo. But Flight 007 did not cross over the Kuril Islands. It did not fly to Tokyo. Williams concluded, "Yes, a definite turn away from a Great Circle route would have to be made to reach Kamchatka." The turn to the north put Flight 007 on a course directly toward some of the Soviet Union's most sensitive military facilities (see map at end of chapter 3).[38]

This turn almost certainly occurred within range of the Air Force radars located on the Alaskan coast at Cape Newenham, Cape Romanzof, and Tin City—the radars whose data were destroyed. The lawyers representing the next of kin concluded, "Consequently, an adverse inference may be raised that the destroyed data, solely in the possession and control of the defendant, contained information which was detrimental to the United States."[39]

On August 2, 1985, Judge Aubrey Robinson dismissed the lawsuits against the Soviet Union. In a seventeen-page opinion, he said that the Soviet Union could not be held liable because of the "act of state" doctrine that bars U.S. courts from judging the actions of other governments which occur on foreign soil or from interfering in the political conduct of foreign affairs. In a separate action, Robinson also dismissed charges against the Boeing Company and Litton Industries. According to the judge's nineteen-page opinion, the two companies could not be held liable for equipment failure in the incident. "No jury in the land," Robinson wrote, "could reasonably find that this chain of events, assumed to have begun with equipment failure and ended with an act of military aggression by a world power against a commercial airliner, was foreseeable to the airplane and equipment manufacturers."[40] Who assumed that Flight 007's deviation began with equipment failure, and on the basis of what evidence? But that was the operative assumption of the civil case.

In the meantime, attorneys representing the families of those who died on Flight 007 continued to experience difficulties in their efforts to obtain information from the government. Documents they requested were never produced. For example, it was only by accident that the lawyers discovered the Air Force regulations requiring military personnel to warn civilian planes about to enter the buffer zone. Witnesses were uncooperative. The lawyers who had questioned people who had been on duty the night of the downing at the Air Route Traffic Control Center and the Regional Operations Control Center at Elmendorf Air Base said in court: "Global amnesia seems to have affected the personnel who were on duty. . . . No one remembers any specific events of the evening in question."[41]

What could the Anchorage air traffic controllers have wanted to forget? A possible answer emerged on August 30, 1985, in the form of an affidavit from a veteran air controller, Raymond Yeager, who had listened to a copy of the communications among controllers in the Air Route Traffic Control Center and asserted that someone had said, "We should warn him."[42]

In a roundabout way, my colleague John Keppel and I were responsible for Yeager's claim. We had hired acoustic expert Lawrence L. Porter, at that time a consultant to Aviation Safety Associates International, to do an analysis of the communications recorded at the Air Route Traffic Control Center on the night Flight 007 was shot down. He heard a background voice on the tapes of communications between U.S. air traffic controllers and KAL Flights 007 and 015 at 1434:04 GMT, the time Flight 007 was entering the Soviet buffer zone. At first he rendered the voice as saying "[unintelligible] should warn him." His best guess for the unintelligible portion was "persons" or "first we." Since it is unlikely that a native English speaker would say "persons should warn him," Porter leaned toward the second rendering.

We immediately wrote to attorney Donald Madole, who asked our principal acoustic consultant at the time, Malcolm Brenner, to make a sworn deposition regarding the new material. Brenner told Madole that "[unintelligible] should warn him" was a "plausible interpretation" made by an extremely able air-crash investigator. (We weren't naming Larry Porter at that time.) But because Brenner had not himself spent much time with the new material and was reluctant to give away the material for which we, his clients, had already paid thousands of dollars, he refused to make a sworn statement. But Keppel and I agreed to give Madole a copy of the enhanced, filtered tape, and Madole had it flown to Washington for copying.

In August 1985, just after the Justice Department attorneys asked for a dismissal of all charges against the United States, the tape reappeared. Plaintiffs' council had given the tape to former air traffic controller Raymond Yeager to analyze. Yeager heard pretty much what Larry Porter did: "We should warn him." Madole submitted Yeager's affidavit to counter the Justice Department's motion to have the U.S. Government dismissed as a defendant in the case. Milton Sincoff, co-chairman of the plaintiffs' steering committee, said, "The government knows the identity of the person who said those words and is concealing it. . . . The concealment of the identity of the person who spoke those words and the destruction of the [radar] recordings indicate the obvious."[43]

Tom Wicker picked up this story in the first of a two-part column on September 3. If "these words, in fact, can be heard," wrote Wicker, ". . . they contradict the Reagan administration's repeated, if hard to believe, claim that no American knew Flight 007 was in trouble during more than five hours when it flew off course by hundreds of miles across skies in which the United States deploys a vast array of electronic sentinels."[44] Given a news peg by the second anniversary of the tragedy, other major media decided it might be worth taking another look at the story.

But the tape didn't do much good in the courtroom. On May 7, 1986,

Robinson dismissed the suits brought against the U.S. Government by the families of those who died on Flight 007. The judge said that "neither the Federal Aviation Administration nor the Defense Department had failed to perform any required duties in connection with the flight" and that there was nothing on the tape to support the assertion that air traffic controllers knew Flight 007 was off course. (However, if Flight 007 had been observed heading for the buffer zone, Robinson was mistaken. Air Force personnel are required to notify civilian air traffic controllers if a plane is heading toward the zone. Information about the relevant Air Force regulation was not volunteered by government witnesses and was discovered only by accident.) Judge Robinson also asserted that "the Soviets' unnecessary act of aggression against KAL 007 was a superseding cause of harm insulating the United States from any liability." [45]

The Federal Aviation Administration announced it was "pleased" by Judge Robinson's decision. Agency spokesman Robert Buckhorn told the press, "It has always been the position of the FAA that our traffic controllers at the Anchorage Air Route Traffic Control Center had no knowledge of Korean Air Lines 007's departure from its flight-plan course and that they had no means of ascertaining that the flight had strayed from its assigned course." [46]

20

THE INVESTIGATION CONTINUES

Most of those who questioned the official U.S. account of the downing of Flight 007 called for a congressional inquiry. My original *Nation* article, for instance, concluded, "Congress owes it to the passengers of KAL 007, their families, the people of the United States and the world community to conduct a full and thorough investigation, to let the truth be known." In an op-ed piece on the first anniversary, John Keppel and I repeated the point.[1]

The Administration used Congress the way it used the ICAO. It provided limited information to the investigators and then claimed that an adequate review had been conducted. Within days of the downing, the House Permanent Select Committee on Intelligence made what it described as an inquiry into the facts of the case, obtaining "detailed information from the intelligence community." The committee's chief counsel, Michael O'Neill, said that the Administration's account was "accurate and leaves out no relevant details." Asked whether the House Committee had access to critical information such as the radar data showing Flight 007's passage over Kamchatka and Sakhalin, O'Neill replied, "We had access to everything there was to have access to." However, a House aide who was familiar with the inquiry has been quoted as saying, "I wouldn't really dignify it by calling it an investigation." What the inquiry amounted to was a parade of Administration officials repeating the official version of events. As Edward P. Boland, the committee's chairman at the time, said, "The committee obtained testimony only from U.S. officials." Interviewing Administration officials is a necessary step, but relying exclusively on their testimony hardly constitutes an investigation.[2]

But the article in *The Nation* stirred things up, and Boland's committee made another round of calls to the intelligence community and the Department of State. In closed-door hearings in early 1985, Boland reported to Congress on his committee's findings. Once again relying exclusively on the word of precisely those officials whose testimony should have been examined, examining no documents or physical evidence, Boland announced, "The committee found nothing to indicate that U.S. intelligence knew the KAL 007 was off track." But finding nothing might mean only that nothing was provided.

The Senate Intelligence Committee also conducted an inquiry, but there are questions about just how thorough and independent it actually was. In its 1984 year-end report, the committee explained how its inquiry was conducted: "Shortly after the event, the Committee was briefed on the KAL 007 tragedy by the appropriate U.S. intelligence agencies. Subsequently, committee staff received periodic updates. Individual committee members also pursued the matter in separate meetings with intelligence and State Department officials." Not surprisingly, the result of these briefings was that "the committee concludes that there was no direct or indirect involvement by the U.S. Intelligence Community in the events leading to the KAL 007 disaster." As David Corn noted in *The Nation*, "No public hearings were held, and the committees will not release the names of the government officials they questioned or even a summary of the material on which they based their conclusions."[3]

The Administration soon proclaimed these limited, closed-door reviews as the reason why there should be no additional inquiry into the downing: "The intelligence committees of both houses have looked into the incident." Right-wing members of the media said that "the Intelligence Committee has exposed the fraudulent nature of the charges." But no independent investigation, with access to all relevant information, had yet been done.[4]

Independent investigators of the case encountered many obstacles. One of the few ways a private citizen or group can compel government agencies to open their files is the Freedom of Information Act. Claiming that FOIA has weakened law-enforcement and become burdensome to enforce, the Reagan administration has done its utmost to limit the scope of the act, supporting bills that would exempt the CIA, the FBI, and the Secret Service. On the Administration's initiative, the classification system has been expanded and attempts have been made to "reclassify" some previously public information. To make information more difficult to obtain, the Administration has reversed the earlier policy of giving fee waivers or reductions to writers, journalists, and scholars. Now, a waiver cannot be granted unless the release of the material in question "meaningfully contributes to the public development or understanding of the subject." "The effect of the new guidelines," Floyd Abrams pointed out, "was to permit the government to decide what information about its conduct—or misconduct— was 'meaningful.' "[5]

After the downing of Flight 007, many people, including me, filed requests under the Freedom of Information Act. Although many agencies of government were targeted, the agencies referred most requests to the Department of State. For a long time the only response was that the department's information and privacy staff was busy reviewing the agency's files to determine what could be released. Not until April 1985 did State finally release over 1,066 pages of documents.

But the documents that were finally released were almost worthless. These 1,000-odd pages were not directly responsive to a single request for specific information. Instead, they consisted almost entirely of reports by U.S. posts abroad on foreign press reaction to the downing. The documents noted that "President [Luis] Monge and Foreign Minister [Fernando] Volio have signed executive order declaring September 8 as day of national mourning in Costa Rica"; that "Greek Cypriot and Turkish Cypriot newspapers have given both heavy factual and editorial coverage to the shooting down of the Korean airliner"; and that the "Peruvian Senate passed resolution September 6 which condemned 'criminal Soviet attack' on KAL airliner." This was the material State had requested following the shootdown, Jack Anderson pointed out, "to know just how big a black eye the Soviets had given themselves." Texts of statements by U.S. officials, which could be found in any newspaper, were also included. As David Sobel, an attorney with the Washington firm of Dobrovir & Gebhardt, remarked, the material "seems to comprise the 'diplomatic history' of the incident and does not address the specifics of what actually happened during the flight." The cost was 10 cents per page.[6]

Sobel, an attorney specializing in FOIA cases, had himself filed a request with the Department of State on behalf of the Fund for Constitutional Government on February 22, 1985. He asked for "all records relating to the crash of a Korean Air Lines Boeing 747 aircraft, operated as Flight 007 from Anchorage, Alaska, to Seoul, Republic of Korea, on August 31, 1983, that were provided to the International Civil Aviation Organization (ICAO) by the government of the United States."[7] A list of what information the United States supplied to ICAO, a United Nations agency, should have been readily available.

In mid-April, State released its first batch of documents, none of which were at all responsive to Sobel's request. Sobel continued to press for the material, but State responded that it did not have the information Sobel wanted. "I find it incredible," Sobel remarked, "that State doesn't have a record of documents it provided to an international organization." Strikingly, the ICAO also claims not to have such a list either.[8] There was little Sobel could do except file an appeal. If this proved unsuccessful, his client would have to take the matter to court, an expensive process. As government agencies are well aware, this is an effective barrier to all but the wealthiest and most persistent of questioners.

On August 16, Sobel appealed State's handling of his request. He objected to State's claim that its large batch of documents were "responsive" to his specific request, for under the Freedom of Information Act, State lacks authority to reformulate requests in this manner. Sobel also objected to the failure to provide the requested information in a timely manner, since FOIA requires that requested documents be provided within ten working days. As of this writing, Sobel has not received the materials he requested.[9] In the meantime, State has released two larger and equally worthless batches of documents.

The Department of State is by no means the only unresponsive government agency when it comes to Flight 007. If one takes literally a response to a FOIA request I filed with the Department of Defense, the vessels involved in the search for the black box were almost totally incommunicado for months. The Department of Defense thus says it cannot make available any information about the ships' role in the recovery effort.

On February 5, 1985, Anne Hurley, a free-lance journalist from California, visited the U.S.S. *Wichita,* one of the ships that had participated in the recovery effort in the Sea of Japan. She was shown around the ship by one Lieutenant Commander Skirm. As Hurley recalled, Skirm "took me to his office, and the conversation about the plane continued there in the presence of a young sailor. . . . At some point the ship's commander Woody Sprouse joined us. I asked, in Sprouse's presence, if there was a written summary of the recovery effort. All three of them said that there was. According to Sprouse and Skirm, they had made such a report at the end of the recovery mission and it was called an 'End of Operation Report.' They said I could get it by writing to the Pentagon. They both felt, however, that it would be considered 'classified.' "[10]

Hurley provided me with a copy of her notes, and on the basis of her account, I filed several FOIA requests for End of Operation Reports for a number of vessels involved in the recovery operation, including U.S.N.S. *Narragansett,* U.S.S. *Badger,* and U.S.S. *Wichita.* The requests were mailed to the Department of Defense on March 17, 1985. On June 19, W. I. Lewis, Jr., the deputy chief of staff for management/inspector general for the commander-in-chief, U.S. Pacific Forces, responded: "No end of operations reports or summaries of operations exist from U.S.N.S. *Narragansett,* U.S.S. *Badger,* or U.S.S. *Wichita.* Therefore, no reports or summaries of operations will be provided in regard to your Freedom of Information Act request."

Anne Hurley reaffirmed the specifics of her conversation on the *Wichita,* and at my request drafted a sworn statement attesting to her meeting with

Sprouse and Skirm. The statement was submitted with a reformulation of the FOIA request on July 3. On July 26, I received a reply. According to Lewis, "An exhaustive search has produced three messages, two from U.S.N.S. *Narragansett* and one from U.S.S. *Wichita*. . . . No messages were found from U.S.S. *Badger*. The executive officer of U.S.S. *Wichita* was contacted as a result of your letter. He stated that the ship did not have any information of reports of the type to which your associate referred in her statement." The message from the *Wichita*, dated October 10, 1983, was a routine twelve-line communication about logistics. The messages from the *Narragansett* were both brief. The first dealt with spare parts and returning personnel to San Diego. The second consisted of one sentence: "KAL FLT 007 SALVOPS TERMINATED 050600z NOV 83."

According to several naval sources, it is impossible that three vessels would have sent a total of three messages over two months. Where were the messages about the Soviet harassment of the search operations? Where were the messages confirming arrangements for the international visitors who boarded the *Wichita* in late September 1983? Where were all the ship-to-shore and ship-to-ship communications necessary for coordinating the many activities and phases of the operation? I was not told that the Department of Defense was not releasing information—the very existence of the information was denied. The officers of the *Wichita*, who recommended that a journalist ask for a specific report, now deny that there is such a document. This was neither the first nor the last time that officials would deny their own statements.

By the spring of 1985, a new line of inquiry was opening up. An article by investigative reporter Duncan Campbell in the British journal *New Statesman* examined the turns made by Flight 007 over Sakhalin. "The data needed to prove KE007 was misleading air traffic control," Campbell began, "was, ironically, first published on the day of the shootdown itself, in the evening edition of the Tokyo newspaper *Asahi Shimbun*." Several hours after the downing, the Japan Defense Agency had posted on the wall of its press room a large map of Sakhalin showing the path of Flight 007 as a broad arc as it crossed the island. Japanese journalists reported this, although they did not consider the implications of a curving course. In the United States, the curve over Sakhalin was reported twice, in the September 12 and 19 issues of *Aviation Week & Space Technology*.[11]

One of the few reporters in the United States who carefully examined the transcripts of the Soviet pilots' communications was Knut Royce of the Hearst newspaper group. Royce recalled that President Reagan had claimed in his September 5 address to the nation that Flight 007 "flew a straight line course" and recalled that an identical claim had been made by Ambassador Kirkpatrick in the Security Council chamber. But as Royce correctly observed, Flight 007 was initially reported by the Soviet pilots to have been on a course of 240 degrees.[12] Then they said it had changed course, and then that it had resumed its original heading. Royce concluded, "What this means according to defense sources is that the plane must have made at least one other turn to have taken it off the 240-degree course to begin with." This suggested that Flight 007 had turned twice as it approached Sakhalin Island, first to the right—taking it deeper into Soviet territory—and then back to the left. This was precisely what Tass had claimed on September 2.[13] Royce's report was ignored in the heated atmosphere of September 1983.

Duncan Campbell noted that Japanese radar operators at Wakkanai claimed to have first picked up the airliner at 1812 GMT, when it was traveling on a course of about 260 degrees, just south of due west. "During the seventeen minutes or so that it was tracked," Campbell said, "this heading changed continuously to the left, by about 20 degrees."[14] The two turns described by the Soviet interceptor occurred just before 1812 GMT —when the Japanese government alleges that Wakkanai radar operators were not tracking Flight 007.

The problem with this explanation is that the range of the Japanese military radars on northern Hokkaido is far greater than the official account suggests. Even using conservative estimates of their range—about 250 miles for an airliner at Flight 007's altitude of 32,000 feet—the radars at both Wakkanai and Abashiri would have picked up Flight 007 before 1800 GMT. If the theoretical maximum range of the radars is considered —about 300 miles for an object at that altitude—the airliner should have been picked up many minutes earlier. The weather was good, so there was nothing to interfere with radar tracking. But when several members of the Diet requested the radar tapes, the JDA refused "because this would reveal the capabilities of our nation's radar."[15]

The ICAO inquiry team had considered the turn "and the different theories about it," said Marinus Heijl, a participant in the inquiry. "But we had no real explanation for any turn or any information about that turn." With no information, however, they charged right ahead:

> The track of KE007 as depicted in the USSR preliminary report showed a distinct curve over southern Sakhalin Island, whereas the track shown by the Wakkanai radar followed a smoother curve. Making two assumptions, an explanation could be given as follows. Firstly, assuming that the radar track information is based on memories of radar observers rather than on recorded radar data, the shape of the depicted curve could have been smoothed and a smaller, more distinct bulge could have been displayed by an air defense radar on Sakhalin Island. Secondly, assuming that the airliner could have flown almost overhead the radar antenna, the track would have been distorted by the "slant range effect," which would project the aircraft's height as a horizontal distance on the radar display. Obviously, the track displayed by the Wakkanai radar would not show such a distortion.

In fact, there are several unwarranted assumptions here. The first is that the Soviets did not record the radar data. Second, it is assumed that the radar operators who noted the turn exaggerated the turn they had seen. Third is the assumption that whatever they saw was an artifact of their equipment, the "slant range effect," but the ICAO team did not determine whether Flight 007 had, in fact, passed directly overhead a radar station. Fourth, the ICAO had to discount reports that the Japanese had also recorded a turn—which would not have been subject to the same distorting "slant range effect"—because the Japanese never provided the ICAO with any radar data. Finally, it is necessary to avoid comment on the Russian pilots' transmissions, which clearly show that turns were made.[16]

The implication of these remarks (see Chapter 3) is unmistakable: On approach to Sakhalin Island, Flight 007 turned to the right. Several minutes later it turned to the left, eventually resuming its original course. As a 747 pilot who examined the sequence of Soviet communications concluded, "I feel that the above exchange can be interpreted only one way—as referring to some kind of turn on the part of KE007—and that it is in fact confirmation that the turn described by the Soviets did in fact occur."[17]

The Reagan administration disagreed. Secretary of State Shultz had originally described the Soviet claim that Flight 007 had made turns on approach to Sakhalin as part of a "brazen and elaborate" cover-up. At the United Nations a week after the downing, Ambassador Kirkpatrick presented a map of Flight 007's course: "Derived from intercepted Soviet tracking data, it shows no such turns." The U.S. Information Agency's glossy and highly misleading pamphlet, *The Shootdown of KAL 007: Moscow's Charges—and the Record,* included a map of the Korean airliner's flight path from takeoff to shootdown, but no turns over Sakhalin were shown. Countering Soviet "assertions" with what it said were American "facts," the USIA said that "the pilot evidently was unaware even then of his course deviation or of the Soviet interceptors in the area, so that he would have had no reason to engage in evasive maneuvers." Unofficial supporters of the official line such as Murray Sayle joined in, suggesting that turns—"if in fact they occurred"—were merely the result of the so-called slant effect, a phenomenon whereby "an aircraft passing straight by a radar station . . . looks to an unwary operator to be describing a curve." As to the Soviet pilot's report that the target had executed turns, this is now dismissed by the State Department as "a mistaken report by the interceptor pilot, who was maneuvering himself at the time."[18]

In Japan, some of the most dramatic new evidence in this case was revealed through the efforts of the Japan Association for the Truth into the KAL Incident. On February 15, 1985, Socialist Diet member Shun Oide called on the Japanese government to release the full tapes of the transmissions from the Soviet pilots to their ground controllers that were recorded by Japanese intelligence. Oide was suspicious of the 4-minute time gap between the first and second Soviet transmissions that were recorded and was sure that some information had been omitted. Oide was also dubious about the government's contention that the Soviet ground controllers had not been recorded. Finally, he felt the translations of the Soviet transmissions that had been made public were misleading. The government of Japan refused. In turning down Oide's request, Shinju Yasaki, a Japan Defense Agency official in charge of defense policy, said that to release the tape would compromise Japan's intelligence-gathering capabilities. This is striking, since what was purported to be the entire tape had been released by U.N. Ambassador Kirkpatrick on September 6, 1983. Yasaki again insisted that Japan did not have the ground-to-air recordings from Soviet ground control stations.[19]

Withholding information about the case from members of the Diet was nothing new for the government of Japan. Within two weeks of the downing, parliamentarians had been calling for a release of radar and communications intelligence. The government had refused on national security grounds, even though, as one Diet member noted, the information "has been exchanged with the U.S. military."[20] But the Diet members kept at it. In April 1985, Diet Upper House senators Yutaka Hata of the ruling Liberal Democratic party and Socialist Hideyuki Seya formally submitted a series of questions and requests for information to the government of Prime Minister Nakasone. Some of the questions referred to the altitude, course, and speed of Flight 007 during the time it was monitored by Japanese military radars.

The government's answer came on May 15. Hata received partial altitude and speed data from the radar stations at Wakkanai, Abashiri, and Nemuro. The altitude figures showed Flight 007's altitude for only a few discrete points in time, although Japanese intelligence collected continuous altitude data for the entire Sakhalin period. "More detailed changes in the altitude cannot be known from the radar record," the government assured Hata. The speed data were averages for five-minute periods, although a radar sweeps around about once every six seconds. The effect of averages is to smooth out any variations, like sharp reductions or accelerations in speed, effectively removing from the record any abrupt moment-to-moment changes such as would be expected during evasive actions. "We wish to refrain from making public the details of the state of speed," the government's reply said, "but from the radar records, no especially unusual situation, such as a large-scale reduction in speed, can be seen."[21]

These assurances are unconvincing. The Japanese government continued to insist that the airliner had disappeared from radar at 1829 GMT, about 2½ minutes after the missile attack. The nearest Japanese radar was at Wakkanai, only about 70 nautical miles away, meaning there was absolutely no reason why it should have lost Flight 007 at 1829 GMT.

However, there were other Japanese radars within range of Flight 007, including one at Abashiri. From its more distant location, the Abashiri radar would in fact have lost Flight 007 at 32,000 feet at about 1829. This suggests that the government of Japan gave Senator Hata information that was technically correct but intentionally misleading. Data up until the time of Flight 007's disappearance from radar were indeed provided—from Abashiri. Data subsequent to 1829 GMT—from Wakkanai—were withheld.

Other evidence also indicates that the Japanese data are misleading. Hata was told that at 1815 GMT, almost precisely the moment Flight 007 entered Soviet territory over Sakhalin, it descended from an altitude of 32,000 feet down to 29,000 feet. It flew at 29,000 feet until just before 1821, it was said, when it began ascending, reaching 32,000 feet at 1823, where it remained until it was lost from radar. There are two reasons to doubt this account. First, the Soviet pilot mentioned no changes in altitude. He reported to his ground controllers at 1821:40 and 1823:10, both during and after the alleged climb, that "the target is flying at 10,000 [meters]." [22]

The second reason to doubt the Japanese data is that they fit so conveniently into the official explanation of the downing. Not only are Flight 007's approach to Sakhalin and final minutes of flight cut from the record, but the alleged climb just before 1821 GMT conveniently explains how Captain Chun—who reported to Tokyo that he was ascending at this time —could have been "decreasing speed," as the Soviet pilot reported and not have seen the cannon bursts. Let's take a closer look at this:

In a radio call to Tokyo at 1815:05, Flight 007 requested permission to climb from 33,000 to 35,000 feet. Tokyo gave the go-ahead at 1820:10, and Flight 007 immediately called back to say it was leaving its present altitude. Tokyo received another call from Flight 007 at 1823:05 reporting: "We're at three five zero"—35,000 feet. Thus it is on record that Flight 007 reported making a 2,000-foot climb.

During this time, the Soviets made their final attempts to intercept the intruder. At 1820:40, pilot 805 reported, "I am firing cannon bursts." Just over a minute later he announced, "The target is reducing speed. I am going around. I'm already moving in front of the target." For a moment the pilot wondered aloud whether it was his own momentum that was carrying him toward the intruder—"Increasing speed," he said. But a moment later he corrected himself: "Negative. It is decreasing speed." If Flight 007 in fact ascended at that time, all of this might be explained innocently: The cannon bursts were not seen, the State Department argued, because the plane's nose was pointed skyward as it climbed. And the reduction in speed reported by the Russian pilot was a mistake as "the Su-15 simply overshot when the airliner slowed during its climb." [23]

Without the climb, Flight 007's ignoring the cannon bursts and its inflight slowdown can only be explained as evasive actions. More important, without the climb, Flight 007 stands indicted for making false reports to Tokyo air traffic controllers. (There are other, equally serious possibilities. One is the transmissions were made by another plane—Flight 015—in

Flight 007's name. Another is that the tape of Flight 007's transmissions was altered.) Did a climb take place? The Russian pilot in close pursuit reported to his ground controllers that the intruder was maintaining the same altitude throughout this period. Was he wrong? Or did the Japanese government intentionally release fragmentary data which appeared to support the climb in order to buttress the U.S.'s official version of events?

The closer one looks, the less credible official Japanese explanations seem. The newly released data show that Flight 007 maintained an altitude of 32,000 feet until 1829 GMT, over 2½ minutes after the Soviet pilot reported to his ground controller, "The target is destroyed." This contradicted an earlier Japanese announcement that said the airliner had descended to 30,000 feet by 1829. Hata inquired about this discrepancy. The government's reply did not inspire confidence: "In making public the altitude of the KAL plane at 3:29 A.M. . . . the expression of generally 30,000 feet, which gave some leeway, was used for the sake of caution."[24] This "cautious" figure created the false impression that Flight 007 had followed emergency procedures and descended after the Soviet attack.

The government's "cautious" figure also matched the ICAO's version of the final radio transmission from Flight 007:

> Korean Air zero zero seven . . . (unintelligible) . . . rapid
> compressions . . . (unintelligible) . . . descending to one zero
> thousand.

This message was said to have been addressed to air traffic controllers in Tokyo about 40 to 50 seconds after the missile attack. It is standard emergency procedure to descend to a lower altitude. So eager was the U.S. to put the plane quickly in the water, thus avoiding questions about its final minutes of flight, that the U.S. delegation to ICAO tinkered with the words in the final transmission to make the point. Since "no positive translation of the last transmission could be made," they recommended that the words "rapid compressions" (which the U.S. delegation believed to be "rapid decompression") be deleted and replaced with "rapid descent."[25]

But the new Japanese radar data showed that over 2½ minutes after the attack, no descent had taken place at all. If true, this means that at least one of the airliner's engines was functioning and that the crew was able to maintain at least partial control. A working engine also means that the jet's electrical system was working, which indicates in turn that there was power for the two HF and three VHF radios. Yet no emergency calls were made, and the crew did not turn the airliner's transponder to the emergency code of 7700. This is, to say the least, unusual.

After receiving the information on May 15, Senator Hata called a press conference. The data released by the government made front-page news in Japan, where they were called "a significant addition to the small stock of facts on the incident." "This is no mistake," said journalist Yoshitaro Masuo. "Pilots know when they are going up and down—and that it is illegal and dangerous not to report all changes." In the United States, by contrast, the story was given cursory coverage. The *Washington Post*'s article appeared on page A19 under the subhead "Significance of Incorrect Altitude Unclear." The *New York Times* made no mention of the story at all.[26]

Whatever its shortcomings, the information about altitude and speed, available from the very beginning to the governments of both Japan and the United States, was not given to the ICAO inquiry team despite Administration claims to have "cooperated fully" with the investigation. "We were never aware of any descent in that phase of the flight," said Marinus Heijl, a technical officer at ICAO's Air Navigation Bureau. The ICAO has made a standing request for all information relevant to the case. "If new information came in, we would scrutinize it," Duane Freer, the director of the Air Navigation Bureau, told investigative reporter David Corn. "The ICAO is willing to elaborate upon the investigation." But months after the Japanese information was publicized around the world, the ICAO had not received it. Nor was the information made available to the House and Senate Intelligence Committees when they queried Administration officials about the downing.[27]

The State Department responded to questions about the new information by denying its significance:

> Fragmentary radar data released by the Japanese government . . . show neither a descent nor a climb, however, but only disconnected segments of level flight. The reason for this is not clear but is probably related to the type of radar used and the general inaccuracy of height-finding radars, particularly at long ranges. . . . At ranges between 100 and 200 miles, similar U.S. radars could show variations in height up to about 6,000 feet.[28]

By this logic, the fact that the Japanese government refused to release all of their data is used to discredit what they did release.

While the State Department may have a point about the "general inaccuracy" of height-finding radars, accuracy depends upon such factors as radar type, power, weather conditions, and when the radar was most recently calibrated. If all three radars used by the Japanese show a change in altitude at the same time, it can be said with confidence that the airliner changed altitude, even if the absolute height is known with less precision.[29] In fact, Yutaka Hata learned from the Japan Defense Agency that the discrepancies in altitude seen for Flight 007 could not be accounted for by the radar's margin of error.[30]

The second anniversary was in many ways a repeat of the first, but in miniature. About forty people, accompanied by about a dozen reporters, camera crews, and about twenty members of the Reverend Sun Myung Moon's Unification Church, gathered in Lafayette Park, across from the

White House. As before, 269 paper tombstones were set up on the grass. For those on the Right, Flight 007 had become an enduring symbol of the evil of the Soviet system. As columnist Jeffrey Hart put it, the downing was "another revelation about a system that is based upon the normalization of sheer brutality, a system that knows no restraint upon such brutality." It was a moral obligation, Hart concluded, "to exploit the crime for political warfare."[31]

There were no ferry boats traveling to Sakhalin two years later. Instead, the anniversary brought the unveiling of a cenotaph—an empty tomb in memory of their loved ones who died elsewhere—built by twenty-three bereaved Japanese families. The twenty-meter-high memorial is in the shape of a crane, made of concrete, with sixteen feathers representing the number of nations with passengers on board the doomed flight. The cenotaph sits on a hill near the town of Wakkanai, overlooking the sea in the direction of Sakhalin Island.[32]

At the time of the second anniversary of the downing, John Keppel and I published another article in *The Nation* reviewing the new evidence that had come to light during the past year. At the same time, a piece by the State Department's Thomas Maertens appeared in the *Foreign Service Journal*. Maertens' article was a remarkably complete compendium of every argument the Administration had issued to date on the case. (These included the "extensive" ICAO investigation; the Air Navigation Commission's "support" of the ICAO report's conclusions; the canard that Flight 007 could not have been modified for cameras; that it was "unclear if the cannon shots were 'along the path' as a warning . . . or at the plane in an attempt to shoot it down"; that the RC-135 "never came within a thousand miles of where the downing occurred"; the turn to the north-northwest as Flight 007 approached Sakhalin was a "Soviet claim"; the second turn back toward the south "appears to be a mistaken report by the interceptor pilot, who was maneuvering himself at the time"; the *Der Spiegel* account "did add at least one new theory to the conspiracy lore"; the altitude and speed changes over Sakhalin were "radar inaccuracies"; and a congressional inquiry was not needed because there had already been one.) As to the claims of the Administration's critics, Maertens wondered how "such charges gained credence in the first place, given their obvious conflict with well-known facts." Maertens concluded, "It is unlikely that we will ever know with any certainty why the aircraft went off course." At taxpayers' expense, the United States Information Agency sent copies of Maertens' article to press agencies, news media, and television stations throughout the world. The *New York Times* dubbed Maertens' article "Required Reading."[33]

It was during the storm of publicity created a year later by the publication of Seymour Hersh's book *The Target Is Destroyed* that the families of Flight 007's American victims held a memorial service at the Cathedral

Church of St. John the Divine in New York City. Prayers were offered by rabbis, ministers, and priests, and tearful testimonies of remembrance were given by those who had lost children, parents, and brothers on the doomed airliner. The names of Flight 007's 269 victims were then read, slowly, and as the names of children were spoken, they were followed by the word "child." Two hundred and sixty-nine candles were lit in their memory.

"The Families of American Victims of the KAL 007 Tragedy, a support group formed in 1983, held a memorial service today to commemorate the dead on the third anniversary of the disaster," Nan Oldham, whose son John had died on Flight 007, told a press conference afterwards. Before several dozen reporters and the blinding television lights, Oldham and other bereaved family members issued their call for an investigation by Congress. "How many nights have we lain awake imagining the horror of their final moments? With no bodies recovered, we have been deprived of the healing ritual of a funeral service, and the intangibility of this unseen event keeps us in perpetual mourning," Oldham said. "It is the unanswered questions about the flight, however, that intensify our pain, and while nothing can ever mitigate our condemnation of the Soviets' inhuman act, these questions suggest that some responsibility for the tragedy may lie closer to home. . . . As long as these questions remain unanswered, no citizen who travels the skies is safe, and the memory of 63 Americans and their 206 fellow human beings will have been gravely violated. The Families of the American Victims of the KAL 007 Tragedy call on the American people to join us in demanding a thorough congressional investigation into the flight and destruction of KAL 007." [34]

While the call was sincere and moving, the story of the downing of Flight 007 was now three years old. Accounts describing the doubts of the still-grieving families were soon replaced by other, timelier stories. One of these was the Iran-contra affair, showing a pattern of White House involvement in illegal financing and organizing of covert operations accompanied by considerable deceit. As Bob Woodward of the *Washington Post* noted, "There was an elaborate effort to keep the operation secret from the press, the Congress and various people in the Administration." The *New York Times* reported that journalists working in Washington who cover government institutions could not get the story because information was restricted within the bureaucracy. In addition, the *Times* noted, the Administration's conduct "was protected from disclosure because it was so improbable that few journalists would have suspected it." "The press was lax in this case," said Michael G. Gartner, the president of the American Society of Newspaper Editors. "The press failed. . . . Part of this scandal must be laid at the doorstep of the press." [35]

Although cracks had appeared, three years after the downing the wall of silence had not yet been breached.

21

THE THEORIES

A number of conflicting theories about Flight 007's fatal deviation from course appeared in print during the three years following the shoot-down. A host of experts, both genuine and self-proclaimed, academicians, government officials, and others argued their points and counterpoints, often in impenetrable technical jargon. Information in the public domain was interpreted and misinterpreted in dramatically different ways; lies, obfuscations, and errors abounded. It was not surprising, then, that members of the press and public had a difficult time understanding the case. Consequently, many have taken the easy way out, embracing the theory —or theories—that best accords with their preconceptions. Those who saw the Soviet Union as the embodiment of darkness and the United States a paragon of virtue, for instance, gravitated toward those theories which confirmed that view. Those with more liberal leanings who deplored the history of abuses by the intelligence community tended to accept suggestions that Flight 007 was on an intelligence mission.

There are two broad theories of the flight—that Flight 007 innocently strayed from course, and that the deviation was intentional. Explicitly or otherwise, all theories also addressed a related issue—whether U.S. intelligence personnel knew the airliner was off course prior to the shootdown. Let's begin with the theories that claim the deviation from course was accidental.

Perhaps the least well supported of the theories of innocence is that the airliner was drawn into Soviet territory by electronic signals emitted by the Russians. The most vocal advocates of this explanation have been officials of Korean Air Lines, who repeatedly claim that because of the Soviet "meaconing" the company should not be held liable for the tragedy. KAL found some support in Jeffrey St. John's tribute to Larry McDonald, *Day of the Cobra: The True Story of KAL Flight 007,* which concluded that the Soviets lured KAL 007 off course. St. John cited what he considered to be three telling pieces of evidence. The first was the caution on navigational charts of the area, "Warning: Unlisted Radio Emissions From This Area May Constitute a Navigation Hazard or Result in Border Overflight Unless Unusual Precaution is Exercised." The other two pieces were drawn from a Jack Anderson column on September 20, 1983. There, Anderson asserted that "the Soviets routinely try to lure U.S. military and intelligence aircraft into Soviet airspace so they can 'legally' shoot them down." He also hinted that the 1978 incident involving KAL Flight 902 may have been caused by an on-board Soviet agent who was "instrumental in electronically disorienting the aircraft's navigation system." [1]

The problems with this theory are many. Most important, Flight 007 began deviating from course immediately after takeoff, well before it came within the Russians' "luring" range. Next, the crew of Flight 007 repeatedly reported themselves to be on Romeo-20, although the navigation equipment on an airliner being lured off course would still have told the crew something was amiss. Finally, there is the question of motive. Why would the Soviets bother? To kill Larry McDonald? As Alexander Dallin, author of *Black Box: KAL 007 and the Superpowers,* noted, "Considering the panoply of possible enemies—and victims—of the Soviet Union worldwide, it is hard to believe that Moscow would choose Congressman McDonald for such unique and costly victimization (even assuming that it would have known of his travel plans sufficiently in advance to get its own agents aboard)." [2] McDonald's plans would have been hard to ascertain; as we saw in Chapter 1, the congressman was a passenger on Flight 007 only because he had missed an earlier flight. If they were not out to kill McDonald, perhaps the Soviets intended to create a provocation? St. John unconvincingly argues that the Russians believed that this show of brutality would so intimidate and terrorize America's NATO allies that the deployment of Pershing II and Cruise missiles in Europe would be cancelled. As was seen in Chapter 11, the result was precisely, and predictably, the reverse.

The other theories of innocence that gained widespread public attention all claimed that Flight 007's deviation from course was the result of "finger trouble"—faulty programming of the inertial navigation system. Most of these were variations on the several scenarios presented in the ICAO report. For instance, in a series of articles in London's *Sunday Times* and *The New York Review of Books,* Australian journalist Murray Sayle argued with energy and considerable emotion in support of one of the ICAO scenarios—that the INS was incorrectly set in the "heading mode," and that the plane was directed to its destruction by its magnetic compass on a heading of 246 degrees. Members of the Reagan administration also publicly praised the ICAO report, while being careful not to endorse any particular scenario. The numerous problems with the theory of the 246-degree magnetic heading—in particular, its failure to account for the plane's position at Bethel and its flight over Sakhalin—as well as the other ICAO scenarios are discussed in detail in Chapter 17.

Most of the theories that the airliner was innocently off course also required a belief that U.S. intelligence personnel did not monitor the flight. Consequently, proponents of such theories minimize U.S. capabilities in the Far East. When it is pointed out that a number of intelligence assets had the capability to detect the errant plane, the response is that having capabilities does not guarantee that they will be used. When it is pointed out that some of the assets did in fact collect information about the plane, the response is that the situation must have been misunderstood, or that the relevant data were only analyzed when it was too late. (There is another logical possibility: U.S. personnel detected the innocently off-course plane, but decided to let it enter Soviet territory to see how the Russians would react. However, because most writers who see the flight as innocent go to considerable lengths to exonerate the United States from responsibility for the tragedy, none has advanced this "target of opportunity" argument.)

On the other side of the explanatory fence were theories that explained the course flown by the Korean airliner as deliberate. Yet these theories differ on two key points, the reason for the flight and what American personnel knew about it.

The most innocuous of these theories, which implicitly assumes that there was no U.S. monitoring of the flight, is that the crew of Flight 007 deliberately overflew Soviet territory in order to save fuel. This explanation is based on allegations that KAL president Harry Cho instituted a policy of cutting corners to save on flight time, and hence fuel costs, after his company suffered substantial financial losses in 1980–81. Canadian Maj. Gen. Richard Rohmer has been perhaps the most vocal proponent of this theory. "A Boeing 747 costs on the average some $8,000 an hour to operate or about $130 a minute," he wrote in his book, *Massacre 747: The Story of Korean Air Lines Flight 007*. "As a matter of company policy, if out of the 130 international flights it operated each week, one hundred minutes a day were saved throughout the system, the value to the company would be in the range of $4 million a year." Even if the time-saving was only 20 minutes a day, he said, "the money saving would be close to a million dollars a year, a highly respectable saving for a company trying to survive."[3]

If this were the case, shortcuts by KAL flights would be relatively common, but neither Japanese nor American air traffic controllers appear to have any record of such deviations. Also running counter to this theory is the fact that by 1982, the tide had turned in KAL's sea of red ink and the company showed a modest profit. Most important, the actual course flown by Flight 007 belies the fuel-saving speculation. The most fuel-efficient way to fly from Anchorage to Seoul would have been on a direct Great Circle course, but the airliner's course was nowhere near this. In addition, the crew changed the plane's speed throughout the flight, consuming additional fuel in the process. Both Soviet claims and Japanese radar data also suggest that Flight 007 was at times operating at lower, unauthorized, and less fuel-efficient altitudes.[4]

Again there is a problem of motivation. How might Korean Air Lines induce its flight crews to risk their lives by overflying Soviet territory? Money is the obvious possibility. Had Flight 007 flown a Great Circle route between Anchorage and Seoul, it has been estimated that the savings would have amounted to approximately $2,500. Given the airliner's actual course, however, the savings would have been considerably less, by some estimates about $1,500. (Because of its changes in speed and altitude, even this is certainly overstated.) General Rohmer suggested that, "a bonus of 50 percent of the saving would not be unreasonable, but perhaps one-third of the saving might be what a prudent, cost-cutting company would offer." If one accepts this argument, KAL risked a multimillion-dollar aircraft, the lives of hundreds of passengers and crew, the reputation of the company, and its potential for future sales, for about $1,000. Had they lived, Flight 007's three-member crew would have split $500 among them.[5]

Another theory that the overflight was intentional but not on an intelligence mission was advanced by Captain Park Young-man, the pilot of KAL Flight 015. Although Park initially did not appear during the discovery phase of the victims' families' suit against KAL (see Chapter 19), in the fall of 1986 he secretly traveled to Washington intending to give testimony in Federal District Court. Why Park did this is not clear—according to some sources he was forced by the Korean government—but his stay was brief. Saying he "feared for his life" in the United States, he returned to South Korea without giving testimony. In a lengthy interview in the December 1986 issue of Seoul's government-controlled *Monthly Chosun*, Park finally had his say. Explaining why he had decided to speak out, Park said, "While I maintained my silence, so many absurd articles have surfaced . . . I have decided the time has come to remedy misunderstandings."[6]

But Park did not clarify much. Saying that the course flown by Flight 007 for the first 200 miles after takeoff was meandering and off the regular route, Park told an interviewer, "I cannot help but conclude that either 007 had run into a situation where it could not rely on the INS, or it relied on malfunctioning INS devices." Park said he had spoken with Captain Chun by radio and had detected trepidation and concern in his voice. Park said he believed Chun knew his plane was experiencing difficulties, but "to return to the airport of origin because of mistakes in inertial navigation will not only inflict a loss of millions of wons [the South Korean currency] on the company, but also become a dishonor and stigma to the pilots." Park described a Korean Air Lines company so strict in its policy of punishing those who make mistakes that pilots are kept "in mortal fear" of admitting error. This fear, he said, made the crew of Flight 007 "carry out a risky flight." Park gave several examples of KAL flights in the past in which pilots who had made navigational errors had turned back and were severely disciplined. He also told of a flight where the crew continued despite a navigational error because they feared reprisals if they turned back.

Park's story, however, is confusing and runs directly counter to some existing evidence. For instance, the radar plots for Flight 007 during the early part of its journey were not "meandering and off the regular route," as he claimed, but instead corresponded perfectly to an INS-directed Great Circle track, as described in Chapters 1 and 17. In addition, had the crew noted an INS malfunction, they would surely have paid particular attention to other instruments and navigational aids to confirm their course, such as the beacons at waypoints Bethel and NEEVA. The fact that the plane passed 12 miles to the north of Bethel is evidence that the VOR was not used. Given Park's "face-saving" scenario, the crew should also have been attentive to their weather radar, which would have provided them with information about what they were flying over. Finally, Park's account of a fearful KAL pilot corps conflicts with a highly publicized incident in which a pilot went off course, losing his plane and several passengers in the process, but was subsequently promoted—Flight 902.

In spite of its contradictions, Park Young-man's story does not paint a flattering picture of Korean Air Lines or its pilots. With KAL designated as the official carrier for the 1988 Olympics in Seoul, why did the South Korean government, normally intolerant of such criticism, permit publication of such a damaging interview in its controlled press? Perhaps, as some of the bereaved family members believe, the purpose was to try to resolve the litigation in Federal District Court in Washington. They suggested that the United States, not wanting the case to go to trial, had pressured KAL and the South Korean government to admit negligence on the part of the crew of Flight 007, and to allow some criticism of KAL company policies, in order to bring the case to a speedy conclusion.

The remaining theories of intentionality all claim that Flight 007 was on a mission for the United States. There have been no serious suggestions that the plane was on a mission for the Republic of Korea, since the areas of the Soviet Union over which the airliner passed were of keen interest to the United States, not South Korea, and because it was the United States that had the intelligence assets to monitor the Russians as the airliner intruded. The theories of intentional overflight differ only in what they consider to have been the purpose behind Flight 007's intrusion.

What would the United States hope to gain by sending a "duck" so deep into Soviet territory? A number of possibilities have been suggested. The most unlikely is that the United States intended the airliner to get shot down in order to heighten tensions between the superpowers and poison the international atmosphere. While farfetched, such suggestions find at least some circumstantiation in reports linking U.S. intelligence to the destruction of commercial airplanes in the past. For example, William Stevenson wrote in his book, *Intrepid's Last Case*, that in 1955 a CIA-manufactured pencil-bomb was placed aboard the Air India plane *Kashmir Princess*, chartered to fly foreign minister Chou En-lai and other Chinese Communist officials to a Third World conference in Indonesia. (The plane exploded over the Java Sea killing all on board, but warned beforehand, Chou had taken another flight.) Another example concerns Bay of Pigs veteran Luis Posada, who, under the pseudonym Ramon Medina, recently played a major role in supplying arms to the Nicaraguan contras. Posada, who has a long history of ties to the CIA, has been identified as the person responsible for the 1976 bombing of a Cubana Airlines plane which killed seventy-three people,[7] although there is no evidence that the agency sponsored it.

One step behind this are theories, notably from the Russians, that posit an intelligence mission which, if things went awry and the plane was downed, would then serve a useful political purpose for the United States. Marshal Nikolai Ogarkov claimed that a civilian plane was deliberately chosen for the "thoroughly planned intelligence mission . . . disregarding or, possibly, counting on the loss of human life." This suggestion was echoed by Akio Takahashi, the Japanese author of *President's Crime: Who Ordered the Espionage Flight of KAL 007?*, who wrote that the primary goal of the flight was intelligence collection, but in the event the intruder was shot down, "another pretext would become available for a further aggravation of the international situation."[8]

Another possibility is that Flight 007 carried reconnaissance equipment, such as cameras or gear for collecting signals intelligence from the Russians, but this is unlikely for two reasons: First, there is little, if anything, that an airliner could collect that the nearby intelligence ground stations, aircraft, satellites, and ships could not. Second and more important, any plan for an overflight of Soviet territory must have taken into account the possibility that the plane would be forced down. If there was spy equipment on board, the aircraft would almost certainly be seized, its crew imprisoned for espionage, and the Soviets would gain an enormous propaganda victory. But if there was no equipment on board, the flight crew could shake their heads in apparent bewilderment at how they went off course. After a few days of angry accusations, the Russians would have to let everyone go, as they have done on several occasions in the past. It seems likely, then, that both the safety of the crew and the plausible deniability of the mission would demand that there be no reconnaissance equipment on the plane.

It is of some interest that it was primarily Administration officials who raised the possibility of on-board reconnaissance equipment—so they could then deny it. As Sugwon Kang, writing in the *Bulletin of Concerned Asian Scholars*, noted, "The officials became so insistent on carrying on this strange debate that even ICAO's Air Navigation Commission felt obliged to insert a statement in its report saying that none of the airport handling staff, who 'had free access to all parts of the aircraft,' had ever 'reported any unusual equipment or structural changes.' " *The New York Times* went so far as to estimate how much it would cost to equip an airliner with photographic equipment and discussed the problems such an appropriation would face in the Congress. The suggestion that Flight 007 carried reconnaissance equipment appears to have been a straw man, a weak argument advanced so that it could then be struck down, apparently demonstrating Flight 007's innocence.[9]

Other scenarios have Flight 007 stimulating Soviet air defense activity, radar systems, communications traffic, and other types of electronic activity so these could be monitored by the U.S. and Japan. Some of the theories advanced along these lines have been quite general. For instance, in his book *KAL Flight 007: The Hidden Story*, Oliver Clubb concluded that Flight 007 was "instigated by U.S. intelligence for the evident purpose, perhaps among others, of studying the operation of the air defenses guarding vital Soviet naval installations." Sugwon Kang suggested that the flight was designed "to activate Soviet radar to enable the National Security Agency to analyze the reactions." In another account, an intelligence source claimed that the flight was designed to collect information about super-secret space defense research then being conducted by the Soviets on southern Sakhalin Island.[10]

More specific theories have also been advanced. Writing in *Queen's Quarterly*, David Cox speculated that the intrusion was designed to collect information about the Soviet microwave transmission network. While not subscribing to this theory, Alexander Dallin noted that "to date, the only plausible idea [for a deliberate intrusion] has been the suggestion that the Kamchatka-Sakhalin-Vladivostok line of flight followed the path of a data link used in the open transmission of Soviet missile test data from Kamchatka back to regular (and more secure) land lines of communication from the Maritime Province to the European USSR." Both the RC-135 and the U.S.S. *Observation Island*, in operation as Flight 007 approached Soviet territory, were equipped to intercept Soviet microwave transmissions.[11]

Still another possible intelligence target was the secret new Soviet surface-to-air missile, the SA-12. This missile was considered by some in the Administration to be useful against incoming nuclear missiles as well as aircraft, and thus a violation of the 1972 Anti-Ballistic Missile treaty. Deployed on both Kamchatka and Sakhalin, the SA-12 reportedly had become the focus of "extravagant" American intelligence efforts to learn more about it. According to the *San Francisco Examiner & Chronicle* work on the missile had been "shrouded—sometimes with sliding roofs and tarpaulins—to conceal it from U.S. spy satellites." The targeting radars for the SA-12, including a major system on southern Kamchatka, were seldom turned on by the Russians so as not to disclose their capabilities to the ever-present U.S. watchers and listeners.[12]

The most detailed theory of why Flight 007 might have deliberately overflown Soviet territory was offered by R.W. Johnson of Oxford University. In *Shootdown: Flight 007 and the American Connection*, Johnson pointed out that five weeks before Flight 007's intrusion, U.S. intelligence had been "electrified" by the discovery of a huge new radar under construction at Abalakova, in central Siberia. The Russians maintain that the radar was designed to track objects in deep space, but some U.S. officials worried that its location, near SS-11 and SS-18 ICBM complexes, might give it a capability against ballistic missiles that was forbidden by the ABM treaty. Other officials suggested that it might be a forbidden early-warning radar. (The two superpowers had agreed that all early-warning radars would be built on the periphery of the two countries, facing outward, and the Abalakova radar was nowhere near the periphery of the Soviet Union.) Hoping to pin arms control violations on the Russians, thus obviating the need to make concessions at the upcoming arms talks in Geneva, the Administration had a keen interest in determining the capabilities of the new system, Johnson argued. But how, in 1983, could the United States evaluate the performance of a radar that would not be completed until 1988? "What was needed," he said, "was a thorough testing of the capabilities of the whole Soviet radar line pointing towards the north Pacific. If there was a gap in the early-warning line which [the radar] might fill, this would be powerful evidence that the new facility was indeed an early-warning radar." This is the role Johnson believes Flight 007 was intended to play.[13]

While many of these theories suggest plausible targets for an intelligence mission, it is impossible at the present time to determine which, if any, of them are correct. One especially energetic supporter of the Reagan administration's official line once told me, "Anyone who claims that the 007 flight was on a covert mission is obligated to suggest what kind of a mission would be sensible and useful for such an aircraft under the circumstances." But he is wrong. Why should investigators be expected to come up with a sensible and useful motive for a mission when it is entirely possible that the whole affair could have been ill-conceived? The main task of critics of the Administration's case has always been to show that there is no plausible innocent explanation for Flight 007's deviation from course, not to speculate about motives.[14]

Many of those who question the credibility of accounts suggesting an intelligence role for Flight 007 also claim that something so heinous, presumably involving so many people, would certainly have leaked out by now. Since it hasn't, they say, there must be nothing there. They make the argument that our political institutions are sufficient, as they were during Watergate, to catch such egregious abuses of power.

This reasoning is flawed on several counts, the Watergate analogy in particular. "The system" had little to do with uncovering the numerous deceits and abuses of the Nixon administration. Instead, as Robert Nisbet wrote, it was not the genius of our political institutions but a bungled break-in—an "almost incredible piece of political cretinism"—that led to the unraveling of the scandal. There was also the fortuitous appearance of the White House tapes, "their mere existence a heavy strain on the imagination, their public disclosure happenstance of the highest order." And far from an inclination to engage in investigation and self-analysis, the system exhibited a remarkable tendency to avoid both. Watergate was not brought to its culmination by a vigilant Congress, a body that engaged in a great deal of initial foot-dragging. Nor was the decisive factor an ever-vigilant press or public, both of whom resisted the story for many months. "As for the judiciary," Nisbet concluded, "this branch of government would not even have come into the matter had it not been for the accident of the bungled break-in." [15] Our democratic system survived, but fortuitousness had more to do with it than did built-in institutional mechanisms for constraining abuses of power by the Executive branch.

Why should the system be expected to perform any better now? For those who engage in secret operations, the enduring lessons of Watergate have been quite different than might be hoped—redoubled efforts to enhance their "plausible deniability" and to restrict the possibilities for exposure to a minimum. In practical terms, this means tighter, more effective deceptions and cover-ups. Should information about the operation begin to leak out, Watergate's lessons are to deny everything; give up nothing; keep your mouth shut; shred the documents; destroy the tapes. It should hardly be surprising, then, that information has not been readily forthcoming about KAL Flight 007. If the plane was on an intelligence mission, the number of knowledgeable insiders would have been severely restricted. Because of their intimate involvement, these people would be the least likely to talk. Of course there would be others who were exposed to information of relevance—the military personnel at Elmendorf and Misawa, for example—but by design their image of events would be highly fragmentary. As novelist Tom Clancy accurately described the nature of large secret operations:

> At most a handful of people would ever know the entire story; the others would only see disjointed fragments that later might be thought parts of any number of other operations. Any Soviet agent [or, we might add, American citizen] trying to determine what this mission had been would find himself in a maze with dozens of blank walls. [16]

Even if someone suspected that the official version of events was incomplete and misleading, what could be done? Without hard evidence, members of the public would find it difficult to effectively voice their concerns. Military personnel, those most likely to have seen relevant pieces of the puzzle, would be forbidden to discuss the subject. The threat of heavy fines and imprisonment for disclosing classified information effectively serves to keep most tongues from wagging. Those who suggest, therefore, that there would be "hundreds" of people in the know, ready and willing to go public if Flight 007 had been on an intelligence mission, are being either naive or disingenuous.

It was in this sea of claims, counterclaims, and conflicting explanations that the press and public foundered, only to run hard upon the shoals of the most improbable theory to date.

"I've broken the hearts of the conspiracy theorists," investigative reporter Seymour M. Hersh told *People* magazine's Montgomery Bower. "That plane wasn't doing anything other than being lost." Hersh was referring to the surprising conclusion of his most recent book, *"The Target Is Destroyed": What Really Happened to Flight 007 And What America Knew About It.* Released in September 1986, at the time of the third anniversary of the tragedy, and summarized in an article in *The Atlantic* that appeared at the same time, the book was destined to receive more, and more favorable, coverage than any work on the incident to date.[17]

The Reagan administration itself was responsible for some of the attention that the book received. Two months prior to publication, newspapers across the country reported that CIA director William J. Casey had telephoned both Hersh himself and his editor at Random House, the book's publisher, alleging that the forthcoming book might contain classified information and thus violate U.S. security laws. When reporters queried the Agency about the call, a CIA spokesman quickly refused to "confirm or deny allegations concerning the director's private phone conversations." A few days later Random House chairman, Robert L. Bernstein, spoke with Casey, and the CIA director repeated his warning that the book might violate "that law dealing with communications intelligence." Apparently unruffled, Bernstein told the *New York Times* that "although Mr. Casey and other Government officials may be embarrassed by Mr. Hersh's book, I am satisfied that its publication is in the national interest."[18]

When the book finally appeared, it was clear that the story it told depended almost entirely upon leaks of information from unnamed sources in the intelligence community. Hersh focused on the questions of whether the Russians identified Flight 007, and whether the U.S. Government chose to ignore evidence of that failure. Contrary to official accounts, he said that the United States had information that the plane was in danger, but because of a lengthy series of intelligence snafus and bureaucratic oversights failed to use it in an effective and timely way. Also contrary to official claims, he agreed with intelligence reports from the time of the downing that the Soviets believed they were shooting down an intelligence aircraft, not a commercial jetliner. Hersh then criticized the Administration for ignoring this information and excoriating the Russians to advance its Cold War agenda.

However, Hersh all but ignored a more important issue—whether the flight was intentional and whether there is evidence of U.S. complicity in its deviation. Hersh asserted that the flight "had its beginnings not in international intrigue but in the ordinary human failings of the Korean Air Lines crew members." He brushed off the question of U.S. complicity in a footnote, saying that he found none.[19]

Having dismissed the possibility of an intentional flight, Hersh then presented an ingenious and highly technical theory for how the plane could have gone off course accidentally. The new theory was worked out by Harold H. Ewing, a flight captain for Flying Tigers—an airline reportedly with connections to the Central Intelligence Agency—who sent it unsolicited to the ICAO. By his own account, Ewing never examined all the evidence in the case. Rejecting from the outset what he termed "outlandish plots and conspiracies," Ewing's only objective was to see if he could produce a scenario of navigational errors that was consistent with Flight 007's actual course, no matter how many assumptions it was necessary to make in the process.[20]

It is worth briefly entering Flight 007's cockpit, as Harold Ewing envisions it, to understand the assumptions he asks us to make. In Anchorage prior to takeoff, Captain Chun Byung-in hand-scrawled a series of numbers on his computerized flight plan suggesting that he had decided to modify it. Ewing claims these represented calculations designed to delay the plane's normal ascent to a higher altitude, calling Chun a pilot "looking under all the rocks" in his effort to be fuel-efficient. Delaying an ascent seems an unusual way to do so, since normally pilots are concerned with getting to the higher, more fuel-efficient altitudes as rapidly as possible. The only reason to remain lower would be if there were adverse weather conditions above, but the winds that night were favorable. In fact, Flight 007 requested an increase in altitude from 31,000 to 33,000 feet at 1444 GMT, an hour and a quarter before the time specified on its computerized flight plan.[21]

Yet it was these last-minute revisions by Chun, Hersh says, which "led him and his crew to rush through the other, more routine, preflight checks," although he failed to mention that Flight 007's departure was delayed by some 40 minutes, presumably obviating any need for such haste. These checks included one of considerable importance: calculating the plane's weight and balance. In the Ewing scenario, Captain Chun did not notice that the plane's flight release sheet showed 10,000 pounds less than the weight-and-balance manifest. Such an oversight is the kind of error that could have led to a disaster upon takeoff. "It's not hard to get it right," Ewing said, "but they did not. It's a mistake—a big mistake."[22]

But assuming big mistakes in preflight calculations was just the beginning. Hersh says it was the responsibility of Flight Engineer Kim Eui-dong to enter the coordinates for the plane's "ramp position"—Anchorage— into the three INS computers. "It was at this point," the scenario goes, "that he made the fatal finger error"—entering W 139 degrees as the longitude for Anchorage into the pilot's INS instead of the correct W 149 degrees. When Kim moved over to the copilot's INS and entered the correct coordinates, an amber warning light immediately illuminated. But "human nature then took over," according to Hersh. The flight engineer "assumed—as many crew members would—that his problem was in INS number two. It couldn't be number one; that INS was loaded and ready to go."[23] So, Hersh says the flight engineer just "cleared" the machine by pressing a button, making the problem go away.

This is confusing when one considers that the whole point to the redundant navigational systems on an airliner like Flight 007 is for *comparison* of the information they contain. If the warning light comes on this indicates, by definition, that a discrepancy exists between the coordinates entered into two different INS's. Thus, there is no way that Kim or anyone else could have assumed that the problem was solely "in INS number two," as Hersh claims. The light meant that the the coordinates entered into INS number two did not match those entered into INS number one. When the coordinates in number two were checked and found to be correct, this indicated, again by definition, that the error was in the other INS.

The next assumption is that upon arrival in the cockpit Captain Chun disregarded company regulations by failing to double-check the coordinates entered into the INS. The whole crew had to then disregard the required procedure for them to individually confirm the aircraft's present position coordinates—this in spite of the fact that they had 40 additional minutes to do so. The explanation that "such checking is not always done" is not reassuring.[24]

Although Hersh does not mention it, there is an additional assumption that has to be made immediately after the allegedly forgotten checking procedures—that is, when the INS was switched from "align" to "nav" (navigate) mode. Given the error the INS was said to contain, the moment the switch to "nav" was made an INS action malfunction code number would have begun flashing and a red warning light come on, according to Professor James Brazell, who interviewed Litton officials about the characteristics of the INS. The warning light is there to alert the crew that a malfunction has occurred and the flashing number indicates its type. When this happens, the crew looks up the code number in a handbook, for neither the number nor the red warning light will go off until the malfunction has been corrected. It seems unlikely that the crew could have missed such warnings for hours.[25]

The scenario of a completely innocent flight ran into difficulties at Bethel, Alaska, Flight 007's first waypoint, because there was simply no way that the crew could have failed to realize they were off course. So in his effort to find an explanation consistent with the facts, Ewing was forced to introduce intentionality, but of the blandest possible sort: to save fuel. Ewing hypothesized that Captain Chun did not want to fly to Bethel as directed. Instead, he wanted to fly farther south, toward an arbitrarily selected point on Romeo-20 somewhere between waypoints Bethel and NABIE, in effect trying to fly the hypotenuse of a triangle rather than the other two sides. (As Ewing acknowledges in his report, this maneuver would actually have cut only about 1 minute's flying time from a planned flight of 8 hours, but the befuddled Captain Chun is supposed to have believed the savings to be greater.) The scenario requires that Chun correctly entered the latitude for his new corner-cutting waypoint, but for some reason did not enter the longitude. "Captain Chun could have been interrupted while inserting the new waypoint and not have returned to the task of entering the longitudinal coordinates," Hersh summarized Ewing's surmise; or the INS malfunctioned.[26]

Ewing claims that the result of this error was the creation of a so-called hybrid waypoint toward which the INS began to fly the plane. By this ingenious solution, a plane which should have flown six miles to the south of Bethel instead flew twelve miles to the north.[27] Upon passing Bethel, this would have been obvious to the captain. Because of the alleged original 10-degree error in entering the coordinates for Anchorage, equally obvious to him would have been that INS was showing that he still had some 300 miles to go before arriving at Bethel. How could he have disregarded all these discrepancies? Ewing said that one of KAL's best pilots had left the cockpit to spend the next 5 hours chatting with Congressman McDonald and with his "dead-heading" pilot friends in the first class cabin: "If the captain had been in the cockpit," Ewing said, "he would undoubtedly have realized something was wrong." In other words, because of the *a priori* assumption that the flight over Soviet territory was unintentional, and an unintentional overflight required Chun not to look at his instruments, he was simply removed from the cockpit.[28]

How likely is Chun's absence from the cockpit for such an extended period of time? Korean Air Lines required the captain to greet on-board dignitaries such as Congressman McDonald, and it is likely that Chun also spoke to his colleagues in the first class section of the plane. But for five hours? Several pilots and air traffic controllers who were questioned on this point dismissed such a conjecture as "unthinkable" and "absurd." And although his testimony may be questionable, Captain Park Youngman of Flight 015 claimed that he had been in communication with Chun, who was using the radio in the cockpit, some three hours into the flight.[29]

The other two crew members had obvious indications that they were off course at Bethel, but Ewing claimed they must have ignored them because of the corner-cutting maneuver: "Of course it [Flight 007] did not go right over Bethel," Ewing wrote in his report, "but this was of no concern to the F/O [First Officer] because he knew that it was not intended that it should." This required First Officer Sohn to falsify his position report at Bethel, saying the plane passed overhead the VOR beacon when it did not, but this was an inescapable part of a corner-cutting maneuver that Ewing considered only a minor infraction, "consistent with KAL's reputation."[30]

Ewing made two additional assumptions to explain how the plane flew off course for hours more after the captain left the cockpit. The first was that Chun did not bother to inform his crew of the precise nature of his shortcut. Second, Ewing assumed that no matter what their instruments displayed in the hours to come, the crew would do and say nothing. In support of this latter assumption, Hersh repeated stories of the "acquiescence" of Korean crews who don't "second-guess the pilot." "They just sit there like vegetables," an American pilot was quoted as saying. And even if they suspected that something was amiss in the hours to come, Hersh wrote, "neither the copilot nor the flight engineer would dare ask for an explanation nor question what the captain did." [31]

The Korean crew would indeed have had to be "vegetables" to ignore the staggering number of warnings they encountered throughout the rest of the flight. At all waypoints after Bethel there were discrepancies between the times the plane was scheduled to arrive and when it actually did. However, according to Ewing's scenario, these were close enough not to cause alarm. The fact that the crew had to relay messages through Flight 015 because they themselves were not able to communicate with air traffic controllers on their very-high-frequency radios was "a common-enough occurrence." The plane's failure to receive the signal from the Shemya VORTAC (Ewing incorrectly says in his report that there was "no requirement to make any position check" with it) would have been viewed by the crew simply as "an indication of the inoperability" of the navigational aid.[32] The unusual returns from the plane's weather radar showing the Commander Islands and the Kamchatka Peninsula would "by no stretch of the imagination . . . be interpreted as in any way valid." As to the discrepant readings appearing on the "cross track distance/track angle error" display of the INS, the Horizontal Situation Indicators, and other instruments in the cockpit, these would presumably all be ignored. These are considerable assumptions about a crew that is supposed to have just gone off course intentionally in an illegal maneuver.[33]

Although the State Department, the CIA, and others had insisted that the airliner had not turned on its approach to Sakhalin, attributing such reports to Soviet propaganda, the "slant-range effects" of radars, radar operators' faulty memories, the incompetence of Soviet pilots, and so on, Ewing knew the turns had occurred because the transcripts of the Soviet pilot flying in pursuit clearly described them. Hersh also knew that the turns were real, noting that, "Members of the Electronic Security Command who were directly involved that morning insist that . . . Flight 007 did turn before reaching Sakhalin." But the Ewing scenario explained the turns as the result of the first officer deciding at just that time to reprogram his INS with additional waypoints for the remainder of the flight to Seoul. Because of the electronic muddle that all the earlier errors had allegedly created inside the INS, "Flight 007 abruptly began to turn right, to the northwest, as it searched out its new route" when he remote-loaded the new waypoints into the other two units. This took the plane on a course between the Dolinsk-Sokol and Smirnykh air bases, coincidentally avoiding surface-to-air missile batteries in the process. "Still," Hersh writes, "there was no cause for alarm. Such mistakes in reprogramming happened often enough and were invariably recognized for what they were." However, judging by the remarks of the Soviet pilot, the turn took place over a longer period of time than would have been the case if Ewing's speculation was correct.[34]

Hersh's reliance on this scenario as his evidence that the flight was innocent was late in coming. Harold Ewing finished work on his report in December 1985. By then, *The Target Is Destroyed*" was nearly complete. Hersh did not mention this issue of timing, thereby implying that the Ewing scenario had informed his judgment throughout his inquiry into the tragedy. But in truth, Hersh's basis for claiming the innocence of the flight had only become available at the last minute. Thus it is reasonable to ask what evidence would have been presented had Ewing not fortuitously appeared on the scene? Ewing himself answered this question: "Had I not come along, Hersh would indeed not have had a credible scenario for the overflight . . . which would not have made the slightest difference in his book (with the possible exception of length) because he had already reached his conclusions through completely different channels."[35] But if the different channels were so convincing, why did Hersh not present their evidence instead, thereby informing readers of the process by which such important conclusions were reached? The issue is of considerable importance because many of the conclusions in the remainder of Hersh's book depend upon—indeed, require—an innocent flight.

How much faith did Hersh have in the Ewing scenario? Hersh was careful to distance himself from the theory, at several points referring to it as "highly speculative" and requiring at least one "leap of faith." Asked about the theory's plausibility in an interview with Mark Ackerman of Thames Television, Hersh said, "I'm not trying to suggest that this is what happened. *Of course this isn't what happened. Nobody's saying this is what happened* [author's emphasis]. The only point is to say that you can devise a means, you're trying to explain something very difficult for this plane, which is how a pilot could not know where he was and it's possible. It is possible. Through a series of admittedly . . . one in particular involves a leap of faith, but it is possible to fuck up the system in such a way that you wouldn't get very many warnings and that's all Ewing was showing."

But that is not all Ewing was showing. He began his report by saying that he believed the events of August 31, 1983, were "a close approximation" of his model. By making the Ewing scenario the focus of the section "The Flight" in *The Target Is Destroyed*," as well as the entirety of his article in *The Atlantic*, entitled "What Really Happened to Flight 007," Hersh gave it visibility and credibility. By pointing out that Ewing's scenario was consistent with the plane's known flight path and with secret information he claimed to have obtained from intelligence agencies, Hersh appeared to give the theory his stamp of approval. And some members of the press and public accepted it as what really happened: "We finally have a carefully researched, reasonable, readable explanation for how Korean Air Lines Flight 007 came to be shot down," wrote Douglas B. Feaver in the *Washington Post*.[36]

Both Ewing and Hersh seem to believe that if an accidental explanation can be devised for a phenomenon then it must be true, no matter how numerous and incredible its assumptions. Yes, Ewing came up with a theory that is consistent with the facts, but since that was his expressed intention this should come as no surprise, and when Hersh congratulates Ewing for so doing, he is only stating the obvious. But being consistent with the facts says nothing about plausibility, as the "strayed NASA weather plane" explanation for the 1960 U-2 flight or Rosemary Woods' "accidental" creation of the famous 18-minute gap on the Watergate tapes makes plain. While it might be possible to believe that several of the errors and oversights Ewing imagines could have taken place, the redundant navigational aids available to the crew made it highly implausible that so many of them could have occurred, in such perfect concert, and with such results. If this convoluted and outlandish theory is the only alternative to a deliberate flight, then it becomes far easier to entertain the idea that Flight 007 intentionally deviated from course.

In making the case that Flight 007 went off course accidentally, Hersh moved from the Ewing scenario to argue that the major Soviet air defense flap it caused went unnoticed by the numerous U.S. intelligence facilities in the area. To do so, he downplayed the capabilities of U.S. and allied intelligence in the Far East and assumed a series of blunders, oversights and failures reminiscent in their scope and implausibility of Ewing's scenario about the flight itself. Operators at Elmendorf Air Force Base in Alaska were said to have misinterpreted all the activity they monitored as the Russians simply "taking advantage of the quiet of the overnight shift to break in a new radar operator or to work on tracking technique by simulating an American intrusion into their airspace." The communication intelligence station on Shemya Island was said to have been closed since 1975. The RC-135, said to be of the Cobra Ball type, saw nothing because it "flies blind." No mention was made of the U.S.S. *Observation Island,* and the ferret satellite was erroneously said not to have passed over the area. The huge U.S. intelligence facility at Misawa was said to have intercepted signs of Soviet air defense activity in real time, but U.S. personnel believed it was just an unusually large-scale Soviet air defense exercise, tracking a "mythical intruder." An intelligence operator at Project Clef, a secret new U.S. intelligence unit at Wakkanai, also intercepted information in real time, but "was not paying that much attention to it." The Japanese at Wakkanai monitored and recorded the Soviet air defense activity, but their "skeleton crew"—"lax" by American standards—was said not to have listened to it, or relayed it, for hours.[37] Proceeding systematically, Hersh thus described every one of the U.S. and allied intelligence platforms either unable to detect or understand what was happening in front of their electronic eyes and ears.

On almost all of these points, it is not possible to evaluate Hersh's account. The story he tells is largely based on unverifiable information from unnamed, but surely hardly disinterested, intelligence sources whose "act of faith in helping to tell this story," he says, "is one that now has to be shared by the reader." But should their account be accepted? Despite the sources' portrayal of the intelligence community as unable to understand what was happening to Flight 007 in real time, that community is generally presented in a favorable light: U.S. personnel monitored Soviet activity, as they were supposed to. After the shootdown, they quickly figured out what happened, again, as they were supposed to. It was the Administration that ignored intelligence reports in order to excoriate the Russians over the downing. Most important, underlying the entire story is the assumption that neither the Administration nor the intelligence community had a hand in sending the Korean airliner over the Soviet Union. Perhaps this self-serving presentation is the truth, and perhaps not. I have tried to compare the testimony of Hersh's sources with information obtained elsewhere whenever possible, and they do not always match up, but not until someone who was at one of these intelligence facilities goes public will we be able to evaluate the claims more fully. In the meantime, it seems important to maintain an appropriate degree of skepticism. Clearly, if U.S. intelligence officials had been involved in a mission for Flight 007, they would have a keen interest in helping a journalist to portray them as unaware of what was going on.[38]

Hersh also neglected to discuss indications of a cover-up by the U.S. Government—the withholding, falsification, and destruction of evidence, the use of pressure to prevent government employees from discussing the case, the attempted intimidation of critics, and the misuse of national security prerogatives to stultify the efforts of victims' families to find out the facts of the case. Of course, we do not know what is being covered up —a U.S. role in directing Flight 007, or further evidence of the Administration's cynical use of the incident for political ends, as Hersh would have it. Still, Hersh's lack of interest in this aspect of the government's response leaves a serious gap in his story of the meaning of the flight.

It seems fair to conclude that contrary to the claim his publisher emblazoned on the cover of "The Target Is Destroyed," Hersh has not told "what really happened" to Flight 007. Instead, he has presented the account of unnamed members of the U.S. intelligence community of how it failed to note Flight 007's initial deviation from course and how it handled information afterwards, an account that is unverifiable and has to be accepted on faith. That account assumes an innocent flight, but with the exception of an absurdly speculative theory, Hersh offers nothing to convince the reader of that innocence. In short, the story of what really happened to Flight 007 remains to be discovered.

22

THE NEW EVIDENCE

Lawrence L. Porter is an independent air-crash investigator specializing in air traffic procedures, including enhancement and analysis of voice tapes and radar computer data. He spent four years in the U.S. Air Defense Command, twenty-two years with the Federal Aviation Administration, and seven years as an independent aviation consultant. I visited Porter in Spokane, Washington, in February 1985, on the way to Anchorage, Alaska, as part of my investigation into the Flight 007 case.

Porter had been retained as an investigator and expert witness by a legal firm that represented one of the defendants in the Flight 007 litigation and agreed to meet with me under the ground rule that any information which he discovered while working for the firm could not be disclosed to me. Throughout his inquiry, it seemed to Porter that the law firm was not interested in having him conduct an aggressive investigation. The firm did not make available to him much of the material it had assembled in the case, and he had been called off several hot leads. In one instance, Porter had traveled to Anchorage, looking for the acoustic materials which are his specialty, and he began to turn up evidence of some importance. He returned to Spokane to make a deposition in another case, planning to return to Anchorage at the earliest opportunity. Describing his progress to the law firm, he was instructed not to return to Alaska. He was quite frustrated and willing to talk to me to the extent that his legal obligation permitted.

We discussed the case for seven hours in the coffee shop of Spokane's Davenport Hotel. My conversation ranged over the details of the case, motivations, and theories about what might have taken place and why. Porter provided a general discussion of radar and its properties, and a description of the responsibilities of the FAA and its relationship to the job of the military. While not providing me with any specific information about the work he had done for the firm, Porter made suggestions as to how I might go about my inquiry. When we spoke about the transcripts of the tapes of air traffic controllers' conversations in Anchorage, Porter insisted that his experience had taught him never to trust other people's renderings because of deliberate tampering, sloppy work, errors in judgment, poor equipment, the bias of the listener, or his lack of background in aviation communications. He described cases on which he had worked where an independent analysis of tapes had yielded a new interpretation, allowing the case to be solved.

The entire seven hours had come down to this. I asked him how much the work he was suggesting would cost. "They charge about $100 an hour," he replied. "The whole analysis would probably take as much as 100 hours." I said that $10,000 was a lot of money to spend for an analysis if it was not decisive, using up most of my remaining funds. "Would it be worth my while," I asked, "to spend my $10,000 for the analysis?" "Yes, it would," he replied. With a Freedom of Information Act request in hand, I flew to Anchorage to get the tapes from the Air Route Traffic Control Center.

I then traveled to San Francisco to meet with Dr. Malcolm Brenner, whom Larry Porter had recommended to perform the acoustic analysis of the tapes. (Porter's connection, through the law firm, to one of the parties in the victims' suit meant that he could not do it himself.) Brenner is one of four principal members of a group called Aviation Safety Associates International (ASAI), described in its brochure as able to provide "technical analysis of flight data recorders and cockpit voice recorders, including state-of-the-art enhancement of CVR [Cockpit Voice Recorder] and control tower voice tapes."[1] I asked Brenner to examine several areas of the tapes that struck me as likely to contain interesting information, and to do an enhancement and analysis of Flight 007's final transmission, a taped version of which I had obtained from ABC television. Laughing, we agreed to call the project "1010 Delta."

The first mention of "1010 Delta" in the KAL case came on September 16, 1983. The Japanese radio and television giant NHK had managed, through its contacts in the Nakasone government, to obtain a section of the radio transmissions from Flight 007 containing the final transmission. Matsumi Suzuki, director of the Japan Acoustic Research Center, was NHK's chief consultant on the project and his rendering of the final message, as reported by the *Los Angeles Times,* was:

Korean Air zero zero seven ... Rapid ... [unintelligible] ... all
engine ... a rapid decompression ... one zero one zero delta.

Times reporter Sam Jameson pointed out that nobody had any explanation
for the final "one zero one zero delta."[2]

The number "1010" again came to my attention when, in 1985, I spent
a day in London with *Defence Attaché* editor Rupert Pengelley. In the
midst of describing his magazine's legal troubles with Korean Air Lines,
Pengelley showed me an envelope he said had been sent to him with no
cover letter or return address. In the envelope were three photocopies of
published materials, with an underlined sentence in each one. The first was
Jameson's article from the *Los Angeles Times,* with "one zero one zero
delta" underlined. The second was an article from the *Christian Science
Monitor* in 1960 about Francis Gary Powers and the U-2 incident. "Mr.
Powers," the underscored sentence read, "served in unit 10-10 which
came under the National Aeronautics and Space Research Board 'only as
a cover.' " The 1010 unit, the article continued, "engages in military intelligence at great altitudes." The final item was a page from James Bamford's book *The Puzzle Palace,* about the National Security Agency. Here,
the underlined sentence was: "The second of the low-altitude surveillance
platforms (LASPs) is the Code 1010, or KH-11 satellite, code-named Keyhole."[3] Apparently "1010" is a number with a distinguished history in the
intelligence community.

Several weeks after my meeting with Brenner, a Department of Defense
official told him that he was examining a subject that was important to
national security, and reminded that his firm did a great deal of work for
the government. The official, Brenner reported to me later, asked him if
he "really knew" the source of the tapes, suggesting that the analysis
could be a Soviet plot. I observed how remarkable it was that such attention would be paid to an analyst working on a technical evaluation of a
flight the government had repeatedly described as innocent. Surely a competent analysis could only confirm that position. "It's important for a
company like ASAI to maintain its connections and guard its reputation,"
Brenner responded, requesting written verification of the sources for all
the tapes I had provided to him. He was obviously shaken: "I felt like the
person who has just received a visit from the Bad Fairy and suddenly
everything is changed," he said. "The streams all run dry and the crops
no longer grow in the fields."

ASAI's fees quickly piled up. My associate John Keppel and I received
additional financial support for the analysis from the Washington, D.C.-
based Fund for Constitutional Government, and we hoped to receive the
results of project "1010 Delta" in time to write a *Nation* article on the
second anniversary of the downing. But it was apparent that Brenner's
initial enthusiasm for the undertaking had been replaced with caution.
Consequently, I asked him to assemble a panel of experts to evaluate the
final message. As a result, a flight captain from a major U.S. airline and

several independent acoustic analysts were brought in as consultants. One of these was Larry Porter.

Members of the panel approached the very difficult acoustic material of the final message in two ways. The first, favored by the outside analysts and Porter, was to try to ascertain precisely what words were spoken, whether they seemed to make sense or not. Brenner, however, took the opposite approach—to try to make sense out of the message in spite of what is seemed to say. This necessitated his making a large number of assumptions. The apparently most audible passage in the final transmission was rendered in the ICAO report as "rapid compressions," and Brenner accepted this. But "rapid compressions" makes no sense, since an airplane just hit by a missile would not gain pressure, and might well lose it. Therefore, Brenner assumed that the pilot must have meant to say "rapid decompressions." Brenner also assumed that the final message actually came just a few seconds after the missile attack. This belief rested on two transcripts—one of the Soviet fighter pilots' communications over Sakhalin Island as prepared by the U.S. Government, and another of Flight 007's communications with Tokyo air traffic controllers as prepared by the Japanese government. (The tape of the Soviet pilots, in Russian, had been distributed by Ambassador Kirkpatrick at the U.N. in September 1983, but the tape of Tokyo controllers was not yet available in the summer of 1985.) Implicitly, Brenner assumed that these transcripts were accurate, and the tapes on which they were based were authentic. Since Brenner's clients had hired him because they did not believe the official version of events, he should have been testing, not accepting, these premises.

Brenner's supposition that rapid decompression had taken place in Flight 007's cabin led to a whole series of additional assumptions. At high altitudes rapid decompression is extremely serious, as the warm artificial climate in the cabin is explosively sucked out and replaced by freezing airlessness. So Brenner next posited that an emergency descent must have followed the decompression. The ICAO report had rendered part of the final message as "descending to one zero thousand" and Brenner accepted this as a "plausible rendering," although he admitted he did not hear those words. These assumptions left Brenner with an interpretation of the final message similar to that of the ICAO.

Although he had sent us to Brenner, Larry Porter violently disagreed with his rendering. "Those words are just not there," he said. He also criticized Brenner's technical handling of the audio material. Brenner had sent the recording of the final transmission to the acoustic laboratory at Brigham Young University for filtering and enhancement. BYU has one of the best audio labs in the world, but Brenner was not present to supervise all of the technical procedures. As Porter pointed out, dozens of different techniques, and combinations of techniques, must sometimes be applied by an analyst to effectively remove noise and "bring out" portions of speech, and the results from one technique suggest the next steps to be taken. But the BYU technicians, working on instructions from afar, applied only those techniques that had been requested. As a result, the enhancement, though competent, was limited.[4] We dropped Malcolm Brenner as our consultant, and turned over the acoustic work to Larry Porter, who had by this time extricated himself from his commitment to the law firm.

After the second anniversary of the tragedy, we obtained the tape of communications between Flight 007 and Tokyo air traffic controllers from Senator Yutaka Hata of the Upper House of the Japanese Diet, who had gotten the tape from the Japanese government under parliamentary procedures. Larry Porter set to work. Practically inaudible material was enhanced by using computer equipment, vocal stressors, parametric equalizers, and filters of various types. The electronic equipment, however, could not do it all. Deciphering difficult acoustic material requires experience, extraordinary patience, and hard work. On first hearing, such material is often utterly incomprehensible. Even after state-of-the-art electronic enhancement, hundreds, sometimes thousands of listenings by an experienced analyst are required. The analyst in effect creates hypotheses in his mind about what was said, and then tests them by repeated listenings. In time, the words begin to make sense. By the end of the process, material that was impossible to make out at first can be completely clear.

Even so, such material does not make good evidence in court. Judges and juries think that if something is said to be on a tape it should be audible to them, and easily audible. They are forced to accept expert testimony without being able to evaluate it. In addition, experts often disagree. Other professionals might dispute Porter's rendering of Flight 007's various messages, or give contradictory testimony to a congressional committee. However, no other acoustic analyst has spent the time on this material that Larry Porter has.

For Flight 007's final transmission, for instance, Porter estimated he had dedicated a minimum of 20 to 30 hours for each second of the audio material, which is 19 seconds in length. "I've got hundreds and hundreds of hours in this thing," Porter said. Porter was assisted in many of the technical aspects of the analysis by Professors Les Atlas and Alan Reich of the University of Washington, and by Rex Andrew, a graduate student. Porter pointed out that the University team, like himself, put in hundreds of hours of work for "pitiful compensation." Many of the ideas about which techniques to try came from Dr. Atlas, who also reviewed and evaluated all of the work. Although Porter's investigation is still in progress, his analysis of the tapes has produced important results.

Porter's most dramatic finding came from the tapes of Flight 007's conversations with air traffic controllers in Anchorage. He had been the first to pick out a background voice in Anchorage's Air Route Traffic Control Center saying, "a person should warn him," which had made something of a splash in Federal District Court in Washington. (Alan Reich had signed an affidavit attesting to the audibility of the passage, but when it was introduced, government witnesses declared the passage "unintelligible," and accused the next-of-kin's lawyers of making "scurrilous allegations" and "manipulating the evidence.") But that was only part of a longer conversation that took place in the Air Route Traffic Control Center: *

1434:01	Okay, you guys got someone bumping into the Russians' air defenses over here.
1434:06	Oh, you're kidding.
1434:08	A person should warn him.
1434:10	That's why you should've given the information here, instead of waiting.
1434:16	[I] can't believe * * * * [give him his position through Radio].

Porter said the first of the remarks had a metallic sound, characteristic of words coming over a loudspeaker. Air traffic controller Kevin DeGarmo had a loudspeaker at his position that night, able to convey messages to him from elsewhere in the ARTCC, as well as from other facilities such as the Regional Operations Control Center at Elmendorf Air Force Base. "The guy's microphone was obviously open," Porter said. "I picked him up tapping his pencil and whistling. . . . You get within a certain range and the noises and words will be picked up." Porter said he is absolutely certain of what was said in the unbracketed passages, and identified three different voices in the conversation.

The implications of these words having been spoken in the Air Route Traffic Control Center are staggering: Air traffic controllers would have been fully aware of Flight 007's deviating course when it entered the Soviet buffer zone, some two hours before it entered Russian airspace. Since only military radars could have observed Flight 007 "bumping into the Russians' air defenses" (civilian radar coverage does not extend nearly that far), U.S. military personnel also must have known of the airliner's deviation. Although Larry Porter heard Kevin DeGarmo, or someone near him, suggesting that a high-frequency radio call be placed to the airliner via "Radio," the privately run International Flight Service Station, no warnings were issued by either civilians or the military. This could explain why FAA personnel were not allowed to comment on the case, why military radar tapes were destroyed, and why none of the controllers who testified in Federal District Court could remember what happened on the night of August 31, 1983.

There are two reasons why the message Porter heard could have escaped

---

* Bracketed words represent best interpretation; asterisks indicate an unintelligible syllable or word.

attention until now. First, on most of the tapes distributed by the FAA, the "dead space" between messages—including these voices—was removed. Second, even on tapes including the dead space, the voices were very faint. Only on a copy made directly from the master tape could most of the words be discerned, and only Porter had made copies directly from the master tape. It is important to remember that the discussion about an airplane about to enter Soviet territory was not broadcast on the radio, and was only picked up accidentally.

Porter believes that there is a great deal of additional information about Flight 007 to be found on tapes of what are known as interphone communications. Some air traffic controllers work the radar scopes, some work the radio, and still others work the interphone. These controllers use direct phone lines to talk to other relevant personnel in the communications net —other controllers at their own facility, controllers at airport control towers in their sectors of responsibility, personnel at the International Flight Service Station, and so on. By pressing a few buttons they also can communicate with liaison personnel at nearby military installations such as Elmendorf Air Force Base. The most important of the interphone communications take place at what are called the supervisory positions. The interphone communications are as integral to air traffic control as radio messages and, like them, are recorded. Thus an entire class of important communications from the night of the downing were never broadcast over the radio, and never made public. "I find it incredible," Porter said, "that they'd release an accident report of this nature and magnitude [the ICAO report] that doesn't include these interphone communications. Normally, we always have the interphone side of the controlling positions on the tape and we have a transcript of what was said. It's just second nature. . . . That's where all the conversations are that would fill in the gaps. That's where all the action is." The ICAO never examined any of this material, and the FAA now claims the most important of the interphone communications, from the supervisory positions at the Air Route Traffic Control Center, were not recorded.

Porter's next finding had to do with a series of the transmissions between Flight 007 and Tokyo air traffic control:

TIME	SOURCE	TRANSMISSION
1815:00	FLT 007	Hey, Tokyo Radio Korean Air zero zero seven.
1815:03	TOKYO	Korean Air zero zero seven Tokyo.
1815:05	FLT 007	[They're at] three zero zero zero zero, request [immediate] climb to three five zero.
1815:12	TOKYO	Requesting three five zero?

TIME	SOURCE	TRANSMISSION
1815:14	FLT 007	That is affirmative [and presently I'm] at three three zero, Korean Air zero zero seven.
1815:16	TOKYO	Roger, stand by [and] call you back.

Starting with these transmissions by Flight 007, Porter detected a continuing rise in the excitement and inflection of the speaker's voice, suggesting that he may have been excited or in a hurry. Several minutes later, he heard the following words:

| 1823:05 | FLT 007 | Test . . . Tokyo Radio, Korean Air zero zero seven's now at three five zero |
| 1823:08 | TOKYO | Korean Air zero zero seven Tokyo, roger. |

Reading a transcript is very different from listening to a tape. For instance, it is easy to overlook the word "test" at 1823:05 or to consider it meaningless unless one actually hears the sucking sound immediately before and after the word. Porter says it was produced when someone donned an oxygen mask and spoke the word "test" into the mask's built-in microphone. "I've had a lot of experience over the years with people talking through oxygen masks," Porter said, "and I've worn them myself and so I know that sound. The mike has specific, identifiable properties that you can pick out." If he is right, it might mean that crew members were aware of the Soviet interception in progress, and had donned oxygen masks some three minutes before the missile attack.

Then Porter turned to the "final message" from Flight 007. This was presented in the ICAO report as "Korean Air zero zero seven . . . [unintelligible] . . . rapid compressions . . . [unintelligible] . . . descending to one zero thousand.[5] The transmission as Porter rendered it, however, was radically different:

1827:00	FLT 007	[They don't] * * Anchorage
	FLT 007	Tokyo Radio, Korean Air zero zero seven.
1827:05	TOKYO	Korean Air zero zero seven, Tokyo.

| 1827:10 | FLT 007 | That was Korean Air zero zero seven repeating. Hold your [bo*ie [n]orth]. Repeat conditions. * * had a bloodbath real bad. |

This strange message raises many questions. Why would Flight 007 make a standard call to Tokyo and then wait for a response? This does not seem to fit with the supposed urgency of the situation. Other questions were equally troubling. Why would Flight 007 mention Anchorage when he was supposed to be speaking to Tokyo? "Hold your [bo*ie [n]orth]"—a passage that was exceedingly difficult to understand—could suggest that somebody had been designated a "bogie," a military term for an unidentified aircraft. Toward the end of the transmission, however, it seems clear that someone was aware that things were going wrong. "Repeat conditions. * * had a bloodbath, real bad" does suggest a severe problem, although there is no indication just what conditions the pilot was "repeating," or to whom. Nevertheless, this is not a "Mayday" message, and as Porter pointed out, it does not discuss the condition of the aircraft or the actions of the crew. An odd message indeed as Captain Chun Byung-in and Flight 007 approached the moment of their destruction. Is it possible that some or all of these transmissions did not originate with Flight 007?

Air traffic controllers in Tokyo overheard, but did not understand the final message. They placed a series of calls to Flight 007:

1827:26	TOKYO	Korean Air zero zero seven, and that's unreadable, unreadable. Radio check on one zero zero four eight.
1828:12	TOKYO	—SELCAL—
1828:30	TOKYO	—SELCAL—
1828:45	TOKYO	—SELCAL—
1828:57	TOKYO	Korean Air zero zero seven Tokyo.
1829:15	TOKYO	Korean Air zero zero seven Tokyo.
1830:01	?	*[seven].

A selcal consists of two tones, the first higher than the second, which activate both an audio and visual signal in the cockpit. Pilots are supposed to acknowledge receipt of the signal, but Flight 007 answered neither the selcals nor the radio queries from Tokyo.

Tokyo then requested that Flight 015 try to contact the unresponsive Flight 007:

1831:35	TOKYO	...Ah, would you attempt to contact ah, ah, Korean Air zero zero seven, Korean Air zero zero seven please, and ah, ah...h, relay his position please.
1831:54	FLT 015	Roger, stand by.
1831:58	FLT 015	Zero zero seven.
1832:21	FLT 015	Zero zero seven.
1832:32	FLT 015	Zero zero seven, zero one five.
1833:10	[FLT 015]	Five.
1833:11	TOKYO	Korean Air zero one five, go ahead.
1833:13	FLT 015	Unable contact Korean Air zero zero seven.

Immediately following this apparently normal exchange between Flight 015 and Tokyo air traffic controllers, Larry Porter detected another background conversation, although, as the brackets indicate, this represents his "best interpretation" of what was said:

1834:50	?	[He was our control].
	?	[Zero zero seven go].
1834:53	?	[He doesn't have him].
1835:02	?	[He doesn't show up here. [Is it] normal...]
	?	* *

Porter believes that most if not all of these background words were not intended for Tokyo air traffic controllers to hear—nor were they heard—and they appeared on the tape because of the sounds "bleeding through" from different sources, such as communications land lines.[6]

Porter, as well as other researchers who have worked closely with the tapes, suspect that they may have been tampered with. There was certainly time to do so. It was only after an inexplicable two-year delay that the government of Japan released the tapes of high-frequency and very-high-frequency communications from the night of the shootdown, and what was eventually produced is strange indeed. First, there are questions of completeness. Following the above transmissions, the tape of HF communications ends. The tape of VHF transmissions does not begin until 1842:17, meaning that there is a seven-minute gap in radio coverage surrounding the critical time 1838 GMT when, according to all early reports, both Soviet and American, the Korean airliner disappeared from radar. Next, there are inexplicable difficulties with audibility. "Every time you have a place where a word could affect your thinking one way or another, you have problems," Porter told me. Sometimes, noise would suddenly obscure only a single, critical word from Flight 007. None of the transmissions from other aircraft on the tapes were so affected. "I've never seen anything like it," he concluded.

The best example of the peculiarities of the tapes, and the doubts they raise, is Flight 007's final transmission. Examining the frequency of the radio message, Porter discovered that the latter part—"That was Korean Air zero zero seven repeating. Hold your [bo*ie [n]orth]. Repeat conditions. ** had a bloodbath real bad"—was shifted upwards in frequency by 800 hertz, while the first part of the transmission was not. Had this abnormality been caused by damage to the plane during the missile attack, the entire transmission would have been off frequency. One possible interpretation is that the two parts of the tape do not belong together. "I have absolutely no faith in the integrity of this tape," Porter concluded. "It seems I've been dealing with a bogus tape all along."

Other researchers have had similar questions about the tapes of the Soviet interceptors recorded by Japan.[7] As Flight 007 approached Sakhalin Island, the fighters were in the air by 1742 GMT, at the latest. Although the Japanese intelligence facilities at Wakkanai and Abashiri were both within range to intercept the Russians' radio transmissions from the start, the tape does not begin until 1756:58. Since there must have been transmissions by the pilots during the first fifteen minutes of flight, when they were ascending and being directed toward the target, where are they?

On September 5, 1983, the White House issued a statement saying that U.N. Ambassador Kirkpatrick would release a tape covering 55 minutes of transmissions by the Soviet pilots. The tape released in the Security Council the following day covered only 49 minutes and 11 seconds, suggesting that it had been edited. What was on the tape was sometimes puzzling. At one point, Soviet pilot 805 said "I see it," but 2 minutes later did not know if Flight 007 had turned to the left or right. At another point, pilot 163 told Karnaval, his ground controller, that he had just dropped both of his wing fuel tanks. Five minutes later he reported, "My wing tanks lit up," suggesting he was still carrying them. However 13 minutes later, he again reported, "I dropped my [wing] tanks." But the MiG-23 flown by pilot 163 had only two wing tanks, and he could not have dropped them twice. Pilot 163 also reported at 1834:02: "Fuel remainder two [thousand]" liters. But 2 minutes later he reported that he could continue searching for the target until he got down to 2,000 liters of fuel. And, as mentioned in Chapter 17, there were serious discrepancies in the fighters' fuel consumption. They burned more fuel in the later stages of their flight, when they were lighter and flying relatively level, and should have used less. It also seems hard to believe that the Soviet pilot in close pursuit of the intruder made no comment on the "glowing orange-colored expanding fireball'' that was seen by the Japanese fishermen several minutes after the missile attack. Finally, where were the transmissions from Soviet ground control stations? The tape released by Ambassador Kirkpatrick did include several transmissions from the ground controller Trikotazh (although the ICAO report later erroneously attributed them to one of the Russian pilots). If some ground-based transmissions could be recorded, then where were the rest? All of this supports the hypothesis that these tapes were cut and spliced.

Japanese investigative reporter Yoshitaro Masuo agrees: "The sound quality of the tape was so poor that it shocked Japan's amateur radio buffs, who could on a very accessible radio band listen in regularly to the communications of Soviet fighters . . . as clearly as if they were listening to the FM band of the radio," he pointed out. Masuo believes that the governments of Japan and the United States released "a kind of counterfeit tape that has been subjected to a variety of operations—in order to erase vital information.[8]

Larry Porter's new findings coupled with a strong possibility that the tapes have been altered suggest a hypothesis about the final minutes of the Korean airliner's flight. The hypothesis begins with two reports which were filed in the hours following the downing. The first of these was Flight 007's position report from waypoint NOKKA. Virtually all early press accounts of Flight 007's disappearance said that the airliner had made a position report at NOKKA, where it was due at 1826 GMT—ironically, the time of the missile attack. Many of these reports were highly specific: The Japan Transport Ministry told the press that "the aircraft reported in its last message that it was passing over a point 42.23 degrees north longitude, 147.28 degrees east latitude"—the coordinates for NOKKA. The *Los Angeles Times* said that Flight 007 had reported passing the waypoint, and that the pilot "gave no indication of any trouble and that the weather was reported good in the area at the time." The Japan Maritime Safety Association seemed to believe that a position report had been made at NOKKA, since search and rescue vessels and aircraft flew there after Flight 007 was reported missing. But when transcripts and tapes of Flight 007's radio transmissions were made public, they contained no such report.[9]

The second story was that Flight 007 vanished from radar at 1838, some 11 or 12 minutes after the missile attack. Announcing the downing of the airliner on the morning of September 1, 1983, Secretary of State George Shultz said, "At 1838 hours, the Korean plane disappeared from the radar screen." This was repeated by Charles Lichenstein at the United Nations a day later. A secret State Department cable on September 1 advised U.S. diplomatic posts abroad that "early today we received confirmation . . . at 1838 hours it disappeared from the radar screen."[10] But the 1838 disappearance from radar itself soon disappeared. Within a few days of the downing, U.S. officials adopted the Japanese story that Flight 007 disappeared from radar at 1829.

With these two stories in mind, we can approach the question of what happened over Sakhalin. Despite the problems with the tape of the Soviet pilots' communications—apparently impossible sequences of events and the deletion of material that was certainly recorded, errors in translation obscuring the Soviet use of standard interception procedures and gratuitous interpolations that made Flight 007's crew appear unaware of the interception—the basic chronology of events described in the Soviet transmissions is probably more or less accurate. The tinkering that appears to have taken place with this tape took the form of selective deletions. Both the United States and the Soviet Union agree that certain events occurred at the same time—the cannon bursts at about 1820 GMT, for instance. No such confidence, however, can be placed in the tapes of communications between Flight 007 and Tokyo air traffic controllers. These were in the sole possession of the U.S. and its allies for two years after the downing, and the tapes that were released did not cover a crucial period of time.

My hypothesis is based on several assumptions, most of them about the role of Flight 007's sister aircraft KAL Flight 015. It is an undisputed fact that Flight 015 flew at an accelerated speed during the first legs of its journey, which put it very close to where Flight 007 was supposed to have been on Romeo-20. This minimized the distance between the two airliners on their diverging courses, permitting them to maintain VHF radio contact with one another for the maximum amount of time. It might also have been a means of deceiving the Russians. The Soviets, like the Americans, use high-frequency radio direction-finding to track aircraft beyond radar range. As Flight 007 approached the Kamchatka Peninsula and came close to the RC-135, routine high-frequency messages ostensibly from Flight 007 were received by the civilian International Flight Service Station—Anchorage Radio. The Soviets are fully aware of which civilian flights come down the NOPAC routes each night, and thus certainly must have entertained the notion that the intruder was Flight 007. Imagine their surprise, then, when they used their HFDF to locate the source of Flight 007's radio messages and discovered that it was way out on Romeo-20! It is possible that all the radio traffic purportedly from Flight 007 was actually from Flight 015, a suggestion of some interest in light of Captain Park Young-man's peculiar later behavior.

Flight 015, if it was indeed sending messages in Flight 007's name, would not have been immediately aware of the attack on its sister plane at 1826:22. Knowing that Flight 007 was scheduled to arrive at waypoint NOKKA at 1826, Flight 015 would have permitted a few extra minutes to elapse for verisimilitude before sending in Flight 007's NOKKA report. I am hypothesizing that the NOKKA report may in fact have been made, but *after* the time when Flight 007 was attacked. Since a radio report from an airplane hit by a missile would normally mention that fact, and this one did not, U.S. and Japanese officials found it necessary to get rid of the NOKKA report.

But not completely. Part of the report consisted of a request for a higher altitude, and this could serve a useful purpose. U.S. intelligence knew that Flight 007 had slowed down, and they knew that the Russian had fired cannon bursts. Some explanation would be necessary both for the slow-down and the obliviousness to the brilliant tracer ammunition. For this, a climb was a perfect.

I postulate that most of the NOKKA report may have been removed from Flight 007's taped transmission. In addition, I suggest that it was made to appear that the reported climb from 33,000 to 35,000 feet began just before the cannon bursts and the slowdown. Air traffic control tapes consist of two channels—one of the voices of pilots and controllers, and the other of a continuous time signal. The time signal, in either voice or digital form, allows the time of every radio communication to be determined. It would be easy to shift the time signal channel with respect to the voice channel, making all transmissions appear to have taken place a fixed amount of time earlier or later. What would be the result if the time signal had been shifted so that all of Flight 007's communications recorded by the Japanese seemed to have taken place about 11½ minutes earlier than they actually did?

If that happened, the "nervousness" perceived by Larry Porter at 1815:00 actually took place only seconds before the missile attack at 1826:22. It means the report of a climb at 1820:20 was actually sent 11½ minutes later, about the time when Flight 015 would have been expected to send a NOKKA report in Flight 007's name. It means that the word "test" would have been spoken into an oxygen mask's microphone at 1834:30—after the missile attack and as the airliner approached its destruction. It means that Flight 007's "final message" would have been broadcast not at 1827, but just after 1838—about the time when the airliner disappeared from radar screens in an apparent explosion and the Soviet pilot in close pursuit of Flight 007 suddenly increased his altitude from 7,000 to 9,000 meters, possibly to get out of the way of debris. It means that the confusing transmissions Larry Porter thought he heard beginning at about 1835—"[he was our control. Zero zero seven go. He doesn't have him. He doesn't show up here [is it] normal . . .]"—took place at about 1847. This was almost precisely the time when Flight 007 should have, but did not, appear on Japanese civil air traffic controllers' radars.

A single shift of the tape's time signal with respect to Flight 007's trans-missions could create a new chronology that supported the official version of events.[11] Flight 007's mid-air slowdown and failure to respond to cannon bursts became the result of a climb. The final message now came, logically, shortly after the missile attack, distracting attention from early statements that gave the time for the disappearance from radar as 1838. It precluded questions about why, twelve minutes after the attack, Flight 007 exploded, and why it sent no emergency messages before then.

The hypothesis of an 11½-minute shift is consistent with a number of the known facts of the case and clears up some of its central mysteries. It explains why reports which apparently once existed no longer do. It also makes far more chronological sense than the materials we have been offered from official sources. Yet it is only a hypothesis, and the claims about the tapes from Flight 007 that I have presented in this chapter do not require that it prove accurate in every detail. There may be other, more compelling interpretations for the evidence before us, and I would welcome them.

The inquiry into the downing of Korean Air Lines Flight 007 has never been like an ordinary investigation. Usually, something happens that investigators consider to be suspicious. They assemble the available evidence, and from that generate a series of possible motives, means, and suspects. The working assumption is that guilt is a possible explanation for the event in question. Hypotheses emerge, and, if they are good, lead to additional evidence. In the process, certain explanations and suspects are dismissed from consideration because they do not fit the growing body of evidence. The range of possible suspects is progressively narrowed. The investigators need not produce unequivocal evidence, nor do they have to assemble an absolutely airtight case. They establish what they call probable cause. And that is enough to initiate the next step in the legal process.

The investigation into the downing of Flight 007 should proceed in a similar fashion. Independent investigators have assembled a large body of logical, circumstantial, inferential evidence. They have shown that the scenarios explaining Flight 007's deviation from course in an accidental way are not credible. They have demonstrated that virtually the entire official version of events is obfuscatory, deficient, or just plain wrong. With the new evidence in this book, including Larry Porter's important finding about conversations in the Anchorage Air Route Traffic Control Center that, if accurate, means that civilian and military personnel were aware of Flight 007's deviation from course hours before the shootdown, a serious investigation is surely called for. The next stage is for an appropriate congressional body—a subcommittee of the Intelligence or Public Works and Transportation committees, or a special group similar to the Warren Commission with the power of subpoena—to consider all the available evidence.

There is a great deal the members of Congress could do. They could require executive orders or approvals concerning intelligence operations in the Kamchatka/Sea of Okhotsk/Sakhalin area that were in force on the night of August 31, 1983. They could demand tapes of all relevant communications and radar monitoring by the National Security Agency and the Department of Defense. They could require the data originally on the radar scope at Elmendorf Air Force Base, said to have been destroyed but in all likelihood preserved elsewhere in the national system, to be produced. The Japanese and American tapes of communications between the Soviet pilots and their ground controllers on Sakhalin could be requested and independently translated, as could intercepted communications from the time of the Kamchatka overflight. The Congress could demand to see the radar data showing Flight 007's disappearance at approximately 1838 GMT. All of this might shed light on the question of whether Flight 007 was on a mission for U.S. intelligence services.

For witnesses, Congress could find out the names of the watch officers on duty that night who might have had access to information about Flight 007; at the White House, the Departments of State and Defense, the CIA, the NSA, NORAD, CINCPAC, Elmendorf AFB, Misawa Air Base, and Wakkanai. The names of the crews involved in monitoring Soviet radar and communications from Elmendorf, Shemya, on the RC-135, on board the U.S.S. *Observation Island* and U.S.S. *Badger,* and at Wakkanai and Misawa could be ascertained. All of these officers and enlisted men could then be subpoenaed and questioned under oath. The air traffic controllers on duty at the FAA Air Route Traffic Control Center in Anchorage could be questioned again.

Congress could also examine information relating to the search for wreckage from the airliner. If Flight 007 fell in international waters, did the U.S. recover any wreckage, and if so, where is it? The wreckage could provide information about the destruction of the airliner, and the flight recorders would solve many mysteries about the flight itself. Alternatively, if the plane fell into Soviet waters and the Russians recovered both wreckage and bodies, as other evidence suggests, why has the U.S. concealed this? Officers and crews from the vessels involved in the search could be summoned and questioned on these matters, under oath.

An inquiry by the Congress is one possibility, and the one we must take. If, on the other hand, we accept the Administration's word for it that the case should not be further investigated, what shall we be saying about the nature of our government? From the founding of our nation it was intended that the Congress should have the right, indeed the duty, to review acts of the Executive which appear improper. When Congress has acted, much of the impetus has come from the press and the public, who, from the beginning, were also considered part of the governmental process. That we have a reasonably open society in the United States today is because individuals in the past have been willing to ask hard and occasionally inconvenient questions, and persist until they got answers. It is time we do so again in the case of KAL Flight 007. If we do not, our silence will be a vote for a kind of government quite different from the one envisioned in the Constitution. It will be one conferring, in effect, all power on the Executive and its most influential backers, institutional and individual. Such a government will be constantly tempted to act arbitrarily and in secret, to manipulate the public with managed news, and to commit the nation to arbitrarily chosen lines of action by presenting it with accomplished facts. We will be its subjects, not its citizens.[12]

The evidence suggests that Flight 007's deviation was known to its crew. It suggests that U.S. civilian and military personnel knew the plane to be headed toward the Soviet Union hours before the shootdown and did nothing to direct it back to course. And it is clear that the Administration has tried from the beginning to limit inquiry into the downing. How are serious observers to interpret this state of affairs? It is essential, therefore, that Congress demand the facts; that it take steps to insure that "national security" remains consonant with responsible government; and that the public learn the truth, whatever that truth might be, before something like the tragedy of Korean Air Lines Flight 007 happens again.

NOTES AND REFERENCES

INTRODUCTION

[1] Charles Perrow, *Normal Accidents: Living with High-Risk Technologies,* 1984, Basic Books, New York, p. 4.

[2] U.S. Congress, House, *Review of Department of Defense Worldwide Communications,* Committee on Armed Services, 10 May 1971, Washington, DC, p. 10; James Bamford, *The Puzzle Palace: A Report on America's Most Secret Agency,* 1983, Penguin Books, New York, pp. 140–41; U.S. Congress, Senate, *Recent False Alerts from the Nation's Missile Attack Warning System,* Committee on Armed Services, 9 October 1980, Washington, DC; and John H. Cushman, Jr., "Pentagon Study Faults Planning on Grenada," *New York Times,* 12 July 1986, pp. 1–4.

[3] William J. Broad, "Philosophers at the Pentagon," *Science,* 24 October 1980, pp. 409–12.

[4] Thorstein Veblen, *Absentee Ownership and Business Enterprise in Recent Times: The Case of America,* 1923, Beacon Press, Boston, p. 444.

[5] Thanks to Tom Gervasi, director of the Center for Military Research and Analysis, for pointing out these issues.

[6] Charles Perrow, *Normal Accidents: Living with High-Risk Technologies,* 1984, Basic Books, New York, pp. 89–100.

PROLOGUE

1. Masagu Ogawa, "Terrorism in Northern Skies," *Japan Times,* 4 September 1983, pp. 1–5; *Aviation Week & Space Technology,* "Washington Roundup," 5 September 1983, p. 13; *Foreign Broadcast Information Service* (hereafter *FBIS*), Japan, "Official: SS-20s in Far East to Increase to 135," 4 October 1983, p. C2; Clyde Haberman, "Challenge in the Pacific," *New York Times Magazine,* 7 September 1986, pp. 26–113; and Robert Gillette, "Soviets Admit Interception but Not Shooting," *Los Angeles Times,* 2 September 1983, Part I, pp. 1–4.

2. The fleet includes the aircraft carrier *Minsk,* equipped for antisubmarine warfare, 85 major surface combatants, and 312 other combat and support vessels. The fleet operates 330 aircraft, including 120 bombers, at least 30 of which are Backfires. Finally, there is an 8,000-man marine unit, the largest such unit in the Soviet armed forces.

3. Brad Knickerbocker, "Why Soviets Are Sensitive About Northern Pacific Coast," *Christian Science Monitor,* 6 September 1983, p. 3; Drew Middleton, "Stragetic Soviet Region," *New York Times,* 2 September 1983, pp. A1–7; Thomas B. Allen and Norman Polmar, "The Silent Chase: Tracking Soviet Submarines," *New York Times Magazine,* 1 January 1984, pp. 13–27; *Aviation Week & Space Technology,* "Washington Roundup," 28 November 1983, p. 17; and Robert Gillette, "Soviets Admit Interception but Not Shooting," *Los Angeles Times,* 2 September 1983, Part I, pp. 1–4.

4. Brad Knickerbocker, "Why Soviets Are Sensitive About Northern Pacific Coast," *Christian Science Monitor,* 6 September 1983, p. 3; Drew Middleton, "Strategic Soviet Region," *New York Times,* 2 September 1983, pp. A1–7; and Fred S. Hoffman, "Russian Security Paranoia Seen Guiding Sakhalin Island Attack," *San Francisco Examiner & Chronicle,* 2 September 1983, p. A7.

5. Michael R. Gordon, "Officials Say Navy Might Attack Soviet A-Arms in Nonnuclear War," *New York Times,* 7 January 1986, pp. A1–14.

6. Michael Klare, "Asia: Theatre of Nuclear War," *South,* November 1983, pp. 9–13.

7. *The Washington Spectator,* "Russian Roulette in the North Pacific," 15 May 1984, pp. 1–3; Michael Klare, "Asia: Theatre of Nuclear War," *South,* November 1983, pp. 9–13; and Brad Knickerbocker, "Why Soviets Are Sensitive About Northern Pacific Coast," *Christian Science Monitor,* 6 September 1983, p. 3.

8. William E. Burrows, *Deep Black: Space Espionage and National Security,* 1986, Random House, New York, pp. 179–80; Jeffrey T. Richelson, *The U.S. Intelligence Community,* 1985, Ballinger, Cambridge, MA, pp. 145–47; Martin Streetly, "Air Electronic Order of Battle 1985," *Jane's Defence Weekly,* 22 June 1985, pp. 1234–42; Malcolm D. Browne, "Submarines Are Foiling Detection Despite Advances in Technology," *New York Times,* 1 April 1986, pp. C1–3; and Thomas B. Allen and Norman Polmar, "The Silent Chase: Tracking Soviet Submarines," *New York Times Magazine,* 1 January 1984, pp. 13–27.

9. Geoffrey Murray, "Under Soviet Eyes, U.S. and Japan Hold Sea Exercises," *Christian Science Monitor,* 22 September 1983, p. 6.

10. The main function of the BMEWS system is to track Soviet missiles and determine their number and likely targets. The Clear site is equipped with AN/FPS-50 and AN/FPS-92 radars, complementing the two other BMEWS facilities at ule, Greenland, and Fylingdales Moor, in Great Britain.

11. Jeffrey T. Richelson, *The U.S. Intelligence Community*, 1985, Ballinger, Cambridge, MA, p. 154; and Desmond Ball, *Code 647: Australia and the U.S. Defense Support Program*, July 1982, Strategic and Defence Studies Centre (unpublished manuscript).

12. Desmond Ball, *Code 647: Australia and the U.S. Defense Support Program (DSP)*, July 1982, Strategic & Defence Studies Centre, (unpublished manuscript); James Bamford, *The Puzzle Palace*, 1983, Penguin, New York, p. 208; and *Los Angeles Times*, "U.S. Eavesdropped as Jetliner Was Attacked," 1 September 1983, Part I, p. 1.

13. Built by Lockheed, the Orion is a four-engined turboprop capable of flying over 1,500 miles, patrolling for 4 hours, and returning to base. The P-3C is equipped with a digital computer that coordinates the returns from its sensor systems— active and passive sonobuoys, magnetic anomaly detectors (which detect large masses of metal such as submarines), forward-looking infrared sensors, and radar—and presents them in visual form on cathode ray visual displays for the crew. The sonobuoys are underwater hydrophones attached to floating buoys. In addition, the Orion is equipped for radar signals collection, communications interception and analysis, and other intelligence functions.

14. Robert Whymant, "Spy in the Sky Island," *The Guardian*, 18 September 1983, p. 7; and Robert R. Ropelewski, "SR-71 Impressive in High-Speed Regime," *Aviation Week & Space Technology*, 18 May 1981, pp. 46–56; and William E. Burrows, *Deep Black*, 1986, Random House, New York, pp. 160 and 169.

15. Robert Lindsey, *The Falcon and the Snowman*, 1979, Simon and Schuster, New York, p. 54; James Bamford, *The Puzzle Palace*, 1983, Penguin, New York, pp. 254–55; Thomas Karas, *The New High Ground*, 1983, Touchstone, New York, pp. 111–12; and Jeffrey T. Richelson, *The U.S. Intelligence Community*, 1985, Ballinger, Cambridge, MA, pp. 121–22.

16. James Bamford, *The Puzzle Palace*, 1983, Penguin, New York, pp. 254–55.

CHAPTER 1

1. Korean Air Lines, the flag carrier of the Republic of Korea, began passenger service between Seoul and New York in March 1979, supplementing its daily flights between Los Angeles and Seoul. Flight 007 was a Boeing 747 200-B aircraft, its tail number HL-7442. Boeing delivered the air frame to Condor, a West German charter subsidiary of Lufthansa, on March 31, 1972. It was the 186th 747 aircraft built by Boeing. KAL purchased the aircraft from Condor in 1979. (*Sources:* Clyde Haberman, "Korean Jetliner with 269 Aboard Missing Near Soviet Pacific Island," *New York Times*, 1 September 1983, pp. A1–D19; and *Aviation Week & Space Technology*, "Soviet Su-15 Shoots Down Korean 747," 5 September 1983, pp. 25–27.)

2. *Washington Post*, "Soviet Diplomats Take a Commercial Flight to Attend U.N. Session," 20 September 1983, p. A11.

3. *Washington Post*, "House Votes Condemnation of Soviet Union," 15 September 1983, pp. A1–19; *Daily Yomiuri*, "IPU Conference Now in Jeopardy," 18 September 1983; *New York Times*, "List of Passengers Aboard Downed Jet," 2 September 1983, p. A6; and David Shribman, "Korean Jetliner: What Is Known and What Isn't," *New York Times*, 8 September 1983, pp. A1–12.

4. International Civil Aviation Organization (ICAO), *Destruction of Korean Air Lines Boeing 747 over Sea of Japan, 31 August 1983: Report of ICAO Fact-*

Finding Investigation, December 1983, Montreal, Canada, p. 4 (hereafter referred to as "ICAO Report").

5. According to a spokesman for Litton Industries, the aircraft was equipped with triply redundant Litton LTN-72R inertial navigation systems in 1982. (*Source:* Douglas B. Feaver, "FAA Suspends Use of Route Korean Airliner Had Been Assigned," *Washington Post,* 3 September 1983, p. A22.)

6. According to Korean Air Lines, the four passengers were Robert Sears, an employee of Alaska International Air, his wife, and two children. They were reportedly returning to Anchorage after a vacation in New York. (*Source:* David Treadwell, "Fate of Korea Jet: Questions Linger," *Los Angeles Times,* 2 October 1983, Part I, pp. 1–29.)

7. ICAO Report, p. 10.

8. McDonald became the second chairman of the John Birch Society in spring 1983, succeeding Robert Welsh, the group's founder. McDonald was himself the founder and first chairman of Western Goals, a private, right-wing, tax-exempt research foundation in Alexandria, Virginia. The organization had its own 6,000-volume library and maintained a mailing list of several thousand supporters. One of its publications was apparently the source of Ronald Reagan's 1982 remark that the nuclear freeze movement was being manipulated by the Soviet Union. Western Goals' Public Disorder Intelligence Division engaged in private spying on the political left in the United States. A Los Angeles police detective named Jay Paul later had charges brought against him for illegally concealing and using confidential police intelligence files and channelling them to McDonald's group.

9. Paul Houston, "Ultimate Irony Ends McDonald's Career," *Los Angeles Times,* 2 September 1983, Part I, p. 4.

10. *San Francisco Examiner & Chronicle,* "Congressman Missed His Earlier Flight," 1 September 1983, p. A21.

11. ABC "20/20 Newsmagazine," 30 August 1984; and Helen Dewar and Vivian Aplin-Brownlee, "Rep. McDonald Hailed as Right-Wing Martyr," *Washington Post,* 2 September 1983, pp. A1–16.

12. Also attending the conference were Ronald Mann, from the White House security advisory staff; Dr. Donald Stims, Undersecretary of Defense for nuclear planning; William Schneider, Jr., Undersecretary of State for security questions; and Robert McCormick, Schneider's assistant.

13. Wilhelm Bittorf and Anthony Sampson, "Sinken Auf Eins-Null Tausend . . ." *Der Spiegel,* 24 September 1984, pp. 144–61.

14. Ivan Sharpe, "Korean Jet Mystery Baffles Pilots," *San Francisco Examiner & Chronicle,* 4 September 1983, pp. A4–5; Murray Sayle, "Charge and Countercharge," *Far Eastern Economic Review* 22 September 1983, pp. 27–30; ICAO Report, pp. 7–8.

15. *New York Times,* "Korean Plane's Pilot Was Air Force Veteran," 6 September 1983, p. A14; Bruce Roscoe, "South Korea's 'Most Trusted Pilot,' " *Daily Yomiuri,* 18 September 1983, p. 5; ICAO Report, p. 8.

16. Ivan Sharpe, "Korean Jet Mystery Baffles Pilots," *San Francisco Examiner & Chronicle,* 4 September 1983, pp. A4–5; Richard Rohmer, *Massacre 747: The Story of Korean Air Lines Flight 007,* 1984, Paperjacks, Markham, Ontario, p. 25; *People,* "The Career of an 'Infallible' Pilot Ends in the Debris of Flight 007," 26 December 1983, p. 41; and attorney Charles Herrmann of Tacoma, WA, personal communication.

17. ICAO Report, p. 8.

18. *New York Times,* "Korean Plane's Pilot Was Air Force Veteran," 6 September

1983, p. A14; interviews with Charles Herrmann of Tacoma, WA, and Melvin Belli; and *Playboy* (Japan), "New Findings About the Shootdown of Flight 007," 3 December 1985.

19. ICAO Report, p. 9.

20. ICAO Report, p. 9.

21. ICAO Report, pp. 1 and 10; and *Newsweek*, "Why the Russians Did It," 19 September 1983, pp. 22–33.

22. ICAO Report, pp. 4, 8, and 35.

23. According to the ICAO Report, the Anchorage VOR/DME went out of service at 0139 GMT on August 31, 1983. It has been suggested, although without supporting evidence, that the outage was intentional so that when Flight 007 began deviating from course it would not be a cause for alarm for the air traffic controllers in Anchorage; after all, the navigational aid was not working! The navigational aid was returned to service at 0039 GMT on September 2, but not for long, and the outage was subsequently extended until 2217 GMT on September 23. Although such an account seems farfetched, military sources have told me that VOR beacons have been used in the past to trick Soviet aircraft and for other nonstandard purposes.

24. ICAO Report, pp. 4 and A-11; and Murray Sayle, "Flightpath to Disaster," *The Sunday Times*, 20 May 1984, pp. 33–34.

25. ICAO Report, p. 12; *Japan Times*, "Navigational, Radio Problems Aboard KAL Jet Were Reported," 11 September 1983, p. 4; and Anthony Sampson, *Empires of the Sky*, 1984, Random House, New York.

26. ICAO Report, pp. 4–5.

27. Air Navigation Commission (ANC), *1818th Report to Council by the President of the Air Navigation Commission*, International Civil Aviation Organization Council, 111th Session, C-WP/7809, 16 February 1984, p. 21 (hereafter referred to as "ANC Report"); Richard Rohmer, *Massacre 747*, 1984, Paperjacks, Markham, Ontario, p. 27; and Ivan Sharpe, "Korean Jet Mystery Baffles Pilots," *San Francisco Examiner & Chronicle*, 4 September 1983, pp. A4–5.

28. Richard Witkin, "Korean Airliner Carried Extra Navigational Aids," *New York Times*, 3 September 1983, p. 6; Michael Goodman, "Questions Raised on Why Plane Strayed," *Los Angeles Times*, 7 September 1983, Part I, pp. 1–6; *Aviation Week & Space Technology*, "747 Carried Litton LTN-72R Navigation System," 12 September 1983, p. 21; and Douglas B. Feaver, "Flaws Cited in Technology on Korean Jet," *Washington Post*, 11 September 1983, pp. A1–15.

29. ICAO Report, pp. 30 and A-13.

30. ICAO Report, p. A-14; R.W. Johnson, *Shootdown: Flight 007 and the American Connection*, 1986, Viking, New York, p. 8; and Sugwon Kang, "Flight 007: Was There Foul Play?" *Bulletin of Concerned Asian Scholars*, 1985, Vol. 17, No. 2, pp. 30–48.

31. Thomas Maertens, "Tragedy of Errors," *Foreign Service Journal*, September 1985, pp. 25–31; and Seymour M. Hersh, *"The Target Is Destroyed,"* 1986, Random House, New York, p. 197.

32. R. W. Johnson, *Shootdown: Flight 007 and the American Connection*, 1986, Viking, New York, pp. 7 and 31.

33. ICAO Report, p. C-1.

34. Because events occurred in numerous time zones and Flight 007 crossed the international date line, times will be standardized using Greenwich Mean Time.

35. Murray Sayle, "Flightpath to Disaster," *The Sunday Times*, 20 May 1984, pp. 33–34; and Harold Ewing, personal communication.

36. Interview with attorney Charles Herrmann of Tacoma, WA; and private communication.

37. U.S. District Court for the District of Columbia, *Statement of Genuine Issues of Material Fact and Plantiffs' Steering Committee's Opposition to the Government's Motion for Summary Judgment,* 30 August 1985.

38. This is 6.9 statute miles; a nautical mile is 6,076.1 feet in length, or about 1.15 statute miles.

39. U.S. District Court for the District of Columbia, *Statement of Genuine Issues of Material Fact and Plantiffs' Steering Committee's Opposition to the Government's Motion for Summary Judgment,* 30 August 1985; and ICAO Report, p. 5.

40. Testimony of Douglas L. Porter, U.S. District Court for the District of Columbia, 6 October 1984.

41. U.S. District Court for the District of Columbia, *Statement of Genuine Issues of Material Fact and Plantiffs' Steering Committee's Opposition to the Government's Motion for Summary Judgment,* 30 August 1985; ANC Report, p. 6; and Wilhelm Bittorf and Anthony Sampson, "Sinken Auf Eins-Null Tausend . . ." *Der Spiegel,* 24 September 1984, pp. 144–61.

42. Charles Perrow, *Normal Accidents: Living with High-Risk Technologies,* 1984, Basic Books, New York, pp. 93–96.

43. Eric Naider, " 'Stay Awake, Watch Radar,' Says North Pacific Ex-Pilot," *Seattle Times,* 3 September 1983, p. 8; and *New York Times,* "What It's Like in a Cockpit on the North Pacific Route," 11 September 1983, p. 16.

44. Murray Sayle, "KE007: A Conspiracy of Circumstance," *New York Review of Books,* 25 April 1985, pp. 44–54; ICAO Report, p. 11.

45. ICAO Report, p. 17; ANC Report, p. 22; David Pearson, "The Fate of KE007: An Exchange," *New York Review of Books,* 26 September 1985, pp. 47–51; and Robert Allardyce, remark to bereaved families, 1 September 1986.

46. Flight 015, departing 14 minutes after Flight 007, was also cleared "direct Bethel." The airliner passed directly overhead the VOR transmitter.

47. ICAO Report, p. 5.

48. ICAO Report, p. 11.

49. David Pearson, "The Fate of KE007: An Exchange," *New York Review of Books,* 26 September 1985, pp. 47–51.

50. ICAO Report, p. A-10.

51. Congress of the U.S., Committee on Science and Technology, House of Representatives, *Aircraft Navigation Technology and Errors,* 19 September 1983, Washington, DC, p. 33.

52. Richard Rohmer, *Massacre 747,* 1984, Paperjacks, Markham, Ontario, p. 30; and Henk Hanssen, "Het Doel Is Vernietigd," *Panorama* (The Netherlands), 18 January 1985, pp. 42–51.

53. U.S. District Court for the District of Columbia, *Statement of Genuine Issues of Material Fact and Plantiffs' Steering Committee's Opposition to the Government's Motion for Summary Judgment,* 30 August 1985.

54. ICAO Report, p. 5; and District Court for the District of Columbia, *Statement of Genuine Issues of Material Fact and Plantiffs' Steering Committee's Opposition to the Government's Motion for Summary Judgment,* 30 August 1985.

55. U.S. District Court for the District of Columbia, *Statement of Genuine Issues of Material Fact and Plantiffs' Steering Committee's Opposition to the Government's Motion for Summary Judgment,* 30 August 1985.

56. Douglas B. Feaver, "Dangers of Violating Soviet Airspace Well-Known to Pilots . . . But How Flight 007 Strayed Is a Puzzle," *Washington Post,* 2 September

1983, pp. A8–9; and Clarence A. Robinson, Jr., "U.S. Says Soviets Knew Korean Air Lines 747 Was Commercial Flight," *Aviation Week & Space Technology,* 12 September 1983, pp. 19–21.

[57.] Rudolf Braunberg, "Exploiting the KAL Tragedy," *Counterspy,* December 1983–February 1984, pp. 17–18.

[58.] U.S. District Court for the District of Columbia, *Statement of Genuine Issues of Material Fact and Plantiffs' Steering Committee's Opposition to the Government's Motion for Summary Judgment,* 30 August 1985; and ANC/AAC Regulation 60-1, Paragraph 2.

[59.] Langhorne M. Bond, "Simple Science Could Have Saved KAL 007," *Washington Post,* 2 October 1983, p. C7; Christopher Wain, "The Last Flight of 007," *The Listener,* 8 September 1983, pp. 5–17; and David Rogers, "The Transponder Question," *Boston Globe,* 8 September 1983, pp. 1–8.

[60.] "*Half* of the sections of Reg. 60-1 Order that relate to the duties of the radar surveillance personnel (as opposed to flight crews) refer to civil aircraft or communications with the Federal Aviation Administration. The trackers are required to have significant interrelationship with the Federal Aviation Administration under both Reg. 60-1 and the National Search and Rescue Plan. Under Reg. 60-1, all operations personnel at the ROCC are required to have continual training on FAA coordination procedures, and the trackers are to receive *monthly* tests on the Buffer Zone and applicable procedures, including FAA coordination, on which a noncorrectable score of 100% is mandatory." (*Source:* U.S. District Court for the District of Columbia, *Statement of Genuine Issues of Material Fact and Plantiffs' Steering Committee's Opposition to the Government's Motion for Summary Judgment,* 30 August 1985. Also see Wilhelm Bittorf and Anthony Sampson, "Sinken Auf Eins-Null Tausend . . ." *Der Spiegel,* 8 October 1984, pp. 205–221; and Marilyn Silcox, "Southeast ROCC Marks Beginning of New Air Defense Era," *National Defense,* July/August 1984, pp. 42–46.

[61.] U.S. District Court for the District of Columbia, Deposition of Odis A. Carmon, 4 April 1985.

[62.] Tapes of Flight 007's communications with air traffic controllers were obtained by me in Anchorage, Alaska. Translations of the Korean sections were done by Professor Sugwon Kang of Hartwick College, Oneonta, New York, and Kapheon Kim of Yale University, New Haven, Connecticut.

[63.] ICAO Report, pp. 19–20.

[64.] Harold Ewing, *An Analysis and Scenario of Probable Cause of the Course Deviation Incident Involving FLT KE007, PANC—RKSS, 31 August 1983,* 1985 (unpublished manuscript).

[65.] ICAO Report, p. 17.

[66.] U.S. Department of State telegram, 3 September 1983, No. 204; and Robert D. McFadden, "U.S. Says Soviet Downed Korean Airliner; 269 Lost; Reagan Denounces 'Wanton' Act," *New York Times,* 2 September 1983, pp. A1–4.

[67.] FBIS, Soviet Union, "USSR Chief of Staff Ogarkov's Statement," 9 September 1983, pp. DD1–3.

[68.] Philip Taubman, "U.S. Says Intelligence Plane Was on a Routine Mission," *New York Times,* 5 September 1983, p. 4; *Boston Globe,* "U.S. Spy Planes Reportedly Trail Civilian Jets," 5 September 1983, p. 12; and Tom Bernard and T. Edward Eskelson, "U.S. Plane Capable of Interceding in Attack on Korean Jet," *Denver Post,* 13 September 1983, p. B3.

[69.] Donald E. Fink, "U2s, SR71s Merged in One Wing," *Aviation Week & Space Technology,* 10 May 1976, pp. 83–89; Duncan Campbell, "Spy in the Sky," *New*

Statesman, 9 September 1983, pp. 8–9; *New York Times,* "U.S. Reconnaissance Plane and the 747: A Comparison," 5 September 1983, p. 1; and Bruce G. Blair and Garry D. Brewer, "Verifying SALT Agreements," in William C. Potter (ed.), *Verification of SALT: The Challenge of Strategic Deception,* 1980, Westview Press, Boulder, CO, pp. 7–48.

70. Donald E. Fink, "U2s, SR71s Merged in One Wing," *Aviation Week & Space Technology,* 10 May 1976, pp. 83–89; Duncan Campbell, "Spy in the Sky," *New Statesman,* 9 September 1983, pp. 8–9; *Aviation Week & Space Technology,* "Electronic Opposition Sampled Regularly," 10 May 1976, p. 90; *Boston Globe,* "U.S. Spy Planes Reportedly Trail Civilian Jets," 5 September 1983, p. 12; James Coates, "Aerial Cat-and-Mouse," *Washington Tribune,* 11 September 1983, pp. 1–5; and George C. Wilson, "U.S. RC-135 Was Assessing Soviet Air Defenses," *Washington Post,* 7 September 1983, p. A12.

71. David M. Alpern, Nicholas M. Horrock, and Frank Gibney, Jr., "How the U.S. Listened In," *Newsweek,* 12 September 1983, p. 25; David Kahn, "Radar Wars: The Eerie World of Invisible Radio Waves, Satellites," *Japan Times,* 14 September 1983, p. 11; Duncan Campbell, "Spy in the Sky," *New Statesman,* 9 September 1983, pp. 8–9; and *IEEE Spectrum,* "Continuum: The KAL Tragedy," December 1983, p. 22.

72. Robert L. Borosage and John Marks, *The CIA File,* 1976, Grossman, New York, p. 114; and Philip Taubman, "U.S. Says Intelligence Plane Was on a Routine Mission," *New York Times,* 5 September 1983, p. 4.

73. David Kahn, "Radar Wars: The Eerie World of Invisible Radio Waves, Satellites," *Japan Times,* 14 September 1983, p. 11; James Coates, "Aerial Cat-and-Mouse," *Washington Tribune,* 11 September 1983, pp. 1–5; and *IEEE Spectrum,* "Continuum: The KAL Tragedy," December 1983, p. 22.

74. Tom Bernard and T. Edward Eskelson, "U.S. Spy Plane Capable of Interceding in Attack on Korean Jet," *Denver Post,* 13 September 1983, p. B3; U.S. Department of State telegram, 2 September 1983, No. 52; and James Bamford, *The Puzzle Palace,* 1983, Penguin Books, New York, pp. 140–41.

75. Philip Taubman, "U.S. Says Intelligence Plane Was on a Routine Mission," *New York Times,* 5 September 1983, p. 4.

76. James Bamford, *The Puzzle Palace,* 1983, Penguin, New York, pp. 233–34; *Ramparts,* "U.S. Electronic Espionage: A Memoir," August 1972, pp. 35–50; and Tom Bernard and T. Edward Eskelson, "U.S. Spy Plane Capable of Interceding in Attack on Korean Jet," *Denver Post,* 13 September 1983, p. B3.

77. David Reid, "Korean Plane: Informational Guinea Pig?" *Hartford Advocate,* 14 September 1983.

78. Ian Ball, "Cat-and-Mouse Game of the 'Straying' Spy Aircraft," *Daily Telegraph,* 6 September 1983, p. 4; *Japan Times,* "Soviet Union Admits Firing at Aircraft," 4 September 1983, pp. 1–4; *FBIS,* Soviet Union, "Kirkpatrick's 'Lack of Knowledge' at UN Blasted," 8 September 1983, p. CC8; T. R. Reid, "U.S. Routinely Turns Back Soviet Planes Testing Defense Zone," *Washington Post,* 3 September 1983, p. A28; and Charles W. Maynes, "The Soviets Shot Down More Than Just an Airplane," *Los Angeles Times,* 4 September 1983, Part IV, p. 1.

79. *Boston Globe,* "U.S. Spy Planes Reportedly Trail Civilian Jets," 5 September 1983, p. 12; Rudolf Braunberg, "Exploiting the KAL Tragedy," *Counterspy,* December 1983–February 1984, pp. 17–18; *IEEE Spectrum,* "Continuum: The KAL Tragedy," December 1983, p. 22; *FBIS,* Soviet Union, "RC-135 Use of Civilian Aircraft as Cover Cited," 6 September 1983, p. C11; and *FBIS,* Soviet Union, "President's Plane Used for 'Spying,' " 8 September 1983, p. A7.

80. Recently, a Royal Air Force Nimrod surveillance plane used the call sign of a civilian airliner in order to avoid detection by Soviet ships that were involved in naval exercises off the coast of Ireland. The Nimrod kept up the charade until it was quite close to the Soviets, then dove down from 29,000 feet to 1,500 feet to take pictures. The incident alarmed civilian air traffic controllers at Dublin's Shannon Airport, who believed the Nimrod to be a civilian flight from London to New York. (*Source:* Joe Joyce, "Nimrod Spied on Soviet Vessels by Posing as a Civil Airliner," *The Guardian,* 22 July 1985.)

81. *Jane's Weapons Systems: 1983–1984,* Jane's Publishing Company, London, England, p. 637; *IEEE Spectrum,* "Continuum: The KAL Tragedy," December 1983, p. 22; Richard Halloran, "President Says Spy Jet Landed Before Incident," *New York Times,* 6 September 1983, pp. A1–16; and James Bamford, "The Last Flight of KAL 007," *Washington Post Magazine,* 8 January 1984, pp. 4–8.

82. George C. Wilson, "U.S. RC-135 Was Assessing Soviet Air Defenses," *Washington Post,* 7 September 1983, p. A12; Philip Taubman, "U.S. Says Intelligence Plane Was on a Routine Mission," *New York Times,* 5 September 1983, p. 4; Tom Bernard and T. Edward Eskelson, "U.S. Spy Plane Capable of Interceding in Attack on Korean Jet," *Denver Post,* 13 September 1983, p. B3; and *The Guardian,* "The Russians Come Clean—or Do They?" 10 September 1983, p. 10.

CHAPTER 2

1. *FBIS,* Soviet Union, "Izvestia on Ground Control Role in KAL Incident," 12 September 1983, pp. DD37–39; *FBIS,* Soviet Union, "USSR Chief of Staff Ogarkov's Statement," 9 September 1983, pp. DD1–3; John F. Burns, "Soviet Says Order to Down Jet Came at Local Level," *New York Times,* 10 September 1983, pp. 1–4; and Department of State telegram, No. 2367, 1 March 1984.

2. Andrew Cockburn, *The Threat: Inside the Soviet Military Machine,* 1983, Random House, New York, p. 222; David M. North, "Soviet Advances Spurring Western Aircraft Upgrades," *Aviation Week & Space Technology,* 21 July 1986, pp. 42–45; Yitzhak Tarasulo, "Is Soviet Radar Really That Bad?" *Armed Forces Journal International,* February 1984, pp. 70–74; and *FBIS,* Japan, "Diet Discussion Centers on KAL Incident, Tanaka," 19 September 1983, p. C5.

3. ICAO Report, p. 17.

4. The *Review* reported that precisely such an incident took place in the United States, where "on a missile-testing range a fighter aircraft unwittingly flew outside of but in line with a target drone and a missile control radar; the radar saw only one target during the crucial time, and the fighter was shot down instead of the drone."

5. *New York Times,* "Transcript of Soviet Official's Statement and Excerpts from News Session," 10 September 1983, pp. 4–5; *Far Eastern Economic Review,* "The Ghost of KAL 007 Still Stalks Washington's Corridors," 24 January 1985, pp. 53–55; Yitzhak Tarasulo, "Is Soviet Radar Really That Bad?" *Armed Forces Journal International,* February 1984, pp. 70–74; *IEEE Spectrum,* "Continuum: The KAL Tragedy," December 1983, p. 22; and Ralph McGehee, "A U.S. Deception," *Muse,* Fall 1984, pp. 11–27.

6. Former RC-135 crew member Tom Bernard was told this by a confidential source; John F. Burns, "Soviet Says 747 Used 'Tricks' Like Spy Planes," *New York Times,* 14 September 1983, p. A12; and *Japan Times,* "KAL Jetliner Ma-

neuvered 'Wildly' to Evade Interceptors: Soviet Pilots," 15 September 1983, p. 4.

7. The U.S. also said, "This aircraft never came closer than 400 nautical miles to KAL 007 and had no connection or communication with it. There were no other reconnaissance aircraft airborne north of 40 degrees north latitude in the North Pacific region during the period in question." However, these are quite limited statements. There is no mention of just where "over international waters north of 40 degrees north" the P-3 Orion was. As to the apparent denial that there were any other intelligence aircraft airborne, this is not necessarily so. Just what is included in the "North Pacific region"? The Sea of Japan? The Sea of Okhotsk? And just what is meant by the "time in question"? (*Source:* Department of State telegram, No. 2440, 21 July 1984.)

8. *FBIS,* Soviet Union, "Soviet Pilots Describe 'Tricks' of KAL Plane," 14 September 1983, pp. DD14–18; and Wilhelm Bittorf and Anthony Sampson, "Sinken Auf Eins-Null Tausend," *Der Spiegel,* 8 October 1984, pp. 205–21.

9. David Rogers "The Transponder Question," *Boston Globe,* 8 September 1983, pp. 1–8; Richard Rohmer, *Massacre 747,* 1984, Paperjacks, Markham, Ontario, p. 31; David Rogers, "Automatic Signal Marked 747 as Civilian," *Boston Globe,* 10 September 1983, p. 4.

10. Source for the number of personnel on Shemya is Tom Gervasi, director of the Center for Military Research and Analysis.

11. Orr Kelly, "The Big Ears of Uncle Sam," *U.S. News & World Report,* 12 September 1983, p. 4; Tom Gervasi, *America's War Machine: The Pursuit of Global Dominance,* 1984, Grove Press, New York; Philip J. Klass, "U.S.A.F. Tracking Radar Details Disclosed," *Aviation Week & Space Technology,* 25 October 1976, pp. 41–46; and Jeffrey T. Richelson, *The U.S. Intelligence Community,* 1985, Ballinger, Cambridge, MA, p. 155.

12. Philip J. Klass, "U.S.A.F. Tracking Radar Details Disclosed," *Aviaton Week & Space Technology,* 25 October 1976, pp. 41–46; and *Aviation Week & Space Technology,* "News Digest," 14 February 1977, p. 23.

13. Personal correspondence; private source; and Tom Gervasi, *America's War Machine: The Pursuit of Global Dominance,* 1984, Grove Press, New York, p. 31.

14. Tom Gervasi, *America's War Machine: The Pursuit of Global Dominance,* 1984, Grove Press, New York, p. 31.

15. Robert L. Borosage and John Marks (eds.), *The CIA File,* 1976, Grossman, New York, p. 114; Stephen Cohen, "KAL 007 in Perspective: Confusion and Cover-Up on Both Sides," *Hartford Courant,* 28 November 1983, p. B7; *Jane's Defence Weekly,* "Upgrade for Cobra Judy Radar," 1 June 1985, p. 1011; *Air Force Magazine,* "The United States," December 1983, p. 72; Tom Gervasi, *The Myth of Soviet Military Supremacy,* 1986, Harper & Row, New York, pp. 249–50; and James Bamford, "The Last Flight of KAL 007," *Washington Post Magazine,* 8 January 1984, pp. 4–8.

16. David Cox, "The Aftermath of the Korean Airline Incident: Gathering Intelligence About Intelligence Gathering," *Queen's Quarterly,* Vol. 92, No. 1, Spring 1985, pp. 37–50.

17. Walt Crowley, "Following Flight 007: The Major Media Begin to Sniff the Trail," *The Weekly* (Seattle), 5–12 December 1984; private source; John Keppel and David Pearson, "A Misguided, Deadly Flight—KAL's 007," *Hartford Courant,* 2 September 1984, pp. C1–4; and Tom Gervasi, *America's War Machine: The Pursuit of Global Dominance,* 1984, Grove Press, New York, p. 31.

18. U.S. Department of Defense, *Soviet Military Power 1984,* 1984, Washington,

DC; and Fred S. Hoffman, "Russian Security Paranoia Seen Guiding Sakhalin Island Attack," *San Francisco Examiner & Chronicle*, 2 September 1983, p. A7.

19. The headquarters of the Far Eastern Theater is at Chita.

20. Clarence A. Robinson, Jr., "U.S. Says Soviets Knew Korea Air Lines 747 Was Commercial Flight," *Aviation Week & Space Technology*, 12 September 1983, pp. 18–21.

21. Frank Grove, "Soviets Trying to Hide New Missile System in Area of Jet Incident," *San Francisco Examiner & Chronicle*, 11 September 1983, p. A5.

22. On September 3, 1949, a U.S. RB-29 reconnaissance aircraft flying from Japan to Alaska on a routine intelligence flight off the Kamchatka coast picked up radioactive debris in the air. When matched with later samples, this provided confirmation that the Soviets had exploded an atomic device. (*Source:* Walter Pincus, "40 Years of the Bomb," *Washington Post National Weekly Edition*, 5 August 1985, pp. 6–11.)

23. Rudolf Braunberg, "Exploiting the KAL Tragedy," *Counterspy*, December 1983–February 1984, pp. 17–18.

24. Peter Garrison, "Hugging the Soviet Coast," *Flying*, December 1983, pp. 84–86; and *Washington Post*, "Soviet Specialist Says Pilots Told to Challenge," 2 September 1983, p. A18.

25. David Shribman, "Korean Jetliner: What Is Known and What Isn't," *New York Times*, 8 September 1983, p. 1; *Los Angeles Times*, "Soviet Radar Failure Claimed in Jet Downing," 11 October 1983, Part I, p. 1; Alexander Dallin, *Black Box: KAL 007 and the Superpowers*, 1985, University of California Press, Berkeley, CA, p. 59; and private source.

26. Yitzhak Tarasulo, "Is Soviet Radar Really That Bad?" *Armed Forces Journal International*, February 1984, pp. 70–74.

27. Michael Dobbs, "Soviets Say Local Order Downed Jet," *Washington Post*, 10 September 1983, pp. A1–10; and *FBIS*, Soviet Union, "USSR Government Statement on 'Intruder Plane,' " 7 September 1983, pp. C1-2.

28. ICAO Report, pp F3–4.

29. David Shribman, "Korean Jetliner: What Is Known and What Isn't," *New York Times*, 8 September 1983, p. 1; David Shribman, "U.S. Experts Say Soviet Didn't See Jet Was Civilian," *New York Times*, 7 October 1983, pp. A1–10; Philip Taubman, "U.S. Had Noticed Activity by Soviet," *New York Times*, 14 September 1983, p. A12; *Aviation Week & Space Technology*, "Mission 9 Astronauts Photographed Soviet Submarine, Fighter Bases at Petropavlovsk," 19 March 1984, p. 17; Robert C. Toth, "Airliner Reportedly Glided 12 Minutes Before Crash," *Los Angeles Times*, 8 September 1983, Part I, pp. 1–12; and Department of State telegram, No. 2440, 21 July 1984.

30. Seymour M. Hersh, "*The Target Is Destroyed*," 1986, Random House, New York, pp. 44–45.

31. On September 18, *Pravda* editor Viktor Afanasiyev said that a number of "military people convinced me that the Korean pilot sent intelligence data."

32. *FBIS*, Soviet Union, "Moscow Radio on Ogarkov Statement," 12 September 1983, pp. DD8–9; *Los Angeles Times*, "News Agency Telex Repeats Soviet Stand," 9 September 1983, p. 6; John Miller, "Soviet Editor 'Justifies' Plane Destruction," *Daily Telegraph*, 19 September 1983; Department of State telegram, No. 2296, 2 February 1984; and *FBIS*, Soviet Union, "PVO Aviation Chief Moskvitelev Interviewed," 12 September 1983, pp. DD34–37.

33. Clarence A. Robinson, Jr., "U.S. Says Soviets Knew Korea Air Lines 747 Was Commercial Flight," *Aviation Week & Space and Technology*, 12 September

1983, pp. 18–21; ICAO Report, pp. F3–4; and R. W. Johnson, *Shootdown: Flight 007 and the American Connection*, 1986, Viking, New York, p. 19.

34. *Japan Times*, "Soviets' Impatience May Have Led to Attack," 6 September 1983, p. 2; Jack Anderson, "KAL Downing Casts Doubt on Need for the B-1," *Washington Post*, 10 January 1984, p. B13; and private source.

35. Clyde Haberman, "U.S. and Japanese Find No Trace of Korean Plane," *New York Times*, 3 September 1983, p. 5; and *Japan Times*, "Soviets Reportedly Find Wreckage of KAL Plane," 5 September 1983, p. 1.

CHAPTER 3

1. Sam Jameson, "Disclosures on Russian Pilots Costly to Japan," *Los Angeles Times*, 19 September 1983, Part I, pp. 13–15; and *Newsweek*, "How the U.S. Listened In," 12 September 1983, p. 25.

2. Jeffrey T. Richelson, *The U.S. Intelligence Community*, 1985, Ballinger, Cambridge, MA, p. 126.

3. *Ramparts*, "U.S. Electronic Espionage: A Memoir," August 1972, pp. 35–50; and James Bamford, *The Puzzle Palace*, 1983, Penguin, New York, p. 212.

4. Bhupendra Jasani and Geoffrey E. Perry, "The Military Use of Outer Space" (Chapter 5), *World Armaments and Disarmament: SIPRI Yearbook 1985*, Taylor & Francis, London, pp. 133–58.

5. Edward A. Gargan, "Island a Focus of Russia-Japan Disputes," *New York Times*, 2 September 1983, p. A4; *Los Angeles Times*, "Sakhalin: Wild, Windy Isle Is Soviet Outpost," 2 September 1983, Part I, p. 4; and *San Francisco Examiner & Chronicle*, "Island's Importance to Soviets," 1 September 1983, p. A21.

6. Drew Middleton, "Strategic Soviet Region," *New York Times*, 2 September 1983, pp. A1–7; *The Times*, "Questions Which Must Be Answered About the Destruction of Flight 007," 6 September 1983; *Wall Street Journal*, "Downing of Korean 747 by Soviet Union Chills East-West Diplomacy," 2 September 1983, pp. 1–6; Daniel Southerland, "Attitudes Toward Moscow Expected to Harden," *Christian Science Monitor*, 2 September 1983, pp. 1–8; G. S. Cooper, " 'Flagon' Fired Missile," *Daily Telegraph*, 3 September 1983, p. 7; and *Japan Times*, "Soviets May Have Fired 3 Missiles at ROK Jumbo," 4 September 1983, p. 4.

7. Viktor Belenko, "What *Really* Happened to KAL Flight 007," *Reader's Digest*, January 1984, pp. 72–78; Seymour M. Hersh, *"The Target Is Destroyed,"* 1986, Random House, New York, p. 56; and *San Francisco Examiner & Chronicle*, "U.S. Intelligence Experts Say Order to Shoot Jet Came from Moscow," 4 September 1983, p. A6.

8. *Newsweek*, "Rules of Engagement," 12 September 1983, p. 22; James Ott, "ICAO Studying Its Rules on Interceptions," *Aviation Week & Space Technology*, 12 September 1983, pp. 24–25; and Richard Witkin, "Rules for Pilots on Interceptions," *New York Times*, 2 September 1983, p. A7.

9. *Washington Post*, "Soviet Specialist Says Pilots Told to Challenge," 2 September 1983, p. A18; and U.S. Department of State, *Department of State Bulletin*, October 1983, Vol. 83, No. 2079, p. 18.

10. *Japan Times*, "Soviets' Impatience May Have Led to Attack," 6 September 1983, p. 2; David Shribman, "U.S. Experts Say Soviet Didn't See Jet Was Civilian," *New York Times*, 7 October 1983, pp. A1–10; and Duncan Campbell, "What Really Happened to KE007," *New Statesman*, 26 April 1985, pp. 8–10.

11. The Su-15 first made its appearance with the Soviet armed forces in 1967.

Throughout the 1970s the plane was continually improved, with modern aviation electronics and up-to-date armaments added. The combat radius of a MiG-23 is somewhat better—about 530 NM.

12. G. S. Cooper, " 'Flagon' Fired Missile," *Daily Telegraph,* 3 September 1983, p. 7; and *Der Flugleiter,* "Korean 007, Do You Read?" March 1984.

13. As Sugwon Kang wrote, "I fail to see any evidence . . . to support the contention that in these critical statements the pilot was talking about the lights on the intruding aircraft, although such a possibility cannot be ruled out. Just as likely, given the sequence of the pilot's remarks, is that he was talking about lights atop his own Su-15 fighter that he had been instructed to switch on. (*Source:* Sugwon Kang, "Flight 007: Was There Foul Play?" *Bulletin of Concerned Asian Scholars,* 1985, Vol. 17, No. 2, pp. 30–48.)

14. Translation by Sugwon Kang, "Flight 007: Was There Foul Play?" *Bulletin of Concerned Asian Scholars,* 1985, Vol. 17, No. 2, pp. 30–48.

15. Yoshitaro Masuo, "Some Research into the Record of Communications of the Soviet Fighters Which Intercepted KAL 007," 1986 (unpublished manuscript).

16. Michael Dobbs, "Soviet Military Chief to Meet with Press," *Washington Post,* 9 September 1983, pp. A1–8.

17. *Japan Times,* "Soviets Reportedly Find Wreckage of KAL Plane," 5 September 1983, p. 1; Clyde Haberman, "U.S. and Japanese Find No Trace of Korean Plane," *New York Times,* 3 September 1983, p. 5; George C. Wilson, "Electronic Spy Network Provided Detailed Account," *Washington Post,* 2 September 1983, p. A15; and *Los Angeles Times,* "Soviet Radar Failure Claimed in Jet Downing," 11 October 1983, Part I, p. 1.

18. Yoshitaro Masuo, "The Korean Airline Incident and the Self-Defense Forces of Japan," *Sekai,* May 1985, pp. 270–89.

19. Duncan Campbell, "What Really Happened to KE007," *New Statesman,* 26 April 1985, pp. 8–10; Murray Sayle, "Charge and Countercharge," *Far Eastern Economic Review,* 22 September 1983, pp. 27–30; David Pearson and John Keppel, "New Pieces in the Puzzle of Flight 007," *The Nation,* pp. 17–24 August 1985, pp. 104–10; David Pearson, "The Fate of KE007: An Exchange," *New York Review of Books,* 26 September 1985, pp. 47–51; ICAO Report, p. 42; and ANC Report, p. 8.

20. Department of State telegram, No. 2367, 1 March 1984.

21. As *Newsweek* later said, "By some reports, Captain Chun blinked his plane's navigational lights on and off, an international distress signal." The French newspaper *Le Monde* reported that Flight 007 turned on its lights only at the last minute, having flown before with its lights extinguished. Much of this confusion could be cleared up by making available the content of the Soviet ground controllers' conversations, something neither the U.S., Japan, nor the Soviet Union has done. The Soviets claimed that commands from ground controllers "such as '805, flash the lights on and off,' '805, force to land at an aerodrome,' and others are not presented" in Western accounts. "The pilot's responses 'roger' and 'executing' and others taken in isolation from the ground commands become meaningless and create a wrong impression of the interception process," the Soviets say. (*Sources: Newsweek,* "A Ruthless Ambush in the Sky," 12 September 1983, pp. 16–30; Alain Jacob, "Circonstances Attenuantes?" *Le Monde,* 10 September 1983; and Department of State telegram, No. 2367, 1 March 1984.

22. John F. Burns, "Jet Incident Adds Insights About Russian Military," *New York Times,* 18 September 1983, p. 16; and Viktor Belenko, "What *Really* Happened to KAL Flight 007," *Reader's Digest,* January 1984, pp. 72–78.

23. Department of State telegram, No. 2367, 1 March 1984.

24. *FBIS*, Soviet Union, "Intervision Carries Press Conference," 12 September 1983, pp. DD10–43.

25. Brad Knickerbocker, "Ex-Pilot's View of What Occurred over Sakhalin Island," *Christian Science Monitor*, 16 September 1983, p. 2.

26. Robert Levey, "Turner Thinks Soviets 'Told Us the Truth.' " *Boston Globe*, 15 September 1983, p. 12A; Murray Sayle, "Believing the Unbelievable," *The Spectator*, 10 September 1983, pp. 7–10; and David Shribman, "U.S. Experts Say Soviet Didn't See Jet Was Civilian," *New York Times*, 7 October 1983, pp. A1–10.

27. *Der Flugleiter*, "Korean 007, Do You Read?" March 1984; Robert C. Toth, " 'Black Box' Could Hold Vital Answers to Many Questions," *Japan Times*, 14 September 1983, p. 11; Alexander Dallin, *Black Box: KAL 007 and the Superpowers*, 1985, University of California Press, Berkeley, CA, p. 83; and *Los Angeles Times*, "Soviet Radar Failure Claimed in Jet Downing," 11 October 1983, Part I, p. 1.

28. William F. Wright, " 'Smart' Missiles Downed Korean Jetliner," *Los Angeles Times*, 22 September 1983, Part I, p. 7.

29. ICAO Report, p. C-10.

30. It was perhaps because of this untidy business of the cause of the airliner's final destruction that Japan Defense Agency sources told the press on September 6 that "information obtained from monitoring Soviet jets on radar and radio waves strongly indicated that the Boeing 747 was hit by two missiles instead of one as reported earlier."

31. *The Economist*, "Murder First, Lies Later," 10 September 1983, pp. 33–39; Jack Anderson, "KAL Downing Casts Doubt on Need for the B-1," *Washington Post*, 10 January 1984, p. B13; *Asahi Evening News*, "Two Missiles Hit KAL Jet," 7 September 1983; and *Japan Times*, "Soviets May Have Fired 3 Missiles at ROK Jumbo," 4 September 1983, p. 4.

32. Wilhelm Bittorf and Anthony Sampson, "Sinken Auf Eins-Null Tausend . . ." *Der Spiegel*, No. 39, 24 September 1984, pp. 144–61.

33. Douglas B. Feaver and David Hoffman, "Plane's Tragic Odyssey Mysterious," *Washington Post*, 4 September 1983, pp. A1–12; Robert C. Toth, "Airliner Reportedly Glided 12 Minutes Before Crash," *Los Angeles Times*, 8 September 1983, Part I, pp. 1–12; ANC Report, p. 8; and Drew Middleton, "Strategic Soviet Region," *New York Times*, 2 September 1983, pp. A1–7.

34. Malcolm Brenner, *KE007: The "Final Message,"* 1985, Aviation Safety Associates International, Inc. (unpublished report).

35. Analysis by Wolfgang Heim, spokesman for the German Air Traffic Controllers' Association.

36. *Washington Post*, "Third Body Found off North Japan Coast," 13 September 1983, p. A15; Daniel Southerland, "Attitudes Toward Moscow Expected to Harden," *Christian Science Monitor*, 2 September 1983, pp. 1–8; and Robert D. McFadden, "U.S. Says Soviet Downed Korean Airliner; 269 Lost; Reagan Denounces 'Wanton' Act," *New York Times*, 2 September 1983, pp. A1–4.

CHAPTER 4

1. James Bamford, *The Puzzle Palace*, 1983, Penguin, New York, p. 181; and *New York Times*, "Ex-CIA Man Accuses Dulles," 6 September 1983, p. A11.

2. David Kahn, "Radar Wars: The Eerie World of Invisible Radio Waves, Satellites," *Japan Times*, 14 September 1983, p. 11.

3. James Bamford provides an excellent description of the incident. See *The Puzzle Palace*, 1983, Penguin, New York, p. 234.
4. Michael R. Beschloss, *Mayday: Eisenhower, Khrushchev and the U-2 Affair*, 1986, Harper & Row, New York, pp. 121–24.
5. The previous year, the Soviets had charged that Bodø was used as a staging site for British and American reconnaissance flights. Norway denied the charge.
6. L. Fletcher Prouty, *The Secret Team: The CIA and Its Allies in Control of the United States and the World*, 1973, Prentice Hall, Englewood Cliffs, NJ, p. 377.
7. Michael R. Beschloss, *Mayday: Eisenhower, Khrushchev and the U-2 Affair*, 1986, Harper & Row, New York, p. 43.
8. David Wise, *The Politics of Lying: Government Deception, Secrecy, and Power*, 1973, Random House, New York, p. 34.
9. *Christian Science Monitor*, "Moscow Says Pilot Caught Spying; U.S. Doubt Voiced on 'Confession,' " 7 May 1960, p. 1.
10. *Christian Science Monitor*, "Moscow Says Pilot Caught Spying: U.S. Doubt Voiced on 'Confession,' " 7 May 1960, p. 1.
11. Davis Wise, *The Politics of Lying: Government Deception, Secrecy, and Power*, 1973, Random House, New York, p. 35.
12. Thomas Maertens, "Tragedy of Errors," *Foreign Service Journal*, September 1985, pp. 25–31.
13. Arthur J. Olsen, "Arctic Search Is Pressed for U.S. Plane Carrying 6," *New York Times*, 3 July 1960, pp. 1–2; Jack Raymond, "North Korean Jets Attack U.S. Plane," *New York Times*, 29 April 1965, pp. 1–8; and Paul Grimes, "U.S. Planes a Familiar Sight at Pakistan Base Linked to U-2," *New York Times*, 6 July 1960, p. 6.
14. Akio Takahashi, *President's Crime*, 1985, Ningensha, Tokyo, Japan, p. 73.
15. Jack Raymond, "U.S. Says Soviet Shot Down Jet," *New York Times*, 30 January 1964, pp. 1–12; and Andrew Wilson, "British Expert's Radar Clue to Flight 007 Riddle," *The Observer*, 17 June 1984, p. 2.
16. Arthur J. Olsen, "U.S. Jet Lost in East Germany: It May Have Been Shot Down," *New York Times*, 29 January 1964, pp. 1–12; and Arthur J. Olsen, "U.S. to Recover 3 Fliers' Bodies in East Germany," *New York Times*, 31 January 1964, p. 3.
17. Arthur J. Olsen, "U.S. Reconnaissance Jet Downed in East Germany," *New York Times*, 11 March 1964, pp. 1–10.
18. William Beecher, "U.S. Scout Plane with 31 Is Lost, Reported Downed by 2 North Korean MiGs," *New York Times*, 16 April 1969, pp. 1–14; and Jack Raymond, "North Korea Jets Attack U.S. Plane," *New York Times*, 29 April 1965, pp. 1–8.
19. William Beecher, "U.S. Scout Plane with 31 Is Lost, Reported Downed by 2 North Korean MiGs," *New York Times*, 16 April 1969, pp. 1–4; James Bamford, *The Puzzle Palace*, 1983, Penguin, New York, pp. 239–40; U.S. Congress, House, Committee on Armed Services, *Review of Department of Defense Command, Control and Communications Systems and Facilities*, 1977, GPO, Washington, DC, p. 14; and private source.
20. Edgar Ulsamer, "A Strategic Blueprint for the '80s," *Air Force*, September 1978, pp. 47–59.
21. Private source.
22. Victor Marchetti and John D. Marks, *The CIA and the Cult of Intelligence*, 1974, Knopf, New York, p. 137; and Jeff McConnell, "The CIA and Airlines," *Counterspy*, December 83–February 84, pp. 19–27.
23. Southern Air Transport, the former CIA airline involved in the recent arms

shipments to Iran and the Nicaraguan *contras,* is a case in point. As the crisis was brewing in October 1986, Southern Air's board chairman and sole owner James H. Bastian distributed an internal bulletin claiming that the airline "is not owned by the CIA and is not performing any services for the CIA and to the best of my knowledge is not performing any services for any company connected with the CIA." As the scandal broke the following month, the last two of these claims were quickly shown to be false. As to the airline's links to the Agency, Southern Air was sold by the CIA to Stanley G. Williams, its president and chief operating officer, who had run it for the CIA since 1962. Bastian, the company's current owner (as well as owner of the CIA-connected Caribbean Air Services), was Southern Air's attorney when the CIA owned it. Bastian was also vice-president of Pacific Corp., the holding company for Air America and Air Asia when they were CIA properties. Southern Air's current vice-president, Hugh Grundy, was president of Air Asia until 1975, when the CIA sold the airline to E-Systems, a Dallas-based CIA contractor.

24. David B. Ottaway, "The Big Business of Flying the Not-So-Friendly Skies," *Washington Post National Weekly Edition,* 5 January 1987, pp. 15–16; and Jeff McConnell, "The CIA and Airlines," *Counterspy,* December 83–February 84, pp. 19–27.

25. Knut Royce, "Aviation Experts Don't Rule Out Possibility KAL Jet Was Spying," *San Francisco Examiner & Chronicle,* 4 September 1983, p. A22; *Miami Herald,* "Soviets Figured: Our Jetliners Spy, So Must Theirs," 11 September 1983, pp. 1–22A; and Jeff McConnell, "The CIA and Airlines," *Counterspy,* December 83–February 84, pp. 19–27.

26. Department of State telegram, No. 635, 8 September 1983; *Japan Times,* "Soviet Jetliners Said to Spy with Hidden Cameras," 23 September 1983, p. 3; U.S. Department of State telegram, No. 269, 5 September 1983; and Ian Ball, "Cat-and-Mouse Game of the 'Straying' Spy Aircraft," *Daily Telegraph,* 6 September 1983, p. 4.

27. T. R. Reid, "U.S. Routinely Turns Back Soviet Planes Testing Defense Zone," *Washington Post,* 3 September 1983, p. A28; U.S. Department of State, *Department of State Bulletin,* October 1983, Vol. 83, No. 2079, p. 6; and U.S. Department of State, "Ambassador Lichenstein's Statement, UN Security Council, Sept. 2, 1983," *KAL Flight #007: Compilation of Statements and Documents,* 1–16 September 1983, p. 4.

28. *Washington Post,* "Russians Intercept Plane with 214 GIs," 1 July 1968, pp. A1–5; and James Bamford, "The Last Flight of KAL 007," *Washington Post Magazine,* 8 January 1984, pp. 4–8.

29. Interview with Lawrence Guernon, July 1984; *Washington Post,* "Russians Intercept Plane with 214 GIs," 1 July 1968, pp. A1–5; and Sylvan Fox, "Jet with 214 Servicemen Intercepted by Russians: Forced to Land in Kuriles," *New York Times,* 1 July 1968, pp. 1–6.

30. *Washington Post,* "Russians Intercept Plane with 214 GIs," 1 July 1968, pp. A1–5.

31. *New York Times,* "U.S. Bids Moscow Return Troop Jet," 2 July 1968, pp. 1–4; and Sylvan Fox, "Jet with 214 Servicemen Intercepted by Russians: Forced to Land in Kuriles," *New York Times,* 1 July 1968, pp. 1–6.

32. Interview with Lawrence Guernon, July 1984.

33. James Bamford, "The Last Flight of KAL 007," *Washington Post Magazine,* 8 January 1984, pp. 4–8.

34. *Ramparts,* "U.S. Electronic Espionage: A Memoir," August 1972, pp. 35–50.

35. James Bamford, "The Last Flight of KAL 007," *Washington Post Magazine,* 8 January 1984, pp. 4–8.

36. Interview with Jerry Fresia, 20 November 1984; and *Washington Post,* "Pilot Denies Flying into Soviet Area," 4 July 1968, pp. A1–15.

37. Sylvan Fox, "Jet with 214 Servicemen Intercepted by Russians: Forced to Land in Kuriles," *New York Times,* 1 July 1968, pp. 1–6; *Washington Post,* "Russians Intercept Plane with 214 GIs," 1 July 1968, pp. A1–5; and Jeff McConnell, "The CIA and Airlines," *Counterspy,* December 1983–February 1984, pp. 19–27.

38. *New Haven Journal Courier,* "214 GIs Arrive in Vietnam After Delay by Soviets," 4 July 1968, p. 1; interview with Lawrence Guernon, July 1984.

39. Walt Platteborze, "State Fliers Recall '68 Incident," *New Haven Register,* 9 September 1983, pp. 1–14; and Bob Poos, "Pilot Denies Violating Air Space," *New Haven Register,* 3 July 1968, pp. 1–2.

40. Robert Trumbull, "Americans Are Weary," *New York Times,* 3 July 1968, p. 4; and Bob Poos, "Pilot Denies Violating Air Space," *New Haven Register,* 3 July 1968, pp. 1–2.

41. Walt Platteborze, "State Fliers Recall '68 Incident," *New Haven Register,* 9 September 1983, pp. 1–14; Wilhelm Bittorf and Anthony Sampson, "Sinken Auf Eins-Null Tausend . . ." *Der Spiegel,* 1 October 1984, No. 40, pp. 190–213.

42. Yoshitaro Masuo, "The Korean Airline Incident and the Self-Defense Forces of Japan," *Sekai,* May 1985, pp. 270–89; *New York Times,* "Radar Contact Reported," 2 July 1968, p. 4; and *New Haven Register,* "U.S. Asks Russia Free Captured Troop Plane," 1 July 1968, pp. 1–2.

43. Sylvan Fox, "Jet with 214 Servicemen Intercepted by Russians: Forced to Land in Kuriles," *New York Times,* 1 July 1968, pp. 1–6; *Washington Post,* "Russians Intercept Plane with 214 GIs," 1 July 1968, pp. A1–5; and interview with Lawrence Guernon, July 1984.

44. *Washington Post,* "Pilot Denies Flying into Soviet Area," 4 July 1968, pp. A1–15; *Washington Post,* "Russians Intercept Plane with 214 GIs," 1 July 1968, pp. A1–5; and *New Haven Register,* "U.S. Asks Russia Free Captured Troop Plane," 1 July 1968, pp. 1–2.

45. Warren Unna, "Exchanges over DC-8 Marked by Restraint," *Washington Post,* 2 July 1968, pp. A1–8; *New Haven Journal Courier,* "214 GIs Arrive in Vietnam After Delay by Soviets," 4 July 1968, p. 1; and *Washington Post,* "Pilot Denies Flying into Soviet Area," 4 July 1968, pp. A1–15.

46. Sylvan Fox, "Jet with 214 Servicemen Intercepted by Russians: Forced to Land in Kuriles," *New York Times,* 1 July 1968, pp. 1–6; *New York Times,* "U.S. Bids Moscow Return Troop Jet," 2 July 1968, pp. 1–4; Felix Belair, Jr., "Soviet Releases Plane Carrying GIs to Vietnam," *New York Times,* 3 July 1968, p. 1; and *New York Times,* "U.S. Concedes Intrusion," 4 July 1968, p. 2.

47. Bob Poos, "Pilot Denies Violating Air Space," *New Haven Register,* 3 July 1968, pp. 1–2; and *New Haven Register,* "Airline Fined in Flight Forced Down in Soviet Union," 11 December 1968, p. 3.

CHAPTER 5

1. This discussion of the history of Korean Air Lines is adapted, with some additions, from David Corn, "The Strange History of K.A.L.," *The Nation,* 14 June 1986, pp. 822–27. Used with permission.

2. *Morning Calm* (the inflight magazine of Korean Air), Vol. 9, No. 5, 1985, p. 99;

and *Business Week,* "Korean Air's Charley Cho Steps Out of His Brother's Shadow," 9 December 1985.

3. *New York Times,* 13 September 1983, p. A11.

4. Steve Lohr, "South Korea's Airline and Its Pilots Have Reputation for Being Aggressive," *New York Times,* 13 September 1983, p. A11.

5. *Korea Times,* 10 January 1962, 28 November 1962, and 19 December 1962; and William M. Leary, *Perilous Missions: Civil Air Transport and CIA Covert Operations in Asia,* 1984, University of Alabama Press, University, AL, pp. 109 and 176.

6. *New York Times,* 18 September 1966, p. 86.

7. Kim left South Korea for self-imposed exile in the United States in 1973. He later disappeared while in France. One rumor widely circulated among Koreans is that Kim was kidnapped by South Korean agents, taken back to Seoul on a KAL plane, and confronted in the presidential Blue House by Park, who personally executed him.

8. *Miami Herald,* "Soviets Figured: Our Jetliners Spy, So Must Theirs," 11 September 1983, pp. 1–22A; the East Berlin case is referred to in the Koreagate report and in Robert Boettcher, *Gifts of Deceit: Sun Myung Moon, Tongsun Park and the Korean Scandal,* 1980, Holt, Rinehart and Winston, New York; and *Boston Globe,* 19 September 1983.

9. *Korea Times,* 1 March 1969; and *New York Times,* 26 October 1969.

10. Donald Raynard, who was the chief of the U.S. State Department's Korean desk in the early 1970s, told the Tokyo newspaper *Asahi Shimbun* that between April 1970 and November 1974 he saw U.S. intelligence reports indicating a vast South Korean campaign to promote the country's interest by distributing payoffs to Japanese politicians. Raynard said that the bribes were often dispensed by KCIA agents stationed in Japan. "The Korean name most frequently mentioned in the secret reports he read," the newspaper reported, was Cho Choong-hoon, the president of KAL. (*Sources:* U.S. Congress, House, Subcommittee on International Organizations of the Committee on International Relations, *Investigation of Korean-American Relations,* 31 October 1978, also known as the "Koreagate Report"; *Boston Globe,* 19 September 1983; and *Asahi Evening News,* 18 February 1977, p. 1.)

11. *New York Times,* 22 September 1974; *Wall Street Journal,* 24 March 1975; John D. Williams, "Korean Air Lines Had Achieved Stability After Losing Money Since Its Formation," *Wall Street Journal,* 2 September 1983, p. 6; *New York Times,* 30 March 1976; and *Wall Street Journal,* 15 September 1976, p. 33.

12. "An Insight into Korean Air," a promotional brochure distributed by KAL; *Business Week,* 30 July 1979, p. 39; *Wall Street Journal,* 17 August 1979; *Wall Street Journal,* 19 November 1980; and *Asia Monitor,* 3 May 1981.

13. KAL also participates in modifying Air Force F-16s based in South Korea, according to Joe Thornton, public affairs officer at General Dynamics, the manufacturer of the F-16.

14. This growth has paid off well for the Cho brothers. A *Forbes* survey in 1983 listed Harry Cho as one of South Korea's wealthiest men.

15. *Forbes,* 19 December 1983; *Morning Calm,* 1985, Vol. 9, No. 5; *The Times,* "Disaster Happened on One of the Busiest Air Routes," 3 September 1983, p. 4; *Aviation Week & Space Technology,* "Soviet Su-15 Shoots Down Korean 747," 5 September 1983, pp. 25–27; and *Aviation Week & Space Technology,* 2 September 1985.

16. The satellites were said to be two ferrets, identification numbers 74085-3 and

78029-3, and a Low Altitude Surveillance Platform (LASP) satellite, identification number 78029-1.

17. Conn Hallinan, "The Curious Flight of KAL 007," U.S. Peace Council, November 1984, p. 6; and Seymour M. Hersh, *The Target Is Destroyed,* 1986, Random House, New York, pp. 3–4.

18. Milton R. Benjamin, "2 Dead in Russia as Korean Plane Mystery Deepens," *Washington Post,* 22 April 1978, pp. A1–10; and *Time,* "The Mystery of Flight 902," 1 May 1978, p. 35.

19. *Aviation Week & Space Technology,* "Korean Pilot, Navigator Held by Soviets," 1 May 1978, p. 34.

20. *Japan Times,* "U.S., Soviet Finish Details on KAL Passenger Shift," 23 April 1978, p. 1; *New York Times,* "Airline Survivors in Tokyo and Seoul; Park Thanks Soviet," 25 April 1978, p. 11; and William Chapman, "Plane's Relieved Passengers Welcomed in Tokyo, Seoul," *Washington Post,* 25 April 1978, p. A14.

21. Kevin Klose, "Soviets: Moscow Wanted Plane Downed," *Washington Post,* 25 April 1978, pp. A1–22; *New York Times,* "Korean Airliner Is Forced Down by Soviet Union," 21 April 1978, pp. A1–13; Richard Halloran, "Flight of South Korean Airliner 'Very Puzzling' to U.S. Officials," *New York Times,* 22 April 1978, p. 5; and *Time,* "The Mystery of Flight 902," 1 May 1978, p. 35.

22. Robert G. Kaiser and Don Oberdorfer, "South Korean Jetliner Down in Soviet Union," *Washington Post,* 21 April 1978, pp. A1–5; and Milton R. Benjamin, "2 Dead in Russia as Korean Plane Mystery Deepens," *Washington Post,* 22 April 1978, pp. A1–10.

23. Kevin Klose, "The Agony of Flight 902," *Washington Post,* 23 April 1978, pp. A1–20; Steve Lohr, "Pilot in the '78 Incident Recalls His Experience," *New York Times,* 9 September 1983, p. A11; *Time,* "Aboard Flight 902: 'We Survived,' " 8 May 1978, p. 43; Kevin Close, "Jet Survivors Say 2 Died in MiG Attack," *Washington Post,* 23 April 1978, pp. A1–18; and Kevin Klose, "Pilot of Korean Jet Downed in Russia Fails to Explain Incident," *Washington Post,* 30 April 1978, p. A18.

24. Oliver Clubb, *KAL Flight 007: The Hidden Story,* 1985, The Permanent Press, Sag Harbor, NY, pp. 97–99; *Time,* "Aboard Flight 902: 'We Survived,' " 8 May 1978, p. 43; and Kevin Klose, "Odyssey Ends but Mystery Doesn't," *Washington Post,* 25 April 1978, pp. A1–14.

25. Kevin Klose, "Soviets: Moscow Wanted Plane Downed," *Washington Post,* 25 April 1978, pp. A1–22; *Aviation Week & Space Technology,* "Korean Pilot, Navigator Held by Soviets," 1 May 1978, p. 34; Kevin Klose, "Plane Incidents Contain Eerie Similarities," *Washington Post,* 4 September 1983, p. A11; and Seymour M. Hersh, *The Target Is Destroyed,* 1986, Random House, New York, pp. 83–84.

26. *Washington Post,* "U.S. Plane in Murmansk Is First in Sensitive Area," 23 April 1978, p. A18; R. W. Apple, Jr., "Airliner's Survivors Reach Finland, Tell of Soviet Jet Attack," *New York Times,* 23 April 1978, pp. 1–3; *Time,* "The Mystery of Flight 902," 1 May 1978, p. 35; Donald Bremner, "Korean Jet Shadowed, Brought Down in 1978," *Los Angeles Times,* 2 September 1983, Part I, p. 5; and Richard Halloran, "Flight of South Korean Airliner 'Very Puzzling' to U.S. Officials," *New York Times,* 22 April 1978, p. 5.

27. William E. Burrows, *Deep Black: Space Espionage and National Security,* 1986, Random House, New York, pp. 179–82.

28. Kevin Klose, "Soviets: Moscow Wanted Plane Downed," *Washington Post,* 25 April 1978, pp. A1–22; *Time,* "The Mystery of Flight 902," 1 May 1978, p. 35;

Seymour M. Hersh, *"The Target Is Destroyed,"* 1986, Random House, New York, pp. 4–5; *Japan Times,* "KAL 5th Civilian Plane Forced Down," 3 September 1983, p. 9.

[29.] Steve Lohr, "Pilot in the '78 Incident Recalls His Experience," *New York Times,* 9 September 1983, p. A11; and Kevin Klose, "Soviets: Moscow Wanted Plane Downed," *Washington Post,* 25 April 1978, pp. A1–22.

[30.] *Time,* "Aboard Flight 902: 'We Survived,' " 8 May 1978, p. 43; *San Francisco Examiner & Chronicle,* "U.S. Intelligence Experts Say Order to Shoot KAL Jet Came from Moscow," 4 September 1983, p. A6; and Andrew Cockburn, *The Threat: Inside the Soviet Military Machine,* 1983, Random House, New York, p. 227.

[31.] *San Francisco Examiner & Chronicle,* "U.S. Intelligence Experts Say Order to Shoot KAL Jet Came from Moscow," 4 September 1983, p. A6; Seymour M. Hersh, *"The Target Is Destroyed,"* 1986, Random House, New York, p. 7; and Kevin Klose, "Soviets: Moscow Wanted Plane Downed," *Washington Post,* 25 April 1978, pp. A1–22.

[32.] *Time,* "Aboard Flight 902: 'We Survived,' " 8 May 1978, p. 43; and *Japan Times,* "Thousands of S. Koreans Protest Against USSR," 4 September 1983, p. 1.

[33.] Kevin Klose, "Soviets: Moscow Wanted Plane Downed," *Washington Post,* 25 April 1978, pp. A1–22; *Aviation Week & Space Technology,* "Korean Pilot, Navigator Held by Soviets," 1 May 1978, p. 34; and *Time,* "The Mystery of Flight 902," 1 May 1978, p. 35.

[34.] Steve Lohr, "Pilot in the '78 Incident Recalls His Experience," *New York Times,* 9 September 1983, p. A11; and *Aviation Week & Space Technology,* "Washington Roundup," 8 May 1978, p. 11.

[35.] Kevin Klose, "Agony of Flight 902," *Washington Post,* 23 April 1978, pp. A1–20; R. W. Apple, Jr., "Airliner's Survivors Reach Finland, Tell of Soviet Jet Attack," *New York Times,* 23 April 1978, pp. 1–3; A. D. Horne, "U.S. Says Soviet Shot Down Airliner," *Washington Post,* 2 September 1983, pp. A1–17; and *Wall Street Journal,* "Downing of Korean 747 by Soviet Union Chills East-West Diplomacy," 2 September 1983, pp. 1–6.

[36.] *Time,* "Aboard Flight 902: 'We Survived,' " 8 May 1978, p. 43; *Aviation Week & Space Technology,* "Korean Pilot, Navigator Held by Soviets," 1 May 1978, p. 34; Kevin Klose, "Soviets: Moscow Wanted Plane Downed," *Washington Post,* 25 April 1978, pp. A1–22; Kevin Klose, "Agony of Flight 902," *Washington Post,* 23 April 1978, pp. A1–20; and Steve Lohr, "Pilot in the '78 Incident Recalls His Experience," *New York Times,* 9 September 1983, p. A11.

[37.] *Time,* "Aboard Flight 902: 'We Survived,' " 8 May 1978, p. 43.

[38.] The distance from the point of attack to the 707's landing spot is only about 180 miles in a straight line. At a 707's cruising speed, it would cover this distance in about 20 minutes, not an hour and 42 minutes.

[39.] Milton R. Benjamin, "2 Dead in Russia as Korean Plane Mystery Deepens," *Washington Post,* 22 April 1978, pp. A1–10; and *Time,* "Aboard Flight 902: 'We Survived,' " 8 May 1978, p. 43.

[40.] Kevin Klose, "Agony of Flight 902," *Washington Post,* 23 April 1978, pp. A1–20; Kevin Klose, "Jet Survivors Say 2 Died in MiG Attack," *Washington Post,* 23 April 1978, pp. A1–18; and *Aviation Week & Space Technology,* "Korean Pilot, Navigator Held by Soviets," 1 May 1978, p. 34.

[41.] Robert G. Kaiser and Don Oberdorfer, "South Korean Jetliner Down in Soviet

Union," *Washington Post,* 21 April 1978, pp. A1–5; *New York Times,* "Korean Airliner Is Forced Down by Soviet Union," 21 April 1978, pp. A1–13; and *Japan Times,* "U.S., Soviet Finish Details on KAL Passenger Shift," 23 April 1978, p. 1.

42. Steve Lohr, "Pilot in the '78 Incident Recalls His Experience," *New York Times,* 9 September 1983, p. A11; *Time,* "Aboard Flight 902: 'We Survived,'" 8 May 1978, p. 43; and Kevin Klose, "Pilot of Korean Jet Downed in Russia Fails to Explain Incident," *Washington Post,* 30 April 1978, p. A18.

43. Kevin Klose, "Pilot of Korean Jet Downed in Russia Fails to Explain Incident," *Washington Post,* 30 April 1978, p. A18.

44. The lesson was that Soviet airspace could be penetrated with the greatest of ease. This was not, of course, something the Air Force wanted to make known, given its persistent lobbying for newer, faster, more sophisticated and expensive aircraft. The result was that the recordings of the Soviet air defense fiasco have never been released. As Andrew Cockburn noted, "A senior but iconoclastic adviser to the Secretary of Defense made himself unpopular with the Air Force by suggesting that it replace the B-1 bomber cancelled by President Carter a year before with a 'B-707' and crew it with Koreans."

45. ABC News "Nightline," "Korean Air Tragedy," 1 September 1983, Show No. 604, p. 11; Seymour M. Hersh, *"The Target Is Destroyed,"* 1986, Random House, New York, p. 14; Andrew Cockburn, *The Threat: Inside the Soviet Military Machine,* 1983, Random House, New York, p. 227; and Anthony Sampson, "What Happened to Flight 007?" *Parade Magazine,* 22 April 1984, pp. 12–23.

46. *San Francisco Examiner & Chronicle,* "U.S. Intelligence Experts Say Order to Shoot KAL Jet Came from Moscow," 4 September 1983, p. A6.

47. James R. Schlesinger, "Let's Keep Cool," *Washington Post,* 4 September 1983; Kevin Klose, "Plane Incidents Contain Eerie Similarities," *Washington Post,* 4 September 1983, p. A11; and Alexander Dallin, *Black Box: KAL 007 and the Superpowers,* 1985, University of California Press, Berkeley, CA, p. 118.

48. Steve Lohr, "Pilot in the '78 Incident Recalls His Experience," *New York Times,* 9 September 1983, p. A11; and private source. The particulars of this story were later confirmed through other informed Korean contacts.

49. Private source; Jeffrey T. Richelson, *The U.S. Intelligence Community,* 1985, Ballinger, Cambridge, MA, p. 127; and *Ramparts,* "U.S. Electronic Espionage: A Memoir," August 1972, pp. 35–50.

50. U.S. Department of State, "President's Address to the Nation, Sept. 5, 1983," *KAL Flight #007: Compilation of Statements and Documents,* 1–16, September 1983, Washington, DC, pp. 6–8.

CHAPTER 6

1. *FBIS,* Japan, "Fishermen Report 'Mid-Air' Flash," 2 September 1983, p. C1; *Los Angeles Times,* "Japanese Saw Fireball, Heard Explosion," 4 September 1983, Part I, p. 8; *Japan Times,* "Fishermen Witnessed Explosion over Sakhalin, MSA Reports," 3 September 1983, p. 2; *FBIS,* Japan, "Oil Slick off Sakhalin," 2 September 1983, p. C2; and Sam Jameson, "Two Explosions Heard by Japanese Fishermen," *Los Angeles Times,* 3 September 1983, Part I, p. 8.

2. *FBIS,* Japan, "Oil Slick off Sakhalin," 2 September 1983, p. C2.

3. ICAO Report, p. 32.

4. Subsequent reports on Japan's national television network NHK said that "Japanese intelligence forces had tape-recorded conversations between Soviet fighter jets and ground control stations for the entire two and a half hours that the Korean airliner was reportedly being tracked." Reports in the *Washington Post* and elsewhere confirmed NHK's account. The information collected by Japanese intelligence was quite specific. It was known that four Soviet fighters had scrambled to intercept an intruding airliner over Kamchatka but that they had "failed to complete the mission." It was known that the Soviets "appeared to have lost track of the airliner" as it passed once again into international airspace over the Sea of Okhotsk. By using radar and intercepting voice communications, the Japanese monitored the scrambling of six fighters over Sakhalin, their failed effort at interception, and the intruder's final moments.

5. Clyde Haberman, "U.S. and Japanese Find No Trace of Korean Plane," *New York Times,* 3 September 1983, p. 5; A. D. Horne, "Soviets: Spy Plane," *Washington Post,* 3 September 1983, p. A23; *Japan Times,* "Soviets' Impatience May Have Led to Attack," 6 September 1983, p. 2; and Japan Defense Agency, Defense Bureau, First Transport Section, "The Locus of 10,000 Scrambles," *Boei Antena,* August 1983 (quoted in Yoshitaro Masuo, "The Korean Airline Incident and the Self-Defense Forces of Japan," *Sekai,* May 1985, pp. 270–89).

6. Reply from the Nakasone government to the President of the House of Counselors, 23 July 1985, Question 3, p. 5.

7. ICAO Report, p. 32; and Wilhelm Bittorf and Anthony Sampson, "Sinken Auf Eins-Null Tausend . . . " *Der Spiegel,* 15 October 1984, pp. 196–222.

8. David Shribman, "Korean Jetliner: What Is Known and What Isn't," *New York Times,* 8 September 1983, pp. A1–12.

9. John Keppel interview with Kunio Yanagida, July 1984; *Japan Times,* "U.S. Says KAL Jet Downed by MiG–23," 2 September 1983, pp. 1–4; and ICAO Report, pp. 32–33.

10. ICAO Report, p. 33.

11. Clyde Haberman, "Korean Jetliner with 269 Aboard Missing near Soviet Pacific Island," *New York Times,* 1 September 1983, pp. A1–D19; *Los Angeles Times,* "Soviets Deny Missing 747 Landed on Island," 1 September 1983, Part I, pp. 1–16; ABC News "Nightline," "Lebanon: Sorting the Factions/U.S.S. Monitor/Korean Airliner," Show No. 603, 31 August 1983; Douglas B. Feaver and David Hoffman, "Plane's Tragic Odyssey Mysterious," *Washington Post,* 4 September 1983, pp. A1–12; and U.S. Department of State, "President's Address to the Nation, Sept. 5, 1983," *KAL Flight #007: Compilation of Statements and Documents,* September 1–16, 1983, Washington, DC, pp. 6–8.

12. ABC News "Nightline," "Lebanon: Sorting Out the Factions/U.S.S. Monitor/Korean Airliner," Show No. 603, 31 August 1983; *Los Angeles Times,* "Soviets Deny Missing 747 Landed on Island," 1 September 1983 (early edition), Part I, pp. 1–16; and private source.

13. Douglas B. Feaver and David Hoffman, "Plane's Tragic Odyssey Mysterious," *Washington Post,* 4 September 1983, pp. A1–12.

14. Wilhelm Bittorf and Anthony Sampson, "Sinken Auf Eins-Null Tausend . . . " *Der Spiegel,* 15 October 1984, pp. 196–222.

15. Wilhelm Bittorf and Anthony Sampson, "Sinken Auf Eins-Null Tausend . . . " *Der Spiegel,* 15 October 1984, pp. 196–222.

16. Private source; and interview with Adm. Eugene Carroll, 11 December 1984.

17. Bernard Gwertzman, "An Angry Shultz Says He Can 'See No Excuse,' " *New York Times,* 2 September 1983, p. A5; and A. D. Horne, "U.S. Says Soviets Shot Down Airliner," *Washington Post,* 2 September 1983, pp. A1–17.

18. Thomas Maertens, "Tragedy of Errors," *Foreign Service Journal*, September 1985, pp. 25–31.

19. Former CIA deputy director George Carver, on Connecticut Public Radio in September 1984; and Seymour M. Hersh, *"The Target Is Destroyed,"* 1986, Random House, New York, pp. 143–44.

20. David Shribman, "Korean Jetliner: What Is Known and What Isn't," *New York Times*, 8 September 1983, pp. A1–12; interview with Robert Cramer of CNN, October 1984; and interview with Adm. Eugene Carroll, 11 December 1984.

21. *New York*, "Intelligencer: Top Reagan Officials Mulled P.R. Value of Korean Air Crash," 12 November 1984, p. 16.

22. Wilhelm Bittorf and Anthony Sampson, "Sinken Auf Eins-Null Tausend . . ." *Der Spiegel*, 15 October 1984, pp. 196–222.

23. David Shribman, "Korean Jetliner:What Is Known and What Isn't," *New York Times*, 8 September 1983, pp. A1–12; interview with Robert Cramer of CNN, October 1984; and Jack Anderson, "Japanese Tape Was Crucial in Pinning KAL-007 Blame," *Mainichi Daily News*, 8 April 1984.

24. Later, KAL would not discuss its announcement that the plane was safe on Sakhalin other than to say it was apparently based on premature information that proved false, as well as a desire to comfort the relatives gathered at Kimpo Airport.

25. David Shribman, "Korean Jetliner: What Is Known and What Isn't," *New York Times*, 8 September 1983, pp. A1–12; *The News American* (Baltimore), "Korean Jet Sought on Soviet Isle: U.S. Congressman Believed on Flight," 1 September 1983, pp. A1–6; *Los Angeles Times*, "Soviets Deny Missing 747 Landed on Island," 1 September 1983 (early edition), Part I, pp. 1–16; *Los Angeles Times*, Shultz Says Missile Downed Plane near Sea of Japan," 1 September 1983, Part I, p. 1; and John Keppel interview with James Kim, July 1984.

26. Wilhelm Bittorf and Anthony Sampson, "Sinken Auf Eins-Null Tausend . . ." *Der Spiegel*, 15 October 1984, pp. 196–222; and Clyde Haberman, "Korean Jetliner with 269 Aboard Missing near Soviet Pacific Island," *New York Times*, 1 September 1983, pp. A1–D19.

27. Wilhelm Bittorf and Anthony Sampson, "Sinken Auf Eins-Null Tausend . . ." *Der Spiegel*, 15 October 1984, pp. 196–222.

28. Toshio Kojima, "Loss of KAL Jumbo Spotlights Japanese Intelligence Work," *Asahi Evening News*, 27 September 1983; John Keppel interview with Kunio Yanagida, July 1984; and *Asahi Evening News*, "SDF Played Important Role in Finding Facts About KAL Case," 3 September 1983.

29. L. Fletcher Prouty, "The Last Flight of 007," *Gallery*, May 1985, pp. 46–101; and Clyde Haberman, "Korean Jetliner with 269 Aboard Missing near Soviet Pacific Island," *New York Times*, 1 September 1983, pp. A1–D19.

30. *San Francisco Examiner & Chronicle*, "South Korea Families Stunned," 1 September 1983, p. A21; and *Los Angeles Times*, "Soviets Deny Missing 747 Landed on Island," 1 September 1983 (early edition), pp. 1–16.

31. Rudy Abramson, "30 Americans on Korean Plane in Russian Airspace," *Los Angeles Times*, 2 September 1983, p. 1; *Washington Post*, "Missing Airliner Reported Safe on Soviet Island," 1 September 1983, pp. A1–18; and James Kim, "Korean Air Lines Jet Forced to Land on Soviet-Held Isle," *Hartford Courant*, 1 September 1983, p. 2.

32. Robert W. Lee and Captain Joe Ferguson, "Mysteries of Korean Air Lines Flight 007," *Conservative Digest*, October 1985, pp. 79–86.

33. David Corn interview with Tommy Toles, April 1985.

34. *New York Times*, "Georgia Democrat on Flight," 1 September 1983, p. D19;

David Hollander and Steven Saint, "Safe on Sakhalin," *L.A. Weekly,* 26 October–1 November 1984, pp. 15–29; and Douglas B. Feaver and David Hoffman, "Plane's Tragic Odyssey Mysterious," *Washington Post,* 4 September 1983, pp. A1–12.

[35.] David Corn interview with Tommy Toles, April 1985.

[36.] David Corn interview with Tommy Toles, April 1985.

[37.] The State Department never formally issued the "safe on Sakhalin" story. When asked later why the story had not been issued simultaneously with the South Korean Ministry of Foreign Affairs, State Department officials refused to comment. (*Source:* David Hollander and Steven Saint, "Safe on Sakhalin," *L.A. Weekly,* 26 October–1 November 1984, pp. 15–29.)

[38.] ABC News "Nightline," "Lebanon: Sorting the Factions/USS Monitor/Korean Airliner," Show No. 603, 31 August 1983, p. 12.

[39.] James Kim, "Korean Air Lines Jet Forced to Land on Soviet-Held Isle," *Hartford Courant,* 1 September 1983, p. 2; and John Keppel interview with Clyde Haberman, July 1984.

[40.] Douglas B. Feaver and David Hoffman, "Plane's Tragic Odyssey Mysterious," *Washington Post,* 4 September 1983, pp. A1–12; David Corn interview with Tommy Toles, April 1985; and *Washington Post,* "Missing Airliner Reported Safe on Soviet Island," 1 September 1983, pp. A1–18.

[41.] David Corn interview with Tommy Toles, April 1985.

[42.] ABC News "Nightline," "Korean Air Tragedy," 1 September 1983, Show No. 604, p. 2.

[43.] Handwritten notes of Kunio Yanagida, July 1984; and Wilhelm Bittorf and Anthony Sampson, "Sinken Auf Eins-Null Tausend . . . " *Der Spiegel,* 15 October 1984, pp. 196–222.

[44.] Yoshitaro Masuo, "The Korean Airliner Incident and the Self-Defense Forces of Japan," *Sekai,* May 1985, pp. 270–89; and Wilhelm Bittorf and Anthony Sampson, "Sinken Auf Eins-Null Tausend . . . " *Der Spiegel,* 15 October 1984, pp. 196–222.

[45.] ICAO Report, December 1983, p. 33.

[46.] Yoshitaro Masuo, "The Korean Airliner Incident and the Self-Defense Forces of Japan," *Sekai,* May 1985, pp. 270–89; and Wilhelm Bittorf and Anthony Sampson, "Sinken Auf Eins-Null Tausend . . . " *Der Spiegel,* 15 October 1984, pp. 196–222.

[47.] Douglas B. Feaver and David Hoffman, "Plane's Tragic Odyssey Mysterious," *Washington Post,* 4 September 1983, pp. A1–12; Robert C. Toth, "Airliner Reportedly Glided 12 Minutes Before Crash," *Los Angeles Times,* 8 September 1983, Part I, pp. 1–12; U.S. Department of State telegram, No. 121, 2 September 1983; Rudy Abramson, "30 Americans on Korean Plane in Russian Airspace," *Los Angeles Times,* 2 September 1983, Part I, p. 1.

[48.] Robert C. Toth, "Airliner Reportedly Glided 12 Minutes Before Crash," *Los Angeles Times,* 8 September 1983, Part I, pp. 1–12; *New York,* "Intelligencer: Top Reagan Officials Mulled P.R. Value of Korean Air Crash," 12 November 1984, p. 16; and private source.

[49.] Department of State telegram, No. 817, 9 September 1983; and interview with James Michelangelo, Chief Federal Air Safety Inspector, Anchorage Field Office, National Transportation Safety Board, 21 February 1985.

[50.] Interview by Michael Chrisman with James Michelangelo, 15 July 1984.

[51.] *Federal Register,* "Rules and Regulations," Title 49—Transportation: Chapter VIII National Transportation Safety Board, Vol. 44, No. 116; private source;

and David Corn, "Fear and Obstruction on the K.A.L. Trail," *The Nation,* August 17/24, 1985, pp. 110–13.

52. U.S. Department of State telegram, No. 121, 2 September 1983; Ian Ward, " 'Cold-Blooded Murder' Anger," *Daily Telegraph,* 2 September 1983, p. 1; *Japan Times,* "U.S. Says KAL Jet Downed by MiG-23," 2 September 1983, pp. 1–4; and Department of State telegram, No. 123, 2 September 1983.

53. John F. Burns, "Moscow Confirms Tracking of Plane," *New York Times,* 2 September 1983, pp. A1–4; Rudy Abramson, "30 Americans on Korean Plane in Russian Airspace," *Los Angeles Times,* 2 September 1983, Part I, p. 1; *New York Times,* "Transcript of Soviet Official's Statement and Excerpts from News Session," 10 September 1983, pp. 4–5; Douglas B. Feaver and David Hoffman, "Plane's Tragic Odyssey Mysterious," *Washington Post,* 4 September 1983, pp. A1–12; and Bernard Gwertzman, "An Angry Shultz Says He Can 'See No Excuse,' " *New York Times,* 2 September 1983, p. A5.

54. John F. Burns, "Moscow Confirms Tracking of Plane," *New York Times,* 2 September 1983, pp. A1–4; *FBIS,* Japan, "Soviet Ministry Denies Plane Landed," 1 September 1983, p. C2; *FBIS,* Soviet Union, "Denial Jet in USSR Territory," 1 September 1983, p. C1; and Robert Gillette, "Soviets Admit Interception but Not Shooting," *Los Angeles Times,* 2 September 1983, Part I, pp. 1–4.

55. Quoted in Alexander Dallin, *Black Box: KAL 007 and the Superpowers,* 1985, University of California Press, Berkeley, CA, p. 2.

56. *FBIS,* Soviet Union, "Landing at Sakhalin Denied," 1 September 1983, p. C1.

57. Clyde Haberman, "Korean Jetliner with 269 Aboard Missing near Soviet Pacific Island," *New York Times,* 1 September 1983, pp. A1–19; and *Los Angeles Times,* "Soviets Deny Missing 747 Landed on Island," 1 September 1983 (early edition), Part I, pp. 1–16.

58. *FBIS,* South Korea, "Government Criticized on Handling Incident," 7 September 1983, pp. E12–13; A. D. Horne, "U.S. Says Soviets Shot Down Airliner," *Washington Post,* 2 September 1983, pp. A1–17; *FBIS,* South Korea, "Government Statement Issued on KAL Jet Incident," 1 September 1983, p. El; *FBIS,* South Korea, "Korea Times Editorial," 2 September 1983, pp. E9–10; and *Los Angeles Times,* "Soviets Deny Missing 747 Landed on Island," 1 September 1983 (early edition), Part I, pp. 1–16.

59. Clyde Haberman, "Korean Jetliner with 269 Aboard Missing near Soviet Pacific Island," *New York Times,* 1 September 1983, pp. A1–D19.

60. *New York Times,* "Tokyo Reacts with Caution," 2 September 1983, p. A6; *FBIS,* Japan, "Abe: Soviet Shootdown Probable," 1 September 1983, p. C1; and *Los Angeles Times,* "Shultz Says Missile Downed Plane near Sea of Japan," 1 September 1983, Part I, p. 1.

61. David Corn interview with Tommy Toles, April 1985.

62. John Keppel interview with Hans Ephraimson, May 1985.

63. Steven Weisman, "President Demands Explanation for 'Horrifying Act of Violence,' " *New York Times,* 2 September 1983, pp. A1–5; Douglas B. Feaver and David Hoffman, "Plane's Tragic Odyssey Mysterious," *Washington Post,* 4 September 1983, pp. A1–12; and Bernard Gwertzman, "An Angry Shultz Says He Can 'See No Excuse,' " *New York Times,* 2 September 1983, p. A5.

64. Douglas B. Feaver and David Hoffman, "Plane's Tragic Odyssey Mysterious." *Washington Post,* 4 September 1983, pp. A1–12.

65. David Hoffman, "Airliner, Lebanon Crises Cut Short President's Stay in California," *Washington Post,* 2 September 1983, p. A14; and Lou Cannon and

Michael Getler, "Reagan Calls for 'Calm but Firm' Response," *Washington Post,* 4 September 1983, pp. A1–10.

66. Steven Weisman, "President Demands Explanation for 'Horrifying Act of Violence,' " *New York Times,* 2 September 1983, pp. A1–5.

CHAPTER 7

1. Robert D. McFadden, "U.S. Says Soviet Downed Korean Airliner; 269 Lost; Reagan Denounces 'Wanton' Act," *Washington Post,* 2 September 1983, pp. A1–4; and U.S. Department of State, "Secretary's News Briefing, Sept. 1, 1983," *KAL Flight #007: Compilation of Statements and Documents* 1–16 September 1983, Washington, DC, pp. 1–2.

2. Douglas B. Feaver and David Hoffman, "Plane's Tragic Odyssey Mysterious," *Washington Post,* 4 September 1983, pp. A1–12; and U.S. Department of State, "White House Statement, Sept. 1, 1983," *KAL Flight #007: Compilation of Statements and Documents* 1–16 September 1983, Washington, DC, p. 2.

3. The item was given no particular significance, coming after several routine reports about Soviet salutes to the Vietnamese people and after a film of a state-sponsored peace rally.

4. Robert Gillette, "Soviets Admit Interception but Not Shooting," *Los Angeles Times,* 2 September 1983, pp. 1–4; and *New York Times,* "Tass Statement on Incident," 2 September 1983, p. A4.

5. Robert Gillette, "Soviets Admit Interception but Not Shooting," *Los Angeles Times,* 2 September 1983, pp. 1–4; John F. Burns, "Moscow Confirms Tracking of Plane," *New York Times,* 2 September 1983, pp. A1–4; and Nigel Wade, "Warning Only, Say Russians," *Daily Telegraph,* 2 September 1983, p. 1.

6. Department of State telegram from Moscow, 2 September 1983; and Robert Gillette, "Soviets Admit Interception but Not Shooting," *Los Angeles Times,* 2 September 1983, pp. 1–4.

7. Department of State telegram, No. 204, 3 September 1983; George Skelton, "President Demands Explanation," *Los Angeles Times,* 2 September 1983, pp. 1–9; and Steven Weisman, "President Demands Explanation for 'Horrifying Act of Violence,' " *New York Times,* 2 September 1983, pp. A1–5.

8. *Newsweek,* "A Ruthless Ambush in the Sky," 12 September 1983, pp. 16–30.

9. George Skelton, "President Demands Explanation," *Los Angeles Times,* 2 September 1983, pp. 1–9; and Douglas B. Feaver and David Hoffman, "Plane's Tragic Odyssey Mysterious," *Washington Post,* 4 September 1983, pp. A1–12.

10. Reagan would not actually cancel a vacation outright until June 1985, when the passengers and crew aboard TWA Flight 847 from Athens to New York were taken hostage by Shiite Moslem extremists.

11. *Newsweek,* "A Ruthless Ambush in the Sky," 12 September 1983, pp. 16–30; David Hoffman, "Airliner, Lebanon Crises Cut Short President's Stay in California," *Washington Post,* 2 September 1983, p. A14; and Steven Weisman, "President Demands Explanation for 'Horrifying Act of Violence,' " *New York Times,* 2 September 1983, pp. A1–5.

12. U.S. Department of State, "Secretary's Statement, Sept. 2, 1983," *KAL Flight #007: Compilation of Statements and Documents,* 1–16, September 1983, Washington, DC, p. 5.

13. Tim Ahern, "Full Flight 007 Story Still Mystery," *New Haven Register,* 26 August 1984, pp. A19–20.

14. *San Francisco Examiner & Chronicle,* "FAA Bars Use of Flight Path by U.S. Planes," 2 September 1983, p. A7; *Aviation Week & Space Technology,* "FAA Suspends Use of Route R20," 12 September 1983, p. 25; Douglas B. Feaver, "FAA Suspends Use of Route Korean Airliner Had Been Assigned," *Washington Post,* 3 September 1983, p. A22; *New York Times* "Air Route Is Closed," 3 September 1983, p. 6; and *Los Angeles Times,* "Jet on Downed Plane's Route," 1 September 1983, Part I, p. 1.

15. U.S. Department of State, "President's Statement, Sept. 1, 1983," *KAL Flight #007: Compilation of Statements and Documents,* 1–16 September 1983, Washington, DC, p. 2; and U.S. Department of State telegrams from Ottawa, Canada, and Seoul, South Korea, 2 September 1983.

16. Douglas B. Feaver and David Hoffman, "Plane's Tragic Odyssey Mysterious," *Washington Post,* 4 September 1983, pp. A1–12; David Hoffman and John Goshko, "A Heinous Act," *Washington Post,* 3 September 1983, pp. A1–22; George Skelton and Rudy Abramson, "Reagan Blasts 'Barbaric Act,' Wants Truth," *Los Angeles Times,* 3 September 1983, Part I, pp. 1–6; and *Washington Post,* "President Reagan's Statement," 3 September 1983, p. A22.

17. U.S. Department of State, "Ambassador Lichenstein's Statement, UN Security Council, September 2, 1983," *KAL Flight #007: Compilation of Statements and Documents,* 1–16 September 1983, Washington, DC, pp. 3–5; Douglas B. Feaver and David Hoffman, "Plane's Tragic Odyssey Remains Mysterious," *Washington Post,* 4 September 1983, pp. A1–12; George Skelton and Rudy Abramson, "Reagan Blasts 'Barbaric Act,' Wants Truth," *Los Angeles Times,* 3 September 1983, Part I, pp. 1–6; and David Hoffman and John Goshko, "A Heinous Act," *Washington Post,* 3 September 1983, pp. A1–22.

18. *Daily Telegraph,* "Russia Admits Shots at Jet," 3 September 1983, p. 1; and *Los Angeles Times,* "Text of Soviet Statement Issued by Tass," 3 September 1983, Part I, p. 11.

19. *Los Angeles Times,* "Russians Say Jetliner Was Cover for Spying Mission," 2 September 1983, p. 1.

20. Richard Owen, "Senior Military Commanders Took Decision to Open Fire," *The Times,* 5 September 1983, p. 1.

21. U.S. Department of State, "Secretary's Statement, September 2, 1983," *KAL Flight #007: Compilation of Statements and Documents,* 1–16 September 1983, Washington, DC, p. 5.

22. U.S. Department of State, "U.S. Letter to President, U.N. Security Council, September 1, 1983," *KAL Flight #007: Compilation of Statements and Documents,* 1–16 September 1983, Washington, DC, p. 3; U.S. Department of State telegram, 1 September 1983.

23. Joining the U.S. in explicitly condemning the Soviet action were the envoys of Japan, the Netherlands, Great Britain, Australia, and Canada.

24. *Japan Times,* "U.S. Urges U.N. Security Council to Meet on Jet," 3 September 1983, p. 1; Ian Black, "U.S. Accuses Moscow of 'Murder,' " *Washington Post,* 3 September 1983, p. A23; and Don Shannon, "Trade Harsh Words over Jet at U.N.," *Los Angeles Times,* 3 September 1983, Part I, p. 1.

25. *Los Angeles Times,* "Tantrums at the U.N.," 21 September 1983, Part II, p. 6; Richard Bernstein, "General Assembly Opens at the U.N.," *New York Times,* 21 September 1983, p. A11; Bernard D. Nossiter, " 'Murder' and 'Massacre' Charged as U.N. Council Starts Its Debate," *New York Times,* 3 September 1983, pp. 1–6; U.S. Department of State, "Ambassador Lichenstein's Statement, U.N. Security Council, September 2, 1983" *KAL Flight #007: Compila-*

tion of Statements and Documents, 1–16 September 1983, Washington, DC, pp. 3–5; and United Nations Security Council, *Provisional Verbatim Record of the Two Thousand Four Hundred and Seventieth Meeting,* S/PV.2470, 2 September 1983, New York, pp. 25–26.

[26.] Don Shannon, "Trade Harsh Words over Jet at U.N.," *Los Angeles Times,* 3 September 1983, Part I, p. 1; and Bernard D. Nossiter, " 'Murder' and 'Massacre' Charged as U.N. Council Starts Its Debate," *New York Times,* 3 September 1983, pp. 1–6.

[27.] United Nations Security Council, *Provisional Verbatim Record of the Two Thousand Four Hundred and Seventieth Meeting,* S/PV.2470, 2 September 1983, New York, p. 72.

[28.] Douglas B. Feaver, "FAA Can Warn Soviets of Stray Planes, Court Told," *Washington Post,* 24 February 1984, p. A20.

[29.] South Korea, unable to get satisfaction in the Security Council because of the Soviets' veto power, planned to raise the issue again before the U.N.'s legal committee during the General Assembly.

[30.] *FBIS,* South Korea, "More on Foreign Minister's Remarks," 6 September 1983, p. E3; and U.S. Department of State telegram, No. 215, 3 September 1983, pp. 1–11.

[31.] *Los Angeles Times,* "Outrage Expressed Around World over Downing of Jetliner," 2 September 1983, Part I, p. 2.

[32.] *Los Angeles Times,* "Leaders in Congress Outraged; Canceling of Grain Pact Urged," 1 September 1983, Part I, p. 1; and ABC News "Nightline," "Korean Air Tragedy," Show No. 604, 1 September 1983.

[33.] David Hoffman and John Goshko, "A Heinous Act," *Washington Post,* 3 September 1983, pp. A1–22; *Washington Post,* "Soviets Purchase More Grain Under New U.S. Agreement," 9 September 1983, p. A9; and Sugwon Kang, "Flight 007: Was There Foul Play?" *Bulletin of Concerned Asian Scholars,* 1985, Vol. 17, No. 2, pp. 30–48.

[34.] Leslie H. Gelb, "Plane Tragedy Poses Tough East-West Issues," *New York Times,* 4 September 1983, p. E1.

[35.] ABC News "Nightline," "Punishing the Soviets—What Options?" Show No. 605, 2 September 1983, pp. 2–3.

[36.] ABC News "Nightline," "Punishing the Soviets—What Options?" Show No. 605, 2 September 1983, pp. 2–3; Steven R. Weisman, "Leaders of Congress Briefed," *Los Angeles Herald Examiner,* 5 September 1983, pp. A1–4; Steven R. Weisman, "U.S. Says Soviet Continues 'to Lie to the World' on Jet," *New York Times,* 7 September 1983, p. A14; Douglas B. Feaver, "New Right Disappointed by Reagan's Reaction," *Washington Post,* 6 September 1983, p. A4; and *Los Angeles Times,* "Reagan May Lose Conservative Aid over Jet Reaction," 14 September 1983, Part I, p. 2.

[37.] *Washington Post,* "Angry Protesters Storm Soviet Compound," 5 September 1983, p. A6; Department of State telegram, No. 257, 4 September 1983; and *FBIS,* Soviet Union, " 'Mob' Attacks Residence of Soviet U.N. Mission," 5 September 1983, p. A1.

[38.] *Washington Post,* "Angry Protesters Storm Soviet Compound," 5 September 1983, p. A6; *Los Angeles Herald Examiner,* "Incident Has 'em Seeing Red from Coast to Coast," 5 September 1983, p. A4; and Department of State memorandum, No. 2530, 4 September 1983.

[39.] Richard Owen, "Russians Hint at Error but Not Shooting Down Jet," *The Times,* 6 September 1983, p. 1; Serge Schmemann, "Moscow Steps Up Attack on U.S. over Downing of Korean Airliner," *New York Times,* 4 September 1983, pp. 1–16; *New York Times,* "Text of Statement on the Airliner Incident," 4 September 1983, p. 16; and Robert Gillette, "Tass Accuses U.S. of 'Provocation,' " *Washington Post,* 4 September 1983, pp. A1–14.

40. John F. Burns, "Kremlin Hints at Concern over Domestic Reaction," *New York Times,* 4 September 1983, p. 18; and Robert Gillette, "Tass Accuses U.S. of 'Provocation,' " *Washington Post,* 4 September 1983, pp. A1–14.

CHAPTER 8

1. John F. Burns, "Soviet Officer in Plane Case Is Dead at 62," *New York Times,* 23 May 1984, p. A5; and Robert Gillette, "Reconnaissance Jet Suspected, Moscow Says," *Los Angeles Times,* 5 September 1983, Part I, pp. 1–10.

2. Richard Owen and Nicholas Ashford, "Airliner 'Was Mistaken for American Spyplane,' " *The Times,* 5 September 1983, p. 1; and Robert Gillette, "Reconnaissance Jet Suspected, Moscow Says," *Los Angeles Times,* 5 September 1983, Part I, pp. 1–10.

3. Robert Gillette, "Reconnaissance Jet Suspected, Moscow Says," *Los Angeles Times,* 5 September 1983, Part I, pp. 1–10; and John F. Burns, "A Soviet General Implies Airliner May Have Been Taken for Spy Jet," *New York Times,* 5 September 1983, pp. 1–4.

4. Another Tass report appeared later that Sunday night, repeating the earlier demand for the U.S. to explain how and why the airliner went off course. Again, the report quoted from the foreign press in noting that the incident had strengthened President Reagan's hand in arms-control negotiations, defense issues, and in Central America.

5. Nigel Wade, "Korean Jet 'Stalking in Darkness,' " *Daily Telegraph,* 5 September 1983, p. 1; and *Japan Times,* "Impossible to Mistake Jet Identity: White House," 7 September 1983, p. 4.

6. Richard Beeston, "U.S. Seeks Allied Support," *Daily Telegraph,* 5 September 1983, pp. 1–28; and Steven R. Weisman, "U.S. Says Spy Plane Was in the Area of Korea Airliner," *New York Times,* 5 September 1983, pp. 1–6.

7. *Japan Times,* "Reagan Plays Recorded Intercepts of KAL Jet," 5 September 1983, p. 1.

8. Steven R. Weisman, "U.S. Says Spy Plane Was in the Area of Korea Airliner," *New York Times,* 5 September 1983, pp. 1–6; and Richard Beeston, "U.S. Seeks Allied Support," *Daily Telegraph,* 5 September 1983, pp. 1–28.

9. George Skelton and Paul Houston, "White House Rules Out Soviet Error," *Los Angeles Times,* 5 September 1983, Part I, pp. 1–10.

10. After the call, Wright said in a telephone interview with the *Washington Post* that the Soviets referred to Flight 007 either as "an RC-135 or a target needing identification" during the intrusion into Soviet territory over Sakhalin.

11. Steven Weisman, "U.S. Says Spy Plane Was in the Area of Korea Airliner," *New York Times,* 5 September 1983, pp. 1–6; and Michael Getler, "U.S. Air Force Plane Crossed Path of Jet," *Washington Post,* 5 September 1983, pp. A1–9.

12. No reporter asked how the U.S. knew the Soviets were tracking both the RC-135 and Flight 007 or how it was learned that they had misidentified the Korean airliner "well in advance" of the downing.

13. Michael Getler, "U.S. Air Force Plane Crossed Path of Jet," *Washington Post,*

5 September 1983, pp. A1–9; and Steven Weisman, "U.S. Says Spy Plane Was in the Area of Korea Airliner," *New York Times,* 5 September 1983, pp. 1–6.

14. Philip Taubman, "U.S. Says Intelligence Plane Was on a Routine Mission," *New York Times,* 5 September 1983, p. 4.

15. U.S. Department of State document, Comments on the Air Navigation Commission Report, p. 9; and Department of State telegram, No. 369, 6 September 1983.

16. U.S. Department of State, "White House Statement, Sept. 4, 1983," *KAL Flight #007: Compilation of Statements and Documents,* 1–16 September 1983, Washington, DC, p. 6.

17. Steven R. Weisman, "U.S. Says Spy Plane Was in the Area of Korea Airliner," *New York Times,* 5 September 1983, pp. 1–6; and *Boston Globe,* "U.S. Spy Planes Reportedly Trail Civilian Jets," 5 September 1983, p. 12.

18. Steven Weisman, "U.S. Says Spy Plane Was in the Area of Korea Airliner," *New York Times,* 5 September 1983, pp. 1–6; and Michael Getler, "U.S. Air Force Plane Crossed Path of Jet," *Washington Post,* 5 September 1983, pp. A1–9.

19. Two other discussants that day were former Ambassador to the Soviet Union Malcolm Toon and retired Adm. Eugene Carroll, the deputy director for the Washington-based Center for Defense Information. As Carroll later remarked, "I was amazed at the attitude of Burt and Toon. They were convinced we had the Russians down and now we could kick them."

20. David Hollander and Steven Saint, "Safe on Sakhalin," *L.A. Weekly,* 26 October–1 November 1984, pp. 15–29.

21. David Hoffman, "Tone of Reagan Speech Was Delicately Balanced," *Washington Post,* 6 September 1983, p. A4; and Lou Cannon, "Reagan Announces Mild Sanctions on Soviets," *Washington Post,* 6 September 1983, pp. A1–5.

22. Admiral Carroll made much the same point: "I think he used that phrase six or seven times in his television address. And I remember him referring in one case to 'the massacre of men, women, children, and infants.' Now, you really have to be demagogic and hateful to stretch out the blame to where you distinguish between the killing of children and infants, but he did. I was in London that night . . . and the BBC announcer, when it was all over, summed it up and said in all the years he had covered international news, covered the White House specifically, he had never heard a president of the United States speak as a demagogue before." *Newsweek,* "Inquest on a Massacre," 19 September 1983, pp. 18–22; George Skelton and Rudy Abramson, "Limited U.S. Sanctions Invoked by President," *Los Angeles Times,* 6 September 1983 (early edition), Part I, pp. 1–6; and interview with Adm. Eugene Carroll, in Washington, DC, 11 December 1984.

23. *New York Times,* "Transcript of President Reagan's Address on Downing of Korean Airliner," 6 September 1983, p. A15.

24. Reagan also talked about the Soviet pilot launching missiles—plural—the first time it was mentioned that more than one missile had been fired. While breaking new ground in the official line, the speech also was the last hurrah for at least one earlier story. Reagan mentioned for the last time that "the Korean pilot gave Japanese air control his position as east of Hokkaido, Japan, showing that he was unaware they were off course by as much as or more than 100 miles." The "100 miles" business was also misleading. At the end, the airliner was about 350 miles off course.

25. *Los Angeles Times,* "Text of Reagan's Demand for Soviet Apology and Com-

pensation," 6 September 1983, Part I, p. 8; and George Skelton and Rudy Abramson, "Limited U.S. Sanctions Invoked by President," *Los Angeles Times,* 6 September 1983 (early edition), Part I, pp. 1–6.

26. Steven R. Weisman, "President Sets Further Limits on Cultural and Other Exchanges," *New York Times,* 6 September 1983, pp. A1–14; and Karen E. House, "Reagan Condemns Jet's 'Massacre' by Russia, but Shuns Tough Moves," *Wall Street Journal,* 6 September 1983, p. 3.

27. In spite of the apparent clarity of the language, a U.S. statement issued in conjunction with the President's speech suggested something quite different, that the Soviet pilots "made no serious effort to identify the aircraft."

28. Steven R. Weisman, "President Sets Further Limits on Cultural and Other Exchanges," *New York Times,* 6 September 1983, pp. A1–14; *Los Angeles Times,* "Text of Reagan's Demand for Soviet Apology and Compensation," 6 September 1983, Part I, p. 8; and ICAO Report, p. 16.

29. The definition of a nation's airspace is established by international agreement, not some ambiguous "claim."

30. *New York Times,* "Transcript of President Reagan's Address on Downing of Korean Airliner," 6 September 1983, p. A15.

31. Lou Cannon, "Reagan Announces Mild Sanctions on Soviets," *Washington Post,* 6 September 1983, pp. A1–5.

32. *Los Angeles Times,* "Text of Reagan's Demand for Soviet Apology and Compensation," 6 September 1983, Part I, p. 8.

33. *Los Angeles Times,* "Reagan: Forceful Restraint," 6 September 1983, Part II, p. 4; and *Christian Science Monitor,* "A Balanced Response," 7 September 1983, p. 24.

34. *Los Angeles Times,* "U.S. Accused of Exploiting Tragedy," 6 September 1983, Part I, p. 2; and *FBIS,* Soviet Union, "Reagan Speech on Plane Incident 'Slanderous,' " 6 September 1983, p. C11.

35. James Reston, "The Politics of Fear," *New York Times,* 7 September 1983, p. A23.

36. George Kennan, "Breaking the Spell," *The New Yorker,* 3 October 1983, pp. 44–51; Walter Lippmann, *Public Opinion,* 1965, Free Press, New York, p. 150; and *Los Angeles Times,* "U.S. Says It Has Further Jet Evidence," 7 September 1983, Part I, p. 2.

37. Jeffrey T. Richelson, *The U.S. Intelligence Community,* 1985, Ballinger, Cambridge, MA, p. 125; George C. Wilson, "U.S. RC-135 Was Assessing Soviet Air Defenses," *Washington Post,* 7 September 1983, p. A12; Harold Jackson, "U.S. Wants Straight Answers on Flight 007," *The Guardian,* 8 September 1983; and Clarence A. Robinson, Jr., "U.S. Says Soviets Knew Korea Air Lines 747 Was Commercial Flight," *Aviation Week & Space Technology,* 12 September 1983, pp. 18–21.

38. There was also a third story that received substantially less attention. This was that the RC-135 in question was an ELINT aircraft that began its mission in Dutch Harbor on Unalaska Island near the mainland end of the Aleutian Islands chain. As far as can be determined, however, Dutch Harbor does not have an airport large enough to accommodate an RC-135.

39. Richard Halloran, "President Says Spy Jet Landed Before Incident," *New York Times,* 6 September 1983, pp. A1–6; George Skelton and Paul Houston, "White House Rules Out Soviet Error," *Los Angeles Times,* 5 September 1983, Part I, pp. 1–10; and Robert Whymant, "Spy in the Sky Island," *The Guardian,* 18 September 1983, p. 7.

[40.] Richard Halloran, "President Says Spy Jet Landed Before Incident," *New York Times,* 6 September 1983, pp. A1–6.

[41.] Military officers quoted in the *New York Times,* acknowledged that the RC-135 would routinely have "painted," or registered with radar, the Korean plane as a matter of aerial safety. "It could not be determined," the sources said, "if the reconnaissance plane spotted the Russian fighters on its radar." And when the high-value reconnaissance plane's radar told the crew that a large aircraft was heading toward them, the first thing they would do is identify it as rapidly as possible in order to ensure their safety.

[42.] ABC "20/20 Newsmagazine," 30 August 1984; Richard Halloran, "President Says Spy Jet Landed Before Incident," *New York Times,* 6 September 1983, pp. A1–6; and Seymour M. Hersh, *"The Target Is Destroyed,"* 1986, Random House, New York.

[43.] William Safire, "Sticks and Stones," *New York Times,* 8 September 1983, p. A23.

[44.] Ian Ball, "Korean Plane 'Interrupted Missile Test,' " *Daily Telegraph,* 9 September 1983; and personal communication from William Safire, 11 October 1984.

[45.] *Los Angeles Times,* "President Invokes New Sanctions," 8 September 1983 (late edition), Part I, p. 1.

[46.] Charles Mohr, "U.S. and Soviet Discuss Whether Moscow Violated Terms of 2 Arms Pacts," *New York Times,* 5 October 1983, p. A8; and *Aviation Week & Space Technology,* "Washington Roundup," 16 January 1984, p. 13.

[47.] The "SS" stands for a surface-to-surface missile and the "X" denotes that it is still experimental and not yet operational. When testing of the missile was completed, its designation was changed to "SS-25."

[48.] Eugene Kozicharow, "Soviet Union Continues Military Buildup," *Aviation Week & Space Technology,* 23 April 1984, pp. 53–56; John P. Wallach, "How Secret Soviet Missile Test May Have Spelled Doom for Jet," *Los Angeles Herald Examiner,* 25 September 1983, p. A4; and Charles Mohr, "U.S. and Soviet Discuss Whether Moscow Violated Terms of 2 Arms Pacts," *New York Times,* 5 October 1983, p. A8.

[49.] Frank Grove, "Soviets Trying to Hide New Missile System in Area of Jet Incident," *San Francisco Examiner & Chronicle,* 11 September 1983, p. A5.

[50.] Philip J. Klass, "U.S. Scrutinizing New Soviet Radar," *Aviation Week & Space Technology,* 22 August 1983, p. 19; and *New York Times,* 20 July 1983.

[51.] Unlike the suspect SS-X-25, this new MIRVed missile—the Soviet version of our MX—is allowable under the terms of the unratified SALT II treaty, although some in the Administration felt that this too represented a violation of strategic arms limitation agreements.

[52.] *Aviation Week & Space Technology,* "Washington Roundup," 26 September 1983, p. 25; Andrew Cockburn, "Pentagon Fantasies," *New York Times,* 21 September 1983, p. A27; Michael Getler, "Soviets Held Test of New Missile Three Days After Jet Downed," *Washington Post,* 16 September 1983, p. A28; and John P. Wallach, "How Secret Soviet Missile Test May Have Spelled Doom for Jet," *Los Angeles Herald Examiner,* 25 September 1983, p. A4.

[53.] William A. Dorman, "Soviets Seen Through Red-Tinted Glasses," *Bulletin of the Atomic Scientists,* February 1985, pp. 18–25; Anthony Marro, "When the Government Tells Lies," *Columbia Journalism Review,* March/April 1985, pp. 29–41; and Alfred Tennyson, "The Grandmother," *The Poetical Works of Alfred Tennyson,* 1870, Harper & Brothers, New York, p. 198.

CHAPTER 9

1. This message, presumably a misquote of the airliner's NIPPI position report, apparently did not exist.

2. Robert Gillette, "Admit They Downed 747, Blame U.S.," *Los Angeles Times,* 7 September 1983, Part I (early edition), pp. 1–6; and John F. Burns, "Russians' Version," *New York Times,* 6 September 1983, pp. A1–16.

3. *The Guardian,* "Pravda: Provocators Are Now Trying to Foul the Trail," 7 September 1983, p. 8; and Robert Gillette, "Admit They Downed 747, Blame U.S.," *Los Angeles Times,* 7 September 1983, Part I (early edition), pp. 1–6.

4. Robert Gillette, "Admit They Downed 747, Blame U.S.," *Los Angeles Times,* Part I (early edition), pp. 1–6; and John F. Burns, "Russians' Version," *New York Times,* 6 September 1983, pp. A1–16.

5. This type of denial is uncomfortably reminiscent of the child who emphatically denies that he stole ten dollars from his father's wallet. In fact, he stole eleven.

6. Writing in the *Columbia Journalism Review,* Anthony Marro described this approach as an attempt "to define the question as narrowly as possible and then answer it that way." As an example, he cites the following exchange: "Q.: Has the assistant secretary of state beeen invited to China? A.: No. (Meaning: He will go to China as an adviser to the vice-president. It is the vice-president who has been invited. Therefore, I am not lying.)"

7. Anthony Marro, "When the Government Tells Lies," *Columbia Journalism Review,* March/April 1985, pp. 29–41; Stanley Karnow, *Vietnam: A History,* 1983, Viking, New York, p. 414; and John F. Burns, "Russians' Version," *New York Times,* 6 September 1983, pp. A1–16.

8. U.S. Department of State telegram, No. 668, 8 September 1983; and John L. Hedges, quoted on BBC, "Panorama," 7 November 1983.

9. *Japan Times,* "UNSC Hears Tapes of Conversations Between Soviet Pilots, Ground Control," 8 September 1983, p. 1; and U.S. Department of State telegram, No. 668, 8 September 1983.

10. BBC, "Panorama," November 1983; U.S. Department of State telegram, No. 668, 8 September 1983; and letter from Lawrence S. Eagleburger to Charles Z. Wick, 8 September 1983.

11. Clyde Haberman, "At Hub of Plane Search, Town Yearns for Peace," *New York Times,* 21 September 1983, p. A10.

12. *Newsweek,* "A Ruthless Ambush in the Sky," 12 September 1983, pp. 16–30; and Wilhelm Bittorf and Anthony Sampson, "Sinken Auf Eins-Null Tausend . . . " *Der Spiegel,* 15 October 1984, pp. 196–222.

13. As the *Far Eastern Economic Review* pointed out, "Such reticence by the U.S., coupled with the hints from officials that more is known, engenders suspicion whether valid or not."

14. *Far Eastern Economic Review,* "The Ghost of KAL 007 Still Stalks Washington's Corridors," 24 January 1985, pp. 53–55; Anthony Sampson, "What Happened to Flight 007?" *Parade Magazine,* 22 April 1984, pp. 12–13; Anthony Sampson, *Empires of the Sky: The Politics, Contests, and Cartels of World Airlines,* 1984, Random House, New York; *Japan Tiimes,* "U.S. Senate Praises Japan on KAL Tragedy Efforts," 22 September 1983, p. 1; and Sam Jameson, "Disclosures on Russian Pilots Costly to Japan," *Los Angeles Times,* 19 September 1983, Part I, pp. 13–15.

15. Bernard D. Nossiter, "U.N. Council Hears a Tape in Russian," *New York Times,* 7 September 1983, pp. A1–15.

16. U.S. Department of State, "Ambassador Kirkpatrick's Statement, U.N. Security Council, Sept. 6, 1983," *KAL Flight #007: Compilation of Statements and Documents,* 1–16 September 1983, Washington DC, pp. 8–10.

17. Ian Ball, "U.N. Hears Tape of Massacre," *Daily Telegraph,* 7 September 1983; and Don Shannon, "Security Council Hears Voices of Soviet Pilots," *Los Angeles Times,* 7 September 1983, Part I, p. 6.

18. *Los Angeles Times,* "Russia Admits Downing Jet," 6 September 1983, Part I, p. 1; *Japan Times,* "UNSC Hears Tapes of Conversations Between Soviet Pilots, Ground Control," 8 September 1983, p. 1; and *New York Times,* "Troyanovsky Leaving; He'll Return to Moscow," 12 February 1986, p. A11.

19. Bernard D. Nossiter, "U.N. Council Hears a Tape in Russian," *New York Times,* 7 September 1983, pp. A1–15; and U.S. Department of State telegram, No. 557, 7 September 1983.

20. Ian Ball, "U.N. Hears Tape of Massacre," *Daily Telegraph,* 7 September 1983; Don Shannon, "Security Council Hears Voices of Soviet Pilots," *Los Angeles Times,* 7 September 1983, Part I, p. 6; U.S. Department of State telegram, No. 558, 7 September 1983; *Los Angeles Times,* "Russia Admits Downing Jet," 6 September 1983, Part I, p. 1; *Japan Times,* "UNSC Hears Tapes of Conversations Between Soviet Pilots, Ground Control," 8 September 1983, p. 1; and *The Guardian,* "U.S. Displays Jet Video to Security Council," 7 September 1983, p. 8.

21. Ian Ball, "U.N. Hears Tape of Massacre," *Daily Telegraph,* 7 September 1983; Michael J. Berlin, "Hushed U.N. Chamber Hears Recording of Stalking Pilots," *Washington Post,* 7 September 1983, pp. A1–14; Yoshitaro Masuo, "Some Research into the Record of Communications of the Soviet Fighters Which Intercepted KAL 007," 1986 (unpublished manuscript); and U.S. Department of State telegram, No. 558, 7 September 1983.

22. *FBIS,* Japan, "More on Released Transcripts," 7 September 1983, p. C2; and *Japan Times,* "Chances of Japanese Sanctions Growing," 7 September 1983, pp. 1–4.

23. *FBIS,* Japan, "Late Report: Soviets Call Tapes 'Fabrication,' " 6 September 1983, p. C9; and U.S. Department of State telegram, No. 1161, 13 September, 1983.

24. Richard Owen, "Moscow Finally Confesses: We Shot Down Jumbo," *The Times,* 7 September 1983, p. 1; Michael Dobbs, "Moscow Admits Shooting Down Korean Plane," *Washington Post,* 7 September 1983, pp. A1–12; and Robert Gillette, "Admit They Downed 747, Blame U.S.," *Los Angeles Times,* 7 September 1983 (early edition,) Part I, pp. 1–6.

25. John F. Burns, "Moscow Concedes a Soviet Fighter Downed Airliner," *New York Times,* 7 September 1983, pp. A1–16; Michael Dobbs, "Moscow Admits Shooting Down Korean Plane," Washington Post, 7 September 1983, pp. A1–12; *FBIS,* Soviet Union, "USSR Government Statement on 'Intruder Plane,' " 7 September 1983, pp. C1–2; Harold Jackson, "US Wants Straight Answers on Flight 007," *The Guardian,* 8 September 1983; Nigel Wade, "Russia Admits 'Stopping 747,' " *Daily Telegraph,* 7 September 1983, p. 1; and Robert Gillette, "Admit They Downed 747, Blame U.S.," *Los Angeles Times,* 7 September 1983 (early edition), Part I, pp. 1–6.

26. U.S. Department of State telegram, No. 560, 7 September 1983.

27. Richard Witkin, "Japan's Civil Radar Too Far Away to Pick up 747," *New York Times,* 8 September 1983, p. A11.

28. Michael J. Berlin, "Hushed U.N. Chamber Hears Recording of Stalking Pilots,"

Washington Post, 7 September 1983, pp. A1–14; Don Shannon, "Security Council Hears Voices of Soviet Pilots," *Los Angeles Times*, 7 September 1983, Part I, p. 6; and Department of State telegram, No. 2578, 6 September 1983.

29. *FBIS*, Japan, "Soviet Pilot's Conversation Reported," 2 September 1983, p. C1; *New Haven Journal Courier*, "U.S. Flays Soviets for Air Atrocity," 2 September 1983, pp. 1–9; *The Times*, "U.S.–Soviet Crisis over Jumbo Jet," 2 September 1983, p. 1; and Sam Jameson, "Two Explosions Heard by Japanese Fishermen," *Los Angeles Times*, 3 September 1983, Part I, p. 8.

30. Accounts identical to the Kyodo report appeared in the United States on CBS News and in *The Times* of London. A slightly more elaborate version appeared in the *Los Angeles Times*, after which veteran Tokyo correspondent Sam Jameson noted that some samples of the monitored conversations had been given to newsmen by "Defense Agency officials":

"I am within two kilometers. He has not noticed me."
"Continue pursuit."
"I have the plane in target."
"Fire!"
"I have fired."

31. *FBIS*, Japan, "SDF Monitored Ground-Air Communications," 6 September, 1983, p. C5; and *FBIS*, Japan, "Official Denies Monitoring Statement," 6 September 1983, p. C6.

32. Steven R. Weisman, "U.S. Denies Having Soviet Ground-Station Tapes," *New York Times*, 8 September 1983, p. A12; *The Sunday Times*, "The Airliner: Not Such a Cold-Blooded Kill," 11 September 1983, p. 18; and Clyde Haberman, "Seas off Japan Yielding Grim Flight 7 Debris," *New York Times*, 12 September 1983, pp. A1–10.

33. *FBIS*, South Korea, "Japanese Diet Delegation Interviewed," 7 September 1983, p. E9.

34. *The Sunday Times*, "The Airliner: Not Such a Cold-Blooded Kill," 11 September 1983, p. 18; Sam Jameson, "Japanese Military Says Korean Pilot May Have Erred on Jet's Location," *Los Angeles Times*, 2 September 1983, Part I, p. 5; *Asahi Evening News*, "SDF Played Important Role in Finding Facts About KAL Case," 3 September 1983; and Ralph McGehee, "A U.S. Deception?" *Muse*, Fall 1984, pp. 11–27.

35. U.S. Department of State, "Secretary's News Briefing, Sept. 1, 1983," *KAL Flight #007: Compilation of Statements and Documents*, 1–16 September 1983, Washington, DC, pp. 1–2; David Shribman, "Korean Jetliner: What Is Known and What Isn't," *New York Times*, 8 September 1983, p. 1; David Shribman, "U.S. Experts Say Soviet Didn't See Jet Was Civilian," *New York Times*, 7 October 1983, pp. A1–10; Philip Taubman, "U.S. Had Noticed Activity by Soviet," *New York Times*, 14 September 1983, p. A12; *Newsweek*, "Inquest on a Massacre," 19 September 1983, pp. 18–22; and *Aviation Week & Space Technology*, "Mission 9 Astronauts Photographed Soviet Submarine, Fighter Bases at Petropavlovsk," 19 March 1984, p. 17.

36. U.S. Department of State telegram, No. 665, 8 September 1983; Steven R. Weisman, "U.S. Says Soviet Continues 'to Lie to the World,'" *New York Times*, 7 September 1983, p. A14; Michael Getler, "U.S. Air Force Plane Crossed Path of Jet," *Washington Post*, 5 September 1983, pp. A1–9; and U.S. Department

of State, "Secretary's News Briefing, Sept. 1, 1983," *KAL Flight #007: Compilation of Statements and Documents,* 1–16 September 1983, Washington DC, pp. 1–2.

37. *Los Angeles Times,* "U.S. Eavesdropped as Jetliner Was Attacked," 1 September 1983 (final edition), Part I, p. 1; Walt Crowley, "Following Flight 007: The Major Media Begin to Sniff the Trail," *The Weekly* (Seattle), 5–12 December 1984; and Steven R. Weisman, "U.S. Denies Having Soviet Ground-Station Tapes," *New York Times,* 8 September 1983, p. A12.

38. Philip Taubman, "U.S. Analysts Say Airliner May Have Taken Short Cut," *New York Times,* 4 September 1983, p. 18; and Michael Getler, "Reagan Demands an Explanation," *Washington Post,* 2 September 1983, pp. A1–17.

39. *New York Times,* "Text of Statement by the State Department," 7 September 1983, p. A14; and Steven R. Weisman, "U.S. Says Soviet Continues 'to Lie to the World' on Jet," *New York Times,* 7 September 1983, p. A14.

40. U.S. Department of State telegram, No. 668, 8 September 1983; and Bernard D. Nossiter, "U.S. Encounters Political Snag in Security Council," *New York Times,* 8 September 1983, p. A10.

41. Zoriana Pysariwsky, "Pressure on Moscow at the UN," *The Times,* 8 September 1983; *FBIS,* Soviet Union, "Socialist Countries 'Rebuff' U.S. 'Cover-Up,' " 9 September 1983, pp. DD4–5; and Bernard D. Nossiter, "U.S. Encounters Political Snag in Security Council," *New York Times,* 8 September 1983, p. A10.

CHAPTER 10

1. *Washington Post,* "KAL to Pay Compensation, Official Says," 5 September 1983, p. A6; and *FBIS,* Japan, "KAL Victims' Relatives Sail for Crash Site," 7 September 1983, p. C4.

2. *Japan Times,* "Boats Continue to Search Area Where KAL Jetliner Shot Down," 4 September 1983, p. 2; *Japan Times,* "Relatives Throw Flowers in Sea near Korean Airliner Crash Site," 5 September 1983, p. 2; and Clyde Haberman, "With Flowers and Cries of Grief, Japanese Honor Those Who Died," *New York Times,* 5 September 1983, p. 5.

3. Interview with Andy Donovan, November 1984.

4. *Japan Times,* "14 Patrol Boats Continue Searching for Jet Debris," 6 September 1983, p. 2; and *Japan Times,* "Objects Found Not Those of KAL Plane," 7 September 1983, p. 2.

5. *Los Angeles Times,* "Soviets Overfly Rites for Jet Victims," 6 September 1983, Part I, p. 2.

6. *FBIS,* Japan, "Oil Slick off Sakhalin," 2 September 1983, p. C2; *Japan Times,* "Fishermen Witnessed Explosion over Sakhalin, MSA Reports," 3 September 1983, p. 2; and *FBIS,* Japan, "Rescue Efforts Detailed," 2 September 1983, pp. C1–2.

7. *Japan Times,* "Fishermen Witnessed Explosion over Sakhalin, MSA Reports," 3 September 1983, p. 2.

8. *FBIS,* Soviet Union, "USSR Envoy to Japan on 'Signs' of Plane 'Crash,' " 2 September 1983, p. C1; and Clyde Haberman, "U.S. and Japanese Find No Trace of Korean Plane," *New York Times,* 3 September 1983, p. 5.

9. This account appears to agree with Larry Speakes's statement on September 2 that the United States had received reports that bodies had been recovered in

the area where Flight 007 went down but had not been able to confirm them at that time.

10. Information from Shozo Takemoto, August 1985; George Skelton and Rudy Abramson, "Reagan Blasts 'Barbaric Act,' Wants Truth," *Los Angeles Times,* 3 September 1983, Part I, P. 1; and Department of State Operations Center, Situation Report No. 5., Document No. 2528, 3 September 1983.

11. A. D. Horne, "Soviets: Spy Plane," *Washington Post,* 3 September 1983, p. A23; *Los Angeles Times,* "U.S. Ships Supporting Search," 5 September 1983, Part I, p. 10; *New Haven Journal Courier,* "U.S. Flays Soviets for Air Atrocity," 2 September 1983, pp. 1–9; and Seymour M. Hersh, *"The Target Is Destroyed,"* 1986, Random House, New York, p. 74.

12. *Aviation Week & Space Technology,* "Soviet Su-15 Shoots Down Korean 747," 5 September 1983, pp. 25–27; *Los Angeles Times,* "U.S. Ships Supporting Search," 5 September 1983, Part I, p. 10; *Japan Times,* "14 Patrol Boats Continue Searching for Jet Debris," 6 September 1983, p. 2; and U.S. Department of State telegram, No. 176, 3 September 1983.

13. William Chapman, "South Koreans Deny Charge That Missing Plane Had Spy Role," *Washington Post,* 4 September 1983, p. A12; *Japan Times,* "Boats Continue to Search Area Where KAL Jetliner Shot Down," 4 September 1983, p. 2; and Clyde Haberman, "Debris of a Plane Found, Soviet Says," *New York Times,* 4 September 1983, p. 17.

14. *Los Angeles Times,* "Russians Say Jetliner Was Cover for Spying Mission," 2 September 1983 (early edition), Part I, p. 1; *Japan Times,* "Boats Continue to Search Area Where KAL Jetliner Shot Down," 4 September 1983, p. 2; Clyde Haberman, "Debris of a Plane Found, Soviet Says," *New York Times,* 4 September 1983, p. 17; Clyde Haberman, "With Flowers and Cries of Grief, Japanese Honor Those Who Died," *New York Times,* 5 September 1983, p. 5; and *Japan Times,* "Fishermen Witnessed Explosion over Sakhalin, MSA Reports," 3 September 1983, p. 2.

15. *Japan Times,* "Relatives Throw Flowers in Sea near Korean Airliner Crash Site," 5 September 1983, p. 2; *FBIS,* Japan, "Possible Debris Found," 6 September 1983, pp. C7–8; A. E. Cullison, "Japanese Recover Debris," *Daily Telegraph,* 6 September 1983, p. 1; *FBIS,* South Korea, "Search Continues for Wreckage," 6 September 1983, pp. E13–14; *Japan Times,* "Objects Found Not Those of KAL Plane," 7 September 1983, p. 2; and *Japan Times,* "14 Patrol Boats Continue Searching for Jet Debris," 6 September 1983, p. 2.

16. *Japan Times,* "14 Patrol Boats Continue Searching for Jet Debris," 6 September 1983, p. 2; and *Los Angeles Times,* "Increase in Soviet Vessels May Signal Jet Debris Sighting," 7 September 1983, Part I, p. 2.

17. *FBIS,* Japan, "Soviets Deny Recovering Bodies," 6 September 1983, p. C6; Michael Getler, "Moscow Keeps a Strong Alert near Flight 007's Crash Site," *Washington Post,* 8 September 1983, pp. A1–26; and *FBIS,* Japan, "No 'Substantial' Debris Found," 6 September 1983, p. C8.

18. *Japan Times,* "Objects Found Not Those of KAL Plane," 7 September 1983, p. 2; and *FBIS,* Japan, "No 'Substantial' Debris Found," 6 September 1983, p. C8.

19. *Japan Times,* "Soviets Reportedly Find Wreckage of KAL Plane," 5 September 1983, p. 1; and *FBIS,* Japan, "Soviets Finish Recovering Wreckage," 6 September 1983, p. C7.

20. During the previous year in New Hampshire, Stolichnaya had accounted for only $130,000 in total sales.

21. *Los Angeles Times,* "N.H. Liquor Stores Say 'Nyet' to Russian Vodka," 6

September 1983, Part I, p. 2; *Japan Times,* "Russian Vodka Banned in N.H. Stores," 8 September 1983, p. 6; *Washington Post,* "New Hampshire Takes a Stand," 7 September 1983, p. A14; and ABC News, "Nightline," "Punishing the Soviet—What Options?" Show No. 605, 2 September 1983.

22. Doyle McManus, "Americans Get Revenge with Vodka," *Los Angeles Times,* 9 September 1983, Part I, p. 6; *New York Times,* "Los Alamos Curbs Travel to Soviet," 8 September 1983, p. A10; *Los Angeles Times,* "Assemblyman Seeks Boycott of Russian Vodka over Jet Incident," 7 September 1983, Part I, p. 24; and Theresa Walker, "L.A. Protest Condemns Soviet 'Barbarism,' " *Los Angeles Times,* 3 September 1983, Part I, p. 7.

23. *New York Times,* "Los Alamos Curbs Travel to Soviet," 8 September 1983, p. A10; *New York Times,* "Head of Charter Agency Ends Travel Talks with Russians," 5 September 1983, p. 5; Doyle McManus, "Americans Get Revenge with Vodka, Video," *Los Angeles Times,* 9 September 1983, Part I, p. 6; Kevin DuPont, "Downing of Jet Has Tangled Soviet–U.S. Sports Exchange," *New York Times,* 21 September 1983, pp. A1–B15; *San Francisco Examiner & Chronicle,* "California-Soviet Meeting Postponed," 2 September 1983, p. A9; and *Los Angeles Times,* "Jesse Jackson Cancels Plan for Soviet Visit," 3 September 1983, Part I, p. 7.

24. Frank J. Prial, "Protesters March on Soviet Mission," *New York Times,* 3 September 1983, p. 6; and Ivan Sharpe, "Anti-Soviet, Cops Clash at Consulate," *San Francisco Examiner & Chronicle,* 4 September 1983, p. A6.

25. *Los Angeles Times,* "Korean Air Lines Cancels Ads About 'Shorter' Flights," 10 September 1983, Part I, p. 22.

26. *FBIS,* South Korea, "Student, Worker Demonstrations Reported," 2 September 1983, p. E5; *FBIS,* South Korea, "Mass Rallies Denounce USSR," 8 September 1983, p. E8; *Japan Times,* "Thousands of S. Koreans Protest Against USSR," 4 September 1983, p. 1; and Sam Jameson, "Koreans React to Loss with Grief, Rage, Stoicism," *Los Angeles Times,* 5 September 1983, Part I, pp. 1–12.

27. *FBIS,* South Korea, "Korean Lawmakers Urge Retaliation," 7 September 1983, pp. E9–10; and *FBIS,* South Korea, "Further Report on Lawmakers' Reaction," 7 September 1983, p. E11.

28. *FBIS,* South Korea, "Korea Herald Editorial," 7 September 1983, pp. E4–5; *FBIS,* South Korea, "*Kyonghyang Sinmun* Editorial," 7 September 1983, pp. E5–6; and *FBIS,* South Korea, "Sanctions Deemed 'Lukewarm,' " 8 September 1983, pp. E3–4.

29. On the international front, the Republic of Korea had been working hand in hand with the United States, doing its best to ensure condemnation of the Soviets at the United Nations and by the European Economic Community.

30. *FBIS,* South Korea, "Diplomatic Efforts Against Soviets," 8 September 1983, p. E5; *Los Angeles Times,* "50,000 S. Koreans Protest; Soviet Apology Demanded," 2 September 1983, Part I, p. 2; and William Chapman, "Seoul Eyes Soviet Ties Despite Jet Disaster," *Washington Post,* 6 September 1983, p. A6.

31. U.S. Department of State telegram, No. 193, 3 September 1983; Steve Lohr, "100,000 at Seoul Memorial Service for 269 Victims," *New York Times,* 8 September 1983, p. A11; *FBIS,* South Korea, "Chun Chairs Meeting, 4 Sept.," 6 September 1983; Sam Jameson, "South Korea's President Chun Faces Problems on the Domestic Front Too," *Los Angeles Times,* 16 September 1983, Part I, pp. 4–5; *FBIS,* South Korea, "Memorial Service Held for Victims of KAL Tragedy," 7 September 1983, p. E1; *Japan Times,* "Koreans Mourn Victims Aboard Plane," 8 September 1983, p. 4; *Los Angeles Times,* "100,000 Rally in Seoul,

Mourn Jetliner Victims," 7 September 1983, Part I, p. 2; and Sam Jameson, "Memorial to Be Held in Seoul Today, and Protests Will Go On," *Los Angeles Times*, 7 September 1983, Part I, p. 12.

[32.] In addition to the families of the Korean victims, KAL had given passage to Seoul to ninety-seven family members of foreign Flight 007 passengers so they could attend the memorial. They came from Canada, the United States, the Philippines, and elsewhere.

[33.] Steve Lohr, "100,000 at Seoul Memorial Service for 269 Victims," *New York Times*, 8 September 1983, p. A11; *New York Times*, "Memorial Service Set for Flight 7 Victims," 4 September 1983, p. 16; *Japan Times*, "Koreans Mourn Victims Aboard Plane," 8 September 1983, p. 4; *Los Angeles Times*, "100,000 Rally in Seoul, Mourn Jetliner Victims," 7 September 1983, Part I, p. 2; *Mainichi Shimbun*, "Chun Renews Demand for All Facts," 8 September 1983; and Sam Jameson, "Memorial to Be Held in Seoul Today, and Protests Will Go On," *Los Angeles Times*, 7 September 1983, Part I, p. 12.

[34.] *Los Angeles Times*, "100,000 Rally in Seoul, Mourn Jetliner Victims," 7 September 1983, Part I, p. 2; and Steve Lohr, "100,000 at Seoul Memorial Service for 269 Victims," *New York Times*, 8 September 1983, p. A11.

CHAPTER 11

[1.] Don Oberdorfer, "Security Talks Ending in Air Disaster's Shadow," *Washington Post*, 7 September 1983, p. A12; and John Darnton, "Plane's Downing May Shadow Talks," *New York Times*, 6 September 1983, p. A14.

[2.] Bernard Gwertzman, "Reagan Sees Need for World Action in Plane Incident," *New York Times*, 4 September 1983, pp. 1–16; and George Skelton, "Reagan's Caution in Crisis Belies Image," *Los Angeles Times*, 10 September 1983, Part I, pp. 1–27.

[3.] U.S. Department of State telegram, No. 485, 7 September 1983.

[4.] John Darnton, "Gromyko Defends Actions of Soviet in Plane Incident," *New York Times*, 8 September 1983, pp. A1–10; Richard Wigg, "Gromyko Insists Jet Was Spying," *The Times*, 8 September 1983, p. 1; and Hella Pick, "Attack Leaves East-West Relations in the Balance," *The Guardian*, 3 September 1983, p. 4.

[5.] Richard Wigg, "Gromyko Insists Jet Was Spying," *The Times*, 8 September 1983, p. 1; and Oswald Johnston, "Gromyko Angrily Puts Blame on U.S.," *Los Angeles Times*, 8 September 1983, Part I, pp. 1–14.

[6.] John Darnton, "Gromyko Defends Actions of Soviet in Plane Incident," *New York Times*, 8 September 1983, pp. A1–10; U.S. Department of State telegram, No. 665, 8 September 1983; and Jonathan Steele, "Gromyko Accuses US of Lying over Jet," *The Guardian*, 8 September 1983, p. 1.

[7.] Department of State telegram, No. 2628, 7 September 1983; and *Los Angeles Times*, "No One Can Judge Us, Soviet Says," 7 September 1983, Part I, p. 1.

[8.] Karen Elliott House, "Violators of Soviet Territory Must Assume Blame for Retaliation, Gromyko Declares," *Wall Street Journal*, 8 September 1983, p. 3; U.S. Department of State telegram, No. 679, 8 September 1983; and Jonathan Steele, "Gromyko Accuses US of Lying over Jet," *The Guardian*, 8 September 1983, p. 1.

[9.] U.S. Department of State telegram, No. 665, 8 September 1983; *Los Angeles Times*, "Shultz Meets Gromyko, Denounces Soviets' Explanation of Jet Downing," 8 September 1983 (late edition), Part I, p. 2; and Karen Elliott House, "Shultz Cuts Off Meeting with Gromyko, Denounces Soviet Stance on Korean Jet," *Wall Street Journal,* 9 September 1983, p. 2.

10. Peter Osnos, "Gromyko Threatens Further Soviet Violence," *Washington Post,* 8 September 1983, pp. A1–26; Don Oberdorfer, "Shultz Denounces Gromyko's Response," *Washington Post,* 9 September 1983, pp. A1–8; and Bernard Gwertzman, "Shultz Confronts Gromyko Directly on Plane Incident," *New York Times,* 9 September 1983, pp. A1–10.

11. Harold Jackson, "Reagan Goes It Alone with Jet Reprisals," *The Guardian,* 9 September 1983, p. 1.

12. Karen Elliott House, "Shultz Cuts Off Meeting with Gromyko, Denounces Soviet Stance on Korean Jet," *Wall Street Journal,* 9 September 1983, p. 2; *Los Angeles Times,* "Shultz Meets Gromyko, Denounces Soviets' Explanation of Jet Downing," 8 September 1983 (late edition), Part I, p. 2; and Harold Jackson, "Reagan Goes It Alone with Jet Reprisals," *The Guardian,* 9 September 1983, p. 1.

13. Harold Jackson, "Reagan Goes It Alone with Jet Reprisals," *The Guardian,* 9 September 1983, p. 1; Karen Elliott House, "Shultz Cuts Off Meeting with Gromyko, Denounces Soviet Stance on Korean Jet," *Wall Street Journal,* 9 September 1983, p. 2; and *Los Angeles Times,* "Shultz Meets Gromyko, Denounces Soviets' Explanation of Jet Downing," 8 September 1983 (late edition), Part I, p. 2.

14. *Los Angeles Times,* "Shultz Calls Russ 'Danger' to the World," 9 September 1983, Part I, p. 2; William Drozdiak, "Mitterand Tells Soviets to Renounce Use of Force Against Civilian Planes," *Washington Post,* 10 September 1983, p. A15; Don Oberdorfer, "U.S. Attacks Soviets at Madrid Finale," *Washington Post,* 10 September 1983, p. A15; and Bernard Gwertzman, "Shultz Assails the Russians but Asks 'Serious Dialogue,' " *New York Times,* 10 September 1983, p. 6.

15. Kevin Klose, "Aeroflot—a Curious Creation," *Japan Times,* 17 September 1983, p. 14; and *U.S. News & World Report,* "Why the West Won't Keep Aeroflot Down," 26 September 1983, p. 35.

16. Aeroflot was still permitted to use the Gander refueling facility for what Canadian Transport Minister Lloyd Axworthy called "odd, occasional" stops by Soviet diplomatic flights.

17. *Los Angeles Times,* "Canada Halts Soviet Airline's Landing Rights," 6 September 1983, Part I, p. 7; and U.S. Department of State telegram from Ottawa, Canada, No. 351, 6 September 1983.

18. *Daily Telegraph,* "Ground Staff Black Aeroflot," 3 September 1983, p. 1; *Japan Times* "London Ground Crews Boycott Aeroflot Jets," 4 September 1983, p. 5; and *Los Angeles Times,* "U.S. Could Shut Air Traffic to Soviets, Union Chief Says," 2 September 1983 (early edition), Part I, p. 1.

19. Jon Nordheimer, "International Pilots' Group Asks 60-Day Ban on Flights to Moscow," *New York Times,* 7 September 1983, pp. A1–16; *Los Angeles Times,* "World Pilots Ask 60-Day Ban on Airliner Flights to Moscow," 6 September 1983, Part I, p. 2; *Daily Telegraph,* "Soviet Air Space May Be Boycotted," 3 September 1983, p. 1; and G. S. Cooper, "Moscow Ban Sought," *Daily Telegraph,* 7 September 1983, p. 1.

20. *Daily Telegraph,* "Call for 'Air Ban' on U.S.S.R.," 6 September 1983, p. 4; *Los Angeles Times,* "More Nations' Pilots Join Boycott of Flights to Russia," 7 September 1983, Part I, p. 1; and *The Guardian,* "Aeroflot Is Vulnerable Target," 7 September 1983, p. 8.

21. David K. Willis, "West Europe Angry over Airliner but Reluctant to Retaliate," *Christian Science Monitor*, 7 September 1983, p. 3; *Los Angeles Times*, "World Pilots Ask 60-Day Ban on Airliner Flights to Moscow," 6 September 1983, Part I, p. 2; Jon Nordheimer, "International Pilots' Group Asks 60-Day Ban on Flights to Moscow," *New York Times*, 7 September 1983, pp. A1–16; and Jon Nordheimer, "European Pilots Join Ban on Moscow," *New York Times*, 8 September 1983, p. A11.

22. David K. Willis, "West Europe Angry over Airliner but Reluctant to Retaliate," *Christian Science Monitor*, 7 September 1983, p. 3; and William Drozdiak, "Allies Shy Away from Curbs on Aeroflot Flights," *Washington Post*, 7 September 1983, pp. A1–12.

23. *Japan Times*, "Pilots Join Ban," 9 September 1983, pp. 1–4; and Harold Jackson, "Reagan Goes It Alone with Jet Reprisals," *The Guardian*, 9 September 1983, p. 1.

24. Karen Elliott House, "Shultz Cuts Off Meeting with Gromyko, Denounces Soviet Stance on Korean Jet," *Wall Street Journal*, 9 September 1983, p. 2; *Japan Times*, "NATO Allies to Ban Soviet Air Travel," 10 September 1983, p. 1; Priscilla Painton, "NATO Countries Fail to Take Joint Action Against Soviets," *Washington Post*, 10 September 1983, p. A14; *New York Times*, "Most NATO Allies Said to Agree on Ban of Soviet Civilian Flights," 10 September 1983, p. 6; and *Los Angeles Times*, "Ban by 12 NATO Nations on Soviet Flights Reported," 10 September 1983, Part I, p. 27.

25. William Drozdiak, "Pilots Seek Action Against Soviet Union," *Washington Post*, 8 September 1983, pp. A1–26; G. S. Cooper, "BA Halts Flights to Moscow," *Daily Telegraph*, 9 September 1983; and Timothy D. Schellhardt and John D. Williams, "President Orders Aeroflot to Close Its 2 U.S. Offices," *Wall Street Journal*, 9 September 1983, pp. 2–16.

26. *Japan Times*, "Gov't Bares Civil Aviation Sanctions Against Soviets," 10 September 1983, p. 1.

27. In 1982, Aeroflot flew only fourteen nonscheduled flights between the Soviet Union and Japan. Japan Air Lines flew just one. Most of these were tourist flights during the summer. By the end of the summer of 1983, Aeroflot had already flown fifteen charter flights and JAL one. With the ban intended to last for only a limited time, few flights would be affected.

28. *FBIS*, Japan, "More Government Measures," 9 September 1983, pp. C1–2; *FBIS*, Japan, "Nakasone: KAL Downing Could Have Been 'Accidental,' " 9 September 1983, p. C1; *Japan Times*, "Kin of Downed KAL Jet Victims Silent About Gov't Sanctions Against Soviets," 10 September 1983, p. 2; Sam Jameson, "Japan Bans Aeroflot Charters, Urges Citizens to Boycott Airline," *Los Angeles Times*, 9 September 1983, Part I, p. 6; William Chapman, "Soviets to Turn Over Plane Debris," *Washington Post*, 9 September 1983, p. A8; and *FBIS*, Japan, "Retaliatory Measures Against USSR Announced," 9 September 1983, p. C1.

29. *New York Times*, "Status of Flights to Soviet Union," 14 September 1983, p. A13; *Aviation Week & Space Technology*, "Pilot Groups Considering Effects of Boycott Action," 26 September 1983, pp. 42–43; William Drozdiak, "Pilots Begin Soviet Boycott; Bonn, Madrid, Tokyo Set Ban," *Washington Post*, 13 September 1983, p. A15; and *New York Times*, "More Europeans Plan Boycotts of Flights to Soviet," 11 September 1983, p. 15.

30. *Daily Telegraph*, " 'Measured Sanctions' by Reagan," 9 September 1983, p. 1; U.S. Department of State telegram, No. 815, 9 September 1983; *New York*

Times, "Text of Reagan Letter to C.A.B. Chairman," 9 September 1983, p. A10; Michael Getler, "U.S. Closes Aeroflot's Two Offices," *Washington Post,* 9 September 1983, pp. A1–8; *Aviation Week & Space Technology,* "U.S. Actions Estimated to Cost Soviets $1.5–2 Million Annually," 19 September 1983, pp. 18–19; and George Skelton and Rudy Abramson, "Breaking All Business Ties with Aeroflot," *Los Angeles Times,* 9 September 1983, Part I, pp. 1–6.

31. Timothy D. Schellhardt and John D. Williams, "President Orders Aeroflot to Close Its 2 U.S. Offices," *Wall Street Journal,* 9 September 1983, pp. 2–16; and George Skelton and Rudy Abramson, "Breaking All Business Ties with Aeroflot," *Los Angeles Times,* 9 September 1983, Part I, pp. 1–6.

32. The full body of the ICAO meets only once every three years, whereas the thirty-three-member council is more or less continuously in session.

33. *Japan Times,* "ICAO to Probe KAL Case," 8 September 1983, p. 6; *Daily Telegraph,* "Call for 'Air Ban' on USSR," 6 September 1983, p. 4; U.S. Department of State telegram, No. 411, 7 September 1983; and Lou Cannon, "Reagan Announces Mild Sanctions on Soviets," *Washington Post,* 6 September 1983, pp. A1–5.

34. Bernard Gwertzman, "Flight Ban Sought," *New York Times,* 3 September 1983, pp. 1–4; and *Japan Times,* "Press Comments," 3 September 1983, p. 16.

35. *FBIS,* South Korea, "ROK to Press Case at UN," 6 September 1983, pp. E8–9; Michael Getler, "U.S. Closes Aeroflot's Two Offices," *Washington Post,* 9 September 1983, pp. A1–8; and *FBIS,* Soviet Union, "Reagan Orders Aeroflot Offices in U.S. Closed," 9 September 1983, p. DD3.

36. *The New Republic,* "Let's Make a Deal," 7 October 1985, p. 4; Robert C. Toth, "Reagan Close to Decision on New Missile Proposals," *Los Angeles Times,* 1 September 1983, Part I, p. 1; and Hella Pick, "Attack Leaves East-West Relations in the Balance," *The Guardian,* 3 September 1983, p. 4.

37. It was reminiscent of how, in early 1978, the Carter administration set up a CIA program to influence Western European media coverage of the NATO decision to deploy the controversial neutron bomb. The program included a plan to have U.S. sympathizers and agents in the European press corps give more favorable press coverage to the bomb, either for money or for free. By March 1978, the CIA reported, "It does appear that the combination of public statements by European officials, along with covert action program, had a marked effect on Western press coverage."

38. Tom Gervasi, *The Myth of Soviet Military Supremacy,* 1986, Harper & Row, New York, p. 152; *Japan Times,* "Carter Used CIA to Influence European Media," 5 November 1984; and Strobe Talbott, *Deadly Gambits: The Reagan Administration and the Stalemate in Nuclear Arms Control,* 1984, Knopf, New York, p. 59.

39. Elizabeth Pond, "NATO Missiles Damaging W. German Democracy?" *Christian Science Monitor,* 2 September 1983, pp. 1–16; and Tom Gervasi's Introduction in Darrell Garwood, *Under Cover: Thirty-Five Years of CIA Deception,* 1985, Grove Press, New York, p. 19.

40. Michael Farr, "Missiles 'Will Act as Incentive' to Talks," *Daily Telegraph,* 3 September 1983, p. 7; and *Los Angeles Times,* "Arms Protests Escalate in West Germany," 3 September 1983, Part I, p. 1.

41. Tyler Marshall, "2,000 W. Germans Protest U.S. Nuclear Missiles," *Los Angeles Times,* 2 September 1983, Part I, p. 11; interview with Adm. Eugene Carroll, December 1984; and Tom Gervasi, *The Myth of Soviet Military Supremacy,* 1986, Harper & Row, New York, p. 141.

42. Elizabeth Pond, "NATO Missiles Damaging W. German Democracy?" *Christian Science Monitor,* 2 September 1983, pp. 1–16; and David Halloway, *The Soviet Union and the Arms Race,* 1983, Yale University Press, New Haven, CT, p. 76.

43. This lack of concern with public opinion was reminiscent of Richard M. Nixon's response to the anti-war moratoriums held in the fall of 1969. Saying that policy "made in the streets" was equal to anarchy, Nixon declared that "under no circumstances will I be affected."

44. Elizabeth Pond, "NATO Missiles Damaging W. German Democracy?" *Christian Science Monitor,* 2 September 1983, pp. 1–16; and Stanley Karnow, *Vietnam: A History,* 1983, The Viking Press, New York, p. 399.

45. Tyler Marshall, "2,000 W. Germans Protest U.S. Nuclear Missiles," *Los Angeles Times,* 2 September 1983, Part I, p. 11.

46. Hendrick Smith, "A New Uneasiness About Soviet Tactics," *New York Times,* 3 September 1983, pp. 1–4; Michael Dobbs, "Europeans Stress Threat to East-West Ties," *Washington Post,* 3 September 1983, p. A24; U.S. Department of State telegram, No. 90, 2 September 1983; and *The Times,* "Be Firm, Be Skeptical," 5 September 1983.

47. Karen E. House, "Reagan Condemns Jet's 'Massacre' by Russia, but Shuns Tough Moves," *Wall Street Journal,* 6 September 1983, p. 3.

48. Paul Nitze seemed an unlikely choice for arms control negotiator. One of the principal architects of the Cold War and a man linked both professionally and personally to a large number of major American defense contractors, Nitze had compiled a career-long record of advocacy for increased defense spending, opposition to arms control, and intransigence toward the Soviet Union. Decades ago, he played a key role in gaining public support for increased defense spending by publicizing the famous, and fictitious, "missile gap." More recently, Nitze and other members of the Committee on the Present Danger were instrumental in making the equally fictitious "window of vulnerability" a campaign issue in 1980.

49. David Halloway, *The Soviet Union and the Arms Race,* 1983, Yale University Press, New Haven, CT, p. 72; *Los Angeles Times,* "U.S., Soviets Renew Talks on Missiles," 6 September 1983, Part I, p. 2; Hella Pick, "Attack Leaves East-West Relations in the Balance," *The Guardian,* 3 September 1983, p. 4; *Los Angeles Times,* "Geneva Talks Hinge on 162 Missiles," 6 September 1983, Part I, p. 8; Lou Cannon and Michael Getler, "Reagan Calls for 'Calm but Firm' Response," *Washington Post,* 4 September 1983, pp. A1–10; Bruce Vandervort, "U.S.: Geneva Arms Talks to Proceed Despite Plane Incident," *Washington Post,* 6 September 1983, p. A7; Department of State telegram, No. 1135, 13 September 1983; and George Skelton and Robert C. Toth, "Arms Talks Will Go On, Reagan Says," *Los Angeles Times,* 4 September 1983, Part I, pp. 1–22.

50. Hella Pick, "Attack Leaves East-West Relations in the Balance," *The Guardian,* 3 September 1983, p. 4; Bruce Vandervort, "U.S.: Geneva Arms Talks to Proceed Despite Plane Incident," *Washington Post,* 6 September 1983, p. A7; and James M. Markham, "Bonn Hopeful on Arms Talks," *New York Times,* 6 September 1983, p. A14.

51. *New York Times,* "Nitze Is Still Determined," 6 September 1983, p. A14; and Bruce Vandervort, "U.S.: Geneva Arms Talks to Proceed Despite Plane Incident," *Washington Post,* 6 September 1983, p. A7.

52. Hella Pick, "Forced Smiles as Geneva Talks Resume," *The Guardian,* 7 September 1983, p. 8; *New York Times,* "Smiles Curt in Geneva as Arms Talks

Restart," 7 September 1983, p. A16; *Los Angeles Times*, "U.S., Soviets Renew Talks on Missiles," 6 September 1983, Part I, p. 2; and *Japan Times*, "Next-to-Last Pershing 2 Flight Test Successful," 9 September 1983, p. 4.

53. *Los Angeles Times*, "Text of Soviet Statement Issued by Tass," 3 September 1983, Part I, p. 11; *New York Times*, "Text of Statement on the Airliner Incident," 4 September 1983, p. 16; *FBIS*, Soviet Union, "Unanswered Questions," 7 September 1983, pp. C12–14; and *FBIS*, Soviet Union, "U.S. 'Poisoning' Talks with KAL 'Provocation,' " 7 September 1983, pp. AA1–2.

54. Nicholas Ashford, "Americans Clamour for Retaliation," *The Times*, 3 September 1983, p. 4; Richard Owen, "Senior Military Commanders 'Took Decision to Open Fire,' " *The Times*, 5 September 1983; and Richard Pipes, "After Death in the Skies, What Now?" *Los Angeles Times*, 6 September 1983, Part II, p. 5.

55. Some have argued the mirror image of reality, saying that Flight 007's intrusion was actually a Soviet intelligence bonanza and a U.S. intelligence loss. For example, Paul C. Roberts of Georgetown's right-wing Center for Strategic and International Studies said of the Soviets, "Their gains are large and permanent. From what our government has revealed, and without losing a single agent of their own, the Soviets now know a great deal more about our intelligence capabilities. . . . It is a tragedy that the downed airliner may turn out to be a Soviet coup. In addition, this incident provides a testing and honing of their network of apologists."

56. Paul C. Roberts, "Again the Soviets Will Reap the Benefits," *Los Angeles Times*, 7 September 1983, Part II, p. 5; and Dusko Doder, "Kremlin Politics: An Inside Story of Three Soviet Leaders," *Washington Post National Weekly Edition*, 26 August 1985, pp. 6–10.

CHAPTER 12

1. Drew Middleton, "Strategic Soviet Region," *New York Times*, 2 September 1983, pp. A1–7; and Robert Gillette, "Soviets Accuse U.S. of Plot to Disrupt Talks," *Los Angeles Times*, 6 September 1983 (early edition), Part I, pp. 1–6.

2. Peter McGill, "Soviet Union Admits It Shot Down Jumbo," *Daily Telegraph*, 6 September 1983, p. 1; Richard Owen, "Senior Military Commanders 'Took Decision to Open Fire,' " *The Times*, 5 September 1983, p. 1; and Michael Getler, "U.S. Air Force Plane Crossed Path of Jet," *Washington Post*, 5 September 1983, pp. A1–9.

3. Hendrick Smith, "A New Uneasiness About Soviet Tactics," *New York Times*, 3 September 1983, pp. 1–4; and *Japan Times*, "U.S. Officials Speculate That Kremlin Had Not Ordered Downing of ROK Plane," 3 September 1983, p. 4.

4. Daniel Southerland, "Attitudes Toward Moscow Expected to Harden," *Christian Science Monitor*, 2 September 1983, pp. 1–8; Lou Cannon and Michael Getler, "Reagan Calls for 'Calm but Firm' Response," *Washington Post*, 4 September 1983, pp. A1–10; private source; and *Japan Times*, "U.S. Officials Speculate That Kremlin Had Not Ordered Downing of ROK Plane," 3 September 1983, p. 4.

5. Richard Owen, "Senior Military Commanders 'Took Decision to Open Fire,' " *The Times*, 5 September 1983, p. 1; and Robert Gillette, "Soviets Accuse U.S. of Plot to Disrupt Talks," *Los Angeles Times*, 6 September 1983 (early edition), Part I, pp. 1–6.

6. Govorov may have ordered the downing, but he was not one of those held responsible for the poor performance of the air defense forces. To the contrary,

less than a year later he was promoted to a deputy defense minister of the USSR. (*Source:* Radio Liberty Publications, RL, 86/84, 21 February 1984. Quoted in Alexander Dallin, *Black Box: KAL 007 and the Superpowers*, 1985, University of California Press, Berkeley, CA, p. 121.)

7. *Japan Times,* "Soviets Report Pilot Involved in 747 Downing," 8 September 1983, p. 4; and *FBIS*, Soviet Union, "Air Defense Forces Command," 7 September 1983, pp. C8–9.

8. Robert Gillette, "Soviets' Public Relations Disaster a Propaganda Coup at Home," *Los Angeles Times,* 8 September 1983, Part I, p. 15.

9. Serge Schmemann, "Pilot Who Shot Down Korean Jet Is Interviewed on Soviet Television," *New York Times,* 11 September 1983, pp. 1–16; and Peter Calvocoressi, "How Russia Hit an 'Own Goal,' " *The Sunday Times,* 11 September 1983, p. 1.

10. *FBIS*, Soviet Union, "Moscow Television Interviews Interceptor Pilots," 12 September 1983, pp. DD32–34; and Patrick Forman and Robin Morgan, "I Received a Precise, Definite Order to Destroy the Plane," *The Sunday Times,* 11 September 1983, p. 1.

11. In the continuing Soviet effort to convince the world that the KAL airliner had been a hostile intruder, the interview with the pilots was sold abroad even before it was shown to domestic audiences. The Kremlin apparently wanted to convey the image that the country was beset on all sides and was simply protecting itself from intrusions. The Russians seemed to think that the rest of the world would derive the same message and draw like conclusions from the film, but the rest of the world did not see it quite that way. Shortly thereafter, the words of the pilots were echoed by another military man of considerably greater stature. Three-star Col. Gen. Nikolai Moskvitilev, the commander of aviation under the Soviet air defense forces, appeared on Moscow's regular Sunday morning military program aimed at Soviet youth. In a performance described by the *Washington Post,* as "stilted and clearly rehearsed," Moskvitilev emphasized how similar an RC-135 is to a Boeing 747. According to the general, the two aircraft have "identical form and geometric dimensions." They have "analogous radar signatures." They have "an identical flight speed." "They can be distinguished in the air only during the day, visually and from a close distance. To do this at night is totally impossible for a pilot."

12. *FBIS*, Soviet Union, "Tass Report," 12 September 1983, pp. DD34; Serge Schmemann, "Reactions of Kremlin: How It Sees Itself and the World," *New York Times,* 14 September 1983, p. A13; Robert Gillette, "Soviet General Says RC-135 and 747 Identical in Size, Shape," *Washington Post,* 12 September 1983, p. A9; and Nigel Wade, "Planes 'Identical' to Soviet Pilots on Interception," *Daily Telegraph,* 12 September 1983.

13. Nigel Wade, "747 'Tried to Elude Fighters,' " *Daily Telegraph,* 14 September 1983.

14. Nigel Wade, "Red Army Chief to Face World Press," *Daily Telegraph,* 9 September 1983; John F. Burns, "Reporter's Notebook: Some Doubts Among Russians on Downing of Jet," *New York Times,* 2 October 1983, p. 14; and *Newsweek,* "The Army's 'Main Brain,' " 19 September 1983, p. 30.

15. Michael Dobbs, "Soviet Military Chief to Meet with Press," *Washington Post,* 9 September 1983, pp. A1–8; John F. Burns, "Crisis Brings Out the Worst in Moscow," *New York Times,* 11 September 1983, p. E2; and Robert Gillette, "Certain That Jet Spied, Soviets Say," *Los Angeles Times,* 10 September 1983, Part I, pp. 1–22.

16. Michael Dobbs, "Soviets Say Local Order Downed Jet," *Washington Post,* 10

September 1983, pp. A1–10; and Serge Schmemann, "An Extraordinary Event in Moscow," *New York Times*, 10 September 1983, p. 5.

[17.] Interview with CNN personnel in Atlanta, April 1984.

[18.] Nigel Wade, "Red Army Chief to Face World Press," *Daily Telegraph*, 9 September 1983.

[19.] *Japan Times*, "District Commander Ordered Jet Downed: Soviet Military Chief," 10 September 1983, pp. 1–4; and Richard Owen, "Moscow Admits That Missiles Destroyed Korean Airliner," *The Times*, 10 September 1983.

[20.] Serge Schmemann, "An Extraordinary Event in Moscow," *New York Times*, 10 September 1983, p. 5; and *New York Times*, "Transcript of Soviet Official's Statement and Excerpts from News Session," 10 September 1983, pp. 4–5.

[21.] *New York Times*, "Transcript of Soviet Official's Statement and Excerpts from News Session," 10 September 1983, pp. 4–5.

[22.] John F. Burns, "Soviet Says Order to Down Jet Came at a Local Level," *New York Times*, 10 September 1983, pp. 1–4; and Serge Schmemann, "An Extraordinary Event in Moscow," *New York Times*, 10 September 1983, p. 5.

[23.] *FBIS*, Soviet Union, "USSR Chief of Staff Ogarkov's Statement," 9 September 1983, pp. DD1–3.

[24.] *FBIS*, Soviet Union, "USSR Chief of Staff Ogarkov's Statement," 9 September 1983, pp. DD1–3; and *Los Angeles Times*, "News Agency Telex Repeats Soviet Stand," 9 September 1983, p. 6.

[25.] *FBIS*, Soviet Union, "USSR Chief of Staff Ogarkov's Statement," 9 September 1983, pp. DD1–3.

[26.] *FBIS*, Soviet Union, "USSR Chief of Staff Ogarkov's Statement," 9 September 1983, pp. DD1–3; *National Defense*, "Soviet Strategic Defense Programs," November 1985, pp. i–xxiv; and *New York Times*, "Transcript of Soviet Official's Statement and Excerpts from News Session," 10 September 1983, pp. 4–5.

[27.] Michael Dobbs, "Soviets Say Local Order Downed Jet," *Washington Post*, 10 September 1983, pp. A1–10; and *New York Times*, "Transcript of Soviet Official's Statement and Excerpts from News Session," 10 September 1983, pp. 4–5.

[28.] *New York Times*, "Transcript of Soviet Official's Statement and Excerpts from News Session," 10 September 1983, pp. 4–5.

[29.] *New York Times*, "Transcript of Soviet Official's Statement and Excerpts from News Session," 10 September 1983, pp. 4–5.

[30.] Personal communication from Victor Litvinski, 25 July 1984.

[31.] *New York Times*, "Transcript of Soviet Official's Statement and Excerpts from News Session," 10 September 1983, pp. 4–5; Nigel Wade, " 'Disbelief' at Soviet Claim of Interception on Doomed Plane," *Daily Telegraph*, 10 September 1983; and *Aviation Week & Space Technology*, "U.S. Intercepts Soviet Fighter Transmissions," 12 September 1983, pp. 22–23.

[32.] Michael Dobbs, "Soviets Say Local Order Downed Jet," *Washington Post*, 10 September 1983, pp. A1–10; *Los Angeles Times*, "Army Chief Defends Downing," 9 September 1983, Part I, pp. 1–2; and John F. Burns, "Soviet Says Order to Down Jet Came at a Local Level," *New York Times*, 10 September 1983, pp. 1–4.

[33.] Michael Dobbs, "Soviets Say Local Order Downed Jet," *Washington Post*, 10 September 1983, pp. A1–10; Nigel Wade, " 'Disbelief' at Soviet Claim of Interception on Doomed Plane," *Daily Telegraph*, 10 September 1983; and *New York Times*, "Transcript of Soviet Official's Statement and Excerpts from News Session," 10 September 1983, pp. 4–5.

34. *New York Times,* "Transcript of Soviet Official's Statement and Excerpts from News Session," 10 September 1983, pp. 4–5.
35. Serge Schmemann, "An Extraordinary Event in Moscow," *New York Times,* 10 September 1983, p. 5.
36. Robert C. Toth, "Soviet Charges on Airliner 'Absurd,' White House Says," *Los Angeles Times,* 10 September 1983, Part I, pp. 1–25; David Shribman, "U.S. Experts Say Soviet Didn't See Jet Was Civilian," *New York Times,* 7 October 1983, pp. A1–10; and David Fairhall, Michael Simmons, and Harold Jackson, "Kremlin Not Told Before Attack on Airliner," *The Guardian,* 10 September 1983, p. 1.
37. Juan Williams, "President Eschews Vengeance," *Washington Post,* 10 September 1983, pp. A1–16; and *Los Angeles Times,* "U.S. Disputes Soviets, Denies Spy Jet Charge," 9 September 1983, Part I, p. 1.

CHAPTER 13

1. U.S. Department of State telegram, 4 September 1983; and Blaine Harden, "Reagan Joins Mourners of Flight 007 Dead," *Washington Post,* 10 September 1983, p. A16.
2. Juan Williams, "President Eschews Vengeance," *Washington Post,* 10 September 1983, pp. A1–16; Department of State telegram, No. 256, 7 September 1983; Robert C. Toth, "Soviet Charges on Airliner 'Absurd,' White House Says," *Los Angeles Times,* 10 September 1983, Part I, pp. 1–25; Francis X. Clines, "Reagan Responds to Conservatives," *New York Times,* 10 September 1983, p. 6; and Blaine Harden, "Reagan Joins Mourners of Flight 007 Dead," *Washington Post,* 10 September 1983, p. A16.
3. Francis X. Clines, "Reagan Responds to Conservatives," *New York Times,* 10 September 1983, p. 6.
4. Blaine Harden, "Reagan Joins Mourners of Flight 007 Dead," *Washington Post,* 10 September 1983, p. A16.
5. Richard Beeston, "Moscow Version Scorned," *Daily Telegraph,* 10 September 1983; *Japan Times,* "Reagan Selects Sunday as Nat'l Day of Mourning," 11 September 1983, p. 4; U.S. Department of State, "Proclamation, Sept. 9, 1983," *KAL Flight #007: Compilation of Statements and Documents,* 1–16 September 1983, Washington DC, pp. 12–13; *Los Angeles Times,* "Reagan Declares Sunday Day of Mourning for Airliner Victims," 9 September 1983, Part I, p. 1; and Blaine Harden, "Reagan Joins Mourners of Flight 007 Dead," *Washington Post,* 10 September 1983, p. A16.
6. Francis X. Clines, "Reagan Says Russians 'Stonewalled the World,' " *New York Times,* 11 September 1983, p. 16; and Juan Williams and Don Oberdorfer, "President Castigates the Soviets," *Washington Post,* 11 September 1983, pp. A1–16.
7. U.S. Department of State, "President's Radio Address, Sept. 10, 1983," *KAL Flight #007: Compilation of Statements and Documents,* 1–16 September 1983, Washington, DC, p. 13.
8. Laurien Alexandre, "Propaganda Coup," *The Nation,* 17/24 August 1985, p. 106; U.S. Department of State telegram, No. 666, 8 September 1983; and *New York Times,* "Voice of America Is Telling Russians of Plane Incident," 5 September 1983, p. 4.
9. U.S. Department of State telegram, No. 668, 8 September 1983; Laurien Alex-

andre, "Propaganda Coup," *The Nation*, 17/24 August 1985, p. 106; Richard L. Strout, "U.S. Uses World Airwaves to Counter Soviet Rhetoric About KAL Incident," *Christian Science Monitor*, 26 September 1983, p. 3; and *New York Times*, "Voice of America Is Telling Russians of Plane Incident," 5 September 1983, p. 4.

10. Arik Bachar, "Nations Battle for Space on Airwaves," *Los Angeles Times*, 11 September 1983, Part I, pp. 2–12; and U.S. Department of State telegram, No. 668, 8 September 1983.

11. U.S. Department of State, "President's Radio Address, Sept. 10, 1983," *KAL Flight #007: Compilation of Statements and Documents*, 1–16 September 1983, Washington, DC, p. 13; and Laurien Alexandre, "Propaganda Coup," *The Nation*, 17/24 August 1985, p. 106.

12. The text was introduced by the Netherlands, on behalf of itself and a number of other countries, including the United States, Britain, France, Japan, Australia, New Zealand, Canada, Malaysia, and Fiji. The resolution's sponsors on the Security Council itself were the U.S., Britain, France, and the Netherlands.

13. Michael J. Berlin, "U.N. Motion Deplores Destruction of Plane, Faces Veto by Soviet," *Washington Post*, 9 September 1983, p. A9; and Bernard D. Nossiter, "U.S. and Allies Agree on a Reproach at U.N.," *New York Times*, 9 September 1983, p. A11.

14. Bernard D. Nossiter, "U.S. Postpones Vote in Security Council on Rebuke to Soviet over Airliner," *New York Times*, 10 September 1983, p. 5

15. Bernard D. Nossiter, "U.S. Postpones Vote in Security Council on Rebuke to Soviet over Airliner," *New York Times*, 10 September 1983, p. 5.

16. Michael Getler, "U.S. Closes Aeroflot's Two Offices," *Washington Post*, 9 September 1983, pp. A1–8; Kenneth Bredemeier, "Conservatives Plan Service for Airliner Victims," *Washington Post*, 10 September 1983, p. A13; and Mary McGrory, "Image of Andropov as a Shrewd Propagandist Has Dissolved," *Washington Post*, 13 September 1983, p. A3.

17. Also attending were such conservative luminaries as Senator Jesse Helms and former Georgia Governor Lester Maddox. South Korean Ambassador Lew Byong-hion led a delegation that included several other members of the embassy staff, a member of the South Korean Supreme Court, and the Korean Church Choirs of Washington.

18. William E. Farrell, "Conservatives Gather to Remember Georgian," *New York Times*, 12 September 1983, p. A10; and Ronald D. White, "3,700 Memorialize Airliner Victims; Soviets Condemned," *Washington Post*, 12 September 1983, p. A10.

19. Ronald D. White, "3,700 Memorialize Airliner Victims; Soviets Condemned," *Washington Post*, 12 September 1983, p. A10.

20. Ronald J. Ostrow, "McDonald Rites Turn Into Anti-Soviet Rally," *Los Angeles Times*, 12 September 1983, Part I, p. 16.

21. Elton Manzione, "The Private Spy Agency," *The National Reporter*, Summer 1985, pp. 34–39.

22. James Barron, "Outspoken General Raises Money for Contras," *New York Times*, 8 October 1986, p. A8; Ronald J. Ostrow, "McDonald Rites Turn Into Anti-Soviet Rally," *Los Angeles Times*, 12 September 1983, Part I, p. 16; and William E. Farrell, "Conservatives Gather to Remember Georgian," *New York Times*, 12 September 1983, p. A10.

23. *FBIS*, Japan, "New Transcripts in KAL Incident Released," 12 September 1983, p. C1; U.S. Department of State, "Department Statement, Sept. 11, 1983," *KAL*

Flight #007: Compilation of Statements and Documents, 1–16 September 1983, Washington, DC, pp. 13–14; U.S. Department of State, "Ambassador Kirkpatrick's Statement, U.N. Security Council, Sept. 6, 1983," *KAL Flight #007: Compilation of Statements and Documents,* 1–16 September 1983, Washington, DC, pp. 8–10; and *Los Angeles Times,* "Text of Soviet Statement Issued by Tass," 3 September 1983, Part I, p. 11.

24. *FBIS,* Soviet Union, "USSR Chief of Staff Ogarkov's Statement," 9 September 1983, pp. DD1–3.

25. Even this was incorrect. Properly translated, what was said was, "She is turned on. The strobe is flashing. . . . They do not see me."

26. ICAO Report, p. 31.

27. For a discussion of the correct translation for these passages, see Sugwon Kang, "Flight 007: Was There Foul Play?" *Bulletin of Concerned Asian Scholars,* 1985, Vol. 17, No. 2, pp. 30–48.

28. The correct translation was, "I am firing a burst from the cannons."

29. Cooper had remarked in other articles that an Su-15 fighter fired cannon bursts at KAL Flight 902 back in 1978, an inconsistency that escaped everyone, including Cooper himself.

30. Michael Getler, " 'An Incredibly Stupid' Decision Seen in Soviet Downing of Korean Airliner," *Washington Post,* 7 September 1983, p. A11; G. S. Cooper, " 'Flagon' Fired Missile," *Daily Telegraph,* 3 September 1983, p. 7; Department of State telegram, No. 951, 11 September 1983; Richard Burt quoted on BBC, "Panorama," 7 November 1983; and Clyde Haberman, "Flight 7's Final Moments: Did It Survive 12 Minutes?" *New York Times,* 13 September 1983, p. A10.

31. *Daily Yomiuri,* "New Assessment of KAL Incident Given," 18 September 1983.

32. Philip Taubman, "Korean Jet Signaled Russians, U.S. Says," *New York Times,* 3 September 1983 p. 6; and Alain Jacob, "A Criminal Act, Whichever Way You Look at It," *Le Monde,* 10 September 1983.

33. *Vancouver Sun,* "U.S. Revises Transcript of Soviet Pilot's Tapes," 12 September 1983, p. 1; John F. Burns, "Moscow Says Pilot Transcript Revision Proves U.S. Is Lying," *New York Times,* 13 September 1983, p. A10; and *FBIS,* Soviet Union, "Tass: U.S. Admits Lying in KAL Airliner Affair," 12 September 1983, pp. DD39–40.

34. Two changes were made in the document. One was simply changing the order of a paragraph. The other was more substantive, recognizing the importance of the principle of territorial integrity and the need to follow international procedures in response to violations of sovereign territory. This change was a nod to the undecided countries that felt the resolution's sponsors were slighting the concept of national sovereignty in their efforts to condemn the Russians. Ambassador Kirkpatrick and National Security Adviser William Clark had approved the text. (*Source:* Department of State information memorandum, No. 2936 [undated; probably 12 September 1983].)

35. These were Portugal, Venezuela, the Ivory Coast, Sudan, and Canada.

36. United Nations Press Release, "Security Council Fails to Adopt Draft Resolution Calling for Secretary General to Investigate Downing of Korean Airliner," SC/4556, 12 September 1983; and U.S. Department of State telegram, No. 1161, 13 September 1983.

37. Don Shannon, "U.N. Approves but Soviets Veto Airliner Inquiry," *Los Angeles Times,* 13 September 1983, Part I, pp. 1–10.

38. U.S. Department of State telegram, No. 1394, 17 September 1983; Michael J.

Berlin, "Kirkpatrick's Miracle at the United Nations: America Is Back," *Washington Post National Weekly Edition,* 7 January 1985, p. 18; and Bernard Gwertzman, "Aid to Zimbabwe Suspended by U.S.," *New York Times,* 10 July 1986, p. A5.

39. *Aviation Week & Space Technology,* "U.S. Intercepts Soviet Fighter Transmissions," 12 September 1983, pp. 22–23.

40. U.S. Department of State, "Acting Secretary Eagleburger's Statement, Sept. 6, 1983,"*KAL Flight #007: Compilation of Statements and Documents,* 1–16 September 1983, pp. 10–11; and U.S. Department of State, "Ambassador Kirkpatrick's Statement, U.N. Security Council, September 6, 1983," *KAL Flight #007: Compilation of Statements and Documents.* 1–16 September 1983, pp. 8–10.

41. BBC, "Panorama," 7 November 1983; ICAO Report, p. D-1; and Sugwon Kang, "Flight 007: Was There Foul Play?" *Bulletin of Concerned Asian Scholars,* 1985, Vol. 17, No. 2, pp. 30–48.

42. BBC, "Panorama," 7 November 1983; *Japan Times,* "Relatives Throw Flowers in Sea near Korean Airliner Crash Site," 5 September 1983, p. 2; ICAO Report, p. 31; and Michael Dobbs, "Soviet Military Chief to Meet with Press," *Washington Post,* 9 September 1983, pp. A1–8.

43. Yoshitaro Masuo, "Some Research into the Record of Communications of the Soviet Fighters Which Intercepted KAL 007," 1986 (unpublished paper).

44. *Los Angeles Times,* "Soviets Brush Off U.S. Claim for Jetliner Compensation," 12 September 1983, Part I, p. 2.

45. U.S. Department of State telegram, No. 1370, 16 September 1983.

46. *FBIS,* Australia, "Moves Against USSR over KAL Incident Discussed," 15 September 1983, p. M1; *Washington Post,* "Soviets Refuse Canada's Claim," 16 September 1983, p. A29; *FBIS,* Japan, "Soviet Envoy Refuses KAL Victim Compensation Note," 14 September 1983, p. C1; *FBIS,* Japan, "KAL Compensation Demands 'Rejected Outright,' " 15 September 1983, pp. C1–2; Sam Jameson, "Difficult to Identify 747 at Night, Japanese Says," *Los Angeles Times,* 15 September 1983, Part I, p. 14; and *FBIS,* Soviet Union, "USSR Embassy Rejects KAL Compensation Note," 19 September 1983, p. C3.

47. Helen Dewar, "Foreign Crises, Political Issues Top Hill Agenda," *Washington Post,* 11 September 1983, pp. A1–16; Hendrick Smith, "Soviet Has Handed Reagan a Powerful Argument for MX," *New York Times,* 11 September 1983, p. E4; Julia Malone, "More Congressmen Back Reagan on Defense in Wake of Jetliner Downing," *Christian Science Monitor,* 7 September 1983, p. 3; and Helen Dewar, "Foreign Crises, Politics Will Top Crowded Agenda as Congress Returns from Recess," *Los Angeles Times,* 11 September 1983, Part I, pp. 10–11.

48. Brad Knickerbocker, "Scowcroft: U.S. Needs Consensus on Arms if It Wants Pact with USSR," *Christian Science Monitor,* 2 September 1983, pp. 1–17; and *Los Angeles Times,* "Weak Case for the MX," 11 September 1983, Part IV, p. 4.

49. Rowland Evans and Robert Novak, " . . . A Mandate to Talk Tough," *Washington Post,* 5 September 1983, p. A17; Julia Malone, "Curtain Rises on a Congress Beset by Foreign Policy Issues," *Christian Science Monitor,* 13 September 1983, p. 3; Julia Malone, "More Congressmen Back Reagan on Defense in Wake of Jetliner Downing," *Christian Science Monitor,* 7 September 1983, p. 3; Richard Beeston, "Reagan Impresses Both Parties," *Daily Telegraph,* 8 September 1983; and Helen Dewar and T. R. Reid, "Incident to Bolster President's Hand, Congressmen Say," *Washington Post,* 7 September 1983, p. A13.

50. Binary weapons contain two gasses that are inert until mixed in flight in artillery shells or bombs. Then, the inert gasses become incredibly lethal. Production of nerve gas had been halted in 1969 by President Nixon. At the time of the downing of Flight 007, the U.S. had 38,000 tons of chemical warfare agents stored at nine sites in the U.S., Germany, and on Johnston Island in the Pacific. The Pentagon considered this insufficient, however, and had been lobbying for $6 billion over five years to replenish the nation's chemical warfare stockpile.

51. Richard Halloran, "House Approves Bill Ending Moratorium on Chemical Arms," *New York Times,* 16 September 1983, pp. A1–9; *U.S. News & World Report,* "Coming: Nerve Gas That Is 'Safer,' " 26 September 1983, p. 17; and *Japan Times,* "Senate OKs Defense Bill, but Fight Seen in House," 15 September 1983, p. 4.

52. Julia Malone, "Congress Returns to Face a Stronger Ronald Reagan," *Christian Science Monitor,* 12 September 1983, pp. 1–8.

53. Julia Malone, "Congress Returns to Face a Stronger Ronald Reagan," *Christian Science Monitor,* 12 September 1983, pp. 1–8; *Newsweek,* "A Ruthless Ambush in the Sky," 12 September 1983, pp. 16–30; and Steven R. Weisman, "Reagan Rides the Crest of an Anti-Soviet Wave," *New York Times,* 25 September 1983, p. E1.

54. Richard Beeston, "Reagan Impresses Both Parties," *Daily Telegraph,* 8 September 1983; and John Dillin, "Thunder on Reagan's Right," *Christian Science Monitor,* 16 September 1983, pp. 1–21.

55. Steven R. Weisman, "Reagan Rides the Crest of an Anti-Soviet Wave," *New York Times,* 25 September 1983, p. E1.

56. Daniel Southerland, "Restrained U.S. Reaction May Earn Political Points," *Christian Science Monitor,* 7 September 1983, pp. 1–7; John M. Goshko, "Reagan Confronting His Longtime Soviet Foes on Three Fronts," *Washington Post,* 12 September 1983, p. A8; Walter Pincus, "U.S. Drops Soviet Talks to Continue A-Arms Testing," *Washington Post,* 8 September 1983, p. A3; and Rowland Evans and Robert Novak, " . . . A Mandate to Talk Tough," *Washington Post,* 5 September 1983, p. A17.

57. *Los Angeles Times,* "Congress Ends Recess, Denounces Jet Downing," 12 September 1983, Part I, p. 1; and Martin Tolchin, "In Congress, Bitter Words and Demand for Sanctions," *New York Times,* 13 September 1983, p. A10.

58. Among other things, the bill allotted $4.8 billion for the MX, $430 million for Pershing II missiles, $340 million for research on laser weapons as part of the Star Wars program proposed by Reagan the previous March, and $144.6 million for chemical weapons.

59. Helen Dewar, "$187.5 Billion Bill for Defense Wins Approval in Senate," *Washington Post,* 14 September 1983, p. A2.

60. *Aviation Week & Space Technology,* "House Condemns Soviets for Attack on 747," 19 September 1983, p. 24; Don Irwin, "U.S. Seeks New Censure of Soviets," *Los Angeles Times,* 15 September 1983, Part I, p. 15; and Martin Tolchin, "House Condemns Soviet in 416–0 Vote," *New York Times,* 15 September 1983, p. A3.

61. Helen Dewar, "Senate Votes Soviet Condemnation but Bars Sanctions," *Washington Post,* 16 September 1983, p. A28; Martin Tolchin, "Shultz Tells Senate Reprisals Against Soviet Require World Support," *New York Times,* 14 September 1983, p. A12; and *Japan Times,* "Senate Conservatives Demand Further Sanctions on Moscow," 15 September 1983, p 4.

62. Martin Tolchin, "Senate, 95–0, Condemns Moscow; Sanctions Rejected," *New York Times,* 16 September 1983, p. A8.

63. Martin Tolchin, "Shultz Tells Senate Reprisals Against Soviet Require World Support," *New York Times*, 14 September 1983, p. A12; Helen Dewar, "Conservatives Seek Tougher Soviet Sanctions," *Washington Post*, 14 September 1983, p. A16; and Helen Dewar, "Senate Votes Soviet Condemnation but Bars Sanctions," *Washington Post*, 16 September 1983, p. A28.

64. Paul Houston, "Senate Condemns Attack on Korea Jet, Shuns Retaliation Call," *Los Angeles Times*, 16 September 1983, Part I, pp. 1–7; and Martin Tolchin, "Senate, 95–0, Condemns Moscow; Sanctions Rejected," *New York Times*, 16 September 1983, p. A8.

65. U.S. Department of State telegram, No. 1396, 17 September 1983; and Doyle McManus, "Pilots End Soviet Sanctions Early," *Los Angeles Times*, 1 October 1983, Part I, pp. 1–22.

66. Helen Dewar, "House Passes Defense Bill," *Washington Post*, 16 September 1983, pp. A1–29; and Eleanor Rudolph, "House Approves Record $187 Billion for Defense," *Los Angeles Times*, 16 September 1983, Part I, pp. 1–18.

67. The resolution called for a Soviet apology and asked Prime Minister Nakasone to make maximum efforts to ease world tensions and to do everything possible to promote arms reductions worldwide.

68. *FBIS*, "Further Sanction Levied Against USSR over KAL," 13 September 1983, pp. C1–2; Sam Jameson, "Japan Cuts Off Soviet Air Ties for 2 Weeks," *Los Angeles Times*, 13 September 1983, Part I, p. 1; *FBIS*, Japan, "Diet Resolution Condemns Downing," 12 September 1983, pp. C6–7; and U.S. Department of State telegram, No. 1214, 14 September 1983.

69. William Raspberry, "Arms and the Airliner," *Washington Post*, 23 September 1983, p. A17.

70. U.S. Department of State telegram No. 1364, 16 September 1983; *FBIS*, Japan, "Airliner Downing Draws Retaliation," 12 September 1983, p. C2; *Japan Times*, "Additional Anti-Soviet Sanctions Expected," 12 September 1983, p. 1; *FBIS*, Japan, "Further Sanction Levied Against USSR over KAL," 13 September 1983, pp. C1–2; and Michael Dobbs, "Moscow Airport Hit by Air Ban Begun by West," *Washington Post*, 16 September 1983, pp. A17–26.

71. In many respects, the Soviet response paralleled actions taken in the U.S. and other Western countries: They cancelled a performance of the thirty-member Buryat Ballet troupe that was to have begun a ten-day performance tour of Japan. Soviet scientists who were to have presented six technical papers on particle beam research at the Fifth International Conference on High-Power Particle Beams in San Francisco cancelled their appearance. Twenty Soviet scholars who had recently arrived in the U.S. for a year of study were called home, according to a spokesman for the Soviet embassy, because they might otherwise be subject to harassment, intimidation, and physical abuse. The Soviets withdrew from an international figure-skating competition to be held in Rochester, New York. Two Soviet players withdrew from the International Tennis Federation's world junior championships in Buena Vista, Florida. The Soviets also announced that they would not send a team to a pre-Olympic rowing and canoeing competition at Lake Casitas, California, the site of the rowing events for the 1984 Los Angeles Olympics.

72. William Drozdiak, "Pilots Begin Soviet Boycott; Bonn, Madrid, Tokyo Set Ban," *Washington Post*, 13 September 1983, p. A15; *FBIS*, Japan, "Soviet Ballet Troupe Forced to Cancel Tour," 14 September 1983, pp. C1–2; *Aviation Week & Space Technology*, "Soviet Scientists Cancel U.S. Appearance," 19 September 1983, p. 25; *Japan Times*, "Soviet Scholars Ordered Home to Avoid

Trouble," 18 September 1983, p. 4; Kevin Dupont, "Downing of Jet Has Tangled Soviet–U.S. Sports Exchange," *New York Times,* 21 September 1983, pp. A1–B15; *Japan Times,* "USSR to Boycott Rowing 'Due to Circumstances,' " 20 September 1983, p. 12; and *Los Angeles Times,* "Aeroflot Bars Tickets Issued by U.S. Lines," 14 September 1983, Part I, p. 1.

73. Richard Witkin, "Japan's Civil Radar Too Far Away to Pick Up 747," *New York Times,* 8 September 1983, p. A11; and *Globe & Mail,* "Tapes Suggest Mistakes by Pilots," 13 September 1983.

74. *Daily Yomiuri,* "Jet Signaled After Attack," 14 September 1983; and *FBIS,* South Korea, "Pilot Said to Have Made Contact After Missile Attack," 14 September 1983, p. E1.

75. Douglas B. Feaver, "Soviet Envoy Refuses to Accept U.S. Demand for Compensation," *Washington Post,* 13 September 1983, p. A15; and U.S. Department of State telegram, No. 1300, 15 September 1983.

76. U.S. Department of State telegram, No. 1311, 15 September 1983.

77. Philip Taubman, "U.S. Had Noticed Activity by Soviet," *New York Times,* 14 September 1983, p. A12; and Richard Halloran, "Soviet's Defenses Called Inflexible," *New York Times,* 18 September 1983, p. 17.

78. Philip Taubman, "U.S. Had Noticed Activity by Soviet," *New York Times,* 14 September 1983, p. A12.

79. Philip Taubman, "U.S. Had Noticed Activity by Soviet," *New York Times,* 14 September 1983, p. A12.

80. *Japan Times,* "Newsweek Poll," 12 September 1983, p. 1; and Adam Clymer, "Poll Finds Country Confused on Jet Downing," *New York Times,* 16 September 1983, pp. A1–8.

81. U.S. Department of State telegram, No. 1299, 15 September 1983; and *Japan Times,* "KAL Tragedy Dominates U.S. News," 18 September 1983, p. 3.

CHAPTER 14

1. The Soviet coordinates were later said to be:

46.15 N	140.15 E
47.10 N	140.15 E
47.10 N	141.35 E
46.35 N	141.25 E

2. The Soviet Union would deliver the debris to Japan rather than to the Republic of Korea because there were no diplomatic relations between Seoul and Moscow.

3. *New York Times,* "Soviet Envoy Pledges to Give Jet Debris to Japan," 9 September 1983, p. A11; *FBIS,* Japan, "Debris, Documents Reportedly Found," 9 September 1983, pp. C2–3; and *Los Angeles Times,* "Soviets Find Jet Debris, Say They'll Give It to Japan," 8 September 1983 (late edition), Part I, p. 2.

4. The coordinates for the find were said to be 45.12 N, 140.35 E.

5. *FBIS,* South Korea, "Paris Report on Debris Found," 9 September 1983, pp. E3–4; *FBIS,* South Korea, "DPA Further Reports on Find," 9 September 1983, p. E3; and *New York Times,* "Soviet Envoy Pledges to Give Jet Debris to Japan," 9 September 1983, p. A11.

[6] The site where the body was found was about 250 miles from where Flight 007 was believed to have crashed.

[7] *Japan Times,* "Debris from Downed KAL Jet Found, Police Say," 10 September 1983, pp. 1–2; *Boston Globe,* "747 Section, Child's Body Found off Japanese Island," 10 September 1983, p. 4; *Los Angeles Times,* "Body of Child, Piece of Downed Jetliner Found," 9 September 1983, Part I, p. 1; William Chapman, "Japan Says Recovered Body Could Be Airliner Victim," *Washington Post,* 10 September 1983, p. A14; and Clyde Haberman, "Japanese Recover Pieces of Airliner," *New York Times,* 10 September 1983, p. 4.

[8] Clyde Haberman, "Japanese Recover Pieces of Airliner," *New York Times,* 10 September 1983, p. 4; and *Boston Globe,* "747 Section, Child's Body Found off Japanese Island," 10 September 1983, p. 4.

[9] *Washington Post,* "ID Card and Body Found off Japan," 12 September 1983, p. A9; Sam Jameson, "KAL Passenger's ID Card Found by Japan Searchers," *Los Angeles Times,* 12 September 1983, Part I, p. 16; Clyde Haberman, "Seas off Japan Yielding Grim Flight 7 Debris," *New York Times,* 12 September 1983, pp. A1–10; *FBIS,* Japan, "KAL Search Continues: USSR Compensation Viewed," 12 September 1983, pp. C4–5; and *Japan Times,* "Coordinated Search Recovers More Debris from KAL Plane," 11 September 1983, p. 2.

[10] *FBIS,* Japan, "KAL Search Continues: USSR Compensation Viewed," 12 September 1983, pp. C4–5; Sam Jameson, "Fragments of Plane Tell of Fiery Deaths," *Los Angeles Times,* 11 September 1983, Part I, p. 25; and *Japan Times,* "Coordinated Search Recovers More Debris from KAL Plane," 11 September 1983, p. 2.

[11] Judith Timson, "A Death in the Family," *Saturday Night,* October 1984, pp. 23–33.

[12] *Los Angeles Times,* "S. Korea Will Seek More Sanctions Against Soviets," 14 September 1983, Part I, p. 8; Shigehiko Togo, "Japanese Gather Gruesome Debris of KAL Flight 007," *Washington Post,* 15 September 1983, pp A1–18; *Japan Times,* "Last Aeroflot Jet Leaves Narita Before Suspension," 15 September 1983, p. 2; *Los Angeles Times,* "Japanese Find 1st American ID from Airliner Wreckage," 15 September 1983, Part I, p. 1; and Clyde Haberman, "On the Sea of Japan, 20 Ships Comb for the Wreckage," *New York Times,* 20 September 1983, p. A10.

[13] Richard Beeston, "Moscow Version Scorned," *Daily Telegraph,* 10 September 1983; and *Los Angeles Times,* "Soviets May Fake Jet Evidence, Weinberger Says," 9 September 1983, Part I, p. 2.

[14] Lou Cannon, "Clark Accuses Soviets of 'Mass Murder,'" *Washington Post,* 15 September 1983, p. A17; *Japan Times,* "Soviets May Forge Data on Plane Espionage: U.S.," 18 September 1983, p. 3; and Michael Getler, "Soviet Disinformation Tactics Get Bolder, State Department Says," *Washington Post,* 17 September 1983, p. A9.

[15] The DFDR on board Flight 007 was made by Sundstrand Data Control, Inc., of Redmond, WA; model number 573A. It had received its last overhaul on 2 June 1983. The voice recorder was model 642C-1 made by Collins, Inc., a division of Rockwell International, based in Cedar Rapids, IA.

[16] ICAO Report, p. 28; Richard Witkin, "Search Narrowed for Wreckage of Jet," *New York Times,* 29 September 1983, p. A16; Peter Grier, "KAL 7's 'Black Box' Isn't Black—but It May Tell a Lot," *Christian Science Monitor,* 21 September 1983, pp. 1–4; *Japan Times,* " 'Black Boxes' Might Solve Puzzle of KAL Plane," 25 September 1983, p. 3; and *Aviation Week & Space*

Technology, "Search for Flight 007 Yields Bodies, Debris," 19 September 1983, pp. 22–23.

17. *Japan Times,* " 'Black Boxes' Might Solve Puzzle of KAL Plane," 25 September 1983, p. 3.

18. U.S. Department of State telegram, No. 679, 8 September 1983; *FBIS,* Japan, "Search Continues," 9 September 1983, p. C3; *Japan Times,* "12 Soviet Vessels Seen in Apparent Search for KAL Jet," 8 September 1983, p. 2; and *FBIS,* Japan, "Patrol Ships Search Waters," 8 September 1983, p. C2.

19. Normally operated by a crew of seventeen civil service mariners, the ship's crew had been doubled by adding additional civilian and military personnel, including four military communications specialists.

20. *Los Angeles Times,* "Aeroflot Bars Tickets Issued by U.S. Lines," 14 September 1983, Part I, p. 1; Skye Dent, "Sailors Recall the Futile Search for Korean Plane's 'Black Box,' " *The Tribune* (Oakland), 22 January 1984, p. C5; and Michael Getler, "Black Box Beeps Heard by Crews Seeking Wreckage," *Washington Post,* 20 September 1983, pp. A1–11.

21. Michael Getler, "U.S. Says Soviet Ships Harass Plane-Data Searchers," *Washington Post,* 21 September 1983, pp. A1–27; *Visnews News Service,* "New Underwater Device Is Used in Search for the Flight Recorder from the Downed Korean Airliner," 30 September 1983; and *Japan Times,* "U.S. Navy Sounding Sea of Japan for Black Box," 15 September 1983, p. 5.

22. *Japan Times,* "Coordinated Search Recovers More Debris from KAL Plane," 11 September 1983, p. 2; and *Washington Post,* "ID Card and Body Found off Japan," 12 September 1983, p. A9.

23. *FBIS* South Korea, "Factfinders to Japan, U.S.," 14 September 1983, p. E1; *FBIS,* South Korea, "Minister Pledges Efforts for Soviet Reparations," 15 September 1983, pp. E1–2; *Aviation Week & Space Technology,* "Soviets Harass Searchers for 747 Debris," 12 September 1983, p. 28; A. E. Cullison, "Russians Bring in Submersible to Seek Jetliner," *Daily Telegraph,* 16 September 1983, p. 6; and *Boston Globe,* "Soviets May Have Found Jet Wreckage," 15 September 1983, pp. 1–2A.

24. Clyde Haberman, "Search Goes On for Jet's 'Black Box,' " *New York Times,* 23 September 1983, p. A3.

25. *Japan Times,* "Soviets Remove Unidentified Object from Sea of Japan," 18 September 1983, p. 2; *FBIS,* Japan, "Object Reportedly Recovered," 19 September 1983, p. C4; and *Japan Times,* "Soviets May Have Found Important KAL Jet Parts," 17 September 1983, p. 2.

26. Clyde Haberman, "Search Goes On for Jet's 'Black Box,' " *New York Times,* 23 September 1983, p. A3.

27. *Washington Post,* "Technicians Recapture More of Airliner's Last Message," 17 September 1983, p. A12; and Clyde Haberman, "On the Sea of Japan, 20 Ships Comb for the Wreckage," *New York Times,* 20 September 1983, p. A10.

28. Clyde Haberman, "On the Sea of Japan, 20 Ships Comb for the Wreckage," *New York Times,* 20 September 1983, p. A10; *Japan Times,* "Soviet Sumbersibles Searching for Jet," 20 September 1983, p. 2; and *FBIS,* Japan, "Submersibles Involved in Effort," 19 September 1983, pp. C3–4.

29. Michael Getler, "U.S. Says Soviet Ships Harass Plane-Data Searchers," *Washington Post,* 21 September 1983, pp. A1–27; and Michael Getler, "Black Box Beeps Heard by Crews Seeking Wreckage," *Washington Post,* 20 September 1983, pp. A1–11.

CHAPTER 15

1. Robert D. McFadden, "2 Airports Closed to Russians," *New York Times*, 16 September 1983, p. A9; and *Washington Post*, "The Gromyko Plot," 20 September 1983, p. A14.

2. In an editorial, the *New York Times*, denounced the governors' action as the "Glen Cove Disease," an infirmity where local politicians imagine themselves to be Secretary of State or President, and take charge of diplomacy in a fit of demagoguery.

3. Don Oberdorfer and David Hoffman, "Public and Political Sentiment Seen Key to the Gromyko Episode," *Washington Post*, 22 September 1983, p. A18; Robert D. McFadden, "How 2 Governors Reached Decision," *New York Times*, 18 September 1983, p. 19; Robert D. McFadden, "2 Airports Closed to Russians," *New York Times*, 16 September 1983, p. A9; and *New York Times*, "Earfuls, Eyefuls," 18 September 1983, p. E18.

4. *Los Angeles Times*, "Speakes Says States Had Right to Block Gromyko," 19 September 1983, Part I, p. 2; Bernard Gwertzman, "Reagan Asserts Downing of Jet Isolates Moscow," *New York Times*, 18 September 1983, pp. 1–18; and Harry B. Ellis, "Long-Range Outlook for US–Soviet Relations," *Christian Science Monitor*, 20 September 1983, pp. 1–10.

5. Oswald Johnston, "Gromyko May Land in U.S. but Not on Aeroflot," *Los Angeles Times*, 17 September 1983, Part I, pp. 1–16; *Washington Post*, "Soviet Statement Assails 'Violation . . . of Norms,' " 18 September 1983, p. A28; and Michael Dobbs, "Gromyko Cancels Trip to U.N. After Flights Restricted," *Washington Post*, 18 September 1983, pp. A1–28.

6. Don Oberdorfer and Juan Williams, "Administration Shows No Sign of Regret," *Washington Post*, 18 September 1983, pp. A1–29; and *New York Times*, "At U.N., Some Still Hope for a Reversal," 18 September 1983, p. 18.

7. *New York Times*, "U.N. Disagrees with U.S.," 17 September 1983, p. 3; Department of State Operations Center, Situation Report No. 32, No. 2883, 16 September 1983; and Bernard Gwertzman, "U.S. Officials See Crisis with Soviet Lasting into 1984," *New York Times*, 19 September 1983, pp. A1–8.

8. *Los Angeles Times*, "Speakes Says States Had Right to Block Gromyko's Landing," 19 September 1983, Part I, p. 2; and Department of State telegram, No. 2888, 17 September 1983.

9. *Washington Post*, "Soviet Statement Assails 'Violation . . . of Norms,' " 18 September 1983, p. A28; *Los Angeles Times*, "Tantrums at the U.N.," 21 September 1983, Part II, p. 6; George Skelton, "U.N. 'Double Standard' to Be Reagan Target," *Los Angeles Times*, 24 September 1983, Part I, pp. 1–24; and *Japan Times*, "Soviet U.N. Envoys Land in New York via Belgium Airliner," 21 September 1983, p. 3.

10. *FBIS*, Japan, "NHK Analyzes KAL Pilot's Communication," 19 September 1983, pp. C2–3.

11. The *Los Angeles Times* quoted Suzuki as saying that at the end of the transmission the pilot's voice suddenly rose in pitch to 240 hertz, "which was probably as loud a voice as he could make." (*Sources: FBIS*, Japan, "NHK Analyzes KAL Pilot's Communication," 19 September 1983, pp. C2–3; and Sam Jameson, "Downed Plane's Pilot Told of Engine, Pressure Loss," *Los Angeles Times*, 17 September 1983, Part I, pp. 1–14.)

12. *Japan Times*, "KAL Jet Sent Last Message," 17 September 1983, pp. 1–4.

13. *New York Times*, "Soviet Asserts Korean Pilot Boasted of Spying for C.I.A.,"

17 September 1983, p. 3; and Sam Jameson, "Downed Plane's Pilot Told of Engine, Pressure Loss," *Los Angeles Times,* 17 September 1983, Part I, pp. 1–14.

14. Michael Dobbs, "Soviets: 747 Was Part of Spy Network," *Washington Post,* 20 September 1983, pp. A1–11.

15. ABC News "Nightline," "Korean Air Tragedy," Show No. 604, 1 September 1983, p. 7; and *Asahi Evening News,* "SDF Played Important Role in Finding Facts About KAL Case," 3 September 1983.

16. *FBIS,* Soviet Union, " 'Direct Involvement' of CIA in Aircraft Case," 6 September 1983, pp. C11–12; *FBIS,* Soviet Union, "Tass Reports KAL's 'Deliberate Provocation,' " 6 September 1983, pp. C6–8; and *FBIS,* Soviet Union, "U.S. 'Poisoning' Talks with KAL 'Provocation,' " 7 September 1983, pp. AA1–2.

17. Such to-the-minute coordination between Flight 007 and the satellite hardly seems necessary. If the goal was collection of signals intelligence, all that the satellite had to do was pass over while Flight 007 was somewhere over Soviet territory. The airliner was over Kamchatka, for example, for more than half an hour.

18. All references to the Kirsanov article are from: *FBIS,* Soviet Union, "U.S. 'Strategic, Political Objectives' Seen," 20 September 1983, pp. DD1–4; and *Globe and Mail,* "Jet's Route Linked to Satellite's Path, Soviet Report Says," 20 September 1983, p. 8.

19. Michael Getler, "U.S. Says Soviet Ships Harass Plane-Data Searchers," *Washington Post,* 21 September 1983, pp. A1–27; Michael Dobbs, "Soviets: 747 Was Part of Spy Network," *Washington Post,* 20 September 1983, pp. A1–11; Serge Schmemann, "Soviet Cites Role of U.S. Satellite," *New York Times,* 20 September 1983, p. A8; *Asahi Evening News,* "Charge Jet, Satellite," 20 September 1983; and *Aviation Week & Space Technology,* "Soviets Charge U.S. Aligned 747 with Satellite, Aircraft," 26 September 1983, pp. 42–43.

20. *Los Angeles Herald Examiner,* "U.S. May Have Found 'Crucial Portions' of Jet," 22 September 1983; and *Japan Times,* "NBC Says KAL Jet Off Course Leaving Alaska," 23 September 1983.

21. John F. Burns, "Soviet Starts Making Some Admissions," *New York Times,* 24 September 1983, p. 3; *Aviation Week & Space Technology,* "Washington Roundup," 26 September 1983, p. 25; *Washington Post,* "Soviet Official Acknowledges Pilots Erred," 22 September 1983, p. A18; and *FBIS,* Soviet Union, "Soviet Official Denies Statement Made to BBC," 22 September 1983, p. DD1.

22. *FBIS,* Soviet Union, "Soviet Official Denies Statement Made to BBC," 22 September 1983, p. DD1; and *FBIS,* Soviet Union, " 'Very Angry' at BBC Interview," 22 September 1983, pp. DD1–2.

23. Headlines appeared in Western newspapers trumpeting the supposed admission of Soviet guilt. "Soviet Official Acknowledges Pilots Erred," wrote the *Washington Post.* "Soviet Delegate Admits Error in Plane Incident," said the *New York Times.* Since a story admitting the BBC had misquoted Linnyk was by no means as newsworthy as Linnyk saying the Soviets had made an error in downing Flight 007, the obvious follow-up story—that an error had been made—received practically no media attention at all.

24. Such an action is extraordinary. That the Department of State would disclose that U.S. intelligence was reading Soviet bloc embassy codes just to prove a trivial point is, one former diplomat noted, unthinkable.

25. *The Washington Spectator,* "Russian Roulette in the North Pacific," 15 May 1984, pp. 1–3; and John Keppel, personal communication.

26. The President's speech was heard in Moscow at 8:00 p.m., when many city people are out at their country *dachas*. According to a VOA official, this was helpful because jamming is much less effective in the country than in the city. (*Source:* Richard L. Strout, "U.S. Uses World Airwaves to Counter Soviet Rhetoric About KAL Incident," *Christian Science Monitor,* 26 September 1983, p. 3.)

27. Don Irwin, "Reagan Aims Talk at Soviet People," *Los Angeles Times,* 25 September 1983, Part I, pp. 1–16; *Japan Times,* "Reagan's Radio Broadcast Beamed into Soviet Union," 26 September 1983, p. 1; and Serge Schmemann, "Soviet Denounces Reagan's Address," *New York Times,* 26 September 1983, p. A7.

28. *FBIS,* Japan, "Patrol Boat Sent to Sakhalin," 21 September 1983, p. C1; and *Japan Times,* "Bereaved Persons," 21 September 1983, p. 2.

29. *FBIS,* Japan, "Patrol Boat Sent to Sakhalin," 21 September 1983, p. C1; U.S. Department of State telegram, No. 1501, 21 September 1983; *Japan Times,* "Japan–U.S. Team Will Go to Sakhalin to Get KAL Objects," 25 September 1983, p. 2; and *Japan Times,* "Soviets Will Turn Over KAL Items on Monday," 22 September 1983, p. 1.

30. Clyde Haberman, "Soviet Hands Over Debris from Korean Plane," *New York Times,* 27 September 1983, p. A9; and Michael Weisskopf, "Soviets Give Over Jet Debris, but Cargo Barren for Mourner," *Washington Post,* 27 September 1983, p. A14.

31. Michael Weisskopf, "Soviets Give Over Jet Debris, but Cargo Barren for Mourner," *Washington Post,* 27 September 1983, pp. A14; and *Los Angeles Herald Examiner,* "Black Box May Be Located," 27 September 1983, p. 1.

32. All the structural material turned over by the Soviets appears to have been flotsam—floating debris—with one exception. One piece of metal was later put into water, and it promptly sank.

33. Clyde Haberman, "Soviet Hands Over Debris from Korean Plane," *New York Times,* 27 September 1983, p. A9; *Life,* "The Infamous Downing of Korean Air Lines Flight 007," January 1984, pp. 99–108; ICAO Report, p. 29; and Department of State telegram, No. 2920, 24 September 1983.

34. Clyde Haberman, "Soviet Hands Over Debris from Korean Plane," *New York Times,* 27 September 1983, p. A9.; and *FBIS,* Japan, "Japanese Official: USSR 'May Have Recovered' Bodies," 29 September 1983, pp. C1–2.

35. During the period December 19–21, 1983, a second expedition to Sakhalin was undertaken to collect additional items from the Soviets. Ten articles were picked up, which were turned over to the Hokkaido prefectural office on December 23 for display with the other items still there. In the second batch of items were seven rolls of textiles, a vinyl shower curtain, a pamphlet published by the Gale Corporation of New Jersey on soundproofing materials, and a book entitled *Banking in London,* published by Peat, Marwick, Mitchell, and Co. None of the items had any markings identifying the owners. This second trip to Sakhalin received no publicity whatever in the U.S. press.

36. Michael Weisskopf, "Soviets Give Over Jet Debris, but Cargo Barren for Mourner,"*Washington Post,* 27 September 1983, pp. A14; U.S. Department of State telegram, No. 2231, 29 December 1983; and *FBIS,* Japan, "Officials Receive 76 Items," 27 September 1983, pp. C3–4.

37. ICAO Report, p. 28; and *Japan Times,* "KAL Jet Items to Be Displayed," 30 September 1983, p. 2.

38. *FBIS,* Japan, "KAL Debris Airlifted from Hokkaido to Seoul," 6 October 1983, p. C2; and *FBIS,* Japan, "Remnants of KAL Airliner to Be Sent to South Korea," 4 October 1983, p. C2.

39. Geoffrey Murray, "Under Soviet Eyes, U.S. and Japan Hold Sea Exercises," *Christian Science Monitor,* 22 September 1983, p. 6.

40. Richard Halloran, "Tokyo Aides Worry About Missile Offer by U.S. to Russians," *New York Times,* 25 September 1983, p. 19; and David Wood, "Japan Tells Weinberger It Fears for Security in U.S.-Soviet Arms Pact," *Los Angeles Times,* 25 September 1983, Part I, p. 8.

41. Michael Weisskopf, "KAL Downing Spurs Japanese Defense Boomlet," *Washington Post,* 8 October 1983, p. A28.

42. It was in order to be able to bottle-up the Soviet fleet that the Pentagon requested, and Congress approved, $17 million for FY 1984 to base U.S. F-16 fighters at Misawa Air Base on the island of Honshu. Eventually, between forty and fifty of the F-16s were deployed at Misawa.

43. *FBIS,* Japan, "Japan–U.S. Joint Sealane Defense Exercise Begins," 27 September 1983, p. C8; *Japan Times,* "U.S. House Approves F-16 Deployment in Misawa," 25 September 1983, p. 1; and Geoffrey Murray, "Under Soviet Eyes, U.S. and Japan Hold Sea Exercises," *Christian Science Monitor,* 22 September 1983, p. 6.

44. *Japan Times,* "Carrier Will Refrain from Naval Maneuver," 26 September 1983, p. 1; Geoffrey Murray, "Under Soviet Eyes, U.S. and Japan Hold Sea Exercises," *Christian Science Monitor,* 22 September 1983, p.6; and *FBIS,* Japan, "Five Soviet Warships Sighted Around Japan," 4 October 1983, p. C2.

45. The agreement was reached because of the dangerous tactics used by both Soviet and American naval vessels and aircraft. They would follow each other all over the world, often coming perilously close. In the late 1960s and early 1970s, this practice had turned into a conscious game of chicken on the high seas. Intimidating tactics were often employed, such as aiming a ship's guns and missiles at the adversary. Acknowledging the inherent potential for military confrontation in this situation, the Incidents at Sea Agreement established rules for conduct between vessels and aircraft, set up procedures for communications between commanders, and established meetings that were to take place twice a year to review the whole process.

46. Michael Getler, "U.S. Says Soviet Ships Harass Plane-Data Searchers," *Washington Post,* 21 September 1983, pp. A1–27; *FBIS,* Soviet Union, "U.S. Accused of Hampering KAL Debris Hunters," 28 September 1983, p. DD1; William Ury, "Beyond the Hotline," *Parade Magazine,* 24 February 1985, pp. 8–17; and Richard Halloran, "U.S. Search Vessels Pick Up Black-Box Signals," *Los Angeles Herald Examiner,* 21 September 1983, p. A5.

47. *Los Angeles Times,* "Weather Snarls Hunt for 'Black Boxes,' " 25 September 1983, Part I, p. 5.

48. David Wood, "Possible 'Black Box' Beeps No Longer Heard, U.S. Says," *Los Angeles Times,* 21 September 1983, Part I, p. 15; and Skye Dent, "Sailors Recall the Futile Search for Korean Plane's 'Black Box,' " *The Tribune* (Oakland), 22 January 1984, p. C5.

49. *Los Angeles Herald Examiner,* "U.S. May Have Found 'Crucial Portions' of Jet," 22 September 1983; *Washington Post,* "Soviet Official Acknowledges Pilots Erred," 22 September 1983, p. A18; and Clyde Haberman, "Search Goes On for Jet's 'Black Box,' " *New York Times,* 23 September 1983, p. A3.

50. *FBIS,* South Korea, "Soviet Refusal of ROK Entry to Sakhalin Noted," 26 September 1983, pp. E1–2; *The Times,* "Armada Hunts for Black Box," 23 September 1983, p. 6; U.S. Department of State telegram, No. 1553, 22 September 1983; and *Japan Times,* "Search Suspended," 25 September 1983, p. 2.

51. Seven U.S. ships had assembled off Moneron Island in a search area that had

been narrowed to 15 square miles—down from the 3,000-square-mile area of a week before.

52. *FBIS*, Japan, "ICAO Experts Arrive," 27 September 1983, p. C9; *FBIS*, Japan, "Black Box Search Narrows; Gotoda on USSR Attitude," 27 September 1983, p. C2; *Globe and Mail* (Toronto), "U.S. Search for Black Box 'Narrowed,' " 28 September 1983; Michael Getler, "Navy Narrow Search for Two Black Boxes from Korean Airliner," *Washington Post,* 28 September 1983, p. A14; and Richard Witkin, "Search Narrowed for Wreckage of Jet," *New York Times,* 29 September 1983, p. A16.

53. *FBIS*, Japan, "Late Report: U.S. Said to Find Black Box," 27 September 1983, p. C9; *Microwave Systems News,* "Has 007's 'Black Box' Been Found?" November 1983, p. 48; and private sources.

54. How can the numerous stories that the flight recorders were recovered be reconciled with the evidence that they were not? One source speculated that while the U.S. did not recover the black boxes, it wanted certain people to believe it had. The reason was to prevent inquiry into the incident. Many members of Congress were well aware of the flimsiness and contradictions in the Administration's official version of events, and it would be necessary to keep them from delving too deeply into the matter. How could this be done? One answer, turning Caspar Weinberger's suggestion on its head, might be to produce "some black box dripping with seaweed." A black box that, when queried, showed our allies the Koreans to be wholly responsible.

In this scenario, the Navy pretended to recover the flight recorders while making denials to the press. Stories then appeared saying that Washington was privately approached by Seoul with the request that the discovery of the black box be kept secret, to which the U.S. agreed. Such an elaborate charade would have served two purposes with respect to Congress. First, it would obviate the need to make the black box public, since it was necessary to protect an important American ally. This also ensured that no outside investigators would examine the black box and find it to be a fake. Second, the manufactured evidence it contained would simultaneously explain any evidence of the flight's intentionality while convincing members of Congress not to probe too deeply into the matter. (Yes, the flight was guilty, and that's why there's evidence to that effect. But the Koreans did it, and we have to protect our ally.) Such a scenario absolves the U.S. of guilt and forecloses investigation at a cost of only making the Koreans appear unsavory to a few key members of Congress.

55. *FBIS*, Japan, "Gotoda Denies Rumors of KAL Black Box Discovery," 28 September 1983, p. C1; Michael Weisskopf, "Soviets Give Over Jet Debris, but Cargo Barren for Mourner," *Washington Post,* 27 September 1983, p. A14; *Los Angeles Times,* "Black Box Find Denied," 27 September 1983, Part I, p. 1; and *Los Angeles Herald Examiner,* "High Winds Slow Sea Search for Jetliner Wreckage," 28 September 1983, p. A4.

56. *New York Times,* "Text of President's Address at U.N.," 27 September 1983, p. A16; and *Los Angeles Times,* "U.N. Assembly to Hear Reagan," 9 September 1983, Part I, p. 1.

57. Leon Wieseltier, "President Alters Arms-Control Rhetoric in Search of a New Deal," *Los Angeles Times,* 2 October 1983, Part IV, pp. 1–6; and Steven R. Weisman, "Reagan Says U.S. Is Willing to Cut Back on Warheads It Wants to Base in Europe," *New York Times,* 27 September 1983, pp. A1–17.

58. Richard Bernstein, "Reagan at the U.N.: Cheers and Folded Hands," *New York Times,* 27 September 1983, p. A15.

59. *FBIS*, Japan, "Ban Not to Be Extended," 27 September 1983, p. C3; *New York Times*, "As Boycotts End, Soviet Flights Return to Normal," 2 October 1983, p. 13; and U.S. Department of State telegram, No. 2061, 4 November 1983.

60. Richard Witkin, "Pilots Urge End to the Boycott of Soviet Flights," *New York Times*, 1 October 1983, pp. 1–5.

61. Doyle McManus, "Pilots End Soviet Sanctions Early," *Los Angeles Times*, 1 October 1983, Part I, pp. 1–22; and Roger Fontaine, "U.S. Rhetoric Tough, but Action Fell Short," *Washington Times*, 31 August 1984, pp. A1–9.

62. *New York Times*, "As Boycotts End, Soviet Flights Return to Normal," 2 October 1983, p. 13.

63. United Nations Press Release, *ICAO Council Examines Follow-Up of Korean Air Lines Incident*, ICAO/699, 24 October 1983; Congress of the U.S., House of Representatives, *Aircraft Navigation Technology and Errors*, Hearing Before the Subcommittee on Transportation, Aviation and Materials of the Committee on Science and Technology, 19 September 1983, Washington, DC, p. 23; *Aviation Week & Space Technology*, "Carriers Say R20 Closing Causing Delays," 26 September 1983, p. 43; and *New York Times*, "Pacific Air Corridor to Reopen Sunday," 28 September 1983, p. A3.

64. *Aviation Week & Space Technology*, "Carriers Say R20 Closing Causing Delays," 26 September 1983, p. 43; *New York Times*, "Pacific Air Corridor to Reopen Sunday," 28 September 1983, p. A3; Douglas B. Feaver, "FAA Seeks New Route Rules," *Washington Post*, 6 September 1983, p. A4; Douglas B. Feaver, "KAL Jet's Path Strewn with Lawsuits and New Tracking Policies," *Washington Post*, 31 December 1983, p. A6; and *Aviation Week & Space Technology*, "Northern Pacific Radar," 3 October 1983, p. 33.

65. In the next few months, the FAA would take a series of other steps. Tracking data from the Air Force radar at King Salmon would be actively monitored instead of merely being available to controllers at their discretion. Air Force personnel at Cape Newenham were instructed to inform air traffic controllers if a deviation in an airliner's course exceeded 10 miles. U.S. airliners were ordered to use the VOR/DME on Shemya, as opposed to having the option (Korean Air Lines required its crews to use the navigational aid). FAA controllers began temporary duty on Shemya Island to monitor the progress of flights on the NOPAC routes, at a cost of $8,300 every two weeks. Air Force personnel had done this for the first six weeks subsequent to the downing but asked the FAA to take over.

66. *Globe & Mail* (Toronto), "U.S. Search for Black Box Narrowed," 28 September 1983; *New York Times*, "Pacific Air Corridor to Reopen Sunday," 28 September 1983, p. A3; *Japan Times*, "FAA Will Reopen Air Corridor Closed After KAL 007 Incident," 30 September 1983, p. 3; and Douglas B. Feaver, "KAL Jet's Path Strewn with Lawsuits and New Tracking Policies," *Washington Post*, 31 December 1983, p. A6.

67. *Japan Times*, "Andropov's Image Dented," 21 September 1983, p. 11; Robert Gillette, "Andropov Ends 3-Week Silence," *Los Angeles Times*, 21 September 1983, Part I, pp. 1–15; *Japan Times*, "Andropov Dismisses U.S. Arms Proposals," 30 September 1983, p. 1; and John F. Burns, "Andropov Attacks U.S. Missile Plan as Unacceptable," *New York Times*, 29 September 1983, pp. A1–14.

68. *FBIS*, Soviet Union, "Andropov Statement on U.S. Policy, KAL, INF Talks," 29 September 1983, pp. A1–2; and Serge Schmemann, "Antiwar Marches Are Held in Soviet," *New York Times*, 2 October 1983, pp. 1–12.

CHAPTER 16

1. Asa Baber, "Killing Us Softly with Their Song," *Playboy,* December 1983, pp. 50–51.

2. Leslie H. Gelb, "Korean Jet: Points Still to Be Settled," *New York Times,* 26 September 1983, p. A6; Ken Lawrence, "Flight 007 Aptly Named," *Covert Action,* Winter 1984, pp. 40–42; and Sugwon Kang, "Flight 007: Was There Foul Play?" *Bulletin of Concerned Asian Scholars,* 1985, Vol. 17, No. 2, pp. 38–40.

3. Donna A Demac, *Keeping America Uninformed: Government Secrecy in the 1980's,* 1984, The Pilgrim Press, New York, p. 144; and Floyd Abrams, "The New Effort to Control Information," *New York Times Magazine,* 25 September 1983, pp. 22–73.

4. Anthony Marro, "When the Government Tells Lies," *Columbia Journalism Review,* March/April 1985, pp. 29–41.

5. Anthony Marro, "When the Government Tells Lies," *Columbia Journalism Review,* March/April 1985, pp. 29–41.

6. George W. Luhrmann, "The KAL 007 Shootdown: A Symbol in the Search for Evil," *Journal of Psychohistory,* Vol. 12, No. 1, Summer 1984, pp. 79–120.

7. Asa Baber, "Killing Us Softly with Their Song," *Playboy,* December 1983, pp. 50–51.

8. David Shribman, "U.S. Experts Say Soviet Didn't See Jet Was Civilian," *New York Times,* 7 October 1983, pp. A1–10.

9. Douglas B. Feaver and David Hoffman, "Plane's Tragic Odyssey Mysterious," *Washington Post,* 4 September 1983, pp. A1–12; Michael Getler, "U.S. Air Force Plane Crossed Path of Jet," *Washington Post,* 5 September 1983, pp. A1–9; and Stephen S. Rosenfeld, "Flight 007: What We Know Now," *Washington Post,* 21 October 1983, p. A19.

10. Edward S. Herman, "Gatekeeper Versus Propaganda Models: A Critical American Perspective," in Peter Golding, Graham Murdock, and Philip Schlesinger (eds.), *Communicating Politics: Essays in Memory of Philip Elliott,* 1986, University of Leicester Press, England, pp. 171–95.

11. William Pfaff, "How U.S. Distorted Jet Crisis," *Los Angeles Times,* 16 September 1983, Part V, p. 1; *Los Angeles Times,* "Letters to the Times," 23 October 1983, Part IV, p. 1; and Stephen S. Rosenfeld, "Flight 007: What We Know Now," *Washington Post,* 21 October 1983, p. A19.

12. Dusko Doder, "Soviet Officers Reportedly Fired for Air Defense Lapse," *Los Angeles Times,* 5 October 1983, Part I, pp. 1–10; and Richard Halloran, "Soviet Is Said to Shake Up Far East Air Command," *New York Times,* 8 October 1983, p. 3.

13. *Newsweek,* "Why the Russians Did It," 19 September 1983, pp. 22–23; *Far Eastern Economic Review,* "Soviets' Murderous Military Bungling," 19 January 1984, pp. 62–64; Alison Smale, "Soviets Still Trumpeting Their Version," *Asahi Evening News,* 31 August 1984; and *Mainichi Daily News,* "Soviet Union Promotes KAL-Downing Figure," 3 November 1984.

14. John F. Burns, "Soviet Officer in Plane Case Is Dead at 62," *New York Times,* 23 May 1984, p. A5; and confidential source.

15. *Mainichi Daily News,* "Ogarkov Demoted over KAL Incident?" 18 September 1983.

16. One possible interpretation is that the independent Ogarkov, whose main base of support was the military rather than the Communist party, was chosen to

carry the ball about Flight 007, a potentially damaging role, to ensure that he would not succeed Dimitri Ustinov as defense minister, a position that almost guarantees membership in the Politburo.

17. Steven R. Weisman, "The Influence of William Clark," *The New York Times Magazine,* 14 August 1983, pp. 17–47; *The Economist,* "The Guard Changes, the Issues Stay the Same," 22 October 1983, pp. 21–22; and *New York Times,* "Reagan Is Tightening Grip on Arms-Control Policy," 20 July 1983, p. A3.

18. R.W. Johnson, *Shootdown: Flight 007 and the American Connection,* 1986, Viking, New York, p. 216.

19. It is strange that the search was abandoned so quickly, because the acoustic pinger is guaranteed for 30 days at a minimum. In waters as cold as the Sea of Japan, the life could be considerably longer. The shift in emphasis could suggest, official denials notwithstanding, that the flight recorders were recovered by either the U.S. or the Soviet Union.

20. Skye Dent, "Sailors Recall the Futile Search for Korean Plane's 'Black Box,' " *The Tribune* (Oakland), 22 January 1984, p. C5; *New York Times,* "Hopes Dim for Finding Jet's Flight Recorder," 4 October 1983, p. A7; and *Los Angeles Times,* "The World," 19 October 1983, Part I, p. 2.

21. U.S. Department of State telegram, No. 2068, 6 November 1983; B. Drummond Ayres, Jr., "U.S. Calls Off Search for Korean Plane Wreckage," *New York Times,* 6 November 1983, p. 8; and *FBIS,* Japan, "Soviet Vessels Halt Search for KAL Debris," 22 November 1983, p. C3.

22. Department of State telegram, No. 2066, 5 November 1983; and ICAO Report, Para. 1.12.1.

23. R.W. Apple, Jr., "Jet's 'Black Box' Is Raised from Sea," *New York Times,* 11 July 1985, pp. A1–8; and *New York Times,* "Deep and Wide," 12 July 1985.

24. There were other significant differences between the two cases as well. The U.S. National Transportation Safety Board sent observers to the investigation of the Air India crash even though the incident did not involve a U.S. carrier, the flight did not originate in a U.S. Flight Information Region, the incident occurred outside a U.S. FIR, and there were no Americans on board the aircraft.

CHAPTER 17

1. Douglas B. Feaver, "U.S Asks International Group for Strong Censure of Soviets," *Washington Post,* 16 September 1983, p. A27; and William H. Harris and Judith S. Levey (eds.), *The New Columbia Encyclopedia,* 1975, Columbia University Press, New York, p. 1351.

2. Douglas B. Feaver, "U.S. Asks International Group for Strong Censure of Soviets," *Washington Post,* 16 September 1983, p. A27.

3. *Los Angeles Times,* "U.N. Agency Asks Inquiry on Jet Downing," 18 September 1983, Part I, pp. 1–24; and Conor Cruise O'Brien, "U.N. Theater," *The New Republic,* 4 November 1985, pp. 17–19.

4. *FBIS,* South Korea, "ICAO Head Pledges Help," 2 September 1983, pp. E6–7; and *FBIS,* South Korea, "ROK Invited to ICAO Meeting," 8 September 1983, p. E7.

5. James Ott, "ICAO Debates Full Inquiry of Flight 007 Destruction," *Aviation Week & Space Technology,* 19 September 1983, p. 24; *Los Angeles Times,* "Jet Downing Won't Affect Negotiations," 14 September 1983, Part I, p. 1; Department of State memorandum, No. 2848, 14 September 1983; and Don Irwin,

"U.S. Seeks New Censure of Soviets, *Los Angeles Times*, 15 September 1983, Part I, p. 15.

6. Murray Sayle, "Shooting Down the Myths," *The Spectator*, 8 October 1983, pp. 7–10; and U.S. Department of State telegram, No. 1103, 13 September 1983; Department of State telegram, No. 1014, 12 September 1983.

7. Douglas B. Feaver, "U.S. Asks International Group for Strong Censure of Soviets," *Washington Post*, 16 September 1983, p. A27; Stanley Meisler, "U.N. Inquiry on Jet Downing Urged at Aviation Conference," *Los Angeles Times*, 16 September 1983, Part I, p. 6; and Douglas Martin, "World Air Agency Meets on Disaster," *New York Times*, 16 September 1983, p. A9.

8. U.S. Department of State, "FAA Administrator Helms' Statement, ICAO Council, Montreal, Sept. 15, 1983," *KAL Flight #007: Compilation of Statements and Documents, 1–16 September, 1983*, Washington, DC, pp. 17–19; *Los Angeles Times*, "Japanese Find 1st American ID from Airliner Wreckage," 15 September 1983, Part I, p. 1; Stanley Meisler, "U.N. Inquiry on Jet Downing Urged at Aviation Conference," *Los Angeles Times*, 16 September 1983, Part I, p. 6; and Department of State telegram, No. 1241, 14 September 1983.

9. Douglas B. Feaver, "By 26–2 Vote, ICAO Deplores Soviets' Shooting of Plane," *Washington Post*, 17 September 1983, p. A12.

10. The countries voting for the resolution were Argentina, Australia, Brazil, Great Britain, Cameroon, Canada, Colombia, Denmark, Egypt, El Salvador, France, West Germany, Indonesia, Italy, Jamaica, Japan, Madagascar, Mexico, the Netherlands, Nigeria, Pakistan, Senegal, Spain, Uganda, the United States, and Venezuela.

11. Stanley Meisler, "U.N. Body Votes to Probe Plane Downing," *Los Angeles Times*, 17 September 1983, Part I, p. 14; U.S. Department of State telegram, No. 1395, 17 September 1983; Douglas Martin, "U.N.'s Civil Aviation Panel Condemns Soviet Downing," *New York Times*, 17 September 1983, p. 3; and *FBIS*, South Korea, " 'Guaranteeing' Civil Aviation Safety," 19 September 1983, pp. E2–3.

12. Stanley Meisler, "U.N. Body Votes to Probe Plane Downing," *Los Angeles Times*, 17 September 1983, Part I, p. 14; *FBIS*, Soviet Union, "Adopts 'Lopsided Resolution,' " 20 September 1983, p. DD4; and *Wall Street Journal*, "U.N.'s Aviation Group Hears Call for Probe of Jetliner's Downing," 16 September 1983, p. 10.

13. U.S. Department of State, "President's Radio Address, Sept. 3," *KAL Flight #007: Compilation of Statements and Documents, 1–16 September 1983*, Washington, DC, pp. 5–6; U.S. Department of State, "President's Address to the Nation, Sept. 5, 1983," *KAL Flight #007: Compilation of Statements and Documents, 1–16 September 1983*, Washington, DC, pp. 6–8; and U.S. Department of State, "U.S. Letter to President, UN Security Council, Sept. 1, 1983," *KAL Flight #007: Compilation of Statements and Documents, 1–16 September 1983*, Washington, DC, p. 3.

14. *New York Times*, "Tass Report on a Soviet General's Comments About Airliner," 5 September 1983, p. 4; *Washington Post*, "Soviet Statement on Downing of Airliner," 7 September 1983, p. A10; John F. Burns, "Soviet Seems Unwilling to Bar Future Downings," *New York Times*, 9 September 1983, p. A10; and *FBIS*, Soviet Union, "Soviet Jurist Justifies Action over Air Intrusion," 7 September 1983, p. C14.

15. Jim Mann, "Scholars See International Law Violation in Attack," *Los Angeles Times*, 3 September 1983, Part I, p. 7; and John Lawless, "Russians Warned Pilot of 'Right to Shoot,' " *The Times*, 3 September 1983, p. 4.

16. James Ott, "U.S. Eases Pressures on ICAO," *Aviation Week & Space Technology*, 26 September 1983, pp. 40–41; *FBIS*, South Korea, "ICAO to Hear Report on Airliner Downing," 21 September 1983, p. E2; and United Nations Press Release, *ICAO Council Examines Follow-Up of Korean Air Lines Incident*, ICAO/699, 24 October 1984.

17. James Ott, "U.S. Eases Pressures on ICAO," *Aviation Week & Space Technology*, 26 September 1983, pp. 40–41; and *Aviation Week & Space Technology*, "ICAO Considers Replacing Route System on Pacific," 3 October 1983, p. 33.

18. *FBIS*, South Korea, "Full ICAO Endorsement Sought on KAL Resolution," 27 September 1983, p. E2; *Aviation Week & Space Technology*, "ICAO Considers Replacing Route System on Pacific," 3 October 1983, p. 33; *FBIS*, South Korea, "ICAO Fact-Finding Team on KAL Arrives in Seoul," 4 October 1983, p. E1; and United Nations Press Release, *ICAO Council Examines Follow-Up of Korean Air Lines Incident*, ICAO/699, 24 October 1983.

19. *FBIS*, South Korea, "Soviet Lack of Cooperation in KAL Probe Noted," 18 October 1983, p. E8; and Richard Witkin, "Aviation Aide to Discuss Flight 007 in Soviet," *New York Times*, 23 October 1983, p. 13.

20. *FBIS*, South Korea, "ICAO, Soviet Officials Discuss KAL Incident," 22 November 1983, p. E1; and *New York Times*, "Soviet Tells of Air-Traffic Plan," 3 December 1983, p. 3.

21. Richard Witkin, "Panel Bars View Korean Jet Spied," *New York Times*, 8 December 1983, p. A9; *Far Eastern Economic Review*, "Soviets' Murderous Military Bungling," 19 January 1984, pp. 62–64; and *Washington Post*, "Remembering KAL 007," 9 December 1983, p. A22.

22. ICAO Report, pp. 2 and 36; and Alexander Dallin, *Black Box: KAL 007 and the Superpowers*, 1985, University of California Press, Berkeley, CA, pp. 41–42.

23. ICAO Report, p. 38.

24. ICAO Report, p. 3.

25. David Corn, "Fear and Obstruction on the K.A.L. Trail," *The Nation*, 17/24 August 1985, pp. 110–13; and Richard Witkin, "Panel Bars View Korean Jet Spied," *New York Times*, 8 December 1983, p. A9.

26. ICAO Report, p. 3; Department of State Contingency Press Guidance, "Soviet KAL Investigation" (about 1 March 1984); David Pearson and John Keppel, "New Pieces in the Puzzle of Flight 007," *The Nation*, 17/24 August 1985, pp. 104–10; and John Keppel interview with Richard Slater, an ex-RAF captain and British member of the Air Navigation Bureau.

27. ICAO Report, p. 43.

28. ICAO Report, p. D-1.

29. In fact, the final of these, "He doesn't see the target," said to have been spoken by pilot 121 actually was spoken by Trikotazh: "But I see it." The Department of State rendering thus obscures a comment suggesting that Flight 007 was seen at substantial altitude a number of minutes after the missile attack.

30. ICAO Report, pp. D3–4.

31. This suggestion, since confirmed by others, was first made by L. Fletcher Prouty, "The Last Flight of 007," *Gallery*, May 1985, pp. 46–101.

32. Fighter 805 was not the only one to have strange rates of fuel consumption. Things were equally strange for fighter 163, whose rate of fuel burn went as follows:

1806:45–1811:37; 181 lbs./min.
1811:37–1814.41; 360 lbs./min.
1814:41–1830:13; 213 lbs./min.
1830:13–1834:02; 289 lbs./min.

33. ICAO Report, pp. 17 and A-11.

34. ICAO Report, p. 43.

35. *ICAO Bulletin,* "ICAO Council Received Report on KAL-007 Incident," January 1984, p. 22; Fred Hiatt and Rick Atkinson, "Profits Soar in Buildup," *Washington Post,* 1 April 1985, pp. A1–6; and *Aviation Week & Space Technology,* "Electronic Systems Emerge as Costliest Avionic Item," 7 April 1986, pp. 50–55.

36. *Far Eastern Economic Review,* "Soviets' Murderous Military Bungling," 19 January 1984, pp. 62–64; and ICAO Report, pp. 46–47.

37. I discuss these at some length in my letter "The Fate of KE007: An Exchange," *New York Review of Books,* 26 September 1985, pp. 47–51, from which the following discussion is drawn.

38. Harold H. Ewing, *An Analysis and Scenario of Probable Cause of the Course Deviation Incident Involving FLT KE007, PACN–RKSS, 31 August 1983,* 1985 (unpublished manuscript).

39. The radar data were plotted by Robert Williams, Ph.D., the retired director of the Map Studies program at Yale University.

40. Harold H. Ewing, *An Analysis and Scenario of Probable Cause of the Course Deviation Incident Involving FLT KE007, PACN–RKSS, 31 August 1983,* 1985 (unpublished manuscript).

41. Richard Witkin, "Computer Input Error Suspected in Korean Airliner's Bad Course," *New York Times,* 17 November 1983, p. A10.

42. ICAO Report, pp. 51–52.

43. ICAO Report, p. 54; and U.S. District Court, District of Columbia, *In Re: Korean Air Lines Disaster of September 1, 1983,* 28 February 1985.

44. Thomas Maertens, "Aircraft Off Course Are Common; Shootdowns Are Not," *Hartford Courant,* 9 January 1986, p. B13; and ICAO Report, p. 56.

45. Letter from W. Tapley Bennett, Jr., assistant secretary for legislative and intergovernmental affairs, to Representative Daniel R. Coats of Indiana.

46. Department of State telegram, No. 2439, 20 July 1984.

47. Department of State telegram, No. 3138, 14 December 1983; Department of State telegram, No. 3139, 13 December 1983; and Richard Witkin, "Panel Bars View Korean Jet Spied," *New York Times,* 8 December 1983, p. A9.

48. Included as attachments to the fifteen-page report were another eight pages of technical information, including extracts from the Korean Air Lines Boeing 747 operations manual.

49. ANC Report, p. 1; Department of State telegram, No. 3139, 14 December 1983; and Department of State telegram, No. 2297, 3 February 1984.

50. Department of State telegram, No. 2297, 3 February 1984; Department of State telegram, No. 2306, 10 February 1984; statement by Japan on Agenda Item 1, ICAO Council, 110th Session, 12 December 1983; Department of State telegram, No. 2317, 20 February 1984; Department of State, U.S. comments to ANC Report (about 1 March 1984).

51. ANC Report, p. 2.

52. ANC Report, p. 14.

53. Thomas Maertens, "Tragedy of Errors," *Foreign Service Journal,* September 1985, pp. 25–31.

54. *Japan Times,* "ICAO Council Condemns Soviets for KAL Tragedy," 8 March 1984.

55. *New York Times,* "Aviation Council Faults Soviet," 7 March 1984, p. A4; Department of State telegram, No. 2365, 1 March 1984; Department of State tele-

gram, No. 2367, 1 March 1984; and *FBIS*, Soviet Union, "USSR Delegate to ICAO Session on KAL Flight," 6 March 1984, p. C4.

[56.] *Japan Times*, "ICAO Council Condemns Soviets for KAL Tragedy," 8 March 1984.

[57.] *ICAO Bulletin*, "ICAO Assembly Bans Use of Weapons Against Civil Aircraft," June 1984, pp. 10–12; and *ICAO Bulletin*, "39 Opening Statements Made Before the Recent Special Assembly," June 1984, pp. 14–27.

[58.] Mark N. Sills, "State Responsibility for Death or Injury of Aliens: The KAL 007 Incident," *IX Curso de Derecho Internacional, Comite Juridico Interamericano, Organizacion de los Estados Americanos*, Septiembre 1985, Washington, DC, pp. 167–77; Charles Maechling, Jr., "KAL Flight 7—the Legal Aftermath," *Christian Science Monitor*, 14 October 1983, p. 16; and John N. Bradbury, "Interception of Civil Aircraft," *ICAO Bulletin*, August 1984, pp. 9–11.

CHAPTER 18

[1.] P. Q. Mann, "Reassessing the Sakhalin Incident," *Defence Attaché*, 1984, No. 3, pp. 41–56.

[2.] However, as Devereux told the *New York Times*, the airport involved none of the infrastructure normally associated with military airports, such as antiaircraft defenses and underground storage sites for weapons and fuel. The Reagan administration surely knew this. "There's not the least doubt," Devereux concluded, "that if the British government had been unhappy about the nature of the contract, it would not have allowed the Export Credits Guarantee Department to underwrite it."

[3.] P. Q. Mann, "Reassessing the Sakhalin Incident," *Defence Attaché*, 1984, No. 3, pp. 41–56; Adrian Berry, "Risky Flight of Fantasy," *Daily Telegraph*, 6 August, 1984, p. 8; *Newsweek*, "The Cuban Connection," 7 November 1983, pp. 77–79; *New York Times*, "Contractor in Britain Denies Airport in Grenada Is Military," 2 November 1983, p. A17; and interview with Rupert Pengelley, 5 January 1985.

[4.] Andrew Wilson, "British Expert's Radar Clue to Flight 007 Riddle," *The Observer*, 17 June 1984, p. 2; and Michael Getler, "Article in Britain Links Ill-Fated KAL Flight to Intelligence Mission," *Washington Post*, 19 June 1984, p. A14.

[5.] Arthur J. Olsen, "U.S. Jet Lost in East Germany: It May Have Been Shot Down," *New York Times*, 29 January 1964, pp. 1–12.

[6.] Craig Covault, "Shuttle Launch Verifies Thrust Margins," *Aviation Week & Space Technology*, 5 September 1983, pp. 21–23; and John N. Wilford, "Challenger Drops Orbit by 54 Miles," *New York Times*, 3 September 1983, p. 9.

[7.] Some reports question whether the deployment of the Indian satellite was the reason for the night launch, noting that NASA has lied about the reasons for shuttle launch times in the past. According to R.W. Johnson, Mission STS-2 was ostensibly delayed to "settle some launch-team questions that arose on vehicle status." In fact, the delay was so the Columbia could be in position to be viewed by a KH–11 photoreconnaissance satellite. Navy Captain Richard H. Truly, on board that mission, was also on board the Challenger. (*Source:* R.W. Johnson, *Shootdown: Flight 007 and the American Connection*, 1986, Viking, New York, p. 158.)

[8.] Thomas O'Toole, "Crew Works Shuttle Arm in Another Near-Perfect Day,"

Washington Post, 3 September 1983, p. A3; and Lee Dembart, "Ground Station Problems Beset Satellite," *Los Angeles Times*, 7 September 1983, Part I, p. 16.

9. Bill Keller, "Military Studies Alternatives to Shuttle," *New York Times*, 30 January 1986, p. A18; U.S. Congress, Senate, Committtee on Aeronautical and Space Sciences, *NASA Authorization for FY 1977*, 1976, Part 3, pp. 1650–53; Bruce G. Blair and Garry D. Brewer, "Verifying SALT Agreements," pp. 7–48, in William C. Potter (ed.), *Verification of SALT: The Challenge of Strategic Deception*, 1980, Westview Press, Boulder, CO; *Aviation Week & Space Technology*, "Mission 9 Astronauts Photographed Soviet Submarine, Fighter Bases at Petropavlovsk," 19 March 1984, p. 17; and William E. Burrows, *Deep Black: Space Espionage and National Security*, 1986, Random House, New York, pp. 297–302.

10. Department of State telegram, No. 2426, 2 July 1984; Alexander Dallin, *Black Box: KAL 007 and the Superpowers*, 1985, University of California Press, Berkeley, CA, p. 116; *New Haven Journal Courier*, "Report Alleges KAL 007 Was Spy Plane," 18 June 1984, p. 5; *Mainichi Daily News*, "U.S. Knew KAL Jet Would Enter Soviet Airspace," 8 August 1984; *Time*, "World Notes: An Anonymous 007 Theory," 2 July 1984, p. 37; and Andrew Wilson, "British Expert's Radar Clue to Flight 007 Riddle," *The Observer*, 17 June 1984, p. 2.

11. Pengelley said he learned from a source at the U.S. Embassy in London that American corporations had been calling the embassy, inquiring if it was "still all right" to continue subscribing to the magazine.

12. Tina Rosenberg, "Mission Out of Control," *The New Republic*, 14 May 1984, pp. 18–21; and Adrian Berry, "Risky Flight of Fantasy," *Daily Telegraph*, 6 August 1984, p. 8.

13. Charles W. Corddry, "KAL Flight 007: Was It on an Intelligence Mission?" *Baltimore Sun*, 8 July 1984, pp. 1–3C.

14. *Time*, "World Notes: An Anonymous 007 Theory," 2 July 1984, p. 37; and Walt Crowley, "The Unquiet Grave of Flight 007," *The Weekly* (Seattle), 3–9 October 1984, pp. 31–40.

15. *Daily Yomiuri*, "KAL Files Suit Against Journal," 30 August 1984; and *Japan Times*, "KAL Files Suit Against TV, Magazine for 'Spy' Claims," 30 August 1984.

16. *New York Times*, "Around the World: Korean Air Lines Gets an Apology and Money," 20 November 1984, p. A5; *Time*, "Backing Down on Flight 007," 3 December 1984, p. 47; and Department of Defense News Briefing, ASD/PA Michael I. Burch, Tuesday, November 20, 1984, 11:30 A.M.

17. Forwarding a copy of the "apology issue" to me in February 1986, Rupert Pengelley wrote, "My hands are tied on the KAL statement."

18. As Duncan Campbell noted, the satellite was launched on May 1982 accompanying a U.S. Air Force Big Bird KH–9 photoreconnaissance satellite. It was then placed in an independent circular orbit, at an altitude of about 440 miles. At that altitude, the satellite completed an orbit of the earth once every 98.6 minutes.

19. Duncan Campbell, "What Really Happened to KE007," *New Statesman*, 26 April 1985, pp. 8–10; James E. Oberg, "Sakhalin: Sense and Nonsense," *Defence Attaché*, 1985, No. 1, pp. 37–47; and Bhupendra Jasani and Geoffrey E. Perry, "The Military Use of Outer Space," Chapter 5 in *World Armaments and Disarmament: SIPRI Yearbook 1985*, 1985, Taylor and Francis, London, pp. 137–58.

20. "The [Soviet] errors, about the angle and spacing of successive orbits, are so

elementary," Duncan Campbell observed, "that they seem scarcely to be accidental. But they serve no particular purpose." Private sources have suggested, however, that Kirsanov's poorly rendered map could have been quite intentional —containing a cryptic message that the Soviets knew more than they were letting on. For example, the map lists a series of apparently arbitrary times for the satellite's location. For the first orbit, these are 18:45, 18:50, and 18:54. The difference between the first and second time is 5; and between the second and third, 4. These add to 9. Using the same procedure for the times on the second orbit yields a value of 8, and on the third a value of 6. This gives "986." The orbital time for satellite 1982-41C was 98.6 minutes.

21. Thomas Maertens, "Tragedy of Errors," *Foreign Service Journal*, September 1985, pp. 25–31.

22. David Pearson, "The Fate of KE007: An Exchange," *The New York Review of Books*, 26 September 1985, pp. 47–51.

23. Sugwon Kang, "Flight 007: Was There Foul Play?" *Bulletin of Concerned Asian Scholars*, 1985, Vol. 17, No. 2, pp. 30–48; Ed Magnusen, "Fallout From Flight 007," *Time*, 10 September 1984, p. 16; and William Boardman, "Leahy and NBC Didn't Touch Basic Questions About KAL 007," *Valley News* (Lebanon, NH), 30 August 1984.

24. ARD, "Raketen Abgefeuert—Ziel Vernichtet—Der Todesflug der KE 007," 23 August 1984, produced by Andre Libik.

25. Another attorney who was present during this interview said that this statement had been made by the wives of First Officer Sohn Dong-hwin and Flight Engineer Kim Eui-dong.

26. *People*, "The Career of an 'Infallible' Pilot Ends in the Debris of Flight 007," 26 December 1983, p. 41; Canadian Broadcasting Corporation, *The Gary Bannerman Show*, 11 October 1984; interview with Melvin Belli, February 1985; and private conversation.

27. Department of State telegram, No. 2439, 20 July 1984; Department of State telegram, No. 2259, 16 January 1984; Martin Linton, "U.S. Blocking Inquiry into Jet Disaster," *The Guardian*, 28 July 1984; and Department of State telegram, No. 2445, 2 August 1984.

28. *Japan Times*, "British TV Claims KAL 007 on U.S. Spy Mission," 21 July 1984; Department of State Paper on the Report of the ICAO Investigatory Commission, No. 3161 (undated, about 1 December 1983); and Martin Linton, "U.S. Blocking Inquiry into Jet Disaster," *The Guardian*, 28 July 1984.

29. Thames Television, *TV Eye—007—Licensed to Spy?*, 19 July 1984.

30. Court Record: In the High Court of Justice, Queen's Bench Division, "Statement of Claim," 1984–K–No. 886, Between Korean Airlines Co. Limited and Thames Television Limited.

31. ABC, "20/20 Newsmagazine," 30 August 1984.

32. ABC, "20/20 Newsmagazine," 30 August 1984.

33. Henk Hanssen, "Het Doel Is Vernietigd," *Panorama*, 18 January 1985, pp. 42–51; and private source.

34. David Wise, *The Politics of Lying: Government Deception, Secrecy, and Power*, 1973, Random House, New York, p. 274.

35. *Washington Post*, "Koreans to Dedicate Memorial to KAL 007 Victims," 31 August 1984, p. A9; and John Burgess, "KAL Victims' Kin Seek Redress," *Washington Post*, 1 September 1984, pp. A1–22.

36. *Washington Post*, "Koreans to Dedicate Memorial to KAL 007 Victims," 31 August 1984, p. A9; *Japan Times*, "Memorials Mark KAL Incident Anniv.," 3

September 1984; and John Burgess, "KAL Victims' Kin Seek Redress," *Washington Post*, 1 September 1984, pp. A1–22.

[37.] *Mainichi Daily News*, "S. Korea Urges Soviets to Take Responsibility," 2 September 1984; and *Japan Times*, "ROK to Continue Effort for Soviet Compensation," 1 September 1984.

[38.] According to *New York* magazine, Seoul had agreed to provide the film with 10,000 soldiers as extras, three Soviet jets, and two KAL Boeing 707 aircraft, one to sink and one to crash. "Without that," said one of the filmmakers, "an $8 million film is a $20 million one." But just before shooting was to begin, the Korean Ministry of Culture withdrew the offer. (*Source: New York*, "South Korea Withdraws Support for Film About Air Crash," 10 December 1984, p. 14.)

[39.] *Mainichi Daily News*, "Relatives of Victims Travel to Crash Site," 2 September 1984; *Japan Times*, "KAL Families Hold Memorial Service," 2 September 1984; and Eugene Moosa, "Families of KAL Victims Plan to Gather near the Crash Site," *Asahi Evening News*, 27 August 1984.

[40.] Clyde Haberman, "Japanese Kin Assail U.S. on Flight 007," *New York Times*, 2 September 1984, p. 3; and Bill Lueders, "Lessons Not Learned," *North Country Anvil*, Fall 1984, pp. 13–17.

[41.] Michael Marriott, "D.C. Rally Commemorates Downing of KAL Jet," *Washington Post*, 1 September 1984, p. A23.

[42.] *Japan Times*, "Memorials Mark KAL Incident Anniv.," 3 September 1984.

[43.] Nigel Wade, "War of Words on Shot-Down Korean Jet," *Daily Telegraph*, 27 September 1984; Department of State telegram, No. 2442, 27 July 1984; Richard Burt, "The Yearlong Shadow of K.A.L. Flight 007," *New York Times*, 31 August 1984; and *The Nation*, "Balancing Act," 15 September 1984, pp. 196–97.

[44.] Douglas B. Feaver and Don Oberdorfer, "Pacific Flights Watched After KAL Downing," *Washington Post*, 29 August 1984, pp. A1–8.

[45.] Ed Magnusen, "Fallout From Flight 007," *Time*, 10 September 1984, p. 16; *U.S. News & World Report*, "Opening Up the KGB's Bag of Dirty Tricks," 20 August 1984, p. 36; and Roy Godson, "Soviet Fairy Tales and the Flight of KAL 007," *Washington Times*, 31 August 1984, p. C1.

[46.] Richard N. Gardner, "A Reagan Fiasco in the World Court, *New York Times*, 2 July 1986, p. A31; and David M. North, "U.S. Using Disinformation Policy to Impede Technical Data Flow," *Aviation Week & Space Technology*, 17 March 1986, pp. 16–17.

[47.] Sugwon Kang, "Flight 007: Was There Foul Play?" *Bulletin of Concerned Asian Scholars*, 1985, Vol. 17, No. 2, pp. 30–48.

[48.] Wilhelm Bittorf and Anthony Sampson, "Sinken Auf Eins-Null Tausend . . . " *Der Spiegel*, 15 October 1984, pp. 196–222.

[49.] After President Reagan's overwhelming victory, a similar story appeared in the "Intelligencer" column in *New York* magazine. "According to an intelligence source," the article said, "Secretary of State George Shultz; Lawrence Eagleburger, then undersecretary for political affairs; Richard Burt, then State's political-military director; CIA chief William Casey; National Security Adviser William Clark; and presidential counselor Ed Meese decided in a video conference that the incident could be used to quell European opposition to Pershing missiles." I tried to find out the name of the source for this story in order to pass the information to the Congress, but Sharon Churcher, the author of the article, said that her source was a "security agent" who could go to jail if he said anything in public. Having just received a visit from the FBI, her source was scared, she said, and "doesn't want to talk to anyone who might be able to subpoena him." (Fear about this story is rather widespread. Asked about the teleconference story, a State Department official told *The Nation*, "I could find out if this happened, but I would lose my job for asking.") Was Churcher's source the same one used by Bittorf and Sampson? After the appearance of the *New York* article, Bittorf contacted his source, who denied having spoken to *New York*.

50. Walter Karp, "Liberty Under Siege," *Harper's*, November 1985, pp. 53–67; *New York*, "Top Reagan Officials Mulled P.R. Value of Korean Air Crash," 12 November 1984, p. 16; conversation with Sharon Churcher, 22 January 1985; David Corn, "Fear and Obstruction on the K.A.L. Trail," *The Nation*, 17/24 August 1985, pp. 110–13; and private conversation.

51. The use of experts "out of government" is a common practice. Ostensibly private citizens but in fact former officials and others with close contacts to government lend support to official government positions through their role as supposedly disinterested experts. Perhaps equally important, in the event of errors, lies, or particularly egregious gaffes, the government cannot be held accountable. In a "for your information only" message following the "TV Eye" program, for example, the State Department instructed the U.S. Embassy in London to debunk the program's claims by using "someone familiar with the case but not currently in the USG [U.S. Government]."

52. Catto's claim is another limited, yet irrelevant statement. Saying that the U.S. military personnel do not monitor "flight pattern accuracy" for civilian planes tells us nothing about whether they were aware of the off-course Korean airliner. Next, Catto did not tell his readers how we knew the airliner—as much as 300 miles off course—was a "civilian plane" in the first place so that we wouldn't bother to monitor it. There is, of course another possibility, the one favored by the Department of State: Nobody saw anything at all. But a former assistant secretary of defense cannot admit that U.S. defenses don't work.

53. Tom Wicker, "A Damning Silence," *New York Times*, 7 September 1984, p. A27; Department of State telegram, No. 2431, 12 July 1984; Henry E. Catto, Jr., " 'Drivel' About the KAL Flight 007 Incident," *New York Times*, 2 October 1984; and Tom Wicker, "Silence on Flight 007," *New York Times*, 21 October 1984, p. E23.

54. Jonathan Kwitny, "Dealings with Lynn Helms Haunt Couple," *Wall Street Journal*, 1 May 1985, p. 6; and J. Lynn Helms, "It Was Impossible for Us to Monitor Flight 007," *New York Times*, 24 November 1984, p. 22.

55. Frederic Golden, "Seeing a Conspiracy in the Sky," *Discover*, December 1984, p. 8.; and Thomas Maertens, "Tragedy of Errors," *Foreign Service Journal*, September 1985, pp. 25–31.

56. U.S. District Court, District of Columbia, *In Re: Korean Air Lines Disaster of September 1983*, 31 October 1984; Tom Gervasi, *America's War Machine: The Pursuit of Global Dominance*, 1984, Grove Press, New York, p. 31; and interview with James Michelangelo, February 1985.

57. *Jane's Weapons Systems*, "United States of America: Over-the-Horizon Radar," 1979–80, pp. 528–29; Duncan Campbell, "New Spy Station to Look Inside USSR," *New Statesman*, 21–28 December 1984, p. 6; Tom Gervasi, *The Myth of Soviet Military Supremacy*, 1986, Harper & Row, New York, p. 249; Charles Mohr, "New Zealand's Rebuff: A Baffling Furor," *New York Times*, 7 February 1985; *Jane's Weapons Systems*, "United States of America: Shipborne OTH Radar," 1979–80, pp. 580–81; and Leslie H. Gelb, "Korean Jet: Points Still to Be Settled," *New York Times*, 26 September 1983, p. A6.

58. U.S. Department of Defense, *Soviet Military Power*, 1984, Washington, DC,

pp. 32–33; William V. Kennedy, *Intelligence Warfare: Today's Advanced Technology Conflict,* 1983, Crescent Books, New York, p. 189; and *Jane's Weapons Systems,* "United States of America: Shipborne OTH Radar," 1979–80, pp. 580–81.

59. Duncan Campbell, "New Spy Station to Look Inside USSR," *New Statesman,* 21–28 December 1984, p. 6; U.S. Congress, House, *Aviation Navigation Technology and Errors,* Subcommittee on Transportation, Aviation and Materials, Committee on Science and Technology, 19 September 1983, p. 54; and Jacques Ellul, *Propaganda: The Formation of Men's Attitudes,* 1965, Knopf, New York, p. 56.

60. Tom Wicker, "A Red-Faced Review," *New York Times,* 30 December 1984, p. E13.

CHAPTER 19

1. *San Francisco Examiner & Chronicle,* "U.S. Citizens Aboard Korean Air Lines Flight," 2 September 1983; *New York Times,* "Husband of Jet's Passenger Sues Soviet Union and Airline," 3 September 1983, p. 4; and *Washington Post,* "$99 Billion Suit Filed Against Soviets, Airline," 4 September 1983, p. A14..

2. *Washington Post,* "Father Files Suit for $60 Million," 7 September 1983, p. A14; and *Japan Times,* "Suit Filed," 25 September 1983, p. 4.

3. *Japan Times,* "KAL Jet Covered by $35 Mil. Policy," 4 September 1983, p. 5; *Los Angeles Times,* "Airliner Pilot Tried 'Trick,' Interceptor Says," 13 September 1983, Part I, p. 2; *Wall Street Journal,* "Korean Air Lines Gets $26.8 Million from Jet Insurance," 14 September 1983, p. 36; and *FBIS,* South Korea, "Insurance Companies Make Payments for Lost Jet," 16 September 1983, p. E1.

4. *Japan Times,* "Negotiation Group," 12 September 1983, p. 2; and *FBIS,* Japan, "KAL Victim Compensation Sought," 13 September 1983, pp. C2–3.

5. This unlikely explanation for the deviation from course of Flight 007 was the centerpiece of Jeffrey St. John's tribute to Larry McDonald: *Day of the Cobra: The True Story of KAL Flight 007.*

6. *FBIS,* Japan, "KAL Chief, Gotoda Meet on Plane Victims," 27 September 1983, pp. C4–5; Jeffrey St. John, *Day of the Cobra: The True Story of KAL Flight 007,* 1984, Thomas Nelson Publishers, Nashville, TN; Anthony Sampson, *Empires of the Sky: The Politics, Contests, and Cartels of World Airlines,* 1984, Random House, New York; and *FBIS,* Japan, "Meeting with Japanese Families," 27 September 1983, p. C5.

7. By mid-March 1984, an offer of $100,000 in compensation was accepted by the families of forty-three South Koreans, five Taiwanese, and a Filipino.

8. *Mainichi Daily News,* "Victims' Families to File Suit Against KAL in September," 31 August 1984; Clyde Haberman, "Shake-Up at Korean Air Lines," *New York Times,* 21 March 1984, pp. D1–11; Bob Horiguchi, "KAL Victims' Families Turning to Reagan," *Japan Times,* 15 May 1984, p. 10; and John Burgess, "KAL Victims' Kin Seek Redress," *Washington Post,* 1 September 1984, pp. A1–22.

9. James Ott, "ICAO Pushes New Intercept Rules," *Aviation Week & Space Technology,* 6 August 1984, pp. 28–30; Al Kamen and Ed Burke, "Lawyers," *Washington Post,* 12 December 1983, p. D2; *New Haven Register,* "Judge Dismisses Claims in Downing of Flight 007," 3 August 1985, p. 1; and *Lexis Nexis,* "The Associated Press," 3 August 1985.

10. Douglas B. Feaver, "KAL Jet's Path Strewn with Lawsuits and New Tracking Policies," *Washington Post,* 31 December 1983, p. A6; and Al Kamen, "U.S., in Response to KAL Suit, Says It Had No Legal Duty to Alert Jet," *Washington Post,* 23 February 1984, p. A14.

11. U.S. District Court for the District of Columbia, *In Re: Korean Air Lines Disaster of September 1, 1983,* 22 December 1983.

12. Memorandum from Donald H. Boberick, Regional Council, AAL-7, to Public Affairs Officer, AAL-5, Federal Aviation Administration, 23 January 1984.

13. Juanita M. Madole, "Korean Air Lines Memorandum: KAL-11," 24 October 1984; and David Corn, "Fear and Obstruction on the K.A.L. Trail," *The Nation,* 17/24 August 1985, pp. 110–13.

14. U.S. District Court for the District of Columbia, *In Re: Korean Air Lines Disaster of September 1, 1983,* 22 December 1983; and Al Kamen and Ed Bruske, "Lawyers," *Washington Post,* 12 December 1983, p. D2.

15. Department of State information memorandum, 23 September 1983; and U.S. District Court for the District of Columbia, *In Re: Korean Air Lines Disaster of September 1, 1983,* 2 February and 18 April 1984.

16. *Mainichi Daily News,* "Victims' Families to File Suit Against KAL in September," 31 August 1984; and *Far Eastern Economic Review,* "The Ghost of KAL 007 Still Stalks Washington's Corridors," 24 January 1985, pp. 53–55.

17. Two books about the case were published in Japan: Kunio Yanagida's *Shootdown* and Aoki Shoten's *People Who Stage Crises.*

18. Bob Horiguchi, "KAL Victims' Families Turning to Reagan," *Japan Times,* 15 May 1984, p. 10.

19. Both the Japanese and Korean next of kin immediately organized themselves, something that was slow to happen in the U.S. The explanation may be partly cultural, but it is also attributable to the artful use of the Privacy Act by the State Department, which has refused to inform victims' families of the other families' addresses. Several next of kin have remarked that they feel this is a deliberate ploy to preclude the possibility of organization.

20. *Asahi Evening News,* "Fact-Finding Group to Study KAL Incident," 1 September 1984; *Japan Times,* "Private Body to Request Facts About KAL Incident," 1 September 1984; and John Burgess, "KAL Victims' Kin Seek Redress," *Washington Post,* 1 September 1984, pp. A1–22.

21. *Asian Wall Street Journal,* "KAL Victims' Families in Japan Suing for Compensation in U.S.," 10 January 1985; *Mainichi Daily News,* "Plaintiffs Rebuffed by KAL in Tokyo Court Hearing," 13 February 1985; and *Japan Times,* "Victims' Kin Say KAL at Fault in '83 Soviet Attack of Jetliner," 13 February 1985, p. 2.

22. *Mainichi Daily News,* "Japanese File Suit in US Over KAL Crash Incident," 10 January 1985; *Japan Times,* "Half of KAL Victims' Kin to File Suit in U.S.," 23 November 1984; and *Japan Times,* "KAL Shootdown Victims' Kin File Damage Suit in America," 10 January 1985, p. 2.

23. U.S. District Court for the District of Columbia, *In Re: Korean Air Lines Disaster of September 1, 1983,* 31 October 1984.

24. *Aviation Week & Space Technology,* "Washington Roundup: KAL Depositions," 5 November 1984, p. 13; and Richard Witkin, "Pilot Declines to Testify on Flight 007," *New York Times,* 1 November 1984, p. A3.

25. U.S. District Court, District of Columbia, *In Re: Korean Air Lines Disaster of September 1, 1983,* 28 February 1985.

26. George C. Wilson, "Air Force Destroyed Korean Jet Radar Tape," *Washington Post,* 5 March 1985, p. A11; and U.S. District Court, District of Columbia, *In Re: Korean Air Lines Disaster of September 1, 1983,* 28 February 1985.

27. U.S. District Court, District of Columbia, *In Re: Korean Air Lines Disaster of September 1, 1983,* 28 February 1985.

28. Richard Mauer, "King Salmon Radar Saw KAL 007 Stray," *Anchorage Daily News,* 22 January 1984, pp. A1–12; Department of State telegram, No. 1242, 14 September 1983; and Michael Chrisman interviews with FAA personnel in Anchorage, July 1984.

29. Richard Mauer, "King Salmon Radar Saw KAL 007 Stray," *Anchorage Daily News,* 22 January 1984, pp. A1–12; and ICAO Report, p. 5.

30. ICAO Report, p. 39.

31. U.S. District Court, District of Columbia, *In Re: Korean Air Lines Disaster of September 1, 1983,* 28 February 1985.

32. *New York Times,* "U.S. Said It Destroyed Korean Airliner Tape," 6 March 1985, p. A7.

33. The following discussion is based on Danny Schechter's article, "The Least We Can Do," *Intervention,* Winter 1985, Vol. 1, No. 2, pp. 6–23.

34. *New York Times,* "U.S. Says It Destroyed Korean Airliner Tape," 6 March 1985, p. A7; and *Japan Times,* "U.S. Air Force Destroyed KAL Radar Track Tape: Testimony," 7 March 1985, p. 5.

35. Department of State telegram, No. 2367, 1 March 1984.

36. Harold H. Ewing, *An Analysis and Scenario of Probable Cause of the Course Deviation Incident Involving FLT KE007, PANC–RKSS, 31 August 1983,* 1985 (unpublished manuscript).

37. Williams did a linear regression of the radar fixes for the airliner in the area of coverage for the Kenai and King Salmon radars. The resulting product-moment correlation coefficient was $r = 0.9998$, where a perfect straight line has a value of $r = 1.000$.

38. Robert L. Williams, Ph.D., director of Map Studies Laboratory (retired).

39. U.S. District Court for the District of Columbia, *Statement of Genuine Issues of Material Fact and Plaintiffs' Steering Committee's Opposition to the Government's Motion for Summary Judgment,* Filed 30 August 1985.

40. *New Haven Register,* "Judge Dismisses Claims in Downing of Flight 007," 3 August 1985, p. 1; and *Lexis Nexis,* "The Associated Press," 3 August 1985.

41. U.S. District Court for the District of Columbia, *Plaintiffs' Steering Committee's Opposition to the Government's Motion for Summary Judgment,* filed August 30, 1985, pp. 3–4.

42. Richard Witkin, "U.S. Saw Korean Jet Stray, Suit Says," *New York Times,* 1 September 1983, p. 3.

43. Douglas B. Feaver, "U.S. Controllers' Role Questioned in KAL Case," *Washington Post,* 31 August 1985, p. A8; and Richard Witkin, "U.S. Saw Korean Jet Stray, Suit Says," *New York Times,* 1 September 1985, p. 3.

44. Tom Wicker, "A Disintegrating Story," *New York Times,* 3 September 1985, p. A21.

45. Richard Witkin, "Judge Dismisses Suits in Downing of Korean Plane," *New York Times,* 8 May 1986, p. A13.

46. Richard Witkin, "Judge Dismisses Suits in Downing of Korean Plane," *New York Times,* 8 May 1986, p. A13.

CHAPTER 20

1. David Pearson, "K.A.L. 007: What the U.S. Knew and When We Knew It," *The Nation,* 18–25 August 1984, pp. 105–24; and John Keppel and David Pear-

son, "A Misguided, Deadly Flight—KAL's 007," *Hartford Courant*, 2 September 1984, pp. C1–4.

2. Letter from Representative Edward P. Boland to Representative George Brown, 18 October 1984; Jeff Levine, "1 Year After KAL 007 Loss, Doubts Linger," *USA Today*, 29 August 1984, pp. A1–2; and David Corn, "Fear and Obstruction on the K.A.L. Trail," *The Nation*, 17–24 August 1985, pp. 110–13.

3. U.S. Congress, Senate, *Report of the Select Committee on Intelligence, United States Senate: January 1, 1983 to December 31, 1984*, Report 98–665, Washington, DC, pp. 41–42; and David Corn, "Fear and Obstruction on the K.A.L. Trail," *The Nation*, 17–24 August 1985, pp. 110–13.

4. *Human Events*, "House Intelligence Panel Exposes Media Falsehoods," 2 February 1985, pp. 1–8.

5. Anthony Marro, "When the Government Tells Lies," *Columbia Journalism Review*, March/April 1985, pp. 29–41; and Floyd Abrams, "The New Effort to Control Information," *New York Times Magazine*, 25 September 1983, pp. 22–73.

6. Jack Anderson, "Reaction to KAL Downing Aided U.S.," *Washington Post*, 18 February 1984, p. E47; and letter from David Sobel to John Keppel, 21 April 1986.

7. John Keppel, "The Fund for Constitutional Government Appeals Its FOIA Request to the Department of State," *The KAL 007 Information Bulletin & Newsletter*, Number 3, 31 August 1985, pp. 6–7.

8. David Corn, "Fear and Obstruction on the K.A.L. Trail," *The Nation*, 17–24 August 1985, pp. 110–13.

9. John Keppel, "The Fund for Constitutional Government Appeals Its FOIA Request to the Department of State," *The KAL 007 Information Bulletin & Newsletter*, Number 3, 31 August 1985, pp. 6–7.

10. David Pearson, "Silence on the Sea of Japan," *The KAL 007 Information Bulletin & Newsletter*, Number 3, 31 August 1985, pp. 7–8.

11. Duncan Campbell, "What Really Happened to KE007," *New Statesman*, 26 April 1985, pp. 8–10; Clarence A. Robinson, Jr., "U.S. Says Soviets Knew Korean Air Lines 747 Was Commercial Flight," *Aviation Week & Space Technology*, 12 September 1983, pp. 18–21; and Eugene Kozicharow, "FAA Studies Upgraded Pacific Navaids," *Aviation Week & Space Technology*, 19 September 1983, pp. 18–21.

12. Since the Soviet pilots were operating under emergency conditions, there is no reason to believe that they were making up the turns by the intruder. Transcripts of their transmissions, intercepted by Japan and made public by the U.S., are obviously not Soviet propaganda.

13. Knut Royce, "Unanswered Questions in Shooting Down of KAL 007," *San Francisco Examiner & Chronicle*, 15 September 1983, p. A3; and *Los Angeles Times*, "Text of Soviet Statement Issued by Tass," 3 September 1983, Part I, p. 11.

14. Duncan Campbell, "What Really Happened to KE007," *New Statesman*, 26 April 1985, pp. 8–10.

15. Yoshitaro Masuo, "The Korean Airline Incident and the Self-Defense Forces of Japan," *Sekai*, May 1985, pp. 270–89.

16. David Corn, "Fear and Obstruction on the K.A.L. Trail," *The Nation*, 17–24 August 1985, pp. 110–13; and ICAO Report, p. 43.

17. Harold H. Ewing, *An Analysis and Scenario of Probable Cause of the Course Deviation Incident Involving FLT KE007, PANC–RKSS, 31 August 1983*, 1985 (unpublished manuscript).

18. U.S. Department of State, "Secretary's Statement, September 2, 1983," *KAL Flight #007: Compilation of Statements and Documents,* 1–16 September 1983, Washington, DC, p. 5; U.S. Information Agency, *The Shootdown of KAL 007: Moscow's Charges—and the Record,* October 1983; Thomas Maertens, "Tragedy of Errors," *Foreign Service Journal,* September 1985, pp. 25–31; and Murray Sayle, "KE007: A Conspiracy of Circumstance," *The New York Review of Books,* 25 April 1985, pp. 44–54.

19. *Asahi Evening News,* "Gov't Refuses to Release Tape of KAL Jet Shooting Incident," 16 February 1985, p. 1.

20. *FBIS,* Japan, "Political Parties Condemn Soviet Plane Shooting," 15 September 1983, pp. C3–7.

21. Reply of government of Japan to Yutaka Hata, 15 May 1985.

22. David Pearson and John Keppel, "Journey Into Doubt: New Pieces in the Puzzle of Flight 007," *The Nation,* 17–24 August 1985, pp. 104–10; and ICAO Report, p. D-2.

23. Thomas Maertens, "Tragedy of Errors," *Foreign Service Journal,* September 1985, pp. 25–31.

24. Reply of government of Japan to Yutaka Hata, 15 May 1985.

25. ICAO Report, p. 43; and Department of State, Comments on ANC Report (about 1 March 1984), p. 13.

26. John Burgess, "Data for Flight 007 Was Wrong, Japan Says," *Washington Post,* 17 May 1985, p. A19; and Bob Bossin, "The New Mysteries of KAL 007," *MacLean's* 27 August 1985.

27. David Corn, "Fear and Obstruction on the K.A.L. Trail," *The Nation,* 17–24 August 1985, pp. 110–13.

28. Thomas Maertens, "Tragedy of Errors," *Foreign Service Journal,* September 1985, pp. 25–31.

29. Letter from Duncan Campbell to Thomas Maertens, 30 October 1985.

30. It would be easy enough to verify the accuracy of Japan's height-finding radars. The Japanese acknowledged receiving signals from Flight 007's transponder, which was squawking an unauthorized identification code. The code, however, is only one piece of information provided by the transponder; in addition, there is information on course, speed, and altitude. These data have never been made public.

31. *New Haven Register,* "KAL Disaster Anniversary Marked by an Observance in Washington," 1 September 1985; and Jeffrey Hart, "Crime of the 20th Century," *New Haven Register,* 14 June 1985, p. 9.

32. *Asahi Evening News,* "Cenotaph Unveiled for KAL Victims," 2 September 1985.

33. Letter from Douglas Davidson, USIA press attaché, Helsinki, to Olli Kivinen, senior editor, *Helsingin Sanomat;* and *New York Times,* "Required Reading," 1 September 1985, p. 58.

34. Press statement of the Families of American Victims of KAL 007, 31 August 1986.

35. Robert Pear, "Missing the Iran Arms Story: Did the Press Fail?" *New York Times,* 4 March 1987, p. A15.

CHAPTER 21

1. Jeffrey St. John, *Day of the Cobra: The True Story of KAL Flight 007,* 1984, Thomas Nelson Publishers, Nashville, TN, pp. 80–87.

2. Alexander Dallin, *Black Box: KAL 007 and the Superpowers,* 1985, University of California Press, Berkeley, CA, p. 27.

3. Richard Rohmer, *Massacre 747: The Story of Korean Air Lines Flight 007,* 1984, Paperjacks, Markham, Ontario, p. 209.

4. ICAO Report, p. 35; and Alexander Dallin, *Black Box: KAL 007 and the Superpowers,* 1985, University of California Press, Berkeley, CA, p. 38.

5. Murray Sayle, "Charge and Countercharge," *Far Eastern Economic Review,* 22 September 1983, pp. 27–30; Alexander Dallin, *Black Box: KAL 007 and the Superpowers,* 1985, University of California Press, Berkeley, CA, p. 38; and Richard Rohmer, *Massacre 747: The Story of Korean Air Lines Flight 007,* 1984, Paperjacks, Markham, Ontario, p. 209.

6. Private source; and Richard Witkin, "Korean Pilot Offers New Theory on Downed Plane," *New York Times,* 28 December 1986, p. 8.

7. William Stevenson, *Intrepid's Last Case,* 1983, Villard Books, New York, p. 229; and Julia Preston and Joe Pichirallo, "U.S. Envoy Pressed Costa Rica," *Washington Post,* 6 December 1986, pp. A1–18.

8. *New York Times,* "Transcript of Soviet Officials' Statement and Excerpts from News Session," 10 September 1983, pp. 4–5; and Akio Takahashi, *President's Crime: Who Ordered the Espionage Flight of KAL 007?,* 1985, Ningensha, Tokyo, pp. 11–12.

9. Sugwon Kang, "Flight 007: Was There Foul Play?" *Bulletin of Concerned Asian Scholars,* Vol. 17, No. 2, 1985, pp. 30–48; and Leslie H. Gelb, "Korean Jet: Points Still to Be Settled," *New York Times,* 26 September 1983, p. A6.

10. Oliver Clubb, *KAL Flight 007: The Hidden Story,* 1985, Permanent Press, Sag Harbor, NY, pp. 106–7; Sugwon Kang, "Flight 007: Was There Foul Play?" *Bulletin of Concerned Asian Scholars,* Vol. 17, No. 2, 1985, pp. 30–48; and private source.

11. Alexander Dallin, *Black Box: KAL 007 and the Superpowers,* 1985, University of California Press, Berkeley, CA, p. 54; and David Cox, "The Aftermath of the Korean Airline Incident: Gathering Intelligence About Intelligence Gathering," *Queen's Quarterly,* Vol. 92, No. 1, Spring 1985, pp. 37–50.

12. Frank Grove, "Soviets Trying to Hide New Missile System in Area of Jet Incident," *San Francisco Examiner & Chronicle,* 11 September 1983, p. A5.

13. R.W. Johnson, *Shootdown: Flight 007 and the American Connection,* 1986, Viking, New York, p. 258; and William E. Burrows, *Deep Black: Space Espionage and National Security,* 1986, Random House, New York, p. 16.

14. Philip J. Klass, personal correspondence, 29 August 1986; and Alexander Dallin, *Black Box: KAL 007 and the Superpowers,* 1985, University of California Press, Berkeley, CA, p. 53.

15. Robert Nisbet, *Twilight of Authority,* 1975, Oxford University Press, New York, pp. 45–47.

16. Tom Clancy, *The Hunt for Red October,* 1984, Berkley Books, New York, p. 322.

17. Montgomery Bower, "Reporter Seymour Hersh Unravels the Tragic Mystery of Flight 007," *People,* 6 October 1986, pp. 57–58; Seymour M. Hersh, *"The Target Is Destroyed": What Really Happened to Flight 007 and What America Knew About It,* 1986, Random House, New York (hereafter referred to as "Hersh"), and Seymour M. Hersh, " 'The Target Is Destroyed': What Really Happened to Flight 007," *The Atlantic,* September 1986, pp. 46–69.

18. Edwin McDowell, "C.I.A. Said to Warn Publisher on Book," *New York Times,*

25 June 1986, p. C25; and Jay Peterzell, "Can the CIA Spook the Press?" *Columbia Journalism Review,* September/October 1986, pp. 29–34.

19. Seymour M. Hersh, " 'The Target Is Destroyed': What Really Happened to Flight 007," *The Atlantic,* September 1986, pp. 46–69; and Hersh, p. 121.

20. Michael Specter, "KAL and the Search for the Answers," *Washington Post,* 24 July 1986, pp. B1–12; Jeff McConnell, "The CIA and Airlines," *Counterspy,* December 1983/February 1984, pp. 19–27; Harold H. Ewing, *An Analysis and Scenario of Probable Cause of the Course Deviation Incident Involving FLT 007: PANC-RKSS, 31 August 1983,* December 1985, unpublished report (hereafter referred to as "Ewing"); and Harold H. Ewing, personal communication, 5 October 1986.

21. R.W. Johnson, "Secondary Targeting," *London Review of Books,* 23 October 1986, pp. 7–9; Hersh, p. 196; and ICAO Report, pp. A-10 and C-5.

22. Hersh, p. 197.

23. Hersh, p. 200.

24. ANC Report, p. 21; and Hersh, p. 201.

25. ANC Report, p. 22; and research by James Brazell.

26. Hersh, p. 204.

27. Hersh, p. 208.

28. Hersh, pp. 205 and 211.

29. Private sources; and Richard Witkin, "Korean Pilot Offers New Theory on Downed Plane," *New York Times,* 28 December 1986, p. 8.

30. Ewing, p. 18; and Hersh, p. 204n.

31. Hersh, pp. 208 and 210.

32. The KAL Operations Manual explicitly states that "during INS flight on an airway using VOR," the crew is to set its "RADIO/INS switch to RADIO position with the appropriate radio aids tuned and monitor courses selected for the airways being flown." This is to cross-check the performance of the INS: "If there is INS nav. error, initiate INS position update."

33. Hersh, pp. 211–212; Ewing, pp. 20 and 22; and ANC Report, p. 22.

34. Hersh, pp. 226–28.

35. Harold Ewing, personal communication, 5 October 1986.

36. Mark Ackerman interview with Seymour Hersh, 1 October 1986, and Ewing, p. 11.

37. Hersh, pp. 37, 39, 42, 55–57, 59, and 60–65.

38. Hersh, p. xi.

CHAPTER 22

1. Aviation Safety Associates International brochure.

2. Sam Jameson, "Downed Plane's Pilot Told of Engine, Pressure Loss," *Los Angeles Times,* 17 September 1983, Part I, pp. 1–14.

3. *Christian Science Monitor,* "Moscow Says Pilot Caught Spying; U.S. Doubt Voiced on 'Confession,' " 7 May 1960, p. 1; and James Bamford, *The Puzzle Palace,* 1983, Penguin, New York, p. 260.

4. In *The Nation,* John Keppel and I did what we could with the panel's conclusions: "The ICAO Report assumes that the final transmission originated with KAL 007, that it was addressed to Tokyo air traffic controllers, that it reported decompression in the airliner's cabin and that the pilot was following standard emergency procedures to descend. But our five experts disagree with that inter-

pretation. While they do not all agree on the precise wording of the transmission, their analysis allows us to say a number of things with certainty. First, although the ICAO rendering suggests that the final message was directed to air traffic controllers in Tokyo, the consensus of our panel is that the word 'Tokyo' is not discernible. Three of the five experts believe that Tokyo was not the intended recipient of the message. Second, the panelists agree that there are a number of additional words and syllables in the transmission not accounted for by the ICAO. Third, a majority of the experts are confident that part of the passage found to be 'unintelligible' by the ICAO says either 'repeat that' or 'repeating.' Finally, the experts agree with the ICAO that 'rapid compressions' or something similar was said, but not a single member of the panel hears 'descending to one zero thousand.' Three of them hear no number in this final passage." (*Source:* David Pearson and John Keppel, "New Pieces in the Puzzle of Flight 007," *The Nation,* 17–24 August 1985, pp. 104–110.)

5. ICAO Report, p. 43.

6. "There's an awful lot of bleed-through on air traffic tapes," Porter remarked. "You have so many lines and so many sources in a communications net, lines that come in, and one is always bleeding across to another. This can occur on the tape itself, where one track will bleed onto another and it can also happen at a connecting source somewhere in the system. And it can happen from cables which are not shielded properly. . . . But I have no idea as to the source."

7. Yoshitaro Masuo, "Some Research into the Record of Communications of the Soviet Fighters Which Intercepted KAL 007," 1986 (unpublished manuscript).

8. Ibid.

9. *The Times,* 1 September 1983, p. 1; and *Los Angeles Times,* "Soviets Deny Missing 747 Landed on Island," 1 September 1983 (early edition), Part I, pp. 1–16.

10. Department of State telegram, No. 122, 2 September 1983.

11. Transmissions by other aircraft, however, would still appear at their proper chronological locations.

12. Thanks to John Keppel for help in preparing this discussion.

BIBLIOGRAPHY

JOURNALS AND NEWSPAPERS QUOTED IN THE TEXT

Air Force Magazine
Anchorage Daily News
Armed Forces Journal International
Asahi Evening News
Asia Monitor
Asian Wall Street Journal
The Atlantic
Aviation Week & Space Technology
Baltimore Sun
Boston Globe
Bulletin of the Atomic Scientists
Bulletin of Concerned Asian Scholars
Business Week
Christian Science Monitor
Columbia Journalism Review
Conservative Digest
Counterspy
Covert Action
Daily Telegraph (London)
Daily Yomiuri
Defence Attaché
Denver Post
Der Flugleiter

Der Spiegel
Discover
The Economist
Far Eastern Economic Review
Flying
Forbes
Foreign Broadcast Information Service
Foreign Service Journal
Gallery
Globe & Mail (Toronto)
The Guardian
Harper's
Hartford Advocate
Hartford Courant
Human Events
ICAO Bulletin
IEEE Spectrum
Jane's Defence Weekly
Japan Times
Journal of Psychohistory
Korea Times
L.A. Weekly
Le Monde
Lexis Nexis
The Listener
The London Review of Books
Los Angeles Herald Examiner
Los Angeles Times
MacLean's
Mainichi Daily News
Miami Herald
Microwave Systems News
Morning Calm
Muse
The Nation
National Defense
The National Reporter
New Haven Journal-Courier
New Haven Register
The New Republic
The News American (Baltimore)
New Statesman
Newsweek
New York
The New Yorker
New York Review of Books
New York Times
New York Times Magazine
North Country Anvil
The Observer
Panorama (The Netherlands)

Parade
People
Playboy
Playboy (Japan)
Queen's Quarterly
Ramparts
Reader's Digest
San Francisco Examiner & Chronicle
Saturday Night
Science
Seattle Times
Sekai
South
The Spectator
The Sunday Times (London)
Time
The Times (London)
The Tribune (Oakland)
U.S.A. Today
U.S. News & World Report
Valley News (Lebanon, NH)
Vancouver Sun
Visnews News Service
Wall Street Journal
Washington Post
Washington Post Magazine
Washington Post National Weekly Edition
The Washington Spectator
Washington Times
Washington Tribune
The Weekly (Seattle)

BOOKS QUOTED IN THE TEXT

James Bamford, *The Puzzle Palace: A Report on America's Most Secret Agency,* 1983, Penguin Books, New York, NY.

Michael R. Beschloss, *Mayday: Eisenhower, Khrushchev, and the U-2 Affair,* 1986, Harper & Row, New York, NY.

Robert Boetcher, *Gifts of Deceit: Sun Myung Moon, Tongsun Park, and the Korean Scandal,* 1980, Holt Rinehart and Winston, New York, NY.

Robert L. Borosage and John Marks, *The CIA File,* 1976, Grossman, New York, NY.

William E. Burrows, *Deep Black: Space Espionage and National Security,* 1986, Random House, New York, NY.

Tom Clancy, *The Hunt for Red October,* 1984, Naval Institute Press, Annapolis, MD.

Oliver Clubb, *KAL Flight 007: The Hidden Story,* 1985, Permanent Press, Sag Harbor, NY.

Andrew Cockburn, *The Threat: Inside the Soviet Military Machine,* 1983, Random House, New York, NY.

Gregory R. Copley and Clifford M. Weiss (eds.), *Defense & Foreign Affairs Handbook*, 1986, The Perth Corp., Washington, DC.

Alexander Dallin, *Black Box: KAL 007 and the Superpowers*, 1985, University of California Press, Berkeley, CA.

Donna A. Dernac, *Keeping America Uninformed: Government Secrecy in the 1980's*, 1984, The Pilgrim Press, New York, NY.

Jacques Ellul, *Propaganda: The Formation of Men's Attitudes*, 1965, Alfred A. Knopf, New York, NY.

Darrell Garwood, *Under Cover: Thirty-Five Years of CIA Deception*, 1985, Grove Press, New York, NY.

Tom Gervasi, *America's War Machine: The Pursuit of Global Dominance*, 1984, Grove Press, New York, NY.

Tom Gervasi, *The Myth of Soviet Military Supremacy*, 1986, Harper & Row, New York, NY.

Peter Golding, Graham Murdock, and Philip Schlesinger (eds.), *Communicating Politics: Essays in Memory of Philip Elliott*, 1986, University of Leicester Press, Leicester, England.

David Halloway, *The Soviet Union and the Arms Race*, 1983, Yale University Press, New Haven, CT.

William H. Harris and Judith S. Levey (eds.), *The New Columbia Encyclopedia*, 1975, Columbia University Press, New York, NY.

Seymour M. Hersh, *"The Target Is Destroyed": What Really Happened to Flight 007 and What America Knew About It*, 1986, Random House, New York, NY.

Jane's Publishing Company, *Jane's Weapons Systems: 1983–1984*, London, England.

R.W. Johnson, *Shootdown: Flight 007 and the American Connection*, 1986, Viking, New York, NY.

Thomas Karas, *The New High Ground*, 1983, Touchstone, New York, NY.

Stanley Karnow, *Vietnam: A History*, 1983, Viking, New York, NY.

William V. Kennedy, *Intelligence Warfare: Today's Advanced Technology Conflict*, 1983, Crescent Books, New York, NY.

William M. Leary, *Perilous Missions: Civil Air Transport and CIA Covert Operations in Asia*, 1984, University of Alabama Press, University, AL.

Robert Lindsey, *The Falcon and the Snowman*, 1979, Simon and Schuster, New York, NY.

Walter Lippmann, *Public Opinion*, 1965, The Free Press, New York, NY.

Victor Marchetti and John D. Marks, *The CIA and the Cult of Intelligence*, 1974, Knopf, New York, NY.

Robert Nisbet, *Twilight of Authority*, 1975, Oxford University Press, New York, NY.

Charles Perrow, *Normal Accidents: Living with High Risk Technologies*, 1984, Basic Books, New York, NY.

William C. Potter (ed.), *Verification of SALT: The Challenge of Strategic Deception*, 1980, Westview Press, Boulder, CO.

L. Fletcher Prouty, *The Secret Team: The CIA and Its Allies in Control of the United States and the World*, 1973, Prentice Hall, Englewood Cliffs, NJ.

Jeffrey T. Richelson, *The U.S. Intelligence Community*, 1985, Ballinger, Cambridge, MA.

Richard Rohmer, *Massacre 747: The Story of Korean Air Lines Flight 007*, 1984, Paperjacks, Markham, Ontario, Canada.

Anthony Sampson, *Empires of the Sky: The Politics, Contests, and Cartels of World Airlines*, 1984, Random House, New York, NY.

Arthur M. Schlesinger, Jr., *The Imperial Presidency,* 1973, Houghton Mifflin Co., New York, NY.

Jeffrey St. John, *Day of the Cobra: The True Story of KAL Flight 007,* 1984, Thomas Nelson, Nashville, TN.

Stockholm International Peace Research Institute, *World Armaments and Disarmament: SIPRI Yearbook 1985,* Taylor & Francis, London, England.

Akio Takahashi, *President's Crime,* 1985, Ningensha, Tokyo, Japan.

Strobe Talbott, *Deadly Gambits: The Reagan Administration and the Stalemate in Nuclear Arms Control,* 1984, Knopf, New York, NY.

Alfred Tennyson, *The Poetical Works of Alfred Tennyson,* 1870, Harper & Brothers, New York, NY.

Thorstein Veblen, *Absentee Ownership and Business Enterprise in Recent Times: The Case of America,* 1923, Beacon Press, Boston, MA.

David Wise, *The Politics of Lying: Government Deception, Secrecy and Power,* 1973, Random House, New York, NY.

OTHER REFERENCES QUOTED IN THE TEXT

ABC, "20/20 Newsmagazine."

ABC News, "Nightline."

Air Navigation Commission, *1818th Report to Council by the President of the Air Navigation Commission,* International Civil Aviation Organization Council, 111th Session, C-WP/7809, 16 February 1984.

Desmond Ball, *Code 647: Australia and the U.S. Defense Support Program,* July 1982, Strategic and Defence Studies Centre.

Malcolm Brenner, *KE007: The Final Message,* 1985, Aviation Safety Associates International, Inc.

Department of Defense, *Soviet Military Power 1984,* Washington, DC.

Department of State, *Department of State Bulletin,* GPO, Washington, DC.

Department of State, *KAL Flight #007: Compilation of Statements and Documents,* 1–16 September, 1983.

Harold Ewing, *An Analysis and Scenario of Probable Cause of the Course Deviation Incident Involving FLT KE007, PANC–RKSS, 31 August 1983,* 1985.

Federal Register, "Rules and Regulations," Title 49—Transportation: Chapter VIII, National Transportation Safety Board, Vol. 44. No. 116, Washington, DC.

Conn Hallinan, *The Curious Flight of KAL 007,* November 1984, U.S. Peace Council.

International Civil Aviation Organization, *Destruction of Korean Air Lines Boeing 747 over Sea of Japan, 31 August 1983: Report of the ICAO Fact-Finding Investigation,* December 1983, Montreal, Canada.

KAL 007 Information Bulletin & Newsletter

John Keppel, *The Case of Korean Air Lines Flight 007 and Constitutional Government,* 13 January 1985.

Yoshitaro Masuo, *Some Research into the Record of Communications of the Soviet Fighters Which Intercepted KAL 007,* 1986.

Organizacion de los Estados Americanos, *IX Curso de Derecho Internacional, Comite Juridico Interamericano,* Septiembre 1985, Washington, DC.

United Nations Security Council, *Provisional Verbatim Record of the Two Thousand Four Hundred and Seventieth Meeting,* S/PV.2470, 2 September 1983.

U.S. Congress, House, *Review of Department of Defense Worldwide Communications,* Committee on Armed Services, 10 May 1971, Washington, DC.

U.S. Congress, House, *Investigation of Korean-American Relations,* 31 October 1978, Washington, DC.

U.S. Congress, House, *Aircraft Navigation Technology and Errors,* Committee on Science and Technology, 19 September 1983, Washington, DC.

U.S. Congress, Senate, *NASA Authorization for FY 1977,* Committee on Aeronautical and Space Sciences, 1976, Part 3.

U.S. Congress, Senate, *Recent False Alerts from the Nation's Missile Attack Warning System,* Committee on Armed Services, 9 October 1980, Washington, DC.

U.S. Congress, Senate, *Report of the Select Committee on Intelligence,* United States Senate, 1 January 1983 to 31 December 1984, Report 98–665, Washington, DC.

U.S. Information Agency, *The Shootdown of KAL 007: Moscow's Charges—And the Record,* October 1983.

INDEX

A-90 air route, 138
ABC, 123–24, 143, 229, 243, 293
Abe, Shintaro, 126, 131, 190, 298
Abrams, Floyd, 259, 317
Ackerman, Mark, 292, 342
acoustic locator beacons, 236
Acree, Edward, 89
Addabbo, Joseph P., 223
Ad-Hoc Coalition to Commemorate the Korean Airline Massacre, 295
ADIZ (Aerospace Defense Identification Zone), 42–43, 62, 67, 88
Adweek, 179
Aeroflot:
   boycott of, 126, 139–40, 143, 154, 185–87, 188, 189, 226–27, 240–241, 255–56
   overflights by, 87, 88, 248, 268–69
"Aftermath, The," 294
Ahn Sang-jeon, 30
Air Control and Warning radars, 42, 43
Air Defense Command, 92
Air Force, 86
Air Force Special Security (AFSS), 22
Air France, 187, 189
Air India Flight, 265
Air Lines Pilots Association (ALPA), 186, 256

Airman Information Publication (AIP), 68
Air Navigation Commission (ANC), 281–82, 326, 334
Air Route Traffic Control Center (ARTCC), 36, 40, 41, 45, 46, 114, 115, 127, 292, 312, 313, 314, 346, 349–50, 351, 359, 360
Alaskan Air Command, 35, 43–44
Alexandre, Laurien, 211–12
Alitalia, 187, 189
America's War Machine (Gervasi), 300
Anab AA-3 missiles, 76, 107, 217
Anchorage Radio, 64
Anchorage VOR beacon, 31, 37, 38
Anderson, Jack, 77, 168–70, 317, 329
Andrew, Rex, 349
Andropov, Yuri V., 135, 140–41, 178, 195, 196, 197, 198, 256–57
Anti-Ballistic Missile treaty (1972), 334, 335
AP (Associated Press), 138, 147, 175, 243, 252
Army Security Agency, 65
Asahi Evening News, 170, 243–44, 319
Ashwood, Thomas, 255
Asiatic Research Center, 29
Aspin, Les, 223
Association for Inquiry into the Truth of the KAL Incident, 306, 321–22

Association of British Pilots, 188
Atlas, Les, 349
Attu Island, 35
Aubert, Pierre, 183
Aviation Safety Associates
    International (ASAI), 346, 347
Aviation Week & Space Technology,
    102, 169, 238, 246, 286, 319
AWACS (Airborne Warning and
    Control System) planes, 35, 65,
    175–76, 245

B-1 bomber, 221
B-29 patrol bombers, 81, 82
B-47 bombers, 82, 85
B-57 bombers, 82
Baber, Asa, 261
Backfire bombers, 21, 67
BADGE (Base Air Defense Ground
    Environment) system, 114, 166
Badger, U.S.S., 176, 238, 245, 251,
    318, 319, 360
Bailey, F. Lee, 304
Baker, Howard H., Jr., 223, 225
Baker, James A., III, 148
Ballistic Missile Early Warning System
    (BMEWS), 22, 58
Baltimore Sun, 136
Bamford, James, 23, 43, 49, 51, 66, 90,
    156, 293, 347
Barnes, Michael D., 222
Bastian, Gerd, 193
Batitsky, Pavel, 263
BBC, 246–47
Belenko, Viktor, 67, 73
Belli, Melvin, 30, 291–92, 302
Bernard, Tom, 50
Bernstein, Robert L., 337
Bessmertnykh, Aleksandr, 129
Bethel VOR beacon, 35, 36, 37, 39, 40,
    41, 55, 278, 279, 280, 292, 308,
    309, 311, 332, 339–41
Bihoro, 177
binary nerve gas, 222, 226
Bissell, Richard M., 82
Bittorf, Wilhelm, 117–18, 297–98
*Black Box: KAL 007 and the
    Superpowers* (Dallin), 329
Block, John R., 143
Bodø listening station, 105, 107
Bodstrom, Lennart, 143
Boeing Company, 99, 276, 302, 304,
    312
"bogies," 353
"bogus tracking," 62–63
Boland, Edward P., 316

Boland Amendment, 222
Böll, Heinrich, 193
Boston Globe, 50, 99
Bower, Montgomery, 337
Braun, Alexander, 292
Braunberg, Rudolf, 50
Brazell, James, 339
"breakouts," 157
Brenner, Malcolm, 77–78, 313, 346–49
Brezhnev, Leonid, 102, 185
Brigham Young University, 348–49
British Airways, 187, 188
Brockman, Orville, 122
Bronco hydrophones, 21
Brown-Spier, Kathy, 235
Bruu, William, 246
Bryant, Clyde, 101
Brynner, Yul, 67
Brzezinski, Zbigniew, 107
Buckhorn, Robert, 314
Buckley, James, 212
Bugayev, Boris, 185
Burch, Michael I., 289, 309
Burnley, James H., 138
Burrows, William, 22, 287
Burt, Richard, 117, 118, 119, 123, 126–
    127, 129, 136, 151–52, 158, 216,
    220, 241, 258, 264, 296, 297
Bush, George, 222
Business Week, 96
Byrd, Robert C., 223, 270

C5A aircraft, 309–10
C-130H aerial recovery plane, 176, 177
Cairn Mountain beacon, 36, 38
Campbell, Duncan, 319, 320
Campbell, Frank, Jr., 92
Camp Fuchinobe, 23
Canadian Defense Forces, 103
Carl Vinson, U.S.S., 251
Carmon, Odis A., 44
Carroll, Eugene, 121, 192–93
Carter, Jimmy, 102, 108, 143, 144, 194
Casey, William J., 101, 117, 118, 119,
    222, 297, 337
Catto, Henry E., Jr., 299
CBS, 119, 120, 151, 229
CDAA (circularly disposed antenna
    array), 66
Celeste, Richard, 178
Central Intelligence Agency (CIA), 83,
    87, 97, 109, 162, 338
    KAL 007 shootdown reported by,
    117, 118–19, 120, 121–22, 123–24,
    298
Chamberlain, Neville, 144

Cha Soon-do, 102, 103, 107
"chatter frequencies," 44, 54
Chekhov, Anton, 66
Cheysson, Claude, 185
Chicago Convention on International
    Civil Aviation (1944), 270, 283
Chidori Maru, 113–14
Cho, Charley, 96–99, 120–21, 122, 130,
    173, 174, 177
Cho, Harry, 96–99, 101, 303, 330
Cho Chin-u, 250
"chokepoints," 20
Chou En-lai, 333
Chrisman, Michael, 292
Christian Science Monitor, 156, 224,
    241, 251, 347
Chun Byung-in:
    insurance policy for, 30, 79, 291–
        92
    as intelligence officer, 36, 44, 245
    navigational skills of, 30, 33–34, 38,
        39, 277, 338, 339
    as pilot, 29–30, 32, 35, 78, 79, 217,
        236, 237, 279, 323, 331–32, 339–
        340, 341
Chun Do-hwan, 29, 30, 180–81, 213
Church Committee, 87
CIA and the Cult of Intelligence, The
    (Marchetti and Marks), 87
Civil Aeronautics Board (CAB), 189–
    190
Civil Air Transport, 97
Clancy, Tom, 336
Clark, David, 289
Clark, Reed, 122, 123
Clark, William P., 117, 118, 119, 132,
    139, 158, 191, 235–36, 245, 247,
    264, 297
Clubb, Oliver, 16, 104, 334
CNN, 119, 120, 202, 205–6
Cobra Dane radar, 57–58
Cobra Judy radar, 59
Cobra Mist radar, 300
Cobra Talon radar, 58, 300
Cockburn, Andrew, 54, 259
Cockell, William A., 238, 252
Cold Witness radar system, 300
Collins, Inc., 236
Commodity Credit Corporation, 224
compasses, magnetic, 37, 330
comprehensive test ban (CTB) treaty,
    223
Conference on Issues and Media, 229
Conference on Security and
    Cooperation in Europe, 166, 182–
    185

Conservative Caucus, 213
Conserver, 237, 239, 251, 252
Continental Airlines, 31–32, 87
Continental Computer Services, Inc.,
    31–32
Contract Maintenance Center, 100
Cooper, G. S., 216
Corn, David, 316, 325
Cox, David, 334
Crehan, Paul, 179
Critical Intelligence Communications
    System (CRITCOM), 49
Cruise missiles, 126, 191, 195, 257,
    329
Cubana, 87
Cuomo, Mario M., 241
Customs Service, U.S., 100
Czechoslovakia Air Lines (CSA), 87,
    88

Daily Telegraph, 164, 216, 284
Daily Yomiuri, 227
Daisetus, 238
Dallin, Alexander, 75, 272, 329, 334
D'Amato, Alfonse, 144, 295
*Day of the Cobra: The True Story of
    KAL Flight 007* (St. John), 329
"deadheading," 31, 90, 340
Deaver, Michael K., 139
"Deepening Doubts on the ICAO
    Report," 306
Defence Attaché, 284–90, 293, 347
Defense Mapping Agency, 286
Defense Week, 100
DeGarmo, Kevin, 41, 45, 46, 350
"Deputat," 69–76, 78, 274
détente, 143, 185, 193, 196, 223
Dickinson, William, 143
Dicks, Norman, 222
Dillman, James, 305
Discover, 299
DME (Distance Measuring
    Equipment), 39, 55
Dobrynin, Anatoly, 94
Dolan, Terry, 144
Dole, Elizabeth H., 191, 268
Dolinsk-Sokol Air Base, 67
Dombroff, Mark, 304
Doppler radars, 102
Dorman, William, 159
"007—Licensed to Spy?", 292–93
Dougherty, Russell E., 48
Downey, John T., 81
Duffy, Henry A., 186, 301
Dulles, Allen, 83
Dulles, John Foster, 83

Dunlop, Harry, 120
Dunsmore, Barry, 123

Eagleburger, Lawrence S., 117, 118,
    119, 129, 138, 150, 158, 162, 171,
    220, 258, 264, 297
EC-121 reconnaissance planes, 85–86
EC-130 electronic intelligence planes,
    82
Economist, 76
Egorov, Evgeny, 213
Eielson Air Force Base, 22, 23
Eisenhower, Dwight D., 83, 84
El Al, 87, 88
electronic security squadrons, 47
Elias, Hank, 308
Elliot, Benjamin, 152
Elliot, U.S.S., 176, 177, 251
Ellsberg, Daniel, 193
Ellul, Jacques, 260, 301
Elmendorf Air Force Base, 22, 35, 61,
    80, 310, 343, 351, 360
Enders, Thomas O., 184
Ephraimson, Hans, 131–32, 302
Eskelson, Ed, 50
E-Systems, 247
Etomo, 238
Etorofu Island, 91, 94
ETP (Equal Time Point), 34
Evans, Rowland, 223
Evans, William, 94
Ewing, Harold, 278, 338–43
"executive privilege," 259
Export-Import Bank, U.S., 101

F-4 fighters, 100
F-5 fighters, 100
F-15 fighters, 175, 238, 259
F-16 fighters, 65
"Face the Nation," 151
"Facts Expose Washington, The"
    (Kirsanov), 244–45
Falwell, Jerry, 214
Far Eastern Economic Review, 55–56,
    271, 276
Farrar, Fred, 138
Farrell, George E., 304
Faurer, Lincoln, 247
Feaver, Douglas B., 343
Federal Aviation Administration
    (FAA), 40, 41, 42, 43, 92, 103, 127,
    138, 256, 304, 305, 307, 308, 314,
    350–51
Federal Trade Commission, U.S., 99
Feldman, Dennis, 256
Fellwock, Perry, 50

Ferraro, Geraldine A., 27
Finnair, 87, 187, 189
First Regional Maritime Safety
    Headquarters, 174
Flight Information Regions (FIR), 64,
    127
Flying Tigers, 92, 93, 94, 338
Ford, Gerald, 185, 309
"fox and hounds," 49–50, 60
FPS-117 radars, 43
Franklin, Anson, 245
Freedom of Information Act (FOIA),
    305, 316–19, 346
Freer, Duane, 273, 325
Friend, Peter, 161
Fujinami, Takao, 250
Fund for Constitutional Government,
    347
fuses, proximity, 76, 107

Gabriel, Charles A., 229
Gair, George, 186
Gamble, Jack, 236
Gartner, Michael G., 327
Gelb, Leslie, 258–59
Genscher, Hans-Dietric, 187
Geodetic satellites, 286
Georgi Kozumin, 237, 238, 239
Gervasi, Tom, 58, 191, 192, 300
"ghosting," 56
Gingrich, Newt, 143
Glennan, T. Keith, 83
Goldmark, Peter C., Jr., 240
Goodman, Julian, 294
Gotoda, Masaharu, 121, 125, 131, 167–
    168, 189, 253, 254
Govorov, Vladimir I., 197, 198, 199
"grandmother fuel," 34
Green Party, 194
Gromyko, Andrei, 166, 182–85, 210,
    240–42, 261
Guardian, 155, 183, 292
Guernon, Lawrence, 90, 92, 93
Gumble, Bryant, 291

Haberman, Clyde, 124
Haig, Alexander M., Jr., 192
Hall, Sam B., Jr., 224
Frank B. Hall & Co., 303
Hanguk Ilbo, 252
Hanjin Transportation, 96–97, 98
Hanks, Robert J., 20
Hart, Jeffrey, 326
Hartman, Arthur, 185, 212
Hartnett, Thomas, 143
Hassayampa, 237

Hata, Yutaka, 322, 323, 325, 349
Hawk missiles, 100
Hedges, John L., 161, 262
Heijl, Marinus, 320, 325
Helms, Jesse, 29, 36, 120, 121, 143, 224–225
Helms, J. Lynn, 138, 267–69, 279, 281, 299
Hendrie, Mary Jane, 235
Hersh, Seymour, 15, 326, 337–44
Hersom, Lyle, 178
HF (high-frequency) radio, 45, 46, 324, 350, 354
HFDF (high-frequency direction-finding) net, 66
Hitler, Adolf, 193, 214
Hoggard, Kim, 217
"horizontal escalation," 20
Horizontal Situation Indicator (HSI), 32, 38, 39, 277, 341
"hot spare," 33
Howe, Geoffrey, 143
Hubbard, Carroll, Jr., 29, 36, 120
Hughes, John, 137, 241, 245
Hughes Aircraft, 100–101
Hulse, Merrill, 96
Hurley, Anne, 318–19
Hutchinson, Robert, 77
Hwang, Duk-sun, 307
hydrophones, 21

Iberia, 189
Identification Friend or Foe (IFF) system, 43, 70, 164, 218–19, 220
IEEE Spectrum, 48
Illiac 4 computers, 22
Imura, Isamu, 174, 176
Incidents at Sea Agreement (1972), 251
Incident Victims Association, 295
Independent Society of Literary Representatives, 293
inertial navigation system (INS):
  distance/time readings of, 277–78, 279
  heading mode of, 276, 329–30
  navigation by, 32–33, 35–36, 39–40, 72, 152, 243, 276–80, 305, 311–12, 331, 338–43
  redundancy in, 13, 17, 28, 32, 33, 37, 339
  waypoints set by, 32–41, 44–46, 54–55, 61, 64, 66, 116, 117, 203, 256, 276, 277–80, 311–12, 332, 338–43, 356, 357–58
Inman, Bobby, 109
Insat-1B satellites, 286

intelligence:
  aerial reconnaissance in, 23–24, 81–95, 158
  delays in receipt of, 113, 118, 119, 125–26, 132–33, 261–62, 297–98, 313
  electronic (ELINT), 48, 288
  in Far East, 21–24
  Japanese operations in, 22, 64, 125–126, 130–31, 162–63, 167–68, 170, 171, 244, 321–22
  Soviet operations in, 61, 87, 88, 161, 248, 268–69
  U.S. operations in, 21–24, 48–51, 59–66, 80, 104–6, 109, 110, 138, 140, 142, 145, 167, 168–71, 196, 198, 228–29, 243–45, 306, 328, 330, 334–335, 337, 343–44, 360
  see also radar; satellites
Intelligence and Security Command (INSCOM), 22
Intermediate-range Nuclear Forces (INF), 192, 194, 195–96, 205, 223
International Civil Aviation Organization (ICAO), 128, 140, 141, 186, 252, 253
  flight scenarios of, 276–80, 329–30, 338
  investigation by, 151, 172, 188, 189–190, 210, 250, 266–83, 320–21, 325
  report of, 125, 273–83, 292, 299, 307, 308–9, 311, 315, 317–18, 326, 334, 348, 351, 356
  resolution passed by, 282–83
  Soviet responsibility determined by, 268, 269, 271–72, 273–74, 281, 282–283
  U.S. support for, 280–81
International Federation of Airline Pilots Associations (IFALPA), 140, 186–87, 189, 255
International Flight Service Station, 45, 46, 64, 350, 351, 357
Intrepid's Last Case (Stevenson), 333
"ionospheric modification," 300
Ishihara, Shintaro, 251
Izvestia, 201, 205

Jackson, Henry "Scoop," 223–24
Jackson, Jesse, 178
Jackson, William, 263
Jameson, Sam, 243, 347
Jane's Weapons Systems, 300
Jangnai Sohn, 119
Janka, Les, 245

Japan:
　　Diet of, 227, 251, 322–23
　　intelligence operations of, 22, 64, 125–
　　　126, 130–31, 162–63, 167–68, 170,
　　　171, 244, 321–22
　　press coverage in, 130, 131
　　radar units of, 114, 160, 166–67, 320–
　　　324, 325, 343, 349–54, 355
　　response to shootdown in, 71–72,
　　　160, 188–89, 244, 249–51
　　sanctions imposed by, 188–89
　　search and rescue efforts by, 115,
　　　128, 131, 174–75, 234–35, 237, 238
Japan Air Lines, 31, 101, 255, 306
Japan Broadcasting Corporation, 130
Japan Defense Agency, 19, 64, 69, 72,
　　79, 114–15, 118, 123, 126, 127–28,
　　132, 168, 169, 170, 215, 251, 319,
　　320, 325
Japan Maritime Safety Agency
　　(JMSA), 114, 116, 126, 175, 176,
　　177, 234, 237, 239, 295
Japan Self Defense Force, 65, 92, 168
Japan Times, 64, 75, 174, 177, 198
Jasani, Bhupendra, 290
Jeppesen charts, 32, 304
Jeppesen Sanderson, Inc., 304
John Birch Society, 28
Johnson, Lyndon B., 88–89, 161
Johnson, R. W., 16, 33–35, 335
Jong Jin Lim, 27

Kaisch, John R., 223
KAL Flight 007: The Hidden Story
　　(Clubb), 334
Kamchatka Peninsula, 42, 53–54, 59–
　　60, 62, 64, 71, 80, 117, 135, 148,
　　158, 160, 161, 169, 199, 200, 203
Kaplan, Fred, 97
Kashmir Princess, 333
Kato, Masayoshi, 252
Kato, Yoshiya, 133, 222, 233
Kawana, Yasukaza, 303
Kazmin, Vasily Konstantinovich, 69–
　　76, 78, 172, 199–201, 218
Kean, Thomas H., 241
Keegan, George, 219
Kelley, John H., 220
Kendon, Anthony, 290
Kennedy, Edward, 223
Kennedy, William, 20–21
Keppel, John, 16, 313, 315, 326, 347
Kerr, Donald, 180
"Keyhold" satellites, 102, 286, 347
Khrushchev, Nikita S., 83–84, 201
Kim, James, 120
Kim Chang-hun, 267

Kim Chang-kyu, 102–3, 104, 105, 106–
　　109, 110
Kim Dae-jung, 99
Kim Eui-dong, 31, 338–39
Kim Hyung-wook, 97, 98
Kim Kyung-won, 141, 142
Kimpo Airport, 119, 122, 130
Kim Sang-hyup, 130
Kim Shu-hwan, 180
Kirkpatrick, Jeane J., 142, 151, 161–
　　165, 170, 204, 213, 214, 218, 227,
　　241, 258, 261, 274, 319, 321, 322,
　　348, 355, 356
Kirsanov, Piotr, 244–45, 285, 290
Klare, Michael, 21
Klemstine, James, 98
Kobysh, Vitaly I., 146
Koch, Ed, 178
Kohl, Helmut, 194
Kola Peninsula, 104–5
Koldunov, Aleksandr, 197, 198, 263
Kole, Michael, 302
Koppel, Ted, 124–25, 144
Korea, Republic of:
　　anti-Soviet demonstrations in, 179–
　　　182, 294
　　official government response of, 130,
　　　191, 270–71
Korea Herald, 179–80
Korean Air Force, 100
Korean Air Lines:
　　as arm of KCIA, 98, 99
　　arms trading by, 100–101
　　flight procedures of, 31, 39, 46–47,
　　　55, 331–32, 339
　　government connections of, 97–101
　　lawsuits against, 302–4, 306, 331, 332
　　lawsuits by, 289–90, 292–93, 347
　　operations of, 15, 27, 96–98, 179
　　overflight bonuses paid by, 291, 331
　　response to shootdown by, 115, 119–
　　　121, 122, 138, 173, 187, 294
　　Special Projects Division of, 99–100
Korean Air Lines Flight 007:
　　airframe of, 302–3
　　altitude of, 35, 41, 46, 53, 64, 77, 80,
　　　130, 201, 203, 204, 243, 245, 322,
　　　323, 324–25, 326, 331, 348, 358
　　automatic pilot of, 33, 276
　　bodies recovered from, 175, 206, 233–
　　　235, 249–50, 254, 327
　　communications between Flight 015
　　　and, 44–45, 54, 61, 66, 227, 323–
　　　324, 331–32, 341, 353–54
　　course of, 15, 30, 35–52, 56, 68, 69–
　　　70, 71, 72, 79, 129, 164–65, 203,
　　　204, 207, 227, 236, 245–46, 272,

276–80, 290, 292, 307, 322, 328, 335, 338–43, 344

crew of, 28, 29–35, 56–57, 75–76, 77–78, 79, 80, 127, 245, 338, 340, 341, 360

decompression in, 77, 155, 275, 348, 352, 358

delayed takeoff of, 32, 35–52, 102

destruction of, 65–80, 155, 161, 200, 204, 216–17, 275–76, 309, 353

distance between Flight 015 and, 46, 54, 80, 114–15, 357

as "duck," 86, 87, 332–33

electronic equipment on, 247–48, 333–334

evasive maneuvers by, 74–75, 170, 200–1, 204, 217, 245, 321, 323

explosion of, 113–14, 130, 234, 355–56
  final transmission of, 77, 78, 80, 242–243, 324, 346–47, 349, 352–54, 355, 358

Flight 902 compared with, 102, 106, 107, 109, 110, 152, 263, 332

flight plan for, 31–32, 34–35, 43, 79–80, 87, 114, 277, 279, 280, 314, 338

flight recorders of, 129, 152, 235–39, 251–54, 264–65, 270, 280, 292, 318–319, 346

flight release sheet for, 128, 338

fuel capacity of, 33–34, 79, 127–28, 278, 330–31, 338, 339–40

Great Circle route of, 278, 311–12, 331, 332

headings altered by, 56, 68, 69–70, 71, 72, 80, 140, 160, 199, 201, 311, 319–20, 321, 341–42

head winds for, 32, 34, 55

"hybrid waypoint" of, 340–41

identification of, 70, 75, 117–18, 134, 148, 149, 151, 153, 166–67, 169, 228, 246, 261–62, 337

INS of, see inertial navigation system (INS)

insurance for, 302–3

intelligence mission of, 15, 17, 19–24, 63, 76, 146, 154, 166, 184, 199, 202, 203, 218, 225, 243, 246, 247–248, 267, 270–71, 284–90, 333–37

interceptor pursuit of, 51, 61, 67–77, 80, 105–8, 109, 116, 126, 146–47, 151, 155, 163–64, 166, 197–201, 204, 214, 215–17, 228, 236, 272–275, 282, 321, 323, 324, 341, 352, 355

maintenance of, 28, 32

navigational aids for, 17, 36, 38, 47, 60, 94, 277, 343

navigational equipment of, 17, 32, 37–38, 39, 60, 72, 102, 120–21, 277, 330, 341

navigational lights of, 73, 135, 140, 164, 165, 166, 171, 199, 205–6, 207, 215–16, 274

overflight by, 15, 20, 61–64, 68, 69–76, 148, 150, 167, 169, 199, 203, 244–45, 262, 269–70, 272, 282–83, 319–20, 332

passengers on, 16, 27–29, 77–78, 127, 130, 134, 171

position reports of, 44–45, 54, 116, 117, 227–28, 279, 280, 340, 356

radio communications of, 44–45, 63, 68, 70–71, 107, 161, 164, 166, 171, 217, 219–20

RC-135 aircraft confused with, 47, 50–57, 62–63, 64, 68, 80, 147, 148–51, 153–61, 166, 169, 198, 203, 205, 207, 215, 228, 245, 268, 285, 287, 305, 326, 334

refueling stopover of, 27–35

safe landing on Sakhalin Island by, 113–33, 298

satellite coordinated with, 102, 243–245, 285, 288, 290, 343

search and rescue efforts for, 115–117, 128–29, 131, 141, 169, 173, 174–77, 206, 233–39, 248–54, 264–265, 282, 318–19, 360

serial number of, 234, 247

"short, coded bursts" of information sent by, 199, 203

silhouette of, 151, 153

Soviet attempts to communicate with, 63, 68, 70–71, 107, 140, 164, 166, 171, 199, 203, 207, 218–20, 258

Soviet tracking of, 53, 55–57, 60–63, 64, 80, 160–61, 207

speed of, 40, 41, 46, 75–76, 79, 200–201, 204, 243, 245, 268, 322, 323, 325, 326, 331

as "target," 69, 148, 151, 164, 330

tracking and surveillance of, 17, 35, 36–37, 40–44, 51, 53, 54–59, 60–64, 79, 80, 114, 115, 130, 134, 140, 160–61, 166–67, 169, 207, 273, 278, 307–11, 320–21, 354, 356

transponder of, 43, 50, 56–58, 68, 72, 78, 79, 166, 220, 324

as unarmed civilian aircraft, 87–88, 137, 152, 199, 229, 296

visual sighting of, 70, 134

warning bursts fired near, 72–74, 80, 135, 140, 142, 160, 164, 200, 204,

Korean Air Lines Flight 007:
  warning bursts fired near (cont.)
    207, 214, 216–17, 218, 258, 262,
    274, 323, 326, 357
  weight and load manifest of, 33, 127,
    128, 338
  wreckage of, 174–75, 177, 233–39,
    249–50, 264, 265, 360
Korean Air Lines Flight 007
  shootdown:
  as accident, 13, 14, 17, 33, 34, 80,
    151, 152, 280, 328–32, 338–43
  anniversary of, 290, 294–96, 325–26,
    349
  arms control issues and, 59, 85, 95,
    119, 126, 143, 144, 157–59, 191–
    196, 221–25, 248, 254–55, 257,
    329, 335
  author's articles on, 14–15, 290–91,
    298–99, 315, 316, 326
  CIA reports on, 117, 118–19, 120,
    121–22, 123–24, 298
  classified information about, 259,
    305, 316–19, 336–37, 343–44, 346
  as complex systems failure, 13–14,
    17, 37, 102
  congressional investigation of, 15,
    18, 315, 316, 326, 327, 359–61
  congressional reaction to, 143, 147,
    221–26, 262, 270
  conservatives' response to, 144, 196,
    224
  "conspiracy theories" about, 296,
    299, 300, 326, 337, 338
  cover-up of, 16–18, 40–41, 141, 211,
    229, 344, 360
  diplomatic maneuvers on, 129, 220–
    221, 248
  disinformation on, 150, 159, 167,
    192, 245, 247, 259–60, 287, 296,
    298, 299, 301
  documents on, 127–28, 305, 317–18
  evidence on, 16, 17, 147–48, 150,
    153, 158–59, 227, 235–36, 272–74,
    283, 336–37, 349–50, 359, 360–61
  "face-saving" scenario for, 331–32
  Freedom of Information Act (FOIA)
    requests on, 305, 316–19, 346
  inaccurate versions of, 116–17, 155–
    159, 247–48
  international law and, 269–70
  lawsuits as result of, 41, 174, 206,
    220–21, 224, 302–14, 331, 332,
    345, 349–50
  "magnetic heading" theory of, 276–
    278, 280, 330

  as "massacre," 154, 210, 211, 226,
    269
  "meaconing" as cause of, 303, 306,
    329
  memorial services for, 173–74, 180–
    181, 209–10, 213–14, 248, 294–95,
    325–27
  national security issues and, 16, 304,
    361
  navigational errors as cause of, 15,
    17, 33, 34, 35–40, 46–47, 60, 145,
    153, 191, 262, 271, 276–80, 306,
    329–30, 332, 337–44
  obfuscation of, 113, 131–32, 138,
    229, 297, 326, 328, 359
  official investigations of, 127–28,
    151, 172, 188, 189–90, 202, 210,
    212, 224, 250, 266–83, 320–21, 325
  political repercussions of, 14, 136,
    144–45, 182–85, 193–94, 196, 198,
    207–8, 222–23
  press coverage of, 15–18, 119, 120,
    122–30, 134–38, 148, 151, 156, 167–
    170, 179–80, 181, 201–2, 228, 229,
    246, 247, 258–61, 271, 280, 291–
    294, 297, 298–99, 304, 310–11,
    313, 327
  propaganda value of, 118, 126–27,
    142, 143, 159, 164, 183, 202, 210–
    212, 248, 260, 263, 269, 296
  as provocation, 195–96, 202–4, 257,
    272, 280, 291–92, 293, 328, 330–
    333, 338, 343, 360–61
  public disclosure of, 14, 118, 152,
    155, 168, 170, 171, 192–93, 196,
    200, 211–12, 223, 225, 229, 259–
    260, 297, 336
  Soviet missile testing and, 155–59
  Soviet press conference on, 201–8,
    217–18
  Soviet press reports on, 129–30, 135–
    136, 140, 146, 154, 160–61, 199–
    207, 244, 257
  Space Shuttle Challenger's mission
    and, 285–87, 288–89
  as symbol, 154–55, 326
  tapes of, see tapes, shootdown
  television programs on, 291–93
  theories about, 328–44, 359
  truth as concept in, 211, 295, 344
  U.N. debate on, 143–45, 163–69,
    172, 173–74, 192, 213–19
  unofficial investigations of, 284–301,
    315–27, 359
  unresolved questions about, 16–17,
    79–80, 290–91, 327

U.S. official version of, 14, 15–16, 40–
    41, 80, 126–28, 136, 137–59, 161,
    170, 196, 207–8, 211–12, 229, 258–
    259, 261, 283, 284, 290, 295–96,
    299, 315–16, 335, 360, 361
  victims' families and, 137, 154, 171,
    173–74, 186, 187–89, 206, 210,
    212, 220–21, 224, 250, 269, 293,
    294–95, 300, 302–14, 326–27, 332
  Watergate scandal compared with,
    335–36
Korean Air Lines Flight 015:
  altitude of, 36, 41, 61
  arrival in Korea of, 120
  communications between Flight 007
    and, 44–45, 54, 61, 66, 228, 323–
    324, 331–32, 341, 353–54
  distance between Flight 007 and, 46,
    54, 80, 114–15, 357
  passengers on, 29, 36
  position reports of, 46
  speed of, 41, 357
Korean Air Lines Flight 902:
  course of, 102–3, 108
  Flight 007 compared with, 102, 106,
    107, 109, 110, 152, 263, 332
  interception of, 102–10, 120, 152
Korean Anti-Communist League, 294
Korean Association of New York, 144–
  145
Korean Broadcasting System, 120, 123
Korean Central Intelligence Agency
  (KCIA), 97, 98, 109, 118, 119, 120
Korean National Airline (KNA), 97
Korean National Assembly, 179
Kornienko, Georgy M., 202, 205, 206
Kornilov, Yuri, 217
Kosygin, Aleksei, 106
Kotaite, Assad, 267, 269
Kotikovo Air Base, 67
Krasnaya Zvezda, 56, 200, 251, 263
Kulikov, Viktor G., 263
Kun Park, 268
Kuroda, Mizuo, 166–67
Kutakhov, Pavel, 197, 198
Kvitsinsky, Yuli A., 194, 195
Kwon Jung-dal, 27–28
Kyodo News Service, 130, 167–68,
  221
Kyonghyang Sinmun, 180

Lagerhus, Otto, 186
Lambert, Yves, 270, 271, 273, 281
La Perouse Strait, 20, 68
Latham, Donald C., 286, 301
launch "windows," 285–86

Leahy, Patrick J., 143, 291
Leath, Marvin, 226
Lee, Y. S., 122
Lee Bum-suk, 106
Lee Han-ki, 179
Lee Hu-rak, 97
Lee Jin-hee, 130
Lee Kun-shik, 102, 103, 105, 108, 109
Lee Won-kyung, 294
Lehane, James, 178
Lewis, W. I., 318
Lichenstein, Charles M., 141, 142, 242,
  269, 356
Lim, Betty, 302
Linnyk, Viktor A., 246–47
Lippmann, Walter, 154–55
Literaturnaya Gazeta, 195, 199–200,
  244
Litton Industries, 276, 280, 302, 304,
  312, 339
Litvinski, Victor, 205, 206
Lloyds, 302–3
Lockheed Corporation, 99, 309–10
Lodge, Henry Cabot, 162
Long, Robert, 21
LORAN (Long-Range Navigation)
  system, 102
Los Angeles Times, 28, 60, 124, 152,
  154, 163, 178, 181, 183, 243, 255,
  286, 356
Lufthansa, 187
Luns, Joseph, 188, 192

M65 missile system, 100–101
McClosky, Robert J., 94
McCormick, Bryce, 77
McDonald, Harold P., Jr., 123
McDonald, Kathryn, 125, 209, 213
McDonald, Lawrence Patton, 28–29,
  116, 120, 122–23, 131, 144, 209,
  213–14, 329, 340
McDonald, Tryggvi, 209, 213
McDonnell Douglas Corporation, 15,
  100, 288
McFarlane, Robert, 148, 264
McGehee, Ralph, 56
Mack, Rob, 100
McKinnon, Daniel, 189
Madole, Donald W., 300, 304, 307–8,
  313
Maertens, Thomas, 15, 326
Mann, P. Q., 284–90
Mansfield, Mike, 188
Marchetti, Victor, 87
Marks, John, 87
Marro, Anthony, 159, 259

MARS (Minimally Attended Radar System), 44
Massacre 747: The Story of Korean Air Lines Flight 007 (Rohmer), 330–31
Masuo, Yoshitaro, 71, 219–20, 324–25, 356
Meese, Edwin, III, 117, 119, 134, 139, 297
Meesman, Johan H., 217
Michelangelo, James, 127–28, 300
Microwave Systems News, 253, 292
Midgetman missiles, 221–22
MiG-17 fighters, 85, 92
MiG-21 fighters, 238
MiG-23 fighters, 61, 67, 78–79, 163, 219, 355
MiG-27 fighters, 67
Mikhail Mirchinsk, 238
"minimum candor" policy, 161
MIRVS (Multiple Independently-targeted Reentry Vehicles), 221
Misawa Air Base, 22, 23, 65–66, 115, 125, 343, 360
"Missiles Launched—Target Destroyed: The Deathflight of Flight 007," 291
Mitterand, François, 185
Monde, Le, 88, 217
Moon, Sun Myung, 29, 325
Moorer, Thomas H., 214
Moran, Fernando, 183
Moscow Radio, 129
Moskvitelev, Nikolay I., 63
Mossad, 88
Mugabe, Robert, 218
Munroe, 177, 239
Murmansk naval headquarters, 104–5, 110
MX missiles, 221, 222, 226

Nakagawa, Ichiro, 106
Nakasone, Yasuhiro, 125, 130, 162, 250, 251, 298, 322
Narita International Airport, 93
Narrangansett, U.S.N.S., 237, 239, 251, 252, 318, 319
NASA (National Aeronautics and Space Administration), 286–87, 288, 290, 305
Nation, 14–15, 98, 128, 296
National Command Authorities, 13
National Conservative Political Action Committee (NCPAC), 144
National Defense, 43
National Military Command Center, 123

National Security Agency (NSA), 22, 35, 49, 65, 82, 105, 109, 117, 121, 170, 243, 297, 347, 359
National Security Council, 133, 139, 210
National Transportation Safety Board (NTSB), 127–28, 273, 292, 307
NATO (North Atlantic Treaty Organization), 105, 108, 126, 187, 188, 192, 193, 197, 198, 226, 295
Natsume, Haruo, 165, 168
Naval Security Group, 21–22, 65, 86
Navasky, Victor, 14–15
NBC (National Broadcasting Company), 119, 120, 169, 229, 245–246
NDB/DME (nondirectional beacon/distance measuring equipment), 47, 55, 277, 280
Neary, Ralph, 89, 90, 93
Nelson, Orvis, 87
Neptune P–2V reconnaissance planes, 82
Neuhart, Mark, 252
Newsweek, 136, 169, 222, 229
New York, 119
New York Times, 38, 49, 51, 79, 97, 124, 131, 142, 143, 145, 148, 151, 154, 168, 169, 171, 181, 194, 201, 207, 213, 217, 223, 224, 228, 234, 241, 242, 252, 257, 261, 263, 265, 270, 289, 325, 326, 327, 334, 337
NHK, 242, 346
Nibu Besshitsu, 65, 164
Nickell, Judy, 40–41, 55
"Nightline," 123, 143, 229, 243, 293
Nippon Telegraph and Telephone, 227
Nisbet, Robert, 336
Nitze, Paul H., 193, 194, 248
Nixon, Richard M., 29, 142, 336
North American Aerospace Defense Command (NORAD), 57, 103
Northern Warning Intelligence Corps, 115
North Pacific composite route system (NOPAC), 30, 31, 42, 115, 256
NOTAM (notice to airmen), 31
Novak, Robert, 223
Novosti, 203, 219

Oakland *Tribune,* 252
Oberg, James E., 15, 288–89, 290
O'Brien, Conor Cruise, 267
Observation Island, U.S.S., 58–59, 61, 80, 334, 343, 360
Observer, 285

Oceanic Transit Route 1, 42
Ogarkov, Nikolai V., 108, 201, 202–5, 206, 207, 211, 214, 215, 217–18, 263, 268, 333
Oglivy & Mather, 179
Oide, Shun, 321–22
Oldham, Ned, 327
Omaha World-Herald, 169
Omipov, Sergey, 53
Onda Pesquera, 233
O'Neill, Michael, 315
Operation Babylift, 309–10
Operation Fleetex, 21
Operation North Pacific Flexible Operations, 21
Operation Urgent Fury, 14
Oriental Fire & Marine, 303
Orlovets, Ivan, 268, 269, 271
Osaka, Mai and Mei, 174, 295
Ovinnikov, Richard, 142, 163, 255
Owada, Hasashi, 129

P-3 Orion aircraft, 23, 56, 65, 176, 177, 202, 245
Pakhomov, Oleg, 53, 54
Pan Am, 99
Panorama, 293
Park Chung-hee, 97, 99
Park Chung-hong, 234
Park Young-man, 36, 44, 307, 331–32, 340, 357
Parlette, Patricia, 94
Pascoe, Lynn, 128, 249
Pavlov, Vladimir Y., 131, 175, 221, 233
Payload Test Flight Article (PTFA), 286
peace movement, European, 193–94, 196, 298
Pengelley, Rupert, 284, 287, 288, 289, 347
Percy, Charles H., 225, 270
Perez de Cuellar, Javier, 212, 241–42
"peripheral missions," 48
Perrow, Charles, 13
Perry, Geoffrey, 290
Pershing II missiles, 126, 191, 195, 257, 329
Peterson, Dale, 124, 131
Petropavlovsk, 239
Petropavlovsk submarine base, 19, 21, 53–54, 59–60, 63, 203
Pfaff, William, 262
Philippines Air, 100
Phillips, Howard, 144, 213
Pinto, Edmund, 138
Pipes, Richard, 196

"plausible deniability," 336
PL-5 missiles, 157–59
"political realism," 260–61
Popov, Victor, 143
Porter, Douglas L., 36–37, 40
Porter, Lawrence L., 313, 345–46, 348, 349, 350–55, 356, 358, 359
Posada, Luis, 333
Powers, Francis Gary, 83–84, 347
Pravda, 136, 147, 160–61, 201, 244–45, 269
President's Crime: Who Ordered the Espionage Flight of KAL 007? (Takahashi), 333
Presse, 194
Project Clef, 343
"Pursuing the Truth of the KAL Affair," 306
Puzzle Palace, The (Bamford), 49, 347
PVO *(protivovozdushnaya oborona),* 54, 69, 146
radar:
    aircraft, 37–38, 102, 277
    for air traffic control, 160, 203, 227–229, 277, 278, 281, 292, 299, 308–309, 312–13, 314, 324
    civilian, 114, 166–67, 228–29, 278, 282–83
    grid systems for, 91
    ground-mapping mode of, 37–38, 277
    Japanese, 114, 160, 167–68, 320–24, 325, 343, 349–54, 355
    military, 40, 43, 167, 228–29, 245–46, 273, 278, 287, 299–301, 309, 310–311, 312
    over-the-horizon (OTH), 299–301
    phased-array, 66, 110, 158
    side-looking (SLAR), 47–48, 237
    slant range effect and, 320–21, 341
    Soviet, 54, 60–63, 67–68, 71, 91, 107, 140, 150, 155, 157, 166, 167–71, 203, 334, 335, 343, 357
    "spoofing" of, 48–49
    surveillance and tracking by, 57–58, 90–92, 155, 166, 167–71, 203
    synthetic aperature, 259
    weather, 37–38, 280, 332, 341
Radio Free Europe, 211, 212
Radio Liberty, 211–12
Radio Moscow, 154
Rappleye, Robert, 124
Raspberry, William, 226
"ravens," 48
RB-47 reconnaissance aircraft, 84
RB-50 reconnaissance aircraft, 81

RB-57 reconnaissance aircraft, 85
RB-66 reconnaissance aircraft, 85, 285
RC-135 reconnaissance aircraft, 23, 47–52
    Cobra Ball, 48, 51, 155, 156, 343
    Flight 007 confused with, 47, 50–57, 62–63, 64, 68, 80, 147, 148–51, 153–161, 166, 169, 198, 203, 205, 207, 215, 228, 245, 268, 285, 287, 305, 326, 334
    mission orbit of, 149–51, 155, 202
    Rivet Joint, 47–48, 51, 104, 109, 155, 156
    surveillance by, 48–51, 91, 155–59, 360
RDF (radio direction finding), 66
Reagan, Nancy, 136, 137, 209
Reagan, Ronald, 88, 110, 193, 223, 268
    as informed of shootdown, 132, 135
    response to shootdown by, 134–35, 136, 137, 139, 143, 144, 147–48, 180, 190, 206, 207–8, 209, 210, 212, 213, 224, 229, 242, 255–56, 269, 306, 344
    speeches by, 116, 151, 152–54, 161, 162, 168, 195, 210–11, 247, 254–255, 319
    tape played by, 151, 153, 162, 168
    U.N. speech of, 210–11, 254–55
Reagan administration:
    military programs of, 20, 152, 154, 191–96, 221–26, 250–51, 257
    response to shootdown by, 15, 84, 110, 117–19, 126–27, 132–35, 139–140, 143, 145, 189–90, 209, 220, 224–25, 246, 321, 335, 337
    restriction of information by, 259–60
    shakeup in, 263–64
"Reassessing the Sakhalin Incident" (Devereux), 284–90
Rebun, 174–75
Red One route, 90
Regional Operations Control Center, 35, 43–44, 67, 308, 312
Reich, Alan, 349
Reichardt, Juergen, 88
"reinformation," 246
Rescue Coordination Center (RCC), 115
Reston, James, 154
Reuters, 121
Rhyolite satellites, 23
Richelson, Jeffrey, 57
"riding a radial," 39
Rishiri, 237
Rivera, Geraldo, 29, 293

Robinson, Aubrey E., Jr., 303, 304, 305, 309, 312, 314
Rock, Patrick, 252
Rogers, Bernard, 192
Rogers, Frank, 126
Rohmer, Richard, 330–31
Romanenko, A. I., 249
Romanov, Seymon F., 148–49, 150, 263
Romberg, Alan, 209, 228
Romeo-20 route, 30, 39, 42, 45, 51, 55, 57, 61, 68, 116, 117, 118, 124, 140, 168, 256, 277, 283, 329, 340, 357
Roos, Michael, 180
Rosenfeld, Richard, 180
Rosenfeld, Stephen, 262
Rossi, Richard, 93
Roundtree, Thomas, 125
Royce, Knut, 319–20
Rusk, Dean, 94
Ryan, Leo, 14
Rygenkov, Boris, 282

SA-12 missiles, 160, 334–35
SA-X-12 missile, 60
Sabih, David, 302
Safire, William, 156–57
St. John, Jeffrey, 329
St. Martine, Dan, 252
St. Paul beacon, 47, 55
Sakhalin Island, 15, 66–69, 71, 78, 80, 135, 148, 158, 160, 169, 274, 319–320, 321, 322, 323, 341
SALT II agreement, 101–2, 108, 159
SAM-5 missiles, 204
Samoteykin, Yevgeniy, 220–21
Sampson, Anthony, 117, 164, 297–98
San Francisco Examiner & Chronicle, 105–6, 157, 334
Sapporo Air Control Center, 114
Sarobetsu, 176
Satellite Data System, 105
satellites:
    ferret, 24, 66, 102, 244–45, 285, 288, 290, 343
    geosynchronous, 23–24, 49
    intelligence, 21, 23–24, 66, 86, 102, 157, 159, 259, 285–86, 288–89, 290, 334–35
    photoreconnaissance, 158
    tactical system for, 289
Satellite Situation Report, 290
Sayle, Murray, 15, 35–36, 278, 321, 329–330
Sazhin, V. I., 268

SCARAB (Submersible Craft for Assisting Repair and Burial), 265
Schechter, Danny, 309–10
Schieffer, Bob, 184
Schlesinger, James R., 110
Schorr, Daniel, 201
Schwaken, Karlheinz, 107
Scott, Earl, 90
Scowcroft, Brent, 222
Seaboard World Airlines Flight 253A, 89–94
Sebastian, Tim, 246–47
secondary surveillance radar (SSR), 43, 57, 68, 72, 78
Security Council, U.N., 141–43, 161, 167, 171–72, 190, 212–15, 217–18
"selcal" transmissions, 353
Senate Intelligence Committee, 109, 316
Senior Arms Control Policy Group, 264
Servair Inc., 28
Seya, Hideyuki, 306, 322
Shemya Island, 57, 61, 90–92, 149, 156, 256, 277, 300, 341, 343, 360
Shiozaki, Seiko, 107
Shootdown: Flight 007 and the American Connection (Johnson), 33–34, 335
Shootdown of KAL 007: Moscow's Charges—and the Record, The, 321
Shribman, David, 261, 262
Shultz, George, 14, 117, 118, 119, 222, 225, 255, 267
    Gromyko's meeting with, 166, 182–185, 210, 261
    response to shootdown by, 137–38, 141, 142, 143, 187, 188, 297, 321, 356
    speeches by, 127, 132, 133, 134, 169, 212
Simes, Dimitri K., 60, 219
Sims, Robert B., 149
Sinclair, Noel G., 141, 213, 217
Sincoff, Milton G., 304, 313
Singlaub, John K., 214
Six Crises (Nixon), 142
6920th Electronic Security Group, 65, 171
6981st Electronic Security Squadron, 22, 35, 90–92
6985th Electronic Security Squadron, 22
Skelton, Ike, 226
Smirknykh Air Base, 67
Smith, Frederic N., 116, 123, 124, 131

Smith, Jack, 243
Sobel, David, 317–18
Sohn Dong-hwin, 30–31, 38, 40, 181, 237, 245, 277, 340
Sokolov, Oleg M., 129, 220, 241
Sorachi, 178
Sound Surveillance System (SOSUS), 21–22
Soviet Military Power, 300
Soviet Pacific Fleet, 19–20
Soviet State Committee for Television and Radio Broadcasting, 136
Soviet Union:
    air defenses of, 50, 58, 61, 64, 75, 80, 105–10, 115, 119, 125, 135, 138, 140, 146, 165, 166, 169, 197–205, 228–29, 244, 262–63, 282, 285, 287–288, 298, 334, 335, 343, 344
    "buffer zones" of, 42–43, 44, 314, 329
    civilian vs. military leadership of, 42, 141, 154, 192, 197–98, 204, 257, 263
    electronic order of battle of, 48, 155
    Far Eastern Command of, 19–24, 60, 67, 197–99, 262–63
    intelligence operations of, 61, 87, 88, 161, 248, 268–69
    international sanctions against, 126, 139–40, 143, 147, 153–54, 177–80, 185–90, 224–27, 240–41, 255–56
    microwave transmission network of, 334–35
    missile tests by, 155–59
    overflights of, 50, 81–95, 102–11, 147
    Politburo of, 135–36, 140–41, 165
    radar installations of, 54, 60–63, 67–68, 71, 91, 107, 140, 150, 155, 157, 166, 167–71, 203, 334, 335, 343, 357
    response to shootdown by, 135–38, 140–41, 142, 145, 146–47, 148, 160–161, 165–66, 183–85, 197–207
    as responsible for shootdown, 128, 134, 139, 147–48, 153, 154–55, 207–208, 268, 296–97, 326, 327
    search and rescue efforts of, 128, 169, 174–76, 177, 206, 233–34, 237–239, 248–50, 251, 254, 282, 319
    U.S. relations with, 143, 182–85, 193, 195, 196, 223, 223–24
    world opinion on, 126, 136, 137, 141–142, 143, 144–45, 165, 166, 171–172, 177–81, 196, 218, 267
Soya Maru, 173–74, 295

Space Shuttle Challenger, 285–87, 288–289
Spadolini, Giovanni, 143
Speakes, Larry, 132–33, 134, 135, 136–137, 148–49, 156–57, 163, 166, 168, 170, 190, 207–8, 210, 217, 242, 245, 253, 254
Speiser, Krause & Madole, 306
Spiegel, 117–18, 119, 122, 126, 297–98, 326
Spriggs, Peter, 100
Sprouse, Woody, 318–19
SR-71 Blackbird aircraft, 23
SS-11 missiles, 335
SS-18 missiles, 158, 335
SS-20 missiles, 19, 60, 193
SS-N-20 missiles, 20
SS-X-24 missiles, 158
SS-X-25 missiles, 157–58
Stark, 239
State Commission for Civil Aviation Flight Safety (Gosavianadzor), 271
State Department, U.S.:
    backchannel communications of, 49, 126, 298
    investigation by, 127–28, 287
    Korean Working Group of, 122–23, 126–27, 132, 211, 298
    official response of, 214, 217, 295–96
Sterrett, U.S.S., 251, 252
Stevenson, William, 333
Stohr, Edmund, 267
Stolichnaya vodka boycott, 177–78
Strategic Air Command (SAC), 47, 56, 88
SU-15 Sukhoi fighters, 61, 67, 69, 73, 75, 106, 107, 163, 171, 193, 216, 219, 238
Suarez, Rafael, 179
submarine-launched ballistic missiles (SLBMs), 20
Sudhoff, Juergen, 143
Sugiura, Takaya, 303
Sugwon Kang, 16, 34, 259, 297, 334
Sunday Times (London), 168, 200, 287
Sun Myung Moon, 29, 325
Sunstrand Data Control, Inc., 236
Superfortress aircraft, 81
Supreme Council for National Reconstruction, 97
Suzuki, Matsumi, 242, 243, 346
Sydney Sun, 49
Symms, Steven, 29, 36, 120

T-39 jet trainers, 85, 285
TACAN (Tactical Air Navigation), 39

Taek Yong-choi, 28, 32
Takahashi, Akio, 333
Takedo, Goro, 75
Takemoto, Shozo, 295
Talbott, Strobe, 191
Tanba, Minoro, 175, 249
Tanikawa, Kasuo, 19, 125
tapes, shootdown:
    air-to-ground communications recorded on, 165, 167–71, 274–75, 310–13, 314, 321–22, 348, 355–56, 357, 359–60
    air traffic controllers recorded on, 227–29, 309, 346, 348, 349–54, 357, 358
    background conversations on, 353, 354
    as evidence, 349–50
    of final transmission, 77, 78, 80, 242–243, 324, 346–47, 349, 352–54, 355, 358
    ICAO version of, 274–76, 283, 348, 351, 356
    independent analysis of, 276, 313, 345–59
    Japanese version of, 162–63, 167–68, 321–22
    tampering with, 165, 206, 354–56, 357, 358–59
    transcripts of, 69–76, 132, 147, 148, 161–64, 167, 214–20
    translations of, 161–62, 171, 322
Tarasulo, Yitzhak, 61
Target Is Destroyed, The (Hersh), 326, 337–44
Tass, 50, 106, 109, 129, 136, 137, 140–141, 142, 144, 145, 147, 154, 165–166, 171, 172, 191, 195, 206, 213, 241, 242, 243, 244, 255–56, 310–311, 320
telemetry, missile, 48, 59, 60, 157–59, 334
Temko, Ned, 205, 206
Tennyson, Alfred Lord, 159
Terry, Burt, 249
Thames Television, 292–93
Thompson, John, 213
Thompson, Llewellyn E., 94
Thrasher, Don, 293
Threat: Inside the Soviet Military Machine, The (Cockburn), 54
Tikhomirov, Aleksandr, 200
Time, 100, 103, 106, 289, 296
Times (London), 165, 194, 195–96, 206, 252
"Today Show," 291

Togo, Kazuhiko, 129
Tokyo Radio, 64, 77
Toles, Tommy, 28–29, 122–23, 124, 131
Tomlinson, Kenneth Y., 248
Tompkins, George N., 304, 307
Toon, Malcolm, 109
Tosolini, Joseph, 90, 92–94
Tracking and Data Relay Satellite (TDRS), 286
Traynor, Dennis, 310
Treger, Henry, 90
"Trikotazh," 274–75, 356
Troyanovsky, Oleg A., 162, 163, 164–165, 166, 214, 217–18, 261
Tsugaru, 177, 248, 249, 250
Tuohy, Denis, 292
Turner, Stansfield, 21, 107
Tweedy, Robert, 186, 187
"20/20 Newsmagazine," 293

U-2 spy planes, 82–85, 106, 298, 343, 347
UHF (ultra-high-frequency) radio, 70, 220
Unification Church, 29, 325–26
UPI (United Press International), 147, 248
U.S. Air Force Security Service, 86
U.S. Information Agency, 161, 287, 320, 326
U.S. News & World Report, 296
U.S. Peace Council, 102
"U.S. RC-135 Was Assessing Soviet Air Defenses," 155
Ustinov, Dimitri, 197, 201

Van Buren, Raymond J., 256
Vance, Cyrus, 101–2, 108
Van Flatern, Jan, 308
Veblen, Thorstein, 16
Vessey, John W., Jr., 147
VHF (very-high-frequency) radios, 32, 45, 46, 55, 103, 277, 324, 341, 354, 357
Viguerie, Richard A., 144
Villarico, Bonnie, 122
Voice of America (VOA), 211, 212, 248
VOR beacons, 31, 38, 55, 275, 280
VOR/DME (Very High Frequency Omni Range/Distance Measuring Equipment), 55, 275, 280

Vremya, 135, 136
Vrevestinik Air Base, 92, 93

Wakkanai Military Base, 22, 65, 72, 79, 115, 125, 166, 167, 320, 323, 343, 355, 360
Walker, John T., 210
Wall Street Journal, 99, 153, 184, 194
War Powers Resolution, 223
Warsaw Convention, 303, 305, 306
Washington Post, 50, 51, 90, 103, 110, 123, 137, 142, 145, 152, 153, 155, 167, 169, 184, 198, 201, 210, 216, 218, 239, 262, 271, 285, 291, 295, 304–5, 308, 325
Washington Times, 296
Watt, James, 264
Wazirzoda, Mohammed Y., 271
Weinberger, Caspar W., 20, 147, 182, 191, 235, 250–51, 287–88, 293
Weisman, Steven, 264
Welles, Benjamin, 239, 251
Western Goals, 131, 214
Westmoreland, William 293
"What Really Happened to Flight 007?" (Hersh), 342–43
White, Lincoln, 83
Wichita, U.S.S., 252–53, 318–19
Wick, Charles Z., 162, 212
Wicker, Tom, 298–99, 301, 313
Wilham, Dennis H., 118, 120, 122, 249
Williams, Robert L., 311–12
Williamson, Elwin, 90–92
Woods, Rosemary, 343
Woodward, Bob, 327
Wooley, Daniel, 246
World Wide Military Command and Control System (WWMCCS), 13–14
Wright, James, 147

Yanagida, Kunio, 79, 121, 125
Yasaki, Shinju, 322
Yeager, Raymond, 312–13
Yu Chi-song, 179

Zamyatin, Leonid M., 202, 205, 206
Zaroubin, Georgi, 83
Zimmerman, Warren, 129